The Blessings of Liberty

From the mural "Adoption of the Constitution," by John Froelich, painted 1934–1935. Based on an original painting by J. Trumbull.

The Blessings of Liberty

A Concise History of the
Constitution of the United States

SECOND EDITION

Michael Les Benedict

Ohio State Universty

WADSWORTH
CENGAGE Learning

Australia • Brazil • Japan • Korea • Mexico • Singapore • Spain • United Kingdom • United States

**The Blessings of Liberty:
A Concise History of the
Constitution of the United
States, Second Edition**
Michael Les Benedict

Publisher: Charles Hartford

Sponsoring Editor: Sally
Constable

Development Editor: Lisa Kalner
Williams

Editorial Assistant: Arianne
Vanni

Project Editor: Reba Libby

Editorial Assistant: Deborah
Berkman

Senior Art and Design
Coordinator: Jill Haber Atkins

Senior Photo Editor: Jennifer
Meyer Dare

Senior Marketing Manager:
Sandra McGuire

Cover Image: U.S. Constitution,
The National Archives

For product information and
technology assistance, contact us at **Cengage Learning
Customer & Sales Support, 1-800-354-9706**

For permission to use material from this text or product,
submit all requests online at **www.cengage.com/permissions**
Further permissions questions can be emailed to
permissionrequest@cengage.com

Library of Congress Control Number: 2002116634

ISBN-13: 978-0-618-35707-9

ISBN-10: 0-618-35707-6

Wadsworth
20 Channel Center Street
Boston, MA 02210
USA

Cengage Learning is a leading provider of customized learning
solutions with office locations around the globe, including
Singapore, the United Kingdom, Australia, Mexico, Brazil, and Japan.
Locate your local office at **www.cengage.com/global**

Cengage Learning products are represented in Canada by
Nelson Education, Ltd.

To learn more about Wadsworth, visit
www.cengage.com/wadsworth

Purchase any of our products at your local college store or at our
preferred online store **www.CengageBrain.com**

Printed in the United States of America
3 4 5 6 7   15 14 13 12 11

FD242

Brief Contents

Table of Contents

Index   467

Preface

In *The Blessings of Liberty*, I have tried to provide a brief, accessible history of our fundamental constitutional commitments as a people. The book is appropriate for a one-semester course; however, it can also serve as the foundation for a more extended course when used with readings or with an anthology of primary documents, such as Kermit L. Hall, *Major Problems in American Constitutional History* or Michael Les Benedict, *Sources in American Constitutional History* (both published by Cengage Learning).

I have sought to recreate the story of how a living idea has influenced the course of American history, rather than to compile an encyclopedia of statutes and court cases. Most studies of constitutional history recount how the formal institutions of American government developed, describe the relationship between the state and federal governments, and especially chronicle the Supreme Court's promulgation of constitutional law. But in recent years legal scholars have begun to stress the important role the people of the United States themselves have played in defining the contours of the constitutional system. This book reflects this insight. It not only covers the traditional subjects of constitutional history but also presents a history of American constitutionalism itself—the development and consequences of Americans' belief that they and their government are bound by fundamental law and guided by basic principles of rights and liberty. It treats constitutional law as only a part of the story—the formal expression of popular understandings, strongly influenced by mingled or conflicting currents of popular thought.

So this book is about the interaction of Constitution and society. It proceeds from the conviction that constitutionalism has meaning only as it affects and is affected by practical political, social, and economic issues. I have tried to explain the context in which Americans have fought to define the central principles of their great effort at self-government, and how they have struggled to apply these principles in particular circumstances. I have tried to clarify the stakes as well as the consequences of the direction we have taken. This second edition of *The Blessings of Liberty* reflects new scholarship throughout, and it pays more attention than the first to issues involving the rights of Native Americans and to the constitutional implications of the rise of the administrative state. It also deals with constitutional issues arising out of the response of the United States to the terrorist attacks of September 11, 2001.

This is a history. Its development is chronological, from the English origins of American constitutional ideas to the present. But within the chronology, I have attempted to deal coherently with different themes. The individual chapters are focused and of manageable length. Each begins with an introductory summary and is then divided into discrete sections. A Timeline at the end of each chapter indicates the most important events and gives brief descriptions of each. The Further Readings sections provide sources for exploring some topics more thoroughly. I have tried to cite the most seminal works as well as the most recent and accessible.

The Blessings of Liberty is the outgrowth of over thirty years of teaching American constitutional history. I owe whatever is good in it to the scholars from whose published research I have drawn; to the colleagues and graduate students who have analyzed and debated that work with me; and to the students who have taken my constitutional history survey classes, asking me new questions, challenging my interpretations, and contributing their own. I am grateful for the insightful, often trenchant comments of the reviewers who read the original manuscript, and especially to those who suggested changes incorporated into the second edition: Lynne Curry, Eastern Illinois University; Kermit L. Hall, Utah State University; Cynthia Harrison, George Washington University; Thomas C. Mackey, University of Louisville; and James Moses, Arkansas Tech University. I am also grateful to Lisa Kalner Williams and Reba Libby of Cengage Learning. Finally, I owe more than I can ever repay to my wife Karen and to our dear friends, who have brought so much joy to our lives.

M. L. B.

INTRODUCTION
The American Constitution and American Constitutional History

The Constitution of the United States was framed in 1787, ratified in 1788, and became operative in 1789. It has changed only slightly since. The document is re-markably terse—far shorter than that of any of the individual states and perhaps the briefest written constitution in the world. The government structure it out-lines seems simple, but on closer inspection the simplicity is illusory.

When they established the Constitution, its framers violated the basic rule that somewhere in every government there must be a "sovereign" authority—a fi-nal, indivisible authority that can make and enforce rules upon all other people and institutions and from which there is no appeal. Instead of establishing such a sovereign authority within the government, the Constitution, in its preamble, recognized the sovereignty of the people of the United States. The Constitution establishes a government no part of which has final authority. The Constitution divides, channels, and limits power, not sovereignty. The Constitution divides governmental power in many ways. A variety of government bodies have enough power to "check" and "balance" the others. Furthermore, the Constitution creates a "federal system" of government—a system in which a central government has final power over some matters and local governments have final power over oth-ers. Finally, to protect rights and to avoid collisions of power in certain areas, the Constitution specifically withholds various powers from the states, or the central government, or both.

The practical workings of the American government are even more complex than the system outlined in the Constitution. Americans have established gov-ernment institutions not mentioned in the Constitution at all. The very brevity of the document has required Americans to interpret the meaning of many of its provisions. This has led to bitter disagreements over what the Constitution re-quires or permits. People often complain that some government activity is "unconstitutional"—that is, that it violates the rules set down in the Constitution. Sometimes these disputes have been settled through ordinary politics, other times by the courts, and at least once by violence.

Constitutional controversies are not merely matters of theory. Few people would expend the resources, and even blood, that Americans have spent over constitutional issues if they did not involve important material interests. Nonetheless, commitment to abstract constitutional principles is a crucial element in the making of public policy in the United States. In the American constitutional system, a claim of a *right* has precedence over the claim of a mere interest.

Take, for example, the issue of censoring the press in order to promote decency and morality. In our system, the constitutional *right* to freedom of the press takes precedence over society's *interest* in maintaining public order or good morals. Naturally, authors, editors, publishers, and broadcasters claim the right to freedom of the press most energetically, because they have a material interest in being able to decide freely what to publish and broadcast. People deeply concerned with maintaining order or good morals, who might be personally offended by the language or images appearing in the media and who might profoundly believe that they undermine the moral and material well-being of society, may argue strenuously for some degree of censorship. But they must reconcile their demand with the Constitution's explicit protection of freedom of the press. The Constitution provides a powerful weapon with which authors, publishers, and broadcasters can appeal for the support of Americans who do not share their material interest in maximum freedom of the press. Even those most sympathetic to imposing some limitations might feel a conflict between their desire to promote order and morality and their own commitment to freedom of the press.

The federal system mandated by the Constitution also affects how material issues are resolved. The balance of power among competing interest groups often is different within individual states than it is in the nation as a whole. Therefore, a state may establish a completely different policy to deal with some problem than the federal government would establish if it had jurisdiction to do so. Throughout American history, different groups have tended to support or oppose "broad construction" of national power, depending on whether they thought the national government or the state governments would be more likely to promote their interests.

The same is true of the separation of powers that the Constitution establishes among the branches of the federal government. Different constituencies have different degrees of influence in Congress, the Executive Branch, and the courts. The shape of public policy on any subject will depend on which branch of government can claim the most authority to establish it. Therefore, people with different interests have often urged greater legislative, executive, or judicial authority depending upon which forum is most likely to promote the policies they want. These constitutional questions add an important element to debates over policy, as those without material interests at stake make their decisions at least in part based on their philosophies of federalism and separation of powers.

For these reasons, a textbook on constitutional history must address the social, economic, and political issues that have precipitated constitutional disputes.

One cannot understand how deeply held constitutional principles led to the American Revolution without understanding the practical interests at stake. One cannot understand how the conflict over slavery led to secession and Civil War unless one understands both the material and the constitutional issues.

People do not expend blood and treasure on constitutional abstractions. But neither do they do so over material interests alone. During and after the Revolution, Americans paid more in taxes than the British ever had required. But they paid those taxes to governments that had the *right* to levy them. In 1861 Southerners had cheaper and safer alternatives than secession to protect their interest in slavery. But they believed with profound conviction that federal policies inhibiting slavery violated their constitutional *right* to maintain and promote it. That right took precedence over what they considered Northerners' mere interest in the matter; they could not be expected to surrender their constitutional rights to satisfy Northerners' interests.

Finally, because the Constitution is law, the American constitutional system gives the courts an important influence over public policy. Judges are affected by their own material interests and their political, economic, and social philosophies. But they are also strongly influenced by their legal training and their commitment to legal reasoning. Moreover, federal judges and, to a large degree, state judges, are insulated from the immediate political pressure imposed by popular elections. They have overturned as unconstitutional policies with powerful political support, profoundly affecting the course of American history. Despite increased scholarly attention to the ways in which the other branches of government and the people themselves influence constitutional interpretation, most Americans nowadays regard the courts, especially the Supreme Court of the United States, as the final authority upon the constitutionality of state and national laws. For that reason some people think that American constitutional history is nothing more than the history of a series of court cases. But court decisions have authority because the American people are committed to adhering to the rules that the Constitution imposes. The judges would not have the power to compel obedience to their decisions if the president, Congress, or the state governments defied them. It is Americans' insistence that the Constitution be observed that makes open defiance too politically dangerous to be undertaken.

This commitment to obeying basic rules of government is called "constitutionalism." It is an application to a constitutional system of the principle of "the rule of law." Without it, there is no way to enforce constitutional rules, and constitutions become meaningless scraps of paper. That is why there are many more constitutions in the world than there are actual constitutional governments. American constitutional history attends not only to constitutional law as expounded by courts but to public understandings of the meaning of the Constitution and public commitment to constitutionalism.

This textbook attempts to convey the history of this complex system of constitutional government, as well as its interaction with social and economic institutions, in a relatively small number of pages. It can only provide an overview. Each chapter begins with a brief summary and then discusses specific topics. The discussion of further readings that follows this Introduction lists works that provide more detailed descriptions of American constitutional history. Neither this discussion nor those that follow each chapter is meant to be comprehensive. The suggested books and articles are either especially important or particularly accessible to the nonspecialist. Subtitles are omitted unless necessary to explain the subject.

This book goes to press as Americans face new challenges that test our fidelity to constitutionalism and the rule of law. Deep divisions within our society have eroded political civility and respect for the democratic process. Thoughtful observers worry that the Supreme Court has become disrespectful of the other institutions of government. The threat of terrorism forces us to ask how far we should go to limit freedom at home and tempts us to bend the rules of international law abroad. We have faced similar challenges in the past. Crises have sometimes led us to drift from our constitutional moorings. But in the end these challenges have served to strengthen our commitment to our fundamental principles, as we have reconsidered decisions made under stress and vowed to do better. Knowing where our ideas of liberty and government came from, how we have fought over them, what we have achieved, and where we have failed seems more important than ever. No textbook can resolve the constitutional controversies now before the American people, but perhaps historical perspective will help us find the answers.

Finally, a note on gendered language: I have generally avoided it but have occasionally reflected contemporary usage where it would be anachronistic to do otherwise. For example, it would be misleading to write of "the rights of English people" in the seventeenth and eighteenth centuries. "The rights of Englishmen" was the common usage, and it reflected the sexist reality.

FURTHER READING

Readers who need a more comprehensive American constitutional history textbook should consult Melvin I. Urofsky and Paul Finkelman, *A March of Liberty* (2d ed., 2002). The encyclopedic work by Alfred H. Kelly, Winfred A. Harbison, and Herman Belz, *The American Constitution* (7th ed., 1991), is now somewhat dated but it is still valuable for its detailed approach. Detailed indexes, tables of cases, and bibliographies make these texts useful for initial research on particular subjects or cases. In *American Constitutional History*, ed. Leonard W. Levy et al. (1989), various authors present thorough essays on successive eras of constitutional history. These are augmented by discussions of the history of the Supreme Court and its decisions, organized by chief justice. The essays provide helpful background information, but the book lacks an index and provides only limited bibliographic help. In *Constitutional Law Stories*, ed. Michael C. Dorf (2004), law professors and political scientists offer essays on fifteen of the most important Supreme Court cases in American history. Historians prepared the essays in an old standard, *Quarrels That*

Have Shaped the Constitution, ed. John A. Garraty (rev. ed., 1987). The essays are engaging but eschewed footnotes and other professional paraphernalia. Those seeking a more scholarly introduction to various aspects of constitutional history might consult the essays in *Constitutionalism and American Culture*, ed. Sandra VanBurkleo et al. (2002), and David Thelen (ed.), *The Constitution and American Life* (1988). As the titles indicate, the authors are careful to link American constitutional development to social, cultural, and other changes. *Crucible of Liberty: 200 Years of the Bill of Rights* (1991), edited by Raymond Arsenault, offers a group of straightforward essays on civil rights and liberties by leading historians.

The two volumes of Bruce Ackerman's *We the People*, entitled *Foundations* (1991) and *Transformations* (1998), integrate American constitutional history and constitutional theory. Leading constitutional historians and lawyers critique and elaborate on Ackerman's thesis in "Moments of Change: Transformation in American Constitutionalism," *Yale Law Journal* 108 (June 1999).

Michael Kammen has written perceptively about the general place of constitutionalism in American culture in *A Machine That Would Go of Itself* (1986). Constitutional theorist J. Jefferson Powell grapples with the relationship between political and constitutional argument in *A Community Built on Words* (2002). The first two chapters of Stephen M. Griffin's *American Constitutionalism* (1996) are especially insightful. Larry D. Kramer recovers the popular basis of American constitutionalism in *The People Themselves* (2004). Keith Whittington likewise draws attention to what he calls "the political constitution" in *Constitutional Construction* (1999). Michael J. Klarman provides a good guide to further reading in the footnotes of "What's So Great about Constitutionalism?" *Northwestern University Law Review* 93 (Fall 1998): 145–194. Herman Belz's collected essays on constitutionalism, *A Living Constitution or Fundamental Law?* (1998), also offer a broad range of information and bibliographic guidance.

A number of works provide overviews of the history of specific constitutional institutions and issues. Sidney M. Milkis and Michael Nelson's *The American Presidency* (4th ed., 2003) and Michael A. Genovese's *The Power of the American Presidency* (2001) are general histories of the presidency. Better is Michael P. Riccards, *The Ferocious Engine of Democracy* (2 vols., 1995). Forrest McDonald is sympathetic to a strong presidency in *The American Presidency* (1994). Compare his view to that of the eminent historian Arthur M. Schlesinger Jr., whose influential *The Imperial Presidency* (1973) lamented the chief executive's overweening power. Supplement McDonald's work with Lewis L. Gould, *The Modern American Presidency* (2003). *The Constitution and the American Presidency* (1991), edited by Martin L. Fausold and Alan Shank, contains scholarly essays on the constitutional history of the presidency. In *Constitutional Conflicts Between Congress and the President* (4th ed., 1997), Louis Fisher provides a historically oriented analysis of clashes over such issues as the control of foreign policy, the appointment and removal of civil servants, and control of expenditures. Donald L. Robinson's more general *"To the Best of My Ability": The Presidency and the Constitution* (1987) uses illustrations from history.

The Origins and Development of Congress (2d ed., 1982), prepared by the staff of Congressional Quarterly, Inc., is a basic survey. Richard Allen Baker sketched a history of the upper house, *The Senate of the United States* (1988), to observe the bicentennial. James T. Currie prepared a companion volume, *The United States House of Representatives* (1988). William S. White's *Citadel: The Story of the United States Senate* (1950) is a readable but now dated survey. Although it too is dated, the best popular introduction to the history of the House of Representatives is still Neil MacNeill, *Forge of Democracy* (1963). Another useful survey is George Galloway's *History of the House of Representatives* (rev. ed., 1976). The staff of the House Committee on Administration later revised it radically, providing much more detail in a less readable volume. See *History of the United States House of Representatives* (1994). Donald C. Bacon et al. (eds.), *The Encyclopedia of the United States Congress* (1995) contains general, chronological essays on the history of Congress, biographical articles, and essays on specific congressional events and issues.

The classic history of the Supreme Court through the Progressive Era is Charles Warren's *The Supreme Court in United States History* (3 vols., 1924). Although dated, it is unrivaled for locating the Court's decisions in contemporary politics. The individually authored volumes of *The History of the United States Supreme Court* (1971–   ), published by the Oliver Wendell Holmes Devise, are full of detailed information. David P. Currie, *The Constitution in the Supreme Court* (2 vols., 1985–86) is an encyclopedic chronicle of Supreme Court constitutional decisions.

There are a number of one-volume histories of the Supreme Court. John E. Semonche's *Keeping the Faith* (1998) is detailed and informative but drifts into a chronicle of cases in the later chapters. The third edition of Robert G. McCloskey, *The American Supreme Court* (2000) brings a concise old standard almost up to date. William Wiecek's *Liberty Under Law: The Supreme Court in American Life* (1988) is probably the best modern overview. Bernard Schwartz, *A History of the Supreme Court* (1993), is designed for nonspecialist readers. Robert W. Langran's *The Supreme Court* (2004) is compressed but a good source for basic information. The *ABC-CLIO Supreme Court Handbooks*, organized by tenure of chief justices, provides useful information on each Court, its personnel, and its decisions, as well as thoughtful essays on the general historical context in which it deliberated and its legacy.

There is no good, complete history of American federalism, and one would be very welcome. Forrest McDonald's *States' Rights and the Union* (2000) is a basic chronicle of disputes over federalism through the Reconstruction era, but it fails to describe the theoretical underpinnings of the rival constitutional interpretations. In *Dreams of a More Perfect Union* (2001), Rogan Kersh offers a much more sophisticated story of how Americans interpreted and applied concepts of the Union from colonial times until the term faded from usage by the end of the nineteenth century. Walter Hartwell Bennett's *American Theories of Federalism* (1964) is an old-fashioned intellectual history that barely goes beyond the Civil War. John R. Schmidhauser, *The Supreme Court as Final Arbiter in Federal-State Relations, 1789–1957* (1958) provides important basic information but, like Bennett, takes a traditional approach. Michael C. Remington, *Federalism and the Constitution* (2002) is a very concise chronological survey.

Harry N. Scheiber in "American Federalism and the Diffusion of Power: Historical and Contemporary Perspectives," *Toledo Law Review* 9 (Summer 1978): 619–677, provides an overview and a modern perspective. Scheiber's classic "Federalism and the Economic Order, 1789–1910," *Law and Society* 10 (Fall 1975): 57–118, is an outstanding example of the new approach to the history of federalism. It combines theory and practice to explain how constitutional principles both reflected and shaped social reality. Donald J. Pisani, "Promotion and Regulation: Constitutionalism and the American Economy," in *The Constitution and American Life*, noted above, is an insightful overview of how constitutional commitments have affected American economic development. The essays in *Federalism and Rights*, ed. Ellis Katz and G. Alan Tarr (1996), relate two of the main themes of American constitutional history.

James McGregor Burns and Stewart Burns provide a broad political history of civil rights and liberty in the United States in *A People's Charter: The Pursuit of Rights in America* (1991). Eric Foner's *The Story of American Freedom* (1998) studies freedom broadly defined. Michael Kammen's *Spheres of Liberty: Changing Perceptions of Liberty in American Culture* (1986) is a cultural history of the subject. Paul L. Murphy offers a balanced chronicle of both freedom of speech and religion in *The Shaping of the First Amendment* (1992). John Nerone has published a chronicle of *Violence Against the Press in United States History* (1994). Mark DeWolfe Howe's *The Garden in the Wilderness: Religion and Government in American Constitutional History* (1965) is a classic, brief account. Philip Hamburger, *Separation of Church and State* (2002) is an excellent history of the subject. Edwin S. Gaustad, *Proclaim Liberty Throughout All the Land* (2003) is a compressed survey that begins with an informative overview but shifts attention almost entirely to the Supreme Court with the advent of the twentieth century. Anson P. Stokes's *Church and State in the United States* (3 vols., 1950) is a good source for detailed information. Melvin I. Urofsky's *Religious Freedom* (2002) is a concise survey with documents, attending mainly to Supreme Court cases. Students might compare John Webb Pratt, *Religion, Politics, and Diversity: The Church-State Theme in New York History* (1967), with J. William Frost, *A Perfect Freedom: Religious Liberty in Pennsylvania* (1993). Louis Fisher's *Religious Liberty in America* (2002) argues that Americans have protected religious liberty primarily through the political process rather than reliance on courts.

Lawrence M. Friedman's magisterial *Crime and Punishment in American History* (1993) presents a general history of crime and law-enforcement in the United States that goes far beyond discussions of criminal procedure and defendants' constitutional rights; he limns the relationship among crime, punishment, society, and culture. Samuel Walker's *Popular Justice* (2d ed., 1998) is shorter, well written, and informative. Herbert Johnson's *History of Criminal Justice* (2d ed., 1996) ranges from ancient origins through modern America with remarkable compression. David J. Bodenhamer, *Fair Trial: Rights of the Accused in American History* (1992) is a good survey.

Donald G. Nieman's *Promises to Keep: African-Americans and the Constitutional Order* (1991) is an outstanding synthesis. It should be supplemented by Adam Fairclough's excellent *Better Day Coming: Blacks and Equality, 1890–2000* (2001), while John Hope Franklin and Alfred A. Moss's *From Slavery to Freedom* (8th ed., 2000) is the standard history of African Americans and their struggle for racial justice. For the history of women's rights, see Sandra VanBurkleo's comprehensive synthesis *"Belonging to the World": Women's Rights and American Culture* (2001). Linda K. Kerber stresses how relieving women of constitutional obligations undermined their constitutional status in *No Constitutional Right to Be Ladies* (1998). Joan Hoff's legal history of American women is a trenchant account of *Law, Gender, and Injustice* (1991). John R. Wunder tells the story of Native Americans and the Constitution in *"Retained by the People"* (1994). Rogers M. Smith's *Civic Ideals: Conflicting Visions of Citizenship in U.S. History* (1997) is an influential general assessment of traditions of inclusion and exclusion in the American community. Judith N. Shklar's *American Citizenship: The Quest for Inclusion* (1991) is a briefer assessment based on a series of lectures. Alexander Keyssar's *The Right to Vote* (2000) covers this important aspect of citizenship and belonging.

Research in American constitutional history should start with Leonard W. Levy and Kenneth L. Karst (eds.), *The Encyclopedia of the American Constitution* (6 vols., 2d ed., 2000). Kermit L. Hall's (ed.) *The Oxford Companion to the Supreme Court of the United*

States (1992) is an immensely useful guide to Supreme Court decisions and doctrines. The standard bibliographic aid for research in American constitutional history is Hall (comp.), *A Comprehensive Bibliography of American Constitutional and Legal History* (5 vols., 1982) and its 1991 supplement. The bibliography in Kelly, Harbison, and Belz's *The American Constitution*, noted above, is also an outstanding research aid for secondary sources published before 1990. Augment the foregoing sources with searches in electronic databases and library catalogues, which have reduced the demand for general bibliographies.

1
English Origins of American Constitutionalism

Understanding the origins of the American constitutional system requires knowledge of its English background. Especially significant are the "common law" of England and the bitter constitutional struggle of the seventeenth century that shaped English and American understandings of British liberty and the British constitution. By the seventeenth century, when most of the North American colonies were established, English people had come to see themselves as entitled to liberty, which meant essentially freedom from arbitrary power. They identified this liberty with the common law, which protected their lives and property from private threats and limited the king from infringing on subjects' rights without securing the consent of their representatives in Parliament.

During the seventeenth century, this system of liberty was threatened. Both Parliament and the king claimed larger areas of power, leading to a bitter conflict between them. If the king won, English liberty might give way to royal absolutism, as happened in much of Europe. The liberty that Englishmen* were so proud of meant much more to the elite than to most English people, who still lived in poverty and ignorance in the countryside and in the teeming slums of London. But the conflict was real. Its outcome was crucial to the constitutional history of both England and America.

The Common Law and the Rights of Englishmen

The settlers who colonized British North America during the 1600s and 1700s, displacing Native Americans through war and disease, came from many nations. Tens of thousands had been torn from Africa and imported as slaves. Most had come from Europe. Some arrived from Germany, the Netherlands, and Scandinavia, others from France, Ireland, and Scotland. By far the largest number came from England. Because the colonies were British possessions and because most of the settlers shared an English heritage, English cultural institutions predominated.

*Please see the Introduction for an explanation of the use of masculine words in various parts of this text.

Nearly all Americans lived under an essentially English legal system. Early American law, established in the first colonies in the early 1600s, was strongly influenced by the customs of local English courts. In Puritan New England, the Bible was another important source of law, although not of procedure. New Englanders also seem to have adopted many of the ideas of Puritan legal reformers, simplifying procedures and reducing the number of crimes punishable by death. But the greatest influence on American law was the "common law" of England. This body of rules had developed over the centuries in the royal courts known as the King's Bench, which dealt with crimes; in the Court of Common Pleas, which dealt with disputes over property and personal injuries; and in the Court of Exchequer, which had jurisdiction over disputes arising out of tax collection. These courts maintained records of their procedures and decisions; judges treated these records as establishing the rules for deciding similar later cases. The origins of some of the procedures of the common-law courts, such as jury trials and the right to call witnesses, dated to the 1300s. Others had developed more recently. Although they often complained about them, Englishmen saw these royal, common-law courts as a source of government protection against the encroachments of the rich and powerful.

Of particular importance to English people was the common law's use of juries in cases involving property or serious criminal offenses. Less serious criminal cases were generally tried before justices of the peace, influential local figures who received royal commissions to act as magistrates and county administrators. In serious criminal cases one generally had to be indicted by a grand jury before being brought to trial. At the trial itself, a petit jury determined guilt or innocence. Although one had to possess a certain amount of property to sit on a jury, the requirement was set at a level that permitted farmers, tradesmen, and craftsmen to serve. In a nation where only a small minority was entitled to vote, the jury was the main way in which ordinary people participated in governance. Juries traditionally could modify law enforcement by finding defendants guilty of lesser crimes than charged or by acquitting them altogether. In extreme cases, the jury system enabled ordinary people to obstruct the enforcement of unpopular laws.

The common law—the law of most of the royal courts—was not England's only legal system. There were other courts. Local courts on manors and in other localities handled minor disputes. English kings issued special charters to various towns, groups, and institutions authorizing them to establish courts to enforce their own rules. Other royal courts served special purposes, with jurisdiction sometimes overlapping that of the common-law courts. The Courts of Chancery, for example, provided justice in cases where the common-law courts were not empowered to act or where their remedies would not solve the problem. Instead of the common law, Courts of Chancery followed rules and procedures called "equity." Equity was supposed to achieve justice in the particular case, and not be bound by precedents. However, it soon developed its own body of rules. These courts were administered by "chancellors" rather than judges, and they empaneled no juries. Church courts governed matters relating to religious doctrine and the sacraments, such as marriage. They punished heresy and had jurisdiction over crimes involving morals. At the beginning of the seventeenth century, they still claimed the right to resolve disputes over church property. Special courts were set up to administer particular unruly localities. Serious crimes against the king and the state and crimes by government officers were tried in the Court of Star Chamber, where defendants could be subjected to torture, might not be informed of the exact charges against them, had no right to cross-examine witnesses, and received no jury trials.

Each of these courts or groups of courts developed its own rules of procedure and substantive law, which differed from the "common law" that had developed in the main royal courts. Many had their own groups of lawyers, feeling a degree of rivalry with other courts and systems.

Despite the existence of these other courts and legal systems, English people in England and America believed that they had a right to traditional common-law procedures and rules, such as the right to a trial before a neutral judge and jury; the guarantee that one's life, liberty, and property could be taken only through proper legal processes; the right to know the charges levied against one; the rule that one was innocent until proven guilty; and the right to be represented by counsel and to present witnesses. They believed these rights to be guaranteed by the *Magna Carta,* or Great Charter, to which King John had agreed in 1215 and which had been confirmed many times since. The common law was the law that applied to English people most generally—hence its name. Other courts were considered exceptional. English people considered the common law to be the source and guarantee of their liberties, the great inheritance of the freest people in the world.

The common law, like the other institutions of English government, had developed slowly over many centuries out of customs, royal charters, legislation, and judicial precedents. There was no written code detailing the law or the structure of government that could simply be transplanted to the infant colonies of the New World. American settlers landed in a wilderness, far from the king, Parliament, or the nearest English court. Some had charters from the king, sketching a system of government, but the charters generally proved incomplete or inappropriate. Massachusetts, one of the most influential of the colonies, struggled for years to produce an acceptable statement of government and rights. Other colonies, such as the Pilgrim colony at Plymouth, as well as Rhode Island and Connecticut, founded by exiles and dissidents from Massachusetts, did not have charters. They had to establish written rules to govern themselves.

Colonists repeated the process of establishing written frames of government as they spread from their first settlements and established new communities in the wilderness. In those documents they listed their common-law rights—both the traditional ones and variations urged by English reformers. Those rights included fair legal procedures, jury trials, legal counsel, and freedom from barbarous punishments and from torture used to obtain confessions. Like English people at home, those settling America thought of these rights as fundamental, a basic element of English governance.

This conviction was strengthened by a great burst of common-law pride and expansiveness in the late sixteenth and early seventeenth centuries, fueled by Sir Edward Coke (pronounced Cook), one of the greatest figures in the history of English and American law. Coke served as Queen Elizabeth I's attorney general, as chief justice of the Court of Common Pleas, and finally as chief justice of the King's Bench. Under his leadership, the common-law courts attacked the jurisdictional claims of rival courts. Taking up controversies under consideration in other courts, they issued writs ordering them to stop proceedings. In one famous case, Coke overturned a penalty levied by the College of Physicians of London against a competitor, Dr. Bonham. Parliament had given the College a monopoly on medical practice in London and authorized it to jail any nonmember practicing medicine. In *Dr. Bonham's Case* (1610), Coke and the other judges of the Court of Common Pleas ruled that the proceedings were void because they violated the common-law maxim that no man could be a judge in his own case. Although this case looks like an early instance of judicial review of the constitutionality of legislation, it is unlikely that Coke intended to challenge the power of Parliament to grant whatever privileges it wished. Rather, he was imposing a common-law rule on the College and at the same time cutting in on its jurisdiction. He was also putting the common law on the side of the growing number of Englishmen who opposed monopolies for the privileged few. Under Coke's leadership, the common-law courts undertook similar excursions against other courts. By the time James I succeeded Elizabeth in 1603, relations between the common-law judges and lawyers and those of other courts had become acrimonious.

To strengthen the position of the common law after he left the bench, Coke published many of his opinions. He also prepared his monumental *Institutes of the Common Law*, which summarized the rules and procedures. Coke stressed the common law's connection to the *Magna Carta* and its protection of the rights of Englishmen, providing a crucial reference work for lawyers, judges, and laypeople. It remained the standard guide to the common law for more than a century, making the law accessible to more people and reconfirming it as a bastion of subjects' rights.

The Constitutional Crisis of the Seventeenth Century

English political rights were closely linked to legal rights; both were considered a part of the common law. Well into the nineteenth century, most English people believed in a semi-mythical version of their political and legal history. They believed that their Anglo-Saxon ancestors had lived in near-perfect freedom under an "ancient constitution." The Norman conquest of England in 1066 had introduced French despotism, the "Norman yoke," to the realm. For centuries Englishmen had labored to reestablish the liberties of the ancient constitution. Winning the *Magna Carta* in 1215 had been the most important victory in the fight, which continued as Englishmen struggled to secure the power of Parliament, reestablishing the old Anglo-Saxon right to participate in government.

The real story was different. British legal and political institutions had developed slowly over the centuries. Except for brief periods, only a small minority of elite Englishmen participated in the conflicts over law and government. English political rights originated in feudal law, which dominated Europe in the medieval period and was introduced into England by the Normans. Feudal law secured great freedom for the landed nobility, limiting the authority of monarchs. Royal authority eroded further when kings granted "liberties"—special privileges—to particular people, towns, institutions, or regions, often in the form of charters detailing special rights or immunities. Power was so diffuse in this system that it proved necessary to establish representative assemblies in which powerful nobles and delegates from semi-independent institutions, towns, and regions joined to advise the king and agree to royal policies. Such gatherings enabled capable monarchs to develop the influence necessary to secure obedience to government. Often representatives of ordinary freemen were called to witness these august proceedings, to be awed by the royal majesty and to manifest their loyal subordination. In England, where the king and nobility descended from Norman French conquerors, these assemblies were called "parliaments," from the French words *parler* and *parlmenter*, meaning "to speak" and "to negotiate."

Like other European lands, England was periodically racked with strife among the great landed aristocrats and between them and the king. The *Magna Carta* was extorted from King John during one of these bitter struggles. In reality, its main purpose was to protect the landed aristocracy. During other times of turmoil, powerful lords used Parliament to impose limits on the king or as a weapon against rivals. By the 1500s it was understood that the king could levy taxes only with Parliament's consent. After the long, bitter, and bloody Wars of the Roses (1455–1485), a new royal dynasty, the Tudors, used Parliament to reinforce its own authority, making Parliament one of the strongest representative assemblies in Europe. The Tudors especially relied on parliamentary legislation when they broke with the Roman Catholic Church early in the sixteenth century and established the Church of England.

As the first English settlers reached America in the early 1600s, events on the continent of Europe foretold rising tensions between Parliament and the English monarchy. Bitter conflicts were developing all across Europe as monarchs claimed greater powers to govern nations of growing size and complexity. In most European states people who wanted progress, stability, and order rallied behind their monarchs against the special privileges claimed by selfish aristocrats, powerful institutions, and narrow-minded localities. Intellectuals articulated an ideology of royal absolutism, based on a new understanding of "sovereignty." Sovereignty, these political philosophers wrote, was the final, indivisible source of law and authority in any state. Theorists of absolutism argued that monarchs could not be bound by laws whose very authority arose out of their sovereign will. In nation after nation, monarchs suppressed their unruly nobility, abrogated charters granted by earlier kings, and abolished representative assemblies or transformed them into subordinate organs of local administration.

In England a new dynasty, the Stuarts, succeeded to the English throne upon the death of Queen Elizabeth in 1603. Like other European monarchs, the Stuarts attempted to expand royal authority and to centralize governmental power. James I (1603–1625) tried to take advantage of the long history of cooperation between king and Parliament to buttress his attempts to modernize. Usually he was successful, but on several occasions disagreements led to sharp conflicts.

Moreover, some Stuart policies proved profoundly unpopular. Unlike other European kings the Stuarts never gained the support of the nonaristocratic classes. James and his son Charles I (1625–1649) tried to purge the Church of England of Puritan reformers, who wanted to reshape it to reflect Calvinist ideals of faith, simplicity, and the priesthood of all believers. More radical religious dissenters, known as Separatists because they wanted to leave the Church of England altogether, were persecuted more harshly than the reformers. James and Charles allied with conservative church leaders, who stressed the importance of ritual, awe-inspiring majesty, and the Church of England's hierarchy of bishops and archbishops, with the king at its head.

As leader of church and state, the king combined both temporal and spiritual authority, a firm platform from which to claim the expanded powers that characterized royal absolutism developing elsewhere in Europe. Favoring a church structure and canon halfway between radical Protestantism and Roman Catholicism, the Stuarts were disinclined to participate on the Protestant side in the great wars that raged between Protestants and Catholics in the rest of Europe, to the despair of most English people, who sympathized strongly with the Protestants.

Working to enhance their authority, the Stuarts tried to weaken the common-law courts and strengthen rival courts. Early in his reign, James I called the judges of the common-law courts and the church courts together to adjudicate the dispute between them. But Coke questioned James's authority to resolve the conflict. He argued that the common-law courts represented the king's will when they issued their writs and rendered their decisions; there was no room for the king's personal intervention. In other words, Coke tried to distinguish between the monarchy as an institution, operating according to law, and the monarch as a person. This argument infuriated James, who exclaimed that it implied that the king, rather than being the source of all law, was subject to the law—and, he might have added, subject to the judges. Such a claim amounted to treason—a capital offense triable in the Star Chamber. The terrified judges fell to their knees, swearing their devotion. But Coke later claimed that he continued to protest even while lying prone. James ultimately removed the recalcitrant chief justice from the bench.

By the 1620s Parliament was more firmly resisting the Stuarts' unpopular policies by refusing to levy taxes unless they were changed and the advisors responsible for them removed. Leading common-law lawyers and judges, including Coke himself, endorsed Parliament's course, while the king's advocates argued that the monarch had preeminent, sovereign authority over law and public policy. It had always been conceded that the king had the "royal prerogative" to make a wide range of decisions without consulting Parliament, including those involving his family, his feudal estates, foreign policy, choosing advisors, granting special privileges through charters, and protecting the realm from foreign threats. Supporters of royal government interpreted these prerogatives as broadly as possible and denied that Parliament could use its power over taxes to force changes in public policy. Its job had always been to advise the king and inform him of grievances, not to govern. They insisted that Parliament exceeded its authority by even discussing matters within his prerogative.

Parliament, however, began to challenge such expansive definitions of the royal prerogative. James and especially Charles turned to other expedients to raise money. They revived old feudal taxes that did not require parliamentary approval and collected fines for offenses tried before the Court of Star Chamber. They sold charters granting monopolies and other special privileges. They coerced loans from Jews and foreigners. Ultimately, Charles demanded a forced loan from ordinary subjects, imprisoning those who refused to pay. Royal officials tried to get Parliament to recognize these expansive claims of royal prerogative and worked to persuade the judges to recognize them as part of the common law itself. Meanwhile, the king's allies in the church, led by William Laud, the Archbishop of Canterbury, purged Puritans from positions of influence and used the Court of High Commission to establish conservative orthodoxy.

James and Charles's course created an alliance among Puritans, common-law lawyers, and Parliament, all claiming to defend the rights of English subjects against the machinations of the king, royal officials, rival courts, turncoat common-law judges, and conservative churchmen. In exchange for new taxes, Charles agreed to the Petition of Right in 1628, eschewing his right to forced loans and to imprison recalcitrant subjects arbitrarily. But when Parliament insisted on attacking Charles's advisors and foreign policy, matters he insisted were solely within his royal prerogative, he prorogued the assembly and, like rulers elsewhere in Europe, refused to call another. From 1629 to 1640 he ruled alone, returning to his old ways of raising money, filling the common-law courts with sympathetic judges, and jailing opponents, while his ally Archbishop Laud took even firmer control of the Church.

For more than a decade Charles's bold gamble seemed to pay off. In 1638 he won a great victory in the *Ship-Money Case*, which arose when his opponents refused to pay one of the king's special taxes, in this case an ancient feudal tax levied on five old ports in times of war, which Charles now tried to collect from the whole country despite the absence of any credible military threat. Judges from the highest common-law courts—King's Bench, Common Pleas, and the Court of

Exchequer—gathered to hear the case. The majority ruled that the common law recognized the king's prerogative to take whatever steps necessary to defend the realm and that the courts had no authority to question how he did so. The decision seemed to accept the idea that the king was above the law. The Stuarts appeared slowly to be gaining the powers claimed by monarchs elsewhere in Europe.

However, a rebellion in Scotland forced Charles to call a Parliament in 1640. This time it refused essential new taxes until Charles redressed grievances. With the cash-strapped Charles at first acquiescing, Parliament promptly impeached and attainted Charles's advisors, Archbishop Laud, and the common-law judges who had recognized the king's legal claims. (An *impeachment* consists of charges brought by the House of Commons and tried in the House of Lords; a *bill of attainder* is a law pronouncing someone guilty of a crime.) It severely restrained royal power and reformed the Church. Firmly allied with the common-law lawyers, Parliament abolished the Star Chamber and the Court of High Commission.

The hostility between Charles and Parliament grew into a bloody civil war that culminated in Charles's execution in 1649 and the establishment of a short-lived republic. But even before Charles was beheaded, Parliament and the nation were torn by bitter conflict among adherents of different religious sects, some of whom demanded complete religious freedom for all Protestants. The chaos led to a coup d'état by Oliver Cromwell, commander of the parliamentary army. In 1653 Parliament resigned its powers to Cromwell, who took the title Lord Protector. For seven years Cromwell, followed by his son Richard, governed England under the repressive Protectorate, supported by compliant Parliaments, while radical Protestants, like the great poet John Milton and the reformer John Lilburne, made futile pleas for religious toleration, freedom of the press, legal reform, and a more democratic government.

The English people reacted so strongly against the instability and repression of the Republic and the Protectorate that two years after Oliver Cromwell's death in 1658, they invited Charles I's heir, Charles II, to take the throne. Tired of disorder, Parliament followed the Stuart restoration in 1660 with laws requiring all government officials, clergymen, and schoolmasters to recognize the supremacy of the king and to adhere to all the teachings of the Church of England. They suppressed those who rejected the Church's doctrines. In 1673 they passed a somewhat softened Test Act, which required all officeholders to take the sacraments of the Anglican Church.

Charles II and his brother James II, who became king in 1685, soon renewed the conflict with their subjects. Again they allied with conservatives in the Anglican Church, who stressed the duty of English people to obey the king. No matter how much a subject opposed a royal policy, one was obligated by the principle of "nonresistance" to accept it. The Stuarts followed an unpopular pro-French foreign policy, making a secret promise to the king of France to reestablish Catholicism in Britain in exchange for French financial support. As a step in that direction, Charles pressed Parliament to establish religious toleration for Roman Catholics and "dissenters," Protestants who rejected Anglican doctrines.

In fact, Charles had no choice but to follow a pro-Catholic policy because the heir to the throne, his brother James, was a committed Catholic. Working to forge an alliance with dissenters, Charles tried to overcome aversion to Roman Catholicism, which most English people identified with England's French and Spanish enemies. But during the 1670s and 1680s Charles's political opponents, who came to be called Whigs, began to work out legal, constitutional, and philosophical arguments that would justify excluding James from succession to the throne. In his stead they favored James's oldest daughter, Mary, a Protestant who had wed the leading Protestant ruler of Europe, William of Orange, *stadholder* (protector) of the Netherlands. At the same time they urged toleration of dissenters and stronger repression of Catholics.

Challenging the line of succession to the throne, the Whigs flirted with treason. Some of the boldest among them, including the political philosopher Algernon Sidney, were executed. The Stuarts' defenders, who came to be called Tories, responded with even more extreme doctrines than "nonresistance." Some agreed with Sir Robert Filmer, a royalist during the Protestant Revolution, who argued in *Patriarcha* (1660) that monarchs received their mandates from heaven. Kings were like fathers to their subjects. Just as fathers had complete, though loving authority over their wives, children, and servants, the king had complete authority over his subjects. Others looked to the ideas of Thomas Hobbes, another royalist, who argued in his famous exegesis *Leviathan* (1651) that men entered into social compacts in order to escape the "state of nature," in which the strong and ruthless terrorized the weak. Society required the strong hand of the sovereign to control human passions and violence. By the terms of the social compact, people surrendered final authority over their lives to a sovereign in exchange for the protection of government.

Whigs warned that once again English liberty was in danger. They blasted Tories for trying to prosecute leading Whigs for treason and celebrated in the streets when the grand juries refused to indict. They rallied to defend freedom of the press and attacked royalist judges for subverting common-law protections. Whigs won some key victories in the fight, establishing landmarks of civil liberty such as recognition of the principle that defendants could not be forced to testify against themselves. Nor could juries be punished for refusing to follow a judge's instructions about the law. In 1679 Parliament passed the Habeas Corpus Act requiring judges to issue the writ on behalf of anyone who claimed he was wrongfully imprisoned. From now on jailers would have to show cause for any imprisonment; no one could be held at the arbitrary command of the government.

But the Whigs could not prevent James's accession to the throne. Remembering the chaos of the Puritan Revolution, most English people acquiesced to his coronation when Charles died in 1685. Acceptance of James II was made easier by the fact that he had not produced a male heir. It appeared that he would be succeeded by Mary and her husband William. The birth of a son, however, later dashed that expectation.

James tried desperately to force toleration upon his refractory subjects, claiming royal power to dispense with laws like the Test Act in order to bring Catholics into the government and the army. He packed the courts with those who would recognize this "dispensing power." As head of the church, he tried to bring the clergy into line, creating a new church Court of Ecclesiastical Commission to remove churchmen who opposed him. In 1687 he issued a Declaration of Liberty of Conscience, granting religious freedom to all Christian denominations in England and Scotland, ordering all Anglican clergymen to read it to their congregations.

Ironically, most Englishmen considered James's drive to establish religious toleration an attack on liberty rather than an extension of it. They saw it as a plot to reimpose Roman Catholicism, which they identified with Spanish and French despotism. They knew that James's ally Louis XIV of France had revoked the right of French Protestants to worship freely. Even Tories became frightened. The archbishop of Canterbury and six other bishops, hitherto James's allies, publicly petitioned him to withdraw his order to read the Declaration of Liberty of Conscience from the Anglican pulpits. James accused them of seditious libel, imprisoning them in the Tower of London. In June 1688 the men were acquitted in the celebrated *Trial of the Seven Bishops* and escorted through London by cheering crowds.

As excitement built during the trial, Whig aristocrats invited William of Orange to save England from Roman Catholicism. In November 1688 William landed in England with a Dutch army, soon augmented by Whigs. James prepared to oppose them, but he had alienated his backers. They refused to rally to his side, and he was forced to flee. Claiming James had "abdicated," the Tories acquiesced in this bloodless, "Glorious Revolution" of 1688. James was formally deposed and William and Mary enthroned in 1689.

The Glorious Revolution and English Constitutional Thought

On taking the throne in 1689, William and Mary agreed to a Bill of Rights reconfirming the rights that the Stuarts had denied. Englishmen could not be deprived of these rights without their consent, given through Parliament. Many were political rights that reaffirmed the independence and centrality of Parliament. The king was bound to call frequent Parliaments. He could not make or dispense with laws nor levy taxes without its consent. All subjects had the right to petition the king. The king could not punish members of Parliament for anything they said there. All Protestants had the right to bear arms "as allowed by law," and the king was forbidden to maintain a standing army in times of peace without Parliament's approval.

The Glorious Revolution marked the preeminence of the common law and established beyond doubt that the king governed under it. Formerly independent courts were now clearly subordinate to it. The rights associated with the common law had clearly triumphed; many were specifically included in the Declaration of Rights. The Declaration confirmed the right to trial by jury; one could not be subjected to excessive bail or fines, cruel or unusual punishments, nor fines or forfeitures before being convicted of a crime. The triumphant Whigs complemented the Declaration of Rights with the Toleration Act of 1689, extending freedom of worship, but not political rights, to all dissenting Protestants who accepted the divinity of Christ.

In 1694 Parliament refused to renew the system of licensing publications, which had allowed government censorship. Now a publisher could be held responsible for his words—that is, charged with "seditious libel"—only after they appeared in print. This change did not guarantee complete freedom of the press, but it did enable juries to block conviction of persuasive critics of the government. Parliament also strengthened the Habeas Corpus Act.

The Act of Settlement of 1701, by which Parliament settled the throne on the Hanoverian line, formally confirmed the practice of holding royal ministers responsible for royal acts. In effect, this act made the chief ministers of the government responsible to Parliament. It became customary for them to resign if they failed to maintain majority support in the two houses of Parliament. The Act of Settlement also made the judiciary independent by giving judges lifetime tenure unless guilty of misconduct.

Although the Tories tried to maintain the fiction that James II had abdicated, it was clear that Englishmen had overthrown their king and that Parliament had chosen a new line of monarchs. To justify the revolution, Britons had to accept the ideas that the Whigs had developed when they opposed the Stuarts in the 1680s. Toryism persisted, sustained by English people with a variety of grievances; Tories even came to power briefly between 1710 and 1714. But most Englishmen regarded Toryism with deep suspicion because its doctrines inevitably drew the Revolution into question and undermined the legitimacy of William and Mary and their Hanoverian successors. Tories denied any subversive intent, but in fact insurrections in 1715 and 1745 raised the Stuart banner.

The best and most influential statement of Whig beliefs was published after the Glorious Revolution by the great English philosopher John Locke. His *Second Treatise of Civil Government* (1690) not only built upon earlier arguments devised by Whig partisans, but it reflected new ideas developing in Europe. The Enlightenment rejected the notion that supernatural forces continued to operate in the universe. Natural laws governed, and people had to use reason to determine what they were and how they worked. Such ideas undermined claims based on divine authority and exalted human capacity for self-government.

Like Hobbes, Locke posited that people had lived in "a state of nature" before joining together in societies. People established societies and governments as they realized that they could do many things better as a group than they could individually—especially protecting their lives and property from others and resolving disagreements over property among themselves. Upon creating societies, Locke wrote, its members entered a compact to delegate lawmaking power to a "supreme Legislative," which could be a king, a legislature, or any institution agreed upon. People exchanged "natural liberty" for "civil liberty." They gave up the right to do whatever they wanted for the right to live in an ordered society.

It was crucial to define some limit to the power of the supreme Legislative, or else civil liberty would turn into slavery. So Locke argued those who entered the compact could delegate to the supreme Legislative only such powers as they had in the state of nature. There were some rights that people could not give up. No one had the right to take his or her own life, even in a state of nature, and therefore no one could surrender his right to life to the supreme Legislative. Nor did one have the right arbitrarily to take another person's life, liberty, or property. One could only protect oneself from the wrongful acts of others. Government's powers were therefore limited to promoting prosperity and to protecting life, liberty, and property. It could not deprive people of that trinity without their consent. In England this consent was given by the people's representatives in Parliament. Thus "civil liberty" meant the right to live under laws designed to protect one's life, liberty, and property from being infringed upon arbitrarily by others.

According to Locke, if the supreme Legislative violated these rules, as James II had, then the compact that created the government was broken, and the people could make a new agreement creating a new supreme Legislative. That, of course, is how the Whigs conceived of the Glorious Revolution and how they justified it.

British Liberty and the Eighteenth-Century Constitution

By the early eighteenth century, the Whig understanding of the origins and nature of government had become orthodoxy in the British realms, including the American colonies. It implied that sovereignty was located in what the English sometimes called "King-in-Parliament," a concept that combined the fact of parliamentary supremacy with the theory that the king was still the head of the state. During this period, the king chose his ministers from among aristocratic political leaders who could command a majority in Parliament. These ministers sat in the House of Lords and framed much of the legislation Parliament considered. It was customary for them to resign if they could no longer command majority support. Then positions were reshuffled to secure the necessary parliamentary majority. Sometimes this meant a radical shift in leaders and policies, sometimes only a minor one. While the king's views remained the single most important factor in public policy, he had to act through Parliament and could not impose his policies over strong opposition.

With Parliament now supreme, it was no longer clear how such documents as the *Magna Carta,* the Petition of Right, and the Declaration of Rights fully protected English liberty. These declarations had been directed to the king and specified rights that could not be taken away without *the consent of Parliament.* It was uncertain how they limited the power of Parliament, since by definition Parliament gave the people's consent to acts of government.

After the Glorious Revolution most English people no longer looked only to such documents to protect their liberty. They claimed that the whole constitution of the English government guaranteed liberty. By "constitution" they meant the fundamental structure of the system taken as a whole—the way it was "constituted." Not only did such basic ordinances as the *Magna Carta* and the Bill of Rights proclaim the rights of British subjects, but England's "balanced" government also protected liberty. In Parliament, the king, the House of Lords, and the House of Commons acted together. Each represented different elements of the community, providing the virtues of each element while checking its vices. The king, as a single chief executive, provided energy, efficiency, and a clear vision of the general welfare. The Lords provided an educated, intelligent, and conservative elite, trained to leadership and statesmanship. The House of Commons represented the ordinary people, primarily the landed gentry and wealthy townspeople, protecting their liberty and interests against the danger of an overly ambitious king or a greedy aristocracy. In turn, the conservative king and House of Lords promoted stability by checking the impulsiveness of the common people.

English people, whether in the British Isles or in America, were tremendously proud of this "balanced constitution" and the liberty it protected. However, all through the 1700s some Englishmen worried that their great system was in danger of being subverted and their liberty in danger of being lost. This fear would become the central issue in British politics in the 1760s and 1770s, and Americans would be anxious and active participants in the fight.

TIMELINE

1066   According to many eighteenth-century Englishmen, the Norman Conquest ends an age of liberty.

1154–1189   Norman Kings of England establish royal courts and lay the foundations of the common law.

1215   King John grants the *Magna Carta.*

1220s–
1290s   Kings call Councils that emerge as recognizable Parliaments by 1300.

1455–1485   Wars of the Roses, ending with the ascension of the Tudor dynasty to the throne of England.

1509–1603   Henry VIII (1509–1547) and Elizabeth I (1558–1603) utilize Parliament to break with the Roman Catholic church and establish the Church of England, and to enact wide-ranging reforms.

1603–1625	Reign of James I (beginning of the Stuart dynasty).
1606–1616	Sir Edward Coke, Chief Justice of the Court of Common Pleas (1606–1613) and King's Bench (1613–1616), expands the authority of the common-law courts.
1625–1649	Reign of Charles I.
1628	Charles I agrees to the Petition of Right.
1629–1640	Charles I rules without calling a Parliament.
1638	The Ship-Money Case (*King v. John Hampden*).
1640–1649	Charles I calls Parliament; civil war between Charles and Parliament (known as the Puritan Revolution).
1649	Charles I beheaded.
1651	Thomas Hobbes publishes *Leviathan*.
1653	Oliver Cromwell disbands Parliament.
	Cromwell declared Lord Protector of the Commonwealth.
1658	Death of Cromwell; Richard Cromwell declared Lord Protector.
1660	Stuart restoration. Charles II (1660–1685) recognized as King of England.
	Robert Filmer publishes *Patriarcha*.
1679	Habeas Corpus Act.
1670s–1680s	"Whigs" propose legislation to exclude James, Duke of York, Charles's Roman Catholic brother, from the line of succession to the throne.
1685–1688	Reign of James II.
1688	Glorious Revolution.
1689	William (1689–1702) and Mary (1689–1694) are declared King and Queen of England.
	Bill of Rights.
	Toleration Act.
1690	John Locke publishes *The Second Treatise of Government*.
1701	Act of Settlement.

FURTHER READING

For more information on the development of the common law, see T. F. T. Plucknett, *A Concise History of the Common Law* (5th ed., 1956). J. H. Baker's *An Introduction to English Legal History* (4th ed. 2002) is the fullest account but, it is detailed and complex. Norman F. Cantor's *Imagining the Law: Common Law and the Foundations of the American Legal System* (1997) is lively and iconoclastic. Peter Charles Hoffer provides a succinct overview of English courts and procedure at the time the colonies were settled in the first pages of *Law and People in Colonial America* (rev. ed., 1998).

There are many brief surveys of the great constitutional conflict of the 1600s, among them G. E. Aylmer, *A Short History of 17th Century England: 1603–1689* (1963); J. P. Kenyon, *Stuart England* (1978); and Mark A. Kishlansky, *A Monarchy Transformed: Britain 1603–1714* (1996). More detailed is Barry Coward, *The Stuart Age: England, 1603–1714* (3d ed., 2003). Conrad Russell initiated a powerful reassessment of the causes of the English civil war, stressing the desire for harmony that characterized the early Stuart period. His seminal essays are reprinted in *Unrevolutionary England* (1990). But recent studies like Kishlansky's *A Monarchy Transformed*, Coward's *The Stuart Age*, and David L. Smith's *The Stuart Parliaments, 1603–1689* (1999) make the centrality of the constitutional struggle clear. For a review of changing interpretations, see the preface to Coward's *The Stuart Age.*

J. G. A. Pocock describes the myth of an ancient, free Anglo-Saxon constitution in *The Ancient Constitution and Feudal Law* (1987), 30–55. Alan Lloyd explains what the *Magna Carta* really was about in *King John* (1973), a book aimed for a popular audience. James C. Holt's classic *Magna Carta* (2d ed., 1992) is more scholarly but quite readable. Ralph V. Turner discusses the origins, influence, and persistent reinterpretation of the Magna Carta in *Magna Carta: Through the Ages* (2003). James C. Holt has edited thought-provoking historical assessments of the *Magna Carta* and some original documents in *Magna Carta and the Idea of Liberty* (1972), which is especially suitable for student use. Whitney R. D. Jones chronicles the development of the idea of "commonwealth" in *The Tree of the Commonwealth, 1450–1793* (2000).

For the medieval origins of Parliament, consult George O. Sayles, *The King's Parliament of England* (1974). Michael A. R. Graves carries the story through *The Tudor Parliaments* (1985). Smith's *The Stuart Parliaments*, noted above, stresses the continuity between the Parliaments that met under Elizabeth and under James I, arguing that the constitutional crisis began only in the reign of Charles I. The best analysis of the relationship among the common law, parliamentary authority, and the royal prerogative in the crisis leading up to the Puritan Revolution remains Margaret Atwood Judson's classic *The Crisis of the Constitution* (1949). Students may wish to turn to the somewhat more accessible prose of J. P. Sommerville in *Royalists and Patriots* (2d ed., 1999). Another more recent consideration is Charles M. Gray, "Parliament, Liberty, and the Law" in *Parliament and Liberty*, ed. J. H. Hexter (1992). In *The Politics of the Ancient Constitution* (1993) and *Absolute Monarchy and the Stuart Constitution* (1996), Glenn Burgess argues that the constitutional crisis was merely a struggle over the relative powers of king and Parliament within a general consensus that rejected extremes.

G. P. Gooch describes the radical ideas about freedom of the press and religion that circulated during the Puritan Revolution in his classic *English Democratic Ideas in the Seventeenth Century* (1908). Barbara Shapiro describes radical efforts to reform the administration of law in "Law Reform in Seventeenth Century England," *American Journal of Legal History* 19 (October 1975): 280–312. For a more detailed discussion, see Donald Veall, *The Popular Movement for Law Reform* (1970). Leonard Levy describes the establishment of the right against self-incrimination during the seventeenth century in *Origins of the Fifth Amendment* (1958). Levy makes clear the symbiotic relationship among seventeenth-century constitutional politics; freedom of speech, press, and religion; and the common law's procedural rights. In *The Triumph of the Lawyers* (1970), Michael Landon shows how

Whig lawyers linked the common law to liberty in the conflict leading to the Glorious Revolution.

Clayton Roberts, in *The Growth of Responsible Government in Stuart England* (1966), describes how Parliament gained control of ministerial appointments. For British political culture and the constitution in the eighteenth century, see H. T. Dickinson, *Liberty and Property* (1979), and J. R. Pole, *The Gift of Government* (1983). Edmund S. Morgan offers more controversial ruminations on the rise of the idea of responsible government in *Inventing the People: The Rise of Popular Sovereignty in England and America* (1988). John Phillip Reid makes clear how central liberty was to British identity in the eighteenth century in *The Concept of Liberty in the Age of the American Revolution* (1989).

2

Colonial Origins of American Constitutionalism

Although American political ideas were essentially English, much of the American constitutional tradition developed in the colonies themselves. Because England did not have the capacity to administer her colonies closely during the first forty or fifty years of colonization, settlers were left free to develop their legal and political institutions. British influence grew after the 1660s. Political and legal institutions became more anglicized. But the colonies continued to develop a cultural and constitutional heritage of their own. Proudly claiming the rights of Englishmen, Americans identified those rights with their own legal and political institutions, which retained significant differences from England's—especially the absence of a hereditary aristocracy, a greater degree of religious liberty, and wider political participation. Less conducive to liberty was the pervasiveness of slavery in America at a time when various kinds of servitude in England were dying out. Nor were women accorded the same rights as men; they labored under severe disabilities imposed by the common law.

At first the colonies were quite independent of British authority. But by the middle of the seventeenth century the British government began to tighten its control, although administrative mechanisms remained weak. During the 150-year history of colonial British America, a customary pattern grew in which the British government regulated war, foreign policy, trade, and other external matters, while the colonial governments took care of internal concerns. Yet in the middle of the eighteenth century, the formal relationship between the colonies and the British government remained undefined.

The Legal Foundations of Government in the American Colonies

The status of the American colonies in English law was ambiguous. The English treated Native Americans as conquered people, entitled to their own laws unless specifically overridden by the king or Parliament. But where English settlers bought land from the Indians, acquired it by treaty, or simply settled in apparently uninhabited areas, they treated the land as if it were newly discovered.

According to English law, all such newly discovered territory belonged to the king, and its settlers were entitled to the laws of England. Various royal patents and charters issued to explorers and settlers during the late 1500s and early 1600s confirmed this understanding. They almost always provided that settlers would retain the same privileges enjoyed by English subjects at home. Originally, all this meant was that settlers' descendants would be entitled to the rights of Englishmen if they returned to the mother country. But Americans came to think it meant that the common law traveled with them to the New World. English legal authorities thought otherwise, but the predominant view among all but legal experts even in Britain was that the common law of England extended to the colonies.

Ultimately the British government differentiated among three types of colonies in British North America—charter, proprietary, and royal. Charter colonies were settled by companies of merchants and settlers who received formal documents from the king specifying the colony's grants, privileges, and mode of organization. Proprietary colonies were organized by individuals, called *proprietors,* who received similar grants. In both cases, the king had no direct authority to name governors or other officials, although by the eighteenth century appointees had to meet government approval. In royal colonies a charter provided for direct royal appointment of governors and other colonial officials.

The actual establishment of the first colonies was far less orderly than this careful delineation suggests. Some colonies were founded without royal authority. The most famous instance involved a group of Separatists, known to Americans as Pilgrims, who had received permission to settle on land in New England patented to the Virginia Company. Blown off course, they landed at Plymouth Rock in what is now Massachusetts, beyond the boundaries of the Virginia Company's territory. Without a legal charter, they had to establish some basis for government themselves. The result was the *Mayflower Compact* (1620), named for the Pilgrims' ship. According to its terms, the Pilgrims "solemnly and mutually in the presence of God, and of one another," agreed to "covenant and combine ourselves together into a civil body politic, for our better ordering and preservation." The colonies of Rhode Island, Connecticut, and New Haven were founded through similar agreements, as settlers left their original settlements to found new ones. In this way they acted out the Whig idea of the formation of societies and governments even before John Locke wrote his *Second Treatise of Civil Government.*

The other North American colonies were founded through charters granted to companies or individual proprietors. Royal advisors conceived of the earliest settlements as commercial enterprises to promote trade with the Indians, find precious metals, and exploit native labor to raise valuable crops for shipment to Britain and Europe. Companies of "merchant adventurers" received charters to organize these activities; of these, the charters of the Massachusetts Bay Company and the Virginia Company of London proved the most important. Besides designating the company's lands and purpose, the Massachusetts charter established a governor and an advisory council of "assistants" to run the organization, with the general stockholders to meet periodically in a "General Court." The company was empowered to make rules "not contrary to the Laws of England."

The leading stockholders of the Massachusetts Bay Company were Puritans. As they faced increasing persecution under Charles I, some decided to emigrate personally to the colony, where they would establish a godly community. In 1629 those who stayed behind agreed to let the emigrants take the charter with them and govern the company from Massachusetts itself. They selected John Winthrop as governor. He and his assistants, usually called "magistrates," were to make the rules for the colony. Winthrop was a powerful and capable leader, with a religious as well as a secular mission. He and the magistrates governed according to God's biblical ordinances. They not only made the rules to govern the colony but also enforced them as judges. They thus served much like English justices of the peace, also often called magistrates, who held both administrative and judicial authority in English communities. Despite their Calvinist commitments, the Puritans were English to the core, and from the beginning their laws and procedures mixed English precedents and biblical rules.

It soon became apparent that more general participation in decision making was necessary. Disputes arose between Winthrop and the magistrates and ordinary settlers, who claimed that the charter made the General Court the final authority in the colony. In the end, Winthrop had to give way. Without a police force or army to enforce unpopular decisions, Winthrop could secure compliance only by involving the settlers in government. Winthrop, the magistrates, and the original stockholders admitted other Puritan settlers to the General Court, and in 1634 Winthrop recognized the court's final authority and agreed to call regular meetings. Ultimately Massachusetts settlers dispersed, founding many communities. Each established local rules through town meetings, which named town officers ("selectmen") and lesser officials and sent delegates to the General Court. Political rights, however, were limited to members of the local Puritan congregation.

The merchant adventurers of the Virginia Company of London thought of their company more like similar settlements planted at the same time in Ireland. They expected to be more conquerors than colonists, to make money from trade and the exploitation of natives. Therefore the company at first attempted to govern its colony on a disciplined, military basis. But it soon became apparent that they had misjudged; Virginia's future lay in cultivation rather than conquest, and labor would have to be imported rather than native. Even before Winthrop had learned his lesson in Massachusetts, Virginia's leaders found they could not govern by fiat in a country with only the most rudimentary law-enforcement institutions. To broaden their authority, they called a yearly meeting of influential settlers, called the House of Burgesses. After two decades of chaos, the British government persuaded the courts to terminate the company's charter in 1624 on the grounds that it had not lived up to the terms. The government replaced the company charter with a royal charter in 1625, making Virginia the first royal colony. The charter called for a royal governor, who was authorized to appoint an advisory council to represent the settlers. But Virginia's settlers insisted that they could be represented only by a body that they selected themselves. Unable to secure obedience and cooperation otherwise, the governors had to give way and work with the House of Burgesses. After some hesitation, the royal authorities confirmed the legitimacy of the settlers' assembly. The Virginia government of governor, council, and assembly provided the model for royal colonies founded later in the century. Thus the English settlements made the crucial transition from companies to polities.

Other North American colonies originated in proprietary grants to royal favorites and allies, based on the king's feudal right to dispose of his lands as he wished. In 1632 Charles I issued such a grant to George Calvert, Lord Baltimore, a Catholic, who named his domain Maryland. The Calverts experienced the same conflicts with their restive settlers as their corporate predecessors, ultimately conceding legislative authority to a representative assembly. In 1662 Charles II granted a proprietary charter over land named Carolina in his honor. When the British conquered the Dutch colony of New Amsterdam in 1664, Charles granted it to his brother James, the Duke of York, who renamed it New York. James in turn granted part of his land to favorites of his own. This area ultimately became part of New Jersey. In 1681, during his drive for religious toleration in England, Charles granted a huge territory to the influential Quaker William Penn, who established Pennsylvania. Half a century later, in 1732, the British government of George II issued a proprietary charter, limited to twenty years, to James Oglethorpe, who called his new colony Georgia. To make their lands attractive to colonists, all the proprietors promised settlers the privileges of Englishmen. To make them governable, they established representative assemblies.

The First Attempt to Tighten Control over the North American Colonies

During the 1660s the British government began to tighten its control over its burgeoning empire. Parliament passed a series of Navigation Acts and customs laws designed to make the colonies fulfill their original promise as a source of wealth for English people at home. These laws gave the colonists a monopoly in the English market for their leading products. However, they required colonial products to be shipped to England or other ports in the empire, where British traders could make a profit by shipping whatever was not consumed to other purchasers. The Navigation Acts also required the colonists to secure nearly all their imports from British traders, guaranteeing them another profit. Customs laws required Americans to pay duties on imports, providing a source of revenue for the British government.

England had great difficulty enforcing the Navigation Acts and customs laws.

The colonies were virtually independent. Their governors were either selected by the colonists themselves or by a proprietor who often served his interests best by conciliating settlers. The governors, in turn, appointed local customs collectors who connived with colonial merchants to evade the unpopular laws. Massachusetts denied the authority of the British government to impose the Navigation Acts at all. The people of Massachusetts obeyed them only because they received the sanction of the General Court. The colony kept the customs revenue for itself and refused to recognize a new customs collector sent from England to enforce British authority.

In response, the British government decided to terminate the charters held by the Massachusetts Bay Company and the proprietors, and to convert Massachusetts into a royal colony over which it would have more direct authority. The government had already issued royal charters to Connecticut and Rhode Island in 1662 and 1663. The leaders of those colonies had been happy to accept them. Founded upon compacts among their settlers, the colonies' status had been shaky; their leaders readily agreed to royal charters that confirmed their existing governmental structures. These new charters obliged the colonies to obey British customs laws and forbade them from passing laws "repugnant" to those of England. Implicitly the British government could disallow such laws. In 1679 the government separated New Hampshire from Massachusetts and made it a royal colony as well.

Following the precedent set when the courts voided Virginia's charter in 1624, the government inaugurated *quo warranto** proceedings against the Massachusetts Bay Colony, charging that it had violated the company charter by passing laws repugnant to those of England. In 1684 the British government succeeded in having the charter revoked. New York also became a royal colony when its proprietor, the Duke of York, became King James II in 1685.

The drive to secure greater control over the American colonies culminated in an effort from 1685 to 1688 to establish a centralized authority to govern New York, New Jersey, and New England, at the same time that James was trying to expand the power of the monarchy in England. Claiming that royal colonies were the personal domain of the king and, unlike England, subject to the king's absolute control, James's ministers established the Dominion of New England. The Dominion was administered by the bold and overbearing Governor Edmund Andros and an advisory council. Colonial assemblies were abolished, and Andros limited towns to one meeting per year. Following James's example in England, Andros imposed religious toleration and disestablished the Puritans' Congregationalist church.

Naturally Andros's opponents in the Dominion identified with James's Whig

---

*A *quo warranto* proceeding asked by what right ("*quo warranto*") a person claiming official authority acted. It could be used to compel the forfeiture of charters whose terms had been exceeded by those acting under the charter's authority.

opponents in England and watched events there anxiously. When word of the Glorious Revolution reached America, they declared their allegiance to William and Mary, overthrew the Dominion, jailed Andros, and shipped him back to England. Massachusetts accepted a new royal charter. The charters of New York, New Hampshire, Connecticut, and Rhode Island were restored. In Maryland, the colonial assembly declared for William and Mary, overthrew the Catholic Lord Baltimore's proprietorship, and successfully petitioned the British government for recognition as a royal colony. Led by the wealthy colonial elite, settlers overthrew unpopular governors in other colonies as well. The assemblies of Massachusetts, New York, Maryland, Virginia, and South Carolina all passed imitations of the Declaration of Rights between 1691 and 1696.

Thus Americans shared the Glorious Revolution of 1688 and, like Englishmen, perceived it to have saved English liberty. Identifying the new British government with liberty and progress, colonists in every other proprietary colony also sought royal colony status, although some did not achieve it for decades. The Calverts, in fact, regained control of Maryland in 1715, when a new Lord Baltimore converted to Anglicanism. Nonetheless, by the 1760s, only the Calverts and Penns had been able to retain their proprietorships. The British government had assumed authority to name governors and colonial officials in nearly all of the colonies.

By the end of the seventeenth century, the North American colonies shared similar institutions of government. Royal charters gave the king—in reality, the Privy Council and the Board of Trade—the power to appoint governors, provincial councils, colonial judges, and attorneys general; in the royal colonies, the governors directly represented the interests of the British government. The king also had to approve governors named by the proprietors. While these governors were expected to look out for the proprietor's interests, the proprietor could not afford to alienate the British government. The governor usually nominated the council for the Board of Trade's approval. He had the power to appoint justices of the peace and some other colonial officials, although the king's ministers and the Board of Trade kept the power to fill the most important offices. The governor also had the power to call and dissolve the colonial legislature.

The provincial council, a small body of influential men in the colony, advised the governor on policy, acted as the upper house of the colonial assembly, and heard appeals from the courts. In an aristocratic era, the governor's residence was the social center of the colony, and a seat on the council carried great prestige. Members of the council could also expect material benefits, such as other good appointments for themselves and their relatives and friends. In return, they were expected to support the governor and the interests of the British government, using their prestige and connections to bolster the governor's influence over the colonial assembly.

Every colony had a representative assembly. During the eighteenth century the importance of these assemblies greatly increased. The Glorious Revolution had confirmed the principle that legitimate government required the consent of the governed, especially for the imposition of taxes. The colonial assemblies were the only place where colonists were represented, and therefore the only place where colonial governments secured the necessary consent. Because Americans elected no representatives to Parliament, and Parliament did not levy direct taxes upon Americans, more and more Americans thought of their colonial assemblies as colonial Parliaments. The assemblies themselves demanded and secured rights similar to the privileges claimed by Parliament. These included absolute freedom of speech for statements made in the assembly, freedom from arrest while the legislature was in session, and the rights to determine qualifications for members, to decide disputed elections, and to punish anyone who attacked or insulted members or the legislature as a whole.

Conflicts often erupted between assemblies and governors because the governor represented the interests of the British government or the English proprietors, while the assembly reflected the interests of the colonists who elected them. Disagreements arose over the pay of royal officials, legislation governing colonial currency, relations with Native Americans, and British demands for effective enforcement of laws governing trade and customs duties. Colonial assemblies passed laws regulating the tenure of judges; the Board of Trade disallowed them, insisting on tenure at the pleasure of the king. In wartime the British government instructed colonial governors to raise money to support the war effort; colonial assemblies often resisted. The frequency of such conflicts between governors and assemblies made Americans suspicious of the British government's intentions even before the rise of the issues that led to the Revolution.

The Rights of Englishmen in the American Colonies

Settled in the wilderness, far from England, Americans felt compelled to establish their structures of governance and to record their rights in writing. Although at first Massachusetts magistrates tried to enforce "natural equity" according to the Bible and their own consciences, the colonists almost immediately began to complain that such decisions were arbitrary. In response, the General Court worked for decades to codify the "Laws and Liberties" of Massachusetts, finally promulgating the formal document in 1648. Other New England colonies followed Massachusetts' lead. When part of present-day New Jersey became the proprietorship of West Jersey in 1676–1677, the proprietors and settlers promulgated Concessions and Agreements that listed rights. Pennsylvania replaced Penn's original framework of government with another in 1701. Besides instituting processes of government, both listed rights.

Nearly all these written frames of government included some formulation of the common law's rule that no person could be deprived of life, liberty, or property except by due process of law. Some, like the Virginia Company's Ordinance and Constitution (1621), simply required that the colonial government "imitate and follow the Policy of the Form of Government, Laws, Customs, and Manner of Trial, and other Administration of Justice, used in the Realm of *England*." Many reiterated common-law procedural rights such as the right to a jury, to a speedy and local trial, and to know the charges one faced, although not all of them were mentioned in every list. Only New Haven, committed to biblical law, repudiated such basic elements of the common law as jury trials.

Colonial assemblies gave local magistrates or justices of the peace summary power to punish infractions of many minor crimes, or *misdemeanors,* just as similar officers did in Britain. Those accused of more serious crimes were kept in custody or released on bail until a grand jury of men from the community formally indicted them. Their trials took place before county courts, called by different names in different colonies, which also adjudicated civil (noncriminal) disputes between individuals. The most serious crimes were heard in higher courts, which might also retry decisions appealed from lower courts. But despite this evidence of a common-law heritage, neither the procedures nor the substance of the common law was followed very closely before the later 1600s. Justice was rather informal, reflecting the customs of local English courts rather than the technicalities of the common-law courts. Rarely were judges trained lawyers. Before the 1660s few defendants exercised their right to a jury trial, nor did they often employ counsel. Courts did not adhere to the formal requirements of pleading in civil cases. It was the spirit of the common law, not its letter, to which Americans adhered in the early decades of settlement.

This informality may have reflected the widespread criticism of the criminal branch of English common law, especially its arcane technicalities and its harshness. In England, many offenses remained "common-law crimes," defined by obscure court precedents rather than by statute. English punishments were draconian and became more so throughout the seventeenth and eighteenth centuries. More and more crimes were punishable by death, although in practice this rigor was mitigated in a variety of ways. Bail was denied to those accused of more and more different crimes. Parliament authorized justices of the peace, usually substantial local landowners, to punish an ever-greater number of crimes summarily, without jury trials. Inquests before justices of the peace were held in private and the defendant not informed of the charges.

American colonists softened the rigors of English criminal law. Colonial assemblies continued to treat bail as a basic right, excluding only those accused of murder or treason. New Englanders patterned their punishments after those specified in the Bible, which generally were milder than those of the common law. Moreover, they eliminated English rules requiring that the property of convicted felons be forfeited, impoverishing their families. The Quaker William Penn also vigorously advocated reform of the criminal law. Unfamiliar with the technical aspects of the common law and much of its arcane substance in the early years of settlement, colonial governments enacted criminal codes to make the law known to all. In the process they drastically reduced the number of felonies. At the same time, they simplified the complicated procedures of English criminal trials. Several of the colonies legislated a right to counsel in felony cases, a reform not enacted in England until 1836. The relative informality of American courts encouraged broader participation by ordinary people, while service on juries gave them a voice in maintaining security and order.

Lacking church courts, Americans allotted jurisdiction over morals to the ordinary courts, although in some colonies churchwardens and vestrymen (parish officers) had a special obligation to bring offenders to the attention of the civil authorities. Especially in New England, enforcement of morals became one of the courts' most important duties. While New Englanders reduced the number of capital crimes against property, they increased the penalties for moral turpitude. Adultery and blasphemy became death-penalty offenses. Virginia and Maryland's treatment of moral offenses remained similar to England's more relaxed approach. Nonetheless, maintaining moral standards remained the business of government everywhere in England and North America.

After the 1660s, and especially between the 1680s and the 1720s, as communications improved and the British tightened control of the empire, the differences between the common law in England and the law in the American colonies decreased. The new royal charters issued during the period required as much consistency as possible between English and American laws. The British government instructed royal governors to promote such consistency and the colonies created court systems more similar to those of England. More newly arriving settlers and government officials were trained in law, English legal texts became more available, judges began to demand closer attention to legal forms and technicalities, and more people used lawyers to represent them in legal actions. By the middle of the eighteenth century, Americans believed themselves entitled not only to the spirit but to the letter of the common law.

Religious Liberty in the Colonies

American colonists were well aware of the conflicts that rent the motherland in the seventeenth century, and they quickly adopted as their own British ideas about liberty that grew out of the Glorious Revolution. But these ideas were augmented by an indigenous tradition that gave a special quality to the North American heritage.

Differences in religious institutions were among the most important distinctions between the American colonies and Britain. In England, people blamed religious strife for the instability that led to the Puritan Revolution and continued through the interregnum. It had precipitated the civil war, destroyed the short-lived republic, and led to the Cromwellian repression. English people had concluded that religious diversity was dangerous. Peace, harmony, and order depended upon a general consensus about religion and an established, national church that united the community.

After the Stuart restoration in 1660, these convictions had led to the suppression both of Roman Catholicism and dissenting Protestant denominations in Great Britain. Puritanism faded quickly, with the remaining Protestant dissenters and Roman Catholics forbidden from participating in public life or worshiping freely. Whigs had urged toleration of Protestant dissenters, and the passage of the Toleration Act in 1689 marked a new beginning for religious freedom in Britain. But few, if any, Englishmen suggested disestablishing the Anglican Church, Roman Catholicism remained proscribed, and Protestant dissenters were still prohibited from holding public office, although Parliament regularly passed special laws to exempt particular appointees.

The American religious tradition was radically different. Anxious to settle its North American colonies, the Stuarts had encouraged Puritans, more radical Protestant sects, and Catholics to emigrate to the New World. Puritans in New England had made their religion—what became known as Congregationalism—the established church in Massachusetts Bay. Only Puritan ministers could register marriages. Massachusetts chartered Harvard College to train a new generation of Puritan divines, providing land for its support and placing Puritan clergymen in charge. Each settlement was expected to have a single Congregational church, its minister to be paid by taxes levied on everyone in the community. Only church members were permitted to vote and hold office. The Puritans believed that God had pre-chosen a select number of people for salvation. None but these predestined "saints," identified by the already elect, could be admitted to the church and thus participate in public life.

While the Puritans came to the New World in search of religious freedom, their quest was for religious freedom for themselves, not for others. Those who challenged religious orthodoxy in Massachusetts were exiled; if they insisted on returning and continuing their agitation, they might be executed, as were several Quakers. The most famous exiles were Anne Hutchinson and Roger Williams, both driven from Massachusetts Bay in the 1630s. Hutchinson had criticized some of the doctrines promulgated by Massachusetts ministers, claiming that God spoke as clearly to her conscience as to theirs. "If God give me a gift of Prophecy, I may use it," she insisted. Roger Williams did not at first challenge orthodox doctrine so much as he challenged Puritan principles of church governance in Massachusetts. Like radical Protestants in England, Williams denied that ministers could bind all church members in matters of conscience and called for the separation of church and state. Like Hutchinson, he was ordered to leave.

Williams, Hutchinson, and others founded new communities in what became Rhode Island. Many of them ultimately articulated religious doctrines that came to be called Baptist, of which one key principle became separation of church and state. In 1644, as the battle over separation of church and state raged in England, Williams published *The Bloudy Tenet, of Persecution for cause of Conscience* in America. "It is the will and command of *God,* that . . . a *permission* of the most *Paganish, Jewish,* Turkish or Antichristian consciences and worships, bee granted to all men in all *Nations* and *Countries,*" Williams wrote, "and they are onely to bee *fought* against with that *Sword* which is only (in *Soule matters*) *able* to *conquer,* to wit, the *Sword* of *God's Spirit,* the *Word* of *God.*" In Rhode Island, there would be no established church.

Thomas Hooker did not wait for Massachusetts authorities to come calling. In 1636 he migrated to what is now Connecticut and founded Hartford. He was not as critical of Puritan orthodoxy as he was of its antidemocratic character. Connecticut maintained Congregationalism as its official, established church. It sponsored Yale College just as Massachusetts sponsored Harvard. Entitled to community support, its ministers had special privileges and responsibilities. But Hooker insisted on the absolute independence of each congregation and eliminated Puritan restrictions on political participation. Any Protestant man who met other voting qualifications could participate in public life.

By the later 1600s many people in Massachusetts chafed under Puritan intolerance. Anglicans complained to British authorities that Puritan efforts to maintain orthodoxy violated English laws. The ill-fated Dominion of New England, which abolished the Congregational establishment, was in part a response to these complaints. After the Dominion was overthrown, Congregationalism was again established in Massachusetts and Connecticut, but the colonies' leaders had to accept religious toleration as part of the agreement. In many parts of New England after 1690, people no longer looked to common religious beliefs as the cement maintaining harmony and order in the community. Especially in the commercially developing seacoast and river towns, it became more common to believe that harmony and order depended on prosperity.

The Catholic proprietors of Maryland naturally espoused religious toleration. Committed to making Maryland a refuge for persecuted English Catholics, the Calverts nonetheless governed an Anglican majority. Proscription of Protestants had never been an option; the Calverts' main concern became maintaining toleration for Catholics. When Puritans, exiled from royalist Virginia, arrived in Maryland in 1649, Maryland's colonial assembly—at that time still predominantly Catholic—passed an act guaranteeing religious toleration to all who believed in the divinity of Jesus Christ. But Maryland was no Rhode Island. The Maryland Toleration Act still provided "That whatsoever person or persons within this Province . . . shall deny the holy Trinity . . . shall be punished with death. . . ." Moreover, after the Glorious Revolution, Maryland's Protestants succeeded in establishing the Church of England and depriving Roman Catholics of some of their rights.

Like the New England colonies and Maryland, Pennsylvania was founded in part as a refuge for those facing religious persecution in England. Its proprietor,

William Penn, was a Quaker ally of the Catholic James II, who promoted religious toleration in his effort to solidify his hold on the throne. Penn, who strenuously campaigned for toleration in England, insisted that the principle be applied in Pennsylvania. The state's Body of Laws of 1682 provided that no one who professed a belief in one God "shall in any case be molested or prejudiced for his, or her Conscientious persuasion or practice," nor be required to maintain any religious establishment contrary to his or her belief. Penn's 1701 Charter of Privileges guaranteed religious freedom to all who believed in "*One* Almighty God" and the right to hold public office to all Christians.

By the mid-1700s, the Church of England was the established church in New York, New Jersey, Delaware, Maryland, Virginia, the Carolinas, and Georgia. As in Massachusetts and Connecticut, local taxes and rents from lands supported ministers and churches, this time Anglican. As in New England, only ministers of the established church were allowed to register marriages. Anglican ministers were in charge of colony-supported colleges, such as William and Mary in Virginia and King's College (later Columbia) in New York; only Anglicans were engaged as teachers. Students were required to attend Anglican services. Vestrymen were responsible for church maintenance and for keeping an eye on community morals.

Nonetheless, even in colonies with established churches, religious toleration was the rule. Far more religious diversity existed in all the North American colonies than in England. Anxious to increase their population, the colonies welcomed immigrants from any nation, and religious persecution was a prime factor motivating people to make the dangerous and wrenching journey to a new world. By the early 1700s, New York, New Jersey, Pennsylvania, Delaware, Virginia, and the Carolinas were polyglot colonies of Anglicans, Dutch Reformed, Presbyterians, Huguenot, and Quakers from England, Scotland, Ireland, Holland, Germany, France, and even Sweden. Moreover, every predominating religious denomination in one colony was a minority somewhere else. Outside of New England, the dream that an imposed uniformity would create harmony never took hold. On the contrary, any attempt to suppress dissent only led to conflict and instability. However, toleration of religion did not imply toleration of irreligion, especially in the seventeenth century. Toleration extended at most to those who believed in one God and more often was limited to Christians or even only to Protestants. Blasphemy remained a crime. Even Pennsylvania made it illegal for people to work on Sunday "that they may better dispose themselves to read and hear the Holy Scriptures of truth at home, and frequent . . . meetings of religious worship abroad. . . ." Every colony had laws punishing immoral behavior, and the definition of morality rested on religious precepts about sin. During the eighteenth century enforcement of some of these laws waned in various parts of the colonies. But in the 1740s a far-reaching religious revival, the Great Awakening, swept over much of British North America, reinvigorating demands that the state enforce spiritual and moral values.

At nearly the same time as the Great Awakening, the European Enlightenment's rationalist, anticlerical ideas reached America. Enlightenment thinkers turned to science rather than to religion to understand the world. Scornful of mere "superstition," these philosophers called for greater freedom of inquiry and thought. Deism, the idea that God had created an orderly universe governed by natural laws with which he did not interfere, grew attractive to many American intellectuals, who urged the state to abstain from enforcing religious beliefs.

Political Rights and Representation

The North American colonies differed most radically from Britain in the area of political rights. The right to vote for members of the British Parliament was severely restricted. Only men taking Church of England sacraments could vote or hold office, although Parliament often gave prominent dissenters special dispensations. Towns, or "boroughs," generally required their own property or other voting qualifications, either specified by their charters or established by custom. The distribution of parliamentary representation had hardly changed since the Middle Ages. So-called "rotten boroughs" therefore retained representation although they had virtually disappeared. Great cities that had developed in modern times, like Manchester and Leeds, elected no members of Parliament. Their residents, if they met the religious and property qualifications, could only vote for members elected by the counties. The qualification for voting in the counties was ownership of a forty-shilling freehold, another tradition that dated back to the Middle Ages. Forty shillings was no longer very much money and the definition of what qualified as freehold property had become progressively looser. Nonetheless, relatively few Englishmen met the requirement—shrinking from about 20 to less than 15 percent of adult males over the course of the eighteenth century.

In North America conditions encouraged a much broader suffrage. In the early years of settlement, it had been necessary to involve male settlers in government to encourage obedience to law. In the following decades, however, the restriction of voting rights to church members in Massachusetts began to narrow the electorate significantly. Modifying the rigid requirements for church membership with what Puritans called the "half-way covenant" expanded the electorate somewhat but did not reverse the trend. By the mid-1600s a narrow aristocracy monopolized political power in Virginia as well. In both cases the result was growing restiveness among the excluded. In New England Andros sought support from those disfranchised under Puritan domination; in Virginia exclusion from policy-making contributed to an outright insurrection (Bacon's Rebellion) in 1676. The scare they experienced under Andros encouraged Massachusetts leaders to eliminate Puritan voting restrictions after the Glorious Revolution, and Virginia's political system opened up at the same time.

After the 1690s no American colony limited political rights to members of an established church as in England. All extended political privileges to Protestants, while several extended them to all Christians and even to non-Christians who believed in a single creator. As improved communications drew the British empire together in the late 1600s and early 1700s, Americans tended to adopt English property qualifications for voting. Yet the right of suffrage remained much more widespread than in England, because in America land was cheap and held in fee simple, qualifying owners as freeholders. In contrast to Great Britain, most colonial white male heads of households could vote.

Members of colonial assemblies were expected to live in the districts they represented, unlike in Great Britain, where there was no such requirement. Indeed, conflict brewed in many American colonies between long-settled areas and newly settled ones, whose residents demanded reapportionment of the colonial assemblies to reflect changes in population. These controversies encouraged Americans to think of assemblymen as representing the interests and opinions of those who elected them, unlike in Great Britain, where the idea developed that each member of Parliament represented the whole realm rather than his particular constituents.

By the early 1700s both Britain and America had in practice developed fairly wide-ranging freedom of political expression. Newspapers and pamphlets circulated widely—more so in Britain, but the American colonies were catching up—and they freely criticized political leaders and policies as long as they did not traduce the king himself. One who too strenuously advocated the old Tory principle of nonresistance might get into trouble. Such ideas implicitly questioned the legitimacy of the monarchs who had replaced James II and his immediate heirs. But in both Britain and America crowds regularly gathered to protest government decisions, engaging in limited and controlled violence. London crowds even roughed up members of Parliament and government ministers. Sometimes such protests effected changes in government policy. In Britain, the government occasionally called out soldiers, who read the Riot Act, which authorized them to fire on demonstrators who did not immediately disperse. In America there generally were no soldiers to call out, encouraging greater attention to public opinion.

The practices of political freedom ran ahead of the law. Technically, pamphleteers who criticized the government could be charged with seditious libel. According to the common law, freedom of the press meant only the right to publish without prior censorship; both the author and the publisher were criminally liable for anything that brought the government into disrepute. The truth of any charges the critic had levied was no defense. The law recognized no right for masses of people to petition Parliament, to organize public pressure upon it, and especially to invite violence by public demonstrations. In fact, such efforts encroached on parliamentary privilege, implying that Parliament was not the voice of the people. As colonial assemblies came to think of themselves as little Parliaments, they claimed similar privileges.

But the law was rarely enforced. When it was, those accused charged their prosecutors with attacking British liberty. The most famous such case in the colonies was that of John Peter Zenger, hauled into court in New York in 1735 on a charge of seditious libel. Allied with the popular party that opposed New York's royal governor, William Cosby, Zenger's newspaper had blasted away at Cosby's tyrannical inclinations, charging him with a series of malfeasances. Unable to persuade a grand jury to indict him, the colony's attorney general finally used an alternative procedure, bringing an "information" against Zenger for publishing "false, scandalous, malicious, and seditious" libels. Zenger and his allies lambasted this procedure as subverting the rights of Englishmen.

At his trial, Zenger's lawyer, Andrew Hamilton, charged Cosby with attacking freedom of the press, arguing that Zenger could not be convicted if the facts he had published were true. The judge responded that truth was no defense to a charge of seditious libel. Furthermore, whether Zenger's attacks on Cosby had been libelous was a matter of law, for the judge to decide, not the jury. The jury's only responsibility was to determine whether Zenger had in fact published the libel. If he had, the jurors must find him guilty. Although the judge's interpretation of the law was correct, Hamilton denounced it and urged the jurors to acquit Zenger if they believed his charges true. To the dismay of Cosby and the delight of most New Yorkers, the jury did so. The Zenger trial illustrated the gap between the law governing freedom of speech and of the press, and the popular understanding of it. With juries reflecting the popular view, it was virtually impossible to convict polemicists of seditious libel in America.

Enlightenment thinkers reinforced liberal practices in the mid-eighteenth century. These philosophers believed free speech to be essential for the rational discovery of truth and hence for the reformation of society. Their views coincided with those of many Britons who were calling for social and political reform. These citizens criticized the landed aristocracy's dominance of British life and denounced the strange rules that made the common law unintelligible to ordinary people and distorted British political institutions. These distortions included the malapportionment of Parliament and the denial of political rights to dissenters. Many American leaders, watching from a distance, sympathized with the reformers.

But despite the breadth of political participation in the American colonies, they by no means constituted little democracies. A significant number of propertyless men, including indentured servants and slaves, nearly all Native Americans, and all women remained without the franchise. Moreover, in early America the model of governance was the family, with the head of the household—the patriarch—holding final authority. Magistrates and governors held a similar position *vis-à-vis* the governed. Such notions of authority and deference persisted in many places into the Revolutionary era.

The Status of Women in the American Colonies

Patriarchal notions of authority inevitably affected the status of women in England and the colonies. The common law may have been the palladium of liberty for English*men*, but it placed severe restrictions on the rights of English*women*.

In law, women were treated much as children or slaves. Originally the common law was concerned especially with disputes over landed property, and it remained so well into the nineteenth century. Landed property among the rich and powerful in England tended to be held in families, with limits imposed on the ability of its owners to dispose of it outside the family through sale, gift, or inheritance. An important part of marriage was the merging of estates. In the common-law view, a married woman's identity merged into that of her husband, who in turn was perceived to be the head of a household that included his wife, children, servants, and all other dependents. The common law spoke of a married woman's identity as having been "covered" by her husband's; she was a *feme covert*. Judges and lawyers referred to this principle as *coverture*.

Developed with an eye towards the control of landed property, coverture was compatible with the economic realities of early modern Britain and America. In this age the family, rather than the individual, was the principle economic unit. Husband, wife, and children together worked a farm or ran a tavern. The law sought to establish a single voice for families' economic decision making. Given the patriarchal nature of society, it was assumed that the voice would be the husband's.

A *feme covert* had no right to hold property separately from her husband. Any personal property she brought into the marriage became his, as did any money she earned. Her husband also had the right to all income from her real property (Real property is real estate and property treated as real estate.) She had no right to dispose of property or make contracts. Legally, family decisions were his alone to make. Like the rest of his household, his wife had to obey. A husband was conceded the same right to chastise his wife physically that he had to chastise his children. Full divorces, entitling parties to remarry, were nearly impossible to secure, even in cases of outright desertion. More common were divorces *a mensa et thoro* (divorce "of bed and board"), a separation that did not dissolve the marriage. Although this quasi-divorce required men to support separated wives, it presumed that they would retain control of most of the property and the children, whom the law considered the father's dependents rather than the mother's.

Although most Americans distrusted equity law—the law of the chancery courts—as a rival of the common law, equity was far friendlier to women's interests. In some colonies equity was enforced in special courts; in others by the same judges who enforced the common law. Equity's rules and procedures softened the rigors of the common law. For example equity courts enforced prenuptial contracts called "marriage settlements," by which husbands agreed to allow wives to retain control of their property. They also enforced "dower" rights, which gave widows a "life estate," a right to property limited to the life of the holder, in proportion to their husbands' real property. Moreover, a proportion of a man's personal property became his widow's absolutely, to do with as she pleased.

The proportion of a man's property subject to his wife's dower right differed from colony to colony. Only Connecticut eliminated dower completely. Definitions of real and personal property could make a significant difference to what women acquired when their husbands died. Some colonies, for example, considered slaves to be personal property and others considered them to be real property. Since women had absolute dower rights to the former and only a life estate in the latter, the rule made a great difference in a widow's economic security. Husbands could not sell their wives' dower rights or divest them in any other way. If a man wanted to sell some of his property, he had to persuade his wife to surrender her dower right in it. While it was difficult for a woman to refuse, many colonies required her to assure a judicial official privately that she was doing so of her own free will.

Despite the rigors of the common law, some American women were active in commercial life independently of their husbands. Many women engaged in household industries such as spinning, weaving, and dressmaking. Women were often responsible for marketing the surplus production of their gardens and farms, and some worked in service occupations—for example as midwives, who attended births, or as healers. In the early years of settlement, women seem to have brought suits to collect unpaid debts for services they rendered or goods they sold. Many colonies passed laws allowing married women to engage in trade as if they were single, especially in cases of desertion. Moreover, women sometimes represented their husbands in commercial transactions. But despite these facts, the common law clearly placed women in positions subordinate to men. Even unmarried *femes sole* rarely brought lawsuits on their own behalf. Married women nearly always depended on their husbands to do so. In cases where their interests or desires diverged, there was little wives could do.

Given their generally weak legal position, it is not surprising that women played no recognized role in public life. Even single women and widows, who were able to act on their own behalf in law, were denied the privilege of voting, holding office, or sitting on juries.

Although women's legal rights were severely restricted everywhere, these rules were applied more rigorously in some colonies than in others. In New England such rules reinforced the generally patriarchal Puritan society. In early Virginia and Maryland, however, there were few women, and they tended to outlive their husbands. Despite the restrictions of the law, in the early colonial years many women acquired a good deal of property and independence when they were widowed and remarried, often protecting their property with marriage settlements. But as colonial law became more anglicized in the late seventeenth and early eighteenth centuries, the common-law rules of coverture tended to be enforced more strictly everywhere.

Unfree Labor and Slavery

The terrible irony of the American colonies was that a people so proud of their own liberty held slaves. In the New England colonies, the Puritans and Pilgrims attempted to create ideal communities in the wilderness, based on an ethic that was in many ways anti-commercial. But in the early decades of settlement, the more southerly colonies of Maryland, Virginia, and the Carolinas were an outlying part of a great Caribbean colonial system. There planters used slave labor on large plantations to produce exotic goods of great value, including tobacco, rice, indigo, and sugar, for export to the mother country. These colonies were from their beginnings part of an international trading and financial system. Hoping to duplicate the large plantations of the Caribbean, southern colonists settled on the rich land along navigable rivers rather than in towns. But large-scale agricultural production on expansive plantations required labor, and the American colonies were short of workers. Settlers who emigrated to the southern colonies with their own economic resources wanted their own land, not a difficult and tedious job on someone else's.

In the first decades of the Chesapeake settlements, planters tried to solve the labor problem with white "indentured servants." An indenture was a well-established type of labor contract, whereby a worker agreed to serve an employer for a specified period in exchange for sustenance and other benefits. Such an arrangement implied a subordinate and dependent status, even more than the usual employer-employee relationship, which was still referred to legally as one between "master and servant." Parents, for example, often indentured children as apprentices to learn trades. Many male workers who emigrated to America entered into indentures for a period of years in exchange for passage to the New World and sustenance thereafter.

Indentured servitude was more severe in the colonies than in England. In England, law and custom limited masters' control over servants; Virginia and Maryland lacked these constraints. Indentured service lasted much longer than in England—often seven years. Masters extorted more intensive labor and regularly resorted to physical punishments. In England an indenture could not be transferred to another master without the servant's consent. But in colonies like Virginia, indentures could be bought and sold freely, regardless of the servant's wishes; in this way indentured servitude prefigured one of the key elements of slavery. In the early decades of settlement, some Africans seem to have served as servants for a term of years; by the 1640s some had already been released from service. But other Africans were being held as slaves for life.

Indentured servitude proved an unsatisfactory solution to the labor problem. Viciously exploited, indentured servants were sullen and unwilling workers. As the population increased after the 1650s, it became easier for disgruntled servants to run away, melting into distant communities. As a result workers could begin to challenge the authority of masters who made unacceptable demands. It became more common for servants to go to court to force masters to live up to agreements, or even to try to abrogate indentures due to mistreatment. Equally serious, once free of indentures, workers stayed on as dissatisfied wage laborers or gathered into rebellious frontier communities, hoping to establish their own plantations. Jealous of the monopoly the richest settlers had secured over the best land, they challenged the authority of the planter elite. Finally, the supply of indentured servants was limited, or, as economists put it, "inelastic"; one could not simply acquire more indentured servants as one needed them. Southern planters had to compete with potential masters in Great Britain and other colonies, as well as with the growing market for free labor in Great Britain and the northern colonies. The supply of slaves, in contrast, was "elastic." If demand increased, higher prices would lead slave traders to import more of them.

By the 1660s Virginia and Maryland planters, like those of the Caribbean islands, turned to African slavery instead of indentured servitude. South Carolina, newly settled by slaveholding Caribbean emigrants in the 1660s, turned to slavery immediately. It had become clear that slaves were better investments than indentured servants. Slavery was perpetual instead of limited to a term of years, and children inherited the slave status of their mothers. An enslaved work force could be coerced into maximum production at minimum cost. While a runaway indentured servant could blend into a distant community, an African stranger would everywhere be suspected of being an escaped slave. From a social standpoint, African slavery would reduce tensions among whites, replacing the ruthless exploitation of white workers with that of an alien race.

It was the racial distinctiveness of black Africans that made slavery possible, enabling liberty-loving Englishmen to deny rights to Africans that they claimed for themselves. Precedents for race-based slavery in Spanish culture and in the Spanish, Portuguese, and Dutch colonies of the Caribbean and South America provided a pattern that North American colonies could emulate. However, racial categories were quite fluid at first; it was not until it became essential to justify holding human beings in perpetual slavery that white settlers constructed strict categories of race, attributing fixed character traits to them. In doing this, they drew upon their experience with gender—a human categorization that had long been held to define character.

By the 1660s the colonies were developing slave codes unlike anything in English law, based on the codes of British colonies in the Caribbean. The southern colonies slowly changed from a society with slaves into a "slave society"—a society in which slavery defined and shaped all other institutions. Moreover, the southern colonies adapted slavery to a new, commercial economic system, creating a peculiarly harsh institution. In most slave cultures, slavery was a personal status in a hierarchical society. Slaves were at the bottom of these societies, but they remained human beings in a web of community relationships. But British colonial slavery, even more than Spanish and Portuguese slavery, depersonalized the slave and made him or her property to be disposed of, almost like any other property. A slave was a unit of production and trade, like a horse, mule, or an ox. Human relationships could and did develop between slaves and masters, especially where slaves worked as household help or on small plantations. But except for a few basic protections, the law treated slaves as property.

Slaves were denied the right to own or dispose of property or to make contracts. Southern colonial law made no provision for slave marriages and gave slave parents no rights to their children, although laws forbade sale of the very young. The slave codes granted broad discretion to masters to use physical force to discipline slaves. Slaves were essentially unprotected by law. No slave could sue in court for an attack on his person or for damage to his possessions. Although murdering a slave was punishable by death, it is questionable whether the punishment was ever enforced.

Colonial laws rigidly circumscribed slaves' autonomy. They could not carry weapons, gather in groups, or travel without passes. They were subject to inquisition by any white person; it was a crime physically to resist any command or assault. At the same time, the law in effect delegated public authority to masters, requiring them to maintain order, enforce curfews, prevent slave gatherings, and punish runaways. In the 1700s a series of scares about slave uprisings led to a general tightening both of the laws and their enforcement. Colonial assemblies made it illegal to educate slaves or to consort with them. Pass laws and curfews were made more stringent. When slave plots, real or imagined, were uncovered, retribution was swift and brutal. Every slave was suspect and at risk. After discovering a slave conspiracy called the Stono Rebellion in 1740, for example, South Carolinians shot and hanged fifty alleged plotters in five days.

Slavery spread northward in the late 1600s and early 1700s, despite taxes designed to keep slave traders out. By the early 1700s about one half the families in the area around New York City owned slaves. In the 1770s, nearly 15 percent of New Yorkers were black, a proportion higher than that of the African–American population of the United States today. By the early 1700s New York and New Jersey had established slave codes similar to those in the South. These codes authorized masters to punish misdemeanors and petty offenses "att Discretion," providing summary slave courts to try more serious crimes. The New York code even authorized slaves convicted of murder to be tortured "as the aggravation and Enormity of their Crime . . . shall meritt." But even New York had not been transformed into a "slave society."

Except in New York, neither actual conditions nor the laws governing slavery in the North were as harsh as in the South. Even in the southern states the practice of slaveholding, if not the laws themselves, became more humane as time progressed. In the North, slavery augmented free labor and indentured servitude, instead of replacing it. Few northerners owned more than one or two servants, who generally worked alongside masters or as household servants. Moreover, the Great Awakening both Christianized the slaves and humanized many of their masters. Northern slave codes generally recognized slave marriage and thus protected slave families. They allowed greater freedom of movement, and the restrictions on movement that did exist were not rigidly enforced. Punishments were milder and more humane than those imposed by southern slave codes. The laws did not ban slave education. In New England and Pennsylvania it was not unusual to teach slaves basic reading, writing, and math.

Nonetheless, slaves in the North were still essentially without rights. Just as in the South, they could not sue to protect themselves or their possessions and were unlikely to receive the protection of the law. Even in enlightened Pennsylvania, a traveler wrote in the 1750s: "A man who kills his negro is, legally, punishable by death, but there is no instance here of a white man ever having been executed for this crime."

African slavery made race the determinant factor in status. Free black people were an anomaly. Yet, by the eighteenth century a significant number of "free persons of color" existed in the North American colonies—mixed-race children of masters and slave women, who might be freed by their fathers; slaves and their descendants who had been manumitted, or freed, by their masters; and the descendants of black indentured servants who had completed their terms before slavery became the norm. In some cities, mixed-race families began to establish relatively successful places for themselves, representing the beginning of a mulatto elite that persisted through the Civil War.

Most whites regarded free African Americans with ambivalence. They were often suspected of fomenting dissatisfaction among slaves. Many colonies put obstacles in the way of freeing slaves. Laws often required the master to post high bonds guaranteeing that the new freedman would not become an economic burden on the community. In many localities, especially in the South, New York, and New Jersey, free blacks were subject to restrictive laws and barred from voting, holding office, and serving in the militia. But this was by no means true everywhere. Even in the South there were regions where a free person of color was recognized as sharing the rights of citizenship with his or her neighbors.

Imperial Relations

After the 1680s the British government paid much closer attention to affairs in the American colonies than it had before. But this attention took the form of a relatively loose general supervision rather than a tight administration. It was generally accepted in England that final authority over all colonial matters lay in the British government—that Parliament could make regulations to govern the colonies directly if it wished. Supervisory control lay with a group of royal officials called the Board of Trade, which reported to the Privy Council (the chief ministers of the royal government) and to Parliament when called upon to do so. But in fact the sinews of the empire were rather flaccid. Ultimately, the system left Americans believing that they had largely independent authority over local matters, a belief encouraged by British constitutional traditions.

The Board of Trade, established in 1696, was the key institution superintending colonial affairs in London. Its mandate was to take care that the empire was governed properly, serving as the conduit between the colonial governors and the Privy Council and Parliament. It had a good deal of influence upon appointments in the colonies. Receiving regular reports from the governors, the Board advised the British government on colonial affairs. It informed the governors of British colonial policy and instructed them to carry it out.

Doing so was no easy task. The governors had much less influence with the colonial assemblies than the British ministry had in Parliament. They had less patronage to offer and less social prestige. At the same time, America's broader suffrage made the assemblies more subject to popular opinion than was Parliament. Like Parliament, the colonial assemblies controlled taxation and thus the financial resources available to the governor and other royal officials. Customs duties went directly to the British treasury, which doled them out to support some expenses of colonial administration. The assemblies never allotted enough money to pay for the rest, or even for the salaries of the governor and other royal officials. Governors were constantly instructed to have the colonial assemblies establish a permanent tax revenue to make up the difference, but the assemblies stubbornly refused. In the 1720s the exasperated Privy Council prepared to submit legislation to Parliament levying taxes on the colonies; it never carried through its threat.

To maintain a degree of uniformity in the empire and to protect the interests of the mother country, most colonial governors were supposed to send all laws passed in America to the Board for review. (The charters of Maryland, Connecticut, and Rhode Island exempted them from this requirement.) The Board could recommend that laws be disallowed, either as inconsistent with English laws or contrary to the empire's interests. Technically, the determination was recorded as made by the king with the advice of the Privy Council; in reality, the Board itself made the decision. Court decisions also could be appealed from colonial courts to the Privy Council sitting in a judicial capacity; the Council was authorized to reverse decisions repugnant to English law and to overturn laws upon which such decisions were based. Thus a dissatisfied colonist could appeal to authorities in London to override a colonial law or a court judgment as inconsistent with English law. By the early 1700s some were persuading local courts to overturn laws on the same grounds. In effect, Americans were getting experience with what would become known as judicial review. But colonists saw this as a way to evade the authority of their legislatures rather than a protection of liberty; they opposed the idea and used their authority over judicial salaries to discourage it.

Beginning in the 1680s, British economists began to see the burgeoning economic development of the American colonies as endangering British interests, and the British government attempted to bar colonial assemblies from legislating on an increasing number of subjects. In many areas, colonial laws were automatically suspended for two years, while the Board of Trade and the Privy Council decided whether to permit them to go into effect. The Board of Trade nullified nearly four hundred laws passed by colonial legislatures, sometimes to Americans' great displeasure. It is unlikely that any American denied that Parliament too could nullify colonial enactments and hear appeals from colonial courts. When Ireland did so, Parliament responded with a Declaratory Act affirming that it could pass laws "of sufficient force and validity to bind" the recalcitrant island. The British government never tried to *impose* a law on a colony, however. Instead it continued to rely on governors to persuade the colonial assemblies to pass laws that the government wanted and to sidetrack proposals that it opposed. Occasionally governors and other royal officials argued that colonial assemblies were obligated to obey legislative proposals included in the governors' instructions, but the colonists never agreed. In the 1740s Parliament twice considered and rejected legislation giving royal instructions the force of law in the colonies. As a consequence, the colonists assumed that local governing institutions—assemblies, governors, and governors' councils—had the sole power to originate laws regulating colonies' internal affairs. These laws were seen as subject to review by British authorities but not to wholesale replacement.

Despite its general restraint, the British government was quite active in two areas: war and trade. Foreign relations were in England's control. When war broke out, the American militias were made adjuncts of the British army and the colonists helped to supply money and ammunition. But even in this case, colonial assemblies made the arrangements, raising, arming, supplying, and paying military units. Often they tried to control how colonial militias were used, getting into nasty squabbles with their governors and with British military officials. They almost always raised fewer troops than British officers requested and enlisted them for shorter periods of time.

England also clearly controlled trade. Indeed, it was trade in which the British were primarily interested. In the seventeenth and eighteenth centuries, political economists adhered to a commercial philosophy now called *mercantilism*. This philosophy assumed a finite amount of wealth in the world. Nations grew strong and their people prosperous in direct proportion to the amount of the world's wealth they possessed. Ideally, governments promoted and channeled economic activities, and colonies existed to enrich their mother countries.

The British government acted on these suppositions by trying to control the trade and production of its colonies, as well as aspects of colonial financial policy. British officials began to recognize that they had acquired a great and valuable empire, and slowly they adapted existing government institutions to administer it. Through parliamentary legislation, Board of Trade regulation, and nullification of colonial laws inconsistent with British policy, the British government tried to establish a mercantile trading system. In this system the colonies produced agricultural goods for export to Great Britain, while importing finished goods from the mother country and enriching Britain's manufacturers and merchants. The government collected duties on this trade. Any trade with places outside the empire had to go through English middlemen. The government gave monopolies over trade in valuable produce to companies of English merchants, such as the East India Company, which controlled the sale of tea throughout the empire.

All goods produced in the empire had to be transported by British ships, English or colonial.

To carry out these policies, Parliament passed a series of Navigation Acts to regulate trade between the colonies and other parts of the world. It also passed laws barring the production of manufactured goods, such as hats and iron, that might compete with those made in Great Britain. It imposed customs duties and regulated trade with Native Americans. Until the 1760s no one questioned its right to pass such laws, although Americans often criticized their wisdom and fairness.

At the same time, the British tried to prevent colonial financial policy from damaging British interests. Because British coin was rare in the colonies, some, especially the New England colonies and entrepreneurial Virginia, devised creative ways of augmenting metallic currency. Virginia printed paper money based on tobacco or other products. Massachusetts created a "public bank," whose notes circulated like money. The New England colonies paid for goods with notes promising payment later when taxes came in. All sorts of private notes—promises of one person to pay money on the demand of another—circulated as well. They could be assigned to a third party who could assign them to yet another. All these notes circulated like money. The value of such currency and notes fluctuated and was always less than the value of British sterling. British creditors complained that they were unable to collect debts in sterling in colonial courts and that colonial assemblies passed laws excluding slaves and land from the assets that could be seized for nonpayment. In response, the Board of Trade futilely instructed governors to prevent the passage of laws creating paper money.

Parliamentary legislation was somewhat more effective. Parliament passed laws regulating the value of foreign coin, making land and slaves liable for sterling debts, and banning private banks from issuing banknotes. With the Currency Act of 1751, it forbade the New England colonies from issuing promissory notes. The laws provided a basis for the Board of Trade to disallow paper money laws passed by the assemblies against the governors' instructions. Parliamentary legislation and the political acumen of royal governors in New England stemmed the demand for paper currency there, but British officials were unable to stop Virginia from relying on its paper-money system. The House of Burgesses continued to pass legal tender acts, and the governor was often forced to sign them in order to get cooperation on other matters. In 1758, for example, Virginia's assembly passed a law authorizing vestries to pay the salaries of their Anglican clergymen in paper currency instead of in tobacco, at the artificially low rate of two pennies per pound of tobacco owed. In 1760 the Board of Trade and Privy Council disallowed the law, and in 1763, Reverend James Maury sued for his back pay in tobacco. In *The Parson's Cause* young Patrick Henry argued that the Privy Council had exceeded its authority by disallowing a beneficial law. Henry cited Locke as authority that governments were restricted to acting for the good of their people and could never act to their detriment. The result again demonstrated the local jury's ability to frustrate the enforcement of unpopular public policy. Although the jury could not accept Henry's legal argument, it limited its award to the infuriated clergyman to one penny.

Colonial complaints not withstanding, a system of trade regulations benefiting Great Britain seemed a fair exchange for the protection the British army and navy provided against Spain and against the French and their Native American allies in Canada. To represent their interests before the Board of Trade and Parliament, the colonies sent or hired agents. These agents lobbied the government to modify customs duties, to shape trade laws in colonial interests, and to sustain colonial laws against challenges before the Board of Trade; the lobbyists provided the informal grease that kept the wheels of empire turning. Conversely, the officials responsible for administering the empire were flexible and sympathetic to colonial interests. It was widely accepted in England that the empire's prosperity rested upon the colonists' management of their own affairs.

Conceding Parliament's right to pass trade regulations, however, did not mean that Americans obeyed them. Disgusted by arbitrary and extortionate enforcement of the laws by corrupt officials, American merchants regularly avoided British customs duties and traded illicitly with the French and Spanish Caribbean islands. To smooth their operations, they bribed the all-too-willing customs officers. If caught, the smugglers were entitled to jury trials in their home communities. They were rarely convicted.

In reality, British authorities and Americans had developed different ideas about how governmental authority was arranged in the British empire. The British government believed that it was supreme in all matters, but that it had not exercised this supremacy in areas better dealt with by the colonial assemblies. Americans believed that Parliament had not interfered in domestic colonial affairs because it recognized that Americans could give consent to such legislation only in their own assemblies, where they were represented. Without thinking very much about it, Americans had come to believe that the British empire was constituted in a way that divided authority. They presumed a federal system, with the British government taking care of imperial concerns like war and trade and the colonial government handling local matters. Therefore, when the British government began to try to exercise more control after 1763, Americans accused it of attempting to change the constitution of the empire.

TIMELINE

1606	Charter granted to the Virginia Company of London to found colonies in North America.
1607	First permanent English settlement in North America at Jamestown in Virginia.

1619	House of Burgesses is established in Virginia.
	First Africans sold as slaves in North America, at Jamestown.
1620	Mayflower Compact.
	Pilgrims settle at Plymouth in Massachusetts.
1625	Virginia becomes a royal colony.
1628	Settlement of Massachusetts Bay.
1632–1634	Maryland patented (1632) and settled (1634) as a proprietary colony.
1634	John Winthrop agrees to meetings of the General Court in Massachusetts.
1636–1638	Roger Williams and Anne Hutchinson found Rhode Island.
1636	Thomas Hooker founds Connecticut.
1648	The General Court promulgates the *Laws and Liberties* of Massachusetts.
1649	Maryland Toleration Act.
	Parliament passes the first Navigation Act.
1660s	First slave codes established in the Chesapeake colonies.
1660–1663	Parliament passes various Navigation Acts.
1662	Carolina established as a proprietary colony.
1662–1663	Connecticut and Rhode Island accept royal charters, becoming royal colonies.
1664	New York established as a proprietary colony.
1679	New Hampshire separated from Massachusetts and chartered as a royal colony.
1681	Pennsylvania established as a proprietary colony.
1684	The charter of the Massachusetts Bay Company is revoked; Massachusetts becomes a royal colony.
1685	New York becomes a royal colony when its proprietor becomes king of England.
1685–1688	New York, New Jersey, Pennsylvania, and the New England colonies are combined into the Dominion of New England, governed by Sir Edmund Andros.
1689	Andros overthrown in the wake of the Glorious Revolution in England.
1691–1696	Colonial assemblies pass declarations of rights.

1696	Board of Trade established.
	Parliament passes a stricter Navigation Act.
1700–1710s	Slave codes established in northern colonies.
1701	Pennsylvania Charter of Privileges established.
1715	Maryland reverts to proprietorship.
1729	North and South Carolina become royal colonies.
1730s–1750s	The Great Awakening sweeps North America.
1732	Georgia established as a proprietary colony.
1735	Zenger Case in New York.
1751	Parliament passes the Currency Act
1763	Patrick Henry pleads The Parson's Cause in Virginia.

FURTHER READING

Peter Charles Hoffer's *The Brave New World: A History of Early America* (2000) combines attention to institutional and political development with attention to the social and cultural history of the new world. Jack P. Greene's *Pursuits of Happiness* (1988) is a highly comparative study of the development of colonial society. Edmond Wright's *The Search for Liberty* (1995) is engagingly written but more traditional. Both Hoffer and Wright provide good bibliographies. The classic, encyclopedic source of information on constitutional development and public policy is Charles M. Andrews's *The Colonial Period of American History* (4 vols., 1934–1938). Andrews provides an excellent overview in *The Colonial Background of the American Revolution* (1924), another classic reprinted nearly twenty times in succeeding decades. A brief but excellent survey is Keith Mason, "Britain and the Administration of the American Colonies," in *Britain and the American Revolution*, ed. H.T. Dickinson (1998). Robert M. Bliss discusses English politics and colonial administration through the Glorious Revolution in *Revolution and Empire* (1990). Daniel J. Hulsebosch presents a very informative although technical discussion of colonists' rights in "The Ancient Constitution and the Expanding Empire," *Law and History Review* 21 (Fall 2003): 439–82.

Edmund S. Morgan's *The Puritan Dilemma: The Story of John Winthrop* (1958) is a readable account of the development of responsible government in early New England. Jack R. Pole describes how colonial assemblies came to be seen as representative of an electorate in part two of *Political Representation in England and the Origins of the American Republic* (1966). In *The Quest for Power* (1963), Greene describes how colonial assemblies in the South accumulated powers similar to those held by Parliament in Great Britain.

Leonard W. Labaree's *Royal Government in America* (1958) provides basic information on imperial relations. Greene offers an insightful, wide-ranging analysis of the colonial origins of American federalism in Book One of *Peripheries and Center* (1986). Mary

Sarah Bilder describes how challenges to colonial laws before the Privy Council helped define *The Atlantic Constitution* (2004). John J. McCusker and Russell R. Menard's *The Economy of British America* (1985) is a comprehensive analysis of the economic context of American constitutional development. Margaret Ellen Newell describes the conflict over New England economic development and British efforts to control it in a brilliant book, *From Dependency to Independence: Economic Revolution in Colonial New England* (1998).

Donald S. Lutz discusses *The Origins of American Constitutionalism* in a brief survey published in 1988, stressing the role of the concept of covenant theology (mutual promises between God and man and among the religious faithful) and colonial charters in creating a sense of limits upon government. Lawrence Leder, *Liberty and Authority* (1968), describes the centrality of "liberty" to American political thought in the eighteenth century. In *Roots of the Republic* (1974), George Dargo provides a concise history of the trend towards freedom of speech and press, and towards religious toleration in the colonial period.

In the 1950s and 1960s historians debated the degree to which colonial American political culture was democratic. Robert E. Brown's *Middle-Class Democracy and the Revolution in Massachusetts* (1955) and Brown and B. Katherine Brown's *Virginia, 1705–1776: Aristocracy or Democracy?* (1964) stressed the democracy of American political institutions. Bernard Bailyn challenged this notion in "Politics and Social Structure in Virginia," in *Seventeenth-Century America*, ed. James Morton Smith (1959). The dominant view now is that American voters generally deferred to an elite colonial oligarchy, but that this deference was eroding in the decades before the Revolution. Mary Beth Norton describes the patriarchal nature of American society in the seventeenth century in section one of *Founding Mothers and Fathers* (1996). While she says things began to change after the 1670s, Gordon S. Wood describes an essentially hierarchical, patriarchic system persisting into the Revolutionary era in his Pulitzer Prize–winning *The Radicalism of the American Revolution* (1991). For a wonderful study of political structure, religion, and society in Virginia, read Rhys Isaac's *The Transformation of Virginia, 1740–1790* (1982), another Pulitzer Prize winner who finds hierarchy only slowly giving way to new egalitarian ideas. But Jack P. Greene challenges Woods's and Isaac's description, insisting that Americans stressed egalitarianism and openness. See chapter four of his *The Intellectual Construction of America* (1993).

If local elites did dominate American politics, neither the political nor the legal system approached the aristocratic culture of Great Britain. Bailyn makes this point clear in *The Origins of American Politics* (1967). Peter Charles Hoffer in *Law and People in Colonial America* (rev. ed., 1998) stresses that colonial legal institutions empowered ordinary (mostly white male) Americans, and that law was central to American concepts of liberty. Bradley Chapin shows how early American colonists modified English law to secure greater rights for the accused and to moderate the severity of punishments in *Criminal Justice in Colonial America, 1606–1660* (1983). Edgar McManus reinforces Chapin's conclusions in *Law and Liberty in Early New England* (1993).

Thomas J. Curry, *The First Freedoms* (1986), discusses church, state, and the origins of religious liberty in the American colonies. Compare his approach to that of Sally Schwarz in *"A Mixed Multitude": The Struggle for Toleration in Colonial Pennsylvania* (1987). Leonard W. Levy stresses the limited protection English and colonial law gave freedom of speech and press in *Emergence of a Free Press* (1985). Larry D. Eldridge casts doubt on Levy's conclusions in *A Distant Heritage: The Growth of Free Speech in Early America* (1994). For the Zenger case, see Paul Finkelman's introduction to *A Brief Narrative of the Case and Tryal of John Peter Zenger* (1997). Jeffrey A. Smith concentrates on how the ideology of a free press developed in *Printers and Press Freedom: The Ideology of Early American Journalism* (1988), finding that practice was more important than formal law.

Betty Wood describes *The Origins of American Slavery* (1997) in a brief book that stresses the reciprocal role of economics and nascent racism. Edmund S. Morgan brilliantly elucidates the relationship between American liberty and the development of slavery in *American Freedom, American Slavery* (1975). Equally important is Winthrop D. Jordan's prize-winning *White Over Black: American Attitudes Towards the Negro, 1550–1812* (1968). Donald R. Wright's survey *African Americans in the Colonial Era* (1990) introduces readers to the historical literature on the subject. Ira Berlin describes the transition in the South from "societies with slaves" to "slave societies" in his acclaimed *Many Thousands Gone* (1998). Philip D. Morgan's *Slave Counterpoint* (1998) is a monumental study of slavery in colonial America. Berlin's synoptic overview, "Time, Space, and the Evolution of Afro-American Society on British Mainland North America," *American Historical Review* 85 (February 1980): 44–78, provides exhaustive footnotes to the historical literature. Arthur Zilversmit summarizes the northern slave codes in *The First Emancipation* (1967). Edgar J. McManus provides greater detail in *Black Bondage in the North* (1973).

Marylynn Salmon's *Women and the Law of Property in Early America* (1986) is a seminal study of women's rights in colonial society. Lyle Koehler paints a grim picture of Puritan attitudes towards women in *Search for Power* (1980), while Kathleen M. Brown describes the complex relationship among race, gender, and white male authority in *Good Wives, Nasty Wenches, and Anxious Patriarchs* (1996).

3

The American Revolution

The American Revolution was the culmination of a bitter argument over the nature of the British constitution. At home and in the colonies, Britons argued over whether Parliament was sovereign in the modern meaning of the word—that is, whether Parliament had final, complete, unappealable authority over the British empire. They debated whether English subjects who did not vote for members of Parliament were nonetheless represented there. Both in England and America, many Britons worried that the aristocratic forces that controlled the British government were conspiring to deprive Englishmen of liberty.

Although Englishmen fought over these questions vigorously, they had special relevance for Americans, who were convinced that Parliament's authority over the colonies was limited. The source of these limitations were the customs that had grown up over the previous century, the charters American colonists had received from the kings, and the principle that Englishmen could be governed only by their own consent given in representative legislatures. Yet Americans did concede that Parliament had authority over matters that touched the whole empire, like trade and foreign policy. Arriving at a theoretical justification for this division of power proved extremely difficult. Indeed the American Revolution occurred largely because America and Britain diverged on this fundamental constitutional issue. Most Americans continued firmly to believe that Parliament's power was limited by the fundamental constitution of the empire and that it did not represent constituencies that were unable to vote for its members. Most Britons slowly reached the opposite conclusion.

Constitutional issues alone did not lead to the Revolution. People fight to defend their rights only when their violation would have serious practical consequences. No revolution would have erupted if colonial interests had not diverged more and more from those of Great Britain. But if the British and Americans had agreed about Parliament's authority under the constitution, the disputes might have been resolved peacefully. Constitutional issues and practical conflicts over public policy combined to precipitate the war for American independence.

American Colonists and British Constitutional Politics

To eighteenth-century Americans and Britons, the Atlantic Ocean was more a bridge than a barrier. For most of the year, ships traveled between American and British ports almost every day. Every vessel brought not only goods but news and correspondence. To modern observers the crossing's six-week delay may seem like an eternity, but it was the regularity of the communication that was most apparent to the colonists.

Improved transportation resulted in increased immigration and trade, as well as the growing anglicization of the American colonies. English fashions, English ideas, English institutions all grew more influential. A stronger sense developed that the colonies were connected to the British political system, fostered by a growing number of newspapers, the importation of British books and pamphlets, and a new domestic publishing industry. Americans were developing what historians have come to call a "public sphere," where people exchanged ideas, creating what we now call "public opinion."

This growing integration of the British empire led many people to add a new sense of Britishness to their local identities as English people—Scots, Jamaicans, or Virginians. For some, their identity as Britons even supplanted their local identities. This was especially true of capable men from outlying regions, who had been precluded from playing significant roles in English politics, but who could be important in the administration of the empire. Public-spirited members of the English aristocracy also saw it as their responsibility to guide the new empire, with the support of a new generation of young, educated civil servants. To them, the local autonomy that colonists identified with liberty was an old-fashioned, parochial stumbling block to efficient governance. These attitudes fit in well with developments in British society and politics. Britain had grown progressively more aristocratic through the eighteenth century. Great landowners came to dominate Parliament and successive British administrations, or "ministries."* The aristocracy exercised a powerful influence over their local communities, maintaining control through their social prestige, family ties, and commercial connections. British ministries consisted of coalitions of powerful aristocrats who combined their influence with that of the king. They could count on the support of large numbers of conservative, independent members from various rural localities, traditionally supporters of the government.

Nearly all the leading aristocrats considered themselves Whigs. But Whiggism no longer meant suspicion of royal power and trenchant defense of liberty.

---

*In the United States, we refer to governments under different presidents as "administrations," such as the "Washington administration" or the "Reagan administration." In eighteenth-century Britain it was customary to refer to the administrations of successive prime ministers as "ministries" rather than "administrations." (In modern times, it has become customary to refer to successive British administrations as "governments.")

Most of the aristocratic Whig factions became identified with the royal court surrounding the king. They were Whigs in that they supported the Hanoverian dynasty, whose legitimacy depended on acceptance of the Glorious Revolution and the subsequent Act of Settlement of 1701. The Whig aristocrats believed supreme power in Britain lay in Parliament—the House of Commons, House of Lords, and the king acting together—rather than in the king alone. They adhered to the principle of ministerial responsibility, the idea that the king's ministers were responsible for the conduct of government and should be replaced if they lost the confidence of Parliament.

The nation was thus governed by coalitions of aristocrats who held the key ministerial positions of government and who saw themselves as custodians of a great empire. When an alliance broke up, depriving a particular ministry of its parliamentary majority, another replaced it. Occasionally the change meant a modest shift in public policy, when rival groupings took somewhat different positions on public issues. To cement their control of Parliament and their influence, successful leaders would use their power to provide lucrative government offices for their relatives and followers. They would supply pensions for favored allies, paid from money Parliament provided to support the king. Many members of Parliament received such patronage; naturally, they tendered their political support in return. In an age when modern commerce and industry were only beginning to develop, such favors were an important source of wealth. In effect, the British government levied taxes on the whole population for the benefit of those who controlled the government and its offices.

This system of patronage-dominated government was widely criticized by dissidents, often identified as a "Country" party at odds with the "Court" party that surrounded the king and dominated the government. Among the critics in the 1760s was an aristocratic parliamentary faction led by Lord Rockingham, whose members considered themselves the true heirs of the old liberty-loving Whigs. They were loosely allied with "The Great Commoner," former Prime Minister William Pitt, whose admirers considered themselves Patriots with a special commitment to promoting the glory, interests, and liberties of the British empire. Unlike cosmopolitan "Britons," many patriotic Englishmen were hostile to the political domination of what they saw as an effete aristocracy. Many of them saw efforts to improve the administration of empire, especially to secure more efficient sources of revenue, as threats to liberty. As the proliferation of newspapers, printing presses, coffee houses, and theaters expanded the public sphere in England, these concerns spread among a growing number of people. Rockingham and Pitt received the support of more radical critics, many of whom were precluded from direct participation in politics because they lived in unrepresented cities or did not meet the other qualifications required of voters. The "Country Party" charged that corrupt ministers misused the king's influence to subvert English liberty and plunder his subjects. Bought and paid for, the unrepresentative Parliament no longer fulfilled its function of protecting against tyranny.

When George III assumed the throne in 1760, the critics hoped he would be a "Patriot King." But he proved a supporter of the system. When a group of aristocrats that particularly identified itself as "the King's friends" came to power in the late 1760s, the disappointed opposition denounced them as Tories—a name that stuck. Americans were well aware of this criticism of the British system, and it played a significant role in colonial politics. Colonial leaders faced British governors who were instructed to promote policies that often ran against colonial interests. When governors and their allies tried to secure influence over American assemblies, using the same techniques of patronage and influence that the ministry used in Great Britain, colonial leaders echoed the criticisms levied by the opposition in England. Opponents of the British ministries could never secure much support in Parliament. But their American counterparts, identifying themselves as Whigs and Patriots, almost always controlled the colonial assemblies. In part the difference reflected the broader right to vote in America and the more representative nature of the colonial assemblies. But it also illustrated that the colonial elite resembled the sorts of people excluded from power in England much more than it resembled the titled aristocracy of the mother country. While the colonies became more English in most ways, America's political power structure remained fundamentally different. Groups and ideas that characterized the radical political opposition in England controlled key organs of government in North America.

Imperial-minded Court Whigs and their opponents in Britain, Ireland, and the colonies fought bitterly over the British constitution. The conflict centered upon two related issues: the existence of a "fixed constitution" that limited the powers even of Parliament, and the nature of parliamentary representation. The Court Whigs argued that Parliament had complete and absolute governmental authority in the British empire, an authority that they saw as essential to governing it efficiently. To sustain their position, they pointed to the accepted definition of sovereignty: the final, unlimited, indivisible locus of authority in any political system (or "polity"). They insisted that, since sovereignty resided in Parliament, its authority must be unlimited. The *Magna Carta,* Petition of Right, Bill of Rights, and other fundamental ordinances listed rights that the *king* could not infringe unless he received the assent of Parliament; they did not bind Parliament itself. Most of these protections of rights were themselves parliamentary enactments. It was a clear maxim of parliamentary law that no Parliament could bind a successor. So if one Parliament had passed the Bill of Rights, another could repeal it.

To the Court Whigs, the constitution merely described how Britain was governed. Perhaps it suggested principles that ought not to be contravened, but it was up to Parliament to carry them out, and Parliament could do so any way it wished. To say otherwise was to deny that Parliament was sovereign, and if sovereignty did not lie in Parliament, where did it lie? If there were a fixed constitution that limited the power of Parliament, where was its sanction? What institution could determine that a law of Parliament was unconstitutional? No court claimed the power. Of course, there existed the right of popular resistance described by John Locke and exercised in the Glorious Revolution. But that was a right of revolution outside the institutions of government. If it succeeded, well and good; if it failed, the rebels surely would be punished as criminals.

The Rockingham Whigs straddled the issue. They did not want to limit Parliament but to free it of corrupt influence. Pitt and more radical elements of the opposition, however, blasted the argument for such absolute parliamentary sovereignty as importing despotism into the British system. Parliamentary absolutism would make Englishmen slaves as surely as royal absolutism had. Could Parliament abrogate all the rights and privileges granted in the ancient charters promulgated over the centuries? Could it abrogate the *Magna Carta*? Could it abolish itself and surrender all power to the king? That the boldest of the Court Whigs seemed to answer these questions affirmatively was an indication of how far the corruption of the British system had gone; their answers were proof of the ministerial conspiracy to crush liberty.

Although not all opposition critics insisted that Parliament was limited by a fixed British constitution, they all agreed that it was failing its duty to protect liberty. They concluded that Parliament no longer represented the people. The opposition demanded reform. At minimum, it should be illegal for members of Parliament to accept government places and pensions. Radicals demanded more. Real reform required reapportionment, so that unrepresented districts could send their fair share of members to Parliament. A few radicals urged an extension of the right to vote to Protestant dissenters, prosperous tenants who did not have freeholds that qualified them to vote, and to townspeople. In response, ministerial spokesmen insisted that members of Parliament represented the whole empire, not individual districts. It did not matter who actually voted. All Britons were represented in Parliament because its members acted in the best interests of all, a doctrine called "virtual representation."

The Court Whigs dismissed the opposition's complaint that government ministers secured too much influence over Parliament through the use of royal patronage. The system of royal influence in Parliament was part of the balanced constitution that protected British liberty. If the House of Commons became too independent, liberty was likely to turn into license, inviting the chaos that characterized the interregnum. Most of the opposition disagreed. What really protected liberty, they argued, was the character of the population. A virtuous people was willing to make the sacrifices necessary to defend the interests and honor of the nation abroad and to defend liberty at home. In a virtuous community, individuals placed the public welfare ahead of their particular personal, social, or economic interests. By seducing voters and members of Parliament with special benefits, the ministries had introduced corruption into British politics and undermined the virtue necessary to preserve liberty.

In this conflict, the American colonists were firmly on the side of the British radicals. The colonies' history made the concept of a fixed constitution much easier for Americans to accept than it was for Englishmen. No written documents had created the British government, but every American government had been created by a covenant among the colonists or by a charter granted by the king. While the British Parliament itself had passed the great laws protecting liberty and perhaps could repeal them, the American assemblies had always operated under limitations imposed by the covenants and charters that had created them. Although no authority existed in England to which one could appeal a parliamentary decision, American colonial assemblies could not pass laws inconsistent with those of England. Laws violating this restriction had regularly been nullified on appeal to the Privy Council.

The special situation of the colonies vis-à-vis Parliament also led Americans to conclude that there were limits on parliamentary power. Americans were clearly unrepresented in Parliament, and they had come to believe that Parliament could not legislate directly on the colonies' internal affairs. Whether Parliament could directly legislate for the colonies had never become a critical issue, because Parliament had not tried to do it with any consistency. But colonial assemblies had protested the occasional parliamentary effort. In 1760 James Otis, one of the leaders of the popular party in Massachusetts, electrified a courtroom audience with an argument that Parliament had no power to authorize royal officials to issue writs of assistance. He argued that these perpetual search warrants allowing general searches of ships for signs of smuggling violated the British constitution. Otis lost the Writs of Assistance Case, but young John Adams, furiously scribbling down notes on Otis's argument, later declared, "Then and there, the child Independence was born."

So the constitutional issues that led to the American Revolution arose in the context of a general struggle over the nature of the British constitution and of representation in Parliament. Allied with the political opposition in England, Americans referred to themselves as Whigs and Patriots and to their opponents as "Tories." When disputes over the authority of Parliament in the colonies first arose, Americans thought of themselves as fighting in common with other Englishmen for the British constitution and for British liberty.

The British Constitution and the Regulation of the Empire

The events that led to the American Revolution were precipitated by the great war that England and her colonies fought against France from 1756 to 1763. Called the French and Indian War in America, through it Britain ousted the French from nearly all their possessions in North America. But the war was extremely expensive; Parliament was forced to raise taxes in England and to borrow money that would require years of high taxes to repay. Taxes on land, the traditional source of most of the government's income, could not keep up with the expenses of empire. They fell, moreover, on those who could vote. What was needed were taxes on commerce, which now equaled land as the basis of national wealth. An ambitious, imperial-minded new government led by George Grenville determined to shift more of the tax burden to non-landowners at home and to raise money more efficiently from the colonies.

In Britain, the government began its new program by expanding excise taxes on alcoholic beverages, especially apple and pear ciders, which were widely consumed there. The taxes were wildly unpopular in the cider-producing regions, not only because they seemed to impose a special tax burden on these areas, but because they were enforced by special collectors, with special search warrants, in special courts without juries. In other words, the cider taxes raised many of the same issues that would soon arise in America. There the first step in the new program was the passage in 1764 of the American Revenue Act, or Sugar Act, which increased customs duties on molasses, the main ingredient of rum, the most common alcoholic beverage in the colonies. To secure efficient collection of the customs duties, Parliament decided to treat offenses as violations of admiralty law, to be tried without juries before a vice-admiralty court in Halifax, Nova Scotia. By allowing customs officers to seize allegedly smuggled goods, the law shifted the burden of proof. To get his goods back, the merchant had to prove he had obeyed the law. Often using general warrants that allowed unrestrained searches, customs officials—largely placemen, who received one-third of the value of the seized property—began to crack down on colonial merchants. Some officials demanded bribes in exchange for protection from sudden searches and seizures.

Grenville increased American dissatisfaction by passing the Currency Act of 1764, which extended the Currency Act of 1751, which had applied only to New England, to the rest of the American colonies. It forbade colonists from paying debts owed to English creditors in depreciated colonial currency and limited their authority to provide substitutes for gold and silver. At the same time, Americans chafed at the Proclamation of 1763, by which King George closed western lands to European settlement and required costly licenses to engage in the lucrative fur trade. In 1765 the Grenville ministry passed the Stamp Act, which required all legal documents and publications in the colonies to bear a stamp bought from the government.

Americans reacted angrily to the new laws, interpreting them as extensions of the corrupt British governmental system into the American colonies. Not satisfied with taxing the people in England to support pensioners and placemen, Britain intended to fatten on Americans as well. Moreover, the new system for enforcing customs laws deprived Americans of the common-law right to a jury trial and subjected them to general search warrants. Americans concluded that having undermined liberty in England, the British government was determined to do the same in America.

While all the new laws threatened American interests, the Stamp Act posed the greatest danger. By imposing a direct tax unconnected to trade, Parliament claimed authority to govern the colonies directly, although Americans were unrepresented in either of its branches. The colonists protested that as British subjects they could not be subjected to laws and taxation without the consent of their representatives; "no taxation without representation," they declared. The British government replied that members of Parliament represented the whole realm, not the particular districts that elected them. Americans were "virtually represented" in Parliament in the same way as Englishmen who could not vote or who lived in unrepresented cities.

Americans vehemently rejected this argument. At least members of Parliament and those who voted for them shared the burden of taxes levied in Great Britain. Americans well understood that once Parliament turned to America for revenue, the temptation to spare the pocketbooks of British voters would prove irresistible. Past disputes had shown that the interests of British subjects in America did not always coincide with the interests of those in Great Britain. How could it be said that Americans retained the rights of Englishmen if Parliament could decide these questions without American participation?

One colonial assembly after another protested the Stamp Tax and denied its constitutionality. For the first time, the colonies sent representatives to a common meeting, or "congress," which forwarded protest resolutions to the king and Parliament. "It is . . . essential to the freedom of a people, and the undoubted right of Englishmen, that no taxes be imposed on them, but with their own consent, given personally or by their representatives," the Stamp Act Congress declared. Colonial lawyers and political leaders, like Otis of Massachusetts and Daniel Dulany of Maryland, published a stream of pamphlets arguing the American position.

Most Americans conceded that Parliament had the right to pass laws regulating the commerce and defense of the empire. But they insisted that the British principle of consent by the governed, the ancient charters that guaranteed them the rights of Englishmen, and the customary practices of the previous 150 years all precluded Parliament from substituting its laws for those of the colonial assemblies.

An Imperial Constitution

As Americans denied the right of Parliament to tax them, they grappled with how to define their relations with Great Britain. Thinking in terms of the limits the British heritage placed on the English Parliament, they were in fact trying to define an imperial constitution—to analyze how the empire as a whole was governed and should be governed. In effect, Americans were groping towards the idea that the British empire was a federal system in which different governments fulfilled different functions. The central government was empowered to act on matters affecting the empire as a whole, including trade and war, but not on matters internal to the individual parts, which were reserved to their own legislatures.

It was a difficult, frustrating task to come up with a coherent description of the divided power that the colonists were struggling to envision. Everyone knew that there could be only one sovereign power in any polity. If the British empire were a single polity, governed from London, then sovereign power had to lie in Parliament. But if Parliament's power over America was limited because Americans were not represented in it, then where did sovereignty lie? If the colonial legislatures could deny power to Parliament, wouldn't that mean that *they* were sovereign? If so, wouldn't that make the colonies independent states? A few anti–Stamp Act pamphleteers argued that the legislative assemblies of the various parts of the empire *were* independent of one another. England and each of the colonies were united only through the monarchy; the king provided the executive power in each polity. But few Americans yet accepted this idea. They saw the British empire as something more than a mere league of independent states.

Most Americans simply denied Parliament's power to levy internal taxes on the colonists, arguing that taxation without representation was beyond Parliament's authority under the British constitution. The fact that no formal sanction existed to prevent the enforcement of an unconstitutional law made no difference. Parliament might have the naked *power* to enforce such a law, but that did not mean it had the *right* to do so. The remedy was for British subjects to petition and resist until Parliament recognized its error and reversed it. In Britain itself, the cider-producing counties did the same.

To make their point, Americans refused to buy the stamps. Mobs forced the officials responsible for selling the stamps to resign. American leaders agreed to stop trading with England until Parliament repealed the Stamp Act. Some radical merchants joined artisans in secret vigilante organizations, calling themselves "Sons of Liberty," which passed resolutions demanding compliance with the embargo. Merchants who refused to cooperate were mobbed and their businesses destroyed. As the boycott took effect, English merchants who depended on trade with America demanded repeal of the stamp tax. Any effort to divide authority in the empire was anathema to the self-conscious British imperialists struggling to strengthen its administration. But radical critics of English politics generally endorsed the American position. The American argument that Parliament's authority was limited by a fixed constitution and that "virtual representation" was a myth accorded with their own views. Moderate English opponents of the ministry, like the Rockingham Whigs, rejected the American argument but urged government restraint. Still other friends of America, such as Pitt, argued that the colonies were immune from taxation by Parliament but not other regulations of their internal affairs.

The American resistance, combined with public dissatisfaction with the current British ministry (and the fact that King George III personally disliked

Grenville), led to a temporary victory for America's allies in England. Becoming prime minister with a tenuous majority in Parliament, Rockingham cooperated with Pitt (who was made the Earl of Chatham to the dismay of his radical allies) to repeal the Stamp Act and the cider excise. But neither Rockingham nor most members of Parliament were willing to concede that the Americans were right on the question of parliamentary power. When it repealed the Stamp Act in 1766, Parliament passed the Declaratory Act, patterned on the one it had passed asserting power over Ireland almost fifty years earlier. The act announced that Parliament had the power to pass laws binding the colonies "in all cases whatsoever" and declared colonial resolutions to the contrary null and void.

Rockingham's government soon fell, replaced by one technically led by his one-time ally Chatham, as Pitt was now called. But the real leader was Lord Townshend, who still faced the problem of securing adequate revenue to pay the bills of the empire. Relying on Americans' concession that Parliament could pass commercial regulations, he reverted to the earlier policy of collecting customs duties. In 1767 Parliament passed the Townshend Duties, a series of taxes upon colonial imports, including tea, paper, glass, and other items. These were not really "taxes," the English avowed, but merely regulations of trade. The money would pay the salaries of colonial governors and other English officials in the colonies. Once again Americans protested. Not only did they argue that these duties were really taxes, but they denounced using the revenues to pay colonial officials. As long as they had to rely upon the assemblies for their salaries, colonial officials were dependent on Americans' good will. Paying their salaries with import duties would make them independent of the colonists and more sympathetic to English than to American interests.

Again Americans boycotted English goods and formed Non-Importation Associations. Unofficial groups enforced the boycott, once more often calling themselves "Sons of Liberty." These organizations cooperated and established a network of potentially revolutionary organizations.

The British Constitution and the American Revolution

While the Court Whigs, denounced by radicals as "Tories," tried to force Americans to recognize the all-powerful sovereignty of Parliament, they fought a similar battle with America's allies in Britain. The great issue arose around the travails of the demagogic radical John Wilkes. In 1764, pressured by the ministry, Parliament expelled him so that he could be prosecuted for libeling the king. Charged after a questionable search of his premises, Wilkes became a hero to disaffected Englishmen. His trial raised issues of freedom of speech and freedom from searches based on general search warrants that did not allege specific crimes or limit searches to specific places—a process Americans complained about when used to fight smuggling. The judge at his trial denied the jury's right to decide whether Wilkes's language was libelous, insisting that judges must decide such legal issues. Critics of the government pointed to the proceedings as further evidence that British liberty was under attack.

Fleeing the country to escape imprisonment, Wilkes returned in 1768 and was promptly reelected to Parliament. Four times the ministry-dominated Parliament refused to seat him. Each time he was reelected. Finally, in 1769, the ministry persuaded Parliament to seat his defeated competitor. Opposition to the government exploded. Tens of thousands of protestors marched through the streets of London calling for "Wilkes and Liberty!" Replacing an elected member of Parliament with a defeated opponent was clearly unconstitutional, the opposition argued; it violated the right of Wilkes's constituents to representation. The controversy raised the same fundamental issues as American taxation: Was Parliament bound by fundamental law? Could its treatment of Wilkes and his constituents be called unconstitutional? Did Parliament's refusal to seat Wilkes deny his constituents representation, or were they "virtually" represented by Parliament as a whole? Americans rallied to his defense, sending resolutions of support and showering him with symbolic gifts of tobacco, hams, and other American products. In Pennsylvania, settlers named Wilkes-Barre after the great radical and Isaac Barre, another radical proponent of British and American liberties.

In 1770, the Wilkes issue, the American question, and other disputes culminated in a great petition campaign organized by the Rockingham Whigs in a loose alliance with radical opponents of the government. Although the Rockinghamites sought only to harness the widespread dissatisfaction in order to oust their rivals and take power, the implications were radical. The great petition drive gained wide support, largely among men who were not entitled to vote. An attempt to influence the government outside traditional channels, the campaign suggested that Parliament did not represent the nation. As one opposition member of Parliament warned, "the time may come when petitions will be followed by remonstrances, and remonstrances by execution." After the ministry barely survived the challenge, this prediction seemed to come true. Thousands of Londoners descended on the royal palace to deliver an Address, Remonstrance and Petition, calling upon the king to dissolve the current session of Parliament on the grounds that it no longer represented the people.

In the wake of the near victory of the opposition, Lord Frederick North became head of a new ministry. At first taking a conciliatory course, he persuaded Parliament to repeal the Townshend Duties on everything but tea. This concession brought peace punctuated by sporadic flare-ups in individual colonies until 1773. In that year the English government, in another effort to make money, passed a new Tea Act. It reduced the tax on tea, encouraging Americans to relax the boycott, and gave the London-based East India Tea Company special benefits that enabled it to sell tea in America more cheaply than American merchants could. Resisting the temptation of the cheaper tea, Americans warned British authorities not to land it in colonial harbors. But the governor of Massachusetts, Thomas Hutchinson, frustrated by British timidity, decided to force the issue. He ordered the tea to be unloaded at Boston. In response the Boston Sons of Liberty dumped the cargo into the harbor in what came to be known as the Boston Tea Party.

The British reacted with a series of severe laws called the Coercive Acts. Parliament closed the port of Boston until its residents would agree to compensate the Tea Company for its loss. It dissolved the colonial assembly and changed the Massachusetts charter to enable the king to appoint more of the colony's officials and all of its judges. Town meetings, where New Englanders traditionally elected town officers and made policies, were limited to one per year. Parliament passed a Quartering Act permitting colonial officials to station troops among the people whenever necessary, even though this policy violated the express provisions of the Bill of Rights. At almost the same time the British passed the Quebec Act, setting up a government for the territory in Canada conquered from France. It provided for no elected assembly at all and transferred territory from other American colonies to Quebec. Americans feared that the British now intended to impose this sort of government upon the rest of the American colonies.

The Coercive Acts passed by overwhelming majorities in Parliament, and with the apparent approval of most English people. By concentrating on the American issue, the North ministry hit the opposition arguments about representation and a fixed constitution where they were politically weakest. The British empire must be either a unitary polity under the sovereign authority of Parliament, North and his allies insisted, or it must be merely an association of independent states. If Americans were able to enforce their view that the colonial assemblies, and not Parliament, had final authority over their own communities, then sovereignty must lie with those assemblies. The empire was thus no more than an alliance, to be maintained at the sufferance of each colony. The American view meant, in effect, the end of the empire.

Few Englishmen could accept that idea, and certainly not English patriots who might be critical of the Tories but saw the empire as England's crowning achievement. Radicals who continued to defend America were isolated. The notion that Parliament was limited by a fixed constitution receded in Great Britain, as did for a time the demand for reform in representation. This collapse of the opposition in Britain shocked Americans, who saw it as proof that the conspiracy to destroy British liberty had succeeded. But if the spirit of liberty was dying in the Old World, Americans were convinced, it lived on in the New.

In response to the Coercive Acts, the colonies called a Continental Congress. Like the Stamp Act Congress, it sent a formal protest to Parliament, declaring the right of Americans to internal self-government. At the same time, it called for another boycott of British goods. In Massachusetts, many members of the colonial assembly refused to obey the British order to disband, forming a "provincial assembly." This action was a revolutionary step in clear opposition to the British government. Many of the towns defied the Coercive Acts as well. They held illegal meetings, protesting British actions and levying taxes to improve their militias. Even where towns did not take such radical steps, members of the local militias often elected radical leaders and began to drill and to collect armaments. In effect, Americans were establishing revolutionary governments.

As the crisis deepened, Americans continued to struggle to define the rights of the British and the colonial governments. Several American leaders, particularly John Adams and the Pennsylvania lawyer James Wilson, developed the idea that the empire was a league of independent states. Sovereignty lay in the king and each legislature, acting together. Thus in Great Britain, sovereignty lay with King-in-Parliament; in Massachusetts, sovereignty lay with King-in-Assembly, and so on for each colony. Although this arrangement would leave every part of the British empire virtually independent, the colonists argued that sharing the same king would lead to coordination in military affairs, foreign policy, and trade. Of course, this idea was exactly what the British government warned would be the result of denying parliamentary sovereignty. It was not acceptable to the British government, nor to the British people. Besides loosening the bonds of empire, it would strengthen the king and his ministers, who would be responsible for executive administration over the whole empire, while weakening Parliament, which would be responsible only for domestic policy in Great Britain. From the perspective of Englishmen, this would put British liberty at even greater risk than it was.

As a second Continental Congress met in 1775 to consider what more to do, British officials in Boston, buoyed by the anti-American reaction at home, determined to send troops to arrest the leaders of the Massachusetts provincial assembly and confiscate military supplies. As they marched through the towns outside Boston, fighting erupted at Lexington and Concord. Thousands of militiamen from surrounding towns, drove the British troops back to Boston and surrounded the city. Militias from all over New England and as far away as Philadelphia joined the besieging American army. Forced to send a commander to take control of these military forces and to create a "Continental Army," the Continental Congress chose George Washington. All realistic possibilities for a compromise ended and the American Revolution began. In 1776 the Congress formally declared the independence of the American colonies.

To justify their Declaration of Independence, Americans called upon the same ideas about natural rights and the origins and obligations of government that John Locke had articulated to justify the Glorious Revolution. The Congress delegated the job of framing the appropriate language to a committee chaired by Thomas Jefferson, whose original language was revised slightly by the other members, among whom were Adams and Benjamin Franklin. The final version read: "We hold these truths to be self-evident, that all men are created equal, that they are endowed by their Creator with certain unalienable Rights, that among these are Life, Liberty and the pursuit of Happiness.—That to secure these rights, Governments are instituted among Men, deriving their just powers from the consent of the governed,—That whenever any Form of Government becomes destructive of these ends, it is the Right of the People to alter or abolish it, and to institute new Government. . . ." The specific charges included a host of complaints, nearly all of which alleged violations of basic rights inherent in the British constitutional system. Implicit throughout was the assumption that the empire must be governed subject to the customs that had developed into a constitution, and that this constitution transcended the power of Parliament to change or violate it.

The American Revolution was fought, fundamentally, over the definition of constitutional power within the British empire. Of course Americans would never have plunged into the turmoil of resistance and revolution if substantial material interests had not been at stake. But the crucial question was not what the British government was trying to do but whether it had the right to do it. The taxes required to create and maintain state militias and a continental army to fight the Revolution were far greater than the taxes Britain had proposed to support a military establishment in the colonies. The costs that the war imposed on American merchant shipping, largely driven from the sea by the British navy, were far greater than the costs of obeying British customs regulations. Americans fought the war to preserve their constitutional rights. Constitutionalism—the conviction that constitutions imposed limits upon governmental power—lay at the heart of the nation's founding.

TIMELINE

1754–1763   French and Indian War.

1760   George III (1760–1820) crowned King of England.

James Otis argues that the powers of Parliament are limited in the Writs of Assistance Case.

1763–1765   Grenville ministry.

1763   Parliament passes the cider excise.

1764   John Wilkes expelled from Parliament.

Parliament passes the Currency Act and Sugar (American Revenue) Act.

1765   Parliament passes the Stamp Act.

The Stamp Act Congress protests the Stamp Act on behalf of the American colonies; individual colonies also protest; Americans establish a policy of nonimportation of British goods.

1765–1766   Rockingham ministry.

1766   Parliament repeals the cider excise and the Stamp Act but passes the Declaratory Act, reaffirming power to legislate for America "in all cases whatsoever."

1766–1768 Chatham ministry.

1767   Parliament passes the Townshend Duties.

           Colonists revive the non-importation policy.

1768–1769 John Wilkes returns to England, is reelected to Parliament, and is denied his
           seat four times.

1770–1782 North ministry.

1770   Parliament repeals Townshend Duties, retaining tax on tea.

1773   Parliament passes the Tea Act.

           Boston Tea Party.

           Parliament passes the Coercive Acts.

           Parliament enacts the Quebec Act.

1774   First Continental Congress.

           Massachusetts forms a Provincial Assembly.

1775   Second Continental Congress.

1775   Fighting at Lexington and Concord.

           The Continental Congress creates a Continental army, George Washington
           in command.

1776   Declaration of Independence.

FURTHER READING

The simplest account of the events leading to the American Revolution is Edmund S. Morgan's *Birth of the Republic* (1956). Taking into account more recent interpretations is Gordon Wood's brief *The American Revolution* (2002).

The traditional view that the American Revolution was essentially a conflict over governmental institutions and liberty was challenged in the first decades of the twentieth century, the Progressive era, by a new generation of historians. The Progressive historians believed that most human beings are moved by economic interests rather than by ideological or philosophical beliefs. Arthur M. Schlesinger, Sr., presented a classic Progressive interpretation in "The American Revolution Reconsidered," *Political Science Quarterly* 34 (March 1919): 61–78. For a review of this historiography, see the introduction to *The Reinterpretation of the American Revolution*, ed. Jack P. Greene (1968).

In recent decades the emphasis has shifted back toward the role ideological and constitutional differences played in bringing about the Revolution, but the heirs of the Progressive historians still dissent. Compare Bernard Bailyn, *The Ideological Origins of the American Revolution* (1967), and John Phillip Reid, *Constitutional History of the American*

Revolution: The Authority to Legislate (1991), to Edward M. Countryman, *The American Revolution* (1985). Bailyn and his successors stress the influence of British "country" and "commonwealth" ideology on American revolutionaries. This "republican ideology" emphasized public virtue and placed the needs of the community ahead of the rights of the individual. Joyce Appleby, in contrast, argues that social and economic change led Revolutionary-era Americans to adopt a "liberal ideology" that placed individual rights ahead of community needs, leading ultimately to the individual rights–based constitutional system of the United States. Appleby straddles the position of historians who stress the autonomy of ideas and those who see ideas as merely reflecting self-interest. See her essays "Liberalism and the American Revolution" and "The Social Origins of American Revolutionary Ideology" in Appleby, *Liberalism and Republicanism in the Historical Imagination* (1992).

In 1926 Charles M. Andrews offered an excellent, concise statement of the constitutional, social, and political differences between Great Britain and the American colonies that led to the Revolution. See his "The American Revolution: An Interpretation," *American Historical Review* 31 (January 1926): 218–232. One should augment it with Jack P. Greene, "The Colonial Origins of American Constitutionalism," in Greene, *Negotiated Authorities: Essays in Colonial Political and Constitutional History* (1994).

In the past twenty years an exciting historical literature has described how the acquisition of a great empire affected British identity, politics, and government. The seminal works were John Brewer's The *Sinews of Power* (1989), which described the growing efficiency of national and imperial administration in the eighteenth century, and Linda Colley's *Britons* (1992), which illuminated the rise of a governmental system that displaced provincial identities and localism. Eliga H. Gould carries their insights further in *The Persistence of Empire: British Political Culture in the Age of the American Revolution* (2000). But this work should be augmented by studies that describe a more "English" British national identity, like Gerald Newman, *The Rise of English Nationalism* (1997) and Kathleen Wilson's *The Sense of the People* (1995) and *The Island Race* (2003).

H. T. Dickinson explains the British imperialist view of the constitution of the empire in "Britain's Imperial Sovereignty: The Ideological Case Against the American Colonists," in *Britain and the American Revolution*, ed. H. T. Dickinson (1998). For the ideology of liberty that underlay the American reaction to British imperial legislation after 1763, see Bailyn's seminal *Ideological Origins of the American Revolution*, noted above, as well as John Phillip Reid, *The Concept of Liberty in the Age of the American Revolution* (1989). Two review essays summarize the "republican synthesis" that has characterized most historians' understanding of revolutionary ideology since the 1970s: Robert E. Shalhope, "Republicanism and Early American Historiography," *William & Mary Quarterly* 39 (3d ser.) (April 1982): 334–356, and Daniel T. Rogers, "Republicanism: The Career of a Concept," *Journal of American History* 79 (June 1992): 11–38. Rogers pronounced the "republican synthesis" dead. More than a decade later, one should still take his obituary with a few grains—or barrels—of salt.

Andrew C. McLaughlin, "The Background of American Federalism," *American Political Science Review* 12 (May 1918): 215–240, is a straightforward account of how Americans struggled to define the relationship between the central and local governments in the imperial system. By far the best work on this subject is Jack P. Greene, *Peripheries and Center: Constitutional Development in the Extended Polities of the British Empire and the United States, 1607–1788* (1986). In his multivolume *Constitutional History of the American Revolution* (4 vols., 1986–1993), John Phillip Reid brilliantly integrates the dispute over authority within the British empire (the precursor of American ideas of federalism) with the dispute over the power of Parliament to infringe on the liberty of Englishmen at home or abroad (the precursor of American ideas of individual freedom). For a taste, see Reid's "Limits of Supremacy," the fifth chapter of *Constitutional History of the American Revolution: The Authority to Legislate*, noted above.

For the English political context of the American Revolution, see George Rudé, *Wilkes and Liberty* (1962); John Brewer, "English Radicalism in the Age of George III," in *Three British Revolutions*, ed. J.G.A. Pocock (1980); Colin Bonwick, *English Radicals and the American Revolution* (1977); and Kathleen Wilson, *The Sense of the People*, noted above. You can get an overview of Wilson's important work from her essay "A Dissident Legacy: Popular Politics and the Glorious Revolution," in *Liberty Secured? Britain Before and After 1688*, ed. J. R. Jones (1992).

4
Establishing New State and Federal Constitutions

Even before Congress and the American colonies declared independence from Britain, the states had established independent governments. With the formal repudiation of British authority, the states had to restructure their political institutions. Most adopted new, republican constitutions. These not only specified the states' governmental organization but defined the rights of their citizens.

Yet after the first flush of enthusiasm for republican government, many Americans became disillusioned. They were unprepared for the bitter disagreements over public policy that arose with new conditions and that were made worse by the postwar economic slowdown. The travail led many Americans to lose faith in the virtue of the American people. In response some citizens developed new ideas about the need for checks and balances in government and a renewed commitment to constitutionalism. Others saw these movements as efforts by a conservative elite to reassert its authority.

Nor did declaring independence from Britain solve the problem of how to divide authority between local and general governments. In 1781 the states agreed to the Articles of Confederation, which specified the powers of Congress and preserved state sovereignty. But the central government it established proved ineffectual, and many Americans blamed the general deterioration of American political life on its weakness. Dissatisfied leaders called for greater centralization. Others charged that these nationalists were bent on undermining liberty, which depended on local control of government. The nationalists' complaints led to a constitutional convention that met in Philadelphia in 1787 to frame a new constitution. The resulting document was remarkable for how it reconfigured ideas about republican government and federalism. Ratified over the objections of localists in 1788, the Constitution was rounded out with a Bill of Rights in 1791. It established the framework of American government from 1789 to the present.

Republicanism and Virtue

After Congress passed the Declaration of Independence in 1776, individual colonial assemblies quickly declared their own independence. Because the British had appointed many colonial officers, independence required modifications of state government. This process had begun even before 1776 with the ouster of royal officials. Two of the new states, Connecticut and Rhode Island, continued to operate under their old charters, merely changing the way governors and other executive and judicial officers were chosen. But the rest of the state legislatures drafted new constitutions in 1776 and 1777, except Massachusetts, which completed the task in 1780. Every state instituted a republican form of government. In effect, Americans were rejecting the prevailing view that only a "balanced constitution" combining monarchy, aristocracy, and popular representation could provide both stability and liberty. They would rely primarily on the civic virtue of the people.

As they turned to republicanism, American revolutionaries began to stress the fundamental equality of rights among citizens. The repudiation of aristocracy encouraged small farmers, craftsmen, and laborers to demand greater respect from the wealthier elite. Urban craftsmen and workers pointed with pride to the role they played in defending American liberty. New leaders emerged from the "middling ranks" of society. Americans viewed claims of special privileges with ever-greater suspicion and hostility.

It was a bold experiment. For all their criticism of the abuse of royal power, few of even the most radical English reformers favored replacing the monarchy with a republic. History taught them that efforts to establish republics usually proved disastrous. Only in ancient Rome had a republic been successful for long. An almost superhuman degree of public virtue was required for people to govern themselves. In a republic they had to obey the laws and maintain order despite the absence of coercive forces that a monarchy could bring to bear. They would have to maintain due deference despite the absence of hierarchy inherent in aristocratic government. Without a hereditary monarchy and aristocracy, the people would have to select wise and virtuous leaders from among themselves. These leaders would have to act harmoniously for the good of the whole commonwealth. When they disagreed, the minority would have to defer to the majority and the majority would have to respect the minority. The disagreement must always be one of judgment; it must never arise because any of the leaders wanted to promote the interests of a particular group, or "faction." It was a sign of Americans' self-confidence that they took such a risk. Minimizing the number of Loyalists among them, American revolutionaries saw only the courageous way the people had stood up to the power of the corrupt British government, unlike the supine people of the mother country itself.

Americans believed that they had another great advantage over other peoples: They lived on the edge of a great continent blessed with abundant, fertile land and natural riches. With no privileged aristocrats to claim huge tracts of land for themselves, Americans could live comfortably as independent farmers, planters, merchants, and craftsmen for generations. If republican government could succeed anywhere, it was in the virtuous communities of the American states.

The State Constitutions and American Constitutionalism

From the beginning the states rested their new constitutions on the authority of the people. In most cases the revolutionaries called special congresses, often chosen by a broader electorate than the old colonial assemblies, to frame constitutions. Besides legislating, these congresses had the special task of framing a binding constitution. The new state constitutions established governments that reflected colonial experience. Most provided for a governor, a judiciary, and a legislature with two branches. They clearly indicated the revolutionaries' fear of executive power and aristocracy. The constitutions made the lower, popular branch of the legislature stronger than the upper branch, which was designed to represent the propertied elite. Pennsylvania's constitution eliminated the upper branch altogether. Every state required frequent meetings of the legislature and frequent elections, usually every year for the lower house. Americans weakened their governors or even eliminated the office. In some states the legislature selected the governor. To prevent governors from corrupting the legislature, the power of appointment was limited and the legislature given a say in the process. Legislators were forbidden to accept other government positions.

The legislatures themselves were made more representative. Having repudiated the idea of virtual representation, they were forced to reapportion representation to accommodate the demands of underrepresented frontier areas. They also faced demands to broaden the franchise. Pennsylvania and North Carolina gave the right to vote to all men who paid taxes. None of the other states went so far. Americans believed in popular government but not yet in democracy. Most Americans believed that allowing men without property to vote would endanger liberty. America was still a society where a tenant, employee, or borrower owed a degree of loyalty to his landlord, employer, or creditor. If the poor and dependent were allowed to vote, their ballots would enhance the power of the rich. Therefore all the states retained some property requirement for voting and required significant property of officeholders.

The status of the new constitutions was somewhat ambiguous. They had been framed by provincial congresses and state legislatures much like ordinary laws. Yet Americans had come to consider constitutions superior to ordinary law. They had insisted that the British constitution was fixed and could not be changed simply by an act of Parliament. They concluded that every free country must have such a fixed constitution, a system of basic rules that even the government had to obey.

These conclusions comported with the natural-rights philosophy that dominated Europe during the Enlightenment. Advanced European intellectuals held that every man was entitled to natural rights that no government could lawfully abrogate. Americans combined this idea with their British heritage of constitutionalism and their tradition of written charters and frames of government, concluding that every state should be governed by a formal, written constitution. Many of these constitutions specified the natural and common-law rights that government could not take away from the people. Reflecting their British heritage, Americans called these sections of the new constitutions "bills of rights" or "declarations of rights."

Inspired by revolutionary fervor, the Virginia assembly passed a "Declaration of Rights" in June 1776. Although not incorporated into the commonwealth's constitution, it provided a model for many of the other states. Prepared by George Mason, it declared the people to be the source of all power, with the government their trustees and servants. It discounted the creation of "exclusive or separate emoluments or privileges," except for nonhereditary ones in recognition of public services. It prescribed proper principles for the organization of republican government, such as separation of powers among the legislature, executive, and judiciary. It defined rights in criminal trials, declared jury trials in both criminal and civil trials "sacred," and pronounced freedom of the press "one of the great bulwarks of liberty" that was restrained only by "despotick governments." It declared that all were "equally entitled to the free exercise of religion."

Every state made clear that its new constitution was intended to bind all branches of the state government. But despite Americans' commitment to constitutionalism, it was not yet clear how a constitution could be enforced against a law that violated it. The Virginia Declaration of Rights was full of "oughts" and "shoulds" but did not literally forbid infringement of the rights it specified. Instead it depended upon the virtue of the people, formally resolving "that no free government, or the blessings of liberty, can be preserved to any people but by a firm adherence to justice, moderation, temperance, frugality, and virtue. . . ."

Some states began to experiment with institutional sanctions to maintain the supremacy of their constitutions. Pennsylvania elected a Council of Censors every seven years to assess the constitutionality of government action and recommend constitutional amendments to rectify problems. New York's constitution of 1777 created a Council of Revision, made up of the governor, judges, and members of the legislature, with the power to veto laws that violated the constitution.

Liberty and the American States

Among the most important reforms in many American states was the disestablishment of the Anglican Church. Revolutionary ideology held that government should not secure special benefits for particular groups. Members of dissenting religious groups soon pointed to the inconsistency between this principle and the privileges afforded the established churches. Pennsylvania, Delaware, and New Jersey abolished the connection between church and state almost immediately upon the Declaration of Independence. New York, North Carolina, and Georgia followed a year later.

Americans expanded their commitment to religious toleration even where they maintained their religious establishments, as in Virginia, Massachusetts, and Connecticut. Religious minorities everywhere insisted that the principle of equal rights meant that no religion should be burdened by special disabilities. They demanded the repudiation of laws that had limited freedom of worship or imposed penalties on dissenters. They campaigned to be exempted from paying taxes that supported established churches where they still existed. They urged the end of preferences for certain religions to administer colleges and an end to all political disabilities based on religion.

Although opposed by people who believed that a common religious belief was essential to maintaining social harmony, the movement for disestablishment and broad toleration proved inexorable. Toleration did not yet mean full equality, especially for non-Protestants. But in 1783 Archbishop John Carroll, the first official head of the Catholic Church in America, could write Rome with enthusiasm that "in these United States our religious system has undergone a revolution, if possible, more extraordinary than our political one."

The Revolution also led to a growing demand for the abolition of slavery. Quakers had been taking progressively more adamant stands against slavery since the Pennsylvania Meeting began struggling with the issue in the 1710s. The pace quickened after the 1760s. Having discouraged their own people from buying and owning slaves, Quakers began to urge legal action against slavery. Inspired by the Great Awakening, other sects reinforced the Quaker point of view.

The Continental Congress had barred the foreign slave trade as early as 1775 to put economic pressure on Great Britain. Jefferson had included a bitter attack on Britain for encouraging slavery in his original draft of the Declaration of Independence, but the Congress eliminated it for fear of alienating slaveholders. During the war, the British tried to undermine the American military effort by promising freedom to slaves who ran away from disloyal masters; the states and the Continental Congress responded by offering freedom to those who enlisted in the American forces. Slaveholders resisted these efforts, however, and in the end only about 5,000 African Americans, mostly from the North, fought on the American side.

With the Revolution the anomaly of a slaveholding people fighting for liberty became painfully apparent. In 1776 and 1777 Pennsylvania and New York Quakers began to expel slaveholders from their Meetings. A growing number of antislavery societies were founded in the 1770s and 1780s. Northern slaves and free blacks organized antislavery petition campaigns. States liberalized the laws governing manumission. Between 1776 and 1786, eleven states either prohibited the slave trade or imposed heavy taxes on it. Pressure grew for the gradual abolition of slavery itself. The people of Vermont, seeking independence from both New York and New Hampshire, barred slavery in their constitution of 1777. In 1780, Quaker-influenced Pennsylvania became the first state to legislate gradual abolition. The legislature repealed the state's slave code, required slaveowners to register slaves, and it freed slave children when they reached adulthood. Many slaveowners failed to meet the registration requirement, leading to widespread emancipation. In Massachusetts a series of court decisions freed slaves on the grounds that slavery was inconsistent with the state constitution's declaration that all men are born free and equal. With masters unable to enforce slavery in the courts, the institution collapsed. Slavery in New Hampshire seems to have dissipated in the same way. In 1784 Connecticut and Rhode Island enacted gradual emancipation laws. Under such pressure, most slaveowners in New England and Pennsylvania freed their slaves or sold them out of state.

Resistance to the antislavery tide was stronger in New York, New Jersey, and states farther south. In fact, New York enacted a revised, comprehensive slave code in 1788. While the New England states and Pennsylvania generally accorded their freed slaves equal civil and political rights, New York and New Jersey explicitly limited the rights of free black citizens. Not until 1799 would New York pass a gradual emancipation act. Although the act freed children born after July 4 of that year, masters could require boys to continue in service until they reached 28 years of age, and girls until they reached 25. However, most slaveowners released children from this requirement, encouraged by a provision relieving them of financial responsibility for them once freed. New Jersey did not pass a similar abolition measure until 1804.

When Abigail Adams urged her husband John to work for laws to improve the legal status of American women, who were still subject to the oppressive legal rules of coverture, he dismissed her comments as mere banter. "I cannot help but laugh," he wrote in response to her "saucy" letter. But Abigail had been in dead earnest. She quietly complained to friends of John's dismissive reaction and urged them to help organize a campaign for "some laws in our favor upon just and liberal principles."

Although the Revolution did not better women's legal status, it improved their social status. Women were expected to inculcate their children with the virtue necessary to the survival of the Republic. Fulfilling that crucial task implied education. It also suggested a responsibility for maintaining those social institutions, such as churches and schools, that imparted republican virtue.

John Adams's reaction to Abigail Adams's demands indicates how the Revolution undermined hierarchical authority in America. "We have been told that our struggle has loosened the bonds of government everywhere," he wrote Abigail, "that children and apprentices were disobedient; that schools and colleges were grown turbulent; that Indians slighted their guardians, and Negroes grew insolent to their masters." Now, his own wife had given him "the first intimation" that women, "more numerous and powerful than all the rest, were grown discontented" as well. Like many conservative Americans, Adams was troubled by signs that ordinary people no longer deferred to the social, economic, and political elite. He would never accept the degree of equality that people were beginning to demand. But it was a demand that ultimately would prove irresistible.

Disillusionment with Republican Government

Despite their early optimism, many Americans were soon disappointed in their new governments. To their dismay, even before Britain recognized American independence in 1783, it became clear that Americans were no more virtuous than other people who had tried to establish republics.

Divisions soon arose in the states over economic policy. The Revolution broke up the economic relationship between Britain and America that underlay American prosperity. Chaotic financial policies made the situation worse. The Congress and several states had issued paper money to help finance the war. This increased circulation, along with the contending armies' demand for goods, had promoted an artificial boom, fueled by high prices. To increase production, farmers increased their holdings, mortgaging their property to do so. But as the war ended, demand for goods shrank. The states began to contract the amount of money in circulation, while specie flowed out of the United States to pay off debts to British creditors. Prices fell. Farmers and other producers who had borrowed when money was plentiful had to repay their loans when it was scarce. As the economy contracted, borrowers could not repay their debts, and creditors went to court to foreclose mortgages on farms and businesses. To the fury of debtors, these creditors were often not even the people who had lent them the money they owed. In a modern commercial economy, creditors could sell mortgages and notes of indebtedness to third parties. Speculators bought these mortgages and notes at a discount, then sought their full repayment.

To make matters worse, Congress levied large requisitions on the states to enable it to pay off the bonds it had issued to fund the war. The states had to raise taxes to meet the requisitions and to pay off their own debts. Again the people who owned government bonds often were no longer those who had actually lent the money; many of the bonds had been purchased at low prices by speculators. Resistance quickly grew to the high taxes necessary to pay them off at their full face value.

Sympathetic political leaders promised a variety of legislative solutions: "installment laws" to lengthen the time that debtors could take to repay loans, "stay laws" to suspend the collection of debts and delinquent taxes entirely until the economy improved, and proposals to reinflate the currency by printing more money. Connecticut refused to pay the high requisition Congress imposed in 1785. Rhode Island established a carefully drawn system of paper currency and required creditors to accept it in payment of debts. People in other states urged their legislatures to emulate them.

Many Americans, including many of the leaders of the Revolution, were dismayed by such proposals. The Revolutionary leadership was drawn primarily from the wealthiest and most influential men in America, many of whom were creditors, although they often owed money as well. Laws interfering with debt collection deprived them of their property. So, more insidiously, did laws making it easier to repay debts by printing more money. Such legislation showed how easily the morals of the people were corrupted. It was factional activities like these that had always destroyed republics, they warned.

These controversies reflected a deep division in Americans' economic interests and attitudes. The elite leaders of the Revolution, often wealthy planters, merchants, or the lawyers who served them, were more likely than most Americans to be actively involved in the commercial economy. They were convinced that economic development required stability, even at the cost of some individual suffering. It required that mortgages and notes of indebtedness be freely exchangeable. Who would lend money in the future, either to individuals or to governments, if the legislature could change the terms of the loan or stop payment altogether? How could a planter or merchant make business plans if the government artificially changed the value of the money whenever a majority demanded it?

But if a modern commercial economy meant that speculators could take the farms and businesses of decent citizens or profit from speculating in government debt at the expense of hard-working taxpayers, many Americans wanted no part of it. It was the obligation of government to soften the blows of economic adversity, even if a few speculators were inconvenienced. Such actions benefited the whole community by maintaining social stability, order, and harmony. Moreover, placing the interests of creditors ahead of those of debtors put the economy at further risk. If large numbers of people went bankrupt, who would continue to buy goods? What would happen to the price of land as creditors put tens of thousands of seized acres up for sale? All over America, spokesmen for farmers and artisans denounced the aristocratic creditor "faction," which would rather let the whole economy collapse than surrender some of their profits.

Each side bitterly condemned the other. To the men who had led the Revolution, it seemed that their faith in the "virtue" of the American people had been misplaced. Americans seemed unwilling to defer to the wisdom of those who had led the Revolution. New, radical leaders challenged the revolutionary elite, denouncing their aristocratic pretensions to dominance. Discouraged by the first results of the republican experiment, many of the Revolution's leaders began to revive the idea that a proper, balanced institutional arrangement might encourage popular virtue and protect liberty. John Adams of Massachusetts and James Wilson of Pennsylvania, both respected lawyers and revolutionary leaders, provided the intellectual leadership. The American states lacked the social basis for British-style balance among monarchs, aristocracy, and the people, they recognized. So they instead stressed the necessity of enabling the executive and judicial branches of government to check and balance the legislative branch.

The conservative reformers had some success. In the 1780s a series of new state constitutions weakened the legislatures and strengthened the governors and the courts. Adams and Wilson played key roles in securing the most influential new constitutions, those of Massachusetts and Pennsylvania. Most of these constitutions made governors directly elected by the people, so that they would be independent of the legislature. They expanded the governors' power to veto legislation and to make appointments. The new constitutions established independent judiciaries, with judges appointed by governors rather than by legislatures.

To strengthen institutional sanctions against unconstitutional legislation, the reformers also stressed constitutionalism as a constraint on legislative power. Governors should use their augmented veto powers to prevent the passage of unconstitutional legislation, they insisted. Judges should refuse to enforce unconstitutional laws. For the first time, a few courts held state laws unconstitutional. This development angered many legislators and those promoting pro-debtor legislation; they argued that judicial review of the constitutionality of legislation transferred sovereignty from the people's representatives to the judges.

These reforms by no means solved the economic problems. In fact, as many of the state governments came under the control of more conservative influences, the disputes grew worse. In western Massachusetts, farmers and townspeople petitioned an unresponsive state legislature to attend to their problems. Frustrated, the locals moved to close the courts. The ensuing riot escalated into Shays's Rebellion. Although the state militia suppressed the insurrection, a sobered state legislature passed laws to ease the farmers' plight.

The descent towards violence tormented the more conservative leaders of the Revolution. Despite changes in state constitutions, they remained gloomy about the prospects for American liberty and prosperity. As George Washington lamented when he learned about the violence in Massachusetts, "Notwithstanding the boasted virtue of America, we are far gone in everything bad."

Federalism After 1776

Most of the disillusioned revolutionary leaders blamed what they saw as the disintegration of public order in the states on the weakness of the central government. They were convinced that a stronger common government was essential to any solution.

Before the Declaration of Independence, few Americans thought of the various colonial Congresses as being anything more than petitioning bodies, designed to increase the pressure on Great Britain. Previous efforts to organize some sort of intercolonial government, such as Benjamin Franklin's Plan of Union, proposed in 1754 at a conference in Albany, had never gotten off the ground. As the disappointed Franklin had observed in 1760, the colonies "all love Britain much more than they love one another."

But the conflict with Britain had united the colonies to a much greater degree than anyone had thought possible. The First Continental Congress inaugurated the Plan of Association to promote cooperation in 1774. The colonies began to act as if the Second Continental Congress, which convened in 1775, had some kind of governmental power. For example, no single colony was willing to proceed alone to declare independence. Instead, several petitioned Congress to do so, issuing their own declarations only after Congress had acted. Some bold visionaries, such as Thomas Paine, began painting a picture of the transcendent grandeur that would flow from a great, continental union. By 1776 most American leaders had decided that the union among the colonies ought to be made permanent. Nonetheless, no one imagined that Congress embodied a sovereign, national government, and it was no easy task to define just what the relationship among the states ought to be.

One of the greatest obstacles to creating an effective central government was the firm understanding that there could be only one sovereign in a political system—that is, one final authority that everyone must obey and from which there can be no appeal. It seemed clear to all that upon independence, each of the colonies became a sovereign, independent state. This conclusion comported with the common belief that only small countries were suitable for republican government. The acquisition of great empires had always signaled the death of liberty.

Delegates representing each of the states continued to meet in Congress, which the states empowered to act on their behalf in areas that required cooperation. These areas were already clear by 1777, and they did not change much. Fearing that the British might divide and conquer the American states through separate negotiations, the states insisted that Congress be solely responsible for discussions with the British and for establishing relations with foreign nations. Congress staffed and paid the Continental Army. To carry out these obligations, it printed and borrowed money. These responsibilities paralleled those that Americans had always conceded to the British government. In reality, the practice of federalism, both in the empire and during the resistance and the war, had developed ahead of the theory of sovereignty needed to understand it.

For over a year, Congress debated its exact authority in the new governmental system. Some delegates called for greater power. Most resisted. Late in 1777, Congress finally passed the Articles of Confederation. As Article III announced, the Articles united the former colonies in "a firm league of friendship." Since the states were sovereign, each had to agree to the Articles; the last did so in 1781.

The Articles of Confederation established a close alliance of independent states. They referred to the central government as a "confederacy" (Article I), as "a firm league of friendship" (Article III), and as "the united states in congress assembled" (Article IX). This last phrase signified that the government of the confederation, or the federal government, represented the states acting together; it was not a government directly responsible to the American people. Each state was represented in Congress, and each had a single, equal vote. Since each state was sovereign, subject to no higher power, amendments to the Articles required unanimous consent.

The Articles delegated to "the united states in congress assembled" only a few powers: to carry out foreign relations and make war (Articles VI, VIII, and IX); to settle disputes between states, if a state requested such help; to administer a postal department; and to borrow money, raise taxes, and coin money to carry out the other powers (Article IX). The Articles carefully denied the attributes of sovereignty to the federal government, in particular the power to enforce its laws on the people directly. There were no national courts or national law-enforcement officials. Congress assessed levies on the states, which were to contribute their shares to a common treasury (Article VIII). The Articles left it to the states to decide how to secure the money from their own citizens. Article IX provided that if the central government declared war, it was up to the states to provide the soldiers and equipment. The states promised to "inviolably observe" the Articles and to abide by the decisions of Congress (Article XIII), but the Articles provided no sanction to enforce a decision against a recalcitrant state.

Disillusionment with the Articles

The Articles of Confederation created an ineffectual government. With no executive department, government administration floundered. Dependent upon the states to pay their share of federal expenses, Congress was chronically short of cash. Unable to collect its assessments from the states, it had difficulty borrowing. It was barely able to pay the interest due on the money it already owed; paying off the principal seemed hopeless. The value of its notes and bonds plummeted. Speculators bought them from disillusioned lenders at rock-bottom prices. Federal officers went unpaid. Soldiers went without the pensions Congress had promised them during the war. Desperately, Congress printed money to pay its bills. The more money it printed, the less it was worth.

The federal government proved unable to carry out the terms of the Treaty of Paris, which had ended the war. According to the Treaty's provisions, the British recognized the independence of the American states and their authority over land from the Atlantic Ocean to the Mississippi River. British ports were to be reopened to American shipping. In return, the United States agreed to urge the states to return all property confiscated from Americans who had remained loyal to Britain, and to see to it that debts that had been owed to British and Loyalist creditors were paid.

After the war, Loyalists began to try to recover their property and British creditors began to try to collect their debts, or they sold their claims to others. However, the states had confiscated and collected these debts during the war. They had auctioned off confiscated property, and those who had purchased it were not about to give it up. Despite the states' promise to abide by the acts of Congress, their courts found ways to avoid enforcing the treaty. In retaliation, the

British refused to permit American ships into British ports, exacerbating the depression. They also refused to evacuate their forts in the western lands they had recognized as belonging to the United States.

While merchants and laborers in American ports blamed the depression on Congress's inability to enforce the Treaty of Paris, people on the frontier complained about its inability to get the British to leave the west. The British were encouraging the Indians to harass American settlers, while their state governments were neither able to protect them nor authorized to negotiate, they complained. These complaints, the desire for a freer opportunity to exploit the frontier (often at the expense of Native Americans), resentment of absentee landlords, and frustration with state governments controlled by the eastern seaboard led residents of frontier areas to try to secede from their states. They petitioned Congress to recognize their new state governments, but the Articles gave Congress no power to do so. In addition, the idea was plainly inconsistent with state sovereignty.

The federal government seemed unable to establish a western territorial policy. To persuade the smaller states to ratify the Articles of Confederation, the larger ones had ceded their western claims to the federal government. Settlers and land speculators longed for access to the wilderness, but Congress seemed to be paralyzed. Northeastern delegates urged a cautious westward expansion and the slow sale of land at high prices to fill the government's coffers. Southerners, inveterate land speculators, urged quick and easy land sales.

Lacking power to regulate commerce among the states, Congress also proved unable to resolve commercial and boundary disputes among them, or to pass rules necessary for interstate trade. As the economy worsened, states tried to protect their own merchants and artisans by imposing tariffs on goods from other states. States with important seaports, like New York and Pennsylvania, financed their governments through tariff duties, on the theory that residents of nearby states would wind up paying for the increased cost of many of the goods. Although Congress was supposed to be responsible for foreign policy, various states raised money by imposing tariffs on foreign imports. Quarrels developed over boundaries. New Jersey, New York, and Pennsylvania all claimed the right to control shipping on various waterways; Maryland, Virginia, and Delaware struggled for control of Chesapeake Bay.

Without money, without an army of its own, without courts to enforce its laws, there was little Congress could do as the states flouted its authority and quarreled among themselves. The situation humiliated Washington, John Adams, and other revolutionary leaders who had staked their reputations on the character of the American people. Their embarrassment fed their growing conviction that Americans lacked the virtue necessary for republican government. And the fact that many of them were themselves creditors of the federal government hardly soothed their feelings.

"Continentalists" or "nationalists," such as James Wilson, James Madison, and Alexander Hamilton, were convinced that economic prosperity and liberty itself depended on re-establishing stability. They desperately tried to expand the powers of Congress in the early 1780s. In doing so, they insisted that Congress, not the states, was sovereign—that it represented the people of the whole nation, not the individual states. Not only was this argument inconsistent with the language of the Articles of Confederation, it alienated many who agreed that something needed to be done. Few Americans were willing to make their states subordinate to the final authority of what would be a distant government, reigning supreme over a continental empire.

To cope with the financial crisis, the Continentalists proposed amending the Articles to strengthen the federal government. They especially urged an amendment authorizing Congress to raise money by taxing foreign trade. But it proved impossible to secure the required unanimous approval. Nonetheless, most Americans realized that they had somehow misspecified the powers of Congress. The principle was clear: the states should retain control of local and internal matters, while the federal government should have control of general and external matters. But the application was difficult. The problem was how to make the central government strong enough to carry out its responsibilities without making it so strong that it threatened liberty. Leaving sovereignty in the states seemed to lead to chaos. But making the central government sovereign meant converting the United States into a single nation with a unitary government. No government had ever governed so vast an area without degenerating into despotism.

With Congress unable to settle commercial disputes among the states, Virginia invited them to send delegates to an interstate commercial convention to be held at Annapolis, Maryland, in the fall of 1786. Failing to secure a large enough attendance to accomplish their mission, the delegates, led by Hamilton and John Dickinson, called for a new convention to meet in Philadelphia the following year. This convention would have the broader mission of determining how "to render the constitution of the Federal Government adequate to the exigencies of the Union." Congress cautiously endorsed the proposal; the states selected their delegates. In May 1787, they began to gather in Philadelphia at the State House, which later became known as Independence Hall.

Each state chose respected leaders clearly identified with nationalist reform. Men who augmented their landed and slave property with government bonds and other financial instruments were overrepresented, compared to the population as a whole. Many delegates thus reflected the new modern commercial orientation. Among its delegates, Virginia sent Washington, Madison, and Edmund Randolph, a dynamic young lawyer who had served as an aide to Washington during the Revolution and had since served as governor. Pennsylvania's delegation included Franklin and Wilson. New York sent Hamilton. Delaware sent Dickinson. Having complained for years about the weakness of the central government and the lack of "virtue" among the American people, they decided to try to cure both problems at once. Although they had been authorized only to recommend changes in the Articles of Confederation, the delegates resolved to consider themselves a constitutional convention, authorized to propose an entirely new constitution for the American union.

The Constitution of the United States

Led by Virginia's Randolph and Madison, and encouraged by Washington, the first delegates to arrive in Philadelphia agreed to promote the Continentalist program for creating a sovereign, national government. The government's courts and law-enforcement officials would act directly upon individuals rather than on the states. The delegates envisioned a national legislature elected directly by the people, with every representative casting an individual vote, directly representing his constituents rather than his state.

The convention named Washington presiding officer and spent two days establishing rules to govern the proceedings. The delegates kept the rules flexible, promoting creativity by permitting initial decisions to be easily reconsidered. They also resolved to keep the proceedings secret. And the first decisions made clear why, for they would have astounded most Americans.

As soon as the rules were settled, Randolph proposed resolutions embodying specific propositions to create the government the Continentalists envisioned. These propositions became known as the Virginia Plan. They called for a truly national government. Its legislature would have two branches: one elected directly by the people and apportioned according to population, and the second elected by the first. The legislature would be empowered to veto state laws that contravened the articles of the union. Randolph proposed an executive chosen by the legislature and a judiciary to consist of both a supreme court and lower courts. No longer would the central government represent the states and depend on them to enforce its laws. It would represent the people, and its officers would be elected by the people. Its laws would act directly upon the people, who would be tried in national courts for violating them. The nationalists were calling for the repudiation of federalism as Americans understood it.

The following day Randolph, urged on by Gouverneur Morris of New York, moved to postpone his specific propositions in order to decide one fundamental question—"that a *national* Government ought to be established consisting of a *supreme* Legislative, Executive & Judiciary." Morris made the issue clear, distinguishing "between a *federal* and *national, supreme*" government. A federal government, he explained, was "a mere compact resting on the good faith of the parties." A national, supreme government would have "a compleat and *compulsive* operation." Neither Morris nor the other delegates saw any alternative to lodging sovereignty either in the states or in a national government. In supporting his resolution Morris, contended "that in all Communities there must be one supreme power, and one only." The convention accepted the nationalist resolution by a vote of six states to one, with one divided. The delegates had abandoned state sovereignty for a sovereign, unitary state.

Having made the critical decision, the delegates turned to Randolph's other resolutions, debating how the legislative, executive, and judiciary should be organized and selected. They argued over whether the second branch of the legislature should be elected by the first or by the state legislatures; whether there should be a single, chief executive or several; whether the chief executive should be elected by the legislature or the people, how long he should serve, and whether he should be empowered to veto laws. The delegates agreed that the judges should hold their offices during good behavior but argued over how to select them and the scope of their jurisdiction. They also considered whether national laws should be enforced by state courts with appeals to a supreme national court or be enforced in national courts created for the purpose. Throughout, the concern was how to ensure that the officers of the powerful new government would not subvert liberty while still enabling the government to act decisively. A plural executive would reduce the threat to liberty from that source, but a single executive would give the government greater efficiency; a national judiciary would enable the government to enforce its laws quickly and firmly, but enforcing them in the state courts would preserve local control and protect popular liberty against a distant, potentially despotic government.

As the difficulty of the task became clear, a reaction set in against the Virginia Plan. Those who opposed it conceded the necessity of increasing the authority of Congress. But they concluded that preserving liberty required the retention of state sovereignty and limits on central power. Equally important, they worried that a legislature apportioned by population would favor the interests of the larger states to the detriment of the smaller ones. Finally, they were concerned that privileged commercial interests would dominate a powerful, distant government. On June 15, two and a half weeks into the debates, New Jersey delegate William Paterson proposed what became known as the New Jersey Plan.

The first of Paterson's resolutions proposed "that the articles of Confederation ought to be so revised . . . as to render the federal Constitution adequate to the exigencies of Government." Thus the New Jersey Plan explicitly envisioned the continuation of the federal system, which to the delegates still implied state sovereignty. Consequently, each state would continue to be entitled to a single vote in Congress. But the New Jersey Plan gave the central government the power to collect taxes directly. It also created a plural executive to be elected by the federal legislature and a central supreme court to be appointed by the executive. To deal with the states' refusal to honor federal decisions, the New Jersey Plan declared that the acts of the federal government would be "the supreme law of the respective States," binding on the state courts despite any state laws to the contrary. It authorized the federal executive to call out the state militias to compel obedience if necessary.

Nationalists adamantly resisted the New Jersey Plan, voting it down seven states to three. But its proponents resisted the Virginia Plan just as firmly, threatening to refuse to sign a proposal embodying it and to block ratification. A stalemate loomed, but the necessity of doing something was so great that pressure for compromise grew. Agreement was aided by the beginning of a conceptual breakthrough. Several delegates came to realize that no matter what the theory, the states were not fully sovereign even under the Articles of Confederation. New York delegate Rufus King put it best: "[T]he import of the terms 'States' 'Sovereignty' '*national*' 'federal,' had been often used & applied in the discussion inaccurately & delusively. The States were not 'Sovereigns' in the sense contended for by some. They did not possess the peculiar features of sovereignty. They could not make war, nor peace, nor alliances nor treaties. . . . If the States therefore retained some portion of their sovereignty, they had certainly divested themselves of essential portions of it. If they formed a confederacy in some respects—they formed a Nation in others."

King's insight made compromise possible. Suddenly delegates realized that it was possible to create a central government that was something more than a league—a government that contained both federal and national characteristics. On June 20, the delegates voted to eliminate the words "national Government" from Randolph's original resolution and substituted simply "the Government of the United States."

In such a government it would be inappropriate for the federal legislature to have a direct veto over state legislation; it was far preferable to adopt the New Jersey Plan's proposal requiring state courts to enforce federal legislation. The delegates thus ultimately drafted Article VI of the proposed constitution, called the "Supremacy Clause," which read, "This Constitution and the Laws of the United States which shall be made in Pursuance thereof; and all Treaties made . . . under the Authority of the United States, shall be the supreme Law of the Land; and the Judges in every State shall be bound thereby, any Thing in the Constitution or Laws of any State to the Contrary notwithstanding."

The delegates' willingness to seek a middle way between a unitary national state and traditional federalism made possible another crucial compromise. Formally proposed by Roger Sherman of Connecticut and known as the Connecticut Compromise (sometimes as "The Great Compromise"), it resolved the apportionment problem. Nationalists had insisted that the national legislature represent the people directly, confirming the government's national character. Their opponents had insisted equally firmly that the legislature represent the states, confirming the government's federal character. Now delegates felt free to mix the two approaches. According to the Connecticut Compromise, the lower house, or House of Representatives, would be elected directly by the people and apportioned according to population. The upper house, or Senate, would represent each state equally with two senators elected by their state legislatures.

Apportionment raised yet another problem. Southerners argued that slaves should be counted as part of their population. Northerners insisted that only free people should be counted towards representation. The dispute reflected divergent attitudes toward both slavery and toward the relationship between property and representation. Northern delegates disliked the idea of giving white southerners the added voting power of their slaves, but many agreed that basing representation entirely on population put property at risk. The southern states were richer than the northern states. If only the free population were counted toward representation, the northern states might impose taxes that burdened southerners more heavily than northerners. To resolve this problem, eleven states had already agreed to an amendment to the Articles of Confederation. It provided that in apportioning contributions to the federal treasury, Congress should count the slave population in the ratio of three slaves to five free persons. The convention adopted the three-fifths ratio as the basis for representation in the House of Representatives.

Tensions over slavery precipitated other compromises. Several northern delegates wanted the new constitution to ban the further importation of slaves. Some southern delegates, especially South Carolina's, adamantly resisted. They demanded that the slave trade be excluded from any new federal power to regulate commerce. The delegates finally compromised by barring any federal interference with slave imports until 1808 and limiting any customs duties to ten dollars per slave.

At the same time, southerners got another concession from Congress (which was meeting in New York while the Constitutional Convention met in Philadelphia). In July 1787 Congress finally passed the Northwest Ordinance, opening the territories west of Pennsylvania and north of the Ohio River to settlement on the easy terms southerners favored, although slavery was forbidden. The Ordinance provided for the future admission of new states on the same basis as the original thirteen. Thus settlers of all American territories were guaranteed an equal part in the new federal system emerging at Philadelphia.

The delegates completed the proposed constitution on September 17, 1788. Its compromises solved two problems: 1) how to make the central government strong without making it sovereign, and 2) how to create a republic for a people who were not "virtuous." To solve the first problem, the framers invented modern federalism—a system with two governments, each having final authority over different subjects. To solve the second, they created a system with ingenious "checks and balances" designed to prevent any one official or group of officials from securing too much power, as well as to prevent short-term majorities from enacting policies detrimental to the good of the whole.

The Ratification Debates and the Nature of the Federal Government

The character of these solutions became clear in the vigorous debate over ratifying the new document. The Constitutional Convention was unwilling to subject its proposal to the amendment process mandated by the Articles of Confederation, because amendment required unanimous consent. Instead, the Constitution called for special ratifying conventions in each state. A constitution, the delegates declared, ought to rest on the direct authority of the people, not on that of the state legislatures. The new Constitution would go into effect whenever the people of nine states agreed to it. Hopefully any hesitant states would join later.

In the campaigns leading to the ratifying conventions and at the conventions themselves, Americans thoroughly debated the virtues and vices of the proposed Constitution. Influential opponents of ratification, such as Samuel Adams of Massachusetts, Patrick Henry and Richard Henry Lee of Virginia, and Luther Martin of Maryland, denied that there could be two governments with final political authority in a single political system. One or the other had to be sovereign and thus superior in case of a conflict between them. The proposed Constitution gave the central government the power to enforce its laws and treaties as well as to collect taxes directly through its own courts and law-enforcement officers. Therefore, its opponents argued, the framers had abandoned the federal system and made the central government sovereign. They forcefully reiterated the traditional belief that a sovereign government over a nation the size of the United States must prove tyrannical.

Alongside the theoretical objections propounded in pamphlets, newspapers, and at the ratification conventions lay a deep-seated fear on the part of many Americans that the new system was designed to foster the growth of a commercial elite at the expense of ordinary citizens. A sovereign central government, over which ordinary citizens would have less influence than they did over state governments, would overwhelm the ability of local government and local courts to protect them from rapacious creditors; it would impose uniform economic policies that subverted local interests. Many of these critics favored economic development but charged that the Constitution was designed to enable a privileged few to secure all its benefits; they lambasted its aristocratic character—its king-like president, elitist Senate, and formidable Supreme Court. Others scorned the unbridled greed they saw accompanying drive for national prosperity, seeing local prosperity as more consistent with a general equality and republican virtue.

Proponents of ratification claimed that the Constitution would strengthen federalism rather than eliminate it. They thus took the name Federalists, to the dismay of their opponents, who wound up being called Antifederalists. Led by James Wilson, the Federalists offered a radically new interpretation of sovereignty. In European monarchies, they observed, sovereignty is located at the apex of society, in the king or in Parliament. Since sovereignty cannot be divided, all other government institutions in those nations had to be subordinate to the sovereign power. But in a republic, the people themselves were sovereign. Sovereignty came from below and remained with the people, who could delegate power to however many governments they wished, changing the distribution of power, if they wanted, by changing the Constitution. Therefore the preamble to the Constitution declared, "We the People . . . do ordain and establish this Constitution."

In the new federal system created by the Constitution, neither the states nor the national government was sovereign. Each was delegated final authority over different matters by a sovereign people. In exercising that authority, each acted independently and directly upon the people. The federal government had the power to act only in those areas where the Constitution delegated it power; all other matters remained under the control of the states. The people of the United States would be subject simultaneously to two separate governments.

Article I, Section 8, and a few sections of other articles listed the areas where the "federal government" would have final authority: over foreign policy and making war; over foreign trade, trade with the Indians, and commerce among the states; over the postal system, bankruptcy, and the currency system; and over territory and property owned by the national government. The Constitution also specifically denied some powers to the states. They were forbidden to carry out their own foreign policies or make war, to create their own currency systems, to "impair the obligation of contracts" (that is, to stop or delay the collection of debts), to create an aristocracy, to pass *ex post facto* laws (laws making acts criminal after they had already been done), or to pass "bills of attainder" (laws declaring people to be criminals without trial).

Like the states, the new federal government would be republican in form. But the framers had no illusions about the character of the American people. They carefully established a system of checks and balances to create a republican government that did not depend on the frail reed of public virtue. Promoting ratification in the *Federalist Papers,* Hamilton, Madison, and John Jay insisted that the new Constitution would not endanger liberty as Antifederalists charged. Rather, the Constitution would make liberty more secure. They also disagreed with the Antifederalists about where the threat to liberty lay. For Antifederalists, the danger emanated from a powerful government that might deprive the people of their rights for the benefit of the powerful few. The Federalists' experience with stay laws and paper money convinced them that republics posed a different danger. What Antifederalists saw as legitimate policies to protect the interests of ordinary planters and farmers, Federalists saw as a deprivation of individual property rights. Therefore, Federalists agreed with Madison's observations in the seminal *Federalist Number 10*: A republic must guard against the power of a majority bent on securing its own selfish interests in disregard of the general good and the rights of the minority.

There was a deep significance in the Federalist perception. In resisting tyranny, Americans had thought primarily in terms of *popular liberty*—the freedom of the people as a whole against a despotic government. They had been less concerned with *individual liberty*—the right of individuals to be free from the oppression of their own community. The heightened concern for the rights of the minority signified a major development in American political and constitutional ideas. In a radical break with traditional republican thought, Madison abandoned the search for a virtuous people free of factions. In every society, differences in religion,

Alexander Hamilton, nationalist and proponent of "broad construction" of federal power.

James Madison, "Father of the Constitution" and defender of state rights.

education, economic interests, wealth, and other characteristics inevitably lead to factions, Madison wrote. A good republican government should be structured to prevent any one faction—even if it was made up of the majority—from oppressing the rest, so that government would serve only the general welfare.

The Federalists argued that the new government, with its separation of powers and its checks and balances, provided part of the solution to the problem of factions. The Constitution created separate legislative, executive, and judicial branches of government to administer its three great functions. Each branch, and each house of Congress, was selected by a different constituency. The President would be elected by a nationwide "college of electors" selected in a manner determined by each state legislature. The members of the House would be elected directly by the people in separate congressional districts. The Senate would be elected by the state legislatures. The president would nominate the judges, but the Senate would confirm them. The president, each house of Congress, and the judges would serve different, overlapping terms. To assure that the president could not use patronage to corrupt the legislature, the Constitution forbade congressmen from holding any other government office.

These differences in constituencies and terms would preclude any one faction or short-term majority from securing complete control of the government. Passing and enforcing laws required the cooperation of all three branches. Proposals needed the approval of both the Senate and the House to become law. The president could veto any law; it required a two-thirds vote of each of the houses of Congress to override him. Likewise, Congress was given a say in matters generally reserved for the executive branch: the Senate confirmed presidential appointments and ratified treaties; executive departments were created by law. Although the president conducted foreign relations and was commander-in-chief, Congress had the power to declare war and to regulate the armed forces. The judicial branch was also largely independent of the other two branches; judges served for life, removable only for misconduct. Yet Congress had the power to establish and modify the lower court system and to regulate its jurisdiction. The president had the power to appoint the judges themselves and the Senate had the power to confirm them. While the judges would issue writs, such writs would be served by United States marshals appointed by the president and subject to his instructions.

The federal system itself added another safeguard. The federal government had authority in only a limited number of areas. The laws and administration most intimately involved in day-to-day life were the responsibility of the states. Besides capturing all three branches of the federal government, an oppressive majority would have to gain control of the state governments. These too represented different constituencies, elected at different times for different terms.

Another new idea followed from this analysis: A large republic was more likely to maintain liberty than a small one. Antifederalists adhered to the old idea that small nations were best suited for republican government, because their greater uniformity of ethnic, religious, and economic interests discouraged the development of factions. But if factions were an inevitable part of politics, Madison wrote in *Federalist Number 10,* the more factions there were, the better. With many factions, it would be more difficult for any one of them to gain control of government. Therefore people would be more likely to choose leaders devoted to the general welfare. The larger government of the United States would be a safer repository of liberty than the smaller state governments.

Underlying Federalists' perceptions and arguments was a commitment both to individual liberty and to the modern, commercial state that Antifederalists feared. The "faction" that Madison and other Federalists worried about most was made up of those who would disrupt the credit and financial system to relieve pressure during economic downturns, or who would protect local interests obstructing national commercial development. But Madison and other Federalists conceived and expressed their goals in more abstract terms—of protecting minority rights from majority oppression, of creating political processes and institutions to restrain the passions of the moment, of promoting the general welfare rather than special interests. Their ideas transcended mere issues of commerce and development, giving them a power that still resonates today.

The Antifederalists scorned Federalists' new-fangled arguments. Under the Constitution, the federal government overflowed with power, and power destroyed liberty. The president would prove a tyrant; Congress would swallow up the states. But without a viable counterproposal for strengthening the federal government, the Antifederalists were at a serious disadvantage. Nearly all Americans agreed that some change was needed. Lamely, the Antifederalists suggested yet another convention.

The Antifederalists did articulate one strong argument: that the Constitution lacked a Bill of Rights. This oversight, the Antifederalists insisted, demonstrated the Federalists' disregard for popular liberty. Federalists answered that no Bill of Rights was needed, because the Constitution granted the federal government no authority to regulate speech, the press, or religion. The states retained the responsibility for protecting people against ordinary crimes and for adjudicating civil disputes between their residents.

Here the Antifederalists clearly had the better argument. The federal government *could* pass laws that affected speech, the press, or religion in the course of carrying out its delegated powers. It was responsible for the post office. Could it bar disfavored publications from the mail? It was empowered to govern the territories of the United States. Could it establish a religious test for voting or holding office there? The federal government could pass and enforce laws necessary and proper to carry out its responsibilities. Some of these might be criminal laws; others would give rise to rights enforceable in civil cases. Both would entail trials in federal courts. Yet nothing in the Constitution guaranteed jury trials, the right against self-incrimination, the right to call witnesses, or other elements of due process.

The Federalists were particularly powerful in the commercial centers, where merchants and craftsmen believed that stable federal regulation of commerce and finances was essential to prosperity. The newspapers published in these cities, which generally set the tone for provincial papers, were solidly Federalist. Nonetheless, Antifederalists swept the less developed rural areas and were very numerous in the ratifying conventions of several of the most important states. It took intricate political maneuvering and significant concessions to win ratification in Pennsylvania, Massachusetts, Virginia, and New York, all of which were crucial to a new union. Still, by the end of 1788, the Federalists had won ratification in every state except North Carolina and Rhode Island, which resisted giving up its carefully drawn paper-money system. North Carolina ratified the following year; Rhode Island grudgingly followed in 1790.

However, the Federalists were forced to agree to add a Bill of Rights to the Constitution. In its first session, Congress proposed twelve amendments drawn from the many submitted by the ratifying conventions. Ten were ratified by the states in 1791. Madison had hoped to have them apply to the states. But Congress rejected his proposal. Instead, the provisions were aimed at restraining the central government. The Bill of Rights protected freedom of religion, speech, and press; limited federal authority over militias and the right to bear arms; and guaranteed property rights and due process in criminal and civil cases. The Ninth Amendment made clear that listing some rights did not mean that government could infringe on others that were not listed. The Tenth stated that the people gave the national government only those powers delegated in the Constitution. All other powers were left with the states or were not delegated at all. The framers had not created a sovereign national government, with general authority over all subjects, but a federal government of limited jurisdiction.

Ratification did not settle the dispute over the proper balance between state and federal power. In fact, by denying sovereignty to either the state or the federal government, the Constitution encouraged continuing disputes since neither government had the final say on the subject. The Constitution was remarkable for its brevity and generality. It established a skeleton of government to be fleshed out by Congress and succeeding generations of Americans.

TIMELINE

1754	Benjamin Franklin proposes the Albany Plan of Union.
1774	The First Continental Congress passes the Plan of Association.
1776–1777	Most states draft new constitutions.
	Virginia passes the Virginia Declaration of Rights.
	Anglican church disestablished in most states where it was previously established.
1777	The as yet unrecognized state of Vermont abolishes slavery.
	The Continental Congress proposes the Articles of Confederation.
1778–1788	The "Critical Period": economic depression, pressure on state governments for stay laws and inflation.
1780	Massachusetts adopts a new state constitution.
	Pennsylvania repeals its slave code and adopts gradual emancipation.
1780s	Series of court decisions abolishes slavery in Massachusetts.
1781	Articles of Confederation ratified.
1783	Treaty of Paris ends the Revolutionary War.
1784–1788	Congress unable to raise enough money to support the government.
1784	Connecticut and Rhode Island pass gradual emancipation laws.
1786	Great Britain refuses to evacuate the Great Lakes region until the terms of the Treaty of Paris are fulfilled.

1786	Annapolis Convention calls for a new convention in Philadelphia to propose changes to the Articles of Confederation.
	Shays's Rebellion breaks out in Massachusetts.
1787	Congress endorses the call for the Philadelphia convention.
	Philadelphia convention convenes and resolves to propose an entirely new constitution.
	Congress passes the Northwest Ordinance.
	The Constitutional Convention proposes a new Constitution of the United States.
1787–1788	All states but Rhode Island and North Carolina ratify the Constitution; many propose amendments declaring rights.
1789	United States government established under the Constitution; George Washington inaugurated as president of the United States.
	North Carolina ratifies the Constitution.
	Congress proposes twelve constitutional amendments declaring rights.
1790	Rhode Island ratifies the Constitution.
	Pennsylvania revises its state constitution.
1791	Ten constitutional amendments, known as the Bill of Rights, ratified.
1799	New York passes a gradual emancipation law.
1804	New Jersey is the last northern state to pass a gradual emancipation law.
1808	Congress abolishes the foreign slave trade.

FURTHER READING

For constitutional developments within the American states during the Confederation period, see Willi Paul Adams, *The First American Constitutions* (1980), Donald S. Lutz, *Popular Consent and Popular Control: Whig Theory in the Early State Constitutions* (1980), and Marc W. Kruman, *Between Authority and Liberty: State Constitution Making in Revolutionary America* (1997). For the movement to separate church and state and secure greater religious liberty in the wake of the Revolution, see Thomas J. Curry, *The First Freedoms* (1986). William Lee Miller offers an account of disestablishment in Virginia, aimed at a general audience in *The First Liberty* (1986). Arthur Zilversmit chronicles the post-Revolutionary emancipation of African Americans in the North in *The First Emancipation* (1967). Ira Berlin discusses abolition in the North and changes in southern slavery in his magisterial history of slavery *Many Thousands Gone* (1998). Donald R. Wright provides a briefer version in *African Americans in the Colonial Era* (1990).

For the development of the ideal of "republican womanhood," see Linda K. Kerber's classic *Women of the Republic* (1980). Mary Beth Norton says that the Revolution was somewhat liberating for American women in *Liberty's Daughters* (1980). But see Joan Hoff-Wilson's contrary view that the Revolution gave only "The Illusion of Change," in *The American Revolution: Explorations in the History of American Radicalism*, ed. Alfred F. Young (1976).

Just as the Progressive historians challenged traditional interpretations of the Revolution, so they challenged the idea that the Constitution was the culmination of the American struggle for liberty. In 1913 Charles A. Beard published *An Economic Interpretation of the Constitution* (1913), suggesting that economic interests rather than ideological commitments motivated the framers. The Beard thesis came under bitter attack in the 1950s. For the most thorough and trenchant criticism, see Robert E. Brown, *Charles Beard and the Constitution* (1956). Forrest McDonald presented a more complex analysis of the relationship between the ratification of the Constitution and economic interests in *We the People* (1958). Important historians continued to argue that economic conflict was central and that the ratification of the Constitution amounted to a conservative counterrevolution. See Merrill Jensen, *The New Nation* (1958) and Jackson Turner Main, *The Antifederalists* (1961). Leonard L. Richards echoes this understanding in his study of *Shays's Rebellion* (2002). Cecilia M. Kenyon, in contrast, saw the issue primarily as ideological in her classic description of the Antifederalists as "Men of Little Faith," *William and Mary Quarterly* 12 (3d ser.) (January 1955): 3–43.

Gordon Wood combined the ideological and economic viewpoints in his brilliant *The Creation of the American Republic* (1969), still the standard account of the transformation of American ideology between the Revolution and the ratification of the Constitution. Various historians have challenged Wood's conclusions. For a smorgasbord of criticisms, see the forum on Wood's book in the *William and Mary Quarterly* 46 (3d ser.) (July 1987): 550–640. In *Between Authority and Liberty*, noted above, Kruman argues that the ideas Wood described as percolating only in the decade following the Revolution were already reflected in state constitutions as early as 1776.

While American historians wrangled over the relationship between social and economic developments and constitutional thought in the Confederation era, McDonald published an outstanding intellectual history of the framers' ideas, *Novus Ordo Seclorum: The Intellectual Origins of the Constitution* (1985). Compare its approach to Wood's effort to integrate a wider range of factors. In *A Revolution in Favor of Government* (2003), Swedish historian Max M. Edling connects the debate over the Constitution to the development of the military-fiscal state in Great Britain and other European nations, arguing that Federalists aspired to such a modern state while Antifederalists resisted it. For a careful analysis of the ideas of the framers and the degree to which they are relevant to present-day constitutional conflicts, see Jack N. Rakove's Pulitzer Prize–winning *Original Meanings* (1996). One example is the controversy over the Second Amendment and gun control. For an insightful historical assessment, see H. Richard Uviller and William G. Merkel, *The Militia and the Right to Arms* (2002).

Jack P. Greene brings his story of the origins of American federalism, *Peripheries and Center* (1986), to a close with the framing and ratification of the Constitution. The eminent political scientist Samuel H. Beer stresses the intellectual heritage of federalism in *To Make a Nation* (1993). For efforts to strengthen the central government under the Confederation, see Jack N.. Rakove, *The Beginning of National Politics* (1979). In *The Origins of the Federal Republic* (1983), Peter Onuf demonstrates that the states needed a stronger central government to settle their own disputes and confer legitimacy on their claims.

The most readable narrative account of the Philadelphia Constitutional Convention is Catherine Drinker Bowen's delightful if hagiographic *Miracle at Philadelphia* (1966). Use it with care. Carol Berkin has written another lively account, *A Brilliant Solution: Inventing the American Constitution* (2002). More detailed but still compelling reading is Christopher Collier and James Lincoln Collier, *Decision in Philadelphia* (1986).

Historians strenuously debate how much the Framers accommodated slavery in the Constitution. Paul Finkelman says the Constitution amounted to "Affirmative Action for the Master Class," *Akron Law Review* 32 (1999): 423–70. Don E. Fehrenbacher disagrees in "Slavery and the Founding of the Republic," chapter 2 of *The Slaveholding Republic* (2001).

The essays in Thomas E. Cronin, *Inventing the American Presidency* (1989) deal with how the structure and powers of the presidency were developed by the framers and the first presidents.

Gary L. McDowell provides the best brief description of Antifederalists' concerns in "Federalism and Civic Virtue: The Antifederalists and the Constitution," in *How Federal Is the Constitution?*, ed. Robert A. Goldwin and William A. Schambra (1982). Saul Cornell discusses the various perspectives from which Antifederalists opposed ratification in *The Other Founders* (1999). Robert A. Rutland describes *The Birth of the Bill of Rights* (1955). Leonard Levy digs deeper into the background in *Origins of the Bill of Rights* (1999), drawn from his many book-length investigations of its provisions. In his highly influential *The Bill of Rights: Creation and Reconstruction* (1998), Akhil Reed Amar forcefully argues that Americans originally conceived of the Bill of Rights as guaranteeing the liberties of the people as a whole rather than the rights of individuals.

5
Constitutional Issues in the Early Republic

When Americans elected their first administration under the new Constitution in 1789, Federalists believed that they had successfully solved the problem of faction and placed the best men in control of government. The electoral college unanimously elected George Washington president. John Adams, another supporter of the Constitution, was elected vice president. Washington named important framers and supporters of the Constitution to leading positions in the government. He nominated Alexander Hamilton to be secretary of the treasury; Thomas Jefferson, identified with the Constitution because of his friendship with James Madison, became secretary of state; and Edmund Randolph was appointed attorney general. John Jay and James Wilson were placed on the Supreme Court, while Madison became the most important leader in the House of Representatives.

Despite their hopes, the Federalists soon found that they were divided among themselves on basic principles of government. By the mid-1790s two loosely organized groups, Federalists and Jeffersonian Republicans,* were fighting for power. Disagreeing on a wide range of issues, each group considered the other to be a mere "faction" and therefore dangerous to liberty. Most Americans could not yet conceive of normal competition between political parties and had little idea that democracy requires toleration of organized political opposition.

Until Americans learned to accept the legitimacy of political competition, the future of the Republic remained uncertain. The crucial test for a democratic system comes when leaders lose elections and must surrender power to their opponents. There was no guarantee that the new nation would pass this test; in fact, the bitter rhetoric of the 1790s made the outcome doubtful. For this reason, the transfer of power from the Federalists to the Republicans after the election of 1800 was a crucial event in American constitutional history.

---

*Republicans of the 1790s through the 1820s are often called "Jeffersonian Republicans" to distinguish them from the antislavery politicians who organized the modern Republican party in the mid-1850s.

The Federalists and Effective Government

The issues that divided the triumphant Federalists arose in response to policies proposed by Hamilton, who quickly became the most influential leader in Washington's administration. Shocked by the strength of the Antifederalist opposition to the Constitution, Federalists feared that the instability of the Confederation period might continue. Most Americans still seemed to owe their first loyalty to their states. The United States might therefore remain a league of jealous localities, powerless against strong foreign nations and plagued by factional conflict at home.

Federalists' desire to strengthen the national government arose partly from their fear that the Revolution had swung America too far towards democracy. They believed that republican society would foster a natural aristocracy of educated, talented people who would secure wealth and high social standing. Ordinary people ought to defer to this "aristocracy of talent" in social and political matters. If every man came to believe he was as good as another, they worried, respect for society's natural leaders would collapse. Demagogues would seek power by appealing to selfish interests. Disorder and tyranny were sure to follow.

To promote respect for authority, Federalists supported the established churches in the states that had them—Congregationalist in New England and Episcopalian in other parts of the country. State-supported churches in America would serve as bulwarks of order and deference in America as they did in Britain. A weak national government encouraged factiousness and disorder; therefore Hamilton and most Federalists were determined to strengthen central authority. Hamilton urged Congress to establish a standing army as a counterweight to the state militias. He proposed that the federal government assume payment of the debts contracted by the states during the Revolution. To pay the combined state and federal debt, he devised a bold financial program. He proposed that the national government borrow money, to be repaid over a long period; advocated a national bank to help administer the program; and submitted a variety of taxes to pay for it. As the government built up its financial reserves, it would deposit the money into the national bank. The bank in turn would lend it out, providing capital for planters and businessmen. A substantial portion of the revenue to pay off the debt would come from high tariffs on imported goods. These tariffs would protect new American industries from cheap foreign competition. Federalists believed that these policies would encourage the development of an orderly, prosperous commercial society—a mercantile utopia. Altogether, this was a system much like that of Great Britain. Hamilton hoped that his program would link the interests of the rich and powerful to the national government, just as similar policies did in England. The support of the social and economic elite would make the national government strong, respected by foreign governments and American citizens alike.

As a natural consequence of these ideas, the Federalists were pro-British.

England had the kind of orderly yet free society that the Federalists admired. At the same time, most Federalists deplored the radicalism that characterized the French Revolution after 1791. Its excesses—killings, civil war, confiscation of property, and anticlericalism—embodied all the horrors they feared would follow if democracy went too far in the United States. Therefore, when Great Britain and France went to war, the Federalists sympathized with the British. In 1795 they ratified a new peace treaty with Britain negotiated by John Jay.

Like the other elements of Hamilton's program, Federalist foreign policy favored the commercial interests of the merchants of New England and the Atlantic ports, at the expense of southern and western farmers, planters, and land speculators. Jay's Treaty secured the right of American vessels to trade with British colonies in East India and the Caribbean, and placed Anglo-American trade on a most-favored-nation basis. But it said nothing about compensation for slaves seized by the British during the war. Although the British agreed to vacate their forts in the northwest, the treaty did not address charges that the British fomented anti-American hostility among Native Americans there. Worse, the British trading concessions were purchased by America's agreement to a joint commission to settle British and Loyalist claims for property seized during the Revolution. Such claims had been resisted in the American state courts, especially in the South.

While working hard to secure New England's commercial interests, the Federalists did little to pressure Spain to open the Mississippi River to American shipping, southerners and westerners complained. Spain controlled New Orleans, at the mouth of the river. Since all rivers beyond the Appalachian Mountains drained into the Mississippi, the great river provided the only route to the sea and world trade. Until the United States secured free, or at least cheap, shipping down the river, its western lands were of little commercial value. Open the area to world trade, however, and one opened the door to booming economic development that would benefit the planter–land speculators of the South and encourage the egalitarian mixed economy that Republicans believed essential to liberty.

The Republicans and Equal Rights

The Federalist program divided Americans along new lines. Many who had supported the Constitution broke with their former allies. The most important were Jefferson and Madison. Most of the Antifederalists joined them in opposition, although a few, like Patrick Henry and Luther Martin, went over to the Federalist side. The dissenters slowly organized, forming "Democratic Clubs" and coalescing into a loosely bound political group whose members called themselves Republicans.

The Jeffersonian Republicans blasted the Federalists for betraying the principles of the Revolution. By giving special privileges to the rich and powerful in order to win their support for the national government, the Federalists were violating the republican tenet of equal rights for all. Such policies had corrupted England and undermined British liberty. Americans had fought the Revolution to prevent the British from imposing similar policies here. Now their own leaders hankered after aristocratic privileges.

Republicans especially criticized Federalist support for the religious establishments that persisted in many states. In Virginia, Jefferson and Madison led the movement to disestablish the Episcopalian church. In 1786, they succeeded in passing the Statute for Religious Freedom, separating church and state, over the objection of Patrick Henry and his allies, who advocated giving state support to all the state's Christian denominations. In the 1790s Jefferson's allies eliminated the church's remaining privileges. A "wall" should exist between church and state, Jefferson would write a few years later, protecting each from the influence of the other. It is doubtful that they would have agreed completely with so trenchant a statement, but the fight made Republicans of most of Virgina's Methodists, Quakers, Presbyterians, and Baptists. In other states too, those who opposed special privileges for religious denominations allied with the Republicans. Supporters of the established churches, like Henry and most of the Congregationalist clergy of New England, gravitated towards the Federalists, who charged that Jefferson and the Republicans were atheists and radicals, bent on destroying both religion and order.

For Republicans, and especially for Jefferson, the fight for religious liberty related to the even more fundamental question of the state's role in governing people's opinions. Reflecting the ideas of the Enlightenment, Jefferson believed one could arrive at truth only through the application of reason. Truth could not be imposed by state or church power. In his 1781 *Notes on Virginia*, Jefferson wrote, "Reason and free inquiry are the only effectual agents against error. Give a loose to them, they will support the true religion by bringing every false one to their tribunal, to the test of their investigation." "It is error alone which needs the support of government," he insisted. "Truth can stand by itself." Jefferson was speaking of religion, but his words could apply to politics as well. They implied not only freedom of religion, but freedom of speech.

Federalists saw things differently. Ordinary people lacked the capacity to determine truth for themselves. They had to rely on the talented minority whose education and intellect fitted them for scientific, religious, and philosophical investigations. To give free rein to popular opinions on such matters was to invite chaos. Religion and education should inculcate due respect for authority, enable people to distinguish good teachers and exemplars from bad, and encourage deference to wise and good leaders. The state was obligated to encourage religion, education, and morality, not to stand aloof from them. By attacking established religion, Jefferson undermined all respect for authority and order, they charged.

Jefferson carried his fight for equal rights into economics and politics. He insisted that republican liberty could exist only where wealth was more or less evenly distributed among independent farmers and planters. Jefferson had no fear that demagogues would seduce the people in such a society. He was much more worried that the rich and powerful would turn government into a machine for securing special privileges, as they had in England. He attacked Hamilton's proposals as encouraging such corruption. Hamilton's program would concentrate wealth in the hands of a few rich planters, merchants, and manufacturers, upon whom other Americans would be dependent. The wealthy minority would use its influence to control the votes of those obligated to them, thereby gaining control of the government.

Just as Federalists' beliefs led them to sympathize with England, Republicans' beliefs led them to sympathize with revolutionary France. More than anything else, Jay's Treaty with England led Republicans to organize against the Federalists. In 1796, when Washington retired from the presidency, the Federalists supported John Adams to succeed him, while the Republicans supported Jefferson. The Federalists were still the stronger group, and Adams was elected. Jefferson, with the next largest number of electoral votes, became vice president.

The Alien and Sedition Acts

To Republicans, Federalists' sympathy for England proved that they had abandoned republican ideals and favored aristocracy over liberty and equality. On the other hand, Republican support for France proved to Federalists that Republicans approved of the murderous anticlerical radicalism of the French Revolution. Each side supposed that the other was a mere "faction," seeking power by appealing to special interests. Denunciations on both sides were bitter. Federalists accused Republicans of being "Jacobins" (the most radical French revolutionaries) bent on making America subservient to France. Republicans accused the Federalists of being monarchists, conspiring to restore British influence over the United States. The ill feeling was exacerbated by the open although undeclared naval warfare that broke out between France and the United States in 1797. The patriotism that war engenders always puts stress on civil liberties, and Federalists could not understand how loyal Americans could continue to criticize their nation's foreign policy in wartime.

Under these circumstances, it is not surprising that the Federalists took steps to suppress the Republican opposition. Looking ahead to the presidential election of 1800, in 1798 they passed the Naturalization, Alien, and Sedition Acts. The latter two were to continue in force only through 1801. The Naturalization and Alien Acts were aimed at newly arriving English, Irish, and French radicals. The Naturalization Act mandated that newcomers live in the United States for fourteen years before they could become American citizens, instead of the five years previously required. During that time, they would be subject to the Alien Act, which authorized the government to deport immigrants whom it considered dangerous.

The Sedition Act made it a crime to falsely criticize government officials.

"Mad Tom in a Rage." This Federalist political cartoon accuses the radical Jefferson of tearing down the pillars of (federal) government.

During the election of 1800, which again pitted Adams against Jefferson, Federalist officials used the new law to prosecute leading Republican newspaper editors and pamphleteers.

Republicans attacked the law bitterly, charging that it confirmed the Federalist threat to liberty. But the act also forced Republicans to reconsider the nature of democratic politics. People began to realize for the first time that political disagreements and rival political parties were inevitable in a democratic country. They concluded that it was more dangerous to liberty to suppress competing organizations than it was to let them operate freely. Consequently, Republicans added calls for "free speech" and "free press" to their demand for religious freedom and equal rights.

Federalists, Republicans, and the Nature of the Union

Since the Federalists controlled the national government, Jefferson and his party tried to limit federal authority and exalt that of the states. But Jefferson also sincerely believed that national power was more likely to be abused than state power and that the Constitution intended the state governments to check federal usurpations.

Jefferson and the Republicans turned to the Constitution to support their position. In 1791, after Congress agreed to Hamilton's proposal to establish a national bank, he and Jefferson debated the idea's constitutionality in separate letters to President Washington, who was uncertain whether to sign the bill. Jefferson, at that time still Washington's secretary of state, advocated strict construction of the powers that the Constitution delegated to the federal government. The Constitution did not authorize the national government to charter a national bank, he argued. The Constitution enumerated a group of powers that were expressly delegated to the national government. It then added that Congress could pass laws "necessary and proper" to carry out these powers (Article I, Section 8). The Constitution did not expressly authorize Congress to charter a bank, nor was a bank necessary to carry out any of the powers enumerated. It might be convenient to have a bank, Jefferson admitted, but it was not *necessary.*

Hamilton responded with an argument for broad construction of national power. When the Constitution delegated power over a subject to the national government, it conveyed the same authority over that subject that any sovereign nation had. The delegation of general powers to Congress necessarily implied the right to pass laws appropriate for exercising them. Article I, Section 8 confirmed this principle by authorizing Congress to enact laws "necessary and proper" for carrying out the enumerated powers. The Necessary and Proper Clause was not a restriction of federal power, as Jefferson argued, but a grant of power. It authorized Congress to pass laws "appropriate" to fulfilling its obligations. These laws did not have to be absolutely essential, but necessary only in the sense of "useful" or "convenient." The real test was whether a law was directly and clearly connected to a delegated power. "The *degree* to which a measure is necessary, can never be a *test* of the legal right to adopt it; that must be a matter of opinion," Hamilton wrote Washington. "The *relation* between the *measure* and the *end* . . . must be the criterion of constitutionality, not the more or less of *necessity* or *utility.*"

Jefferson replied that such a broad construction of federal power effectively eliminated the limits inherent in the federal system. There was no measure "which ingenuity may not torture into a *convenience* in some instance *or other,* to *some one* of so long a list of enumerated powers," he warned. Under such an interpretation, the Necessary and Proper Clause "would swallow up all the delegated powers, and reduce the whole to one phrase." Washington, who had consistently favored a stronger national government, sided with Hamilton, throwing his prestige behind Federalists' constitutional nationalism.

When the Federalist-dominated Congress passed the Alien and Sedition Acts, Jefferson and Madison again argued that Congress had exceeded its constitutional powers. Hoping to sway public opinion in time for the elections of 1800, they offered a detailed argument about the nature of the federal system. To publicize their views, they prepared a series of resolutions and arranged to have them passed by the Kentucky and Virginia state legislatures, where Republicans held a majority.

In the Kentucky and Virginia Resolutions, Jefferson and Madison repudiated the understanding of federalism that James Wilson and other Federalists had articulated during the campaign to ratify the Constitution. They argued that the Constitution was merely a compact among sovereign states by which the states had created a confederation. The "several states composing the United States of America" had delegated a strictly limited number of powers to the general government. The Tenth Amendment confirmed that all other powers remained under state jurisdiction. Since the Constitution provided no arbiter to settle a disagreement over whether a federal law exceeded the powers the states had delegated, each state retained the right to judge for itself. Exercising that right, Kentucky and Virginia pronounced the Alien and Sedition Acts void, instructed their congressmen to work for their repeal, and urged other states to do likewise.

Through pamphlets, court decisions, charges to grand juries, and resolutions passed by Federalist-controlled state legislatures, Federalists responded with a nationalist interpretation of the federal system. Federalists insisted that the *people* of the United States had framed the Constitution. The Constitution was not a compact among sovereign states, creating a confederacy; it was the organic act of the people creating a sovereign national government, although the jurisdiction of that government was limited to certain subjects. With respect to those subjects, the states were not sovereign and therefore retained no power to pronounce national laws void. That was a job for courts, not legislatures.

Federalist Supreme Court justices, led by Wilson, John Jay, and Samuel Chase, incorporated the nationalist argument into some of their earliest decisions. One issue was whether the states could be sued in federal courts by citizens of other states. Article III of the Constitution declared that the judicial power "shall extend to all Cases . . . between a State and a Citizen of another State." It gave the Supreme Court original jurisdiction in any case "in which the State shall be a Party." The Federalists had assured the state conventions that these provisions were designed to enable the states to bring cases as plaintiffs. As sovereign states, they would be immune from suits brought against them. Nonetheless, after ratification citizens began to bring suit against various states. State officials protested that as sovereign entities, the states could not be forced to appear in federal court. But in *Chisholm v. Georgia* (1793), the justices rejected the argument. The people of the United States had ordained the Constitution. Where they had given the federal government authority, they had subjected the states to it.

State officials reacted with outrage. Within a few months Congress proposed a constitutional amendment to bar such suits. The Eleventh Amendment was ratified in 1798, approved by both Federalists and Republicans. For Federalists, the issue was the principle of "sovereign immunity," by which a state was immune from suits brought by its own citizens. The Eleventh Amendment merely extended this doctrine to suits brought by citizens of other states. Republicans, in contrast, took the Eleventh Amendment to confirm their view of the federal system. The Amendment meant that the states retained sovereignty in the Union and could not be subjected to the authority of a branch of the federal government.

The Election of 1800

Federalists and Republicans had divided over fundamental issues about political and civil rights and the nature of the federal system. The bitterly contested presidential and congressional elections of 1800 therefore involved these basic issues of American government. The Federalists renominated Adams, while the Republicans again nominated Jefferson, with Aaron Burr of New York proposed for the vice presidency. Federalists attacked Republicans as atheists and anarchists, subverting order and authority in a frenzy of French-inspired radicalism and threatening to destroy the Union with their exaltation of state sovereignty. Republicans charged Federalists with being aristocrats and monarchists, intent on subverting the liberty of the people and converting the Union into a consolidated empire. Neither side conceded the legitimacy of the other's opposition. Each considered extra-constitutional measures and each feared the other would resort to violence. Each believed that there was only one correct answer to the issues. It never occurred to the Republicans that the courts were the place to settle such issues; it was up to the people to define the contours of American constitutionalism.

The result was a great victory for Jefferson and the Republicans, who won the presidency, control of the House of Representatives, and a tie in the Senate, which could be broken in their favor by the casting vote of Vice President Burr. However, the most crucial test of American democracy remained: Would the defeated Federalists turn power over to their political enemies, whose policies they believed to threaten liberty and the Union? The Constitution provided that the candidate receiving a majority of the votes of the Electoral College would become president, with the candidate receiving the second highest number becoming vice president. If no candidate received a majority, the House of Representatives would elect the president, with each state delegation casting a single vote. All 73 Republicans elected to the Electoral College voted for both Jefferson and Burr. The election therefore went to the House of Representatives, which the Federalists would control until the new Congress met the following year. A deadlock ensued. Through 35 ballots, no candidate secured a majority of the state delegations. Some Federalists conspired to shift the Federalist vote to Burr and place him rather than Jefferson in the presidency, but they never struck a deal. Finally, Delaware Federalists secured a commitment from Jefferson that he would not radically alter the government. They broke the stalemate, and Adams peacefully surrendered the presidency to his old friend and rival.

To prevent repetition of the crisis, Congress quickly proposed another amendment to the Constitution—to have the Electoral College cast separate ballots for the president and the vice president. The states promptly ratified it. In effect, the Twelfth Amendment recognized the inevitability and legitimacy of party competition, a major step in the development of American democracy.

In his inaugural address, Jefferson too recognized the legitimacy of party competition, urging Americans to accept political differences. Both Federalists and Republicans were committed to the basic values of American republicanism, he acknowledged: "We have called by different names brethren of the same principle. We are all Republicans, we are all Federalists." In language reminiscent of his *Notes on Virginia*, Jefferson argued that in a free republic, even the most offensive opinions must be permitted: "If there be any among us who would wish to dissolve this Union or to change its republican form, let them stand undisturbed as monuments of the safety with which error of opinion may be tolerated where reason is left free to combat it." The Republicans allowed the Alien and Sedition Acts to expire in 1802.

Out of power, Federalists quickly came to agree that there could be such a thing as a loyal opposition, which the government should not try to suppress. The idea of political freedom became firmly established in the United States, even as Federalists continued to defend "order" and "religion" and to attack "extreme democracy."

The Rise of Nationalist Republicanism

After the Republican victory in the election of 1800, most people expected Republicans to follow the principle of "strict construction" of national power. But Jefferson and his successors often construed the national government's power broadly, over the opposition of the more radical members of their own party.

Jefferson demonstrated the flexibility of his principles when he purchased the territory between the Mississippi River and the Rocky Mountains from France. The strongest support for Republicanism had come from southerners and westerners, who complained that the Federalists had failed to open the Mississippi River to American shipping. In 1802, during a lull in the wars between France and her European neighbors, Jefferson learned that Spain had secretly transferred ownership of New Orleans and much of the Spanish territory along the Mississippi River and its western tributaries to France. Negotiating intensively for the purchase of New Orleans and a guarantee of free navigation along the rest of the Mississippi, Jefferson was amazed at a French offer to sell all its western American territories, comprising some 828,000 square miles, for about $15,000,000. Jefferson jumped at the deal, closing it in 1803.

The Constitution nowhere plainly gives the national government the power to acquire more territory, and many Americans opposed the acquisition. But despite the absence of clear language on the subject, Jefferson insisted that the power to acquire territory was implicit in the nation's right to carry out foreign policy. This reasoning sounded much like Hamilton's argument that within its jurisdiction national power was sovereign and complete.

Ironically, now that they no longer controlled the federal government, many Federalists began to argue for strict construction of constitutional provisions. They feared that the Louisiana Purchase would shift power permanently from the Federalists' northeastern and Atlantic-coast political base to the South and West. They denied that the mostly French and Spanish residents of the newly purchased territories could become American citizens as the terms of the treaty provided. Since Article I gave the authority to naturalize citizens to Congress, the power could not be exercised by the president and Senate alone in a mere treaty. Republicans argued for a broader construction of the treaty-making power. Overcoming Federalist opposition, the Republican-controlled Senate ratified the purchase. Soon thereafter Congress arranged for the sale of western lands at cheap prices, encouraging frontier land speculation and economic development. Despite the absence of any express delegation of power to do so, Jefferson's secretary of the treasury, Albert Gallatin, proposed that some of the money be used to build roads between the Atlantic seaboard and the Ohio River, linking the West more firmly with the East.

The passage of the Embargo Act of 1807 was an even more extreme example of Jefferson's willingness to construe constitutional provisions broadly. At Jefferson's urging, Congress barred all exports from the United States in an attempt to force England and France, again at war, to allow peaceable trade with both countries. Jefferson and Madison, who succeeded him as president in 1809, defended the embargo as warranted by Congress's power to regulate foreign commerce and the president's power to carry on foreign relations. It virtually destroyed the economy of New England, which was based on trade with Great Britain, and it had a disastrous effect upon the well-being of ordinary citizens.

To most New England merchants and seamen, the federal officials enforcing the embargo were no better than the British officers who had once tried to enforce the Townshend Duties. Continuing their shift towards strict construction of national power, the Federalists, pro-British and with a strong political base in New England, denied that the embargo was a regulation of foreign commerce. The word "regulate" should be strictly construed, they argued; a ban on commerce was not a "regulation" of commerce. Nor did federal authority over foreign policy justify such drastic interferences with the economy.

The tensions between Great Britain and the United States led to war in 1812, encouraged by American expansionists who hoped to annex Canada. The war was devastating to New England, whose state governments adamantly opposed the hostilities. Massachusetts and Connecticut refused to furnish militia to support the war effort. Their merchants supplied British armed forces, leading President James Madison to impose an embargo on all New England trade.

Disaffection in New England was so great that some of the region's Federalists, led by the influential Timothy Pickering, began to call upon the New England states to withdraw from the Union—a proposal that forced them to adopt Jeffersonian views about state sovereignty. The Massachusetts state legislature called for a new constitutional convention to meet in Hartford, Connecticut, on December 15, 1814. The state legislatures of Massachusetts, Connecticut, and Rhode Island sent official delegates, while New Hampshire and Vermont sent representatives selected by local conventions. All were Federalists, but moderates prevented extremists from plunging into secession.

The convention's report echoed the Kentucky and Virginia Resolutions, arguing that "in cases of . . . palpable infractions of the Constitution, affecting the sovereignty of a State and liberties of the people, it is . . . the duty of such a State to interpose its authority for their protection." Its resolutions demanded that the Constitution be amended to apportion taxes and representation according to free population, excluding slaves; to limit the federal government's power to institute embargoes; to require two-thirds majorities of Congress to restrict commerce, declare war, or admit new states; to restrict federal office to native-born citizens; and to limit presidents to one term. Left implicit was the threat to secede if the demands were not met. However, American and British negotiators had signed a peace treaty nine days after the convention began. When the news arrived, preceded by descriptions of a belated American victory at New Orleans, a wave of patriotism condemned the conduct of the Hartford Convention and the Federalist party as treasonous. Remnants of the discredited party competed for office in some parts of the country, but it could no longer mount a national opposition.

As the Federalists turned towards strict construction and doctrines of state sovereignty, more and more Republicans adopted nationalistic constitutional views. By 1812 many Jeffersonian Republicans, especially younger ones like Henry Clay of Kentucky and John C. Calhoun of South Carolina, had virtually abandoned the older Jeffersonian commitment. Enthusiastically patriotic and hostile to England, they favored vigorous national action to develop the American economy, much as the Federalists had in the 1790s. Even Jefferson reluctantly agreed that it was necessary to encourage manufacturing in order to make America independent of England. Madison also reverted to his earlier views and generally shared the nationalist Republicans' vision.

To aid the development of commerce and industry, Clay offered a group of proposals. His "American Plan" included national support for "internal improvements" in transportation facilities—such as dredging rivers and harbors, subsidizing transportation companies, and building roads and canals. These improvements would encourage economic development in the West by making it more accessible to national and international trade. In addition, Clay and his nationalist allies suggested that Congress enact a "protective" tariff to protect American goods from cheap foreign competition. They called for the revival of the national bank, whose charter had expired in 1811, to help establish a stable, uniform currency. The government would deposit its tax receipts there, providing a huge source of capital for investment in commercial and manufacturing enterprises. With authority to open branches throughout the United States, the national bank would bring development capital to the frontier. Madison favored the plan in general, although he doubted the constitutionality of a national bank, having denounced the proposal in the 1790s.

Many Republicans opposed the nationalists' program. Some saw modern commercial development as a corrupting influence that would undermine the virtues of an agricultural society. The nationalist program would encourage speculation in land and stocks; it would foster development of a creditor class, which would live off the interest of loans and the profits of stock speculations instead of working to produce goods of value. The program violated the Jeffersonian ideal of equal rights, opponents charged, primarily benefiting wealthy capitalists, bankers, and merchants, while all Americans would have to pay the costs. It was Federalism in disguise, raising the old danger of the government becoming an engine of corruption.

Old-fashioned Republicans denied the constitutionality of such proposals, repeating the old strict-constructionist Jeffersonian Republican arguments and insisting that the Constitution nowhere delegated such powers to Congress. The Necessary and Proper Clause had to be construed strictly. The Tenth Amendment had guaranteed the right of the sovereign states to regulate their internal affairs. In sum, they denounced nationalist Republican leaders for abandoning the Republican principles of '98.

Nationalist Republicans responded with the Hamiltonian constitutional argument. The Constitution gave the national government jurisdiction over interstate and foreign commerce. It delegated the power to levy taxes and spend money for the general welfare, to establish post roads for the delivery of mail, and to wage war. Where such power was delegated, the government could take any action necessary and proper to carry it out; where the Constitution delegated power to the national government, that power was "plenary" and sovereign. If by levying taxes, the government also protected American industry from foreign competition, the tax was not any less constitutional. If a bank created to help collect and deposit taxes also served to develop industry, the bank was not therefore unconstitutional. If the government wished to use its power to spend money for the general welfare to promote transportation, there was nothing to prevent it.

Radical Jeffersonians disagreed. By reserving undelegated powers to the states, the Tenth Amendment imposed limits on how the national government could exercise its powers. The amendment created areas of state jurisdiction upon which the federal government could not trespass on the pretense that it was carrying out its delegated powers.

Despite these objections, Congress began to enact Clay's program in 1815 and 1816. After vetoing a national bank bill in 1815, Madison announced his conversion. In 1816 Congress passed a bill, sponsored by John C. Calhoun, establishing the second Bank of the United States, with a charter to run for twenty years. A few months later it passed the Tariff Act of 1816, designed to protect American industry from foreign competition by making permanent the steep duties imposed in 1812 to raise money for the war. In 1817 Congress passed another nationalistic bill authored by Calhoun, promoting western economic development by building roads and canals to connect the western hinterlands with the Ohio and Mississippi River systems. But this time Madison vetoed the measure, saying it went beyond the powers delegated to the federal government and urging a constitutional amendment to give Congress the necessary authority.

Although Congress supported the nationalist Republican development program, its opponents predominated in many states. Many Americans felt ambivalent about the modern commercial economy. Most wanted economic development but were uneasy about the tendency towards speculation. A widespread feeling existed that prosperity ought to come from producing goods, whether agricultural or manufactured, and not from merely speculating (we would call it "investing") in land, commodities, or businesses that depended on government subsidies. Many people suspected that speculators were able to get bank and other business charters through special influence and corruption. They worried that banks helped to overheat the economy by encouraging borrowing and issuing too many banknotes, which circulated like money. When the economy cooled, the banks foreclosed on the property of hapless borrowers. Often the banks themselves collapsed, leaving people holding their now worthless banknotes. Such an economic slowdown began with the Panic of 1819, which led to a recession that persisted through the mid-1820s.

Some states refused to charter banks. Others tried to withdraw or modify charters or to establish state-owned banks, especially after the 1819 panic. Many tried to ease the effects of the recession by issuing paper currency to replace withdrawn or worthless banknotes. They passed laws to suspend or stretch out the collection of debts. Blaming the national bank for the hardship and criticizing the special privileges granted to its wealthy incorporators, several states passed laws forbidding it from opening branches within their boundaries. Others levied high taxes upon the bank's branches in order to drive them out of business.

The obvious conflict between the federal law of 1816 establishing the second national bank and state laws designed to suppress its branches raised fundamental questions about the federal system: Where and how would such conflicts be resolved? Which theory of federalism was correct, the nationalist doctrine or strict construction and state sovereignty? What sanction would enforce the Constitution of the United States against violations, whether committed by the states or by the federal government?

TIMELINE

1781	Thomas Jefferson publishes *Notes on the State of Virginia*.
1786	Virginia Statute for Religious Freedom.

1789	Inauguration of the federal government under the Constitution; George Washington inaugurated as president.
1790	Congress adopts Secretary of the Treasury Alexander Hamilton's plan to fund the national debt as well as those of the states.
1791	Hamilton and Secretary of State Thomas Jefferson debate the creation of a national bank in letters to President Washington.
	Congress charters the first Bank of the United States.
1792–1796	"Republican" opposition to Federalist programs coalesces around Jefferson and James Madison.
1793	In *Chisholm v. Georgia,* the Supreme Court rules that states can be sued in federal courts.
1795	Jay's Treaty ratified.
1796	Federalist John Adams elected president, and inaugurated in 1797; Republican Thomas Jefferson elected vice president.
1798	Ratification of Eleventh Amendment, forbidding suits against states in the federal courts.
	Congress passes the Naturalization Act and the Alien and Sedition Acts
	Kentucky and Virginia pass resolutions protesting the Alien and Sedition Acts.
1800	Republican Thomas Jefferson elected president, and inaugurated in 1801; Republicans take control of Congress
1802	Congress repeals the Naturalization Act; the Alien and Sedition Acts are allowed to lapse.
1803	Louisiana Purchase.
1804	Ratification of the Twelfth Amendment, providing for separate election of the president and vice president.
1807	The Embargo Act forbids trade with all foreign nations.
1808	Republican James Madison elected president, and inaugurated in 1809.
1812–1814	War of 1812 with Great Britain.
1814	Federalists hold Hartford Convention to protest Republican war and commercial policy; secession considered.
1816	Congress charters the second Bank of the United States.
	Republican James Monroe elected president, and inaugurated in 1817; Federalist party declines and is unable to mount national political opposition, leading to the so-called Era of Good Feelings.
1819	Panic of 1819 leads to economic depression.

FURTHER READING

Stanley M. Elkins and Eric L. McKitrick's comprehensive account of *The Age of Federalism* (1993) is a magnificent throwback to the days of grand narrative history. James Roger Sharp's *American Politics in the Early Republic* (1993) is more pointed and analytic. In *Adams vs. Jefferson* (2004), John Ferling provides a readable, insightful account of the constitutional issues that created American politics in the 1790s, as well as a thorough account of the critical election of 1800. Joseph Charles described *The Origins of the American Party System* (1956) in a classic study. The best account of the acceptance of the legitimacy of political parties remains Richard Hofstadter, *The Idea of a Party System* (1969).

For a concise discussion of how the Jeffersonian Republicans became the champions of liberty, see Michael Les Benedict, "The Jeffersonian Republicans and Civil Liberty," in Henry E. Huntington Library and Art Gallery, *Essays in the History of Liberty* (1988), 23–41. For the ideology of the Jeffersonian Republicans, see Lance Banning, *The Jeffersonian Persuasion* (1978), which can be augmented by his explanation of "The Great Divergence" between Madison and his old ally Hamilton in *The Sacred Fire of Liberty: James Madison and the Founding of the Federal Republic* (1995). The standard accounts of the Alien and Sedition Acts are John C. Miller, *Crisis in Freedom* (1951) and James M. Smith, *Freedom's Fetters* (1956). In *The Emergence of a Free Press* (1985), Leonard Levy argued that despite wide-ranging practical freedom of the press, until the 1790s most Americans endorsed the legal rule that one could be punished for libeling the government. Recent historians have vigorously challenged that conclusion. See Jeffrey A. Smith, *Printers and Press Freedom* (1988); Michael Warner, *The Letters of the Republic* (1990); and Robert W. T. Martin, *The Free and Open Press* (2001), which relate the development of press freedom to the rise of a "public sphere," where popular opinion was made and made itself felt. Richard D. Brown sets the struggle in the broader context of the bitter fight British ministries and their radical critics had waged over freedom of the press. See "The Idea of an Informed Citizenry in the Early Republic," in *Devising Liberty: Preserving and Creating Freedom in the New American Republic*, ed. David Thomas Konig (1995).

Older interpretations have pictured the Jeffersonian Republicans as state rights-oriented, agrarian champions of negative government. See, for example, Dumas Malone, "Jefferson, Hamilton, and the Constitution," in *Theory and Practice in American Politics*, ed. William H. Nelson (1964). Since the 1980s historians have recognized the nationalism of many Republicans and stressed the connection between their economic ideas and their republican ideology. See Drew R. McCoy, *The Elusive Republic* (1980); John R. Nelson, *Liberty and Property* (1987); Robert W. Tucker and David C. Hendrickson, *Empire of Liberty* (1990); and Lance Banning's excellent overview "Political Economy and the Creation of the Federal Republic," in *Devising Liberty*, noted above. John Lauritz Larson describes Republican visions of national development in *Internal Improvement: National Public Works and the Promise of Popular Government in the Early United States* (2001). Joyce Appleby has suggested that Republicans' ideas were part of a long transition from republican ideology to a more modern economic individualism. See her *Capitalism and a New Social Order* (1984).

John K. Wilson, "Religion Under the State Constitutions, 1776–1800," *Journal of Church and State* 32 (Autumn 1990): 753–773 presents a compendium of state laws on religion in the post-Revolutionary era. For religious liberty and separation of church and state in the Jeffersonian era, see Daniel L. Dreisbach, *Thomas Jefferson and the Wall of Separation Between Church and State* (2002) and the first chapters of Philip Hamburger, *Separation of Church and State* (2002). They challenge the idea that there was strong support for strict separation of church and state in the early republic, as suggested by Thomas Curry's *The First Freedom* (1986). Marc Douglas McGarvie insists that the individualistic values underlying the Constitution made separation of church and state inevitable and that this became apparent early in the history of the republic. See his *One Nation Under Law* (2004). For a thoughtful assessment of the religious issue in national politics, see Robert M.S. McDonald, "Was There a Religious Revolution of 1800?" in *The Revolution of 1800*, ed. James Horn et al. (2002).

Since the 1970s, historians have attended far more to Republican than Federalist ideology. For the Federalists, see Clinton Rossiter, *Alexander Hamilton and the Constitution* (1964); Gerald Stourzh, *Alexander Hamilton and the Idea of Republican Government* (1970); David Hackett Fisher, *The Revolution of American Conservatism* (1965); and Nelson, *Liberty and Property*, cited above. For an effort to restore attention to Federalist ideas, see *Federalists Reconsidered*, ed. Doron Ben-Atar and Barbara B. Oberg (1998). Lance Banning explains the implications for American constitutionalism of rival Federalist and Republican ideas of political economy in "Political Economy and the Creation of the Federal Republic," in *Devising Liberty*, noted above. E. James Ferguson discusses the relationship between financial policy and federalism in *The Power of the Purse* (1961).

Several essays in *The Revolution of 1800*, noted above, make clear how much the election of that year strained the new constitutional system. See especially those by James E. Lewis, Jr. and Joanne B. Freeman. Leonard Levy makes clear how enforcement of the embargo trenched on civil liberties in *Jefferson and Civil Liberties: The Darker Side* (1963).

In the course of discussing the Jeffersonian attack on the courts, to be discussed in the next chapter, Richard E. Ellis limns the division between moderate Republican nationalists and radical Republican defenders of state sovereignty in *The Jeffersonian Crisis* (1971). For agrarian Republican disillusion with nationalist Republican policies, see Norman K. Risjord, *The Old Republicans* (1965); Robert E. Shalhope, *John Taylor of Caroline* (1980); and Larson, *Internal Improvements*, noted above. For the controversy over a national financial system centered on a national bank, see Bray Hammond's standard history *Banks and Politics in America, from the Revolution to the Civil War* (1957).

6
Judicial Review, Nationalism, and State Sovereignty

Those who framed and ratified the Constitution of the United States believed in constitutionalism. They considered the Constitution fundamental law, binding on all the organs of the federal and state governments. Proponents of constitutional liberty in Britain and the American colonies had relied on a vigilant populace to guard against its violation—what historians call "popular constitutionalism." But in time it became clear that treating the Constitution as law implied that courts must refuse to enforce state and federal laws that violated it. This power came to be known as "judicial review."

Over time judicial review would replace popular constitutionalism as the primary sanction against unconstitutional government action. However, the Constitution itself referred to judicial review only in the Supremacy Clause of Article VI, which required state judges to reject inconsistent provisions of state laws and constitutions. It did not expressly endow the federal judiciary with similar authority.

Nonetheless, the Supreme Court not only claimed the authority to rule federal laws unconstitutional in the monumental case of *Marbury v. Madison* (1803), it also claimed the power to void state laws for violating the United States Constitution. In exercising this power, the Supreme Court, led by the great Chief Justice John Marshall, supported and developed the constitutional theories expounded by Hamilton, the Federalists, and the nationalist Republicans. The Court sustained broad national power, encouraged economic development, and protected property rights.

The Court's course was bitterly opposed by those who sustained the Jeffersonian "principles of '98": strict construction of federal power, state sovereignty, equal rights, and a primarily agricultural economy under local control. A reaction against nationalist Republican public policies and the Supreme Court's decisions culminated in the late 1820s with the rise of Jacksonian Democracy. Part of that reaction was a reassertion of the idea that the people themselves, rather than an errant Supreme Court, had the primary responsibility for holding the government to constitutional principles.

Federal Judicial Power and Judicial Review

Not only had the framers tried to structure the government in a way that would encourage responsible politics, the Constitution incorporated several provisions designed to encourage federal and state governments to adhere to its terms. Besides declaring the Constitution the supreme law of the land, Article VI required all federal and state officials to take oaths to support it. Article II specified a special presidential oath to "preserve, protect, and defend the Constitution." These oaths clearly imposed a duty on lawmakers and administrators, both state and federal, to oppose any law contravening the Constitution. Article VI also required state courts to enforce the Constitution of the United States and federal laws "made in Pursuance thereof . . . , any Thing in the Constitution or Laws of any State to the Contrary notwithstanding."

Clearly, Article VI provided for judicial review. It expressly imposed that duty upon the state courts, requiring them to review state actions in order to assure conformity to the federal Constitution, laws, and treaties. Moreover, by requiring state judges to sustain only those federal laws "made in Pursuance" of the Constitution, Article VI implied that they could enforce a challenged state law if it found the federal law to be unconstitutional—that is, *not* "made in Pursuance" of the Constitution.

Nowhere did the Constitution explicitly give the same power to the federal courts. Nonetheless, when the first Congress organized the federal judiciary in the Judiciary Act of 1789, it gave the Supreme Court the final say in most cases where state laws and actions came into conflict with those of the federal government. However, the issue was controversial, and the result had compromised federal judicial authority more than most Federalists had wished.

Article III, section 2 of the Constitution defined the federal judicial power as extending "to all Cases . . . arising under this Constitution, the Laws of the United States, and Treaties made . . . under their Authority," and it went on to give the Supreme Court "appellate Jurisdiction" over all such cases under "such Regulations as the Congress shall make."

Most Federalists urged Congress to establish a complete federal court system, with exclusive authority to try cases arising under federal laws and treaties. Moreover, they interpreted the jurisdiction of the federal courts broadly. When a state law or action was challenged as contrary to the federal Constitution, laws, or treaties, the challenge created a case arising under the Constitution or the laws of the United States, they argued. It should therefore be heard in a federal court. This procedure would remove the obstructions state courts and juries had put in the way of enforcing federal laws and treaties.

Localist congressmen hoped to maintain the power of local juries to protect local interests and popular rights against judges who they expected to be agents of the central government. They saw no need for a system of federal courts. They argued that with the exception of those cases that the Constitution specifically placed under the original jurisdiction of the Supreme Court, all proceedings should begin in the state courts. Cases that involved the federal Constitution, treaties, or laws could be appealed from the highest state court to the Supreme Court. Moreover, the mere fact that a party to a case claimed that a state law was inconsistent with the federal Constitution or federal laws did not make the case one "arising under this Constitution," they argued. Article VI expressly left it to the state courts to decide whether state laws violated the federal Constitution or federal enactments. There should be no appeal to the Supreme Court in such cases.

The result was a compromise. The Federalists secured a complete federal court system of district and circuit courts, with appeals to the Supreme Court. But even where the federal courts were given authority to decide cases, the state courts were permitted to retain concurrent jurisdiction. Cases involving citizens of different states, called "diversity cases," could be brought in either the state or federal courts. Once proceedings began in state courts, however, it was almost impossible to move them to federal courts. The only recourse was a long series of appeals through the state courts and finally to the Supreme Court of the United States.

The biggest Federalist victory was embodied in section 25 of the Judiciary Act. Section 25 provided for an appeal to the Supreme Court whenever a state supreme court upheld a state constitutional provision, law, or action against a claim that it violated the federal Constitution. To the dismay of localists, this provision gave the Supreme Court the final authority to review the constitutionality of state laws. It also gave the Supreme Court a limited power to review the constitutionality of federal laws. If the Court upheld a state court's opinion that a federal law was not in pursuance of the Constitution, the Court would in effect be ruling the federal law unconstitutional. But the power was not complete. Section 25 did not provide for an appeal if the state courts *sustained* a federal law against an inconsistent state provision; in this case, the Supreme Court received no opportunity to review the federal law.

Neither the Constitution nor the Judiciary Act expressly gave the federal courts any other power to review the constitutionality of federal acts. Nonetheless, the supremacy clause and section 25 of the Judiciary Act clearly reflected a growing conviction that judges must review the constitutionality of laws before enforcing them. In the dispute with Britain, Americans had argued that a law passed in violation of the Constitution was not really a law, but merely an act of power. Judicial review followed logically from that postulate. Proponents of popular liberty in England and America had long insisted that juries could protect defendants from "unconstitutional" exercises of power, as they had in the cases of the Seven Bishops, the Zenger case, and the prosecution of John Wilkes. In a free country, should not judges do the same?

Several instances of such "judicial review" came up in the years immediately preceding the Constitutional Convention. The courts were most likely to act when state laws seemed to impinge upon judicial power or to deprive people of procedural rights. But people with a broader concept of judicial review urged judges on; they wanted judges to refuse to enforce laws that arbitrarily deprived people of property rights. A 1787 North Carolina case, *Bayard v. Singleton,* illustrated how the three issues were connected. It arose out of a law that required judges to dismiss lawsuits to recover Tory property confiscated during the Revolution. The North Carolina Supreme Court refused to obey the law. Courts, not legislatures, had to decide the outcome of property disputes; the legislature had invaded the sphere of power the state constitution had reserved to the judiciary.

The members of the Constitutional Convention had been aware of such cases, and several indicated that they expected the courts to refuse to enforce unconstitutional laws. From Europe, Jefferson wrote Madison in favor of adding a bill of rights to the Constitution because it would encourage judges to refuse to enforce despotic legislation. As Federalists lost ground to the Jeffersonian Republicans in the 1790s, they began to look upon the courts, with their Federalist judges, as a bulwark against Republican legislation that might threaten property rights or challenge the powers of the federal government.

The justices of the United States Supreme Court also clearly accepted the doctrine of judicial review. In 1796 the Court sustained the constitutionality of a federal excise against a claim that it violated the constitutional prohibition on direct taxes. But the justices made clear that they would have ruled the tax unconstitutional if it had indeed fallen under the prohibition.

At the same time, the federal courts entertained cases that significantly affected the states' public policies. Article III of the Constitution gave federal courts jurisdiction over controversies between a state and citizens of another state. In the ratifying conventions, the Federalists had assured delegates that the provision was meant only to give the states the benefit of the federal courts when suing citizens of other states. The provision would not authorize individuals to sue the states in derogation of their "sovereign immunity"—the common-law doctrine that the government cannot be sued without its permission.

Despite these assurances, the federal courts immediately began hearing cases brought against the states by foreigners and citizens of other states. Most of the plaintiffs sought to collect debts for which the states denied responsibility. As sovereign states, Massachusetts, New York, Virginia, and Georgia all refused to appear. But in *Chisholm v. Georgia* (1793), the Supreme Court ordered the state to appear or lose the case by default. Justice James Wilson stated bluntly that "as to the purposes of Union, Georgia is not a sovereign state." Although the Eleventh Amendment reversed the decision, it could not erase the conviction that the federal courts ignored local opinion. Moreover, plaintiffs could still sue state officials as individuals, arguing that unconstitutional actions cannot be considered those of the state.

Just as the Antifederalists had feared, the federal courts intervened to secure the rights that the peace treaty of 1783 had given to Britons and Loyalists whose debts and lands had been confiscated during the Revolution. These debts had been paid to the states, and the seized lands had been auctioned off to new owners. Speculators, often Americans, had bought the British and Tory claims, hoping to profit if the courts upheld them. Various states had passed laws to obstruct prosecution of such claims in the courts, and jurors used every excuse to help their neighbors repulse speculators in them. The Constitution had been framed to overcome such obstructions, and speculators quickly brought suits in the federal courts. The states again raised objections based on their sovereignty: A federal treaty could not supersede a state's sovereign power to regulate its internal affairs.

The issue reached the Supreme Court in *Ware v. Hylton* (1796). In that case Virginia insisted that as a sovereign state, it had broad discretion to determine how the treaty's provisions might be enforced in its own courts. All but one justice ruled that the supremacy clause rendered such state laws unconstitutional. Any law that obstructed the operation of a federal law or treaty must fall.

By the 1790s Republicans saw the exaltation of the federal judiciary as yet another element of the Federalist conspiracy against liberty. Federal judges had issued Federalist political harangues from the bench; they had encouraged the prosecution of Republican pamphleteers and newspaper publishers under the Sedition Act. They had intervened on the side of Tories and speculators to undermine land titles in the states and to reactivate old debts. Many Republicans considered the appeals section of the Judiciary Act of 1789 to be a Federalist scheme to enable Federalist judges, protected by lifetime tenure, to nullify Republican state laws on the pretext that they violated the Constitution. They feared that a Federalist Supreme Court would nullify even laws of Congress on the same pretext.

The Republicans were hardly reassured when outgoing Federalist president John Adams named his secretary of state, John Marshall, chief justice of the Supreme Court. They were even less pleased when the lame-duck Federalist majority in Congress passed a new Judiciary Act in 1801.* The new law created sixteen circuit courts with new judges for each, as well as new court clerks, district attorneys, and United States marshals. Marshall stayed up late into the last night of the Adams administration signing commissions for the new officials, all of whom were Federalists, before he himself resigned as secretary of state to become chief justice. A large number of undelivered commissions lay on the desk when the new secretary of state, James Madison, arrived the next morning.

As chief justice, Marshall moved boldly to increase the prestige of the Supreme Court. He ended the tradition whereby each justice presented a separate opinion in every case. From then on, the court majority would speak through a single opinion presented on its behalf. A justice would present a concurring opin-

---

*Until the ratification of the Twentieth Amendment to the Constitution in 1933, the terms of a newly elected president and Congress did not begin until March 4 of the year following their election. Thus the outgoing president and Congress continued in office for four months following the election of their successors. Sessions of Congress that met during this time were popularly called "lame-duck" sessions.

ion only if he disagreed with reasoning although he agreed with the result, or a dissenting opinion if he disagreed with both. Marshall worked successfully to discourage dissents, favoring compromises among the justices and the preparation of opinions that all in the majority could accept. He convinced most of his colleagues to suppress disagreements in order to enhance the impression that the law dictated a single, correct answer to every legal dispute and that the Court had the special expertise necessary to identify it. He undertook to prepare the most important opinions himself, reinforcing their authority. It was clear to Republicans that Marshall intended to make the Supreme Court a bulwark of Federalism.

Reacting against what they saw as Federalist abuse of the judiciary, many Republicans began to resist the notion of judicial review. For a court to rule a law unconstitutional violated democratic principles, they said, because judges generally were appointed and not elected. Judicial review made judges superior to the legislative and executive branches of government, violating the basic American tenet that the three branches of government were equal. Finally, it violated the doctrine of separation of powers, because the power to nullify laws in effect gave the judges a legislative role.

Marshall determined to reconfirm the principle of judicial review and put it beyond dispute. He acted in 1803 in the landmark case of *Marbury v. Madison.* Marbury was one of the "midnight appointees" whose commission Marshall had signed on the last day of the Adams administration. Finding Marbury's commission on his desk, Madison refused to deliver it. Marshall urged Marbury to sue in

John Marshall, the great nationalist chief justice of the Supreme Court.

the Supreme Court for a writ of *mandamus* ordering Madison to deliver the commission.

Speaking for a unanimous court, Marshall ruled that Marbury was entitled to his commission. While the Supreme Court could not order an officer of the executive branch to perform an act over which he had discretion, it could order an officer to perform a merely ministerial duty. Delivery of a signed and sealed commission fell into that category. According to the common law, a writ of *mandamus* was the appropriate remedy, and Congress had given the Supreme Court original jurisdiction to issue writs of *mandamus* in section 13 of the Judiciary Act of 1789. However, Marshall ruled, Congress had exceeded its authority when it did so. Article III of the Constitution specified the original jurisdiction of the Supreme Court; it made all other Supreme Court jurisdiction appellate, with Congress authorized to regulate only the appellate jurisdiction. Article III said nothing about original jurisdiction to issue writs of *mandamus*.

Could Congress authorize the Court to issue writs of *mandamus*? Obviously not, Marshall concluded. The government of the United States is one of limited powers, delegated by the people through a written Constitution. "To what purpose are powers limited, and to what purpose is that limitation committed to writing, if these limits may, at any time, be passed by those intended to be restrained?" he asked. The theory of any government created by a written constitution "must be that an act of the legislature, repugnant to the constitution, is void."

But if section 13 were unconstitutional, did the courts have to enforce it nonetheless? "This would be to overthrow in fact what was established in theory," Marshall answered. It was the plain duty of the courts to refuse to enforce an unconstitutional law. "It is emphatically the province and duty of the judicial department to say what the law is . . . . If two laws conflict with each other, the courts must decide on the operation of each." If inconsistent provisions of a law and the Constitution both applied to a particular case, the Court had to decide which must govern. "This is of the very essence of judicial duty," Marshall observed. Clearly, the Constitution must be preferred in case of such a conflict. So the Supreme Court refused to issue the writ of *mandamus* to which the hapless Marbury would otherwise have been entitled.

There was no way for the infuriated President Jefferson to challenge the decision. If he ordered Madison to deliver Marbury's commission, he would merely be acting in accordance with the Court's statement of his obligation. He could only declaim privately about the perfidy of the Federalist judiciary.

In reality, Marshall had artfully shaped the entire case to create the opportunity for the Supreme Court to endorse the concept of judicial review. If the Supreme Court had no jurisdiction to issue the writ Marbury sought, there was no need to decide whether he was entitled to it. The court could have simply dismissed the case. Although the basis of the dismissal still would have been the unconstitutionality of the *mandamus* provision of the Judiciary Act, the decision would have lost much of its rhetorical force.

But Marshall's strategy involved even more than that. He deliberately misconstrued the meaning of section 13. Congress had not intended it to give the Supreme Court original jurisdiction to issue writs of *mandamus*. It had intended to authorize the Court to issue the writs only to enforce decisions where it did have jurisdiction. But none of that mattered. Providing a firm underpinning for the principle of judicial review, *Marbury v. Madison* is one of the most compelling judicial statements ever issued.

Marshall's concept of judicial review should not be exaggerated. His main concern was to affirm the judiciary's right to decide for itself whether a law was unconstitutional. He did not claim that the Supreme Court had the sole power to decide what was constitutional and what was not. Each department of the government had that obligation and could make its own decision. Nonetheless, laws generally must be enforced by the courts, and enforcement follows legislative enactment and presidential signature. As a practical matter, therefore, the Court would have the final say in most cases. Most importantly, Marshall characterized the Constitution as a legal document rather than a political one. Jefferson and Madison had organized the Republican party to defend what they saw as correct constitutional principles from Federalist abuses. They had relied on a political remedy for constitutional violations, appealing to popular constitutionalism, as had British radicals and American colonists. Marshall separated constitutional law from politics. He had argued powerfully that constitutions were more than popular declarations of basic principles; they were law, to be enforced like other laws. Once Americans accepted this idea, they inevitably would see the courts as the most appropriate forum for enforcing constitutional limits.

The Jeffersonian Republicans and the Courts

Fearing that the Federalists would use the federal courts to overturn Republican legislation and bitterly opposed to judicial "usurpation" under the guise of judicial review, many Republicans determined to eliminate the threat. In several states they moved to impeach Federalist judges, charging that they had abused their judicial authority in order to promote Federalist policies. Although some Federalist judges had been blatantly partisan, the problem actually arose because Americans were only slowly coming to accept the legitimacy of political opposition and the separation of law from politics. When Federalist judges denounced Republicans, they fulfilled the traditional role of magistrates in the British system. In both England and America, judges had traditionally been part of the government apparatus, expected to support the administration that appointed them and to denounce its enemies. Now, with Republicans demanding an end to such activities, judges redefined their role. Slowly judges concluded that they must refrain from open partisanship and not let their party loyalties prejudice their judicial activities.

Yet Federalist judges' beliefs inevitably affected their understanding of the law, even if they strove to control outright partisan bias. Naturally, many Republicans considered their decisions biased, and they deemed such partisanship—especially on the side of aristocracy and oppression—an impeachable offense. Other Republicans disagreed. They accepted the inevitability that Federalists would see things differently from Republicans. If Republicans successfully impeached judges for decisions that reflected Federalist views of the law, then Federalists would impeach Republican judges whenever they returned to power. Instead of eliminating partisanship from the bench, the courts would become completely partisan.

Events followed a similar course on the national level. Republicans immediately repealed the Judiciary Act of 1801, eliminating the judgeships established by the law. Although some judges challenged the repeal's constitutionality, arguing that it deprived them of their positions without charging misconduct, the Supreme Court quickly rejected their contention. The Republicans then moved against the most egregious offenders. House Republicans impeached a mentally ill and alcoholic New Hampshire district court judge who attacked Republicans in his jury charges and berated Republican lawyers from the bench. After the Senate convicted and removed him in 1804, House Republicans moved on to impeach Supreme Court Justice Samuel Chase.

Chase was a violently partisan Federalist who had consistently attacked Republicanism from the bench. He had orchestrated the prosecution of prominent Republicans under the Sedition Acts and presided with blatant bias over their trials. Yet in an age when such activities were commonplace, Chase had at most only slightly exceeded the bounds of accepted judicial decorum.

The impeachment proceedings failed. Moderate Republicans worried that success would lead to the impeachment of Marshall, a step that would be politically dangerous as well as a real threat to judicial independence. Moreover, Chase's conviction would tip the balance in favor of Republicans who were advocating similar assaults on state judges. In the end enough Republican senators bolted to acquit Chase. The House decided against bringing charges against other judges, and the attack petered out. In the states as well, moderate Republicans joined Federalists to block the radical Republican attack. By the 1810s few questioned the power of judges to rule legislation unconstitutional, and it was understood that they could not be impeached for doing so.

The Courts and "Vested Rights"

As president, Jefferson tried to appoint Supreme Court justices who would offset Marshall's Federalism, but he never succeeded. The most capable Republican appointee, Joseph Story, became Marshall's firm ally. Together, they dominated the Court. Both believed in national supremacy and the economic and legal tenets associated with modern commercial society. They considered the United States Constitution a bulwark of liberty against the efforts of misguided majorities to deprive property owners of their rights. The Constitution was intended to guarantee the stability that encouraged trade and commercial development.

Like most Americans, Marshall and Story believed that once a person received actual control of property—that is, once the right to property had "vested"—it could not be taken away by ordinary legislation. A person could be deprived of a vested right to property only as punishment for a crime or if someone else could prove a better claim. Either justification required a court proceeding. Transferring vested rights from one person or group to another was not a proper legislative activity. It therefore seemed unconstitutional in some way that was difficult to articulate.

In the first cases that ruled such legislation unconstitutional, the judges said transferring vested rights violated general principles of justice and natural law. Many observers criticized such reasoning as implying that judges could overturn laws whenever they felt that they were unjust. While Americans were coming to accept the idea of judicial review, they did not believe that judges could rule any law they disliked unconstitutional.

An early example of the controversy occurred in the Supreme Court case of *Calder v. Bull* (1798). This case arose when the Connecticut state legislature passed a law that set aside a probate decision (a case involving issues of inheritance) and required a new hearing. The original winner complained that the law violated the constitutional prohibition against *ex post facto* laws and arbitrarily deprived him of a vested right to property. All the justices agreed that the Connecticut measure was not a forbidden *ex post facto* law, because that term referred only to criminal enactments. But Justice Chase went on to argue that the courts could find a law unconstitutional if it "violated certain vital principles in our free republican government." Such an enactment would be beyond the legislative power. "An act of the legislature . . . contrary to the great first principles of the social compact, cannot be considered a rightful exercise of legislative authority."

Justice James Iredell and the two other justices hearing the case denied that judges could overturn legislation on such vague grounds. A court cannot pronounce a law void "merely because it is, in their judgment, contrary to the principles of natural justice," Iredell insisted. "The ideas of natural justice are regulated by no fixed standard; the ablest and purest men have differed upon the subject." The only objective basis for refusing to enforce a law was its violation of specific constitutional provisions.

By the 1800s most Americans agreed with Iredell's position. Judges soon stopped ruling laws unconstitutional for violating vague notions of natural rights. Instead, state judges interpreted certain phrases of state constitutions to protect vested property rights against legislative action. They began to rule that laws invading vested rights violated constitutional provisions that prohibited taking property without "due process of law" or unless "according to the law of the land."

The Fifth Amendment imposed a due-process limitation on the federal government, but nothing in the United States Constitution imposed a similar limitation upon the states. Thus it remained unclear what the Supreme Court could do if state judges failed to protect vested rights. However, the justices were able to use other language in the federal Constitution to protect some vested rights against state deprivation. In *Fletcher v. Peck* (1810), Marshall and Story persuaded the Court to rule unconstitutional a Georgia law that revoked an earlier sale of state land. The purchasers had bribed the state legislature to sell them lands along the Yazoo River at a fraudulently low price. Georgians had swept the malefactors out of office, replacing them with legislators who promised to get the land back. But the criminals had already sold much of the land to people who supposedly did not know of the fraud. Marshall ruled that the state could not take away the property of those who had bought it in good faith. The first sale amounted to a contract between the state and the purchasers. An attempt to rescind it violated Article I, section 10 of the Constitution, which forbade states from "impairing the Obligation of Contracts."

The decision illustrated not only Marshall's commitment to protecting vested rights but his conviction that economic development required stability. No one would buy public land if the legislature could simply reverse the sale. But to those who opposed the development of a commercial economy dominated by "speculators," banks, and creditors, the Court had protected precisely the sort of corruption they feared.

In *Dartmouth College v. Woodward* (1819), the newly elected Republican legislature of New Hampshire intervened in a dispute between the president and the board of the college. Critical of the special privileges that the original charter gave to the elite Congregationalists who controlled the school, the legislators replaced the old charter with a new one putting the college under state control. The original trustees, represented by the rising young attorney Daniel Webster, failed to convince the New Hampshire Supreme Court that the state had deprived them of property without due process of law. But the U.S. Supreme Court reversed the decision. A charter of incorporation was a contract between the state and the people who received it, Marshall wrote. Changing it without the agreement of its owners impaired the obligation of the contract.

Again more was at stake than property rights. States were beginning to grant charters to entrepreneurs, allowing them to incorporate their businesses. The corporation became a key instrument in economic development, providing businesses with legal personalities separate from their owners. With many people critical of the special privileges that corporate charters gave their recipients, Marshall and Story put the weight of the Supreme Court and the Constitution behind them. Once given, corporate charters could not arbitrarily be rescinded or changed.

The Court continued to enforce the Obligation of Contracts Clause in *Sturges v. Crowninshield* (1819), which ruled state bankruptcy laws unconstitutional. *Green v. Biddle* (1821) upheld the rights of people claiming land under titles that Kentucky had agreed to recognize when it separated from Virginia to become a state.

The Marshall Court's decisions were based on the belief that economic stability and progress depended on the reliability of contracts. This opinion was closely related to the justices' abhorrence of "special legislation" that took vested rights from one group and gave them to another. Such legislation violated the principle that laws must affect all equally. Opposition to "special legislation" recalled the Jeffersonian idea that government ought not to violate the "equal rights" of its citizens by giving special privileges to some at the expense of the rest. By the 1820s it was clear that all Americans opposed "special privileges" and believed in "equal rights"; they disagreed, however, on how to apply the principle.

The Supreme Court and National Supremacy

All these cases disrupted important state policies. The Yazoo land fraud had been a *cause celebre* in Georgia. By ruling its revocation a violation of the Obligation of Contracts Clause in *Fletcher v. Peck*, the Court outraged the overwhelming majority of Georgians. The *Dartmouth College* decision made it impossible for state legislatures to modify old charters that had granted special privileges to favored groups. It also challenged the legislature's ability to rescind or modify charters of institutions that were doing serious damage to the states' economies, including irresponsible banks flooding some of the states with irredeemable banknotes. *Sturges v. Crowninshield* prevented the states from handling terrible economic distress by staying the collection of debts or spreading their collection out over time. *Green v. Biddle* seriously disrupted the stability of Kentucky's land titles, clouding the titles of honest settlers and providing a windfall for speculators who had bought Virginia-based claims cheap.

Although its decisions limited the power of the states to deal with economic problems, the Marshall court supported broad national power to promote the economy. In *McCulloch v. Maryland* (1819), the Court sustained the constitutionality of the second national bank. In what remains the leading case on the power of the federal government, Marshall endorsed the nationalist interpretation of federal government powers. At the same time, he overturned the heavy taxes that states like Kentucky, Maryland, and Ohio had imposed on the bank's branches in order to discourage their operation.

Using language almost identical to Hamilton's, Marshall denied Maryland's contention that the national bank was unconstitutional. Where the Constitution delegated power to the national government, that power was "sovereign." The Necessary and Proper Clause of the Constitution gave Congress wide latitude to pass laws to carry out the delegated powers, including the power to create a national bank to help regulate the currency, to levy and collect taxes, and to fund the national debt. "Let the end be legitimate, let it be within the scope of the constitution, and all means which appropriate, which are plainly adapted to that end . . . are constitutional," Marshall wrote.

If Congress had acted within the scope of its constitutional powers when it created the bank, could a state tax its branches? No, Marshall answered. "The power to tax involves the power to destroy," he wrote, and "may defeat and render useless the power to create." Therefore states could not tax instruments of the national government.

In several other cases, the Marshall court further expanded federal power and limited that of the states. In *Gibbons v. Ogden* (1824), Marshall defined Congress's power to regulate foreign and interstate commerce very broadly. New York had rewarded Robert Fulton, the inventor of the steam-propelled ship, with a monopoly on steam navigation within the state. Ogden, who had received a license from Fulton, tried to prevent Gibbons from competing with Ogden's Manhattan-to-New Jersey line. Gibbons had secured the license Congress required of all people running ships in the coastal waters; his lawyer, Daniel Webster, claimed that this license superseded Fulton's monopoly. New York's lawyers responded that the state had sovereign authority to regulate trade within its boundaries and that Congress's power to regulate interstate commerce extended only to making rules governing commercial exchanges, not to the instruments of trade.

Speaking for a unanimous court, Marshall found for Gibbons. "Commerce" encompassed all aspects of trade, including the instruments by which it was carried on. Congress's power to regulate interstate commerce covered every aspect of trade among the states; it did not end at the state line. Like all powers delegated by the Constitution, it was complete and "plenary." Where Congress exercised it, incompatible state laws fell. The justices recognized that the Constitution left the states with the "police power" to promote safety, health, and morals. But in *Gibbons* as well as in *Brown v. Maryland* (1827), in which Maryland tried to license the importation of alcoholic beverages, the court said that the states could not exercise these powers in ways that burdened interstate commerce.

State authorities objected that since the Constitution left the police power with them, they could pass any regulation necessary to exercise it—at least until Congress passed a law that clearly conflicted with the state rules. But Marshall insisted that the delegation of interstate commerce power to Congress was as much an inhibition upon state action as the express limits the Constitution imposed in Article I, section 10.

The State-Sovereignty Reaction

The interference of the federal courts with popular state policies led to a rearguard defense of state sovereignty in the 1810s and a full-fledged revival of state-sovereignty constitutionalism in the 1820s.

During the 1810s state-sovereignty theorists, such as Spencer Roane, the chief justice of the Virginia Court of Appeals (the state's highest court); Thomas Ritchie, the editor of the state's leading Republican newspaper and the leader of the politically dominant "Richmond Junto"; and the Virginia planter and political philosopher, John Taylor, built upon the old Jeffersonian strictures against broad construction of federal powers. The states had created the federal government, they argued. Therefore the states (or, to be precise, the people of each state) retained sovereignty. The Constitution did not create a national government, but a confederacy of sovereign states. The government of that confederacy was subordinate to the government of the states. No branch of the subordinate government could impose its will upon a sovereign state in a dispute over the meaning of the Constitution and the validity of state laws. Article VI left final decisions over such conflicts to the judiciaries of individual states. Acting on these understandings, state-sovereignty Republicans in Congress tried to repeal section 25 of the Judiciary Act of 1789, which authorized the Supreme Court to hear appeals from the state courts. But nationalist Republicans consistently blocked their efforts.

In several cases, the state courts defied the Supreme Court, ruling that section 25 was unconstitutional and that the Supreme Court had no right to reverse a state court's decision. In the 1810s, the Supreme Court waged a bitter struggle with Roane's Virginia Court of Appeals over the extent of federal judicial authority. The first two cases involved claims of quitrents* owed to the heirs of Lord Fairfax, whose estates were confiscated during the war. John Marshall and his brother James had purchased the claims and sought to have them enforced under the treaty with Britain. The Virginia courts sustained the state law confiscating the Fairfax estate; in *Fairfax's Devisee v. Hunter's Lessee* (1813) the Supreme Court, with Marshall not participating, reversed the decision.

The Virginia Court of Appeals refused to obey the order. The court argued the state-sovereignty position: It was absurd to permit a branch of the government created by the sovereign states to decide the extent of its own powers. Therefore section 25 of the Judiciary Act, which authorized appeals from state supreme court decisions, was unconstitutional. Roane, Ritchie, Taylor, and other critics of nationalist constitutionalism augmented the court's opinion with pamphlets and books defending this state-sovereignty interpretation of the federal system. The Virginia state legislature, recalling the precedent set by the Kentucky and Virginia Resolutions of 1798, formally declared Section 25 void.In *Martin v. Hunter's Lessee* (1816), with Virginia refusing to appear and Marshall still recusing himself, the Supreme Court rejected Virginia's argument, upholding the disputed section of the Judiciary Act. But the Virginia courts continued to thwart the Court's decisions. Marshall and Story were determined to find another case with which to make their points. In *Cohens v. Virginia* (1821), they were able to issue a powerful restatement of the nationalist argument. As in *Marbury v. Madison,* Marshall carefully chose a case that offered Virginia no chance to defy the Court's decision. He found his opportunity when Virginia arrested the Cohen brothers for selling lottery tickets issued across the border in the District of Columbia. The Cohens argued that the law of Congress authorizing the District lottery

---

*A quitrent was a continued payment owed to the original owners of land by those who acquired it from them and by all later purchasers.

superseded Virginia's law against selling the tickets. When the Cohens appealed their conviction to the Supreme Court under section 25, the Virginia Court of Appeals again refused to forward the records of the case and the state refused to send counsel to argue it. Led by Marshall, the Supreme Court took jurisdiction nonetheless and issued a ringing statement of the nationalist position.

The American people, not the people of the individual states, created the Union, Marshall wrote. The United States was no mere confederacy; "the United States form . . . for most important purposes, a single nation." Speaking for a unanimous court, Marshall intoned:

> In war, we are one people. In making peace, we are one people. In all commercial regulations, we are one and the same people . . . , and the government which is alone capable of controlling and managing their interests, in all these respects, is the government of the Union. It is their government, and in that character they have no other. America has chosen to be, in many respects, and to many purposes, a nation; and for all these purposes her government is complete; to all these objects, it is competent. The people have declared, that in the exercise of all powers given for these objects, it is supreme.

Having taken jurisdiction despite Virginia's objections and having made their point, the justices then ruled that Congress had not intended the lottery tickets to be sold outside the District of Columbia, so Virginia could keep the Cohens in jail.

Despite Marshall's clever strategy and powerful rhetoric, no clear winner emerged in these confrontations. Overall, most northern lawyers accepted the Supreme Court's nationalist argument. But in the South, various issues, including the perennial land-title, banking, and bankruptcy issues, inclined people toward the state-sovereignty position.

Other issues also alienated many southerners from nationalist constitutionalism. Among the most important were the controversies over lands within the southern states that still belonged to Native American tribes. In Georgia, Tennessee, Alabama, and Mississippi, the so-called Civilized Tribes—Cherokee, Creek, Choctaw, Chickasaw, and Seminole—held broad expanses of territory, recognized as theirs by treaties signed with the United States. Settled farmers, these Indian nations had developed stable governing and legal institutions. But their legal systems severely restricted the ownership of land, preventing its sale to outsiders, and thus limiting the land speculation that was a cornerstone of the southern and western economy. Motivated both by racism and by the desire to develop their economies, Alabama and Mississippi formally annexed Native American lands in violation of the treaties. In 1828 Georgia declared its laws applicable in the Cherokee Nation and declared Cherokee laws null and void. When lawyers for the Cherokee went to federal court to protect their rights under their treaties with the United States, Georgians and Alabamians echoed the Virginia state-sovereignty school's argument against federal court jurisdiction.

Some southerners, especially in South Carolina, also denounced the protective tariff. By the 1820s, South Carolinians recognized that their economic future lay in the production and sale of cotton and rice to the manufacturing nations of Europe. A protective tariff merely encouraged those nations to retaliate with tariffs on South Carolina's exports. Moreover, the tariff raised the cost of manufactured goods to consumers. Because northerners were interested in developing manufactures, the tariff benefited them at southerners' expense, violating the principle of equal rights. Worse, the money collected through the duties went to develop transportation primarily in the North and West, rather than in the South, which was blessed with many navigable rivers. So powerful was South Carolina's reaction against national economic legislation in the 1820s that even John C. Calhoun, South Carolina's leading politician, who had originally authored much of it, had to give way. By the mid-1820s he, like many other southerners, supported the state-sovereignty interpretation of the federal system.

Finally, many southerners worried that a strong national government might threaten slavery. These fears were kindled by the Missouri statehood controversy of 1819 and 1820. Missouri petitioned to enter the Union in 1819 as a slave state. Dismayed that slavery was spreading across the Mississippi River, a New York representative introduced an amendment to the resolution admitting the new state, requiring Missouri to accept the same sort of gradual emancipation that northern states like New York had recently enacted. The House of Representatives adopted the amendment over furious southern resistance, but the Senate, where slave and free states had an equal number of members, rejected it. Southerners denied that the federal government's power to admit new states included the right to impose conditions in areas traditionally within state jurisdiction. Northerners construed the government's power far more broadly.

The deadlock was resolved by the "Missouri Compromise." Congress balanced the admission of Missouri as a slave state with the admission of Maine as a free state. A line was drawn through the territories of the United States at a latitude of 36° 30'. Settlers could bring slaves into territories south of the Missouri Compromise line, but not north of it.

The crisis reignited when Missouri formally presented its new constitution for acceptance by Congress. The constitution included a provision prohibiting free Negroes from entering the state. Northerners complained that this provision deprived their black citizens of the benefits guaranteed by Article IV of the Constitution, according to which "the Citizens of each State shall be entitled to all Privileges and Immunities of Citizens in the several States." The conflict required a second Missouri Compromise, an ambiguous provision requiring Missouri's legislature to construe the offending clause in a way consistent with the privileges and immunities of United States citizens. By the 1820s these conflicts led to a reaction against constitutional nationalism in the South and West. Many western lawyers and politicians endorsed the state-sovereignty ideas developed by the Virginians. Americans had created two rival theories of federalism that diverged radically on the nature of the Union, the scope of federal power, and the right of the Supreme Court to resolve constitutional conflicts between the state and federal governments. Both the constitutional issues and their practical consequences were beginning to play a significant role in national politics.

TIMELINE

1787 In *Bayard v. Singleton,* the Supreme Court of North Carolina rules a state law unconstitutional in an early instance of judicial review.

1789 Congress organizes the federal judiciary in the Judiciary Act of 1789; section 25 provides for appeals to the U.S. Supreme Court when state courts sustain the constitutionality of local laws challenged as inconsistent with the Constitution, laws, or treaties of the United States.

1798 Justices Samuel Chase and James Iredell debate the nature of judicial review in *Calder v. Bull.*

1801 Federalists pass the Judiciary Act of 1801, creating a new federal circuit court system.

John Marshall becomes the third chief justice of the United States Supreme Court.

1802 Congress repeals the Judiciary Act of 1801.

1803 *Marbury v. Madison* establishes the principle of judicial review of federal legislation.

1805 The Senate acquits Justice Chase of charges brought on impeachment.

1810 The Supreme Court rules that Georgia's repeal of the Yazoo land sale violates the Constitution in *Fletcher* v. *Peck.*

1813–1821 The Supreme Court and the Virginia Court of Appeals clash over the Supreme Court's authority to hear appeals from state court decisions on constitutional questions under section 25 of the Judiciary Act of 1789, culminating in *Cohens v. Virginia* (1821).

1819 In *Dartmouth College v. Woodward,* the Supreme Court rules that legislative revisions of corporate charters violate the Obligation of Contracts Clause of the U.S. Constitution.

McCulloch v. Maryland upholds the constitutionality of the second national bank and overturns state laws taxing its branches.

1819–1821 Missouri Crisis; Congress enacts the Missouri Compromise (1820).

1824   The Supreme Court defines federal power to regulate interstate commerce expansively in *Gibbons v. Ogden.*

1828   Georgia passes legislation, to take effect in 1830, extending the operation of its laws over Native American lands within the boundaries of the state.

FURTHER READING

The first two volumes of Charles Warren's *The Supreme Court in United States History* (1922–1924) and Charles Grove Haines's *The Role of the Supreme Court in American Government and Politics, 1789–1835* (1944) are classic accounts of judicial review in the early years of the republic.William R. Casto's *The Supreme Court in the Early Republic* (1995) is a detailed examination of the framing of the Judiciary Act and the pre-Marshall Supreme Court. The best short survey of the Marshall Court appears in R. Kent Newmyer, *The Supreme Court under Marshall and Taney* (1968). The best recent scholarly assessment is Newmyer's *John Marshall and the Heroic Age of the Supreme Court* (2001). A more traditional and concise account is Charles F. Hobson, *The Great Chief Justice* (1996).

Many of the above works present the conventional view of *Marbury v. Madison* and the origins of judicial review. Compare them to Robert Lowry Clinton's *Marbury v. Madison and Judicial Review* (1989), which argues that Marshall and the framers had a much more restricted concept of judicial review than scholars have ascribed to them. Newmyer provides a powerful rebuttal in *John Marshall and the Heroic Age of the Supreme Court*, noted above, Like Newmyer, William E. Nelson stresses Marshall's separation of law from politics in *Marbury v. Madison* (2000), a book aimed at students and nonspecialists.

For the competition between popular and judicial claims to interpret the Constitution in the early Republic, see part two of Donald G. Morgan, *Congress and the Constitution* (1966). Larry D. Kramer describes "popular constitutionalism" and its subversion by judicial review in *The People Themselves* (2004). Michael W. McConnell, in contrast, sees *Marbury* as a last-ditch, minor victory for judicial review against the popular constitutionalism of the Jeffersonian Republicans. See his "The Story of *Marbury v. Madison*: Making Defeat Look Like Victory," in *Constitutional Law Stories*, ed. Michael C. Dorf (2004). Richard E. Ellis provides the best account of the Jeffersonian attack on the courts in *The Jeffersonian Crisis* (1971). Donald F. Melhorn's *Lest We Be Marshall'd* (2003) and John Phillip Reid's study *Controlling the Law* (2004) address the same theme in Ohio and New Hampshire, respectively.

Mark A. Graber explains the relationship between the Marshall Court's nationalist decisions and the programs promoted by the nationalist wing of the Jeffersonian Republican party in "Federalist or Friend of Adams: The Marshall Court and Party Politics," *Studies in American Political Development* 12 (Fall 1998): 229–266. For specific cases, see C. Peter McGrath's *Yazoo* (1966); Bray Hammond's very readable account of *McCulloch v. Maryland* in "The Bank Cases," in *Quarrels That Have Shaped the Constitution*, ed. John A. Garraty (1962, 1987); and Maurice Baxter's discussion of *Gibbons v. Ogden* in *The Steamboat Monopoly* (1972).

For continuing challenges to federal judicial supremacy, see Hammond's "The Bank Cases," noted above; F. Thornton Miller, *Juries and Judges Versus the Law* (1994); and

Gerald Gunther (ed.), *John Marshall's Defense of McCulloch v. Maryland* (1969). Richard E. Ellis provides a nice overview of the state-sovereignty view of federalism and judicial authority in "The Path Not Taken" in *Virginia and the Constitution*, ed. A.E. Dick Howard and Melvin I. Urofsky (1992). Chapter 3 of Daniel Farber's *Lincoln's Constitution* (2003) provides the clearest comparison between Marshallian nationalism and the competing vision of state sovereignty.

The classic statement of the "vested rights" doctrine that underlay active judicial review in the early nineteenth century is Edward S. Corwin's "The Basic Doctrine of American Constitutional Law," *Michigan Law Review* 12 (February 1914): 248–276. In the chapter "Origins of Police Power Jurisprudence" of his *The Constitution Besieged* (1993), Howard Gillman argues that by the 1820s and 1830s the courts were analyzing questionable legislation in terms of its "special interest" or "class" nature, rather than in terms of its violation of "vested rights." Compare that chapter and Michael Les Benedict's similar observation in "Laissez Faire and Liberty," *Law and History Review* 3 (Fall 1985): 293–331, to Corwin's perception. One of the key cases in which the Marshall Court protected vested rights was *Dartmouth College v. Woodward*. For a discussion of the case aimed at students as well as academics, see Francis N. Stites, *Private Interest and Public Gain* (1972).

The best analysis of the political and constitutional issues of the Missouri crisis is found in an early chapter of Don E. Fehrenbacher's *The Dred Scott Case* (1978). Fehrenbacher discusses the case further in "The Missouri Controversy and the Sources of Southern Sectionalism," in *The South and Three Sectional Crises* (1980).

7

Andrew Jackson, Democracy, and "State Rights"

The late 1820s and the 1830s witnessed the development of a strong belief in the character and intelligence of the common man and woman known as "Jacksonian Democracy." Claiming the heritage of Jefferson, President Andrew Jackson and his followers denounced aristocracy and special privilege. He made the issue concrete by vetoing the bill that rechartered the second national bank.

Despite growing commitment to equality, the treatment of African Americans worsened. To justify the oppression, white Americans became more firmly racist. Although the status of women improved, they too were denied equal rights—their differential treatment justified by the idea that men and women exercised authority in separate spheres: women in the private sphere of home and family, and men in the public sphere of politics and business.

Equally attached to the Union and to state rights, Jackson rejected both nationalist constitutionalism and state sovereignty. In the Nullification Crisis he articulated a third understanding of federalism. At the same time, he exalted the status of the presidency, claiming a special authority to represent the people and defend the Constitution. Jackson's powerful convictions created the political and constitutional issues of the 1830s and 1840s. His actions led Americans to divide into two parties: Jackson's Democratic party, dedicated to state rights and equal rights, and the opposition Whigs, who denounced Jackson's "despotism" and inherited the nationalist Republican commitment to national supremacy and broad federal power. Preeminent in politics, Jackson's ideas ultimately were reflected in constitutional law as the appointees of his party came to dominate the Supreme Court.

Democracy and Equal Rights

Opposition to the economic development program supported by nationalist Republicans grew throughout the 1820s. Disillusioned by hardships caused by an economic slowdown, many Americans blamed the difficulties on the materialism fostered by commercial expansion. They worried that Americans had lost their republican simplicity and spiritual values; too many Americans were concerned only with getting rich with as little work as possible. At the same time, Americans became more democratic and egalitarian, hostile to remaining vestiges of aristocracy and special privilege. Social, political, and economic institutions were democratized. The changes reached their peak in the 1830s and 1840s. By then another era of religious revival, the Second Great Awakening, had democratized churches, opening the ministry to men moved by faith rather than trained by seminaries. Standards for entry into professions, including the law, were eased or eliminated.

American social life became more democratic. During the Revolutionary era and after, Americans had believed that all people, or at least all white males, were entitled to equality before the law and equal opportunity to improve their positions. However, this belief had not meant that all men were socially equal. What Americans meant by equality was equal opportunity to improve one's social standing through hard work and ability. They spoke of replacing the British "aristocracy of birth" with an American "aristocracy of talent." But by the 1810s social distinctions began to break down, especially in more recently settled areas of upstate New York, western Pennsylvania, the hill country of the southern states, and the new states and territories of the West. The feeling grew that people should be treated equally. It became less and less acceptable to "put on airs." It became bad form to dress better than others, to speak differently, or to make a display of one's learning.

Americans became ever more hostile towards discrimination in political rights. Over the next 150 years, opposition to special political privileges would lead to the enfranchisement of African Americans, women, people under 21 years of age, and other groups. But during the 1820s and 1830s the drive to expand political privileges concentrated on eliminating distinctions based on property ownership among white men.

It had been considered dangerous to give the vote to people who were dependent on others for their livelihoods because they would vote as their masters directed. But newer anti-aristocratic ideas suggested that employees need not defer to employers outside the workplace. In the new commercial economy, employment was considered a "contractual relationship" rather than a "status relationship." The employer and employee were no longer considered master and servant but equally independent individuals who had entered a mutually beneficial but limited relationship, defined by the contract between them. It no longer seemed appropriate to withhold political privileges from those without property. In fact, such a rule implied subordination where none ought to exist.

Most western states had never imposed any property qualifications on the exercise of political rights, but the eastern states still did so. Some had property requirements for holding high state offices; others retained property requirements for voting for the upper house of the state legislature. Pressure grew to eliminate all such restrictions. By the 1840s most of them were gone.

Democracy, Race, and Slavery

However, the democratization of public life led to further repression of black Americans. Ordinary working people contrasted their status as free and equal citizens to the degraded status of African Americans, most of whom were slaves in the South or held demeaning positions in the North. Immigrants quickly saw the advantage of stressing their whiteness in seeking civic equality and better jobs.

Growing racism undermined African Americans' status as citizens. In many northern and some southern states, free black men had been able to vote if they could meet the property requirements. But when states eliminated property restrictions in the 1820s and 1830s, they imposed racial requirements. Most Americans still believed that only independent citizens made safe voters, and slavery tainted even free black Americans as "dependents."

The revived vitality of slavery in the South also contributed to the increasing racism throughout the nation. In a nation dedicated to equal rights, slavery could be justified only by differentiating African Americans from everyone else. The ideology of racism that developed to justify the exclusion tainted all black people.

Southerners remained ambivalent towards slavery. Many Southerners were still convinced that it was detrimental to their society and ought to be eliminated. Leading politicians, such as Henry Clay, continued to express moderate antislavery opinions. Antislavery societies existed throughout the South. In the northernmost slave states such as Delaware, Maryland, and Virginia, these antislavery societies hoped to establish gradual emancipation programs like that of New York. In others, they linked gradual emancipation to the colonization of freed slaves in Africa. Nowhere in the South could whites imagine living with African Americans on terms of civil equality. Moreover, white Southerners were adamant that they alone would deal with the problem. Therefore, even antislavery Southerners reacted angrily to northern efforts to force gradual emancipation in Missouri during the crisis of 1819.

Antislavery feeling in the South persisted into the 1830s. Virginians debated gradual emancipation in 1832, after the famous and bloody Nat Turner slave rebellion, only narrowly defeating the proposal. But the growing importance of cotton to the southern economy weakened antislavery sentiment. More and more Southerners, whether slave owners or not, depended on an economic system that turned on the value of land and slaves. Emancipation would destroy the immense capital invested in slaves. It would jeopardize the value of land, whose price rested on the value of the cotton, rice, tobacco, and sugar that Southerners believed could only be grown by slave labor.

Democracy and Gender

As they grew more committed to equal rights, Americans drew a sharper line between male and female roles. It became common to think of men and women as operating in separate spheres of society. Men were responsible for making economic decisions for their families and public decisions for their communities; women were responsible for maintaining the home and promoting the moral and spiritual values that undergirded the family and society. As a result, women continued to be excluded from public life and denied equal opportunity in economic life.

Although few questioned the idea that women had special nurturing and spiritual capacities, some women challenged the conclusion that this justified civil and political discrimination. A small but active number of women demanded greater autonomy in family life, sexual relations, child rearing, and economic matters.

People also recognized that the growing commercialization of the economy made "female emancipation" necessary. The modern economy encouraged more business speculation and consequently led to more business failures. The traditional rule of coverture left women helpless to protect themselves or their children when profligate husbands wasted the family's money and property. As men came to believe women had a special role in nurturing the family, they conceded that economic changes required a modification of the legal rules that left them and their children vulnerable to male incapacity or abuse. Beginning in the 1830s, nearly all states passed Married Women's Property Acts, which recognized married women's rights to own property and to make contracts. Much more slowly, states passed laws allowing married women to control their own income, a reform that did not become widespread until the 1870s and 1880s. At the same time, however, many states weakened women's dower rights to their husband's property, so that all the interests in a property could be sold without her permission. Both the elimination of dower rights and the expansion of women's property rights reflected the nation's growing commercialization, which called for maximum freedom to acquire and dispose of property.

Many states also liberalized divorce laws. The tremendous geographic mobility in the ever-expanding United States enabled, even encouraged, a significant number of men to desert their families and begin anew elsewhere. Liberalized divorce laws were necessary to enable deserted women to make new lives. The problem of physical abuse, often related to alcoholism, also encouraged the easing of restrictions on divorce.

The pervasive idea that women bore a special responsibility to nurture and train children led to changes in custody rules in cases of divorce or separation. Formerly, the law had recognized the husband's primary right to custody of his children. Now the law gave priority to the welfare of the children, and courts assumed that children would be better off with their mothers, who judges assumed were better suited for child care then men.

However, these changes fell far short of what the small band of early feminists wanted. Men continued to dominate women through control of economic resources and legal and political discrimination. The effort of reformers to secure women the full rights of citizenship, including the right to vote, inaugurated in 1848 at a now-famous convention held at Seneca Falls, New York, did not garner much support. Participation in public affairs drew into question the belief that women's first responsibility was to manage the home and care for their husbands and children. Even radical male reformers, like the abolitionists, generally discouraged women from taking an active part in public life. Nonetheless, some women did so, especially in the antislavery movement, which became the training ground for women who led the fight for women's suffrage after the Civil War. Because women were conceded a special role in the areas of health and moral improvement, crusaders like Dorothea Dix were able to campaign for reform in orphanages, hospitals, and mental health institutions. Nonetheless, most of women's social work took place in the private sector, especially in the churches.

Equal Rights and the Economy

Believing that no one should have special social or political privileges, most Americans thought that government ought not to confer special economic privileges either. The Jeffersonian Republicans had preached this concept in the 1790s, making "equal rights" their slogan. By the 1820s nearly all Americans accepted this idea, but they did not agree on how to apply it. Just what kind of government action *did* give people special privileges?

In the economic sphere, many Americans felt that allowing some people a special benefit was justifiable if the community received an equal benefit in return. Many believed it acceptable to give special privileges to a company in exchange for building a road, canal, railroad, bridge, or mill. The benefit might be an exemption from taxes, a monopoly, a government guarantee of company bonds, or even a direct government subsidy. The second national bank's incorporators received the privilege of having all the government's money deposited in their bank; in exchange, the people of the United States received the benefit of central control over the currency, thus stabilizing the economy. The protective tariff helped American businesses by keeping out cheap foreign competition, but it raised prices to consumers. Manufacturers and their employees were able to work and sell goods in an industry that otherwise would have been unable to compete with cheap foreign imports; in return the community benefited from a more diversified, stronger economy.

But many Americans, especially those whose lives and habits were disrupted by what historians call "the market revolution," complained that such laws *did* violate the principle of equal rights by giving special privileges to the favored few. With innovations in communications and transportation, business dealings among strangers began to replace exchanges among neighbors. Credit was controlled by remote bankers. Factory work began to replace craft work, and relations between large employers and a less skilled workforce supplanted relations between masters and journeyman artisans. In the view of many Americans, nationalist economic policies were fostering the development of a new aristocracy of speculators, bankers, and capitalists.

Andrew Jackson, Equal Rights, and Federalism

In 1824 many anti-nationalists supported the candidacies of William H. Crawford or General Andrew Jackson for the presidency, against the more nationalist candidates John Quincy Adams and Henry Clay. Crawford represented the state-sovereignty–oriented South, while Jackson challenged the nationalism of his fellow westerner Clay. The position of John C. Calhoun, slowly shifting away from nationalism, was still ambiguous enough to allow him to run as the vice presidential candidate of both the nationalistic Adams and the state-rights proponent Jackson.

Jackson was a hero of the War of 1812 against Britain. He had commanded American forces against one of the Civilized Tribes, the Seminoles, commending him to the Southerners who craved Indian lands. He seemed to reject the temptations of modern commercial society, manifesting a simple republicanism. He was a slaveholder and an opponent of federal efforts to restrict slavery, yet he was not as clearly identified with state sovereignty as Crawford.

This combination of attractions led more Americans to vote for Jackson in 1824 than for any of his competitors. But no candidate received a majority, and the election was thrown into the House of Representatives, to be decided according to the provisions of the Twelfth Amendment. There the supporters of the nationalist Republicans Clay and Adams joined to make Adams president. In return Adams made Clay secretary of state. Since every secretary of state since Madison had succeeded to the presidency, it was clear to Jackson's supporters that a deal had been made. For the next four years, they charged that Adams and Clay had struck a "corrupt bargain."

Adams proposed a nationalistic program of further internal improvements and government support for the arts and education. But such ideas were no longer popular, and almost none of them passed Congress. However, Congress did pass a steep protective tariff, the "Tariff of Abominations," just before the presidential election of 1828. Several southern state legislatures angrily passed resolutions denouncing the measure as unconstitutional. In South Carolina, Calhoun authored an *Exposition and Protest,* expanding on the doctrines of state sovereignty previously articulated by Roane, Taylor, and other Virginians. In 1828 Jackson and his "Democratic Republicans" defeated Adams and his "Nationalist Republicans." Jackson became president, while his ally Calhoun, now clearly identified with state sovereignty, was reelected vice president.

Upon his election Jackson quickly demonstrated his commitment to the democratic ideas sweeping the country by opening the celebration of his inauguration at the White House to all comers. Newspapers described ordinary citizens, their boots muddy from the unpaved Washington streets, wandering through the great rooms, gaping at the ornate furnishings and the fine art. Jackson rewarded his political supporters with government offices, arguing that no one was entitled to a permanent government sinecure; government positions should be rotated among ordinary citizens. Jackson's supporters pressed for the elimination of property requirements for voting or holding office in the states that still retained them. They argued that the "common sense" of the people was a surer guide to truth than the recondite investigations of philosophers. Jackson came to represent the great movement towards egalitarianism in America known as "Jacksonian Democracy."

Soon after his election, Jackson began to act on his commitment to state rights and a strict interpretation of "equal rights." The practical application of Jackson's principles would precipitate a bitter political struggle, dividing even his early supporters. Jackson would create a new political party division in the United States, based largely on constitutional issues.

The implications of his opposition to nationalist constitutionalism became clear when Jackson vetoed the Maysville Road bill in 1830. This measure provided government support to build a road linking the small Kentucky town to the Ohio River. It was the type of legislation envisioned by Clay's nationalistic "American Plan." Moreover, the road lay in Clay's own state. It presented the perfect opportunity for Jackson to challenge his western rival.

Jackson argued that the bill was unconstitutional. The government could not justify the expenditure as a promotion of interstate commerce because the road lay entirely within a single state. Nor did it meet the requirement of Article I, section 8 that all expenditures be for the general welfare; the road simply was too local. Clay, now serving in the Senate, responded with a nationalistic vision of interstate commerce and the general welfare. Whenever the federal government linked a locality to the great waterways that coursed among the states, it served the general welfare and promoted interstate commerce, he insisted. In contrast to Jackson, Clay articulated a vision of a nation bound together by a web of transportation facilities reaching into the smallest crannies of the country. The Constitution's delegation of power to the federal government must be construed broadly to achieve that goal, he argued. But he was unable to muster the votes necessary to override the veto.

Jackson also displayed his anti-nationalist orientation by the course he followed in the conflict between the southern states and the Civilized Tribes. Almost immediately after Jackson's election, the Georgia state legislature declared that its laws would supersede those of the Cherokee nation on June 1, 1830. It authorized a survey of the Indian lands to facilitate their sale. The Cherokee, who had devised a sophisticated legal strategy with the aid of missionary advisors, appealed directly to the Supreme Court for protection, asking for an injunction to stop the state's proceedings. At the same time, the Court issued a writ of error instructing Georgia's highest court to forward the papers in the case involving a Cherokee named

Corn Tassel, who had been arrested, tried, and sentenced to death in defiance of the Cherokee treaty with the United States. Like Virginia, Georgia denied the Supreme Court's jurisdiction. The state's officials refused to appear and hanged Corn Tassel despite the Court's writ. They also jailed missionaries who refused to take an oath recognizing the state's authority over the Cherokee and their lands.

The Supreme Court hesitated to take up the challenge. In *Cherokee Nation v. Georgia* (1831), it refused to issue the requested injunction, holding that it had no original jurisdiction to do so. But the Court finally took action as criticism of Georgia's aggression grew. In *Worcester v. Georgia* (1832), despite the state's refusal to concede the Court's jurisdiction, the justices reversed the missionaries' convictions and remanded the case to the Georgia Supreme Court for further action.

Georgia remained defiant and refused to release the missionaries. Jackson, whose attorney general supervised the United States marshals who would have to enforce any court order, was reputed to say, "John Marshall has made his decision, now let *him* enforce it!" The missionaries finally dropped their case in exchange for a pardon. Forcefully prodded by Jackson, some Cherokee leaders finally agreed to a new treaty surrendering all their lands, as the other tribes of the southeast had done earlier. Under federal supervision they were moved west in a brutal march known as "The Trail of Tears." It seemed clear that Jackson endorsed state sovereignty and that the Supreme Court no longer had the power to sustain the rival nationalist position.

Another, even more controversial application of Jackson's ideas came in 1832, when Congress passed a bill to renew the charter of the second national bank. Jackson vetoed the bill. Behind the veto lay Jackson's dislike of banks and his distaste for modern commercial society, in which banks played a key role Most of all, Jackson opposed the special privileges the bill gave to the bank's owners, who received the profits made by lending out the millions of dollars the government deposited. In his veto, Jackson presented a ringing statement of his equal-rights credo:

> It is to be regretted that the rich and powerful too often bend the acts of government to their selfish purposes. . . . There are no necessary evils in government. Its evils exist only in its abuses. If it would confine itself to equal protection, and, as Heaven does its rains, shower its favors alike on the high and the low, the rich and the poor, it would be an unqualified blessing.

Jackson doubted the power of the national government to charter a national bank. Nowhere did the Constitution specifically mention such a power. Even if it were true that Congress could pass laws that were "necessary and proper" to levy taxes and spend for the general welfare, Jackson believed that the Tenth Amendment placed limits on what could be done. By declaring that the powers not delegated to the national government were reserved to the states, the Tenth Amendment recognized an area of jurisdiction in which states had final authority. In effect, the amendment created a line between national and state jurisdiction, and the national government could not exercise the powers delegated to it in such a way as to cross that line. But the Bank bill did cross that line, Jackson concluded. Of course, the Supreme Court had explicitly ruled that the bank was constitutional. But Jackson denied that the justices could bind a co-equal branch of the government. He was as much obligated to obey the Constitution as they were, and he had an equal right to interpret it.

Many Americans, however, considered the national bank essential to economic progress and stability. They saw the veto message as a demagogic appeal to reactionary ignorance. The veto's critics, including many who had earlier supported Jackson, began to organize an opposition. Those who agreed with him organized in support, calling themselves "Democratic Republicans," or "Democrats," in contrast to the "National Republicans" who opposed him. This new Democratic party naturally claimed to be the party of "equal rights," while its leaders attacked Jackson's opponents as representing "aristocracy" and "special privilege."

While Whigs and Democrats fought over how far the national, state, and local governments could go to *promote* economic development, both supported wide-ranging local *regulation* of social and economic life. Local communities regulated where and how people could buy and sell goods and store dangerous products. They set standards of quality. They authorized officials to tear down fire traps and bar wooden buildings; build roads and canals; and widen ports despite damage to neighboring property. Every community policed morals, regulating drinking establishments, suppressing prostitution, and controlling entertainment.

These regulations were rarely challenged in the courts. When they were, judges consistently sustained them as valid exercises of the state's "police power"—the authority to regulate persons and property to protect public health, safety, and morals. Despite the example of the Supreme Court's protection of individual property rights, state and local courts rarely interfered to protect individual rights against such community control.

The Nullification Crisis, "State Sovereignty," and "State Rights"

Despite Jackson's vetoes of the Maysville Road bill and the National Bank bill on state-rights grounds, a new crisis erupted in 1832 that demonstrated that he did not believe in state sovereignty. Jackson was forced to present an alternative theory of federalism during the Nullification Crisis of 1832.

The Nullification Crisis grew out of the Southern response to the "Tariff of Abominations" of 1828. In denouncing the tariff as unconstitutional, the protesting southern state legislatures had articulated the theory of state sovereignty developed by the Virginians and endorsed by other opponents of national power: The Constitution was a compact among the states; the Union was a confederacy in which the states retained sovereignty; the powers of the federal government must be construed narrowly; and the states retained final authority to decide when a federal law was unconstitutional. But no one had yet been able to provide

Senator John C. Calhoun, apostle of nationalism in the 1810s and the leading exponent of state sovereignty after the 1820s.

an effective mechanism for a state to enforce its determination that a federal law was unconstitutional. At most, some states had refused to obey a few Supreme Court decisions, and that defiance had only occasionally succeeded.

In the *South Carolina Exposition*, Calhoun, just elected vice president on Jackson's ticket, offered an answer. The "People of the United States" who, according to the Preamble, had ordained the Constitution, were the people of each of the individual states, he insisted. Therefore sovereignty lay in the people of each state. They had exercised their sovereign power by ratifying the Constitution in special state conventions. Acting through the same medium, they could pronounce a federal law invalid and "nullify" it.

In November 1832, the people of South Carolina, led by Calhoun's political organization, acted on his ideas. They held a convention that passed an ordinance "nullifying" the Tariff of Abominations and instructing the state legislature to prevent its enforcement in the state. The legislature complied by declaring it illegal for anyone to enforce the tariff within South Carolina. Anyone who defied the law, including federal officials, would be prosecuted, fined, and imprisoned. The law forbade any appeal to the United States Supreme Court. If the federal government tried to sustain the law by force it would break the compact among the

Henry Clay, one of the young nationalist
Republicans in the 1820s, Whig advocate of federal support for transportation
and economic development in the
1830s and 1840s.

states, and South Carolina would be free to secede from the Union. To prepare for
any confrontation, the legislature authorized the governor to raise and equip an
armed force.

Many people expected President Jackson to agree with the state-sovereignty
doctrine and to support South Carolina's nullification of the 1828 tariff. Jackson
had been elected with the solid support of voters who had opposed the national
bank, the tariff, and the Marshall court, and he had recently refused to support
the Supreme Court against Georgia in the Indian cases.

But Jackson loved the Union too much to endorse nullification. He and his
northern supporters, and many Southerners as well, rejected Calhounite state
sovereignty. Harking back to Madison's earlier formulations—and aided by the
last of the framers himself—they developed an alternative, which provided the
constitutional basis for what we still call "state rights" today. According to this
new doctrine of federalism, the states and the federal government were each sovereign over the different areas within their jurisdiction. The Supremacy Clause
specified that where the Constitution delegated authority to the federal government, its laws were supreme. But the Tenth Amendment guaranteed sovereign
power to the states in those areas under state jurisdiction. In effect, it established

Andrew Jackson tramples on the Constitution in a cartoon that makes clear why his opponents named their new political organization the Whig party.

a line separating the area of national supremacy from the area of state supremacy. The federal government could not exercise final authority on the state side of that line. The state and federal governments were each sovereign and supreme, an idea scholars have referred to as "dual sovereignty" or "dual federalism." According to the advocates of state rights, therefore, the Tenth Amendment, like the Bill of Rights, imposed a limitation on the powers that the Constitution delegated to the government. Just as the First Amendment barred the federal government from using its delegated power to infringe on freedom of the press, the Tenth Amendment barred the government from using its delegated powers to invade areas under state jurisdiction.

According to Jackson's idea of state rights, the Supreme Court, not the state courts or a state convention, determined what lay within state and what lay within federal jurisdiction. If the federal government used a delegated power in such a way as to invade the state's jurisdiction, the Supreme Court must rule the federal law unconstitutional. If the Court too sustained unconstitutional legislation, the remedy lay with the people at the polls. "Let all contested matters be brought to that tribunal, and it will decree correctly," Jackson declared confidently.

Jackson and most of his supporters agreed with Calhoun and the South Carolinians that the protective tariff was an abuse of the federal government's delegated powers. But Jackson denied that South Carolina could unilaterally bar the enforcement of a federal law within the state. If the people of every state made such a claim, the Union would soon fall apart. Nor would Jackson concede that states had the right to secede from the Union.

In December 1832, Jackson issued a proclamation ordering South Carolina not to interfere with the tariff's enforcement. At his urging Congress passed the Force Act, permitting the president to use military force to uphold the law if necessary. But at the same time, Jackson urged Congress to pass a law lowering the tariff. Congress did so, and South Carolina held a second convention rescinding the ordinance of nullification. The compromise of 1832 ended the crisis, but Calhoun and the South Carolinians refused to admit they had been wrong. To reiterate the state's commitment to the state-sovereignty doctrine, the second convention "nullified" the Force Act.

"State rights" and "equal rights" became principal commitments of the Democratic party, which generally controlled both Congress and the presidency between 1836 and 1860. During those years, the federal government retired from the business of regulating banking and the currency. The tariff lost its protective features by the mid-1840s. The government also ended direct subsidies to develop transportation, turning money directly over to the states instead. The people, through their support of the Democratic party, had construed the Constitution as effectively as the Marshall court ever had.

Jackson and the Presidency

A forceful giant of a man, Jackson interpreted the powers of the presidency much more broadly than had his predecessors. The bank veto had established his claim that the president's right to decide whether a law was constitutional equaled that of Congress and the Supreme Court. If the Constitution obligated the courts to refuse to enforce unconstitutional laws, it imposed the same obligation on the president. Jackson acted on this idea in 1833 when he ordered his secretary of the treasury to withdraw the deposits of the United States from the national bank, three years before its charter expired. Even many who disliked the Bank blasted this high-handed action. In 1834 the Senate formally declared that Jackson had "assumed upon himself authority and power not conferred by the constitution and laws, but in derogation of both." But when Jackson's Democratic party gained control, the Senate expunged this censure from its record.

Jackson also increased presidential authority by using the power to appoint federal officials—the "patronage"—to strengthen his Democratic supporters. This program not only strengthened the party, but gave Jackson great influence within it, because he could promise political office to party members who followed his directions and refuse office to those who resisted.

Such claims of broad presidential power revived old fears of tyranny and executive "corruption" of the political system, as well as the old suspicion of political parties. Many people assailed "King Andrew" and organized politically to oppose him. Calling themselves Whigs to identify themselves with the heritage of opposition to executive tyranny, Jackson's opponents ranged from nationalists who supported the national bank and the protective tariff to Calhoun and other southern proponents of nullification. But despite their distaste for party organizations and their declared opposition to the "spoils system" of patronage that sustained them, when Whigs finally did win the presidency, their presidents did the same thing.

The Supreme Court and Jacksonian Jurisprudence

Jackson's ideas were also reflected in Supreme Court decisions, where the anti-nationalist reaction had clearly sobered the justices. As early as 1827, the Court sustained state bankruptcy laws that applied to contracts made after the laws' passage, rejecting Chief Justice Marshall's dissenting argument that the Contracts Clause barred state impairment of any contract, past or future.

Marshall's own opinions seemed now to point towards dual federalism. In the 1820s many state legislatures, spurred by the Second Great Awakening, tried to combat the widespread abuse of alcoholic beverages in America. Regulation of alcohol was well within the states' "police powers" to promote the public safety, health, and moral welfare. But liquor dealers challenged state laws that barred the importation of alcoholic beverages as infringements of the federal government's exclusive power to regulate interstate commerce. In the case of *Brown v. Maryland* (1827), Marshall attempted to resolve the issue with the "original-package rule," which stated that federal jurisdiction ended and state jurisdiction began when goods came to rest in a state, were removed from their packages, and split into smaller packages for local distribution.

In *Barron v. Baltimore* (1833), the Marshall court confirmed that the state police power lay beyond federal intervention. The case involved improvements that Baltimore, like many ports throughout the country, made to its harbor area. These improvements often hurt wharf owners. In Barron's case, Baltimore diverted streams flowing into the harbor in order to improve its roads. As a result the harbor around Barron's wharf silted up, becoming too shallow for ships to navigate. In similar situations, wharf owners had brought suits in state courts, charging that such regulations deprived them of property without due process of law and without compensating them for the loss. However, state courts uniformly held that these regulations were valid exercises of state police power and did not physically deprive the wharf owners of their property.

Barron appealed his case to the Supreme Court, arguing that Baltimore had violated the Fifth Amendment's clause that prohibited the taking of property for public purposes without compensation. In earlier years, the Marshall court had been quick to protect such vested property rights, and it had interpreted constitutional provisions creatively to do so. But now the Court exercised restraint. Although only the First Amendment referred specifically to the federal government, the justices unanimously agreed that the whole Bill of Rights applied only to federal actions. Constitutional provisions that imposed limitations upon the states did so explicitly. For example Article I, section 10 expressly stated "No State shall" undertake the forbidden acts. Such language was missing from the Bill of Rights.

Had the Court decided differently, state residents could have challenged any number of state actions as violations of due process of law or of other provisions of the Bill of Rights. The Supreme Court would then have superseded the state courts as the protectors of citizens' rights against their own governments. Of course making the courts the protectors of individual rights against local majorities was exactly what many old Federalists had hoped for. But by the 1830s such ideas did not have a very wide appeal.

When John Marshall died in 1835, Jackson named Roger Brooke Taney, who strongly agreed with Jackson's political and constitutional views, chief justice. By the 1840s most of Taney's colleagues on the supreme bench were Democrats as well. Believing in "equal rights," the Democrats on the Supreme Court were less likely than their predecessors to protect special privileges against efforts by state legislatures to end them. The Court made this preference clear in the 1837 case of *Charles River Bridge Co. v. Warren Bridge Co.* Many years earlier, the colony of Massachusetts had given the Charles River Bridge Company a charter authorizing it to build a toll bridge linking the towns of Boston and Cambridge. As commerce across the Charles River grew, the bridge became extremely profitable, and the owners of its valuable stock became among the wealthiest people in New England.

By the 1800s many Bostonians bitterly resented the bridge company's monopoly. They demanded that the state legislature build a new bridge, but the Company argued that this action would take away its vested rights by destroying the value of the bridge. In 1828 the antibridge party finally persuaded the Massachusetts state legislature to charter another company to build a second bridge across the Charles, not far from the first. This new Warren Bridge Company would be permitted to charge tolls only until it made a small profit. Then the bridge would be free.

The Charles River Bridge Company challenged the new law in the Massachusetts state courts, arguing that once the Warren Bridge became free, no one would pay to use the original span. In effect, they argued, the legislation authorizing the second bridge deprived the company of property without due process of law, in violation of the Massachusetts constitution. The state judges did not agree and refused to rule the law unconstitutional. The Charles River Bridge Company then retained Daniel Webster to appeal the decision to the United States Supreme Court. Because the Court's decision in *Barron v. Baltimore* had made clear that the Due Process Clause of the Fifth Amendment did not apply against the states, Webster turned instead to the Obligation of Contracts Clause. The *Dartmouth College* decision precluded the state from repealing or changing the charter directly, Webster argued; it could not evade the decision by doing so indirectly.

Justice Story agreed with Webster's argument. If Marshall had still been alive, he might have been convinced as well. But the new chief justice, a committed Jacksonian, had no sympathy for monopolies like the Charles River Bridge Company. "While the rights of private property are sacredly guarded, we must not forget that the community also have rights," Taney wrote, speaking for the majority of the justices. The charter to the Charles River Bridge Company did not specifically say that no other bridge could be built across the Charles River. States should not be considered to have given up such powers unless the charter made such an intention explicit.

Taney recognized that to hold otherwise would dramatically increase the cost of economic development. Companies that had received charters to build turnpikes and canals could have blocked charters to railroads running between the same towns. Chartered ferries could have blocked bridges. Old banks could have blocked the incorporation of new ones. In all these cases, the states or the new companies would have been forced to purchase the old companies' rights. A chartered company's stock would reflect not so much the value of the company as the value of its ability to block competition.

The Democratic justices did not distrust the state governments the way that Marshall had. After Taney became chief justice, the Supreme Court usually sustained the power of states to make economic and other regulations. In a dramatic reversal of the federal courts' hostility towards state efforts to handle currency problems, the Supreme Court upheld the power of the state-controlled Bank of Kentucky to issue banknotes, which circulated as paper money. Article I, section 10, which barred states from coining money or emitting "bills of credit," did not apply to banknotes, the Court ruled, even those issued by a state-controlled bank.

If the Taney Court was willing to let states evade limitations clearly imposed by Article I, section 10, it was unlikely to block state actions on the vague grounds that they infringed on Congress's power to regulate interstate and foreign commerce. In a series of cases, the Court rejected arguments that Congress's power over interstate and foreign commerce was exclusive and negated all state laws that touched on these areas. But having done so, the Court had difficulty establishing a rule distinguishing permissible state regulations from unconstitutional infringements on federal power. In *New York v. Miln* (1837), the Court sustained the constitutionality of state health regulations for immigrants. In the *License Cases* (1847), it permitted states to tax and regulate the sale of liquor imported from other states. But in the *Passenger Cases* (1849), the Court overturned state laws imposing taxes on immigrants. In *Cooley v. Board of Wardens* (1851), which tested the constitutionality of local safety regulations governing ship traffic in ports, the

Court finally arrived at a flexible rule. If the subject of such regulations was local, as were the contested safety regulations, the regulations could stand until Congress passed a law clearly inconsistent with them. If the subject of a regulation was inherently national, the regulation was unconstitutional. This rule is still the law today.

Although the Taney Court in many ways reflected the state-rights philosophy of Jacksonian Democracy, it never formally established the doctrine's key principle of "dual federalism" as a matter of law. However, several justices articulated it in the *Miln, License,* and *Passenger* cases: In areas where the states had primary jurisdiction—as over the health, safety, and morals of the community—a conflicting national law would have to give way, even if passed under what would otherwise be a constitutional power. Likewise, in *Groves v. Slaughter* (1841), Chief Justice Taney declared that states had exclusive control over all aspects of slavery, including the slave trade, Congress's power to regulate interstate commerce not withstanding. But these statements were made in concurring opinions or in *dicta*—that is, in asides that did not pertain directly to the question in point—so they did not have the weight of formal judicial decisions.

The Supreme Court came closest to a formal acceptance of "dual sovereignty" in *Prigg v. Pennsylvania* (1842). There the Court held that the national government could not require state officials to enforce the Fugitive Slave Act of 1793, even though the law itself was constitutional. The state governments and the national government were independently sovereign; neither could require the other's officials to enforce its laws.

There was one great exception to the pro-state tendency of the Taney Court decisions. The Judiciary Act of 1789 had provided that in cases of "diversity jurisdiction" (controversies between citizens of different states or between states and citizens of other states) the federal courts should follow the law of the jurisdiction in which the case arose. But in *Swift v. Tyson* (1842), the justices, following the nationalistic Story's lead, evaded the requirement. The federal courts must follow the statutes of the jurisdiction, the Court held, but not the decisions of its courts. Instead, they should apply general commercial law. Thus the federal courts developed a separate body of economic law, uniformly enforced throughout the nation. This proved immensely important for the economic development of the United States. The federal courts developed rules of commercial law that were much friendlier to business than those in many state courts.

Nonetheless, in most of its decisions and in its *dicta*, the Supreme Court reflected the principles of Andrew Jackson and his Democratic party. Most Americans had accepted the Democratic ideas of "equal rights" and "state rights." The Supreme Court applied these general principles to specific cases. In doing so, the Court generally ended the intervention in state policy that had characterized the Marshall Court. It freed the states to exercise their own police powers to promote safety, health, morality, and economic development.

Within the states, people struggled over how to shape their societies. Moderate Democrats joined Whigs to pass state legislation encouraging and even subsidizing the development of transportation facilities, banking, and commerce. Radical Jacksonians warned that such policies gave special benefits to influential entrepreneurs, encouraged greed and speculation, and restricted personal liberty. A spate of new state constitutions limited the authority of state and local governments to subsidize economic development. Reflecting both a commitment to democracy and to popular constitutionalism, many states made their judiciaries elective. A number of new constitutions strengthened governors, who were seen as representing the whole people more directly than legislators.

The society that emerged from these conflicts stressed the equal opportunity of white men to participate in political and economic life, while it severely restricted the freedom of African Americans and women. The contradiction between liberty and slavery, in fact, was already beginning to strain the system. As time progressed, ever more Northerners questioned whether liberty could survive in a society that tolerated slavery. Southerners wondered whether federalism's balance between the rights of the states and the authority of the federal government insulated them effectively enough from northern pressure to abolish their central institution.

TIMELINE

1820s   State constitutions democratized.

1825   John Quincy Adams elected president by the House of Representatives after no candidate receives a majority in the Electoral College.

1828   Congress passes the "Tariff of Abominations" over widespread southern opposition.

John C. Calhoun authors the *South Carolina Exposition and Protest.*

Andrew Jackson elected president and Calhoun vice president; both inaugurated in 1829.

1830   Jackson vetoes the Maysville Road bill.

Congress passes the Indian Removal Act.

Under a state law passed in 1828, Georgia extends its jurisdiction over lands secured to the Cherokee by federal treaty.

1831   Nat Turner slave rebellion in Virginia.

1832   In *Worcester v. Georgia,* the Supreme Court rules unconstitutional Georgia's takeover of Cherokee lands. Doubting that Jackson would enforce Court decision, the Cherokee agree to move to Oklahoma.

1832	President Jackson vetoes the bill renewing the charter of the second national bank.
	Jackson reelected president.
	South Carolina convention "nullifies" the Tariff Act of 1828.
	Jackson issues a Proclamation to the People of South Carolina repudiating Nullification.
1833	*Barron v. Baltimore* rules that the Bill of Rights applies only to the federal government and not to the states.
	Congress passes the Force Act of 1833 to enforce federal laws against Nullification.
	Congress passes the compromise Tariff of 1833; South Carolina repeals the ordinance nullifying the Tariff of 1828 but nullifies the Force Act of 1833.
	President Jackson withdraws federal funds from the second national bank.
1836	Mississippi passes the first Married Women's Property Act.
	Democrat Martin Van Buren elected president, and inaugurated in 1837.
	Roger Taney becomes chief justice of the U.S. Supreme Court.
1837	In *Charles River Bridge Co. v. Warren Bridge Co.*, the Supreme Court declines to extend the "vested rights" of corporations beyond the explicit terms of their charters.
1842	In *Prigg v. Pennsylvania*, the Supreme Court upholds the constitutionality of the Fugitive Slave Act of 1793 but rules that state officials cannot be required to enforce it.
	Swift v. Tyson enables the federal courts to establish a uniform commercial law for the nation.
1843–1851	The Supreme Court wrestles with the constitutionality of state police regulations affecting interstate and foreign commerce in the *License Cases* (1843) and *Passenger Cases* (1849); *Cooley v. Board of Wardens* affirms state power to establish strictly local rules affecting interstate commerce in the absence of national action.
1848	The Seneca Falls Convention calls for equal civil and political rights for women.

FURTHER READING

Gordon S. Wood concludes his *The Radicalism of the American Revolution* (1992) with a discussion of the developments that led to a "Middle-Class Order"—the title of his last chapter. Alexander Keyssar describes the expansion of voting rights from the Revolution through the Jacksonian era in part one of *The Right to Vote* (2000). Sean Wilentz links the growth of democracy to the market revolution in "Property and Power: Suffrage Reform in the United States," in *Voting and the Spirit of American Democracy*, ed. Donald W. Rogers (1990). The eroding position of African Americans in the North in the Jacksonian era is described by Leon Litwack in *North of Slavery* (1961). David R. Roediger discusses the growth of racism in the North in an already classic exposition, *The Wages of Whiteness* (rev. ed., 1999). A number of essays describe the centrality of racism in antebellum American culture in *Race and the Early Republic*, ed. Michael A. Morrison and James Brewer Stewart (2002). Richard H. Brown, "The Missouri Crisis, Slavery, and the Politics of Jacksonism," *South Atlantic Quarterly* 65 (Winter 1966): 55–72, details the relationship between proslavery sentiment and the rise of the Jacksonian Democratic party.

In her seminal "The Cult of True Womanhood, 1820–1860," *American Quarterly* 18 (Summer 1966): 151–174, Barbara Welter describes how an idealized view of womanhood improved women's status but relegated them to the private sphere of family life. For women's role and rights in antebellum American society, see Nancy Isenberg, *Sex and Citizenship in Antebellum America* (1998) and part two of Sandra F. VanBurkleo, *"Belonging to the World"* (2001). For specific issues, consult Norma Basch, *In the Eyes of the Law: Women, Marriage, and Property in 19th Century New York* (1982); Michael Grossberg, *Governing the Hearth: Law and the Family in Nineteenth-Century America* (1985); and Richard H. Chused, *Private Acts in Public Places: A Social History of Divorce in the Formative Era of American Family Law* (1994).

The most readable narrative survey of public policy in Jacksonian America is Harry L. Watson, *Liberty and Power* (1990), which stresses the interaction between new market forces and the heritage of republican ideology. Daniel Feller, *The Jacksonian Promise* (1995) is a wide-ranging discussion of American life from 1815 to 1840. Gerald Leonard argues that the founders of the Jacksonian Democratic party saw it, and not the Supreme Court, as the vehicle by which the people of the United States would assure fidelity to constitutional principles. Gerald Leonard, "Party as a Political Safeguard of Federalism" *Rutgers Law Review* 54 (Fall 2001): 221–281. Charles Sellers, *The Market Revolution* (1991), is a monumental study of how economic change fueled politics in the Jacksonian era, but see Donald J. Ratcliffe's careful refinement in "The Crisis of Commercialization," in *The Market Revolution*, ed. Melvyn Stokes and Stephen Conway (1996). Tony A. Freyer discusses the constitutional conflicts engendered by the market revolution in *Producers Versus Capitalists* (1994). William J. Novak emphasizes how thoroughly local communities regulated economic and social life in *The People's Welfare* (1996).

For a thorough discussion of the Cherokee cases and state rights, see Tim Alan Garrison, *The Legal Ideology of Removal* (2002). Jill Norgren's *The Cherokee Cases* (1996) is more concise. For Jackson's war on the national bank, see Robert V. Remini, *Andrew Jackson and the Bank War* (1967), and Bray Hammond, *Banks and Politics in America* (1957).

The best study of the Nullification Crisis is Richard E. Ellis, *The Union at Risk* (1987). Keith E. Whittington compares constitutional nationalism to Calhounite "extreme federalism" and Jacksonian "centrist federalism" in an essay in his *Constitutional Construction* (1999). Kenneth M. Stampp argues that the notion of an indissoluble union only developed in relation to the Nullification Crisis in "The Concept of a Perpetual Union," *Journal of American History* 65 (June 1978): 5–33. See also Paul C. Nagle, *One Nation Indivisible* (1964), which stresses Webster's role in promoting a deeper nationalism. For the theoretical bases of the rival theories of federalism that emerged from the Nullification Crisis, see

Michael Les Benedict, "Sovereign Nation or Sovereign States: Federalism Through the Civil War Era," in *Constitution 200: A Bicentennial Collection of Essays,* ed. Mary A. Hepburn (1988), 3–21. Robert Remini describes Jackson's aggressive use of presidential power in his essay on the Jackson era in *The Constitution and the American Presidency*, ed. Martin Fausold and Alan Shank (1991). Carl B. Swisher's *History of the Supreme Court of the United States,* vol. 5: *The Taney Period, 1836–1864* (1974) is a comprehensive account of the Taney Court. A more accessible overview is Timothy S. Heubner, *The Taney Court* (2003), one of the ABC-CLIO Supreme Court Handbooks. Felix Frankfurter, *The Commerce Power Under Marshall, Taney, and Waite* (1937) is a classic study. Stanley I. Kutler's *Privilege and Creative Destruction: The Charles River Bridge Case* (1971) puts the Taney Court's judicial restraint in the context of antebellum American economic development. For the importance of *Swift v. Tyson* (1842), see Tony A. Freyer, *Forums of Order: The Federal Courts and Business in American History* (1979), and *Harmony and Dissonance: The Swift and Erie Cases in American Federalism* (1981).

8
Slavery and the Constitution

The existence of slavery in the United States presented the greatest possible contradiction to the American heritage of liberty and equal rights. Both an economic institution and an instrument of racial control, slavery was a brutal institution that grew ever more intolerable to Northerners. Yet most Northerners accepted slavery as the price of Union and shared the racist attitudes that undergirded it. By the 1830s slavery was so intertwined with American government and society that it characterized the United States as much or more than liberty.

Slavery's opponents, including both abolitionists and less radical antislavery activists, determined to end slavery's sway. They argued that although the Constitution tolerated slavery as a local institution, it committed the national government to freedom. The Bill of Rights prohibited the national government from passing laws to support slavery, while the Constitution's delegation of powers could sustain various actions against it. Slavery's defenders, in contrast, claimed that the Constitution secured *slaveholders'* rights. More and more white Southerners were attracted to state-sovereignty doctrines of federalism, which they interpreted as making the federal government the agent of the states, bound to promote all state interests equally.

The issue came to a head over slavery in the territories. Opponents of slavery argued that the Fifth Amendment's Due Process Clause forbade Congress from allowing slavery in the territories. They also held that Congress's plenary power to regulate the territories authorized it to establish a "free-soil" (no-slavery) policy. In response, most Southerners, relying on state sovereignty, demanded that Congress protect their right to carry slaves to all the territories. With the South's fundamental interests at stake and with each side making its claim as a matter of right, compromise became increasingly difficult. When the Supreme Court ruled in favor of the southern position in the *Dred Scott* case, it became impossible. Northerners turned to the antislavery Republican party and elected Abraham Lincoln president in 1860. The states of the Deep South, again relying on the doctrine of state sovereignty, responded by attempting to secede from the Union. When Lincoln called on the army and state militias to suppress the rebellion, the states of the Upper South joined their slaveholding sister-states as the nation plunged into civil war.

Southerners and Slavery

Americans' commitment to liberty following the Revolution had precipitated a powerful antislavery movement. One state after another had legislated gradual emancipation. But it was a state-by-state development; the Missouri Crisis of 1819–1821 made clear how strongly the states that still had slavery opposed federal action on the subject.

The post-Revolutionary abolition movement traveled from north to south, beginning in New England immediately after the war and reaching Maryland and Virginia in the 1830s. But there it stalled. Virginians debated gradual emancipation in the state constitutional convention of 1832 but rejected it.

It was much more difficult for Southerners to extend freedom to their slaves than it was for Northerners, even in slaveholding New York. The commercialization of the United States led to the end of unfree labor—that is, both slavery and indentured servitude—in the North. Ironically, however, it fixed slavery more firmly on most of the South. The exceptions were Delaware and northern Maryland, where masters freed more and more slaves, until free African Americans outnumbered slaves there. In the rest of the South the wealth that followed increased commercialization was invested in slaves and land. In the 1830s cotton growing emerged as a tremendously profitable agricultural industry. The money to be made from this "white gold" led to a boom in land and slave values, as well as to a great westward movement as ambitious Southerners raced to develop the lands of the southwest. Thousands accepted Mexico's invitation to develop agriculture in Texas, importing slaves to do the work despite Mexico's abolition of slavery. Not only planters but everyone involved in the South's commercial system—merchants, lawyers and other professionals, even urban laborers—depended on slavery to maintain prosperity. By the 1830s there was no way to extricate slavery from the economy, and many Southerners had abandoned the old conviction that slavery was a "necessary evil" that would ultimately die out. In 1860 slaves accounted for nearly 20 percent of the wealth owned by Americans, more than all the investment in manufacturing, railroads, and banks put together.

More than economic considerations recommitted white Southerners to slavery. White racism had made the imposition of slavery upon Africans conceivable in the first place. The more Americans believed in liberty and equality, the more they had to justify excluding African Americans from freedom's benefits. Therefore, as Southerners became more committed to slavery, they became more harshly racist. They believed that Africans were incapable of living in a civilized community, erroneously claiming that there had never been a black African civilization. Racists insisted that Africans lacked the intelligence and self-discipline of the white races and were easily tempted to vice and violence. They would not work unless forced to; if freed, they would sink into pauperism and live by theft.

Accepting this racist ideology, white Southerners viewed slavery not only as a labor system but as essential to race control. As the nineteenth century progressed, they made their slave codes harsher. Although the trend in modern states was to withdraw coercive power from private hands and to concentrate it in the state, the central feature of the slave codes was their recognition of the master's right to control his slaves through force and violence. In turn, the master delegated coercive power to others. The codes included provisions to prevent abuse, torture, and murder. But conviction for violations required proof of guilty intent. It was almost impossible to prove that a brutal master or overseer intended more than the maintenance of order and discipline, especially since neither slaves nor free African Americans were permitted to testify against whites in court. Furthermore, whites were reluctant to punish even the most brutal masters, lest they give slaves the idea that they had rights. The whites most likely to be brought to trial for abusing slaves were those who had leased their slaves or who had assaulted them without specific authority from their masters. In such cases, a master's affection for a servant or her anger at the damage to her property might motivate a prosecution.

The codes recognized no rights for slaves, except the right to life itself implied by the ban on murder. Some courts drew even that right into question by denying that slaves could defend themselves against whites even to save their own lives. Slave marriages were unrecognized by law. Families could be broken up and sold, husbands torn from wives, children from parents. The law did not recognize slaves' rights to own property or make contracts and therefore did not protect slaves from theft or fraud, or provide a forum for resolving disputes among themselves. (This did not stop slaves from accumulating personal property. It meant that they had to devise extra-legal ways to identify what belonged to them, none of which bound whites.)

Fearing insurrection, Southerners barred unsupervised slave gatherings, banned black clergymen from preaching without white permission, and required slaves to carry passes when off their plantations. Most states forbade teaching slaves to read or write. State laws required all able-bodied white men to serve on slave patrols and often gave both the patrols and justices of the peace summary power to inflict punishment, which generally consisted of whipping rather than imprisonment. The system encouraged callousness and brutality.

Southern laws also severely repressed free blacks. Statutes and court cases denied them the status of citizens. Laws limited their right to gather together and to bear arms. African Americans had no political rights. They could testify only in cases in which they were parties and could not sit on juries. They were subject to stiffer penalties than whites for crimes, including enslavement if they could not pay fines. Worried that the very existence of free African Americans encouraged slaves to aspire to freedom, southern states made it progressively harder for their owners to emancipate them. Freed slaves were required to leave the state, abandoning spouses and children, unless they received special permission to remain. By the 1850s, many southern states were considering laws expelling all their free blacks and re-enslaving those who refused to leave.

The rule for determining who was white and who was black varied from state to state. It was common to define as "colored" anyone with a single black grandparent. In appearance, such persons might be white and yet held in slavery. Americans constructed racial identities in such a way that people who objectively were much nearer white than black became black nonetheless, a tendency that continues even today.

Northerners and Slavery

As it became clear in the mid-1830s that the gradual emancipation movement had stalled, a few Northerners became "abolitionists," agitating in newspapers, pamphlets, and in the churches for immediate steps to end slavery. William Lloyd Garrison established *The Liberator,* which promised to be "as harsh as truth and as uncompromising as justice." Theodore Weld used the words of slave owners themselves to condemn *Slavery As It Is* (1839). The great fugitive slave orator Frederick Douglass was a living rebuttal of racist beliefs in black inferiority.

The abolitionists had two goals. First, they hoped to revive the antislavery movement in the South by educating Southerners on the moral evils of slavery, on how it damaged the interests of nonslaveholders, and how it inhibited the region's economic development. Second, they pressed for the federal government to take antislavery action wherever it had the authority to act. They felt morally compromised by federal support for slavery, and they wanted to pressure Southerners by isolating the institution.

Most Northerners strongly opposed abolitionism. Southerners made clear that they would prefer to leave the Union rather than risk abolition. Therefore, most Americans at first identified abolitionism with disunion; they considered it almost treasonous. Moreover, most Northerners accepted the same racist ideas as Southerners. Nearly all the northern states continued to deny political rights to their black residents, including the right to sit on juries or serve in the militia. Many denied them the right to testify against whites in court. Several prohibited African Americans from settling within their boundaries. Everywhere black Americans were discriminated against in employment, and in most places their children could not attend public schools. Many northern judges held that African Americans were not even citizens. Such racism helped northern whites to reconcile African-American slavery with their belief in individual liberty and equal rights for white people.

The northern Democratic view of the federal system also helped Northerners accept slavery in the South. Northern Democrats advocated the idea of "state rights," or "dual federalism," with its strict line separating state and national jurisdiction. Democrats insisted that slavery was on the state side of the line and therefore that the national government had nothing to do with it except for passing the Fugitive Slave Act to help catch slaves who had run away to the North. Even in this case, the Supreme Court had ruled that the national government could not require state officials to enforce the act. Thus northern Democrats were able to argue effectively that Northerners did not share moral responsibility for slavery. It was the responsibility of Southerners alone.

Abolitionists denied the validity of the northern Democrats' argument. First, the national government did in fact return runaway slaves to the South through the Fugitive Slave Act. Second, the national government controlled the District of Columbia, the nation's capital, and allowed slavery there, backed by all the rigors of a typical slave code. Slavery was permitted in the territories south of the Missouri Compromise line. The United States consistently defended the rights of slave owners in disputes with other countries. Federal courts enforced contracts involving slave property. The federal government was heavily involved in slavery, abolitionists argued, and therefore so were all Americans, North and South.

To make this point more clearly, in the 1830s the abolitionists began circulating petitions asking Congress to abolish slavery in the District of Columbia. As these petitions poured into Congress, Southerners reacted angrily. In deference to their feelings, many northern congressmen refused to present them. But former president John Quincy Adams took up the cause and presented petitions from throughout the North. Southerners then combined with northern Democrats to pass a rule requiring all such petitions to be "laid on the table" without even being read. For years Adams risked censure and expulsion from Congress by evading the "Gag Rule" and presenting antislavery petitions under one pretext or another. He did not favor federal action against slavery but insisted that he was defending the right to petition guaranteed by the First Amendment. Over time, a few antislavery congressmen joined his crusade. Ultimately, the struggle convinced many Northerners who were not abolitionists that Congress was taking away the rights of *white* Americans in order to protect slavery.

Defense of freedom of speech became a key argument of Northerners who opposed slavery. For example, southern states made it illegal to say or publish anything that might encourage slaves to revolt. Prosecutors often interpreted such laws to preclude people from advocating abolition at all, on the grounds that any criticism of slavery tended to increase dissatisfaction among slaves. Judges sometimes rejected such a broad interpretation of the law, but these setbacks did not stop local prosecutions, especially in times of excitement. By the 1850s many southern state courts sustained the broader view as a matter of law.

As more Northerners denounced slavery, Southerners became ever more intolerant of slavery's critics. Southerners who opposed slavery were ostracized and sometimes driven from their homes. Antislavery editors, such as Elijah

Lovejoy of St. Louis and James G. Birney of Kentucky, were targeted early. By the 1850s antislavery professors were ousted from colleges. By then criticism of slavery was considered disloyalty to one's neighbors, and few were bold enough to voice it.

Besides suppressing dissent in their own region, Southerners attempted to silence northern abolitionists. Southern postmasters were authorized to withhold antislavery literature from the mail and burn it. Some states required them to give law-enforcement officials the names of people to whom such materials were addressed. Southern state legislatures asked their northern counterparts to make it a crime to advocate abolition in the North, and many Southerners openly threatened the lives of northern abolitionists who came to the South. Southern mobs crossed over into northern states along their borders to burn abolitionist newspaper presses and attack abolitionist speakers.

In the late 1830s, northern mobs, often led by Democratic politicians and government officials, attacked abolitionist speakers and presses. After scattering abolitionists, such mobs generally turned their fury on the local free-black community. Abolitionists were even mobbed in Boston. In 1837 a mob of locals and Missourians murdered Elijah Lovejoy, who had reestablished his antislavery newspaper across the Mississippi River in Alton, Illinois, after having been driven out of St. Louis. Instead of prosecuting the killers, local officials arrested citizens who had tried to protect Lovejoy and his press. The riots led to a powerful reaction among many Northerners, who were appalled at the violent suppression of free speech. By the 1840s, many Northerners had come to believe that slavery threatened the liberty of white people as well as that of black slaves.

Equally troubling were southern efforts to recapture runaway slaves. The Fugitive Slave Clause in Article IV, section 2 of the Constitution required runaway slaves to be returned to their masters, without specifying how it was to be done. Many states passed laws governing the recovery of runaways within their borders, and in 1793 the federal government passed the Fugitive Slave Act as well. To protect their free black citizens from slave catchers, in the 1820s northern states tightened requirements for proving that a person actually was a fugitive slave. The new laws made it illegal to seize alleged runaways without following these procedures, which were much more stringent than those of the Fugitive Slave Act.

Abolitionists and other, less radical antislavery advocates* argued that the federal Fugitive Slave Act was unconstitutional: first because the Constitution did

---

*One could hold antislavery views of varying degrees without being an abolitionist. An abolitionist favored taking immediate steps to begin the complete abolition of slavery. One might favor other antislavery measures, such as ending the slave trade in Washington, D.C., repealing or modifying the Fugitive Slave Act, or barring slavery in the territories, without insisting on the immediate abolition of slavery in the South. In the text, "antislavery" refers to the range of antislavery opinion, including but not limited to abolitionism.

not explicitly authorize Congress to enforce the Fugitive Slave Clause, and second because the act's provisions deprived accused runaways of various rights specified in the Bill of Rights. But in *Prigg v. Pennsylvania* (1842), the Supreme Court upheld the constitutionality of the act. Justice Story, ever the friend of national power, reasoned that the presence of the Fugitive Slave Clause in the Constitution implied exclusive congressional power to enforce it. The clause guaranteed the right of slave owners or slave catchers to seize suspected runaways without going to court at all, Story wrote. State laws punishing such seizures as kidnapping were unconstitutional, as were all state laws requiring procedures stricter than those of the Fugitive Slave Act. The decision was especially bad for African Americans, because most southern states held that being black raised the presumption of slavery. Once in the South, slave catchers would not have to prove that an alleged runaway was a slave; the protesting black prisoners would have to prove that they were free.

People throughout the North strongly opposed both the *Prigg* decision and the Fugitive Slave Act. Story did concede that the federal government could not require state officers to help enforce the unpopular law. Many northern states immediately made it illegal for them to do so, angering Southerners. Fewer and fewer Northerners were willing to help slave catchers find runaways, and many sympathized with black citizens who organized warning systems and escape routes when slave catchers appeared. Captures of runaway slaves regularly reminded Northerners of slavery's reach into the North. Legal efforts to persuade state courts to intervene proved futile, however, in light of the *Prigg* decision.

Slavery's critics constantly pointed out how proslavery forces restricted Northerners' ability to protect their citizens' liberty. They charged that both the South and the federal government were dominated by "the Slave Power"—the concentration of wealth and political influence in the hands of southern planters—which was working to subvert freedom throughout the nation. Slowly, the antislavery movement convinced white Northerners that slavery not only put the liberty of their black neighbors at risk but their own as well. Antislavery became identified with liberty, and "the Slave Power" with oppression.

Southerners insisted, and the Supreme Court agreed, that the Fugitive Slave Clause of Article IV, section 2 authorized the passage of the federal Fugitive Slave Act. But Southerners interpreted the same section's Privileges and Immunities Clause narrowly. That clause provided that "Citizens of each State shall be entitled to all Privileges and Immunities of Citizens in the several States." By the terms of the clause, abolitionists and black citizens of northern states should have been free to travel unrestrictedly through the South, entitled to the same rights as southern citizens. But southern states passed laws forbidding free blacks even to enter their states. Particularly galling to the New England states were Negro Seamen's laws requiring the many African Americans who worked on New England trading vessels to remain on board or be confined to southern jails while their ships were in port. When Massachusetts sent lawyer Samuel Hoar to Charleston, South Carolina, in 1844 to challenge the constitutionality of such laws, leading citizens warned him to leave the state. Informed by local officials that they would not protect him, Hoar fled for his life. Quick to pass a stringent Fugitive Slave Act, Congress never even considered a law to enforce the Privileges and Immunities Clause.

With the exception of the Fugitive Slave Act and judicial intervention to enforce the Obligation of Contracts Clause, Americans had not turned to the federal government to protect their rights in the decades following the Constitution's ratification. Most Americans saw themselves as citizens of both their states and of the United States. But the federal government had only limited powers. Therefore, the obligation to protect citizens from the wrongful acts of their neighbors fell nearly entirely upon the states. No one had catalogued the rights of American citizenship, with the possible exception of a single Supreme Court justice in an obscure federal circuit court case. But this reliance on state governments to protect peoples' rights slowly changed with the rise of the antislavery movement. By the mid-nineteenth century, both slave owners and slavery's opponents claimed that the federal government was obligated to protect their rights, precipitating the greatest constitutional crisis in American history.

The Antislavery Constitutional Argument

Opponents of slavery presented a variety of constitutional arguments against slavery and in favor of national action to curtail it. Some of the most radical abolitionists, disillusioned by the Slave Power's dominance of the federal government, conceded that the Constitution protected slavery. William Lloyd Garrison publicly burned it, declaring it "a covenant with death and an agreement with hell." Wendell Phillips, another leading abolitionist, thundered. "I say, my curse be on the Constitution of these United States!" Such expressions of fury fueled attacks on abolitionists as disunionists.

A few other abolitionists went to the opposite extreme, arguing that the Constitution in effect abolished slavery. Nowhere did it mention slavery, they pointed out. The so-called Fugitive Slave Clause spoke only of fugitives from labor, that is, indentured servants, and did not refer to slavery at all. Moreover, by declaring that no person shall be deprived of liberty without due process of law, the Fifth Amendment made slavery illegal. Every government owed its subjects protection in exchange for their allegiance, and slaves were therefore entitled to the protection of the Bill of Rights. Not only should judges enforce black Americans' constitutional rights, but Congress had the power to secure any right guaranteed by the Constitution as well, including those specified in the Bill of Rights.

Of course, this argument was strained and ran against history. Few Americans, and even fewer lawyers and judges, endorsed it. Even most abolitionists accepted what scholars now call "the federal consensus": It was up to each state to determine whether to countenance slavery, and it was beyond the power of the federal government to interfere with that decision. However, antislavery Americans who accepted the "federal consensus" favored their own interpretation. They stressed a key English decision, *Somerset v. Stewart* (1772), in which the renowned chief justice of Common Pleas, Lord Mansfield, declared that slavery was unnatural and could exist only by positive enactment.

Antislavery advocates, led by the Ohio antislavery lawyer Salmon P. Chase, translated this assertion into the slogan "Freedom National, Slavery Local." The nation's founders had hated slavery and had expected it to wither, Chase insisted. The Constitution avoided the term entirely. The institution of slavery was solely the product of state legislation. Article IV's injunction to return fugitive slaves was aimed at the states alone, the antislavery lawyers argued. It gave Congress no power to enforce it. The Fugitive Slave Act was unconstitutional, both for that reason and because it violated provisions of the Bill of Rights. The recognition of slavery in American territories south of the Missouri Compromise line was likewise unconstitutional, as was slavery in Washington, D.C. The Constitution did not permit the federal government to sustain slavery in any way, Chase and his colleagues claimed. Insofar as they came within federal jurisdiction, all people were free. The federal government could recognize no other condition.

Other antislavery lawyers and politicians cast about for further constitutional arguments. They argued that the Constitution implied the existence of national citizenship separate from state citizenship. The Bill of Rights, sections 9 and 10 of Article I, the Judiciary article (Article III), and Article IV—especially the Privileges and Immunities Clause—all secured rights to Americans, thus defining the rights of American citizenship. This understanding meant that free African Americans had rights as national citizens, whether their states recognized them as state citizens or not. What it meant for slaves remained foggy: How could people be entitled to the rights of national citizenship and at the same time remain slaves under state law? The contradictory nature of the question sustained the proposition that slavery was incompatible with the Constitution and that no more territories should be permitted to join the Union as slave states.

Chase and many antislavery advocates were essentially negative in their approach, denying that the federal government had power to sustain slavery. Others went so far as to demand positive federal action against slavery. Endorsing the nationalist constitutionalism of Hamilton, Marshall, and Clay, they argued that a government dedicated to liberty could make broad use of its delegated powers to promote freedom and restrict slavery. They demanded that Congress ban slavery in the territories and Washington, D.C. They urged it to ban the interstate slave trade. Congress should refuse to admit new states unless they excluded slavery from their boundaries.

Most controversial was the prospect of using the Privileges and Immunities Clause of Article IV against slavery. Nationalist constitutionalism implied broad federal power to enforce that provision. In later years, some antislavery lawyers in Congress would say that they had always believed that Article IV authorized legislation to protect citizens' rights; others said that the article merely laid an injunction on the states, unenforceable by congressional legislation.

The Wilmot Proviso and "Free Soil"

As of 1845, antislavery lawyers and politicians had been unable to persuade state or federal courts or Congress to accept any part of the antislavery interpretation of the Constitution. The antislavery Liberty party won scant electoral support. In fact, radical abolitionists, led by Phillips and Garrison, repudiated political action altogether, criticizing the compromises that always crept into political platforms. But Americans' desire to expand their national territory led to a new controversy over slavery that opened the door to antislavery politics and constitutionalism.

In 1836 the Texans successfully revolted against Mexico, at least in part to preserve slavery against growing Mexican pressure. From 1837 on, the new republic petitioned for admission to the Union, but antislavery Northerners resisted adding another slave state, especially in territory that Mexico had declared free. The antislavery forces were able to prevent pro-expansionist Democrats and southern Whigs from securing the two-thirds vote necessary to ratify an annexation treaty until 1845. In that year, over bitter opposition, the expansionists secured the admission of Texas by a joint resolution of Congress, which only required a majority vote. The following year, the annexation led to war with Mexico over the disputed Texas-Mexico boundary.

Many Northerners believed that proslavery Democrats, led by President James K. Polk of Tennessee, had maneuvered the nation into war in order to acquire more territory suitable to slavery. Such tactics seemed especially objectionable in light of Mexico's abolition of slavery. Therefore, northern congressmen proposed the Wilmot Proviso as an amendment to a bill appropriating money to pay for territory that might be acquired in negotiations to end the war. Echoing the language of the Northwest Ordinance, the Proviso stipulated that "neither slavery nor involuntary servitude shall ever exist in any part of the said territory, except for crime, whereof the party shall first be duly convicted." Any territory acquired from Mexico would be "free soil."

The House of Representatives, where Northerners had a majority, passed the Wilmot Proviso; but the Senate, with an equal number of senators from free and slave states, defeated it. Congress finally passed the appropriation without the Proviso, and the United States acquired the vast expanse of land from southwest Texas to California, including what is now New Mexico, Arizona, California, Nevada, Utah, and parts of Colorado. But Wilmot and his allies renewed their effort when Congress considered legislation to organize the newly acquired land into territories. Congress deadlocked, the House favoring and the Senate opposing the renewed Proviso. Until the issue was resolved, Congress was unable to pass a law creating territorial governments to administer the newly acquired territory.

With Calhoun, who had returned to the Democratic party, still in the vanguard, Southerners insisted that the Wilmot Proviso was unconstitutional. They expanded the state-sovereignty argument. From the axiom that the Union was a compact among the states, they drew a new conclusion: The federal government was merely the *agent* of the states. It must govern for the equal benefit of the people of all the states, without discrimination—a proslavery twist to the Democratic principle of "equal rights." Southerners must be permitted to take their slave property to any territory administered by the United States; not until a territory became a state could its people decide to ban slavery. According to this argument, Congress was barred from declaring future acquisitions "free soil." This reasoning rendered the Missouri Compromise, which still governed the remaining territories acquired in the Louisiana Purchase, unconstitutional as well. The principle of equal rights for all states applied to every power the Constitution delegated to Congress. Federal power must promote and protect slave property equally with any other type of property. It could never be used to restrict or diminish it. Thus abolitionist calls to outlaw the slave trade and ban slavery in Washington, D.C., were unconstitutional.

Guarantees for slave property had been central to the compromise that fashioned the Constitution, Southerners insisted. Any violation of the principle of equal rights for all states would therefore justify secession. The Union was based on mutual accommodation and affection, they warned. Northern attacks on slavery undermined the bonds that held the federation together. State sovereignty was no longer a defensive doctrine, positing a weak federal government in order to protect the South from federal interference; Southerners had converted it into an aggressive doctrine, positing a strong government obligated to act boldly in the interest of slavery.

Supporters of the Wilmot Proviso answered with the nationalist constitutional argument. The people of the United States, not the states, created the federal government. For the purposes specified in the Constitution, they had created a nation, independent of the states. When exercising its constitutionally delegated authority, the federal government's power was complete and plenary. The Constitution gave Congress the right to make regulations for the territory and property of the United States. Therefore, it could ban slavery from any territory. Some of the Proviso's backers went further, insisting that the Fifth Amendment precluded the federal government from sustaining slavery in the territories.

At first most northern Democratic congressmen joined northern Whigs to support the Wilmot Proviso. Their constituents clearly favored it, and the Proviso did not seem to violate state-rights ideas because regulating the territories had always been within national jurisdiction. However, when the issue threatened to break up the Democratic party and even the Union, many northern Democrats looked for a compromise. They found one in the doctrine of "popular sovereignty," or "squatter sovereignty," suggested by Michigan senator Lewis Cass, who was seeking the 1848 Democratic presidential nomination. Cass argued that the Constitution delegated to Congress merely the authority to establish territorial governments through which settlers could govern themselves. This interpretation of the Constitution was the only one consistent with American principles of democracy and local control. It was up to the people in each territory to decide whether or not to permit slavery. Most northern and many southern Democrats accepted this view, which seemed congruent with the party's commitment to state rights, and Cass defeated former president Martin Van Buren for the nomination.

Not all Democrats abandoned the free-soil position, however. Many dissenters joined the Liberty party to form the Free-Soil Democratic party, which nominated Van Buren on a free-soil platform. The Free-Soil party won widespread support, securing a large audience for antislavery interpretations of the Constitution, especially the "Freedom National, Slavery Local" argument associated with Chase. Although the alliance broke up after 1850, antislavery politicians emerged stronger than before, and many of their leaders, including Chase himself, began to secure prominent political offices.

As southern radicals openly advocated secession, Whigs and northern Democrats worked for a compromise. They finally passed the "Compromise of 1850," fashioned by Henry Clay but engineered by the talented and ambitious Democratic senator from Illinois, Stephen A. Douglas. Under the compromise, California entered the Union as a free state; the slavery question in the other territories secured from Mexico would be settled according to "popular sovereignty"; the slave trade was forbidden in the District of Columbia; and Congress passed a much stricter Fugitive Slave law.

Despite stiff opposition from antislavery forces in the North and radical proslavery forces, called Fire-Eaters, in the South, most Northerners and Southerners accepted the compromise. But many people in both regions felt they had paid a very high price. Southerners surrendered what they believed to be their right to take slaves anywhere in United States territories. Northerners gave up the free-soil principle and had to acquiesce in the new Fugitive Slave law.

The bruising fight weakened the Democrats and wrecked the Whigs. Northern Whigs now tended too strongly towards antislavery for Southerners. Many southern Whigs drifted to the Democrats; others supported state Whig organizations. Yet others looked for new parties.

Northerners were particularly troubled by the Fugitive Slave law. The statute authorized special commissioners to help judges enforce it. Professional slave catchers, carrying southern newspaper descriptions of runaway slaves, descended on northern cities. They could ask federal judges or commissioners for permission to seize suspected runaways. If an alleged fugitive tried to escape, every able-bodied man in the community was obligated to help catch him. To receive authority to convey his captive South, a slave catcher had only to establish a *prima facie* case* that the captive was a fugitive. The law denied the alleged runaway the right to testify, present evidence, or have a jury trial. If the judge or commissioner agreed that the required *prima facie* case had been made, he would receive ten dollars. If he released the captive, he received only five.

Almost every procedure of the Fugitive Slave law violated the Bill of Rights, patently depriving its victims of liberty without due process of law. But its defenders argued that the law's determination was not final and therefore did not violate due process. Once an alleged runaway slave arrived in the South, she could sue for her freedom in the state courts. That was cold comfort for the desperate victim.

To many Northerners, it appeared that the Fugitive Slave Act imposed elements of the southern slave codes on the North. Nearly every northern state legislature passed a "personal liberty" law to obstruct the act's enforcement by making it illegal to seize a runaway slave without proving the allegation in a jury trial that accorded due process. Growing ever more hostile to slavery, northern state courts began ruling that slaves became free as soon as they set foot on northern soil. The new rules made it dangerous for Southerners to bring slaves on even short visits.

Tensions developed further in 1854 when Douglas proposed a bill to establish territorial government in the Nebraska territory, part of the Louisiana Purchase lying almost entirely north of the Missouri Compromise line. To satisfy Southerners, Douglas proposed breaking the territory in two, the southern half to be called Kansas and the northern half Nebraska. Arguing that the popular-sovereignty provision of the Compromise of 1850 had repealed the Missouri Compromise, Douglas proposed to let the settlers of each territory vote on whether to permit slavery. Many people expected Kansas to do so, since it bordered Missouri.

Northerners reacted with outrage. Douglas reportedly said that he could travel from Boston to Chicago by the light of his burning effigies. Many Democrats broke with their party, joining former Whigs and supporters of the Liberty party to form a new party dedicated to the policy of "free soil." They called it the Republican party, after the old Jeffersonian party of equal rights. Opposing the Kansas-Nebraska Act and other Democratic legislation, Republicans popularized the "Freedom National, Slavery Local" antislavery argument. Many adopted other elements of the antislavery argument as well, especially the claim that the Fifth Amendment's Due Process Clause barred proslavery legislation. Republicans stressed how the "Slave Power" suppressed freedom of speech and the press in the South, a task made easier when a southern congressman viciously beat Republican senator Charles Sumner on the floor of the Senate.

Republicans carried nearly every northern state in the 1856 elections, almost defeating the Democratic presidential candidate, James Buchanan, just two years

---

*A *prima facie* case is one strong enough to indicate guilt in the absence of any counter-evidence on behalf of the defendant.

SOUTHERN CHIVALRY — ARGUMENT_{versus} CLUB'S.

"Southern Chivalry" (1856). A Republican illustration of Representative Preston Brooks assaulting Republican senator Charles Sumner, while Democratic senators happily look on. Note Sumner's pen—an allusion to freedom of speech and press.

after they organized. Democrats desperately tried to stave off the Republican threat by appealing to Northerners' racism and warning that Republican attacks on slavery threatened the Union.

The Know-Nothings, Legislation of Morals, and Anti-Catholicism

As Americans looked for alternatives to the collapsing Whig and Democratic parties, two new political organizations competed for their support. The first was the antislavery Republican party. The second erupted spontaneously out of local anti-Catholic, anti-immigrant secret lodges organized all over the country in the 1850s. Refusing to divulge information about these lodges, their members became known as "Know-Nothings."

Neither secret social clubs nor anti-Catholicism was new in the 1850s. Clubs with secret membership and rituals, influenced by Masonic lodges, were common, especially among workingmen in various trades. Eventually many of these clubs grew into labor unions. Anti-Catholicism was based in part on prejudice against Catholic immigrants from Ireland, France, and southern Germany. It was reinforced by the hostility of Protestant immigrants from the same nations towards their Catholic compatriots.

Anti-Catholicism was also fueled by democratic criticism of the Catholic church, which strongly supported the reactionary monarchies of Europe against nationalist and liberal opposition. The Church itself was a hierarchy in which the Pope claimed absolute and final authority. It formally condemned freedom of speech and of the press, as well as liberalism in general, and was associated with brutal suppression of dissent in Italy. Moreover, by the 1850s church authorities, with the support of recent immigrants, had succeeded in wresting control of church property and decision making from formerly independent Catholic congregations in the United States. Catholics began withdrawing their children from public schools, newly instituted in the 1840s, because of the justifiable perception that the schools inculcated Protestant beliefs; they pressed for state tax support for their own schools.

Between 1853 and 1855 the Know-Nothing lodges endorsed anti-Catholic candidates for local and state offices—sometimes Democratic, Whig, or independent candidates and eventually nominees from their own American party. In 1854, as the Whigs collapsed and the Democrats alienated their own supporters with the Kansas-Nebraska Act, Know-Nothing candidates swept many elections. They pressed for a naturalization law that would deny citizenship to immigrants for decades. They urged laws excluding the foreign-born from holding political office. They also backed vigorous enforcement of laws that reflected Protestant moral values, such as regulations forbidding work or entertainment on Sundays; laws outlawing dueling, gambling, and activities associated with gambling, like boxing, dogfighting, and cockfighting; and laws prohibiting the manufacture and sale of alcoholic beverages.

The anti-Catholic, anti-immigrant element of such moral reforms should not obscure the fact that these reforms dealt with real social problems in ways that seemed effective during the Victorian age. Gambling, prostitution, and drunkenness were associated with crime, disease, and poverty. In an age where families depended on men for subsistence and children depended on parents for everything, such vices posed serious threats. A drunken, abusive husband was a terror to his wife and children. Addiction to alcohol or gambling meant poverty for the whole family. Although reformers pressed for orphanages for children and more liberal divorce laws for wives, they believed these measures to be merely palliative. The only real solution lay in reforming the character of wayward men and women by supporting the efforts of churches and temperance societies to reform sinners. Prohibition laws and other moral legislation were designed to provide an environment conducive to such efforts.

Know-Nothing support for such measures made them a reform party, an antidote to the corrupt Democrats, that attracted refugees from the collapsing Whigs. Thus the Know-Nothings attracted more than just bigots—or perhaps it is human nature that real social concerns could become entwined with bigotry.

Because theirs was a reform party, the Know-Nothings in the North tended strongly towards antislavery. At the same time, many Republicans resented Catholic immigrant support of the Democratic party and identified the illiberalism of the Church with the illiberalism of the Slave Power. The Republican party was a reform party too; many of its leaders and voters were committed, evangelical Protestants who supported legislation that promoted morality and individual responsibility. Both parties competed for the same sorts of voters. As a result, Know-Nothings and Republicans sometimes worked together to pass moral legislation such as prohibition laws. Such laws continued the long tradition of community regulation of safety and morals.

But economic and social change was leading to much greater heterogeneity in local communities. Not only Catholics and immigrants resented such efforts to dictate their behavior. A significant part of the population, especially urban laborers and artisans, considered gambling and activities associated with saloons among their primary forms of recreation. It was this lifestyle that the reformers sought to suppress with a combination of law, moral suasion, and religious revival. Those who did not succumb complained about the "puritanism" of the reformers and claimed the "personal liberty" to adhere to their own moral standards. Naturally, they turned to the Democratic party, with its Jeffersonian heritage of toleration and sympathy for dissenters. Yet they remained bitterly racist, denying that African Americans were entitled to similar freedoms.

Many Republicans rejected the bigotry of the Know-Nothings, especially as the passions aroused by their leaders led to anti-Catholic riots in cities around the country. They warned that appeals to anti-Catholic, anti-foreigner prejudice would only divert Americans from the evils of slavery. Prejudice against Catholics and immigrants would surely extend to prejudice against African Americans, weakening the antislavery movement. Finally, the antiforeign aspect of Know-Nothingism alienated antislavery German immigrants, who were a powerful voting bloc in states from Ohio to Iowa.

Both Republican and Know-Nothing leaders carefully jockeyed for position, allying against Democrats and fighting one another. In the end, efforts to create a national anti-immigrant political party blew apart as northern and southern Know-Nothings fought bitterly over slavery. In 1856 the Republican party emerged as the major opposition to the weakened Democrats. Among the party's supporters there remained a significant number of people who shared varying degrees of anti-Catholic prejudice, while most Catholic voters maintained their allegiance to the Democrats.

The Constitutional Crisis over Slavery

The controversy over slavery in the territories continued to divide the Democrats themselves. Ever more southern Democrats moved towards the extreme proslavery position, adopting the state-sovereignty constitutional argument associated with it and rejecting the state-rights constitutionalism of Jackson. Only with great difficulty did Douglas and other Democratic leaders persuade the Democratic national convention to endorse popular sovereignty in 1856. The new

Democratic president, James Buchanan, owed his election to southern votes, and he came under strong pressure from Southerners to make sure that settlers in Kansas permitted slavery. This possibility led more Northerners to turn to the Republican party. Under great political pressure, northern Democrats, led by Douglas, insisted that Kansas settlers be allowed to decide the question on their own. But southern Democrats, under pressure from *their* constituents, argued more and more adamantly that the national government was required to protect slavery in all the territories, no matter what the settlers thought.

All the great constitutional issues dividing the nation came together in the great Supreme Court case of *Scott v. Sandford*. Dred Scott had accompanied his master to the Wisconsin Territory, north of the Missouri Compromise line, and then to Illinois, before returning with him to Missouri. Now he claimed that his residence in free territory had emancipated him. Scott brought suit in federal court against his new owner, who lived in New York, under the federal courts' jurisdiction over controversies between citizens of different states. The case raised the question of whether Scott was a citizen who could invoke the diversity jurisdiction of the federal courts; it also raised the constitutionality of the Missouri Compromise. Buchanan, desperate to avoid responsibility for deciding the issues, alerted Americans to the forthcoming decision, insisting it would settle the ques-

Chief Justice Roger Taney, Jacksonian proponent of state rights and judicial restraint—except when defending slavery.

Salmon P. Chase, the influential antislavery lawyer and politician, was appointed chief justice by President Lincoln in 1864.

tion of slavery in the territories. He did not report what he had secretly been told: that the Court would come down on the side of the southern extremists.

The Supreme Court, seven of whose members were Democrats and five of whom were slave owners, promulgated its ruling in 1857. Although most of the justices carefully avoided endorsing the state-sovereignty doctrine, by a majority of 7–2 they came down clearly on the side of the South. Almost every justice wrote his own opinion, but Chief Justice Taney's was taken to embody the majority view, although fewer than half the justices agreed with him on some points.

The majority of the justices agreed that Scott was not a citizen of Missouri and therefore could not bring a case in federal court as a citizen of one state suing a citizen of another. But while most of the proslavery justices held that the laws of Missouri determined Scott's status, Taney was determined to seize the opportunity to repudiate the key elements of antislavery constitutionalism.

Antislavery lawyers and politicians had argued that the Constitution defined rights of United States citizenship separate from state citizenship. Taney agreed. But, he wrote, only those sorts of people who were citizens of the states when the Constitution was ratified in 1788 could be considered citizens of the United States. Taney interpreted citizenship in light of dual federalism. National citizenship and state citizenship, he insisted, were completely distinct. Ignoring the overwhelming evidence that many northern and some southern states had considered their free black residents to be citizens in 1788, Taney held that no state had done so. Black Americans "had for more than a century before been regarded as beings of an inferior order," he wrote, "so far inferior, that they had no rights which the white man was bound to respect." No post-1788 grant of state citizenship to African Americans could make them American citizens. Such a grant would take at least an act of Congress. Until Congress passed such a law, Taney's reading of the Constitution meant that no black American, even the free black citizens of northern states, was entitled to any of the rights of American citizenship. They could not bring suits in federal court. Nor were they entitled to the benefit of the Privileges and Immunities Clause.

The justices had decided that Scott was not entitled to bring his case to the federal courts in the first place. But as was customary, they went on to decide the question of the most immediate political importance—the constitutionality of the Missouri Compromise. On that great issue, the Court ruled flatly that Congress could not bar slavery from any of the territories; the Missouri Compromise was unconstitutional, and so was "free soil," the key plank of the Republican party. Rather than accept the state-sovereignty argument outright, Taney used tortured reasoning to conclude that the Territorial Government Clause of Article IV applied only to those territories in the government's possession in 1789. The federal government had no power of its own to acquire territory; it could do so only on behalf of the people of the individual states, "acting [as] . . . their agent and representative." Therefore, when it came to governing the territories, if nowhere else, the state-sovereignty theory of federalism applied. The government had to administer the territories as "the representative and trustee" of the people of the states, "for their common and equal benefit."

Even if Congress did have general power over the territories, it could not use its authority to bar slavery. Taney pointed out that the Fifth Amendment barred Congress from depriving people of property without due process of law. "And an act of Congress which deprives a citizen of the United States of his liberty or property, merely because he . . . brought his property into a particular Territory of the United States, . . . could hardly be dignified with the name of due process of law," he continued. In this way Taney converted the Fifth Amendment, one of the bulwarks of the antislavery argument, into a bulwark of slavery. What was true of Congress's power over the territories was true of every other power: None of them could be used in a way that deprived slave owners of their property without due process of law.

The *Dred Scott* decision proved a disaster for the country. Instead of reinforcing Democratic resistance to Republicans in the North, it provoked a storm of denunciation. Next, Republicans warned, the Supreme Court would rule that the Privileges and Immunities Clause entitled slave owners to take their slaves into northern states as visitors and long-time sojourners. A case raising that issue was already in the process of being appealed to the Supreme Court.

The Court further demonstrated its aggressively proslavery program by sustaining the constitutionality of the Fugitive Slave Act of 1850 and ruling the northern personal liberty laws unconstitutional in *Ableman v. Booth* (1859). In ringing language that echoed Marshall and Story, the justices denied that states could pass legislation inhibiting the operation of a federal law. It seemed that according to the Supreme Court, the federal government had sovereign power when it came to promoting slavery, but it had no power to obstruct it.

Dred Scott was even more significant in the South than it was in the North. It undercut the position of southern Democratic moderates who had supported popular sovereignty in the territories. The Supreme Court had endorsed the Fire-Eaters' argument that Southerners were entitled to take slaves anywhere in the territories; it was impossible to urge settling for anything less. Southerners now demanded that Congress enact a slave code for all the territories. They denounced northern Democrats, such as Douglas, who attempted to find a way to sustain popular sovereignty despite the decision.

The decision divided the Democratic party. Led by Douglas, northern Democrats insisted that settlers in the territories could prevent slavery from being established there, despite the Supreme Court's ruling, simply by refusing to pass the slave codes necessary to support it. Southern Democrats argued that the national government was required to pass a slave code to apply to all the territories. At the 1860 Democratic national convention, the two sides could not agree, and the convention broke apart over the question. The northern Democrats nominated Douglas for the presidency, while the Southerners, backed by President Buchanan, nominated John C. Breckenridge. As a consequence, the Republicans were able to win the presidential election in November. In four months Abraham Lincoln would become president.

Before becoming a Republican, Lincoln had been a nationalist Whig, a fervent follower of Henry Clay. Although he reassured Southerners that he had no intention of interfering with slavery in the states, they had no reason to doubt that Republicans would press to abolish slavery in the territories and in Washington, D.C. Pressure was sure to grow for a ban on the interstate slave trade and repeal of the Fugitive Slave law.

Equally troubling to Southerners was the prospect of Republican judges serving on the Supreme Court and lower federal bench: What if they repudiated the Taney Court's holding on African-American citizenship, permitting slaves to sue their out-of-state owners in the federal courts and overturning state laws inconsistent with the Privileges and Immunities Clause? What if Congress repealed the ban on black testimony in federal courts?

Finally, slaveholders worried that Republicans would expand their antislavery party into the South, appealing to the nonslaveholding farmers of the hill country and the immigrant workers of such cities as St. Louis and Baltimore. Many of the Southerners in these regions opposed slaveholders' political dominance, if not slavery itself. Delaware and Maryland, where so many slaves had been manumitted already, might prove vulnerable to antislavery arguments. Republicans would appoint local federal officials from among dissatisfied Southerners and try to convert them and others to antislavery positions. Republican-appointed postmasters could hardly be expected to withhold delivery of antislavery materials. State prosecution of federal officials who carried out their duties and expressed their opinions would lead to further conflict and erosion of support for Democrats in the North.

Facing certain defeat, Douglas had traveled through the South urging restraint, breaking his health to save the Union. The Democrats retained control of Congress, he pointed out. They could block antislavery legislation or appointments. In four years Northerners would react against the stalemate and throw the Republicans out. At the same time, Douglas blasted the Republicans for refusing to compromise and thereby risking violence.

But many Southerners no longer trusted Douglas and other northern Democrats. To them the Republican victory and northern Democratic backpedaling from slavery signaled the end to the constitutional system as they had known and understood it—a system in which the federal government reinforced slavery and most Northerners opposed policies that threatened it. The Fire-Eaters, joined now by less radical allies, urged Southerners to act on the state-sovereignty principles of federalism and secede from the Union.

According to the state-sovereignty doctrine as Calhoun and his allies had developed it, the people of the states exercised their sovereignty through popular conventions. They had ratified the compact that created the Union in such conventions; they could withdraw from the compact in the same way. South Carolina was the first state to hold such a convention, which passed an ordinance of secession on December 20, 1860. In the four months between Lincoln's election and his inauguration, six other states of the Deep South followed—Mississippi, Florida, Alabama, Georgia, Louisiana, and Texas. In the other slaveholding states, those who favored immediate secession and those who favored compromise fought to a standstill.

As the seceding states formed a new confederacy, the Confederate States of America, outgoing President Buchanan did nothing. The states had no right to secede, he insisted, but the Constitution delegated no power to the federal government to stop them. Seceding state officials simply took over federal post offices, customs houses, forts, armories, and ammunition. Federal officers, who had all taken oaths to support the Constitution and government of the United States, resigned their commissions and accepted new ones from the Confederacy. State officers, who had taken similar oaths, now took new ones to sustain the Confederate States of America.

Northern and southern conservatives desperately tried to cobble together another compromise. Congress even sent the states a new, thirteenth amendment to the Constitution for ratification. This *unamendable* amendment would have forever guaranteed slavery in the states against federal interference. But Lincoln and most Republicans were unwilling to give up the central plank of their platform, "free soil" in the territories.

Many northern Democrats blamed Republicans for the crisis. Democrats had consistently tried to counteract antislavery sentiment in the North by appealing to unionism, warning that proposals to use federal power to discourage slavery threatened the country. Republicans had dismissed the warnings. Now they resisted proposed compromises. Many Democrats warned that they would not support efforts to restore the Union by force. It would be impossible to maintain democracy and federalism in a country where some of the states were kept in the Union by force alone. Leaders in the slave states that had not yet seceded were even more adamant. Southerners opposing immediate secession urged Lincoln to avoid coercion and work for compromise.

In his inaugural address, Lincoln urged peace and patience, but he also powerfully articulated the nationalist understanding of the Union and developed it further. He denied that the states had formed the Union or that they could secede from it. In fact, he argued, the Union was older than the Constitution. It was formed by actions of the Continental Congress in 1774 and 1775 and matured by the Declaration of Independence, over a decade before its people ratified the Constitution. A few months later, in his first message to Congress, Lincoln pointed out that no state except Texas had ever existed independently outside the Union. None had ever been sovereign. "The States have their status in the Union, and they have no other legal status," the president insisted.

Lincoln promised to take no aggressive action, reassuring northern Democrats and residents of the upper South and the border states that he would not be the first to resort to violence. Yet he took a tougher line than the palsied Buchanan. He would fulfill his duty to enforce the laws only where the federal government still exercised authority, but he would enforce the laws in those places. There would be no more turning over federal property to the seceding states.

In reality, Lincoln was maneuvering to make the fundamental issues clear to the people of the North. Neither the North nor the Republicans were the aggressors, he believed. It was the slaveholders who refused to accept the result of a democratic election; it was they who acted on a theory of federalism that required Northerners to help maintain slavery as a price of Union and who were willing to wreck the Union when Northerners refused.

The United States still exercised authority at Fort Sumter, located on an island squarely in the middle of the harbor of Charleston, South Carolina. By refusing to give the fort up and by promising to enforce the laws of the United States, including customs laws, wherever he could, Lincoln put great pressure on the fiery South Carolinians. Ignoring pleas for restraint from other Southerners, in April 1861 the Carolinians fired on the fort and the flag of the United States, making clear to Northerners that it was the Slave Power, not the Republicans, who threatened the Union.

The attack on Fort Sumter precipitated the American Civil War, temporarily ending divisions among Northerners over how to handle the secession crisis. The ailing Douglas, who died within a month, urged Democrats to rally to the flag. Lincoln, relying on existing laws that were not exactly apposite and on his own authority as president, called upon the northern state militias and the army to enforce the government's authority. As Virginia, North Carolina, Arkansas, and Tennessee seceded and joined the Confederacy, northern Democrats—patriotic state-rights Unionists in the tradition of Jackson—rallied to the flag.

For Northerners, at stake was not only the prosperity and pride associated with the Union, but the conviction that the United States was a beacon of liberty and democracy to the world. All over Europe, Northerners believed, monarchs, aristocrats, and reactionary religious leaders were applauding the evidence that a free people was incapable of governing itself, while liberals and nationalists were in despair. And in fact Confederate leaders did turn to European conservatives for support.

Two and a half years later, in November 1863, Abraham Lincoln summarized both constitutional nationalism and the meaning of the Civil War for liberty in the brief words he delivered at the cemetery dedicated to those who had fallen at Gettysburg. In his Gettysburg Address, Lincoln referred to the United States as a nation, not a federation or even a union, and he dated its founding to the Declaration of Independence of 1776, not to the Constitution of 1789. Echoing Webster's great reply to Hayne, Lincoln insisted the United States was a "government of the people, by the people, for the people," not the states. The war was more than a test of power among the American states. It was a war to assure that such a government "shall not perish from the earth."

In 1861 the slavery issue precipitated a national crisis framed largely in terms of constitutional issues. The crisis developed because both slaveholders and opponents of slavery demanded that the federal government protect the rights of American citizens—rights that each side interpreted in completely opposed ways. The issue was nearly impossible to resolve because each side understood its claim to be a matter of right, not of mere interest.

To some extent it was a contest between different conceptions of liberty. To Southerners, the United States had become an alien government threatening popular liberty—the right to live freely in one's community. To Northerners, especially Republicans, it was a war against people who not only denied basic human rights to African Americans but freedom of speech and press to their own neighbors. As the influential political scientist Francis Lieber put it, it was a national war against "local absolutism and local oppression."

Secession also raised the most basic issues of federalism: What was the nature of the federal system and the Constitution that sanctioned it? Was the Constitution, as Southerners argued, a compact among sovereign states, creating a central government that could act only as their agent? Or did the Constitution create a sovereign nation, as both nationalists and state-rights advocates insisted? The issue would not be decided in the courts but on the battlefield.

TIMELINE

1772   In *Somerset v. Stewart*, the King's Bench rules that the common law of England does not recognize the status of slavery within the kingdom.

1776–1804   Slavery abolished in northern states through gradual emancipation.

1793   Congress passes the Fugitive Slave Act.

1808   Congress bans the foreign slave trade.

1819–1821   The Missouri crisis; the Missouri Compromise of 1820 establishes the Missouri Compromise line, above which slavery is barred from territory acquired from France.

1831   Nat Turner slave rebellion in Virginia.

1832   The Virginia constitutional convention of 1832 rejects gradual emancipation.

1833–1837   Mobs attack abolitionists in northern cities; mobs burn abolitionist literature in southern cities.

1835–1836   Great petition campaign for abolition of slavery in Washington, D.C.

1836   The House of Representatives passes the "Gag Rule," laying all petitions for abolition on the table without a hearing.

1837	Elijah Lovejoy murdered while protecting his press from a proslavery mob in Alton, Illinois.
1842	In *Prigg v. Pennsylvania,* the Supreme Court sustains the constitutionality of the Fugitive Slave Act of 1793 and rules state "personal liberty" laws unconstitutional.
1845	Texas annexed to the United States by joint resolution.
1846–1848	Mexican-American War.
1846	The House of Representatives passes the Wilmot Proviso, barring slavery from any territory to be acquired from Mexico as a result of the war; the Proviso fails to pass the Senate.
1848	Senator Lewis Cass (D-Mich.) advocates "popular sovereignty" in the territories, allowing settlers to decide for themselves whether to permit slavery.
	Democrats nominate Cass for the presidency on a "popular-sovereignty" platform; Free-Soil Democrats nominate Martin Van Buren on a free-soil platform; Whig Zachary Taylor elected president and inaugurated in 1849.
1848–1850	Stalemate over the Wilmot Proviso prevents organization of territory acquired from Mexico.
1850	Compromise of 1850: California admitted to the Union as a free state; the slave trade banned in Washington, D.C.; territory acquired from Mexico to be organized on the principle of "popular sovereignty"; new, draconian Fugitive Slave Act of 1850 enacted.
1853–1855	The "Know-Nothing" movement organizes to oppose Catholic immigration to the United States.
1854	The Kansas-Nebraska Act applies "popular sovereignty" to Louisiana Purchase territory north of the Missouri Compromise line.
1854–1855	The antislavery Republican party organizes.
1856	Republicans carry most northern states but Democrat James Buchanan elected president and inaugurated in 1857.
1857	In *Scott v. Sandford,* the Supreme Court rules that African Americans are not citizens of the United States and that the Missouri Compromise is unconstitutional; the Court denies Congress the power to bar slavery in the territories of the United States.
1859	The Supreme Court rules northern personal liberty laws unconstitutional as violations of national supremacy in *Ableman v. Booth.*
1860	The Democratic national convention divides over the issue of slavery in the territories; John C. Breckenridge nominated for the presidency on a platform calling for a slave code in the territories; Stephen A. Douglas nominated on a "popular-sovereignty" platform; Republican Abraham Lincoln elected president on a free-soil platform.

1860   South Carolina passes an Ordinance of Secession from the Union.

1861   Mississippi, Florida, Alabama, Georgia, Louisiana, and Texas pass secession ordinances and join South Carolina to establish the Confederate States of America.

Inauguration of President Abraham Lincoln.

South Carolina attacks Fort Sumter and President Lincoln calls for troops to suppress the rebellion.

Virginia, North Carolina, Arkansas, and Tennessee pass secession ordinances and join the Confederacy.

FURTHER READING

The best study of the slavery issue and the Constitution appears in Harold M. Hyman and William M. Wiecek, *Equal Justice Under Law: Constitutional Development, 1835–1875* (1982), although it does not discuss the rights of slaves themselves. Arthur M. Bestor's classic "The American Civil War as a Constitutional Crisis," *American Historical Review* 69 (January 1964): 327–352, also places the antislavery controversy in its constitutional context. Don E. Fehrenbacher describes how tightly the United States was bound to slavery before the Civil War in *The Slaveholding Republic* (2001). Leonard L. Richards makes the same point in his trenchantly titled *The Slave Power: The Free North and Southern Domination* (2000). James L. Hutson makes clear the economic stake slave owners had in the struggle in "Property Rights in Slavery and the Coming of the Civil War," *Journal of Southern History* 65 (May 1999): 249–286. Paul Finkelman provides a concise background and relevant documents in *Dred Scott v. Sandford* (1997).

The best study of slavery as a deprivation of human and civil rights remains Kenneth M. Stampp's *The Peculiar Institution* (1956). Mark V. Tushnet raises a host of interesting questions about the relation of the law to the treatment of slaves in *Slave Law in the American South* (2003), which is aimed at a student audience. But neither conveys much information about how legal institutions assimilated slaves into the law of property. Thomas D. Morris's *Southern Slavery and the Law* (1996), somewhat heavy going for nonacademics, provides an eye-opening discussion. In *Roll, Jordan, Roll: The World the Slaves Made* (1972), Eugene Genovese argues that, no matter their legal status, slaves managed to establish *de facto* rights within the slave regime. For slavery as lived, one should turn to John W. Blassingame, *The Slave Community* (rev. ed., 1979). Charles Joyner's *Down by the Riverside* (1984) is a magnificent recreation of slave life in nearly all-black coastal South Carolina. Dylan C. Penningroth explains how slaves established claims to private property outside the law in *The Claims of Kinfolk* (2003).

William Wiecek analyzes *The Sources of Antislavery Constitutionalism in America* (1977) up to 1848. See also Jacobus TenBroek, *The Antislavery Origins of the Fourteenth Amendment* (1951) and Howard Jay Graham, "The Early Antislavery Background of the Fourteenth Amendment," in Graham, *Everyman's Constitution* (1968), 295–336. Eric Foner discusses Salmon P. Chase's crucial role in developing antislavery constitutional arguments in "Salmon P. Chase: The Constitution and the Slave Power," chapter 3 of his influential study of the ideology of the Republican party, *Free Soil, Free Labor, Free Men* (1970).

Robert M. Cover shows how northern judges accommodated slavery in *Justice Accused* (1975). For suppression of abolitionists' civil liberties in the North, see Russel B. Nye, *Fettered Freedom* (1949) and Lionel L. Richards, *Gentlemen of Property and Standing* (1970). Clement Eaton, *The Freedom-of-Thought Struggle in the Old South* (1940) tells the story there.

Leon F. Litwack describes pervasive discrimination against African Americans in the North in *North of Slavery* (1961). Rogers Smith stresses that African Americans were excluded from citizenship and community in antebellum America in *Civic Ideals: Conflicting Visions of Citizenship in U.S. History* (1997). In contrast, Paul Finkelman stresses the clear trend towards greater legal rights in "Prelude to the Fourteenth Amendment: Black Legal Rights in the Antebellum North," *Rutgers Law Journal* 17 (Spring/Summer 1986): 415–482.

Finkelman describes how slavery put increasing stress on the federal system in *An Imperfect Union* (1981). However, it was the issue of slavery in the territories that converted large numbers of Northerners to the antislavery stance and ultimately led to the rise of the antislavery Republican party. Fehrenbacher's Pulitzer Prize–winning *The Dred Scott Case* (1981) is a monumental analysis of the conflict over slavery in the territories. He also addresses it in *The Slaveholding Republic*, noted above. Michael A. Morrison's *Slavery and the American West* (1997) is a detailed account of the politics surrounding the issue. Fehrenbacher's *The Slaveholding Republic* describes the Fugitive Slave Acts. Carol Wilson demonstrates how they encouraged kidnapping in *Freedom at Risk* (1994).

For a comparison of Stephen A. Douglas's state-rights federalism and Abraham Lincoln's nationalism, see Michael Les Benedict, "Abraham Lincoln and Federalism," *Journal of the Abraham Lincoln Association* 10 (1988–1989): 1–43. Garry Wills's *Lincoln at Gettysburg* (1992) is an outstanding discussion of the heritage of Lincoln's constitutional nationalism. Historians disagree over the relationship among Republicanism, nativism, and the Know-Nothing party. Michael F. Holt and William E. Gienapp argue that nativism was central to the origins of the Republican party in Holt, *The Political Crisis of the 1850s* (1978) and Gienapp, *The Origins of the Republican Party* (1987). They imply that the core of Republicanism was intolerance towards Catholic immigrants and white Southerners, rather than humanitarian concern for African Americans, a position taken explicitly by Paul Kleppner in *The Third Electoral System, 1853–1892* (1979). Tyler Anbinder disagrees, arguing that nativism broke apart over the moral issue of slavery. He also provides an excellent description of anti-Catholic sentiment in mid-nineteenth-century United States. See his *Nativism and Slavery* (1992).

9

The Constitution and the Civil War

The Civil War led to the repudiation of the state-sovereignty doctrine of federalism and to strengthened constitutional nationalism. Acting on nationalist constitutional ideas, the Republicans, who controlled the federal government, enacted wide-ranging policies not only to win the war but to promote economic development, education, and social welfare.

The war also led to some restrictions of white Americans' civil liberties. President Lincoln suspended the privilege of the writ of *habeas corpus*, enabling the government to hold suspected Confederate sympathizers without trial. He authorized military trials in occupied Confederate territory and even in the North. The government confiscated the property of rebels. But as the rights of white Americans temporarily contracted, the rights of African Americans expanded. Lincoln and Congress emancipated millions of slaves, and by the war's end, the states were in the process of amending the Constitution to abolish slavery throughout the nation. At the same time, Republicans became progressively more committed to securing basic civil rights to the freedmen.

The war witnessed a dramatic expansion of the power and prestige of the presidency. Lincoln interpreted the Constitution as imposing a special obligation upon the president to preserve and protect the Union. Moreover, his position as commander-in-chief of the armed forces authorized him to take forceful steps to suppress the rebellion. Subject in most instances to the final authority of Congress, the president nonetheless had broad authority to take the initiative. But although they generally cooperated to save the Union, Congress and Lincoln disagreed on how to restore it once victory was won. By 1865 that tension would be clearly evident.

The Civil War and Nationalist Constitutionalism

The rebellion of the South irrevocably tied the doctrine of state sovereignty to disloyalty and treason in the mind of Northerners, discrediting the concept to the present day. No respectable number of Americans has sustained that view of federalism since the South's defeat. At the same time, the war for the Union deepened Northerners' sense of nationalism, leading to the widespread acceptance of an idea growing in Europe: that a nation is defined not by a social contract among its citizens but by the common feelings, customs, language, and culture of its people. Many Northerners now argued that Americans had become a national people through common experience and culture even before they had adopted the Constitution. Lincoln articulated this understanding in his inaugural address. The Union was older than the Constitution, he said. Americans were united not only by a Constitution but by "mystic chords of memory, stretching from every battlefield and patriot grave to every living heart and hearthstone all over this broad land."

This idea of a national people strengthened the nationalist argument about the nature of the federal system. If the people of the United States had become a nation before 1787, then of course the Constitution was created directly by them, not by the states, nor by the people of the individual states. The American people had created a government that expressed their nationality. "This country, with its institutions, belongs to the people who inhabit it," Lincoln said. Of course such a nation had sovereign, plenary power over all subjects within its jurisdiction. During the war, Republicans acted on these principles to greatly expand the power of the central government. Legislating on subjects over which the Constitution gave the national government no direct authority, they justified their actions on the ideas of "implied powers" and "broad construction." Reacting against the strict-construction paralysis of the Buchanan administration in the secession crisis, Republicans discerned a Constitution brimming with power.

Republicans found a deep reservoir of governmental authority in the so-called "war powers" of the Constitution. The expressly delegated powers to declare war, regulate the armed forces, guarantee republican forms of government to the states, and suspend the privilege of the writ of *habeas corpus,* combined with the Necessary and Proper Clause, implied wide-ranging national power to wage war, they insisted. They exercised this power to enact a national conscription law. The government took control of railroads and telegraphs, subordinating them to military authority. Congress passed confiscation laws, seizing the property and freeing the slaves of Southerners; confiscation, they rationalized, would help defeat the rebels and therefore was justified as an exercise of the war power. Both the president and Congress claimed power to "reconstruct" the governments of the rebel states, directly controlling them in all their functions, until peace was restored. Under the "war power," Congress claimed the authority to dredge canals, build railroads, and improve the navigability of rivers and harbors, all necessary, Republicans argued, to improve military transportation.

Republicans undertook programs not directly connected to the war that could be justified only under the nationalist interpretation of the federal system. As an exercise of the war power and also of the power to coin money and "emit bills of credit," Congress in 1862 passed the Legal Tender Act. This law established paper notes, or "greenbacks," issued under government authority as legal currency. Such currency would be "legal tender for all debts public and private," meaning that creditors had to accept it in payment of debts. This financial revolution dramatically increased the power of the national government by giving it the ability to manipulate the supply of money. Increasing the money supply reduced interest rates and encouraged investment and economic activity; reducing the money supply increased interest rates and slowed the economy.

To further strengthen the nation's financial system, the Republicans passed the National Bank Act in 1862. Banks that purchased government bonds became part of a national banking system, authorized to issue banknotes in proportion to the value of the bonds they bought. Like the greenbacks, the banknotes became part of the nation's legal-tender currency. By controlling the total value of bonds available for bank purchase and specifying the regions where they would be sold, the federal government gained further control over the economy. To encourage banks to join the system, the government levied a stiff tax on banknotes issued by local, state-chartered banks. These local banks continued to provide an important source of currency in cash-starved regions of the country, but the tax levied upon them made the situation even worse in areas that were short of money and national banks.

To collect money to pay for the war and help develop American industry, Congress for the first time since the 1840s passed a protective tariff discouraging foreign imports. Republicans cited the "war power," the taxing power, and the power to regulate foreign commerce to justify the law.

These laws made Washington, D.C., the focal point of the nation's economic regulation for the first time since Jackson destroyed the second national bank. For the rest of the nineteenth century, national tariff, banking, and financial policy remained major political issues, concentrating Americans' attention on the national government.

Congress had always exercised its power to dispose of federal property to promote education, setting aside sections of public land to be used for grade schools in the territories and new states. Now it used this power to encourage states to promote higher education. The Morrill Act gave each state a federal land grant to help pay for colleges. The country's great state universities were founded under the auspices of this law. Congress also used its power to spend money for the general welfare to create a Department of Agriculture, authorized to collect and distribute agricultural information and seeds. Immediately after the war, Congress established a Bureau of Education, to collect and disseminate educational information to school officials.

In the same way, the government encouraged transportation development. To help pay for construction, it gave grants of public land to railroad, canal, and telegraph companies. To encourage people to build roads and operate stage coaches in rural areas, the government designated postal "star routes," subsidizing them by paying high fees to carry the mail. It similarly subsidized steamship lines.

The government also greatly expanded its program of dredging rivers and constructing harbors. It fostered economic development by building large and ornate post offices, customs houses, and court buildings in urban centers.

To encourage western settlement, Congress passed the Homestead Act, which offered heads of families 160 acres of public land without charge after five years of continuous residence. After the war, the government built upon the homestead policy, offering land to Civil War veterans, to people who maintained a portion of their land in timber, and to those who irrigated desert lands.

Finally, Congress established a pension system that provided financial help to disabled veterans and to the widows and children of soldiers killed in the war. In the following decades, the pension system provided crucial support to a large number of poor and disabled Americans. Ultimately, it provided small secondary incomes to all northern veterans and their families. (In later years, southern states established similar, smaller programs for Confederate veterans.)

These federal government activities made the central government much more important to ordinary Americans than it had been before the Civil War, reconfirming the emotional commitment to the nation fostered by the great struggle.

People who continued to believe in "state rights," especially northern Democrats, criticized most of these programs as unconstitutional, complaining of the "centralizing tendencies of the age." Some of them exceeded what was necessary and proper to carry out the powers delegated by the Constitution, they insisted. Other programs violated the Tenth Amendment by exercising delegated powers to invade areas within state jurisdiction. Democrats even challenged measures clearly connected to the war. For example they denied the constitutionality of the draft instituted in 1863. Throughout the North, Democratic state judges ruled the draft unconstitutional and issued writs of *habeas corpus* ordering the release of those conscripted.

However, the most crucial controversy over federal power involved the status of the southern states. State-rights Democrats, as good Jacksonians, denied that a state could leave the Union. Only individuals could rebel against the government. Individuals had committed treason and could be punished, but the states remained intact and entitled to their rights. The federal government received no extra war powers beyond those it had in peacetime. From this position northern Democrats assailed proposals of militant Republicans, soon known as "radical Republicans," to abolish slavery as a war measure. The Democratic view also suggested that the southern states were entitled to restoration of normal relations in the Union immediately upon the end of hostilities. Finally, Democrats vigorously denied that the southern states could be excluded from congressional representation or denied other state rights during a period of "reconstruction" after the war.

By continuing to elect Republicans to office, most Northerners seemed to reject state-rights limitations on federal power and the Democratic view of the nature of the rebellion. In the *Prize Cases* (1863), the Supreme Court rebuffed the idea that the rebellion was merely an insurrection by individuals, ruling that the states and all their inhabitants could be treated as belligerents. However, the Court did not clearly define the wartime status of the southern states until it decided the case of *Texas v. White* in 1869. In it the Court held that the rebel states remained in the Union but without governments capable of exercising state rights under the Constitution.

Civil Rights in Wartime

The Lincoln administration restricted civil rights during the Civil War to an extent that shocked Democrats, who lamented the loss of civil liberties for white war resisters that they never conceded to African Americans and had denied to abolitionists. Critics of the war were occasionally mobbed by patriots and some were jailed briefly, but surprisingly in a time of civil war, there were few restrictions on liberty. In general, the war's opponents were left free to try to persuade Americans to end hostilities.

Unity among Northerners began to break down by 1862 as greater numbers of Republicans pressed for laws to abolish slavery and secure rights for African Americans. The Conscription Act of 1863 proved extremely unpopular among Democrats, especially since it followed the Emancipation Proclamation, which made abolition a war aim. As early as 1862 "Peace Democrats" began to urge a ceasefire, to be followed, they hoped, by negotiations for a restoration of the Union. To many Republicans this policy and Democrats' strident criticism of the draft as a denial of liberty verged on treason; they called its advocates "Copperheads," poisonous snakes poised to strike the unwary. Over Democratic objections, Republicans expelled a small number of the most extreme advocates of peace from Congress.

But no one suggested suspending elections and, with very few exceptions, the opposition press remained free to challenge the Lincoln administration. In 1862 Democrats, including a powerful pro-peace wing of the party, nearly won control of the House of Representatives. Democrats controlled key governorships. Lincoln worried that he might be defeated for reelection in 1864 by General George B. McClellan, a Democrat who was committed to the war but whose party was badly divided on the issue.

The Lincoln administration did authorize the military to suppress the distribution of newspapers opposed to government authority. This power was exercised frequently in the parts of the South occupied by Union troops. On the rare occasions it was exercised in the North, the reaction was so strong that the orders were quickly reversed. Even in the South, military authorities were quite tolerant of general opposition to the Lincoln administration. The power was never used simply to stop criticism of the government.

The government also suspended the privilege of the writ of *habeas corpus* throughout the country. As a result, authorities could arrest and hold suspected offenders without trial; suspects had no recourse to the courts. The government went further, establishing military tribunals to hear cases involving war-related offenses, especially in the border states and in occupied southern territory.

For a few months early in the war, the suspension of the privilege of *habeas corpus* was abused, as the government acted on information from overzealous private citizens. But officials soon became more careful. Those accused of treasonous sympathies were released on their promises of good behavior. The suspension was used primarily to enable military officers to ignore the writs of *habeas corpus* that Democratic state judges issued ordering the release of draft dodgers. Nonetheless, in 1863 Congress responded to continuing complaints about arbitrary arrests by sharply limiting the time that a prisoner could be held without trial.

Many Americans, especially Democrats, criticized such war measures and charged Lincoln with moving towards a dictatorship. Still bitterly hostile to any legislation to secure the rights of black Americans, the Democrats continued to identify their organization as the party of personal liberty for whites. In speech after speech and pamphlet after pamphlet, Democrats denounced the wartime excesses of the Republican administration. Democrats also took their case for white men's civil liberty to the courts. When military authorities declared martial law and jailed a Maryland saboteur in the earliest days of the war, lawyers went directly to Chief Justice Taney for a writ of *habeas corpus* to secure his release. Taney ordered the detaining officer to show cause why the prisoner was being held, but the officer refused, citing Lincoln's suspension of the privilege of the writ of *habeas corpus*. Taney issued the writ anyway in *Ex parte Merryman* (1861). The provision for suspending the privilege of the writ was located in Article I of the Constitution, he pointed out; this fact indicated that suspension was a congressional rather than presidential power. Taney went further, denying that the president had any general authority to suppress resistance to federal laws. The president's duty was merely to aid the courts if they were unable to enforce their orders. He must act "in subordination to judicial authority, assisting it to execute its process and enforce its judgments."

Lincoln ordered the army not to obey Taney's ruling, informing Congress that he would abide by its decision. He suggested that in an emergency the president might be justified in violating the law to save the Union. "Are all the laws *but one* to go unexecuted, and the Government itself go to pieces lest that one be violated?" he asked. But Lincoln backed away from this hint that he could ignore the Constitution in an emergency. Instead he forcefully argued that under the Constitution the president shared the power to suspend the privilege of *habeas corpus*. Taney was outraged by Lincoln's defiance of his order, but could do nothing but wait for the issue to come before the whole Supreme Court. If the whole Court declared such acts unconstitutional, Lincoln might not be able to resist.

Still counting on the people themselves to maintain the Constitution, Democrats vigorously challenged the Lincoln administration on this issue. They formed the Society for the Diffusion of Political Knowledge, which published books and pamphlets denouncing arbitrary arrests. Among the most bellicose critics was Clement L. Vallandigham, a Democratic leader from Ohio. He opposed the war so outspokenly that he was finally arrested, tried, and convicted by a military commission for violating a questionable military order that forbade the expression of disloyal sentiments. Lincoln commuted his prison term to expulsion across Confederate lines. When angry Ohio Democrats nominated him for governor, Vallandigham appealed his conviction to the Supreme Court, challenging the legitimacy of the military proceedings in *Ex parte Vallandigham* (1864). But the justices avoided deciding the case on the technicality that the Judiciary Act did not provide for appeals from military tribunals.

Only after the war ended did the Supreme Court finally rule on the constitutionality of authorizing trials by military commission in states not in rebellion. Rather than following the provisions of the Habeas Corpus Act, Lincoln had authorized a military commission to try a pro-Confederate conspirator, doubting that a jury of his southern Indiana neighbors would convict him. By the time the Supreme Court considered his petition for a writ of *habeas corpus* in 1865, Lincoln had named several justices to replace retired or deceased Democrats, including the influential Salmon P. Chase, who replaced Taney as chief justice after his death in 1864. Nonetheless, in *Ex parte Milligan* (1866), a bare majority of the justices held that although Congress could authorize the suspension of the privilege of *habeas corpus*, neither it nor the president could suspend the writ, declare martial law, and authorize military commissions to try civilians where the civil courts were open. Chase and three other justices refused to go this far. They agreed that the army had failed to abide by the Habeas Corpus Act, but they insisted that Congress could have authorized the president's actions even where the civil courts still functioned.

Civil liberties were restricted most dramatically in the border slave states and in areas of the southern states that came under Union occupation. The governments of those states, as well as the provisional governments of occupied Arkansas, Virginia, and Tennessee, faced powerful and dedicated Confederate sympathizers. To distinguish friends from foes, they required loyalty oaths from all voters and candidates. The most stringent of these came to be known as "test oaths" and required the taker to swear that he had never provided aid or comfort to the rebellion, or had not done so since a certain date. To reduce the influence of rebels and rebel sympathizers, some of the loyal governments required test oaths as a condition for practicing law and medicine, or for serving as a clergyman.

Congress also passed laws requiring test oaths of its members, federal officials, and attorneys practicing before the Supreme Court. President Lincoln instructed provisional governors in occupied southern states to require oaths from voters and officeholders trying to restore loyal governments there. These oaths promised future loyalty and acquiescence in the Emancipation Proclamation.

Democrats attacked the toughest oath-taking requirements as violations of civil liberty, designed primarily to keep Republicans in power. The Supreme Court ultimately proved hostile to the oaths as well. After the war it ruled the law requiring a test oath of lawyers practicing before the Court unconstitutional on the grounds that it infringed on the independence of the judiciary. It ruled that state laws imposing test oaths on lawyers, doctors, and clergymen were violations of the Constitution's ban on *ex post facto* laws and bills of attainder.

The Confiscation Acts and the Emancipation Proclamation

Confiscating the property of rebels is a traditional weapon in civil wars, designed to punish traitors and to keep waverers in line. American Patriots had confiscated Tory property in the American Revolution. Congress passed a mild Confiscation Act in 1861, followed by a stricter one in 1862. The new law seized the property and slaves of disloyal residents of the rebel states. Congress also gave soldiers immunity from being sued for anything done under the general direction of army officers and the president, such as confiscating property, seizing deserters and draft evaders, and, later, freeing slaves. This immunity deprived people of the right to go to court to protect their property from the military or to receive compensation for wrongful actions. But it was necessary to protect Union soldiers, who were being harassed by lawsuits instituted in the state courts on behalf of slave owners and Confederate sympathizers.

From the beginning of the war, Republicans like Chase, Senator Charles Sumner, and Horace Greeley, editor of the influential *New York Tribune,* urged the immediate abolition of slavery. As long as the institution continued to exist, they warned, it would sustain the Slave Power and its suppression of liberty. To reestablish permanent peace, the nation had to go to the root of the conflict. Hence, advocates of immediate wartime abolition became known as "radical Republicans."

Lincoln, more conservative Republicans, and most Democrats resisted the radical argument. From a political and strategic standpoint, abolition would estrange unionists in the loyal border states of Kentucky, Missouri, and Delaware. It would alienate unionists in the rebel states, whom Lincoln and other Republicans hoped might organize against the Confederacy and help to restore the Union. Lincoln was most worried that abolition would disaffect racist, state-rights-oriented northern Democrats, upon whom a successful war effort depended. To reassure all these groups, Lincoln successfully encouraged Congress early in the war to pass a resolution denying any intention to interfere with slavery in the states. Lincoln also doubted the constitutional power of the federal government to abolish slavery. Like most Americans, he adhered to the "federal consensus." Slavery lay at the heart of state jurisdiction; the federal government had no power to interfere.

As it became clear that southern Unionists were a weak minority in the Confederacy and that the war would be a long and bloody struggle, sentiment in the North began to change. The 1862 Confiscation Act provided that captured slaves would be given their freedom. Radical Republicans urged Lincoln to recruit African Americans into the armed forces; they were seconded by northern state and local officials, who wanted to substitute black soldiers for their own draftees. The reluctant Lincoln stalled, fearing that arming blacks to kill whites would alienate Democrats and even some Republicans. But as federal forces advanced, tens of thousands of slaves poured into Union army encampments. Lincoln saw that it would be impossible to return them to slavery at war's end. After long hesitation, in the fall of 1862 he finally announced that, as commander-in-chief, he would authorize African-American enlistment and that, as a war measure, he would emancipate the slaves in all territory still resisting the Union's authority. On January 1, 1863, he issued the Emancipation Proclamation. From that day forward, Lincoln announced, the United States would consider all slaves behind enemy lines as free. Radicals complained that the Emancipation Proclamation was too timid, operating only behind enemy lines and therefore not immediately freeing a single slave. Many Democrats and other conservatives, in contrast, criticized its radicalism. The Proclamation repudiated the nearly seventy-five-year-old understanding that slavery was unequivocally a state institution, not subject to federal control. At a stroke, they charged, Lincoln had destroyed the foundation of the southern economy and deprived slave owners of hundreds of millions of dollars of property without due process of law.

Indeed, the commitment to abolishing slavery did revolutionize American constitutionalism. Protection for slavery had become deeply embedded in American law. Lincoln knew how radical the change was— "a new birth of freedom," as he described it in the Gettysburg Address. As the national government moved slowly towards abolishing slavery, support grew, especially among Republicans, for securing fundamental civil rights to black Americans. Pressured by African Americans, abolitionists and the radical wing of their party, in state after state Republicans cautiously moved to eliminate discriminatory laws. They repealed laws prohibiting black immigration. Laws barring African Americans from suing whites or giving testimony in courts were abrogated. Localities established schools for black children, or permitted them to attend schools with whites. Pressure grew to eliminate white-only voting restrictions. Where legislatures did not act, Republican judges sometimes did, ruling that discriminatory laws violated state constitutions or reinterpreting the laws to sustain black rights.

Urged on by radical Republicans like the conscientious Sumner, Congress acted as well. Besides authorizing recruitment of African Americans into the armed services, it eliminated white-only restrictions on other government employment. It also eliminated restrictions against black testimony in federal courts, established schools for black children in Washington, and ended discrimination in the capital's streetcars.

Lincoln and Presidential Power

Abraham Lincoln proved to be a powerful leader, the first president to dominate government since Polk had left office in 1849. He exceeded even Jackson in his claims of presidential authority. Political scientists sometimes refer to Lincoln's vision of power as the "prerogative presidency." In other words, he claimed inherent presidential power to advance the public welfare by assuming quasi-legislative power on some occasions and ignoring legal restraints on others. Lincoln pointed out that the president alone, among all government officers, took an oath specified in the Constitution itself, to "preserve, protect, and defend the Constitution of the United States." Lincoln believed that this oath implied a delegation of power to the president to do whatever necessary to preserve and protect the Constitution. In his response to Taney's *Merryman* opinion and in a few public but unofficial letters, he suggested that the oath might also justify his refusal to enforce a law if necessary.

Lincoln manifested his conception of presidential power on a variety of occasions. Without clear congressional authorization, he called up the militia in 1861 to suppress the rebellion, and without any authorization at all, he called for volunteers to increase the size of the army. On his own authority, he declared a blockade of southern ports and suspended the privilege of the writ of *habeas corpus*. In 1863 he issued the Emancipation Proclamation. He was an extremely active commander-in-chief, working closely with Secretary of War Edwin M. Stanton, personally promoting and demoting one commanding general after another, cajoling and advising each until he found a dogged fighter in Ulysses S. Grant. He closely monitored local commanders in the occupied South, encouraging them to foster loyalty but warning them against excesses. He claimed the power to appoint provisional governors to administer occupied Confederate territory. He created these positions without the sanction of a congressional law, nor, with one exception,* did he seek Senate confirmation of those he appointed. Not only did his appointees preside over provisional civil governments, subject to martial law, but Lincoln instructed them to begin the process of reconstructing permanent, loyal governments that would ultimately be restored to normal relations in the Union, and he kept close tabs on the process.

Where Lincoln claimed a power that was also delegated to Congress, such as the power to suspend the privilege of the writ of *habeas corpus* or to regulate Reconstruction, he acknowledged Congress's primary responsibility. He accepted that he acted subject to Congress's right to modify or even annul his actions. But he also made clear that he would exercise his influence in such lawmaking to the fullest.

Reluctantly, Congress retroactively authorized many of Lincoln's actions. Other actions brought Lincoln into conflict with Congress, especially where his policies differed with those favored by a majority of congressmen. Since the Constitution gives Congress the right to declare war and make rules to govern the armed forces, it claimed the final right to make military policy. Exercising this authority, it appointed a Committee on the Conduct of the War to investigate

---

*When Lincoln appointed Andrew Johnson provisional governor of Tennessee, he simultaneously commissioned him as a brigadier general in the army. The Senate confirmed the military appointment.

military activities and make recommendations for improvements. The committee, led by Ohio's tough Senator Benjamin F. Wade, pressured Lincoln to put favored generals in positions of command, to recruit African Americans into the armed services, and to adopt emancipation as a strategy to win the war. Congress also claimed the primary, if not the sole, right to suspend the privilege of the writ of *habeas corpus,* and it passed laws regulating the length of time and the procedures for holding people without trial.

Republican leaders in Congress doubted that the Emancipation Proclamation alone could free the slaves. Therefore they proposed the Thirteenth Amendment to the Constitution, banning slavery throughout the nation. It was ratified in 1865. Finally, Congress denied that the president could establish a program for restoring loyal governments in the southern states simply by using his power as commander-in-chief. Reconstructing the Union required legislative action, congressional leaders insisted. The seriousness of the disagreement was evident in 1864, when Congress passed a Reconstruction bill authored by Wade and Representative Henry Winter Davis.* Lincoln killed the Wade-Davis Reconstruction bill with a "pocket veto," refusing to sign it before Congress adjourned. Wade and Davis angrily penned a "manifesto" blasting the president and implicitly suggesting that Republicans turn to a radical like Chase rather than renominate him. Party activists swiftly rejected the idea, and Lincoln became the first president since Jackson to win a second term of office. Nonetheless, many members of Congress continued to disagree with him over Reconstruction. As the war drew to a close, Lincoln urged Congress to recognize the legitimacy of new governments established by his provisional governors in Louisiana and Arkansas. He won the support of most Republicans. But radical Republicans, led by Sumner, managed to delay and kill the measure with a filibuster. As the war ended in the spring of 1865, Congress and the president had not yet agreed upon a policy for reconstructing the Union.

However, one should not exaggerate the differences. Lincoln was a Republican through and through, on good terms with his party. He had conceded Congress's final authority over matters like Reconstruction. He was simply determined to exercise as much influence over its decisions as he could, hoping that it would acquiesce in this policy as it had in others. But on April 14, 1865, he was assassinated, bringing to the presidency a very different man, Vice President Andrew Johnson. The resulting conflict over reconstructing the Union would lead to a constitutional crisis almost as serious as the rebellion itself.

---

*Lincoln's policy and the terms of the Wade-Davis bill are discussed more fully in Chapter 10. See p. 188 and succeeding pages.

TIMELINE

1861   Civil War begins with South Carolina firing on Fort Sumter.

President Lincoln calls troops to Washington, D.C., to suppress the rebellion; he suspends the privilege of the writ of *habeas corpus* along a corridor from New York to Washington.

In *Ex parte Merryman,* Chief Justice Roger Taney denies that the president has the constitutional authority to suspend the privilege of the writ of *habeas corpus;* Lincoln refuses to comply.

The first Confiscation Act authorizes seizure of property of rebel sympathizers.

1862   The Legal Tender Act authorizes the issue of paper currency ("greenbacks") to be repaid in gold at an unspecified date.

The Homestead Act grants free, 160-acre homesteads to settlers living on public land for five years.

The Pacific Railway Act grants public land to subsidize construction of a transcontinental railroad.

The Morrill Landgrant College Act grants public land to states to endow agricultural colleges.

The second Confiscation Act confiscates and frees the slaves of rebel sympathizers.

Lincoln issues the Preliminary Emancipation Proclamation, announcing his intention to free slaves in all areas still in rebellion as of January 1, 1863.

1863   The Emancipation Proclamation frees slaves in all areas of the United States still in rebellion.

The National Bank Act establishes a national currency system.

The Conscription Act establishes a national draft.

Congress regularizes military arrest procedures in the *Habeas Corpus* Act.

In the *Prize Cases,* the Supreme Court sustains Lincoln's declaration of a blockade, defining the rebellion as a state of war.

1864   In *Ex parte Vallandigham,* the Supreme Court rejects Vallandigham's petition for a writ of *certiorari* appealing his conviction by a military court.

Lincoln refuses to sign the Wade-Davis Reconstruction Act, preventing it from becoming law with a "pocket veto."

Lincoln reelected president; Andrew Johnson elected vice president.

1864	Salmon P. Chase becomes chief justice of the Supreme Court.
1865	Congress sends the Thirteenth Amendment, abolishing slavery, to the states for ratification; it is ratified in December.
	Confederate armies surrender.
	Lincoln assassinated; Andrew Johnson becomes president.
1866	In *Ex parte Milligan,* the Supreme Court rules that neither the president nor Congress can suspend the privilege of the writ of *habeas corpus* and authorize the trial of civilians by military commissions as long as civil courts are open.

FURTHER READING

The standard narrative history of the Civil War is James M. McPherson, *Battle Cry of Freedom* (1988). More textbook-like is his *Ordeal By Fire* (1982), which is more useful for finding specific information. For a discussion of changing historical interpretations of the Civil War and the Constitution, see Michael Les Benedict, "A Constitutional Crisis," in *Writing the Civil War*, ed. James M. McPherson and William J. Cooper Jr. (1998).

In 1926 James G. Randall published his classic study of the constitutional aspects of the Civil War, *Constitutional Problems Under Lincoln*. Daniel Farber's *Lincoln's Constitution* (2003) is an elegant analysis of the subject, bringing to bear both contemporaneous and present-day understandings. Harold M. Hyman's *A More Perfect Union* (1973) places constitutional Civil War–era constitutional development in a broad social and political context. Less dense is *Equal Justice Under Law* (1982), the survey of constitutional development from 1835 to 1875 that Hyman co-authored with William M. Wiecek. Melinda Lawson describes how American intellectuals and reformers constructed a new nationalism in *Patriot Fires* (2002). See also Garry Wills's very readable *Lincoln at Gettysburg* (1992). For the way the Civil War expanded federal power, see Leonard P. Curry, *Blueprint for Modern America* (1968) and Richard F. Bensel, *Yankee Leviathan* (1990).

In *Constitutional Problems*, Randall concluded that Lincoln's government trod heavily on civil liberties. Dean Sprague explicitly criticizes Lincoln's record in this area in *Freedom Under Lincoln* (1965). Mark E. Neely Jr.'s Pulitzer Prize–winning *The Fate of Liberty* (1991) is a judicious account that concludes that the government's overall record on civil liberties was good in the context of a civil war. Faber arrives at a similar conclusion in *Lincoln's Constitution*. The most comprehensive discussion of the Supreme Court's record on this and other Civil War issues is Carl Brent Swisher, *History of the Supreme Court*, vol. 5: *The Taney Period, 1836–1864* (1974).

Michael Vorenberg, *Final Freedom* (2001) is the definitive account of the abolition of slavery during the Civil War. Herman Belz's *A New Birth of Freedom* (1976) and *Emancipation and Civil Rights* (1978) are solid studies of emancipation and the future status of the freedmen and freedwomen. Allen C. Guelzo's insightful *Lincoln's Emancipation Proclamation* (2004) stresses Lincoln's awareness of the obstacles the Constitution put in the way of emancipation by executive action. In *Military Necessity and Civil Rights Policy* (1977), Mary F. Berry argues that African Americans won their own freedom by successfully demanding inclusion in the federal armed forces. LaWanda Cox chronicles Lincoln's growing commitment to racial justice in *Lincoln and Black Freedom* (1981). See also Don E. Fehrenbacher, "Only His Stepchildren: Abraham Lincoln and Racial Equality," *Civil War History* 20 (December 1974): 293–310.

The best study of Lincoln's use of presidential power is Phillip S. Paludan, *The Presidency of Abraham Lincoln* (1994). Frank J. Williams provides a brief introduction to "Abraham Lincoln and the Changing Role of Commander in Chief," in *Lincoln Reshapes the Presidency*, ed. Charles M. Hubbard (2003). James G. Randall describes a benign "Lincoln in the Role of Dictator," in the *South Atlantic Quarterly* 28 (July 1929): 236–252, as does Clinton Rossiter in *Constitutional Dictatorship* (1948). M. E. Bradford does not view Lincoln so charitably in "The Lincoln Legacy: A Long View," *Modern Age* 24 (Fall 1980): 355–363. In contrast, Herman Belz dismisses the notion that Lincoln was a dictator in *Lincoln and the Constitution* (1984). Michael Les Benedict reaches the same conclusion in his essay on the Lincoln presidency in Martin L. Fausold and Alan Shank (eds.), *The Constitution and the American Presidency* (1991).

The best book on wartime Reconstruction policy is Herman Belz, *Reconstructing the Union* (1969). See also Michael Les Benedict, *A Compromise of Principle* (1974). Both severely modify the old idea that Lincoln and the congressional Republicans were in fundamental disagreement over Reconstruction.

10
Reconstruction and the Constitution

B y 1865, Union forces under the overall command of General Ulysses S. Grant seemed to be moving inexorably towards victory over the Confederacy. Victory would require the federal government to establish a policy for reconstructing the Union, and probably for reconstructing state governments in the South as well, since most Republicans strongly opposed any recognition of the existing Confederate state governments. Reconstruction presented several interrelated and extremely difficult problems of constitutional and social policy: What was the status of the southern people and the southern states? What power did the federal government have to exercise control over the South once the war ended? How long could that power last? Which branch of the federal government, Congress or the president, had the constitutional authority to exercise that power and determine Reconstruction policy? What should be the status of the freed slaves (generally called "freedmen" after emancipation) and other African Americans? What rights should be secured to them? What were the implications for the rights of women? Did the federal government have the power to protect these rights? If not, should the Constitution be amended to delegate this power?

These issues precipitated a bitter struggle between the president and Congress, Republicans and Democrats, nationalists and advocates of state rights, and those who wanted to protect individual and minority rights versus those who worried more about popular rights. Not quite coinciding with this struggle was another—between advocates of women's equality and traditionalists. Over dogged resistance, from 1866 to 1869 Republicans passed Reconstruction Acts and civil rights laws. They passed the Fourteenth and Fifteenth Amendments to secure equal civil and political rights regardless of race. But they faced a president who seemed bent on returning ex-Confederates to power in the South, who used his power and influence to subvert congressional legislation, and who appeared even to threaten violence. Driven to impeachment, they failed to remove him from office by a single vote.

Republicans attempted to enact their Reconstruction program without repudiating the federal system, but their constitutional amendments and legislation

186

nevertheless radically expanded the powers of the national government. The courts were left with the difficult job of interpreting Republican policies in a way that maintained the essentials of federalism. Ultimately, the Supreme Court's interpretation seriously weakened, but did not overturn, the Republican program.

Most southern whites fiercely resisted Republican Reconstruction, turning to fraud and violence to overthrow Republican regimes in their states. Republicans saw themselves as trying to protect individual and minority rights against local oppression; most white Southerners considered their resistance a struggle for popular liberty against despotic governments imposed by an outside power. Over time Northerners slowly lost enthusiasm for the fight. By 1877 every southern state had reverted to ex-Confederate control. The civil and political rights of African Americans eroded in the South and racism revived in the North, leaving the task of securing racial justice to later generations of Americans.

Theories of Reconstruction

The status of the southern states after the Confederate armies surrendered in spring 1865 posed a thorny constitutional problem for Americans. State-rights Democrats argued that the states had never left the Union and continued to exist with all their rights intact. Individual Southerners had committed treason, they concluded, but the states remained. Whenever they sent loyal representatives to Congress, they would be entitled to admission. Whenever they elected loyal officials, they would be entitled to all their rights, including the right to decide the status of African Americans in their societies. Republicans firmly rejected the Democratic view. Loyalty would be easy to avow now that the Confederacy was defeated, and many Confederates would pretend loyalty only to escape the consequences of their actions. Southern unionists who had never aided the rebellion suggested turning authority over to them, but Republicans knew that loyal governments could not be erected on so narrow and undemocratic a basis. Sooner or later ex-Confederates had to be permitted to exercise the rights of American citizens. Yet once the southern states returned to normal relations in the Union, the national government would lose its power over internal state affairs. How would it then protect southern loyalists from ex-Confederate majorities? How could it protect the freed people? How could it even assure that white Southerners did not restore some version of near-slavery? Although Republicans had argued before the war that the national government had the power to protect citizens' rights, neither the courts nor Congress had ever agreed. There was no guarantee that either would accept antislavery constitutionalism once Southerners returned to the Union. Clearly, Republicans insisted, restoration had to be preceded by a program of Reconstruction to instill loyalty, secure the safety of southern unionists, and define and protect the civil rights of African Americans in the South.

The most radical Republicans, like House majority leader Thaddeus Stevens, argued that the seceding states no longer existed. The occupied South was conquered territory, no different from the territory taken from Mexico. Congress had the same power over it as over any property of the United States. It could govern the South directly, or it could erect territorial governments according to the usual pattern—with the president nominating governors, territorial judges, and other officials, and the residents electing a territorial legislature subject to congressional oversight. The radicals advocated a long period of territorialization with both blacks and whites entitled to vote, before new southern states were readmitted to the Union.

Other Republicans took more moderate positions: The states had not escaped their obligations to the Union through secession, but they had forfeited their rights. The influential radical Republican Senator Charles Sumner called this "state suicide." He pointed to Article IV, section 4 of the Constitution, which required the United States to guarantee republican forms of government in the states, as the source of federal power to restore them to life. Sumner and other radicals argued that this provision obligated the federal government to require the states to guarantee equal civil and political rights to all men, regardless of color. They even argued that it authorized Congress to insist on equal rights in all the states of the Union, North as well as South.

A third group of Republicans rejected such an expansive notion of congressional power. Having defeated southern armies, Congress held the southern states "in the grasp of war." According to this theory, the federal government could govern them directly under martial law until their people agreed to the conditions necessary to restore permanent peace. These conditions might include ratifying the Thirteenth Amendment or even enfranchising black Southerners. But once the conditions were met and the southern states were restored to normal relations in the Union, they would be entitled to all the rights of states in the federal system.

Presidential versus Congressional Reconstruction

Related to the issue of the status of the southern states was the question of which branch of the federal government had power to govern them and to set the conditions for restoration. President Lincoln had claimed at least a share of this authority for himself as commander-in-chief and through his power to pardon offenders. Not waiting for congressional legislation, during the war he set in motion a process for restoring southern states to normal relations in the Union. Hoping to weaken the Confederate war effort, Lincoln wanted to create alternative, loyal southern governments even as the war continued. He offered a pardon to any Southerner, except high-ranking Confederate civil and military officers and a few others, who took an oath promising future loyalty and support for the Emancipation Proclamation. Lincoln's plan instructed provisional governors to call state constitutional conventions whenever a number of men equaling 10 percent of the voters of 1860 signed oaths of future loyalty to the United States. The conventions would then establish new free-state constitutions. After the requisite number of voters ratified a new constitution and elected state officials, Lincoln expected Congress to admit the state's representatives, completing the restoration process.

Many Republican congressmen rejected Lincoln's program, preferring to delay Reconstruction until Southerners were thoroughly beaten. The Wade-Davis bill, passed in 1864, required a number of men equaling 50 percent of the voters of 1860 to take loyalty oaths; it permitted only those who had never aided the rebellion to participate in establishing new state constitutions; and it required the new constitutions to ban slavery. Lincoln never denied Congress's power to pass such legislation, but he preferred his own plan and killed the measure with a "pocket veto." But he was unable to persuade Congress to recognize state governments reconstructed according to his plan.

Upon Lincoln's assassination, Vice President Andrew Johnson became president. Johnson had been a Democrat before the war and the only senator from a seceding state to remain loyal to the Union. Lincoln had secured his nomination as vice president to cement the alliance with prowar Democrats in the so-called Union Party. But unlike many other War Democrats, Johnson had never identified himself as a Republican. An old follower of "King Andrew" Jackson and the successor of the equally forceful Lincoln, Johnson tried to be a strong president too. However, his policies differed so radically from those advocated by most Republicans that they precipitated a monumental conflict with Congress.

Following Lincoln's precedent, Johnson claimed the authority to reconstruct the South through his power as commander-in-chief and his authority to pardon rebels. Using these powers while Congress was adjourned in 1865, he followed the Lincoln plan with some modifications. He increased the proportion of men required to take the loyalty oath to 50 percent of the number of voters in 1860, as Congress had wanted in the Wade-Davis bill. Like Lincoln, he mandated constitutional conventions to reinstitute state governments, and he required these conventions to nullify secession ordinances, repudiate war debts, and ratify the Thirteenth Amendment.

Although Johnson's plan resembled Lincoln's, the situation had changed radically. Lincoln had wanted to reconstruct the southern state governments while the war was still raging and an oath of future loyalty really meant something. With the war ended, even rabid Confederates rushed to take the oath in order to receive pardons that would save them from prosecution and the confiscation of their property. In this new context, Johnson's plan was very lenient. He allowed nearly all ex-rebels to participate in the restoration process. Thus when it was finished, former Confederates controlled the state governments.

Johnson did not insist on anything beyond emancipation for African Americans in the South. He rejected the suggestion of half of his Cabinet that at least literate black Southerners and those who had served in the Union military participate in the Reconstruction process. He permitted the new state governments to pass codes defining their status and controlling their conduct. White Southerners thought these new laws were liberating, because they conferred some basic rights, but appalled Northerners called them "Black Codes," because they resembled the antebellum slave codes.

The Black Codes differed in each southern state, but nearly all forbade African Americans from testifying in courts against whites except in their own cases. They barred black Southerners from serving on juries, denied them the right to assemble freely or own weapons, and discriminated against them in the administration of criminal law. Many Black Codes restricted the right to own property and to work in different occupations. Strict "vagrancy" laws permitted government officials to arrest African Americans who had been unable to find work and to hire them out to the highest bidder. Some states passed "apprenticeship" laws that kept black children in virtual slavery until they were eighteen years old. Towns and counties passed local ordinances that restricted the freedom of black Southerners even further.

Republicans denounced the Black Codes and insisted that the federal government secure the civil rights of the freed people before completing Recon-

Columbia.—"Shall I Trust These Men,   **And Not This Man?"**

A pair of Thomas Nast drawings in 1865 advocate voting rights for African Americans during Reconstruction.

struction. Sobered by the Republican reaction, some southern states passed more even-handed laws. But none permitted African Americans to vote or to sit on juries. Vagrancy laws were made to apply equally to blacks and whites, but everyone knew that white law-enforcement officers, judges, and juries would apply them only to African Americans.

By the time Congress met in December 1865, Johnson's program of Reconstruction had been completed in most of the South. The southern states sent senators and representatives to Congress and claimed all the rights of states in the Union. At first the president was vague about Congress's power to modify his program, but he soon made it clear that, unlike Lincoln, he thought Congress had no power over Reconstruction. Only he, as commander-in-chief, had the right to reorganize the southern state governments. Moreover, he had gone as far as any federal officer could go in setting conditions for reentry into the Union. Anything more would invade matters inherently within the states' jurisdiction. Democrats, pleased with the practical results of Johnson's policy and his commitment to state rights, rallied to his support.

But Republicans overwhelmingly rejected Johnson's views. No matter which theory of Reconstruction they adhered to, they insisted that the national government retain control over the southern states until Congress recognized their restoration. Even the most moderate Republicans would not release the South from the "grasp of war" until something was done to secure basic rights to the freed people and southern loyalists.

Reconstruction, Civil Rights, and Federalism

Before the war the term *citizenship* had been filled with ambiguity. In one sense to be a "citizen" merely implied allegiance rather than a right to participate in government. But the term *citizen* was also identified with the privileges and obligations of participating in public life—to debate public policy and vote for those who made it, to accept public office, to sit on juries, to defend the community by serving in the militia. The relationship of citizenship to gender was particularly complex. The fact that black men were denied political rights in many states and by federal laws was cited as proof that African Americans were not citizens at all. But white women clearly *were* citizens, even though they too were excluded from public life.

So would African Americans now be considered citizens? If so, would that imply that black adult males would have the privileges and obligations of public life? Advocates of equal rights for women argued that citizenship itself implied these privileges and obligations. If excluding black men from them meant they were not citizens, excluding women from them implied the same thing. All citizens deserved the right to participate in the making of public policy, they insisted.

Emancipation forced Americans to define citizenship and the rights that went with it. The Black Codes reinforced this determination. But they also reinforced the idea that what citizens shared was an equal entitlement to the *civil* rights that the southern laws denied. Denouncing the Black Codes, Republicans distinguished the civil rights of citizenship from political privileges.

Empowering the national government to protect basic individual rights required a change in the federal system that many Americans were reluctant to undertake. Protection of rights had always been the states' job. During the war, many people had worried that the national government was growing too powerful. Even adherents of the nationalist theory of federalism began to worry that if carried to its logical conclusion, there would be no limit to national jurisdiction. People insisted that a line must exist somewhere that marked the end of the national government's authority and the beginning of the states'.

This concern for federalism was reflected in the court decisions even of Republican judges. Several state courts denied that the national government could tax legal documents issued by states, insisting that state sovereignty limited the national government's power to levy taxes on state activities. The Supreme Court agreed in *Collector v. Day* (1871), holding that the national government could not tax the income of state judges. In *Texas v. White* (1869), which answered the question of whether Texas had ceased to exist when it tried to secede, the Court said that the Constitution created "an indestructible Union, composed of indestructible States." The language suggested an equality between state and national sovereignty and repudiated the "conquered-province" and "state-suicide" doctrines of Reconstruction.

Northerners were forced to balance their desire to empower the national government to protect the rights of Americans, especially the freed people, against their commitment to the basic structure of the federal system. For President Johnson, preserving the old federal system was much more important than protecting the rights of the freed people. Like most Democrats, Johnson not only believed in state rights but in white supremacy. Denying that Congress had the power to protect the rights of black people against state discrimination, he also opposed amending the Constitution to give it such power.

Far more concerned than Johnson with protecting the rights of the ex-slaves, nearly all Republicans agreed that Congress must act to modify Johnson's program. At first they concentrated on securing African Americans the status and rights of citizenship. To accomplish this goal, Congress passed the Civil Rights Act of 1866. It defined as citizens all persons born in the United States, except for Native Americans who did not pay taxes. It went on to declare that all persons had the same rights as white people to make contracts, to dispose of property, and to enforce their rights in the courts; it made all people subject to the same penalties as white people for violations of law. States would retain the primary responsibility for protecting their residents and defining their mutual relations, as long as they did not discriminate in fundamental rights when they did so. The Civil Rights Act implied that all citizens shared civil rights but not necessarily political rights, an ominous sign for advocates of equal political rights for women. More-over, by guaranteeing simply that all persons would have the same civil rights as white persons, it left gender discriminations intact.

Johnson, the Democrats, and a few Republicans, including the influential congressman John A. Bingham, a leading antislavery lawyer, insisted that the Civil Rights Act was unconstitutional. The act invaded the right of the states to define state citizenship, protect rights, and determine the day-to-day relationships among human beings. Breaking with those who had elected him vice president, Johnson vetoed the bill. In response, Republicans argued that the act was justified by a broad reading of Congress's power to enforce the Thirteenth Amendment. That Amendment not only outlawed slavery; its second section authorized Congress to make all laws "appropriate" to enforce the prohibition. Some Republicans argued that the Privileges and Immunities Clause of Article IV of the Constitution also authorized federal legislation to protect rights. The Republicans passed the Civil Rights Act over the president's veto.

To overcome constitutional objections to the Civil Rights Act and to make the recognition of African American citizenship irreversible, Congress passed the Fourteenth Amendment, which was ratified in 1868. Authored by Bingham, the first section declared all persons born or naturalized in the United States and subject to its jurisdiction (thus excluding many Native Americans) to be citizens of the United States and of the states in which they lived. It prohibited the states from abridging the privileges or immunities of United States citizens; taking away life, liberty, or property without due process of law; or denying equal protection of the laws. The fifth section authorized Congress to pass "appropriate" laws to enforce the other sections.

By framing the Fourteenth Amendment this way, Republicans accomplished two goals. First, the language was similar to the restrictions Article I, section 10 imposed on the states. This formulation meant that the state and federal courts could enforce the amendment even without further congressional action, just as they enforced the Obligation of Contracts Clause.

Second, like the Civil Rights Act, the Fourteenth Amendment left the states with the primary authority to govern the ordinary activities of their residents. Only if state action or state officers violated the rights of their people—or perhaps if they failed to protect their rights at all—could the federal government intervene.* By specifying that states could not deny anyone the privileges and immunities of United States citizens and by guaranteeing due process to all, the amendment expanded the power of the national government to protect the rights of all people, not only African Americans. Yet, it did so in a way that preserved the essential character of the federal system.

*Some constitutional scholars insist that the Fourteenth Amendment was intended to empower the federal government to punish individual infringements of rights, not only state actions. For a good statement of that argument, see Robert Kaczorowski, "To Begin the Nation Anew: Congress, Citizenship, and Civil Rights after the Civil War," *American Historical Review* 92 (February 1987): 45–68.

The Fourteenth Amendment treated civil rights as distinct from political rights. While all citizens were entitled to civil rights, the second section of the Amendment confirmed that states could deny political rights as long as their representation in Congress was reduced proportionally.

Congress refused to recognize the governments organized under Johnson's authority until they ratified the Fourteenth Amendment and modified their laws to conform to it. Encouraged by President Johnson, they refused to do so. Breaking the impasse in 1867, Congress passed a series of Reconstruction Acts over his veto. Furiously denounced as unconstitutional by the president, the Democrats, and nearly all white Southerners, the Reconstruction laws divided the South into five military districts. They gave the commanders of each district the power to enforce order, punish offenses, override laws enacted by the Johnson-state legislatures, and replace Johnson-state officials.

The Reconstruction Acts required Southerners to frame new state constitu-

President Andrew Johnson, defender of state rights during Reconstruction, escaped removal through impeachment by only one vote.

Representative John A. Bingham, father of the Fourteenth Amendment.

tions under the supervision of the military. All adult males, black and white, were permitted to vote for delegates to new constitutional conventions, except those who had joined the rebellion after having taken oaths to support the Constitution. The new state constitutions could make no racial distinctions in voting and had to be consistent with the Fourteenth Amendment. The people of each state, without regard to color, had to ratify the new constitutions before they could go into effect. Not until the new state governments ratified the Fourteenth Amendment would Congress finally restore them to normal relations in the Union.

The Reconstruction Acts were the most radical exercise of federal power in the history of the United States. Yet Republicans passed such draconian measures precisely because they felt compelled to restore the traditional federal system, with its limits on federal power. Even with the ratification of the Fourteenth Amendment, Republicans knew that the federal government would be hard-pressed to protect the rights of people against state governments determined to restrict them. The Republicans needed to reestablish state governments that could be trusted to exercise their powers fairly once the federal system was restored.

In effect, Congress reinforced the changes of the Fourteenth Amendment with changes in the political systems of the southern states themselves. They hoped that giving black men the ballot would lead to the election of governments that would protect the rights of all people equally. To fix the change permanently, Republicans passed the Fifteenth Amendment, which was ratified in 1870. It prohibited both the national and the state governments from depriving anyone of the right to vote on account of race, color, or for having once been a slave.

Because it permitted voting discrimination based on sex, the Fifteenth Amendment bitterly disappointed activists who had been working to extend political rights to women as well as African Americans. Furious at the Republicans whom they had supported, radical woman's suffragists, such as Susan B. Anthony and Elizabeth Cady Stanton, broke their alliance with antislavery reformers and began an independent campaign for women's rights. They launched drives to secure the vote in several northern states, but they failed in every case. Although many Republicans were sympathetic, they were unwilling to risk losing one radical measure by adding another.

However, women's rights did continue to expand. Even the most conservative states now passed Married Women's Property Acts. One state after another followed that reform with laws securing married women's rights to control their earnings. Despite these advances, none but the most radical feminists denied that states could discriminate between men and women in their legislation. Such discriminations did not violate the Fourteenth Amendment, the Supreme Court held, neither depriving women of a basic right of citizenship nor denying them equal protection of the laws. In the law's view, such discriminations were reasonable recognitions of sexual differences. Justice Joseph P. Bradley summarized this position in his now-infamous concurring opinion in *Bradwell v. Illinois* (1873).

Opponents of political rights for women lampoon the women's rights movement.

Illinois could refuse to admit Myra Bradwell to the bar, Bradley opined, despite her manifest capacity as a lawyer. "The paramount destiny and mission of woman are to fulfill the noble and benign offices of wife and mother," he wrote. "[I]n view of the peculiar characteristics, destiny, and mission of woman, it is within the province of the legislature to ordain what offices, positions, and callings shall be filled and discharged by men, and shall receive the benefit of . . . that decision and firmness which are presumed to predominate in the sterner sex."

Presidential Power and the Impeachment of President Johnson

The Constitution assigns to the president the job of enforcing the laws. Denying the constitutionality of the Reconstruction laws, Johnson instead used his presidential powers to obstruct their operation. Federal law-enforcement officers did little to enforce the Civil Rights Act. When appointing federal officers in the South, Johnson's cabinet ignored the requirement that they take the test oath. Johnson encouraged the intransigence of the officers of the state governments he had helped to establish. He removed military commanders who vigorously enforced the Reconstruction Acts and replaced them with officers who opposed Congress's Reconstruction policy. Like presidents before him, Johnson removed his political opponents and nominated political allies to replace them.

In response Congress passed laws limiting presidential authority over government officers. The Tenure of Office Act provided that while the Senate was in session, Johnson could remove government officers only upon the confirmation of their successors. While Congress was adjourned, he could only suspend them temporarily. Worried about Johnson's interference with enforcement of the Reconstruction Acts, Congress forbade the president from sending General Ulysses S. Grant out of the country and required that all orders to the army go through the general's headquarters.

Many Republicans, led by Thaddeus Stevens, the bellicose Benjamin F. Butler, and the influential lawyer George S. Boutwell, argued that Johnson's course justified his impeachment under Article II, section 4 of the Constitution. This article states that the president and other government officers may be "removed from Office on Impeachment for, and Conviction of, Treason, Bribery, or other high Crimes and Misdemeanors." The Constitution gave the power to bring impeachments to the House of Representatives and the power to try them to the Senate, where conviction would require the vote of two-thirds of the senators.

Many Republicans argued that by "high Crimes and Misdemeanors" the Constitution meant abuse of power and misconduct in office. Johnson's use of presidential power to obstruct congressional legislation surely qualified. But Democrats and other Republicans insisted that an official could be impeached only for violating a criminal statute. Because Johnson had not clearly violated the law and because impeachment seemed so radical a step, most Republicans rejected the idea. The

House voted it down in December 1867, with Stevens, Butler, Boutwell and their supporters denouncing the timidity of their Republican colleagues.

But early in 1868, Johnson did seem to violate a law in open defiance of Congress. Determined to gain control of the army, and in apparent violation of the Tenure of Office law, he fired Secretary of War Edwin M. Stanton, who had sympathized with Congress. Johnson had brought the issue of his power to resist a program he believed unconstitutional to a head. Nearly all the Republicans in the House voted to impeach him.

Angry as most Northerners were at Johnson, many worried about the precedent that impeachment might set. Chief Justice Chase, whom the Constitution required to preside at the impeachment of a president, successfully forced the adoption of procedures suggesting that the Senate took on the character of a court when it tried impeachments. Aided by the chief justice and a large number of cautious Republican senators, Johnson's lawyers were able to slow the proceedings and minimize the seriousness of the charges.

The most extreme of Johnson's lawyers argued that a president could refuse to enforce a law he believed to be unconstitutional, especially if it trenched upon his own powers, as did the Tenure of Office Act. Others made the more modest argument that a president could refuse to enforce such a law in order to bring its constitutionality before the courts. They described the Tenure of Office Act as a congressional invasion of Executive independence. Surely, they insisted, the president must have authority to name a cabinet that reflected his policies and his constitutional and political philosophy.

The House managers effectively rebutted the idea that a president could refuse to enforce any law he believed unconstitutional. They also demonstrated rather convincingly that Johnson had not defied the law in order to secure a court test, but rather to get control of the War Department. But the most important element of the House's case turned out to be surprisingly weak. The House and Senate had disagreed over whether to include the president's cabinet in the Tenure of Office Act. The compromise language left it unclear whether the law covered cabinet officers whom Johnson had held over from Lincoln's administration. One such officer was Stanton. This uncertainty forced the managers to argue that Johnson should be removed for a general pattern of abuse of power. Many Americans feared that conviction on such grounds would leave all future presidents vulnerable to removal whenever they strongly disagreed with Congress. Consequently, Johnson escaped conviction by one vote. Seven Republicans broke ranks to vote not guilty, nearly all on the grounds that Stanton had not been covered by the Tenure of Office Act.

Johnson served out the last few months of his term quietly, in 1869 giving way to Grant, the successful Republican candidate in the presidential election of 1868. The failure of the Johnson impeachment indicates how difficult it is for Congress to control a president who uses his powers to obstruct Congress, especially if he does not clearly break a law. But Johnson came so close to being removed and was so unpopular, that for many years afterward presidents conceded to Congress the sole responsibility for making laws. Despite a few successful exertions of presidential power, not until Theodore Roosevelt became chief executive in 1901 did a president act as forcefully as Lincoln and Johnson had during the Civil War and Reconstruction.

The Failure of Congressional Reconstruction and the Electoral Crisis of 1876

As a result of the Reconstruction laws and the Fifteenth Amendment, African American voters were able to combine with a few white Republicans to elect Republican state governments in the South from 1868 through the mid-1870s. However, most white Southerners were unwilling to accept their legitimacy. They began to try to overthrow them by intimidating Republican officeholders and preventing freedmen from voting. By 1871 organized bands of night riders, many calling themselves the Ku Klux Klan, terrorized parts of the South.

The national government was forced to act. Congress passed the Enforcement Acts of 1870 and 1871 to punish infractions of the Fourteenth and Fifteenth Amendments. It became a criminal offense not only for persons to violate the rights of United States citizens under the color of law, but for private individuals to do so as well. Democrats and some Republicans argued that these laws exceeded Congress's authority, but most Republicans agreed that Congress could protect rights when states failed to do so.

In order to curb the violence, especially during elections, President Grant sent soldiers into the South. The Enforcement Act of 1871, also called the Ku Klux Klan Act or Force Act, temporarily authorized Grant to suspend the privilege of the writ of *habeas corpus* in counties where violence threatened to overwhelm state law enforcement. In several states, fraud and violence led both Republicans and Democrats to claim victory in elections. Each party then appealed to President Grant to recognize and support its claim under the constitutional clause empowering the national government to guarantee republican government in the states. Several Republican state governments remained in power only through such decisions and the willingness of Grant to use troops to enforce them.

Although their goal was to deprive their black neighbors of equal rights, most white Southerners thought of themselves as resisting tyranny. They considered governments elected primarily by black votes to be unrepresentative regimes, sustained by outside power. They viewed the higher taxes they imposed to provide increased public services to be little better than looting white citizens for the benefit of black ones and the corrupt government officials they elected.

By the mid-1870s, the turmoil in the South created an intense reaction in the North against "centralization" of national power and in favor of state rights. This reaction, evidence of corruption in Congress and the Grant administration, as well as an economic depression, led to a big Democratic victory in the congressional elections of 1874. Their power waning, Republicans passed a new Civil Rights Act in 1875, authored by Sumner but passed after his death, barring racial discrimination by individuals and companies that operated transportation facilities, hotels, and places of amusement.

With northern Republicans reluctant to intervene, by 1876 Democrats had retaken control of all but three of the southern states. Democrats ran bitterly racist, violent election campaigns that led to the murders of Republican leaders and the massacres of black Southerners. In the election of 1876, the fraud and violence led to a national crisis. After elections that again were marred by cheating and intimidation, the results were contested in the three remaining Republican states of the South, South Carolina, Louisiana, and Florida. Both Republicans and Democrats sent electoral votes to Congress to be counted. If Congress counted the votes of the Republican electors, the Republican candidate, Rutherford B. Hayes, would win the election, with 185 electoral votes to 184 for the Democratic candidate, Samuel J. Tilden.

Democrats expected the contested electoral votes to be turned over to the House and Senate for consideration, as similarly contested votes had been in 1868. Since the Republicans controlled the Senate and the Democrats controlled the House, Democrats expected Congress to deadlock on which votes to count, leaving neither Hayes nor Tilden with a majority. In that case the Twelfth Amendment authorized the House to select the president, and Tilden would be elected. However, Republicans insisted that the Constitution required the presiding officer of the Senate to count the officially designated electoral votes, which could be rejected only by a vote of both branches of Congress. Thus Hayes would secure the presidency.

After weeks of stalemate, tension, and threats of violence, Republicans and Democrats finally compromised, appointing a special commission to decide which set of electoral votes were entitled to be counted. The decision could be rejected only by the action of both Houses. To the fury of the Democrats, the Electoral Commission decided in favor of Hayes's electors on a party-line vote. Challenging the decision, Democrats in the House prepared to delay the count beyond the constitutional deadline for inaugurating a new president. But a combination of promises by Hayes's supporters and the refusal of moderate Democrats to risk such a dangerous course killed the proposed filibuster, and Hayes was inaugurated.

The electoral-count crisis of 1876 so frightened and angered Americans that most determined finally to put the Reconstruction issue behind them, even if it meant abandoning the South to Democratic control. President Hayes tried to win support for Republicans in the South by ending military intervention and conciliating moderate whites. Without federal government support, the Republicans surrendered their claims to the contested state offices and Democrats established complete control over the southern state governments.

The Supreme Court and the Reconstruction Amendments

Like most Americans, the justices of the Supreme Court wanted to preserve the federal system after the Civil War. As northern voters began to worry about "centralization" in the 1870s, so did they. The majority of the justices were especially concerned that the Fourteenth Amendment could be interpreted to undermine federalism. In passing the Enforcement Acts, Congress had interpreted the Amendment as authorizing Congress to intervene to protect people whenever it believed that the states had failed to do the job. The justices feared that such an interpretation would give the national government virtually unlimited power in areas traditionally under state jurisdiction.

At the same time, people who objected to various state laws began to turn to the courts to overturn them, claiming that they deprived the plaintiffs of rights protected by the Fourteenth Amendment. These were not black Americans suffering from state oppression, but whites who turned to the courts to win public policy fights that they had lost in the state legislatures. The first important Supreme Court case to test the meaning of the Fourteenth Amendment was brought by butchers from New Orleans, who complained that a law requiring them to slaughter animals in a central slaughterhouse deprived them of the privilege of citizens of the United States to work freely in their chosen occupation. They were sustained by Louisiana Democrats who charged that the law was a typical Republican boondoggle for the benefit of the owners of the slaughterhouse. Of course, Republicans had intended the Fourteenth Amendment to protect the rights of all Americans, not only the freed people, but the butchers' case brought home the enormous constitutional implications of the change. The majority of the justices recoiled from them.

In addressing these new issues, the Supreme Court limited the breadth of the Fourteenth Amendment in two ways. First, it defined the terms *privileges and immunities of citizens of the United States* and *due process of law* narrowly. In the *Slaughter-House Cases* (1873), the Court held that state citizenship and national citizenship entailed different rights. The Fourteenth Amendment protected only the rights associated with national citizenship. These national rights were limited in scope and did not include the ordinary day-to-day rights that people possessed by virtue of their state citizenship. If the butchers had a right to follow their occupations freely, it was a right of state citizenship, not a privilege or immunity of United States citizenship. Four of the nine justices dissented. Yet even they wanted no revolution in federalism. Chief Justice Chase and Justice Stephen J. Field, both of whom dissented, strongly sympathized with localism.

The Court continued to interpret the Fourteenth Amendment narrowly in succeeding cases. In *Bradwell v. Illinois* (1873) the Court reiterated that the right to labor in one's chosen calling was a privilege of state rather than of national citizenship; therefore the Fourteenth Amendment did not preclude Illinois from limiting the right to practice law, and presumably other professions, to men. In *Minor v. Happersett* (1875), the Court dashed woman suffragists' hopes that it would agree that political rights were among the privileges of citizenship that states could not abridge. In *Hurtado v. California* (1884), the Court held that the Fourteenth Amendment did not include the specific provisions of the Bill of Rights among the elements of due process. "Due process" referred to more general ideas than the particular proceedings associated with the common law. These decisions led lawyers and judges to conclude that the Bill of Rights continued to apply only against the federal government. By taking this narrow view of the Fourteenth Amendment, the Court avoided becoming a court of last resort to which anyone dissatisfied with state legislation might appeal simply by claiming that his or her rights had been infringed.

Defining the privileges of American citizenship narrowly, the *Slaughter-House Cases* and succeeding decisions limited the scope of the rights that Congress could protect. The Court reinforced these restrictions when it considered laws protecting southern blacks and Republicans from violence. The Enforcement Acts of 1870 and 1871 made it illegal for state officers and private individuals to deny people the rights protected by the Fourteenth and Fifteenth Amendments. But when federal officers brought cases against southern mobs, the Court—influenced especially by Justice Joseph P. Bradley and a new chief justice, Morrison R. Waite, both of whom held circuit courts in the Deep South—carefully circumscribed national power. It insisted that laws and indictments specify that voting frauds and violence were motivated by the race of the victims; it denied that the rights listed in the Bill of Rights were necessarily privileges of United States citizenship; and it held that deprivation of due process of law referred only to state acts, not to those perpetrated by private citizens.

In the *Civil Rights Cases* (1883), Bradley's Court opinion enunciated the "state action doctrine," the second way the Court limited the scope of the Fourteenth Amendment. The cases involved the refusal of theaters, including the New York Grand Opera, to seat African Americans in the elite "dress circle," as well as a railroad's refusal to allow an African American woman into the car reserved for "ladies." Federal officers prosecuted the theaters for violating the Civil Rights Act of 1875, while the offended woman's husband sued the railroad. The Civil Rights Act was extremely controversial. Many lower-court judges had refused to enforce it, while others had sustained it. Federal officials and African American leaders watched the Supreme Court's proceedings anxiously.

The Court ruled the accommodations sections of the Civil Rights Act of 1875 unconstitutional. The justices held that the Fourteenth Amendment protected people only against violations of rights undertaken by states or state officers, not against actions by private individuals. Only one justice dissented. John Marshall

Harlan, a former Kentucky slaveholder who had converted to Republicanism after the Civil War, argued that such racial discrimination constituted a "badge of servitude" that Congress was authorized to prevent under the Thirteenth Amendment, which did not refer to state action. But although it did accept the idea that Congress could eliminate "badges of servitude" under the Thirteenth Amendment, the majority denied that "mere" social discrimination constituted such a symbol. Not only did the Court limit the enforcement of the Fourteenth Amendment to state actions, but its view that "social discrimination" did not affect fundamental rights suggested that it might tolerate state-enforced segregation.

The Supreme Court rulings demoralized federal law-enforcement officials in the South and made convictions difficult. But the Chase and Waite Courts never accepted the extreme state-rights interpretation of the Fourteenth and Fifteenth Amendments advocated by Democratic lawyers and by Justice Field. This interpretation would have denied Congress almost any power to enforce the amendments, leaving enforcement to the courts alone. The Court sustained the government's power to punish private, race-motivated violations of voting rights in state elections; upheld broad congressional power to punish all violations of voting rights in federal elections; and confirmed convictions of state officials for voting fraud, rejecting state-rights arguments that such convictions impaired state independence. The laws that remained on the books still provide the basis for federal prosecutions of many civil rights violations today.

Racial Segregation and Disfranchisement

The decisions of the 1870s and 1880s made it difficult for the national government to protect the rights of its citizens, but after 1896, the Court made the situation even worse. In the famous case of *Plessy v. Ferguson* (1896), the Supreme Court confirmed the implication of the Civil Rights Cases. It held that states did not violate the Fourteenth Amendment by requiring segregation of the races in facilities serving the public. With few justices remaining from the Civil War era, the Court established the Separate but Equal doctrine: As long as the separate facilities provided for each race were generally equal, segregation did not violate the Equal Protection Clause of the Fourteenth Amendment. Not only did this rule apply to transportation facilities, which were at issue in the case, but to all public institutions, including schools.

Once again Justice Harlan disagreed. Using the pen with which Chief Justice Taney had prepared his tragic *Dred Scott* opinion, Harlan delivered an inspired dissent. The Separate But Equal Doctrine was but a "thin disguise" for racial discrimination, he wrote, inconsistent with the Fourteenth Amendment: "[T]here is in this country no superior, dominant, ruling class of citizens. . . . Our Constitution is color-blind, and neither knows nor tolerates classes among its citizens." Although the Supreme Court sustained segregation on the principle that racially segregated state facilities must be equal, Harlan knew that white Southerners had no intention of creating a separate-but-equal society. They intended to maintain white supremacy, a system in which black people were kept subordinate to whites in all aspects of life.

Freed from the threat of federal intervention, the southern states changed their constitutions and laws to make it extremely difficult for black Southerners to register to vote. For example they required all voters to pay a "poll tax." The amount of the tax was small, but any tax was a burden for the many African Americans in the South who lived in poverty. State officials, hoping to reduce the number of black voters, discouraged African Americans from paying it, while the Democratic party often paid the tax for white voters. Southern states also established literacy tests. These tests were administered in a discriminatory way by the white officials in charge of voter registration. In addition, several states passed "grandfather clauses" exempting people whose ancestors had voted in 1867, before African Americans were enfranchised, from the tests. In several states, the Democratic party restricted participation in primary elections to whites. Since Democrats controlled nearly every southern state, this practice effectively eliminated African American influence from the electoral process. Finally, black Southerners who persisted in voting faced violence that was condoned by state and local officials.

In 1890 Republicans mounted one, last effort to pass federal laws to secure the right to vote in the South. When they failed, white Southerners felt free to incorporate provisions into their state constitutions that enabled white voting registrars to disfranchise black voters, and most southern states did so in a wave of constitutional reforms in the 1890s and 1900s. These policies reduced the number of black voters in all the southern and border states. In the Deep South (South Carolina, Georgia, Alabama, Mississippi, and Louisiana) fewer than 5 percent of black voters remained on the voting rolls. As a result, black officeholders disappeared. Even where African Americans made up overwhelming majorities of the local population, they were governed entirely by white people.

In *Williams v. Mississippi* (1898), the Supreme Court accepted these measures, refusing to rule them unconstitutional as long as they did not openly discriminate on the basis of race. Since jurors were chosen from the voting lists, African Americans disappeared from juries as well. The law-enforcement system was thus entirely in the hands of whites, who used it to maintain white supremacy. African Americans were systematically oppressed and exploited and were unable to speak or organize politically in protest.

With white Southerners controlling all the political power, government officials inevitably spent more money on white public facilities than on black ones. Segregated public facilities were anything but equal, with black schools, state hospitals, prisons, and transportation underfinanced and poorly administered. Black sections of local communities often received hardly any public services. Streets remained unpaved and unlit; communities often went without sewers, sometimes without running water and, in later years, without electricity. In *Cumming v. School Board of Richmond County* (1899), the Supreme Court decided not to challenge such discriminations. Upholding a school board's right to provide a high school for white students but not for black ones, the Court held that local officials could make such "reasonable" decisions.

In the 1890s southern states also began to pass laws excluding African Americans from any facility or business that served white people, unless the two races were physically separated, no matter what the feelings of the people affected. Even people who wanted to serve both races equally were forbidden from doing so. As a result, businesses that served the black community were often shabby and underfinanced. They often exploited their customers with high prices and poor service. The Supreme Court upheld the constitutionality of these exclusionary laws in *Berea College v. Kentucky* (1908), sustaining a law forcing the integrated college to expel either its white or black students. The college administration reluctantly expelled the black students because it had more white students and because more of the whites could afford to pay.

At the same time southern states tightened the legal definition of *whiteness,* adopting the "one-drop" rule that any black ancestry, no matter how remote, defined one as African American. As a result people who had been legally married now were violating laws banning interracial unions; children were forced from white schools to black ones.

White supremacy dictated that black people be kept subordinate in all aspects of life. Although many northern states had responded to the *Civil Rights Cases* by passing civil rights laws of their own, racism revived in many parts of the North as well, especially as poor southern African Americans migrated northwards in the 1890s. A black Southerner could not challenge a white person's word or business practices; he ran a serious risk if he resisted even a physical attack, much less a verbal one. In the South and in many parts of the North, no black person could be placed in a position of authority over a white one, precluding African Americans from holding positions in police forces, government offices, as military officers, or in supervisory positions in any business. In many parts of the country, white workers refused to work on terms of equality with blacks, so that black workers were forced to do only the menial jobs that whites scorned. As labor unions grew stronger, they enforced this policy. Few employers ever resisted it, preferring to threaten to bring in black workers to break strikes rather than to employ them as equals.

By the 1920s, segregation spread to every aspect of life in the South and to many aspects of life in the North. Separate, unequal public facilities served black people throughout the South, the border states, and in parts of many northern states. Such discrimination did encourage African Americans to establish their own businesses and institutions, which in turn could instill pride and enable some to achieve a degree of economic security. They resisted the system where possible, especially by demanding the formal equality that separate but equal was supposed to provide. Black plaintiffs often were successful in suing businesses that failed to meet that requirement. But despite such small victories, African Americans suffered from racial discrimination everywhere.

TIMELINE

1864	President Abraham Lincoln kills the Wade-Davis Reconstruction Act with a "pocket veto."
1865	The Confederate armies surrender.
	Lincoln assassinated; Andrew Johnson becomes president.
	President Johnson promulgates his plan to restore civil government in the former Confederate states.
	States ratify the Thirteenth Amendment abolishing slavery.
1865–1866	Southern states pass the "Black Codes."
1866	Congress refuses to seat congressmen from former Confederate states.
	The Civil Rights Act of 1866 passed over President Johnson's veto.
	Congress proposes the Fourteenth Amendment.
1867	Congress passes the Reconstruction Acts over President Johnson's veto.
	Congress passes the Tenure of Office Act over President Johnson's veto.
	The first impeachment resolution is defeated in the House of Representatives.
1868	President Johnson removes Secretary of War Edwin M. Stanton in apparent violation of the terms of the Tenure of Office Act.
	The House of Representatives impeaches President Johnson.
	Ratification of the Fourteenth Amendment.
	Congress restores most former Confederate states to normal relations in the Union.
	President Johnson acquitted of impeachment charges.
	Ulysses S. Grant elected president.
1869	Congress proposes the Fifteenth Amendment.
	In *Texas v. White*, the Supreme Court says the United States is "an indestructible Union . . . of indestructible states."
1870	Ratification of the Fifteenth Amendment.
1870–1871	Ku Klux Klan violence in the South.

1871	Congress passes the Enforcement (Ku Klux Klan) Act.
1873	The Supreme Court defines the Fourteenth Amendment's Privileges and Immunities Clause narrowly in the *Slaughter-House Cases*.
	The Supreme Court permits states to bar women from practicing law in *Bradwell v. Illinois*.
1874	Democrats win control of the House of Representatives in elections of 1874.
1875	The Supreme Court rules that voting is not among the privileges and immunities of citizenship in *Minor v. Happersett*, dashing the hopes of woman suffragists to secure the vote under the Fourteenth Amendment.
	Congress passes Civil Rights Act of 1875.
1876	Contested presidential election of 1876.
1877	Republican candidate Rutherford B. Hayes declared the winner of the election of 1876 and inaugurated.
	President Hayes ends federal protection of Republican state governments; Democrats take control of the last former Confederate states.
1883	The Supreme Court rules the accommodations section of the Civil Rights Act of 1875 unconstitutional in the *Civil Rights Cases*.
1890s–1910s	Southern states and some northern localities institute racial segregation.
1896	The Supreme Court rules "separate-but-equal" racial segregation constitutional in *Plessy v. Ferguson*.

FURTHER READING

Early histories of Reconstruction severely criticized Republicans. The most readable and trenchant example is Claude G. Bowers, *The Tragic Era* (1929). Compare it to the present standard history, Eric Foner's *Reconstruction* (1988). Claudine L. Ferrell's *Reconstruction* (2003) incorporates recent historiography into its concise account. For Reconstruction from black Southerners' perspective, see part two of Stephen Hahn's Pulitzer Prize–winning, *A Nation under Our Feet* (2003). On constitutional issues, compare John W. Burgess, *Reconstruction and the Constitution* (1902) to Harold M. Hyman's dense but polished *A More Perfect Union* (1973). Michael Les Benedict and Robert J. Kaczorowski disagree about the constitutional radicalism of Reconstruction. See Benedict's "Preserving the Constitution: The Conservative Basis of Radical Reconstruction," *Journal of American History* 61 (June 1974): 65–90, and Kaczorowski's "To Begin the Nation Anew: Congress, Citizenship, and Civil Rights after the Civil War," *American Historical Review* 92 (February 1987): 45–68.

While historians like Foner and Kaczorowski tend to see Reconstruction as a failed revolution, legal scholars Bruce Ackerman and Akhil Reed Amar see the Civil War and

Reconstruction as precipitating a permanent, radical transformation in the nature of the Union and the conception of rights. See Ackerman's *We the People, 2: Transformations* (1998) and Amar's *The Bill of Rights: Creation and Reconstruction* (1998). Earl M. Maltz offers a far more conservative interpretation in *Civil Rights, the Constitution, and Congress* (1990). For the framing and enforcement of the Fifteenth Amendment, see Xi Wang, *The Trial of Democracy* (1997). Benedict reflects the modern understanding of Reconstruction in his *The Impeachment and Trial of Andrew Johnson* (1973). Chester G. Hearn's sympathetic account of Johnson's travails, *The Impeachment of Andrew Johnson* (2000) reflects the older view. Keith E. Whittington's essay on the Johnson impeachment in *Constitutional Construction* (1999) provides the best analysis of its deeper meaning for congressional-presidential relations.

For the relations between the Republicans and the Supreme Court and important changes in federal court jurisdiction during Reconstruction, consult Stanley I. Kutler, *Judicial Power and Reconstruction Politics* (1968), and William M. Wiecek, "The Reconstruction of Judicial Power, 1863–1875," *American Journal of Legal History* 13 (October 1969): 333–359. Kaczorowski accuses the Supreme Court of gutting Reconstruction-Era legislation in *The Politics of Judicial Interpretation* (1985). That remains the dominant view, expressed in such works as Frank J. Scaturro's scathing *The Supreme Court's Retreat from Reconstruction* (2000). Benedict offers a less critical interpretation in "Preserving Federalism: Reconstruction and the Waite Court," *Supreme Court Review* 1978: 39–79. Robert M. Goldman tells the story of the enforcement of Reconstruction-Era laws protecting political rights elegantly in *Reconstruction and Black Suffrage* (2001).

William H. Rehnquist's *Centennial Crisis* (2004) summarizes the crisis over the disputed presidential election of 1876, but it must be augmented by the work of academic scholars, such as Charles Fairman's *Five Justices and the Electoral Commission of 1877* (1988).

C. Vann Woodward ruminates on the origins of segregation in *The Strange Career of Jim Crow* (1955). Charles A. Lofgren indicates that the separate but equal doctrine was widely articulated before *Plessy v. Ferguson* in *The Plessy Case* (1987). In *Recasting American Liberty* (2001), Barbara Welke points out that the doctrine originally was used to guarantee equal accommodations to African Americans rather than to discriminate against them. For the drive to disfranchise African Americans in the South, see Michael Perman, *Struggle for Mastery* (2001). Leon F. Litwack's *Trouble in Mind* (1998) is a comprehensive overview of black life in the segregation era.

Sandra VanBurkleo describes "The Civil War Settlement" regarding women's constitutional rights in chapter 7 of *"Belonging to the World"* (2001). Amy Dru Stanley's "Conjugal Bonds and Wage Labor," *Journal of American History* 75 (September 1988): 471–500, compares African American and women's rights during Reconstruction, while Ellen Carol Dubois' *Feminism and Suffrage: The Emergence of an Independent Women's Movement in America* (1975) discusses the relationship between feminists and Republicans during Reconstruction.

11

The Industrial State, Laissez-Faire Constitutionalism, and State Rights

The second half of the nineteenth century witnessed a remarkable burst of entrepreneurial energy that created the modern industrial state, launching the United States on the course that would make it the most prosperous nation in history. Bringing a previously unimaginable range of goods within the reach of ordinary people, the economic revolution also challenged American egalitarianism, raising fundamental issues of the distribution of wealth and power. The transition caused hardship everywhere, but especially in the South and West. It reduced the proportion of skilled artisans in the workforce and created a huge class of unskilled factory workers, laboring under poor conditions for long hours and low pay. It fostered the growth of festering slums racked by crime and disease. It led to concentrations of economic power that overwhelmed the ability of ordinary individuals to control their destinies.

When reformers tried to secure legislation to counteract the effects of economic change, they ran into the ideology of laissez faire, the conviction that government only stunted prosperity when it tried to interfere with the natural laws that governed economic life. An entrenched sister ideology was laissez-faire constitutionalism, which called on judges to guard vigilantly against "class legislation"—laws that benefited particular groups instead of the community as a whole.

Laissez-faire constitutionalism was sustained by the moral convictions of the Victorian age, which held poverty to be a punishment for vice, laziness, self-indulgence, and other sins. Not only did laissez-faire constitutionalism guard against the use of government to reward the undeserving, but Victorian moralism called upon the state to foster morality. The courts' endorsement of laissez-faire constitutionalism in the 1880s and 1890s led reformers to see the judges as allies of the powerful economic interests that opposed much-needed change.

The Industrial State

The economic system that emerged in the last decades of the nineteenth century had many of the elements that characterize the economy today. Government-aided and privately developed railroads, river shipping, telegraphs, and telephones created a national transportation and communications network, as small transportation and communications companies consolidated into large ones that spanned the continent. This transportation and communications revolution created a national market for goods that slowly created national competition among producers. As never before, events in one part of the nation affected business owners and farmers in other parts. Fewer and fewer producers remained isolated in remote areas of the West and South.

The need to compete in a national market encouraged mechanization of the production process in one industry after another, because companies using large-scale production techniques could sell goods more cheaply than those that continued small production by hand. Improved transportation made it possible for large companies in, say, Connecticut to sell goods more cheaply in California than could small manufacturers in San Francisco. These changes in turn led to the concentration of economic and political power. Larger companies either absorbed smaller ones or drove them out of business. The owners and managers of these large companies exercised greater influence on economic and political life than the owners of smaller businesses had been able to exert. As companies grew larger, there were fewer of them in any one industry. The growing concentration of industry made it possible for the leaders in an industry to know each other, and to cooperate to control the market. As the first well-organized economic interests, big businesses were able to exercise more control over their markets and more influence over government than poorly organized or unorganized groups like farmers, workers, and consumers. The ability of big businesses to control prices and wages contradicted most Americans' ideas about how the economic and political system should work. Most Americans believed in free competition among many employers and producers. Free competition in an open market would lead to the highest wages, lowest prices, and best products. They were dismayed as big businesses began to cooperate to close markets and reduce competition.

The development of mass production led to a steady decline in the prices of goods between 1865 and 1900, a trend encouraged by government policies to be discussed below. This deflationary trend—that is, the increasing value of each dollar—benefited Americans as consumers, fostering a "consumer revolution" that soon complemented the Industrial Revolution, but it damaged businesses that could not increase production to make up for lower prices.

The changes also led to the economic domination of the country by the urban, financial centers of the northeastern United States and elsewhere, such as Chicago in the Midwest and San Francisco on the West Coast. The banks in these financial centers provided low-interest loans to large businesses, encouraging economic development, but the South and most of the West lagged behind. Farmers and business owners there had to import capital from the dominant regions; the interest on the loans went back to the Northeast and to the financial centers. To make matters worse, the national government relied on high tariffs for its revenue. The tariffs protected the industries of the already dominant Northeast at the expense of the other regions, whose residents had to pay higher prices for both American and imported goods.

Labor and the Industrial State

The new economic system caused a crisis in the American labor market. Wages were based on "supply and demand"—that is, the number of workers available compared to the number of jobs that employers needed to fill. Before the mechanization of industry, production required highly skilled workers; such people were in short supply and commanded high wages. They owned their own tools and moved freely from job to job. Many expected to become master craftsmen, employing other skilled workers like themselves. If such perceptions romanticized reality, they were tenaciously held nonetheless.

The mechanization of production eroded the world of the skilled workers, who now could be replaced by semi-skilled or unskilled workers. From the 1880s to the 1920s, millions of poor, unskilled immigrants poured into American cities from Europe and from rural areas of the United States to take factory jobs. Strong downward pressure on wages and working conditions resulted; skilled workers lost their independence; the idea that an artisan could progress from employee to employer faded. Worse, factories were dangerous. The number of industrial accidents soared, in an age when an injury could destroy a family's economic security.

In response to these changes, skilled workers began to organize labor unions. These unions organized nationally into the Knights of Labor, strong in the 1880s, and the American Federation of Labor, which grew as the Knights declined in the 1890s. Besides legislation to improve wages and working conditions, the unions' most effective weapon was the strike. For strikes to be successful, the striking workers had to prevent employers from replacing them. However, the law reflected the traditional view that although workers had the right to refuse to work, they had no right to prevent others from working under the terms that they had rejected. It was against the law to interfere with new employees entering the workplace, and efforts to do so led to the arrest of strikers and often to violent clashes between them and the police.

Because the law put such obstacles in the way of strikes and other labor actions, labor organizations and their sympathizers turned to political action. Some turned to the doctrines of socialism, with the most radical seeking to overthrow the capitalist state. More moderate labor leaders called upon the state and federal governments to help workers in a variety of ways. They pressed lawmakers to repeal laws that made it difficult to organize unions and strikes; they urged new laws friendly to workers' interests to replace anti-labor common-law rules developed in the courts, especially those that made it difficult for injured workers to seek compensation from employers. They called for laws limiting working hours to eight hours per day and six days per week, and for laws to require safe and healthy working conditions. They asked legislators to require employers to pay them in United States currency, rather than scrip good only at company stores.

By the 1890s labor organizations began to call for laws to establish minimum wages and to require equal pay for women, in part to prevent male workers from having to compete with lower-paid female workers. For the same reason, the unions called for laws outlawing child labor. They urged Congress to restrict immigration in order to reduce the number of workers competing for jobs, and they worked for legal changes to make it more difficult for employers to replace striking workers.

Farmers and the Industrial State

The new economic system also caused a crisis for American farmers and for the small towns that relied on them for their own prosperity. The concentration of food processing in the hands of a few large companies made it possible for them to cooperate to reduce the prices they paid farmers for their crops. The concentration of the ownership of railroads and storage facilities in a few big companies enabled them to demand higher prices for transporting and storing farm produce. At the same time, the transportation revolution led to an increased supply of farm products around the world, driving down the prices of American agricultural goods.

The farmers' situation was made worse by the government's policy of reducing the money supply. Between 1875 and 1879, the government withdrew from circulation all the paper money left over from the Civil War, limiting the currency to gold and a small amount of silver. This deflationary policy increased the value of the dollar, further reducing already low prices.

Farmers who had borrowed money to buy land in the previous decades were especially hurt, because they had bought their property when prices were high but had to repay their loans when prices were low and money scarce. Furthermore, farmers generally borrowed money to finance the planting of their crops. Those in the South and West had to pay higher interest rates, because their banks were forced to import capital from the currency-rich Northeast. Consequently farmers' advocates, like labor reformers, called on the government for help. They called on the state and federal governments to regulate prices charged by railroads and warehouses and break up the big railroad companies. They urged the government to replace the protective tariff, which helped the Northeast at the expense of the South and West, with an income tax, which would fall more heavily on the wealthier regions. They supported "free banking," which they hoped would lead to a more even distribution of banking facilities and currency. Most of all, they demanded that the national government put more money into circulation—to "inflate" the currency—so that prices would go up and they could repay their loans more easily. After large amounts of silver were discovered in the western United States, they demanded that it be freely coined as money along with gold, instead of being coined in only small amounts.

Small Business Owners and the Industrial State

Many small business owners also complained about the consequences of the new economic system. Although many benefited from the increased prosperity that development brought to the industrializing parts of the country, the government's deflationary policies made it expensive to borrow money to start new businesses or increase the size of old ones, especially in the capital-starved South and West. This helped big companies, whose financial resources enabled them to undersell new competitors, to prevent new businesses from entering the market. They also used their influence to prevent customers from buying or shipping their competitors' goods. Therefore many small business owners in the West and South joined the calls upon the state and federal governments to regulate unfair business practices and to inflate the currency.

Laissez Faire

State legislators tended to be sympathetic to such reforms, in part because the demand was widespread among voters. The proposals were more divisive in Congress, because they would benefit the South and West at the expense of the Atlantic and northeastern states and because police-power regulations had generally been left to the states.

Despite widespread support, demands for government action met determined and often successful opposition from big businesses, bankers, and employers. But it was not their political influence alone that enabled these interests to prevent such laws from passing. They appealed to the powerful principle of "laissez faire"—the doctrine that government should not interfere in the economy—in which many Americans, especially leading opinion makers, such as journalists, college professors, writers, and clergymen, believed.

There were two arguments for "laissez faire." The first was economic. Its advocates argued that when allowed free play, natural economic laws, especially the law of "supply and demand," led to the most efficient use of resources. As long as people were free to enter any business they wished and to make contracts to buy and sell goods and services, they would produce the goods that people wanted and that they were best equipped to provide. Government interference only distorted the operation of these laws, leading to inefficient use of resources and reducing prosperity.

In the opinion of laissez-faire economists, a society's prosperity was the sum of the prosperity of each of its members. Any society would be most prosperous when its members were free to maximize the benefits they could secure through their own efforts. People should be free to make their own decisions about how to improve their lives and to make any agreement that they thought was to their advantage, as long as they did not deprive third parties of similar rights. The right freely to make contracts was a central principle of laissez-faire ideology.

Of course, such ideas were inconsistent with traditional limitations imposed on women, who were still barred from making a variety of contracts. Reformers harnessed the principle of "freedom of contract" to argue that women should be freed of such restrictions. However, old ideas remained strong. Women only slowly were granted the same freedom to enter agreements as men. Various professions, such as law and medicine, remained mostly closed to them. Nonetheless, progress, though gradual, was steady.

The second argument for laissez faire was essentially moral. People who advocated laissez faire believed that the value of everything was determined by supply and demand. Whatever price people agreed upon in a free bargain was a fair price. The "price" did not have to be in money. For workers, especially, the "price" of their labor was not only their wages but their working conditions, the number of hours they worked, and the way in which they were paid. A law changing any of these elements would interfere with the free bargaining of the parties.

To those who believed in laissez faire, such governmental interference was a kind of theft because it changed the outcome of a free and fair bargain for the benefit of one of the parties and to the detriment of the other. Laissez-faire ideologues, like the influential American sociologist William Graham Sumner and the British philosopher Herbert Spencer, warned that those who wanted to get special benefits would seek to gain control of government to accomplish their nefarious ends. In aristocratic countries, it was the few who sought such power. In democratic governments, it was the many.

A role for government did exist in a laissez-faire system, however. The system could work only if the government protected the right of everyone to bargain freely. Therefore both court decisions and legislation made it illegal for one company to try to prevent another from entering its business or for two companies to conspire together to control the supply of goods. Similarly, the common law considered it illegal for a group of workers to conspire to prevent other workers from offering to work at their jobs for less money. The courts of some jurisdictions considered such interferences criminal. In nearly every jurisdiction, workers and unions that engaged in such activities were held liable for damages to the businesses affected. During the 1880s and 1890s, judges issued labor injunctions, ordering striking workers to desist from interfering with newly hired replacements, blocking entrances to workplaces, or interfering with businesses in any other way. If unions defied the injunctions, judges ordered their enforcement by local police forces. Companies themselves sometimes hired professional strikebreakers to enforce the orders. In a few instances of serious violence, state militias and even federal troops were called in to break the strikes.

Most Americans blamed such violence on workers, and especially on those radicals who accepted socialism and anarchism (the doctrine that government was inherently oppressive and should be eliminated). Many states passed "anti-syndicalism laws," making it illegal to advocate resistance to lawful authority. Courts agreed that individuals could be punished for membership in organizations that encouraged resistance to law, or for giving speeches and publishing language that tended to encourage such resistance, even if they did not directly advocate it or engage in it. After the famous Haymarket Riot of 1886 in Chicago, where a labor rally exploded in violence, the meeting's organizers and speakers were sentenced to death on the argument that they must have known that their actions might lead to bloodshed.

Victorian Morality, Censorship, and Intolerance

The acceptance of what legal scholars now call the Bad Tendency Test of free speech was part of a general movement towards censorship and intolerance in the late-nineteenth century. Nineteenth-century Americans believed that social problems such as crime, immorality, and poverty resulted from individuals' moral shortcomings. Therefore the public welfare obligated government to try to create an environment that encouraged what historians call "Victorian morality." Public schools taught the virtues of hard work, thrift, and self-control. Most required Bible reading and prayers. The courts upheld the constitutionality of such religious activities on the grounds that they served the secular purpose of instilling morality and public virtue. The state and federal governments sponsored chaplains and religious training in prisons; states did the same in orphanages. Legislative sessions opened with prayers, both in the state capitals and Washington, D. C. Governors and presidents proclaimed days of thanksgiving and prayer. Religious symbols decorated statehouses and other public places.

Until the Civil War, many states still punished blasphemy. Later in the nineteenth century, people who publicly blasphemed God or religion often were prosecuted for "disturbing the peace." Many states and localities encouraged observation of the Sabbath by forbidding business, recreation, and the sale of liquor on Sundays. When Jews, who observed a different Sabbath, and others protested, most state courts justified these "blue laws" on secular grounds as encouraging rest and time for self-improvement. But some courts frankly acknowledged the centrality of Christianity to American concepts of morality. In 1892 the Supreme Court encouraged this sentiment. Citing the long history of government support for religious institutions, public prayer, the pervasiveness of Christian organizations and charities, and old court cases declaring Christianity part of the common law, the Court declared that the United States "is a Christian nation."[*] In response to criticisms of such doctrines, and especially in reaction to a few state court cases that called for greater separation of church and state, a strong movement grew in favor of amending the Constitution to recognize formally the primacy of Christianity in the nation. Closely linked to efforts to promote Christianity was a growing anti-vice movement, which led to the outlawing of gambling and prostitution and to the suppression of polygamous marriage among Mormons.

The anti-vice movement was fostered by a long-standing belief that a shadowy underworld of gambling, drinking, prostitution, and other vices existed in the cities. This *demi-monde* challenged family and church for the allegiance of young men. Originally identified with New York, it was spreading its influence into the American heartland through racy novels, periodicals, and advertisements, abetted by the transportation and communications revolution. Exciting even more concern was a growing scientific reform literature urging greater sexual freedom and control over pregnancy to improve physical and mental health.

The anti-vice movement took a number of forms. A drive to prohibit the manufacture and sale of alcoholic beverages gained momentum in the 1870s; by the 1880s and 1890s many states enacted Prohibition. A strong censorship movement also developed. In 1873 the anti-vice crusader Anthony Comstock persuaded Congress to pass the "Comstock law," making it illegal to import, transport, or mail pornography or any "article of indecent or immoral nature, or any article of medicine . . . for causing abortion," unless prescribed by a doctor "in good faith." Many states passed "little Comstock laws," making it illegal to produce or sell pornography, contraceptives, or abortion devices.

Prosecutors defined pornography under the Comstock laws extremely broadly. Local governments barred not only sexually explicit literature, photographs, and art, but often clearly artistic handling of nudity and sex as well. Comstock laws were utilized not only to prosecute utopian advocates of free love and critics of marriage but advocates of birth control, abortion, and sex education. The Comstock laws became weapons not only against pornography but against challenges to conventional Victorian ideas about the role of women and the nature of human sexuality. Victims of the Comstock laws charged that the statutes violated freedom of speech and the press. But judges upheld convictions on the grounds that such publications tended to corrupt the young, who needed special protection from the blandishments of immorality.

The federal crusade against Mormon polygamy reflected similar concerns with sexuality. The founders of Mormonism believed that they had been divinely instructed to emulate the polygamous patriarchal households of the Old Testament. Despite the apparent support for polygamy among Mormon women, most

---

[*]The case was *Holy Trinity Church v. U.S.* (1892). In it the Court ruled that the federal anti-contract labor law, which barred any person or organization from paying the cost of transporting an employee to the United States, could not have been intended to cover religious organizations.

Americans considered the practice akin to slavery and an outrage upon sexual propriety. Congress refused to grant statehood to Utah as long as its Mormon majority condoned it. Outlawing polygamy in all United States territories, from the mid-1870s through the 1880s the government pursued polygamists with grim determination, rounding up hundreds at a time and depriving Mormons of the right to vote in territorial elections. Mormons stubbornly resisted, but they finally gave in when Congress threatened to outlaw the Church itself and seize its property. A new revelation convinced Mormon leaders to forbid polygamy (and disrupted thousands of Mormon families).

The assault on polygamy led to one of the initial challenges to federal action based on the First Amendment's Religious Freedom Clause. In *Reynolds v. U.S.* (1878), jailed Mormons protested that the anti-polygamy law violated their right to exercise their religious beliefs. But the Supreme Court drew a distinction between belief and behavior that remains a key element of First-Amendment law today. Mormons could believe whatever their consciences dictated, the Court ruled, but the First Amendment did not preclude Congress from outlawing behavior that impaired the public interest. The promotion of morals lay well within the traditional scope of the police power, and Congress could exercise that power over the territory and property of the United States.

Women played a leading role in the anti-vice movement. Victorian social ideas made them the guardians of the home and its values of morality, order, harmony, and self-discipline. The saloon stood as the home's great rival for the allegiance of young men, offering the inviting vision of irresponsibility, freedom, sex, and pleasure. Moreover, the vices associated with the barroom and the brothel, which were often intimately connected, directly threatened women. Drunken men were abusive and irresponsible in an age when it was the man's responsibility to provide his family's shelter, food, and comfort.

The activities of such anti-vice organizations as the Women's Christian Temperance Union (WCTU) blurred the line between the private and the public spheres, as did the reform activities of growing numbers of women's clubs. Public policy directly affected the wellbeing of the home, feminists argued. Enfranchising women would strengthen the political forces promoting home values. Frances Willard, long the driving force behind the WCTU, made "home protection" the reformers' slogan. Prohibition and moral reform thus became closely identified with women's suffrage.

To a large degree, the moral behavior that anti-vice crusaders sought to encourage reflected the values of Protestants whose forbears had come to America before the great wave of Irish and German immigration in the 1830s and 1840s. The effort to reinforce traditional Protestant morality after the 1870s intensified in response to a new wave of immigration, largely from southern and eastern Europe. The huge tide of immigration in the decades following 1880 greatly increased the numbers of Roman Catholics in the United States and for the first time led to the presence of a significant number of Jews. Italian, French

Canadian, German, and Irish immigrants objected to Sabbatarian laws and to Prohibition, as well as to the Protestant slant to public education.

As the political influence of Catholics increased, Protestants worried that they might persuade state legislatures to fund Catholic schools or even to take over some public school districts. In 1875 James G. Blaine, a leading candidate for the 1876 Republican presidential nomination, proposed a constitutional amendment barring the use of public money to support sectarian education. What Blaine's amendment really aimed to prevent was government financial support for Catholic schools; its advocates did not intend it to bar Bible reading or nonsectarian prayer. Although Congress never sent the Blaine Amendment to the states for ratification, several states, including New York, added it to their constitutions.

The growing numbers of Jewish and Catholic immigrants fueled a new nativist reaction, linked to quasi-scientific ideas about racial differences that became widely accepted in the United States and Europe. A number of American intellectuals accepted the notion that northern Europeans belonged to a superior racial stock that was hard-working, disciplined, progressive, and alone capable of exercising liberty and democracy. They warned that the United States was losing its Anglo-Saxon character, urged limits on immigration from areas outside northern Europe, and advocated strong measures to "Americanize" immigrants already in the country. Such attitudes reinforced the drive for Prohibition and other moral legislation, which clearly was motivated not only by a commitment to moral reform but also by dislike of immigrant culture. These ideas also reinforced opposition to birth control and abortion, which were more common among middle-class, native-born women than among immigrants. "Scientific" racists worried that the Irish, Jews, and southern and eastern Europeans were out-breeding the native-born population.

Anti-Catholicism, which had been a persistent element of American life for some time was now joined by anti-Semitism. Social clubs and residential neighborhoods openly excluded Catholics and Jews, and anti-Semitic stereotypes became common in literature and journalism. In the 1890s a new anti-Catholic organization, the American Protective Association (APA), expanded dramatically, absorbing many older nativist clubs and secret societies. Members boycotted Catholic merchants, proscribed Catholic workers, and took oaths to vote against Catholic political candidates.

Racism grew stronger in this environment as well. California and Nevada witnessed a series of anti-Chinese riots when white workers, ironically often Irish Catholics, blamed Chinese immigrants for low wages. In the 1870s California workers supported a powerful anti-Chinese political party, led by the labor leader and politician Dennis J. Kearney, that forced the traditional parties to take anti-Chinese positions. State legislatures and local governments in the Far West passed a variety of laws discriminating against Asians. The federal courts overturned much of this legislation as violating the Due Process Clause of the Constitution or conflicting with the federal government's power to regulate immigration. But Congress, pressed by Californians, labor organizations, and racists, acted to stop the immigration of Chinese laborers in the Chinese Exclusion Act of 1882.

In this climate southern states were able to disfranchise their black citizens in the 1890s and 1900s and to institute racial segregation. At the same time, a wave of lynchings swept the South. Strongly affected by growing racism, many, if not most, Republicans acquiesced and even endorsed disfranchisement and segregation. As segregation spread northwards, some cities formally segregated their school systems and other facilities. Others informally encouraged racial segregation, drawing school boundaries to create all-white and all-black schools. Local officials encouraged similar separation of Catholic and Protestant, Jew and Gentile, native-born and immigrant, rich and poor.

At the same time the government altered its policy towards Native Americans. No longer negotiating with Indians as sovereign nations, in the 1860s and 1870s the federal government fought a series of wars to force bitterly resisting Indian nations onto reservations, often unconnected to their homelands. Reformers criticized the reservation policy, insisting that education, allotment of reservation land to individual families, and extension of United States citizenship would enable Native Americans to escape the despair into which reservation life had plunged them. However, "education" meant the suppression of native language and customs and indoctrination into white culture, often by removing children to boarding schools where they would be free of their parents' influence.

In 1887 Congress responded to these calls for reform by passing the Dawes Act, which reformers hailed as "the Indians' Magna Carta." It authorized the president to allot land on Indian reservations to individual Native Americans. To guard against an immediate loss of their land, recipients were precluded from selling their allotments for twenty-five years. All Native Americans who received allotments were declared to be citizens, entitled to the protection of state laws.

While some Native Americans were able to assimilate and improve their lives in accordance with the new individualist regime, the program would prove disastrous for the majority. By extending the jurisdiction of states into the reservations where lands had been allotted, the Dawes Act subjected Indians to the control of governments responsive to the influence of land and resource-hungry westerners. Within forty years, two-thirds of the reservation lands would be lost to Native Americans. Mining, oil, and lumber corporations secured lucrative deals to exploit reservation resources. Most Indians were forced to become sharecroppers or wage earners, suffering high unemployment rates. Subject to the same exploitation and discrimination as other minority groups, unable quickly to adopt alien ways, bereft of native customs and institutions to sustain them, many Indians sank further into poverty and despair.

December 9, 1876

The Ignorant Vote—Honors Are Easy.

In this vicious 1876 cartoon, captioned "The Ignorant Vote,"
Thomas Nast equates African Americans and Irish immigrants
as threats to democracy. Compare the drawing to Nast's
sympathetic characterization of African Americans a decade
earlier, on page 190.

Laissez Faire and "Class Legislation"

Advocates of laissez faire believed that in an economic system free of government
intervention, all people would achieve their potential in life. Those who had talent, worked hard, and exercised self-discipline would succeed; those who lacked
these characteristics would fail. It was natural to believe that the rich had earned
their wealth through hard work and strong character. It was equally logical to
consider poverty the deserved consequence of weak character and incapacity.
Moreover, given the prevalent idea that character was an innate racial characteristic, it seemed reasonable that poverty occurred disproportionately among immigrant groups, Native Americans, and African Americans.

Advocates of laissez faire pointed out that the poor were prone to crime, immorality, and disease, all signs of weak character. To eliminate poverty and the so-

cial problems associated with it, the poor must be encouraged to alter their behavior. If the government tried to reduce poverty simply by equalizing the distribution of wealth, it would reward people who did not deserve success at the expense of those who did. Such an effort was doomed to failure, laissez-faire advocates believed, since the root of poverty was not economic but moral. Worse, the effort would break the natural link between good character and economic success, undermining the moral order. Of course, the community did have a responsibility to those clearly unable to fend for themselves—the injured, the mentally deficient, the decrepit, widows, and deserted wives and children, a categorization that placed many women among the inherently dependent. Payments to them legitimately served the public good. So, perhaps, did pensions for injured and elderly volunteer firefighters, constables, and military veterans. But subsidies to independent businessmen and workers were another thing altogether, no matter the hardship they faced. After the Civil War, advocates of laissez faire perceived an ever growing danger that radicals and demagogues would persuade voters to use their power to redistribute wealth—that is, to secure better economic conditions for themselves than they could get in the free market. Southern and western demands for an increase in the money supply, farmers' demands that the government regulate railroad rates, workers' demands for an eight-hour day, and small business owners' demands that government prevent unfair business practices all exemplified the danger. Even worse was the proposal for an income tax aimed at the wealthy. These ideas were all calls for what advocates of laissez faire called "class legislation"—laws designed to help one group of people at the expense of others. In the opinion of laissez fairists, such "class legislation" violated the rule that government must protect the interests of everyone equally.

Proponents of laissez faire especially opposed "socialism" and "communism," because these doctrines openly urged government action in the interests of the working class against the interests of other classes. Laissez fairists denounced as "socialistic" or "communistic" any government action that would distribute wealth and resources more equally than the free market did. The only equality government could rightfully promote was equality of opportunity. Inequalities in wealth, status, power, and influence were inevitable in a free society. Efforts to reduce or eliminate such differences required the destruction of individual liberty as well. Proposals to intervene on behalf of those suffering under the new economic system were regarded as the result of ignorance compounded by the influence of "foreign" ideologies that had no legitimate place in American life.

The General-Welfare State

Despite the general predominance of laissez-faire ideas among intellectuals and opinion makers, the tradition of using government powers to promote the peoples' welfare persisted. A growing number of reformers argued that the new industrial state had led to such a concentration of economic power that ordinary people could no longer hope to bargain effectively. The results of free-market bargains over wages, railroad rates, and other contracts no longer were fair or even efficient. Big corporations had so much power that they controlled the supply of goods and the demand for labor. Laws that interfered with bargains made under such conditions did not unfairly redistribute resources from the deserving to the undeserving. On the contrary, they protected deserving, hard-working people from unfair exploitation by the rich and powerful. In a complex, closely interconnected world, events beyond individual control often prevented hard-working, able, and moral people from succeeding.

Such a perspective challenged both the idea that poverty was the fault of the poor and that businessmen and wage earners were independent and therefore outside the category of those who could receive public assistance. Immorality, crime, and bad morals did not cause poverty, reformers insisted. It was the other way around: Poverty caused disease, crime, and immorality. Since it was for the good of everyone in the community to combat such social ills, laws designed to reduce poverty were not "class legislation," but on the contrary promoted the general welfare. Such reformers called for the development of a "general-welfare state" that actively used its power to improve the environment of its people rather than relying only on individual action through the free market.

Even before the forces advocating change gathered their full force in the 1890s, farmers, workers, and reformers were strong enough to secure the legislation they wanted in many states, especially in the West, Midwest, and Northeast. Farmers were especially successful because they exerted pressure through new social and political organizations, such as the Patrons of Husbandry, often called "the Grange." In many states they secured the passage of "Granger laws," which established railroad commissions to regulate the charges and practices of shipping companies and grain-storage facilities. Many states also passed laws to protect workers' safety in mines and other dangerous occupations; regulated wages and working hours for women and children, barring them from some industries altogether; and imposed licensing standards on lawyers, doctors, and members of other professions. Localities established health and sanitation commissions, and regulated public utilities. State officials went to court to break up monopolies. Despite the abstract influence of laissez-faire ideas, state and local governments were entering a period of increasing activism. But regulation of the currency supply and banking system, reform of the protective tariff, and reforms affecting interstate commerce were all beyond the effective control of the states. To affect those changes required control of the federal government.

In the 1890s the newly organized People's party, or the "Populists," supported calls for nationwide reform. At the same time, spokesmen for farmers grew stronger in the Democratic party, especially in the West and South. In 1894 the Democrats were able to lower the tariff somewhat and to enact an income tax on those who earned more than $2000 per year. In 1896 southern and western Democrats were able to nominate their candidate, William Jennings Bryan, for president on a platform advocating the free coinage of silver. The Populists nominated Bryan as well, setting the stage for a great struggle in the following presidential campaign. Conservatives believed that they faced a crisis in which radicalism threatened to overthrow traditional American values, while reformers believed that powerful economic interests were struggling to retain control of the American government in order to exploit the people. In the end, Bryan was defeated, and the conservative Republican candidate, William McKinley, was elected president.

Laissez-Faire Constitutionalism

Strongly held among the economic and intellectual elite, laissez-faire ideas affected lawyers and judges. Of particular importance was the conviction that government interferences with prices, wages, and working conditions often amounted to "class legislation." It was easy to argue that by transferring wealth from one group to another, such "class legislation" deprived the losers of their property without due process of law. As early as the 1860s, people appeared in court to demand that such laws be ruled unconstitutional.

The courts had traditionally distinguished between laws appropriately designed for the benefit of the whole community or to aid those unable to take care of themselves, and those that secured illicit special privileges for favored groups or imposed special burdens on disfavored ones. There had always been a general sense that the latter deprived victims of their liberty or property without due process of law. That is, even though the procedures by which the offending law was enforced were fair, the law itself was so flawed that it deprived people of their rights. Lawyers ultimately called this idea "substantive" due process of law. But judges had not usually been rigorous in applying the principle, sustaining states' and localities' exercise of the police power over a wide range of subjects.

At first most courts continued to follow this tolerant pattern. In the *Slaughter-House Cases* (1873), which so limited the scope of the Fourteenth Amendment, the Supreme Court in essence had rejected a claim that the Louisiana law requiring butchers to use a single slaughterhouse was class legislation that deprived them of their privileges as American citizens. In the same case, the Court denied that the law deprived the butchers of rights without due process of law. In cases like *Munn v. Illinois* (1877), the Court upheld Granger legislation that regulated the rates charged by railroads and grain warehouses. Again the Court ruled that the regulations did not deprive the business owners of property without due process of law. Such businesses traditionally were considered to be "affected with a public interest" and therefore subject to regulation. But both decisions drew vigorous dissents from justices such as Stephen J. Field, who wanted the Court to play a more vigilant role.

Although the Supreme Court remained reluctant to disallow allegedly class legislation a number of state courts were less inhibited. They began to rule a variety of state regulations of business and working conditions unconstitutional as violations of the Due Process Clause of the Fourteenth Amendment. Likewise the dissenting Justice Field cooperated with the judges in his circuit to enforce laissez-faire principles in his circuit-court cases. Because such decisions could be appealed to the Supreme Court only if the circuit-court judges disagreed, Field was able to create a body of circuit-court precedents supporting the idea that various regulations of business violated the Fourteenth Amendment's Due Process Clause.

In the 1880s the Supreme Court finally began to accept Field's arguments. The Court started by reviewing state regulations of railroads and other businesses "affected with a public interest" to make certain that the regulations were "reasonable." Soon the justices began to overturn regulations with which they disagreed, ruling them unconstitutional on substantive due-process grounds. An unreasonable regulation violated the Due Process Clause, no matter how fair the procedure by which it was enforced.

As the Populist party and protest movements grew stronger in the 1890s, the Supreme Court moved decisively towards laissez-faire constitutionalism. In the *Income Tax Cases* of 1895, a five-to-four majority ruled the new federal income tax unconstitutional for violating the Constitution's vague prohibition on "direct" taxes. In the same year, it sustained the use of labor injunctions by federal judges in strikes involving interstate commerce, although Congress had passed no law authorizing them. In the key case of *Smyth v. Ames* (1898), the Court unanimously overturned Nebraska's regulation of railroad rates, holding that unreasonably low rates deprived the railroad of property without due process. In *Allgeyer v. Louisiana* (1897), the Court declared that the Due Process Clause protected "liberty of contract." Soon the courts held that freedom of contract could be limited only when the government had compelling reasons to do so.

By accepting the tenets of laissez-faire constitutionalism, the courts did not mean that the state and federal governments were forbidden from enacting any regulations of property or imposing any restrictions upon the right to contract. However, they drew a strict line between those regulations that served the public interest and those that they believed only benefited some special interest. To establish the line, judges drew upon the traditional definition of the "police power," that is, the inherent right of government to regulate private property in order to protect and promote the safety, health, and morals of the community. In the great case *Lochner v. New York* (1905), the Supreme Court explained, "In every case that comes before this court . . . , where legislation of this character is concerned and where the protection of the Federal Constitution is sought, the question necessarily arises: Is this a fair, reasonable and appropriate exercise of the police power of the State, or is it an unreasonable, unnecessary and arbitrary interference with the right of the individual to his personal liberty . . . ?"

This formulation of the Court's responsibility enabled the judges to question the reasonability of every law that interfered with property rights or the right to make a contract. In the *Lochner* case, a majority of the justices concluded that a law limiting the working hours of bakers could not possibly be related to health or safety and was therefore an arbitrary, unconstitutional interference with liberty of contract. Where the courts did find a health, safety, or morals justification for a law, they sustained it. In *Holden v. Hardy* (1898), for example, the Court upheld the constitutionality of a law limiting the working hours of coal miners. The common law traditionally treated mining as a dangerous occupation, and therefore the justices recognized the safety and health benefits of the legislation. Likewise, the courts continued to hold that businesses traditionally "affected with a public interest" were subject to greater regulation than other businesses.

All over the country, state and federal courts reevaluated legislation to see whether it regulated businesses "affected with a public interest" and whether it was reasonably designed to promote the general interest in safety, health, and good morals. The courts sustained most legislation, but ruled many laws unconstitutional, especially legislation designed to help workers and labor unions. The *Lochner* decision became the emblematic example of laissez-faire constitutionalism's mordant concern with "class legislation." In 1908 the great social worker Jane Addams wrote that the one sentiment uniting workers "is a growing distrust of the courts."

The National Economy, Constitutional Nationalism, and State Rights

The development of the national market also created a crisis for federalism. The Supreme Court and most American lawyers had come to accept the principles of constitutional nationalism—the idea that the national government had sovereign, plenary power to act in the areas delegated to it by the Constitution. But the creation of a national market greatly expanded the scope of interstate commerce. From 1789 until the Civil War, most trade had been local. Even goods manufactured out of state were sold by local merchants. The states and not the federal government had made most of the rules that governed the economy. The development of the national market threatened to change this balance of power dramatically, as huge manufacturing corporations began to market their products directly to local merchants or even consumers.

Increasing state regulation raised a problem for the federal system. Businesses that operated across state lines demanded that they be subject to uniform legal rules regarding contracts, liability for injuries and damage, and other legal questions. They complained that local judges and juries were prejudiced against them, and they criticized state and local laws designed to protect local businesses from outside competition.

Such businesses had always received some protection against local prejudice from the provisions of the Constitution and the Judiciary Act of 1789, which permitted them to sue citizens of other states in federal rather than in state courts. In

1875 Congress increased this protection by passing the Judiciary Act of 1875, which permitted out-of-state businesses to remove their cases to federal courts when they were defendants. Furthermore, the act allowed anyone who claimed a right under the Constitution or laws of the United States to bring suits in the federal courts rather than the state courts; it permitted defendants to remove cases to the federal courts if they claimed a similar right. No longer would such cases have to be appealed all the way through the state courts before finally getting to the Supreme Court.

The federal courts proved far more sympathetic to national business interests than local courts did. Although they were supposed to follow state laws in settling legal questions, according to *Swift v. Tyson* (see p. 141) this rule only applied to statutes and not to state judicial precedents. The federal courts established rules about debt collection, corporate liability for injuries and damage, employment, and contract enforcement. These rules were uniform throughout the nation and often inconsistent with state and local regulations. They encouraged economic development by promoting business interests rather than those of consumers, employees, or farmers. The federal courts also overturned state laws protecting small local businesses against big out-of-state competitors, saying such laws violated the Interstate Commerce Clause. The key case establishing the precedent was *Welton v. Missouri* (1876), which overturned a Missouri law requiring a license to sell goods produced outside the state.

But while the federal courts were quick to take jurisdiction over cases involving interstate businesses, they did not want to encourage federal regulation of such businesses. Their attitude reflected that of most Americans, who had already shown during the Reconstruction era that they were uncomfortable with the idea of greatly expanding the power of the national government. Americans had permitted white Southerners to deprive black Southerners of their rights rather than continue the policy of national interference in the southern states. The Supreme Court showed that it shared this concern in cases like *Texas v. White* (1869), *Collector v. Day* (1871), and Reconstruction-era cases that limited the power of the national government to protect the rights of its citizens. In *Twining v. New Jersey* (1908), it reconfirmed that the Due Process Clause of the Fourteenth Amendment did not apply the Bill of Rights to the states. Although the justices abandoned the idea that *none* of the provisions of the Bill of Rights were included in the concept of due process, they held that only the most shocking violations of liberty constituted due-process deprivations. The Court did not want to force uniformity on the states, nor did it want the federal courts to intervene in state law enforcement, except, it seemed, to protect property rights.

However, by the late 1880s and the 1890s, many Americans called on the national government to confront problems arising out of the new national economy. In response, the government began to regulate the economy in new and more vigorous ways. In 1887 Congress created the Interstate Commerce Commission to regulate railroads and steamship lines. In 1890 it passed the Sherman Anti-Trust Act to supplement state monopoly laws by making it illegal to conspire to monopolize interstate commerce. The government also began to use its delegated powers to augment state laws regulating safety, health, and morals. The Comstock law barred pornography from the mail. Congress banned the sale and shipment of lottery tickets through interstate commerce. It levied a heavy tax on the production of oleomargarine colored to look like butter.

In general, the Supreme Court attempted to draw a line distinguishing the federal government's authority over the economy from that of the states. In *U.S. v. E.C. Knight Co.* (1895), it made the distinction between production and commerce. Production was within state jurisdiction, the Court ruled, no matter how it might affect the national economy or that of other states. Therefore the national government could not use the Sherman Anti-Trust Act to break up a company that had gained control of most of the nation's sugar refining. Although the whole country was affected by the monopoly, it was up to the state where the company was located to deal with it. The decision made clear that only the states, not the federal government, could pass laws regulating working conditions and employment on farms, in mines, and in factories.

However, the Supreme Court discerned broad federal power to protect interstate commerce against labor unions. In the same year it decided the *E. C. Knight* case, it decided *In re Debs* (1895), which sustained a contempt-of-court citation against Eugene V. Debs, the leader of the American Railway Union. Debs had refused to obey a federal court order requiring the union to end a boycott of Pullman sleeping cars. The Court had held that the sugar-refining monopoly did not affect interstate commerce directly enough to justify applying the Sherman Anti-Trust Act, but efforts by workers to organize similar industries evidently did. In the so-called *Danbury Hatters* case (1908), the Court found a local labor union liable for damages under the act because it called on people to boycott a company against which it had called a strike. Labor reformers complained that the Court was administering a double standard.

The Supreme Court's laissez-faire, state-rights, and anti-labor decisions angered Americans who favored government action to handle the problems created by the rise of the industrial state. They charged that the Court was sympathetic to powerful corporations and hostile to farm and labor interests. The Populists demanded that Congress take action to curb the power of the Supreme Court. In response, the justices and conservative lawyers became even firmer in their criticism of reformers. As the struggle between advocates of laissez faire and advocates of the general-welfare state intensified, the Supreme Court seemed firmly allied with the former.

TIMELINE

1860s–   Development of a national economy, concentration of business.
1900s

1871   Knights of Labor founded.

Illinois passes the first "Granger law" regulating railroad rates and practices.

1873   The federal Comstock Act bars pornography and birth-control information and devices from the mail and interstate commerce.

In the *Slaughter-House Cases,* the Supreme Court narrowly defines the privileges and immunities of U.S. citizenship.

1875   Congress passes the Resumption Act, providing for the return to the gold standard in 1879.

The Judiciary Act of 1875 broadens jurisdiction of the federal courts.

New York passes a state constitutional amendment (the so-called "Blaine Amendment") barring the use of public money for religious education.

1876   In *Welton v. Missouri,* the Supreme Court rules that state license fees imposed on out-of-state salesmen unconstitutionally impair interstate commerce.

1877   The Supreme Court sustains state regulations of railroad rates and practices in the Granger Cases (*Munn v. Illinois* and others).

1878   In *Reynolds v. U.S.,* the Supreme Court sustains federal enforcement of anti-polygamy laws against Mormons, distinguishing between laws suppressing beliefs and those merely suppressing behavior.

1879   The U.S. returns to specie (gold with some silver) standard.

1880s   States pass anti-syndicalism laws.

1882   Congress passes the Chinese Exclusion Act.

1884   Grover Cleveland elected first Democratic president since 1856.

1886   Haymarket Riot.

1887   Congress passes the Interstate Commerce Act, creating the Interstate Commerce Commission to regulate railroads and other interstate transportation facilities.

Congress passes the Dawes Act, authorizing the president to allot lands on Indian reservations to individual families.

1890s	Decline of the Knights of Labor, rise of the American Federation of Labor.
	Rise and decline of the anti-Catholic American Protective Association.
1890	Congress passes the Sherman Anti-Trust Act.
1892	The Supreme Court declares the United States is "a Christian nation" in *Holy Trinity Church v. U.S.*
	Populists win over 1 million votes in the presidential election of 1892.
1894	Congress reduces tariffs and enacts an income tax.
1895	*U.S. v. E. C. Knight Co.* rules that the Sherman Anti-Trust Act cannot apply to businesses engaged in production rather than interstate transportation.
	The Supreme Court rules the federal income tax unconstitutional in the *Income Tax Cases.*
1896	Republican William McKinley defeats William Jennings Bryan, presidential candidate of both the Democratic party and the Populists.
1897	*Allgeyer v. Louisiana* holds that "liberty of contract" is protected by the Due Process Clause of the Fourteenth Amendment.
1898	*Smyth v. Ames* rules a state law setting railroad rates unconstitutional for denying due process of law in violation of the Fourteenth Amendment.
1905	In *Lochner v. New York,* the Supreme Court rules that a state maximum-working-hour law deprives employers and employees of liberty of contract.

FURTHER READING

The best survey of the so-called Gilded Age period (circa 1865–1900) is Mark Walhlgren Summers's engaging *The Gilded Age* (1997). Maury Klein's *The Flowering of the Third America* (1993) is a more traditional consideration of change from the 1850s to 1920 . Samuel P. Hayes's *The Response to Industrialism* (2d ed., 1995) and Robert H. Weibe's *The Search for Order* (1967) are classic brief overviews that limn the challenges that the rise of the industrial state posed for American society. The best comprehensive study of government in the Gilded Age is Morton J. Keller's outstanding synthesis, *Affairs of State* (1977). Stephen Skowronek, *Building A New American State* (1982), a classic of the political-science literature, sees the whole period of 1877 through 1920 as a time of transition to modern American government. Elizabeth Sanders's *Roots of Reform* (1999) offers an economic interest–oriented interpretation from the perspective of the agricultural periphery. Charles W. Calhoun (ed.) in *The Gilded Age* (1996; 2d ed., forthcoming) presents the latest historical interpretations.

Loren Beth's dated *The Development of the American Constitution, 1877–1917* (1971) is still the standard constitutional survey of the Gilded Age and Progressive Era. Nancy Cohen's *The Reconstruction of American Liberalism* (2002) is an excellent account of the rise of laissez-faire thought in the United States.

For an excellent brief overview of Victorian moralism and its shadowy antithesis in America, read the first chapter of Kevin White, *Sexual Liberation or Sexual License?* (2000). For a brief discussion of its constitutional impact, see Michael Les Benedict, "Victorian Moralism and Civil Liberty and the Nineteenth-Century United States," in *The Constitution, Law, and American Life*, ed. Donald G. Nieman (1992), 91–122. Gaines M. Foster describes agitation for federal morals legislation on a number of areas in *Moral Reconstruction* (2002), while Wayne E. Fuller concentrates on *Morality and the Mail in Nineteenth Century America* (2003). Helen Lefkowitz Horowitz offers a fascinating account of the struggle to control sexual discourse in the nineteenth century in *Rereading Sex* (2002). Alison M. Parker describes the role of women in promoting censorship in *Purifying America* (1997). Kenneth David Driggs surveys "The Mormon Church–State Confrontation in Nineteenth-Century America," *Journal of Church and State* 30 (Spring 1988): 273–289. Sarah Barringer Gordon's *The Mormon Question* (2002) is a fuller discussion.

John Higham describes late-nineteenth-century nativism in his classic *Strangers in the Land* (2d ed., 1988). For the growth of racism in the late-nineteenth century, see Rayford W. Logan, *The Betrayal of the Negro* (1965) and Ronald T. Takaki, *Iron Cages: Race and Culture in Nineteenth-Century America* (1979). The standard account of the reformers and the change in American Indian policy remains Francis Paul Prucha, *American Indian Policy in Crisis* (1964). See also Frederick E. Hoxie, *A Final Promise: The Campaign to Assimilate the Indians* (1984). For a good, brief account, read "Kill the Indian to Save the Man," chapter ten of James Wilson's history of Native Americans, *The Earth Shall Weep* (1998).

Howard Gillman, presents the best analysis of laissez-faire constitutionalism in *The Constitution Besieged* (1993). For a briefer exposition of a similar interpretation, see Michael Les Benedict, "Laissez Faire and Liberty," *Law and History Review* 3 (Fall 1985): 293–331. William M. Wiecek's *The Lost World of Classical Legal Thought* (1998) describes the broader intellectual framework of judicial decision making. Morton J. Horwitz provides an excellent concise description in his chapter "The Structure of Classical Legal Thought," in Horwitz, *The Transformation of American Law, 1870–1960* (1992). Mark Warren Bailey in *Guardians of the Moral Order* (2004) shows how constitutional law reflected the moral ideas that dominated the mid and late-nineteenth century. In *Public Pensions* (2003) Susan M. Sterett describes how courts distinguished between legitimate public support for the dependent and those whose service merited special treatment, from illegitimate subsidies of independent businessmen and workers. William E. Forbath describes the effect courts' application of laissez-faire constitutionalism had on organized labor in *Law and the Shaping of the American Labor Movement* (1991).

Ronald M. Labbe and Jonathan Lurie describe the tension between modern business regulation and laissez-faire constitutionalism that characterized *The Slaughterhouse Cases* (2003). For the classic *Lochner* case, see Paul Kens, *Judicial Power and Reform Politics* (1990). Students can contrast the ideas of the great justices Samuel F. Miller, Stephen J. Field, and John M. Harlan by reading Michael A. Ross's study of Miller, *Justice of Shattered Dreams* (2003); Paul Kens, *Justice Stephen Field* (1997); and Linda Przybyszewski, *The Republic According to John Marshall Harlan* (1999). For an insightful discussion of how the federal courts expanded their ability to intervene in public policy, see chapter 2 of Edward A. Purcell, *Brandeis and the Progressive Constitution* (2000).

12

The Progressive Era

Despite the apparent victory of conservatism in the presidential election of 1896, between the late 1890s and about 1919 the United States entered into what historians have called "the Progressive Era," the first age of general-welfare legislation. Calling upon government to deal with the problems of the modern industrial state, progressives reformed the political process. Led by Presidents Theodore Roosevelt and Woodrow Wilson as well as congressmen and local politicians, they created new government structures to cope with a more complex society. They secured state and national legislation controlling business practices, improving working conditions, protecting consumers, and preserving the environment. The Supreme Court generally upheld the constitutionality of the new laws. It retreated from laissez-faire constitutionalism and sustained the exercise of broad national powers.

Progressives' confidence in the utility of government for regulating the economic and social environment led them to use it to control behavior. Support boomed for Prohibition and government suppression of vice and immorality. So-called scientific understandings of race and genetics encouraged racism, immigration restriction, and population control.

As government became more involved in domestic matters, women played a growing role in public programs; they argued persuasively that government needed their input into public policy. As ever more women entered the work force, activists worked to improve their labor conditions and win access to the professions. In 1920 they finally succeeded in securing the right to vote.

American participation in World War I in 1917–1918 marked a new high in government control of the economy. It also tainted radicalism with disloyalty, since most radicals opposed the war. The Supreme Court upheld the broad exercise of national power to organize the economy for war and to suppress dissent. At war's end a reaction against progressivism set in, setting the stage for a bitter struggle between conservatism and liberalism in the following decade.

Progressivism

Progressivism was more a mood than a movement. It reflected a desire to use government to control the environment and confidence that experts could apply scientific knowledge to do so effectively. Many intellectuals and politicians identified themselves as progressives, favoring government action on a wide range of issues, but support for their endeavors came from a shifting coalition of people who saw the need for reform in differing areas of life.

Progressivism seemed more realistic and practical than Populism, which often appeared to reject the modern industrial economy. Most Americans considered a return to a simpler economy impossible as well as undesirable. Populists had advocated the free coinage of silver to inflate the currency and raise prices. This policy ran against the interests of banks, other influential creditors, and workers in urban centers, whose standard of living rose as prices fell. Progressives succeeded where Populists had failed in part because they rejected the free-silver program, an issue that receded in importance as new discoveries of gold increased the currency supply anyway.

The Populists seemed too "socialistic" and "agrarian," alienating many Americans. Most progressives eschewed radical attacks on the basic economic and political system and, like conservatives, repudiated "class legislation." Instead, they based their calls for reform on an expanded idea of what kinds of laws were in the general interest and a conviction that unbridled competition of business against business, farmer against farmer, and worker against worker hurt all the competitors.

Businesses moved to limit competition by consolidating production and transportation, creating ever-larger corporations with ever-greater economic power. The modern corporation emerged, financed by huge loans and millions of shares of stock and directed by professional managers rather than owners. It integrated into one company the production of raw materials, the manufacture of finished products, and their sale in national and international markets. Workers and farmers responded in parallel ways by forming labor unions and agricultural cooperatives.

Progressives pointed out that corporate power could oppress ordinary citizens as effectively as any government. It was impossible to negotiate a fair contract—whether as a worker, a consumer, or a business associate—on terms of equality when one party was so much stronger than the other. In such circumstances "liberty of contract" simply meant that powerful institutions could secure their interests at the expense of those who were forced to deal with them. Liberty was no longer guaranteed merely by limiting the power of government; it required protection from private power as well, and only government could provide it. As conservatives adhered to laissez faire, progressives charged them with sticking to old dogmas divorced from reality. Progressives were attracted to the "pragmatic" understanding of knowledge popularized by the philosopher and educator John Dewey: An idea had to be tested against reality to see if it were true. Dewey and other pragmatists charged that old-fashioned "formalists" reasoned deductively from a few basic, untested propositions. One could not arrive at truth this way, they insisted. One had to judge an idea by how it worked in practice. And laissez-faire ideas failed that test. Far from increasing the range of liberty that most people enjoyed, their application had led to immense concentrations of private power that had reduced freedom instead.

Progressives concluded that government had to intervene to protect farmers, consumers, small businessmen, and workers. It had to act boldly to assure that powerful interests did not endanger the public welfare by marketing dangerous and unsanitary products, or by forcing employees to work in dangerous and unhealthy conditions. This goal required government to intervene in labor and other contracts. Agreeing that "class legislation" was wrong in a society where every person had an equal opportunity to succeed, progressives argued that in a modern industrial society, government had to act vigorously to assure that such opportunity existed. Until everyone's opportunities truly were equal, it benefited the whole society to shift some of the nation's wealth from the rich to the poor.

Progressive ideas were translated into public policy because such ambitious, young politicians as Theodore Roosevelt of New York, Robert M. La Follette of Wisconsin, and Woodrow Wilson of New Jersey recognized their popularity. Roosevelt tried without much success to use progressivism to challenge the leaders of the Republican machine in New York. In order to get rid of him, they put him in the usually powerless position of vice president. However, when President McKinley was assassinated in 1901, Roosevelt succeeded him. As president the energetic Roosevelt made himself the leader of the progressive movement and gave it a tremendous impetus. Powerful progressive wings developed in both political parties. Roosevelt was succeeded in 1909 by William Howard Taft, who, although relatively conservative, continued many of Roosevelt's policies. In 1912 Roosevelt sought the Republican presidential nomination once again. Losing to Taft, he ran anyway, supported by the newly organized Progressive party. The resulting split among Republicans led to the victory of Democrat Woodrow Wilson, who also championed progressive reform during his administration.

Progressive Reform

Progressive reforms, which began in the 1890s and continued through the 1910s, can be grouped under several headings. First, progressives reformed government to reduce the power of old-fashioned politicians and powerful economic interests. They passed the Seventeenth Amendment to require U.S. senators to be elected directly by the people, instead of by the state legislatures. They established primary elections to free nominations from the control of party bosses. They passed laws providing for referenda on issues, so that people could vote directly to enact proposals that politicians delayed. Progressives established methods to "recall" unpopular officials. They enacted voter registration systems and established the secret ballot to fight election fraud. They reformed the civil service to make government officials more professional and independent. Designed to reduce the influence of old-fashioned politicians, these reforms also increased the power of the educated middle class at the expense of laborers and immigrants.

Progressives also passed state and federal legislation to regulate business. These regulations won some business support by promoting efficiency, providing sources of information, and setting standards, but they were also designed to control the power of large corporations. The Hepburn Act (1906) strengthened the Interstate Commerce Commission. The Federal Reserve Act (1913) regulated banking. The Clayton Anti-Trust Act (1914) expanded the antitrust laws and limited their use against labor unions. In the same year, Congress created the Federal Trade Commission, to prevent big companies from engaging in unfair business practices.

Antitrust activity was central to the progressive ethos. Progressives' first reaction was to break up the immense new concentrations of industrial power. Trust busting played a big role in Roosevelt's Square Deal, as he termed his progressive program. He launched a few, highly publicized antitrust prosecutions. His successor, Taft, pursued an even more active antitrust policy. The two administrations broke up the Northern Securities Company, which controlled three major railroads, the Standard Oil monopoly, and the American Tobacco Company. Yet ultimately Roosevelt, Taft, and many other progressives concluded that business consolidation was both inevitable and beneficial. It created efficiencies of scale that translated into increased production, more jobs, and lower prices. They distinguished between "good trusts" and bad ones that raised prices and engaged in unfair business practices. The Supreme Court endorsed this flexible approach, interpreting the antitrust acts to bar only "unreasonable" restraints of trade.

Although many progressives, including Wilson, criticized this acceptance of big business, there clearly was no returning to the old days of small firms and individual ownership. American government adjusted to the new corporation-dominated economy by regulating rather than combating it. Progressives enacted legislation to protect public health, often regulating business practices to do so. The federal government began to inspect meat and poultry. In 1906 Congress passed the Pure Food and Drug Act, requiring safe and healthful ingredients in products. Local governments passed zoning ordinances. States and local governments passed the first antipollution laws. The state and federal governments moved to protect public safety, especially the safety of workers. The new laws required fire escapes, cleanliness, and ventilation in workplaces, and protective devices for dangerous machinery.

The progressives passed other labor regulations as well. They limited the workday to ten or even eight hours, established minimum wages, forbade the employment of women and children in dangerous jobs and those deemed to pose moral risks, regulated how workers should be paid, and required employers to establish pensions for their employees. The states mandated employer contributions to workers' compensation funds, which provided money to laborers injured on the job. They made it illegal to fire workers who joined labor unions. Of central importance to organized labor were statutory limits placed on the use of injunctions to break strikes and boycotts. The national government passed similar laws to protect workers in Washington, D.C., or employed in interstate commerce. Some states created administrative agencies to resolve labor disputes through arbitration.

The progressives increased the number of national parks and established the National Park Service. They reinvigorated the Forestry Service, originally established in 1887, and created other agencies in the Interior Department to preserve natural resources. To overcome judicial resistance to the graduated income tax, progressives passed and ratified the Sixteenth Amendment, explicitly giving Congress the power to levy it.

All these laws reflected the philosophy of the "general-welfare state." In each instance, the government acted on the principle that the general welfare would suffer if the free market were permitted to determine how resources would be used. For example, if the market were permitted to operate freely in the area of pollution, most companies would simply dump dangerous materials into rivers and lakes, or burn them. This procedure would cost companies very little, but would shift the burden to people who got sick. By forcing business to take antipollution measures, the government imposed the burden on business and removed it from ordinary people.

Progressives were enamored of science and professional expertise. They created boards of trained professionals to propose and administer public policy. They were dubious about the ability of unschooled politicians to deal with modern problems and worried about their susceptibility to corruption. They scoffed at the notion that old legal precedents, administered by judges with no expertise in specialized fields of knowledge, should determine the rules of modern life. They insisted that businesspeople needed to know what was permitted and forbidden, not find out in court after disputes arose.

Moral Reform, Race, and Gender

Despite other differences, conservatives and progressives agreed that government had a responsibility to promote good morals. Social scientists' statistics demonstrated the connection between alcoholism, vice, disease, poverty, and crime. States and localities continued to make it illegal to work on Sundays. Modernized police forces suppressed gambling and other vices, filling the jails with people arrested for the catch-all "disorderly conduct." Growing recognition of the danger of venereal disease—a virtual panic over syphilis—fueled a massive drive to outlaw and suppress prostitution. Progressive governments established specific courts to deal with juvenile crime and special schools to train delinquent children.

Although physicians and social reformers discussed such issues as prostitution with greater openness, their calls for "social hygiene" echoed earlier calls for sexual purity. Government officials continued to link abortion and contraception to vice. But feminist reformers now began to challenge this idea. They linked a woman's right to control pregnancy to women's growing demand for independence in general. This movement among women for greater autonomy led to increasing criticism of sexual repression. Citing the discoveries of the great founder of psychoanalysis, Sigmund Freud, critics of Victorian morality argued that repressing natural sexual instincts left deep psychological scars.

Reformers like Margaret Sanger called for an end to prudery and for the promotion of sex education and birth control. In 1914 Sanger was indicted under the Comstock law for advertising birth control in her magazine *The Woman Rebel*. Socialists, radicals, and left-wing progressives rallied to her defense, creating a grassroots birth-control movement. Although the charges against Sanger were dropped, in 1917 the federal government again indicted her, this time for opening the nation's first birth-control clinic. In response to widespread protest, the government agreed to permit such clinics if physicians prescribed the birth-control devices. Sanger went on to found the Birth Control League, the forerunner

Margaret Sanger, the crusader for women's reproductive freedom who challenged Comstock laws in order to encourage birth control.

of the present-day organization Planned Parenthood, in 1921. With support spreading far beyond socialists and radicals, Sanger and other reformers continued to press for liberalization of federal and state Comstock laws, with growing success.

Because the vices that so troubled Americans were associated with saloons and public drunkenness, the Prohibition movement grew ever stronger. Urban political machines and some political parties were strongly influenced by brewers, distillers, and saloon-keepers, so Prohibitionists backed the progressive reforms designed to break their power: the referendum, direct primary, and secret ballot. They used "local-option" laws to ban saloons in parts of many states, especially in rural areas. By 1916 they had outlawed saloons altogether in twenty-three states, using the referendum procedure in seventeen of them. In 1917 Congress proposed a constitutional amendment prohibiting the manufacture, sale, and transportation of alcoholic beverages. Ratified by the necessary number of states in 1919, it became the Eighteenth Amendment.

Such moral legislation was still aimed largely at immigrant groups and other minorities. Although many progressive reformers were sympathetic to these groups, they shared conservatives' concern about the erosion of Anglo-Saxon Protestant influence over politics and culture. In the South progressives worked to eliminate black voting and to institute segregation. The North did nothing to stop them. President Roosevelt considered the issue a lost cause. To Northerners "the wrongdoing in the South is a matter far off and of little immediate consequence," he lamented. In fact, they were "impatient of any attempt to make things better in any way."

Roosevelt precipitated a raucous controversy shortly after becoming president when he invited the renowned African American educator Booker T. Washington to dinner at the White House. The attacks continued as he continued the traditional Republican practice of naming a few African Americans to low- and middle-level government offices. As if to counteract the criticism, Roosevelt summarily cashiered a black army regiment accused of rioting against whites in Brownsville, Texas, without affording its members any opportunity for defense or explanation. Roosevelt's successor, William Howard Taft, distanced himself from black Republican leaders, cultivating so-called "Lily White" southern Republicans instead. In response to the complaints of white civil servants, he began to segregate the federal work force in Washington. Democratic President Wilson, born and raised in Virginia, completed the process when he came to power in 1913. It was a stunning humiliation for black government workers, banished from canteens, assigned to separate toilets and locker rooms, and moved to segregated work spaces.

To fight such racism, black and white progressives formed the National Association for the Advancement of Colored People (NAACP) in 1909. The National Urban League, organized in 1911 to combat social problems among African Americans immigrating to the North, was another manifestation of the progressive impulse. A few years earlier, in 1906, the B'nai B'rith, a Jewish social and fraternal organization, had formed the Anti-Defamation League to battle anti-Semitism. But despite these first civil-rights organizations, the advancement of civil liberty and toleration was not a part of the progressive agenda.

Labor organizations grew more discriminatory as well. In the South, unions used their power to exclude black workers from jobs. In general the members of the growing American Federation of Labor, mainly skilled workers and craftsmen, saw black and immigrant workers as competitors who enabled employers to keep wages low. Women's labor and child labor also served to depress wages, labor leaders believed. So labor support for child-labor legislation, minimum wages, and exclusion of women from dangerous and unhealthy occupations was based not only on concern for fairness, safety, and health; such laws made black, immigrant, woman, and child labor less competitive.

Scientific racism continued to foster hostility towards eastern and southern Europeans, Jews, and African Americans, and condescension if not antipathy to Native Americans. Many progressives were fascinated by the science of "eugenics," which claimed that intelligence, morality, discipline, and other human traits were genetically determined, with the white northern European races endowed with more good qualities than any other. Race mixing would dilute these qualities, eugenicists warned. In fact, the northern European races could be improved by inhibiting the reproduction of their defective individuals. Such notions encouraged a movement to sterilize women who showed signs of mental or moral defects. The Catholic church led the resistance to such laws. Where it failed to stop them, a number of state and federal judges ruled them unconstitutional as violations of due process or impositions of cruel and inhuman punishment.

Sustained by eugenicists, many progressives, supported by most labor organizations, pressed for the restriction of immigration. In 1908 Japanese laborers were effectively barred from entering the United States, as Chinese had been for over twenty years. In 1917 Congress passed a literacy test for immigrants, overriding President Wilson's veto. The Immigration Acts of 1921 and 1924 reduced immigration dramatically, sharply limited the number of immigrants from places other than northern Europe, and excluded South and East Asians entirely. At the same time (1923) the Supreme Court upheld West Coast laws barring aliens ineligible for naturalization—Japanese, Chinese, East Indian, and other Asian immigrants—from owning land.

Pressure for the assimilation of Native Americans mirrored Progressive-Era efforts to assimilate immigrants and block further immigration of undesirables. In 1903 the Supreme Court ruled in *Lone Wolf v. Hitchcock* that Congress had plenary power over Native Americans and could not be held to treaty commitments. With this, pressure to open reservation lands to white economic development proved irresistible. Thousands of "grafters" bilked Indians out of allotments and acquired "surplus" land, mining, and timber rights. A few Native American "irreconcilables" refused to claim allotments or accept money for surplus land sold by the Indian Bureau, but most acquiesced. Scientific theories of racial inferiority explained away the poverty, disease, and alcoholism that followed the destruction of Native American culture.

The Dawes Act had made recipients of allotments citizens, but the status of Native Americans remained ambiguous. In 1906 Congress amended the Act to delay effective citizenship until Indians received full title to their allotted land; until then they would remain under federal guardianship. Many western states denied such "restricted Indians" the right to vote. In response Congress passed the Indian Citizenship Act in 1924, which finally made all Native Americans citizens, but it was also designed to undermine their allegiance to tribal authorities and traditions. And the law did not stop courts from permitting local communities to mandate segregated schools for Native American children. Nor did it prevent states from barring marriages between Indians and whites.

While the Progressive Era marked a nadir in race relations, it witnessed the emergence of what contemporaries called "the new woman." Medical schools graduated their first woman physicians. Women's colleges began to stress academic subjects, creating a demand for female professors, and leading graduate schools began to produce them. Women began to dominate such professions as nursing, social work, and teaching in primary schools. Female secretaries began to replace male clerks. However, few women were admitted into highly paid professions or into positions in business management. Wages lagged dramatically in work where women predominated. No laws barred such discrimination. States continued to bar women from dangerous or "unsuitable" occupations.

Women's organizations strove to improve the working conditions of women employed in low-paying industrial jobs. Some concentrated on securing equal pay and employment opportunities; others sought special protective legislation that took account of women's roles as wives and mothers and the physical differences between the sexes. Radical women reformers, such as Florence Kelley and Jane Addams, allied with socialists and labor unions to fight for employees' rights. At the same time they pressed for "mothers' pensions"—a government subsidy to all mothers. Women progressives were a prime force behind the push for Prohibition and the regulation of prostitution, gambling, and other vices that particularly harmed women.

The entry of women into the public workplace fueled the drive for woman suffrage, as did its identification with many of the moral reforms enacted in the Progressive Era. The Progressive Era's emphasis on the general welfare led to what historians have called "the domestication of American politics," or even "maternalist politics," creating a political role for women, who had always been seen as less individualistic and more concerned with the welfare of others. By 1917 women had secured the right to vote in thirteen states and the right to vote in presidential elections in two more. Many states enfranchised women in local elections—for school boards, for example, and in "local-option" elections that decided liquor issues.

Demanding a constitutional amendment to enfranchise women throughout the nation, suffragists organized giant marches and rallies. Some engaged in civil disobedience, chaining themselves to the fences of the White House. The National American Woman Suffrage Association (NAWSA), by this time the largest voluntary organization in the country with over two million members, lobbied local, state, and federal officials, bombarding them with petitions, letters, and telegrams. Winning the vote in ever more states, the NAWSA warned legislators of retribution at the polls. In 1918 it persuaded twenty-four state legislatures to send petitions endorsing woman suffrage to Congress. The more militant Woman's Party picketed the White House and challenged President Wilson, who had endorsed the proposal, to act on his words. Arrested, they went on a hunger strike that forced their release. Congress finally sent the woman-suffrage amendment to the states in 1919; it was ratified in less than three years, becoming the Nineteenth Amendment to the Constitution in 1920.

But how far would the Nineteenth Amendment go in securing equality for women? Would conferring the highest right of citizenship be held to confer equal civil rights as well? Many feminists urged state legislatures to repeal laws discriminating between men and women as inconsistent with women's new status as voting citizens, but they had little success. Legislators continued to back legislation that barred women from dangerous or morally compromising jobs and mandated special rules to protect female employees. Most states rejected the idea of a general mothers' pension, instead improving systems to provide payments to mothers in need. The reforms were another progressive victory for the general-welfare state, but they reconfirmed women's dependent status. Half the states still restricted jury duty to men. In most of the rest, women either had to request to serve or were allowed to decline. Hardly anyone suggested that women should participate in the militia—another obligation traditionally associated with full citizenship. From these standpoints, women remained less than full citizens.

Progressivism and the Growth of American Government

Progressive legislation led to a growth of executive power, both in state and national government. An even more active chief executive than Jackson or Lincoln, Theodore Roosevelt developed the "stewardship theory" of the presidency. Because the president represented all the people, while Congress represented only local constituencies, he said, the president had a special responsibility to protect their welfare. Just as the Constitution delegated "implied powers" to Congress, it delegated "implied powers" to the president to enable him to carry out this responsibility. Roosevelt thus took an active role in settling labor disputes. He ordered his subordinates to break up monopolies. He used his position to organize support for progressive policies, giving interviews to newspaper reporters and taking them along on his trips. What Roosevelt did as president, progressives like Robert M. La Follette of Wisconsin, James M. Cox of Ohio, and Woodrow Wilson of New Jersey did as governors.

Presidents and governors had always been responsible for alerting legislatures to matters requiring attention. Department heads had sometimes worked closely with legislators in framing laws. But now for the first time, executive-branch officials began to prepare legislation. Prime responsibility for shaping public policy shifted from the legislative branch to the president and governors. Voters came to expect them to provide such leadership. They credited chief executives for successes and held them responsible for failures.

From the 1890s onward states and localities created ever more new agencies to gather information and make new rules governing a variety of private business activities, public utilities, public health, safety on the job, and employer-employee relations. Planning commissions proposed public parks and zoning to channel urban development. Ohio, for example, had a division of mines, a railroad commission, a dairy and food commission, an industrial commission, an agricultural commission, and many others. The national government followed the states' lead. In 1903 Congress created the Bureau of Corporations to gather statistics and make recommendations about the promotion and regulation of business. The new Federal Reserve Board, established in 1913 to regulate banking, and the Federal Trade Commission, created in 1914 to regulate business practices, were other examples. Commissions and boards enabled the government to cope with the growing complexity of the economy. Commissions were empowered to investigate, regulate, and administer, and they generally contained separate arms to fulfill each function. Congress and the state legislatures passed laws establishing general goals and administrative procedures, and instructed the commissions to establish the details. Commission employees soon became experts in their subjects; they provided a great flow of information to Congress and the state legislatures, enabling them to pass laws much more effectively than in the past.

The power of the national government increased greatly during the Progressive Era. There were two main reasons for the change. First, the growth of a national market and transportation system created more interstate commerce to regulate than ever before. The national government had to regulate railroads, river traffic, telegraph and telephone companies, and banking. By the 1920s trucking, radio, and air traffic were added to the interstate mix of transportation and communication. Second, the development of a national economic system undermined the ability of the states to govern effectively, because of what constitutional scholars now call "federal effects." No state could isolate itself from commerce in the federal system. A state might ban the manufacture and sale of dangerous products, for example, but it could not close its borders to their importation. That was a matter for federal regulation. Therefore Congress came under pressure to ban the interstate shipment of alcohol, lottery tickets, birth-control devices, and other products states wanted to keep out of the hands of their citizens. "Federal effects" also inhibited various reforms. For example, if a state wanted to prohibit child labor, the cost of doing business in that state would be higher than the costs elsewhere. That was a strong argument against enacting the reform. But once such reforms were enacted despite the costs, affected businesses began to pressure the national government to pass similar laws in order to make the rules uniform across the whole country. In this way "federal effects" helped to create the alliance between businessmen and reformers that characterized the Progressive era.

The result was the development of a "national police power." The Constitution nowhere expressly delegates authority to the national government to enact such police regulations, but advocates of progressive national legislation offered two main justifications. Both relied on a nationalist rather than state-rights interpretation of federalism. First, progressives argued that Congress's power over interstate commerce was complete and sovereign; Congress had the power to ban goods from interstate commerce if they did not meet congressional approval. Relying on this broad interpretation of its authority, Congress banned the sale of oleomargarine colored to look like butter and of lottery tickets used for gambling. It forbade interstate transportation of impure drugs in the 1906 Pure Food and Drug Act and of goods made by child labor in the First Child Labor Act (1916). It passed the Mann Act (1910) making it illegal to transport women across state lines "for immoral purposes." To make sure that goods met its requirements, Congress established such agencies as the Meat Inspection Agency and the Food and Drug Administration, both created in 1906. Second, Congress used its taxing power to impose prohibitively high levies on goods it believed dangerous to health and morals, such as phosphorus matches in 1912, narcotic drugs in 1914, and goods made with child labor in the second Child Labor Act (1919).

Progressives also insisted that the federal government regulate employment in interstate commerce, creating the Railway Labor Board in 1919. Congress forbade interstate transportation companies from requiring workers to eschew union membership. It made them liable for all workplace injuries. In 1917 it established an eight-hour workday for interstate railroad employees. These laws were similar to those that progressive state governments passed to help workers employed in their states.

Strengthened by Congress, the Interstate Commerce Commission began to act forcefully, even regulating transportation that took place entirely within the boundaries of one state, since such activities often affected interstate commerce. Presidents Roosevelt, Taft, and Wilson also enforced a strengthened Anti-Trust Act, bringing suits to break up several of the largest companies in the United States.

The Courts and the Progressive Era

At first the state and federal courts resisted progressive legislation. They observed a rigid distinction between purely private businesses and businesses affected with a public interest. In the latter case, the government's regulatory authority was broad. But the courts interpreted governmental authority over purely private business much more strictly. Judges upheld the constitutionality of most of the laws that came before them. But important decisions set definite limits on how far government could go in restricting property rights and limiting freedom of contract. The Supreme Court's decision in *Lochner v. New York* (1905), overturning New York's maximum-hour law for bakery workers, is the most famous example. All over the country state and federal courts used the *Lochner* case as a precedent to overturn general-welfare laws. Even when they upheld progressive legislation, judges often interpreted the statutes narrowly. They remained suspicious of administrative agencies. The courts came to see themselves as the primary protectors of American constitutional rights.

Influenced by the philosophy of pragmatism, legal analysts criticized conservative judges for mechanistically following theoretical precedents, often ruling laws unconstitutional without investigating real circumstances. State court judges like Oliver Wendell Holmes, who moved from the Supreme Judicial Court of Massachusetts to the United States Supreme Court in 1902; legal scholars like Roscoe Pound; and practicing attorneys like Louis D. Brandeis demanded an end to such "mechanical" jurisprudence and its replacement with what Pound called "sociological jurisprudence" and Brandeis called a "living law." This approach to decision making called for judges to apply laws in light of the actual social problems they were designed to remedy. A law's constitutionality was to be decided in terms of its actual operation and effect rather than how it theoretically accorded with constitutional principles and precedents.

Judges must acknowledge that they made policy and that law changed to meet new circumstances, these critics insisted. As early as 1881 Holmes wrote, "The life of the law has not been logic; it has been experience. The felt necessities of the time, the prevalent moral and political theories, intuitions of public policy, avowed or unconscious, . . . have had a good deal more to do than the syllogism in determining the rules by which men should be governed." Judges who thought they were neutrally applying general legal principles to specific cases, discovering law rather than making it, were fooling themselves. "You can give any conclusion a logical form," he warned. Judges must be aware of their own biases and willing to concede differences of opinion.

In particular, Holmes and other critics accused conservative judges of deciding cases according to their laissez-faire beliefs as if these beliefs were incorporated in the Constitution. Holmes believed in laissez faire too, but he knew that others disagreed. He dissented from the Court's decision in the *Lochner* case, writing that the majority had decided it "upon an economic theory which a large part of the country does not entertain." They had no justification for doing so. "[A] constitution is not intended to embody a particular economic theory," he insisted. "It is made for people of fundamentally differing views, and the accident of our finding certain opinions natural and familiar or novel and even shocking ought not to conclude our judgment upon the question whether statutes embodying them conflict with the Constitution of the United States."

Pound and Brandeis insisted that if the constitutionality of a law turned on

Oliver Wendell Holmes (*left*) and Louis D. Brandeis (*right*), the great liberal justices whose dissents established the basis for liberal constitutionalism on the Supreme Court.

whether, for example, it promoted public health or safety, judges must learn the facts. Such an approach meant that courts required the same sort of information that legislatures considered when deciding whether to pass laws. Lawyers thus began to augment their legal briefs with statistics and other information about the social benefits of laws. The most famous example was the brief Brandeis submitted in the case of *Muller v. Oregon* (1907), defending Oregon's law limiting the number of hours that women could work in commercial laundries. Relying on Brandeis's compilation of facts and expert opinion, the Court agreed that the law promoted the general welfare by protecting the health of women workers. Brandeis's brief resonated with the justices because it drew on a long tradition that held government responsible for protecting women in ways that it did not protect men. But progressives believed that modern economic life had rendered everyone more vulnerable to forces beyond their control, blurring the distinction between men and women. Many expected that judges' acceptance of protective legislation for female workers made it more likely they would soon accept it for men as well.

Most progressives therefore considered the Court's decision in *Muller v. Oregon* a great victory. But some women's rights leaders protested it. In order to distinguish the *Muller* case from the *Lochner* precedent, Brandeis had cited social scientists who concluded that women were particularly vulnerable to disease and exploitation; he had stressed the interest of society in maintaining the health of potential mothers. This evidence persuaded the majority of justices to sustain Oregon's law. But it could also be used to justify laws that restricted women's equal access to jobs. In fact, if women alone were protected by minimum-wage laws, employers might replace them with men. Nonetheless, the "Brandeis Brief" became a staple of arguments defending the constitutionality of general-welfare legislation. This development was reinforced by Brandeis's appointment to the Supreme Court in 1916, over the objection of conservatives and anti-Semites.

Even before Brandeis's appointment, it was clear that both state and federal courts had become much more likely to uphold laws regulating businesses and working conditions as reasonably related to the public good. But the use of sociological evidence in briefs confirmed the tendency of judges to identify the constitutionality of legislation with its reasonability. Critics complained that by demanding such evidence, the courts were acting more like legislatures than courts. Such behavior was undemocratic, they argued, because judges were not elected and not authorized to consider the necessity of laws, only their constitutionality. Nonetheless, most observers applauded when the courts accepted sociological evidence and sustained progressive legislation.

The Supreme Court also seemed to relax its defense of state rights against federal legislation. Opponents of national regulation relied on decisions like the *E. C. Knight* case to argue that Congress could not exercise police powers, because that authority was reserved to the states. But the Supreme Court rejected such state-rights arguments in favor of constitutional nationalism. In *Champion v. Ames* (1903), the Court sustained the power of Congress to prohibit the shipment of lottery tickets through interstate commerce. In *McCray v. U.S.* (1904), it upheld Congress's power to suppress the production of goods through the taxing power. In *Hoke v. U.S.* (1913), the Supreme Court sustained the constitutionality of the Mann Act, which punished the interstate transportation of prostitutes, a law that was clearly more a regulation of morals than commerce. The Court forthrightly applied the doctrine of constitutional nationalism to these cases: "The principle established in the cases is the simple one . . . that Congress has power over transportation among the several States, that the power is complete in itself, and that Congress, as an incident to it, may adopt not only means necessary but convenient to its exercise, and the means may have the quality of police regulations." By undercutting the state-rights arguments of those who opposed progressive legislation these decisions encouraged the great wave of progressive regulation that Congress enacted from 1900 to 1919.

The justices also supported the federal government's new efforts to enforce the Sherman Anti-Trust Act. In *Northern Securities Company v. U.S.* (1904), the Court expanded the definition of interstate commerce to allow such antitrust activities. In *Swift & Co. v. U.S.* (1905), the Court ruled that the stockyards and meat-packing houses, where animals were collected and slaughtered for shipment to the rest of the country, were part of "a stream of commerce" and therefore subject to federal regulation. The decision seemed to repudiate the strict line the Court had drawn between production and commerce in the *E. C. Knight* decision. It was difficult to see how the slaughtering of beef to be sent through interstate commerce differed from the refining of sugar for the same purpose. As the Court sustained antitrust prosecutions of other manufacturers and producers, such as Standard Oil and the American Tobacco Company, the way seemed open for general regulation of businesses that produced goods for interstate commerce. With more and more companies producing goods for a national market, this interpretation could sustain federal regulation of virtually all the nation's business.

World War I, Federal Power, and Civil Liberty

In 1917 the United States entered the First World War. The United States government, already strengthened during the Progressive Era, acted forcefully to organize society to win the war. Congress quickly passed a law drafting men to serve in the armed forces. In the *Selective Draft Law Cases* (1918), the Supreme Court unanimously agreed that the law was a constitutional exercise of the government's war powers.

Congress authorized President Wilson to regulate and even take control of railroads and communication as well as to prevent strikes and operate factories producing war material. In 1917 Congress enacted the Lever Act to assure the supply of reasonably priced food during the war. The law made it illegal to fix the price of food, or to monopolize its production or distribution. It authorized the president to issue rules governing food sales, to take over factories and mines, and to set prices. Armed with such authority, Wilson established a series of bureaus to supervise American industry to assure its efficient wartime operation.

In *Northern Pacific Railway Co. v. North Dakota* (1919) and *U.S. v. L. Cohen Grocery Co.* (1921), the justices confirmed the sweeping powers that Congress had exercised during the war. In the Court's view, the Constitution contemplated a radical expansion of the national government's powers in wartime; nothing reasonably related to winning the war was beyond Congress's authority. The Court seemed to have completely abandoned the state-rights idea that the Tenth Amendment preserved areas of state jurisdiction from national action.

The national government claimed equally broad authority to silence those who opposed the war effort. Even during the height of the Progressive Era, many states and localities had prosecuted radicals, especially radical labor unions like the Industrial Workers of the World (I.W.W.). Applying the Bad Tendency Test, state courts sustained the resulting convictions. But many Americans opposed such limits on freedom of expression. The I.W.W. stood in the forefront of the fight for freedom of speech, which was closely related to the right of their organizers to agitate publicly for worker support. The I.W.W.'s fight for freedom to organize workers culminated in the great "Free Speech Fight" in San Diego, California, in 1911. As its organizers were arrested, hundreds of I.W.W. activists converged on the city to take their places. Civil libertarians organized the Free Speech League to defend the so-called "Wobblies" in court. Unable to win an absolute right of free speech, the League did persuade many judges and legal scholars at least to balance the value of free speech against the risk of illegal activity.

The war led to a reaction against freedom of expression. Many German and Scandinavian Americans opposed the decision to enter it; many Irish Americans opposed the alliance with Great Britain, which kept Ireland in subjugation. American socialists sympathized with the Communists who seized power in Russia and pulled it out of the war, and they protested bitterly when the allies sent soldiers there to help reactionaries regain power. Because of their opposition to the war, radicals in general were charged with being disloyal and un-American—a charge that became a staple of American politics. To suppress such dissent, Congress passed the Espionage Acts of 1917 and 1918. These laws authorized President Wilson to censor the mails and made it illegal to do, say, or publish anything that might interfere with the war effort, or use "disloyal, profane, . . . or abusive language" to describe the government. The 1918 law seemed to make almost any criticism of the government illegal; it came to be called the Sedition Act of 1918, because it seemed similar to the law the Federalists had passed in 1798. States passed similar laws. German institutions were specially targeted. States eliminated German from the public school curriculum and suppressed private German-language schools. German-language newspapers and books were burned in the streets.

To enforce federal anti-subversion laws, the Wilson administration created an intelligence division in the Bureau of Investigation of the Justice Department. It also banned certain newspapers and magazines from the mail. The national and state governments arrested leading critics of the war, including Eugene V. Debs, who had received nearly a million votes as the Socialist party's presidential candidate in 1912. Radical labor unions and publishers were crushed, sometimes through prosecutions and other times by the vigilante action of the government-sponsored American Protective League. As intolerance of dissent grew, even innocuous acts and comments brought prosecution. The government successfully prosecuted the producer of a movie about the American Revolution because the film was unabashedly anti-British. He got ten years. A group of South Dakota farmers who petitioned the state government to hold a referendum on the war received one-year jail terms.

Civil libertarians organized the Civil Liberties Bureau to defend people arrested for violating the state and national sedition laws. Ultimately it became the American Civil Liberties Union, one of the nation's most important defenders of civil rights. Despite these efforts, the state and lower-federal courts relied on the Bad Tendency Test to uphold convictions under the challenged laws.

With the end of the war in 1919, civil libertarians hoped that the Supreme Court would overturn the convictions and void the Sedition Act. But they were disappointed. In *Schenck v. U.S.* (1919), the Court upheld the conviction of the secretary general of the Socialist party, who had directed the distribution of anti-war leaflets to draftees in Philadelphia. To the dismay of civil libertarians, Justice Holmes interpreted the leaflets as a direct incitement to refuse to obey the draft law. In the context of war, such a direct appeal went too far. There must be some limit to freedom of speech, he wrote. One cannot yell "Fire!" in a crowded theater, for example. When there is "a clear and present danger" that words may lead to illegal activity, laws may punish those who speak them.

Despite the disappointment of civil libertarians, Holmes apparently had persuaded the Court to tighten the traditional Bad Tendency Test; his opinion suggested that speech could be punished only when it posed a real danger of illegal conduct, not for merely tending to encourage it. But when the Court upheld convictions in *Debs v. U.S.* (1919) and *Abrams v. U.S.* (1919), it interpreted Holmes's words as an endorsement of the old Bad Tendency rule. The government could ban the expression of ideas that tended to make illegal activity more likely or to damage society.

In response, Holmes reconsidered the meaning of "clear and present danger," making it a much more libertarian standard than it first appeared. In the *Abrams* case, the defendants were sentenced to twenty years in prison for publishing a pamphlet calling for a general strike to protest the government's decision to send troops to aid opponents of the Russian Revolution. Although the pamphleteers had not intended to damage the war effort against Germany, as the Sedition Act required, the Court's majority argued that the war effort would have been severely impaired had the strike occurred. They should have known that their pamphlets presented this danger. Even though there was no real chance of a general strike, the Court said that this "bad tendency" was enough to sustain the radicals' conviction.

This argument went too far for Holmes and Brandeis. In ringing language Holmes's dissent attacked the Bad Tendency doctrine for failing his Clear and Present Danger Test. "In this case sentences of twenty years have been imposed for the publishing of two leaflets that I believe the defendants had as much right to publish as the Government has to publish the Constitution of the United States now vainly invoked by them," Holmes wrote. It was clear that the harsh sentences were punishment "not for what the indictment alleges but for the creed that they avow." But, Holmes urged, "when men have realized that time has upset many fighting faiths, they may come to believe . . . that the ultimate good desired is better reached by free trade in ideas—that the best test of truth is the power of the thought to get itself accepted in the competition of the market, and that truth is the only ground upon which their wishes safely can be carried out." With this dissent, Holmes and Brandeis became heroes to American civil libertarians, who began to demand the application of the Clear and Present Danger Test to freedom-of-expression cases in order to protect the right to free speech in all but the most extreme cases.

The suppression of radicalism during World War I and the Supreme Court's endorsement of its constitutionality reflected the declining influence of progressivism. While progressive reforms lived on and the government continued to regulate the economy to a greater extent than it had in the nineteenth century, the reformist commitment to fighting the power of big business, improving the conditions of labor, and protecting the consumer waned. Still, progressives remained numerous and powerful, continuing to dominate in many states. But the justices' differing positions on freedom of speech during the period mirrored fundamental differences over political, social, and constitutional issues that would divide Americans dramatically in the decade that followed the war.

TIMELINE

1895–1900 Various states enact progressive legislation.

1901 President William McKinley assassinated; Vice President Theodore Roosevelt becomes president.

1902 Oliver Wendell Holmes named to the Supreme Court.

1903 In *Lone Wolf v. Hitchcock* the Supreme Court rules that Congress has plenary power over relations with Native Americans and can repudiate Indian treaties.

The Supreme Court upholds congressional power to bar lottery tickets from interstate commerce in *Champion v. Ames.*

The Roosevelt administration brings an antitrust action against the Northern Securities railroad holding company.

1904 The Supreme Court sustains Congress's power to levy prohibitive taxes to suppress the production of goods in *McCray v. U.S.*

The Supreme Court sustains the breakup of the Northern Securities Co. under the Sherman Anti-Trust Act.

1905 State laws limiting working hours in ordinary occupations ruled unconstitutional in *Lochner v. New York.*

The Supreme Court upholds the application of the Sherman Anti-Trust Act to the Swift & Co. meat-packing corporation, ruling that its slaughtering facilities are within a "stream of commerce."

1906 The Hepburn Act expands powers of the Interstate Commerce Commission.

Congress passes the Pure Food and Drug Act.

1906	The B'nai B'rith establishes the Anti-Defamation League to combat anti-Semitism.
1907	The Supreme Court sustains the constitutionality of state laws limiting working hours for women in *Muller v. Oregon*.
1909	National Association for the Advancement of Colored People (NAACP) founded.
1911	International Workers of the World (I.W.W.) "Free Speech Fight" in San Diego, California.
1912	Progressive Democrat Woodrow Wilson elected President and takes office in 1913.
1913	Ratification of the Sixteenth Amendment authorizing the federal government to collect graduated income tax.
	Ratification of the Seventeenth Amendment requiring direct election of United States senators.
	The Federal Reserve Act creates the Federal Reserve Board to regulate banking.
1914	The Clayton Anti-Trust Act strengthens federal antitrust power and exempts organized labor from the provisions of the Anti-Trust Act.
	Congress creates the Federal Trade Commission.
	Margaret Sanger indicted for advertising birth-control information and devices.
1916	Congress bars goods made by child labor from interstate commerce in the first Child Labor Act.
	Louis Brandeis confirmed as Supreme Court justice.
1917	The United States enters World War I.
	Congress passes the Lever Act, establishing wide-ranging controls over the wartime economy.
1918	Congress passes the Sedition Act.
1919	Congress levies prohibitive taxes on goods made by child labor in the second Child Labor Act.
	Supreme Court sustains broad government power to regulate the economy in wartime in *Northern Pacific Ry. Co. v. North Dakota*.
	In *Schenck v. U.S.*, the Supreme Court upholds convictions of war protesters, adopting the Clear and Present Danger Test.

1919   In *Abrams v. U.S.*, the Supreme Court sustains convictions of radicals calling for a strike to protest intervention in Russia, utilizing the Bad Tendency
Test; Holmes and Brandeis dissent.

The Eighteenth Amendment establishes Prohibition.

1920   The Woman's Suffrage Amendment is ratified.

1924   The Immigration Act of 1924 establishes quotas based on the national
origins of Americans as of 1920 and bars immigrants who are ineligible for
naturalization (all nonwhites except those of African descent).

FURTHER READING

There are a number of good general surveys of the Progressive Era, among them
Richard L. McCormick, *Progressivism* (1983); John Whiteclay Chambers II, *The Tyranny of
Change* (2d. ed., 2000); Michael McGerr, *A Fierce Discontent* (2003); and Lewis L. Gould,
America in the Progressive Era (2001). John Burnham insightfully describes the Progressive
ethos in "The Cultural Interpretation of the Progressive Movement," in *Progressivism*, ed.
John D. Buenker et al. (1977).

Martin J. Sklar's *The Corporate Reconstruction of American Capitalism* (1988) argues
powerfully that the Progressive movement was designed to align American government
and law with a corporation-dominated society. Morton Keller provides a sweeping survey
of government social regulation in *Regulating a New Society* (1994). Maxwell Bloomfield
shows how arguments for constitutional change were transmitted through popular culture in *Peaceful Revolution: Constitutional Change and American Culture from Progressivism to the New Deal* (2000). See also two classics: Samuel P. Hayes's *The Response to
Industrialism* (1957) and Robert H. Wiebe's *The Search for Order* (1967). For the role "federal effects" played in promoting progressive legislation, see William Graebner, "Federalism in the Progressive Era: A Structural Interpretation of Reform," *Journal of American
History* 64 (June 1977): 331–357, which does not use the term, however.

The standard discussion of the ideology of the general-welfare state is still Sidney
Fine, *Laissez-Faire and the General-Welfare State* (1956). See also Charles Forcey, *The
Crossroads of Liberalism* (1961). Morton White discusses the assault on *a priori* reasoning
and the rise of pragmatism in *Social Thought in America: The Revolt Against Formalism*
(1975). Thomas Haskell discusses the related and equally important development, *The
Emergence of Professional Social Science* (1977).

Lewis L. Gould, *The Modern American Presidency* (2003) discusses Roosevelt, Wilson,
and Taft's impact on the presidency in the Progressive Era. William Harbaugh describes
increased prestige and power of the office in "The Constitution of the Theodore Roosevelt
Presidency and the Progressive Era," in Martin L. Fausold and Alan Shank (eds.), *The Constitution and the American Presidency* (1991), 63–82. For the development of the administrative state, the standard work is Stephen Skowronek, *Building a New American State*
(1982). For progressive theories of governmental administration, see John A. Rohr, *To
Run a Constitution* (1986).

Richard L. McCormick stresses the Protestant, moral-reform aspect of progressivism
in "Progressivism: A Contemporary Reassessment," in his *The Party Period and Public*

Policy (1986). Norman H. Clark, *Deliver Us from Evil: An Interpretation of American Prohibition* (1976); Alison M. Parker, *Purifying America* (1997); Alan Hunt, *Governing Morals* (1999); and David J. Pivar, *Purity and Hygiene* (2002) all describe the progressives' effort to enforce moral values. David J. Langum, *Crossing over the Line: Legislating Morality and the Mann Act* (1994) and Richard F. Hamm, *Shaping the Eighteenth Amendment* (1995) pay special attention to the constitutional controversies that followed. On the fight over distribution of birth-control information and devices, see Ellen Chesler, *Woman of Valor: Margaret Sanger and the Birth Control Movement in America* (1992) and Linda Gordon, *The Moral Property of Women* (2002).

Paula Baker published the classic description of "The Domestication of Politics" in the *American Historical Review* 89 (June 1984): 620–647. Historical sociologist Theda Skocpol has been especially influential in discerning the link between progressive and "maternalist" politics. See *Protecting Soldiers and Mothers* (1992). For the interaction between constitutional doctrines and gender, see Vivien M. Hart's aptly titled *Bound by Our Constitution* (1994) and Julie Novkov, *Constituting Workers, Protecting Women* (2001).

Alice Kessler-Harris describes how protective labor legislation for women divided feminists in *Out to Work* (1982). Judith Baer echoes arguments that protective legislation discriminated against women in *The Chains of Protection* (1978). See also Nancy Woloch's concise study *Muller v. Oregon* (1996). For traditional accounts of the woman suffrage amendment, see Ann Firor Scott's *One Half the People* (1975) and David Morgan's *Suffragists and Democrats* (1972). Gretchen Ritter, "Jury Service and Women's Citizenship before and after the Nineteenth Amendment," *Law and History Review* 20 (Fall 2002): 479–515 and Reva Siegel, "Collective Memory and the Nineteenth Amendment," in *History, Memory, and the Law*, ed. Austin Sarat and Thomas R. Kearns (1999) discuss the limited impact the Amendment had on women's search for equality. Linda Kerber tells the story of women and jury duty in the decades following the ratification of the Nineteenth Amendment in chapter 4 of *No Constitutional Right to Be Ladies* (1998).

Edward J. Larson, *Sex, Race, and Science: Eugenics in the Deep South* (1995) has a good introductory chapter on the national eugenics movement. For more detail, supplement Mark H. Haller, *Eugenics* (1984) with Donald K. Pickens's *Eugenics and the Progressives* (1968). Roger Daniels links the racism and ethnocentrism of the Progressive Era in *Not Like Us: Immigrants and Minorities in America, 1890–1924* (1997). Mae M. Ngai insightfully discusses the Immigration Act of 1924 as part of her study of illegal aliens *Impossible Subjects* (2004). See also the classic studies of the sorry record of racism during the Progressive Era, Rayford W. Logan's *The Betrayal of the Negro* (1965) and chapter 5 of Daniel J. Tichenor's *Dividing Lines: The Politics of Immigration Control in America* (2002). Tanis C. Thorne sets the fascinating story of *The World's Richest Indian* (2003) against the history of Native Americans and American law from the Progressive Era through the 1930s.

Philip Foner discusses labor-union racism in *Organized Labor and the Black Worker* (1982). See also Warren C. Whatley, "African-American Strikebreaking from the Civil War to the New Deal," *Social Science History* 17(Winter 1993): 525–558, and David E. Bernstein's thought-provoking "Roots of 'the Underclass': The Decline of Laissez-Faire Jurisprudence and the Rise of Racist Labor Legislation," *American University Law Review* 43 (Fall 1993): 85–138. Eric Arnesen, *Brotherhoods of Color: Black Railroad Workers and the Struggle for Equality* (2001) is a study of race relations in a specific industry.

John E. Semonche, *Charting the Future* (1978), is still the standard survey of the Supreme Court's constitutional law decisions in the Progressive Era. The most comprehensive study is Alexander M. Bickel and Benno C. Schmidt Jr.'s massive *The History of the*

Supreme Court, vol. 9: *The Judiciary and Responsible Government: 1910–1921* (1984). For progressive legislation in the state courts, see Melvin I. Urofsky, "State Courts and Protective Legislation during the Progressive Era," *Journal of American History* 72 (June 1985): 63–91.

A number of scholars argue that historians have exaggerated the influence of laissez-faire ideas upon the Supreme Court. See, for example, Melvin I. Urofsky, "Myth and Reality: The Supreme Court and Protective Legislation in the Progressive Era," *Yearbook of the Supreme Court Historical Society* (1983) and Michael J. Phillips, *The Lochner Court: Myths and Reality* (2001). However, it is not the number of decisions overturning progressive legislation that is determinative, but the breadth of those decisions and the parameters they established for considering social and economic legislation.

William G. Ross analyzes progressive and labor-union criticism of the judiciary in *A Muted Fury* (1994). William Wiecek describes the attack on formalist legal thought in *The Lost World of Classical Legal Thought* (1998). Howard Gillman explains how new jurisprudential ideas combined with social and economic change to undermine classical constitutional jurisprudence in *The Constitution Besieged* (1993). Barry Cushman stresses the importance of the private-public distinction in *Rethinking the New Deal Court* (1998). Susan M. Sterett describes how the courts came to accept public pensions and workmen's compensation in *Public Pensions* (2003); John Fabian Witt demonstrates how the problem of industrial accidents undermined the conceptions underlying laissez-faire constitutionalism in *The Accidental Republic* (2004).

For more on the great Justice Oliver Wendell Holmes, consult David H. Burton's concise *Oliver Wendell Holmes, Jr.* (1980). In *Louis D. Brandeis* (1984), Phillipa Strum shows the interaction among Progressive social and economic reform, deeper intellectual currents, and constitutional law. Melvin I. Urofsky describes Brandeis more briefly in *Louis D. Brandeis and the Progressive Tradition* (1981).

The standard survey of civil liberty during World War I is Paul L. Murphy, *World War One and the Origin of Civil Liberties in the United States* (1979). William Preston Jr. puts wartime suppression of radicals in the context of the progressives' general disinterest, if not hostility to, freedom of expression in *Aliens and Dissenters* (1963). For the *Abrams* case and its background, see Richard Polenberg, *Fighting Faiths* (1987).

13

Liberal versus Conservative
Constitutionalism in the 1920s

B y the time World War I ended, the progressive impulse that had dominated American public policy seemed spent. Americans had lived
through political turmoil, reform, and war for over twenty years. The war,
with its intense emotions and rigid controls over business and labor, made
people weary of constant change. A wave of nostalgia for simpler times swept
the nation. The Republican candidate for the presidency in 1920, Warren G.
Harding, captured the mood when he promised a "return to normalcy." Conservatism revived in the years following the war, leading to an era of conflict between rival philosophies of politics, morals, and society, with powerful
implications for civil liberties and constitutional government.

The Red Scare and the Race Riots of 1919–1920

The victory of communism in Russia fueled hostility towards socialism, radicalism, and the labor movement in general. As a series of bitter strikes followed the
end of the war, leaders of the Wilson administration, who had supported progressive reform a few years earlier, charged that socialists and their allies intended
to overthrow the United States government just as the Communists had overthrown that of Russia. In the fall of 1919, Wilson's attorney general, A. Mitchell
Palmer, launched a series of raids on the offices of labor unions, the Socialist
party, and radical organizations and publications. In the Palmer Raids, which
continued into 1920, the attorney general's strike force, led by J. Edgar Hoover,
the young head of the Intelligence Division of the Justice Department's Bureau of
Investigation, arrested thousands of foreign-born Americans and immigrants
and prepared to deport them without trial. The government destroyed the offices
of radical newspapers and periodicals on the pretense of searching for evidence
of illegal activity. In the heated antiradical environment, businessmen used violence to break the strikes of 1919 and 1920.

Many people recoiled from the excesses of the "Red Scare" of 1919, and few
of its victims were actually deported. But the Red Scare, combined with charges

of disloyalty and the wartime prosecutions, broke the power of socialist and other radical political and labor organizations, leaving the United States the only western nation without a viable socialist party. The persecution also wrecked the radical labor unions, leaving the conservative American Federation of Labor as the prime spokesman for American workers.

The Red Scare was not only a reaction against radicalism; it was fueled by hostility towards new immigrants from southern and eastern Europe. American-born workers feared their competition, their potential as strikebreakers, their willingness to work for low wages. Other Americans feared their radicalism and their support for "un-American" political ideologies like socialism and communism. Rural Americans and prosperous city-dwellers now moving to the suburbs viewed the immigrant-filled urban slums with alarm. It was no accident that restrictive immigration laws were passed following the Red Scare, nor that the 1920s were the era of Prohibition. The same years witnessed a surge of racial violence. Emboldened by the "war for democracy," the newly formed NAACP spread southwards, establishing 85 new southern branches and gaining 35,000 new southern members in 1919. They were received with a renewed wave of lynchings and race riots. The violence spread northward. Tens of thousands of black families had migrated north to fill job vacancies created by the war. Competition for jobs and housing at war's end worsened the racism that had been growing in the North since the 1880s. White mobs attacked black neighborhoods throughout the region. The Chicago race riot of 1919 lasted five days, with sporadic violence continuing for another eight, leaving nearly forty people dead, over 500 injured, and a thousand African American families homeless.

Revulsion against the violence bolstered northern membership in the NAACP and the Urban League, although most of the NAACP's southern branches collapsed. The B'nai Brith's Anti-Defamation League, perceiving the similarity between the riots and the anti-Semitic pogroms of Russia, began forging an alliance with African American civil rights organizations, which would be cemented as the antiblack, anti-Semitic Ku Klux Klan grew in power.

The Revival of Conservatism

As Americans recoiled from radicalism, they became more sympathetic to business interests. No longer perceived as a rapacious exploiter of consumers and workers, American business was credited with creating the great prosperity of the 1920s. A "consumer revolution" radically changed the economic expectations of ordinary Americans. Increased literacy and the rise of mass magazines went together. A new technology created the radio. The new mass media was fueled by a new kind of advertising that no longer simply announced the availability of goods but worked to create demand for ever more products, in turn fostering ever greater investment and creating millions of jobs that drew Americans from the countryside to the city.

The new prosperity of the 1920s created practical new freedoms. Household appliances emancipated married women from hours of drudgery. Mass-produced automobiles increased mobility. Movies brought new sights; the radio, new sounds. For many equality and freedom came to mean access to an egalitarian middle-class standard of living, with the freedom to choose from a wide range of products and opportunities. Outside of some western states, Americans gave little support to proposals for further progressive legislation in this buoyant environment.

Businessmen, many of whom had supported various progressive reforms, turned against further regulation. Alienated by the controls that the government had imposed during the war, they particularly opposed those that regulated working conditions and encouraged the formation of labor unions. At war's end, they worked to turn some progressive reforms to their advantage and to eliminate others. Taking advantage of progressivism's acceptance of bigger businesses and economic cooperation, they organized trade associations that set production standards, controlled the cost of labor and raw materials, and coordinated marketing. But the business community took advantage of popular hostility towards socialists and labor radicals to attack labor unions and labor regulation as un-American.

The election of President Warren G. Harding in 1920 led to a decade of Republican control of the federal government and most of the state governments outside the South. Except in a few midwestern states, Republicans became staunchly pro-business, naming pro-business appointees to state and federal regulatory commissions. The commissions continued the progressive tradition of rationalizing markets and business activity, providing information, and defining and suppressing unfair business practices. But their primary goal became the promotion of business interests. Rejoicing in burgeoning economic development, enjoying the practical expansion of individual liberty that economic security made possible, ordinary Americans sustained the party of prosperity. The revival of conservatism took place amidst calls for a renewed commitment to constitutional liberty and state rights. To conservatives, radical calls for government intervention in the economy were incompatible with a true understanding of the American Constitution. However, others were linking freedom to the idea of "social justice"—exercising government power to offset the disparities in power between employers and employees, lenders and debtors, landlords and tenants, planters and sharecroppers. What conservatives denounced as socialistic infringements on property rights, they saw as reasonable enactments for the general welfare.

The Supreme Court and Conservative Jurisprudence

The decisions of the Supreme Court mirrored the conservative reaction that followed World War I. The *Abrams* case, in which the Court adopted the Bad Tendency Test in free-speech cases over the objections of Holmes and Brandeis, was decided in the wake of the first Palmer Raids. The argument among the justices continued through the 1920s, the years in which former president Taft presided as chief justice, with the majority sustaining state laws limiting freedom of speech. In general, these laws made it illegal to advocate the violent overthrow of the government or to belong to organizations that did so. In *Gitlow v. New York* (1925), the Court ruled that the government could imprison socialists under such laws without having to show they actually did anything beyond talking and writing. In *Whitney v. California* (1927), the Court sustained a conviction for merely participating in a convention of the Communist Labor party. To the dismay of Taft, who wanted to "mass the Court" behind conservative decisions, Holmes and Brandeis wrote dissenting opinions, adhering to their Clear and Present Danger doctrine. After 1925, they were joined in dissent by a new justice, Harlan Fiske Stone.

Although the Court continued to support restrictions on freedom of expression and association, civil libertarians won a significant victory simply by persuading the justices to hear such cases. The reasoning of *Hurtado v. California* (1884) had indicated that the Due Process Clause of the Fourteenth Amendment did not cover any of the liberties mentioned in the Bill of Rights. In *Twining v. New Jersey* (1908) the Court had modified its position somewhat, conceding that some of the rights protected by the Bill of Rights were so fundamental that they might also be protected by the Fourteenth Amendment. But the Court had not yet specified such a right. Now, although they sustained Gitlow's conviction, the justices finally announced that "freedom of speech and of the press—which are protected by the First Amendment from abridgment by Congress—are among the fundamental personal rights and 'liberties' protected by the due process clause of the Fourteenth Amendment from impairment by the States."

With this language, the Court repudiated the reasoning of the *Hurtado* case. It was not clear that the Court intended to hold that the Fourteenth Amendment imposed on the states the identical limitations that the First Amendment imposed on the federal government. But that is how the Court would interpret the decision later, so most legal scholars regard *Gitlow* as the first decision to "incorporate" a provision of the Bill of Rights into the Fourteenth Amendment and apply it to the states. As a result of the Court's statement in *Gitlow,* civil-liberties lawyers actively began to seek Supreme Court review of state laws that violated the Bill of Rights.

As most Americans turned against organized labor and radicalism, the Supreme Court became more sensitive to the "class legislation" aspects of progressive legislation. Concerned that state governments might promote consumer interests by regulating prices, the Court ruled such regulations unconstitutional in *Tyson v. Banton* (1927). The case involved a New York law forbidding the resale of theater tickets, enacted to prevent brokers from buying up tickets to popular Broadway shows and selling them at inflated prices. Authorities could only regulate prices charged by businesses "affected with a public interest," a narrow category of businesses long known to the common law.

The Court was especially sensitive to minimum-wage laws. Most of the justices considered them to be the baldest class legislation, simply transferring resources from employers to employees. Nonetheless, many states had passed minimum-wage laws for women, relying on *Muller v. Oregon* to justify them, and Congress had applied similar laws to Washington, D.C. In *Adkins v. Children's Hospital* (1923), the Supreme Court ruled them unconstitutional, over the dissent of Holmes and, surprisingly, of Taft. The law "exacts from the employer an arbitrary payment for a purpose and upon a basis having no causal connection with his business," the justices complained. The minimum wage was based "not [on] the value of the services rendered, but the extraneous circumstance that the employee needs to get a prescribed sum of money to insure her subsistence, health and morals."

The justices concluded that recent moves towards greater equality between the sexes, especially ratification of the Women's Suffrage Amendment, militated against giving women greater protection in work contracts than men—or as the Court saw it, against placing greater restrictions on women's freedom to make contracts than on men's freedom to do so. Compelled to follow the Supreme Court decision, state and federal courts overturned all minimum-wage legislation, some reluctantly and others with enthusiasm. The feminist response to *Adkins v. Children's Hospital* was decidedly mixed. Frustrated at their inability to eliminate state laws discriminating against women, militant feminists, represented by Alice Paul's National Woman's party, demanded an amendment to the federal Constitution to ban all discriminations based on sex. Paul and her allies welcomed the *Adkins* decision, praising it for eliminating the justification for sex discrimination that the Court had accepted in *Muller*. They hoped (futilely as it turned out) that the Supreme Court would now look skeptically at all legislation that treated women differently from men, turning the Nineteenth Amendment into an engine of equality.

Other women's-rights activists were appalled. Having won the right to vote, many had organized the League of Women Voters to use their new power to press for further reforms. "[M]en do not bear children, are freed from the burdens of maternity," Florence Kelley objected. "These are differences so far reaching, so fundamental, that it is grotesque to ignore them." The way to eliminate discrimination in labor contracts was to secure the same protections for men that *Muller* had sustained for women, feminists like Kelley contended. The *Adkins* decision merely secured for women the same right as men to be exploited by low wages. An equal rights amendment would be even worse, they warned. It might nullify all legislation protecting women from exploitation in the free market. It reflected the interests of middle-class and professional women, not working-class women, Paul's feminist critics charged, and they played an important role in blocking it.

The Supreme Court also overturned some of the most important progressive legislation dealing with employer-employee relations. In *Wolff Packing Co. v. Kansas Court of Industrial Relations* (1923), the Court voided an ambitious state law creating a special court to settle disputes between workers and employers in industries "affected with a public interest," such as those producing food, clothing, and fuel. This definition of "affected with a public interest" was too broad, the Court said. No matter how important an industry was, it did not fit into the legal category of "businesses affected with a public interest" unless it had been defined as such by the ancient precedents of the common law. Outside of that limited category of businesses, the state could interfere with freedom of contract only in the valid exercise of the police power.

Even when Progressivism was at its strongest, the Court had overturned state and federal laws banning "yellow-dog" contracts that barred workers from joining labor unions. Now the Court overturned laws banning the use of injunctions in labor disputes. Such laws deprived the employer of the means to protect his property rights, the Court concluded. Consequently, state and federal courts continued to issue injunctions ordering unions to stop picketing and boycotting businesses in labor disputes. At the same time, the Court narrowly construed Congress's Progressive-Era efforts to exempt labor unions from the operation of the Sherman Anti-Trust Act.

Holmes and Brandeis, later joined by Stone, regularly dissented in these cases. Echoing the progressive demand for a "sociological jurisprudence" and reiterating his call for a "living law," Brandeis pointed out again and again that the Court's decisions ignored social realities. "Whether a law enacted in the exercise of the police power is justly subject to the charge of being unreasonable or arbitrary, can ordinarily be determined only by a consideration of the contemporary conditions, social, industrial and political of the community to be affected," he insisted in *Truax v. Corrigan* (1921). A law that might once have been a blatant piece of class legislation could be a valid exercise of the police power under modern circumstances. Attention to actual social conditions would demonstrate that labor injunctions, for example, no longer protected employers' rights against infringement. Instead they "endowed property with active, militant power which would make it dominant over men." Under such circumstances, banning them was a reasonable exercise of the police power. "Nearly all legislation involves a weighing of public needs against private desires; and likewise a weighing of relative social values," Brandeis insisted. A law's constitutionality could not be decided merely by looking at precedents regardless of circumstances.

Holmes went further, continuing to adhere to the position he had taken in his *Lochner* dissent. Unlike Brandeis and Stone, who urged their conservative colleagues to adopt a broader conception of what regulations might reasonably serve the public interest, Holmes rejected the dichotomy between general-welfare legislation and class legislation. "I think the proper course is to recognize that a state legislature can do whatever it sees fit to do unless it is restrained by some express prohibition in the Constitution," Holmes wrote in his dissent in *Tyson v. Banton*.

"The truth seems to me to be that . . . the legislature may forbid or restrict any business when it has a sufficient force of public opinion behind it."

Holmes's position challenged the idea that the courts should assume a special responsibility to protect constitutional liberty from democratic decisions. His main concern remained to assure that the First Amendment preserved the free competition among ideas upon which democracy depended. He was not much concerned with personal liberty for its own sake. His powerful commitment to judicial restraint led him to sustain state laws that, inspired by the "science" of eugenics, permitted the involuntary sterilization of people with transmittable handicaps. A believer in eugenics himself, Holmes had no trouble ruling in *Buck v. Bell* (1927) that such a law served the general welfare. This time most of Holmes's conservative colleagues agreed with him. The decision undercut the widespread opposition to such legislation and led sixteen states to enact sterilization laws in the following decade.

The Supreme Court also began to return to the old state-rights doctrine of "dual federalism," especially in cases involving labor regulations. In *Hammer v. Dagenhart* (1918), the justices revived the Court's former distinction between production and commerce, ruling the Child Labor Act unconstitutional as a violation of the Tenth Amendment. The national government's power to regulate interstate commerce could not be used to control labor conditions in businesses not directly related to transportation. When Congress passed the Second Child Labor Act in 1919, this time imposing a punitive tax on goods made with child labor, the Court ruled it unconstitutional as well in *Bailey v. Drexel Furniture Co.* (1922). Once again the Court held that the Tenth Amendment prohibited Congress from using even its delegated powers to regulate subjects within state jurisdiction.

However, the justices did not want to deprive the federal government of the power to promote morality through federal laws that barred pornography, gambling materials, and prostitution from foreign and interstate commerce and the mail, nor did they want to undermine protections of public health like the Pure Food and Drug Act. So they distinguished between items that were evil in themselves (*mala in se* in legal Latin) from those that were not. Congress could exercise its national police power to ban intrinsically bad or dangerous commodities from interstate commerce, but not others. In effect the Court left standing two competing lines of precedents dealing with interstate commerce, one that justified broad regulation and another that limited federal power, distinguished by the questionable *mala in se* rule. Similarly, the Court had established two lines of precedents dealing with economic regulations—the Progressive-Era cases that took a generous view of what was within the police power and another line of cases that took a more restricted view, especially when it came to regulating prices and wages.

The Supreme Court's justifications of its decisions became ever less persuasive to observers, especially in the nation's finest law schools. A new generation of legal scholars, the "legal realists," moved beyond the criticism of formalistic jurisprudence levied by Pound, Brandeis, and other advocates of sociological jurisprudence. The earlier group had urged the identification and application of legal principles through the careful investigation of social reality rather than through abstract logic. The legal realists scoffed at the idea that judges could find principles of law through any kind of analysis. In reality, judges made policy choices based on their own social, political, and economic beliefs, and their own sense of justice. They applied the law to specific situations in light of those commitments.

Legal realists drew varying conclusions from this insight. Many urged judicial restraint: Since both courts and legislatures made public policy, the legislative will should prevail because it represented the views of the majority. That was the position that Holmes took in most cases, leading him to the awful decision in *Buck v. Bell*, in which a mildly retarded young woman—if she was retarded at all—was forced to undergo sterilization for fear she might transmit her handicap. Other legal realists, accepting the inevitability of judicial policymaking, urged that executives and legislatures openly take judges' social, economic, and political attitudes into account when naming them to office. They wanted judges who would recognize the policy consequences of their decisions and who would fashion law to carry out liberal rather than conservative policies.

Liberalism, Conservatism, and Civil Liberty in the 1920s

The disagreement within the Taft Court mirrored a similar conflict in the nation as a whole. The 1920s were an age of struggle between different ways of looking at society. On one side were people of varying degrees of conservatism who clung to Victorian ideals. They were repelled by the pragmatic idea that there were no absolute truths. They continued to believe that success depended upon morality and character. In the land of equal opportunity, each individual was responsible for his own success or failure. They believed that it was appropriate for government to pass laws designed to encourage morality, but inappropriate to pass "socialistic" laws that would redistribute wealth. Many conservatives welcomed another of the periodic revivals of religiosity that gained strength in the 1920s and reinforced support for Prohibition and other moral legislation. They supported measures to suppress radicals who advocated communism, socialism, or the necessity of revolution to achieve social justice.

On the other side were reformers of varying degrees of liberalism, who believed that conservative ideas were hopelessly anachronistic. Strongest in the large cities, liberals believed that society had become so complex that it was naive to say that people controlled their own destinies. The idea that wealth was the reward for hard work and good morals while poverty was a punishment for bad character was a pernicious myth that prevented society from dealing with its real problems, they insisted. Poverty was the *cause* of crime, ignorance, and degradation, not the result. Not all would go as far as Clarence Darrow, who absolved individuals of almost any responsibility for their actions, but his view was an extreme statement of the general tendency: "Each act, criminal or otherwise, follows a cause," he explained in *Crime: Its Causes and Treatment.* "However much society may feel the need of confining the criminal, it must first of all understand that the act had an all-sufficient cause for which the individual was in no way responsible, and must find the cause of his conduct, and, so far as possible, remove the cause." A more moderate version of such ideas led liberals to advocate laws to shift resources from rich to poor, including minimum-wage laws, maximum-hour laws, and laws mandating employer-funded pensions and insurance against industrial accidents.

Although the modern economy demanded government regulation of business and labor, in other areas liberals wanted maximum individual liberty, which they defined more and more in terms of personal autonomy and self-fulfillment. As a critic of Prohibition put it, one of the great dangers in a democracy was "the temptation of the sovereign individual . . . to regard himself as his brother's keeper, called upon to direct and regulate his brother's habits and morals." By no means did all opponents of Prohibition follow this idea to its logical conclusion, but it was clear nonetheless: If people had the right to decide whether taking a drink was consistent with their moral code, that right must extend to other behavior as well.

Thus liberals sympathized with demands for greater freedom for women, and they were not much troubled by evidence of a revolution in sexual behavior. (Later research would show that women reaching maturity in the 1920s were twice as likely as those born ten years earlier to engage in premarital sexual relations; anywhere from a quarter to one-half of them violated the traditional taboo.) They supported the fight to improve the status of racial and religious minorities. They attacked policies trying to force Native Americans to assimilate, calling for respect for traditional customs and beliefs. This toleration of differing viewpoints and moral values was a prime characteristic of liberalism and one of the most significant ways in which it differed from progressivism. But to conservatives, it appeared that the immoral ideas that had always lurked in the dark corners of city life were threatening to displace traditional morality itself.

The disagreements between liberalism and conservatism came to a head in a series of conflicts in the 1920s that led ever more people to reassess their feelings about these ideologies. Perhaps the single most important conflict arose over Prohibition. Most Americans still believed liquor to be a dangerous drug, ruinous to health and morality. Other Americans continued to charge that Prohibition was simply an effort on the part of intolerant, Anglo-Saxon Protestants to impose their way of life on others. The same was true of "blue laws," which made it a crime to work or to present public entertainment on Sundays.

Prohibition led to the most widespread American resistance to law since Reconstruction. With the government banning legal production and distribution of alcohol, criminals filled the vacuum, giving rise to organized crime in the United States. Ordinary citizens prepared home brews and distilled bathtub gin. Illegal drinking and gambling houses, called "speakeasies," spread through the cities. Bootleggers transported illegal alcohol through the country. By the 1930s many of Prohibition's original proponents preferred repeal to growing (if somewhat exaggerated) disrespect for law. Both the Democratic and the Republican candidates for the presidency in 1932 promised to back a new constitutional amendment revoking it.

Hostility towards radicalism, foreigners, and racial and religious minorities fueled the growth of a new Ku Klux Klan. Inspired by the heroic portrayal of the Reconstruction-Era Klan in the powerful movie *The Birth of a Nation* (1915), the "Invisible Empire," as it sometimes called itself, promised to restore control of the United States to native-born, white Protestants. The Klan supported Prohibition and other laws to defend traditional Victorian morality against the attacks of foreigners, Communists, and other aliens. Its leaders argued that Catholics, Jews, Negroes, and Asians could never become good Americans. Strong in rural areas, small towns, and mid-sized cities, the Klan attacked the moral laxity of the big cities with their speakeasies, jazz, easy women, and crime. Its members reacted violently to evidence that movies, magazines, and the radio were spreading new attitudes to their own towns and farms.

Terrorizing African Americans, Catholics, and Jews, the Klan became politically powerful in the South and Midwest. Northern Democrats, many of whom were Catholics and city-dwellers, traditionally opposed such "puritan" attacks on "personal liberty." In the Democratic presidential nominating convention of 1924, they fought a titanic battle against southern, Klan-influenced Democrats. It took over one hundred ballots to name a presidential candidate, and the party almost broke apart. In 1928 the northern Democrats won a clear victory, nominating the Catholic governor of New York, Al Smith, for president and promising to repeal Prohibition. Smith's nomination was so unpopular in the South that many white Southerners voted for a Republican presidential candidate for the first time in their lives, giving the more conservative Republican, Herbert Hoover, an overwhelming victory. But in the North, Democrats carried many of the large cities for the first time in a generation, foreshadowing the liberal Democratic victories of the 1930s.

Another great symbolic event was the 1921 murder trial of two Italian immigrant anarchists, Nicola Sacco and Bartolomeo Vanzetti. Although there was scant evidence that the men had committed the crime, a conservative judge and jury condemned them to die after the prosecutors stressed their radical political views. All over the country people protested the unfair verdict, charging that Sacco and Vanzetti were being executed for their political beliefs rather than for the crime of which they were accused. Despite the efforts of liberal and radical groups, they were executed in 1927, as weeping men and women picketed the prison and the offices of government officials and judges.

The famous "Scopes Monkey Trial" of 1925 provided another battleground in the ongoing struggle. In this trial, broadcast nationwide by radio, a young teacher, John Scopes, was prosecuted for violating a Tennessee law that forbade educators from teaching the theory of biological evolution because it contradicted the biblical statement that God created the world in six days. Scopes and his famous lawyer, Clarence Darrow, argued that the government could not deny teachers the right to teach theories supported by reputable scholarship. The state prosecutors, aided by former Democratic presidential candidate William Jennings Bryan, argued that the state had the right to promote religion and morality in the classroom.

With such famous lawyers engaged in legal combat, newsmen from all over the country came to report on the trial. Once again those who believed in freedom of expression were pitted against those who believed that the state had the right to impose the beliefs of the majority. In a bold move, Darrow called on Bryan to testify. It seemed to many observers that Darrow's examination made Bryan look foolish and intolerant. In the end Scopes was convicted, but the case was a great moral victory for liberalism.

Similar struggles took place in the courts when the national and state governments tried to suppress books, movies, and art that offended the majority's moral sensibilities or religious values. In response, civil libertarians argued that freedom of speech and of the press protected artistic as well as political expression. Free access to artistic expression helped to develop human potential; to deny it was to cripple the human spirit. As the Supreme Court began to suggest that the Fourteenth Amendment protected free speech against state infringement, artists and their lawyers hoped that judges might hold laws that limited freedom of artistic expression unconstitutional.

By the late 1920s, Americans were divided on a series of issues involving all aspects of society. Many of these issues had constitutional implications. The arguments of Holmes, Brandeis, and Stone seemed persuasive to more and more people, especially to legal scholars teaching in law schools. But it would not be the courts that ultimately decided the great constitutional issues over the power of government to regulate the economy, over free speech, religious and racial toleration, and women's rights. The American people would decide them through the democratic process. Only after the people registered their decision in the 1930s would the courts enshrine it in constitutional law.

TIMELINE

1918   The Supreme Court rules the federal Child Labor Act unconstitutional as an invasion of state rights in the First Child Labor Case (*Hammer v. Dagenhart*).

1919   Eighteenth Amendment ratified, instituting Prohibition in 1920.

Labor strikes and violence continue through 1920.

1919	Chicago race riot.
	Ku Klux Klan grows in power, spreading throughout the South and Midwest.
	Attorney General Palmer launches Palmer Raids against radical organizations; the raids and the "Red Scare" continue into 1920.
	Supreme Court upholds the constitutionality of the Sedition Act in *Abrams v. U.S.*
1920	Warren G. Harding elected president calling for "normalcy."
1921	Sacco-Vanzetti trial.
	Congress restricts immigration into the United States in the Emergency Quota Act.
1923	Supreme Court rules minimum wage laws for women unconstitutional in *Adkins v. Children's Hospital.*
1924	Northern liberal and anti-Prohibitionist delegates battle southern and Ku Klux Klan–influenced delegates at the Democratic national convention.
1925	Scopes "Monkey Trial."
	Supreme Court upholds state sedition laws in *Gitlow v. N.Y.,* but rules that the Fourteenth Amendment protects freedom of speech.
1927	Sacco and Vanzetti executed.
1928	Democrats nominate Catholic New York governor Al Smith for president on an anti-Prohibition platform.

FURTHER READING

The best survey of the 1920s still remains William E. Leuchtenburg's concise and lively *The Perils of Prosperity* (2d ed., 1993). There are a number of other good overviews, including Geoffrey Perrett's more substantial but readable *America in the Twenties* (1982); part one of Michael E. Parris, *Anxious Decades* (1992); David J. Goldberg, *Discontented America* (1999); and Ronald Allen Goldberg, *America in the Twenties* (2003). Lynn Dumenil stresses the Twenties' challenge to Victorian culture in *The Modern Temper* (1995). For a seminal essay on the role of advertising and consumption in fostering a culture of personal self-fulfillment, see T. J. Jackson Lears, "From Salvation to Self-Realization," in *The Culture of Consumption,* ed. Richard Wightman Fox and T. J. Jackson Lears (1983).

Paul L. Murphy's *The Constitution in Crisis Times* (1972) is the standard survey of American constitutional history from World War I through the era of the Warren Court. For the development of the rhetoric of "liberty and justice," see Michael Kammen, *Spheres of Liberty* (1986). For a lively chronicle of the history of civil liberty and civil rights from

World War I to the 1950s, one can't do better than John P. Roche, *The Quest for the Dream* (1963). Robert K. Murphy describes the Palmer Raids and other antiradical activities in *Red Scare* (1955). Harry N. Scheiber is critical but more dispassionate in *The Wilson Administration and Civil Liberties* (1960). Samuel Walker describes the early 1920s as the era of "Civil Liberties in the Wilderness" in his excellent history of the American Civil Liberties Union *In Defense of American Liberties* (1990). Adam Fairclough chronicles the rise of the NAACP, the effect of World War One, and the racial bloodshed of 1919 in his excellent account of the fight for African American rights *Better Day Coming* (2001). Paul Murphy chronicles the rise of civil libertarianism in the 1920s and the response of the Supreme Court in *The Meaning of Freedom of Speech* (1972), while Walker describes "The First Victories" in his history of the ACLU, noted above. See chapter 16 ("Law and Civil Liberties") of Philippa Strum's biography *Louis D. Brandeis* (1984) for an insightful discussion of how Brandeis's personal liberty-oriented support for civil liberties differed from that of Holmes.

The best general account of the Supreme Court's 1920s conservative constitutionalism is found in William F. Swindler, *Court and Constitution in the Twentieth Century: The Old Legality* (1969). "Taft: The Court as Super-Legislature" is probably the best chapter in Alpheus T. Mason's spritely *The Supreme Court from Taft to Warren* (rev. ed., 1968). Robert Post discusses "Defending the Lifeworld: Substantive Due Process in the Taft Court Era," *Boston University Law Review* 78 (December 1998): 1489–1545. Stanley I. Kutler describes the revival of dual federalism in the 1920s in "Chief Justice Taft, National Regulation and the Commerce Clause," *Journal of American History* 51 (March 1965): 651–668. Post analyzes the Taft Court's dual federalism with typical law-review thoroughness and an eye towards the present in "Federalism in the Taft Court Era: Can It Be Revived?" *Duke Law Journal* 51 (March 2002): 1513–1639. William E. Nelson describes the conflict between conservative and reform legalism in 1920s New York in the first section of *The Legalist Reformation* (2001). Michael Kammen describes the state-rights rhetoric that characterized the 1920s in "The Revival of State Rights in American Political Culture," in his *Sovereignty and Liberty* (1988).

Nancy F. Cott describes the break between Alice Paul's radically equalitarian National Woman's Party and the feminists who supported protective legislation in "Feminist Politics in the 1920s," *Journal of American History* 71 (June 1984): 43–68. See also Amy E. Butler's *Two Paths to Equality* (2002). William H. Chafe surveys women's movement into politics and the work force in the seventy years following 1920 in *The Paradox of Change* (1991).

James E. Herget describes legal realism in his history of *American Jurisprudence Since 1870* (1990), while Laura Kalman has written an influential study of *Legal Realism at Yale* (1986). For a compelling retelling of the story behind *Buck v. Bell*, see William Leuchtenburg's "*Buck v. Bell*: 'Three Generations of Imbeciles,'" *Virginia and the Constitution* A. E. Dick Howard and Melvin I. Urofsky (eds.), (1992).

Stanley Coben discusses the *Rebellion Against Victorianism* (1991) in the 1920s, while Kevin White presents a longer-range view, chronicling contested understandings of sexual morality from the Progressive era to the turn of the twenty-first century, in *Sexual Liberation or Sexual License?: The American Revolt Against Victorianism* (2000). Paul Boyer devotes much of *Purity in Print* (1968) to the struggle between anti-vice crusaders and civil libertarians in the 1920s. In a provocative book, John C. Burnham chronicles the final acceptance of *Bad Habits* (1993) in the twentieth century, while Rochelle Gurstein laments *The Repeal of Reticence* (1996) resulting from liberal victories in the legal and cultural struggles over obscenity, art, and sexual behavior. Norman H. Clark describes the resistance to Prohibition in *Deliver Us From Evil* (1976). See also David E. Kyvig's *Repealing National Prohibition* (1979).

David M. Chalmers portrays the Ku Klux Klan's intolerant and racist defense of traditional values in *Hooded Americanism* (1981). For an account of the Sacco-Vanzetti trial aimed at a general audience, see Francis Russell, *Tragedy in Dedham* (1962), and his sequel *Sacco & Vanzetti: The Case Resolved* (1986). Ray Ginger engagingly describes the Scopes Monkey Trial in *Six Days or Forever?* (1958). Edward J. Larson's *Summer for the Gods* (1997) won the Pulitzer Prize for its lucid placement of the trial within the broader history of American civil liberty.

14

The New Deal and the Constitution

The Great Depression, which began with the stock market crash of 1929, led to the transformation of American constitutionalism. Americans turned to Franklin Delano Roosevelt and the Democratic party to save the nation from economic disaster. Roosevelt and the Democrats responded with the New Deal, which used federal authority as never before to regulate the economy, control corporate power, and modify the free market's distribution of economic resources. Constitutional conservatives resisted the change. They charged that the new state and federal programs interfered with property rights and liberty of contract, and that federal New Deal programs invaded the jurisdiction that the Constitution reserved to the states. The Supreme Court ruled the key legislation of the New Deal unconstitutional in a series of cases between 1934 and 1936.

The Republican Party made the elections of 1936 a referendum on the future of American government but the American people endorsed the New Deal. Faced with the popular mandate of 1936, criticized for the inconsistency of its rulings, and threatened by a plan to pack the Court with new justices, the Supreme Court repudiated conservative constitutionalism, ratifying the New Deal transformation of government.

The Great Depression

Despite most Americans' optimism, the economy had been weakening since the mid-1920s. In 1929 investors suddenly lost confidence and the stock market collapsed. People stopped purchasing goods, and soon companies were reducing production and firing workers. The economy spiraled downwards. Businesses were forced to lay off ever more workers, reducing demand still further, leading to further layoffs. With no pension plans, no unemployment compensation, and no government-sponsored system of relief for the poor, people who lost jobs were in desperate situations. As the disaster overwhelmed private charity, the states tried to take over. But without a stable economy, the relief rolls simply kept growing; it was like throwing money down a bottomless hole.

By 1930 the United States had entered the Great Depression. In 1933, 25 percent of the work force was unemployed; an equal number worked only sporadically. Industrial production plunged 50 percent, yet unemployment was so widespread that more goods were being produced than could be consumed. Desperate to increase sales, businesses lowered prices. Competitors were forced to match the reductions, leading to cutthroat rounds of price cutting. Prices collapsed, making it impossible for farmers and businessmen to pay off loans and discouraging new investment.

State legislatures passed debt-moratorium laws to slow the wave of foreclosures on farms, homes, and businesses. They tried to reduce industrial and agricultural production so prices would stop falling and businesses could return to profitability. But the federal system frustrated such state efforts. For example, under its innovative governor Franklin D. Roosevelt, New York regulated levels of milk production and set minimum prices for its sale. But New York could not regulate dairy production in neighboring states. As soon as its milk prices stabilized, the state was flooded with milk from its neighbors, driving prices down once more. The same was true of any similar regulatory effort. If a state tried to raise prices by limiting production, there was no way to stop businessmen and farmers in other states from increasing output, taking up the slack in a desperate effort to stay afloat.

The nature of the problem drove businessmen and farmers to turn to the national government. To stabilize the economy, it was essential to control production, divide up shares of the market, and regulate prices. But if businesses cooperated to do so, they would be violating federal antitrust laws. Moreover, without government enforcement, maintaining industrywide agreements would be difficult or impossible. Voluntary price regulation put a premium on recalcitrance, since a business that did not agree to limit production would still get the benefit of higher prices if its competitors reduced theirs.

At first, President Hoover tried to persuade business, labor, and farm organizations to cooperate to fight the Depression, promising to suspend enforcement of the antitrust laws. To get more money into circulation and increase prices, he urged banks to increase lending. At the same time, he promised to reduce taxes and increase spending on public works. When these voluntary measures failed, Hoover turned to the power of the federal government, especially its authority to spend money. In 1929 Hoover and Congress gave the newly created Federal Farm Board $500 million to lend to farm marketing cooperatives and other joint agricultural ventures that enabled farmers to control production and stabilize prices. Part of the money went to buy surplus crops to keep them off the market. In 1932 Hoover persuaded Congress to create the Reconstruction Finance Corporation, a government-owned bank, to lend two billion dollars to banks, insurance companies, and other businesses. Congress created the Home Loan Bank System to lend money to homeowners. But even the two-plus billion dollars was not enough.

Hoover, appalled at the growing federal budget deficit, was reluctant to spend more. He rejected frantic pleas from the states to take over the relief of the poor and unemployed, both on state-rights grounds and because he believed a massive program of government relief would be "socialistic."

For most Americans, Hoover's inability to combat the Great Depression discredited conservative ideas about economics and government. The crisis demonstrated how factors beyond individual control affected peoples' lives and made it implausible to attribute success and failure entirely to matters of individual character. Some redistribution of wealth would help those in economic trouble through no fault of their own. Moreover, it would benefit everyone by helping the economy.

The Depression also discredited state-rights principles of federalism. The American economy was clearly national; the states could not insulate their citizens from nationwide economic trends. On the contrary, the federal system inhibited such efforts, because no state could afford to cut its own economic production, raise prices, or increase the cost of doing business by improving working conditions unless its neighbors did the same. "Federal effects" necessitated nationwide action.

The New Deal

In 1932 American voters rejected Hoover and elected the Democratic candidate, New York's Roosevelt, to the presidency. Upon taking office in 1933, he began to act on liberal understandings of society and the economy, securing a series of measures between 1933 and 1938 that came to be known as the New Deal, completing the transformation of the United States into a "general-welfare state."

There were four main thrusts to the New Deal. The first was to attempt to restore confidence in the economy, and especially in the banking system, which was on the brink of collapse. Roosevelt declared a "Bank Holiday," ordering all banks to close. In a matter of days he had Congress pass the Emergency Banking Act, under which only banks that met criteria of solvency would reopen. A few months later Congress passed a new banking act, regulating banking practices and guaranteeing depositors' accounts. To restore confidence in stocks and bonds, the government passed the Federal Securities Act in 1933 and a year later created the Securities Exchange Commission to regulate the stock market. To inflate the currency and raise prices, Roosevelt took the United States off the gold standard.

The second thrust of the New Deal was to modify the free market's distribution of resources. Roosevelt first expanded the various programs lending money to businesses and farmers. The government suspended enforcement of antitrust laws and created agencies in which representatives of business, labor, and government joined to set production quotas, prices, quality standards, wages, and working conditions for whole industries. The primary goal was to end the cutthroat competition that had led to the collapse of prices and blocked economic recovery. Businesses could now set minimum prices free of the fear that competitors would undercut them and steal their markets. Unscrupulous or desperate businessmen were prohibited from reducing their costs by lowering quality or working conditions below mandated levels.

The biggest of the new agencies was the National Recovery Administration (NRA), created by the National Industrial Recovery Act of 1933. The NRA created codes for many industries; other agencies were set up to create codes for particular industries, like bituminous coal and steel. The government also passed the Agricultural Adjustment Act, which created the Agricultural Adjustment Administration (AAA) to pass similar codes for farmers. Input came from farmers through their organizations, especially the American Farm Bureau, with farmers sitting on state and local committees that established production quotas for various crops. A majority of affected farmers had to agree to each program. The AAA paid growers who adhered to the quotas, the money coming from taxes on food and textile processors.

Unlike the industrial boards, farm workers had no say in setting up the agricultural codes. Although they regulated prices, production, and quality, the codes said little about the conditions under which farm laborers toiled. Without unions to pressure the government and politicians, farm workers had little clout. Many moved from place to place to harvest crops, with no permanent voting residence. In the South, many farm workers and sharecroppers were black, denied the right to vote or to protest the conditions imposed by white employers and landlords.

The early New Deal programs encouraged cooperation among producers to increase prices and to stabilize wages. In effect they redistributed income from consumers to industrial and agricultural producers and their employees. Prodded by Roosevelt, Congress also created public works programs, hiring unemployed people to help build roads, dams, buildings, and public parks. Young men were recruited into the Civilian Conservation Corps (CCC). Such programs shifted resources from taxpayers to the unemployed.

Later New Deal programs were aimed more clearly at shifting resources from the wealthier parts of the community to the poorer. The Social Security Act (1935) required employers to contribute to a government fund to provide workers with financial support after retirement. It promised federal money to states that established unemployment insurance programs. The Farm Tenant Act of 1937 authorized low-interest loans to sharecroppers and farm laborers to help them buy their own land. In the same year, Congress passed the National Housing Act. It offered low-cost loans to cities and counties to develop cheap public housing. As important as the Social Security Act was the Fair Labor Standards Act of 1938, which established minimum wages and maximum hours in most industries, and forbade child labor.

Third, the New Deal helped control corporate business power. It forced businesses to absorb many of the costs of handling modern economic problems, rather than letting these costs fall on the public. For example, the government began to regulate banks closely, preventing transactions that would have increased profits but put depositors' money at risk. From the New Deal onwards, the government played an increasing role in regulating business practices, passing product-safety laws, requiring honest labeling of products, and protecting worker safety.

Finally, the New Deal encouraged the development of new centers of private power in American society to offset the power of big business. To help labor organize, Congress severely limited the power of courts to enjoin strikes and picketing. The National Labor Relations Act, or Wagner Act, of 1935 created the National Labor Relations Board (NLRB) to prevent unfair labor practices that obstructed union organization. The NLRB could also order and supervise elections to see whether workers wished to join unions. In response labor unions launched a tremendous organizing drive. Between 1935 and 1941 the membership in American labor unions more than doubled from 3,750,000 to 8,700,000 workers. By 1947 membership reached fifteen million.

State governments also expanded their functions. Federal programs did not so much displace state governance as augment it. State social and economic regulations remained in place. Many federal programs relied on the states for implementation. Like the federal government, states increased the responsibility of existing administrative agencies and created new ones, confirming the shift to the administrative state begun in the Progressive Era.

The New Deal and Women

Although a number of women held prominent positions in New Deal agencies, it did not challenge traditional gender roles. Women might work, but the New Deal conceived of men as the breadwinners. It treated women's income as secondary to men's, so occupations in which women predominated were not covered by Social Security or the Fair Labor Standards Act. Housewives earned no social security benefits, received no minimum wage; no laws limited their hours of labor.

The women who helped administer the New Deal had no use for the Equal Rights Amendment. They continued to favor special protections for female workers. Yet the New Deal proceeded on the assumption that all workers were in a weak position versus employers. Arguments that had justified special consideration for women were now used to justify protection of all employees. But the work force to which these laws applied was mostly male. The New Deal left it mostly to the states to continue to care for women, children, the poor, and the disabled—lumping women in with those who could not care for themselves. In sum, the New Deal reinforced traditional assumptions about gender, limiting the ability of women to make the kinds of choices that liberalism secured to men.

The "Indian New Deal"

The New Deal policy towards Native Americans illustrated liberalism's toleration of cultural differences, reversing fifty years of aggressively encouraging assimilation.

Roosevelt named John Collier, the founder of the American Indian Defense Association and the most vociferous critic of assimilation, to be Commissioner of Indian Affairs. Collier aspired to reinstitute Indian self-government through the adoption of new tribal constitutions that would restore communal landholding and promote Native-American culture. However, the Indian Reorganization Act of 1934 was watered down by opponents of autonomous Indian communities and those who still believed in assimilating Indians fully into American society. Moreover, some Native Americans saw the proposal as another example of white condescension, a move "back to the blanket." Most tribes failed to adopt the constitutions that would have made them independent of federal bureaucratic control.

Despite its shortcomings, the so-called "Indian New Deal," marked a significant shift towards appreciation of Indian culture, and it helped revitalize tribes that had kept their institutions alive. It foreshadowed commitments to cultural pluralism that would grow stronger in the last decades of the twentieth century. But Collier's enemies forced his resignation in 1945. Once again advocating assimilation, they called for the termination of tribal authority and reservations. "Termination" meant distributing all of a tribe's resources to individual members and bringing all Native Americans within state jurisdiction. But a general sense that Native Americans had been treated shabbily also led to the creation of a special Indian Claims Commission in 1946 to hear grievances and make restitution. Compensated for past wrongs, assimilationists believed, Indians would at last be ready to be ordinary American citizens.

The New Deal and African Americans

Although many of the people who devised the New Deal were sympathetic to the plight of black Americans, dealing with racial discrimination was not one of the New Deal's priorities. Roosevelt and his advisers knew that making this issue would undermine support for their program throughout the country and especially in the South, where African Americans remained widely disfranchised. Therefore Roosevelt refused to put his prestige behind efforts to secure antilynching legislation in Congress. New Deal industrial codes did nothing to fight segregation or assure African Americans equal access to jobs. The effect of empowering organized labor was often to exclude black workers, who were still barred from many unions and seen as undermining white men's wages. The Social Security Act and the Fair Labor Standards Act excluded occupations dominated by African Americans from coverage. The Civilian Conservation Corps relegated the few African Americans it employed to demeaning jobs.

But Roosevelt opened the White House to a number of black advisors. Liberal members of the Cabinet brought African Americans into their departments at significant levels of authority. Leading northern New Deal congressmen began to support parts of the agenda promoted by African American advocacy groups. First Lady Eleanor Roosevelt made her sympathies for the downtrodden of all races well known. In 1939 President Roosevelt approved the creation of a new section of the Justice Department to protect the rights of American citizens, especially labor organizers and African Americans. In 1941 its name was changed to the Civil Rights Section. Twenty years later it would be the federal agency most active in promoting the civil rights revolution.

Despite the New Deal's concessions to racism, African Americans came to see it as representing their interests. Even if discriminatory, its programs did provide aid and jobs to black Americans. As time went on, discrimination in the programs lessened. Many industrial unions opened their ranks to black workers. As African Americans moved into occupations covered by the Fair Labor Standards Act, Social Security Act, and other regulations of the workplace, they received the same benefits as white workers. The New Deal majority on the Supreme Court began to protect the rights of black southerners. The massive shift of northern black voters into the Democratic party was the natural consequence.

The New Deal, the Growth of Presidential Power, and the Administrative State

The New Deal also marked a great turning point in the history of the presidency and the executive branch of government. During its first one hundred days, Congress passed any law the president wanted to fight the Depression. It became usual to frame legislation within the executive branch and have friendly legislators submit it to Congress. By the 1960s Congress would be more of a forum to consider presidential proposals than to make proposals of its own.

To fulfill its new responsibilities, the executive branch expanded rapidly. In 1933 about 60,000 Washingtonians worked for the executive branch, while about 10,000 worked for Congress. By 1970 290,000 would work for the executive branch, while only 30,000 would work for Congress. Congress became ever more dependent on executive agencies for the information necessary to govern. As if to symbolize the change, Americans elected Roosevelt to a third term in 1940, breaking the precedent of 150 years. In 1944, they elected him again.

The manner of legislating also changed radically. Congressional legislation set goals and procedures but authorized administrative agencies to devise specific rules and apply them to individual cases. The number of special commissions and agencies in the United States government grew dramatically. The New Deal recovery program was run by such agencies as the NRA, AAA, the Works Progress Administration (WPA), and the Civilian Conservation Corps. The Social Security Administration ran the national pension system. The NLRB administered employer-employee relations.

Roosevelt wanted to create a political system in which presidents, with a strong national vision and responsible for efficient government through administrative agencies, mobilized voters against local and parochial interests. This vision required effective presidential control of the government bureaucracy. In 1936 Roosevelt appointed a special committee that recommended that Congress authorize the president to overhaul the bureaucracy by executive orders. Many resisted, fearing a drift towards executive dictatorship as in fascist Germany and Italy. Congress passed a more modest Reorganization Act in 1939, instructing the president to recommend specific changes. Over time, Congress adopted many presidential proposals, slowly reorganizing the system. But Congress retained final authority over the bureaucracy's operations.

Nonetheless, the turn to administrative government, reinforced the president's central position in American politics. Voters paid more attention to the character and philosophies of presidential candidates than they did to the parties that nominated them. In turn, it became as important for congressmen and congresswomen to represent their constituents to the federal bureaucracy as it was to make laws.

The shift towards executive agencies indicated the influence of the legal realists. Waiting for judges to apply laws to day-to-day cases was an inefficient mode of regulating economic relations in the modern world, the realists had pointed out. Businesspeople needed to know the rules before disputes arose. Moreover, setting modern business standards required technical knowledge that ordinary judges did not possess. As James M. Landis, one of the most important advocates of administrative agencies, put it, "The administrative process is, in essence, our generation's answer to the inadequacy of the judicial and legislative processes." Such a wholesale attack on the traditional American legal system was bound to inspire opposition. Critics worried that the replacement of common-law judges with administrative bureaucrats threatened liberty. How could such an administrative system be reconciled with traditional, court-centered American understandings of due process of law?

The New Deal, the Constitution, and the Supreme Court, 1933–1936

The New Deal was based on the liberal jurisprudence that had been developing since the Progressive Era. This jurisprudence was characterized by nationalist constitutionalism, support of the general-welfare state, and legal realism. The New Deal's federal programs were all based on the nationalist theory of national government power. Nowhere did the Constitution expressly delegate the power to undertake most of them. In the first months of the New Deal, Roosevelt and his aides drew an analogy between the crisis engendered by the Great Depression and that created by war. Faced with imminent disaster, the government had to exercise emergency powers without undue regard for constitutional technicalities; the fight against the Depression amounted to an economic war, which justified the use of broad federal war powers.

However, these justifications were unlikely to carry much weight with judges when New Deal legislation was challenged in the courts. Although some of the administration's legal advisors were "legal realists" who dismissed the importance of legalistic arguments about constitutional authority, the Justice Department had no choice but to articulate constitutional justifications for New Deal legislation. Bumbling and confused at first, the administration's lawyers ultimately recognized that New Deal legislation was justified by the two powers used to create a "national police power" during the Progressive Era: the power to regulate interstate commerce and the power to tax. Most New Deal regulations applied to businesses that affected interstate commerce, or they suppressed undesirable activity by imposing prohibitive taxes. To these pillars of the national police power, New Dealers added a third: the power to spend. That is, Congress offered money to people, businesses, and local governments who voluntarily agreed to carry out the government's programs. The Social Security Act relied on such inducements to secure state participation. The national government's powers to regulate interstate commerce, to collect taxes, and to spend money for the general welfare were "sovereign" and "plenary," New Dealers insisted. Their exercise was not limited by their effect on matters within state jurisdiction.

Conservatives bitterly attacked the liberal, "general-welfare state" philosophy of the New Deal. Small businessmen especially supported this opposition because

Left-wing New Dealers lampoon the naysaying Supreme Court.

they felt that New Deal programs strengthened big businesses and big labor unions at their expense. By 1935, after the New Deal had stabilized most industries, big businessmen too came to oppose its programs because they strengthened labor unions and interfered with business autonomy. Unable to prevent the enactment of liberal legislation, conservatives continued to protest, hoping to defeat Roosevelt and other liberals in the election of 1936.

The critics had powerful allies in the state and national courts. While they organized to fight Democrats politically, businessmen brought test cases, asking judges to rule New Deal legislation unconstitutional. National and state New Deal legislation violated the Due Process Clauses of the Fifth and Fourteenth Amendments, corporate lawyers argued, by infringing property rights and by vesting legislative and judicial power in executive agencies. Moreover, the federal laws invaded the jurisdiction of the states in violation of the Tenth Amendment. The state and lower federal courts divided in their responses to this legal offensive. Some sustained challenged state and federal laws; others overturned them and blocked enforcement within their jurisdictions. This inconsistency disrupted the New Deal program and similar state legislation, because businesses in jurisdictions that enjoined enforcement of the regulations undercut those in jurisdictions that upheld them. Everyone's attention turned to the Supreme Court as such cases reached it between 1934 and 1936.

Almost the entire Court had been appointed by Republican presidents. However, it was not as conservative as it had been under Chief Justice Taft's leadership. Taft himself had been replaced by Charles Evans Hughes, the former governor of New York, who had led the opposition to the Red Scare. He and Justice Owen J. Roberts wavered between the liberal justices Brandeis, Stone, and Benjamin N. Cardozo, who had replaced Holmes in 1932, and the conservative McReynolds, George Sutherland, Pierce Butler, and Edward T. Sanford.

Even within the traditional jurisprudence that had characterized the Court's approach to constitutional questions since the 1880s and 1890s, the justices had a wide range of precedents to draw upon. Since the Progressive Era, a number of decisions had taken a broad view of the general welfare. The Court had supported wide-ranging regulations of businesses affected with a public interest. Likewise, a line of cases had taken a capacious view of federal power to regulate activities affecting interstate commerce. Other precedents echoed the more restrictive approaches identified with *Lochner, Tyson v. Banton,* and the Child Labor cases. But when New Deal legislation first came before the Court, the Roosevelt administration's lawyers did not do a very good job of defending it. Comparing the Depression to a wartime emergency, they simply urged the justices to ignore inconvenient precedents. They unpersuasively stressed the voluntary nature of the codes promulgated by the boards and agencies.

As these first challenges to Depression-era legislation came to the Court, Hughes and Roberts proved more sympathetic to state efforts to combat the Depression than to the federal government's New Deal. In *Home Building and Loan*

Association v. Blaisdell (1934), Hughes and Roberts joined the liberal justices to sustain state laws suspending the collection of debts. Writing for the majority, Hughes argued that the Obligation of Contracts Clause must be interpreted flexibly to allow states to protect the interests of their citizens in emergencies as grave as the Depression. "[W]hile emergency does not create power, emergency may furnish the occasion for the exercise of power," he wrote. McReynolds, Sutherland, Butler, and Sanford trenchantly denounced the decision. It amounted to a declaration that the Constitution could be suspended in emergencies, they said.

In *Nebbia v. New York* (1934) Hughes, Roberts, and the liberal justices seemed to explode the underpinnings of laissez-faire constitutionalism by radically expanding the definition of businesses that were "affected with a public interest." The conservative view, reiterated in *Tyson v. Banton* in 1927, had been that only businesses that the common law traditionally recognized as affected with a public interest were subject to pervasive regulation. Upholding New York's regulation of the production, marketing, and price of milk, the majority in *Nebbia* abandoned the old idea and adopted Holmes's dissenting view. Any business vital to the well-being of the community was "affected with a public interest," Justice Roberts held in the majority opinion. A state could regulate it "in any of its aspects," including prices. Echoing Holmes's famous dissent in *Lochner v. New York*, Roberts declared, "[A] state is free to adopt whatever economic policy may reasonably be deemed to promote public welfare, and to enforce that policy by legislation adapted to its purpose."

Although Hughes and Roberts broadened the scope of the states' police powers, they seemed hostile to the New Deal. They worried that Congress was delegating too much power to the executive branch and the commissions and agencies created since the Progressive Era. Hughes and Roberts joined the conservative justices on these questions. In three important cases the Court overturned major New Deal programs on the grounds that they violated "state rights" or the principle of "separation of powers." In *Schechter Poultry Corp. v. U.S.* (1935), the court ruled the National Industrial Recovery Act (NIRA) unconstitutional. All the justices agreed that the law delegated too much authority to the president and the National Recovery Administration, violating the separation of powers ordained by the Constitution. Even the liberal justices believed that the NIRA went too far. "This is delegation run riot," Cardozo wrote. Congress had to set clear goals and guidelines; it could not simply tell commissions to make whatever rules they believed necessary.

Moreover, all the justices doubted that Congress's power over interstate commerce justified regulation of such a small, local business as the Schechter Poultry Company. The more conservative justices believed that only businesses that "directly" affected interstate commerce were subject to federal regulation. They attempted to maintain the old distinction between "production," which did not directly affect commerce, and other aspects of business, like marketing and transportation, that did. The liberal justices rejected that distinction, but they agreed that businesses like Schechter's were too remote from interstate commerce to be subject to federal control.

In *U.S. v. Butler* (1936), the Court overturned the Agricultural Adjustment Act, with Brandeis, Stone, and Cardozo dissenting. The AAA had depended on the government's taxing and spending power to encourage farmers to obey codes limiting production as well as other rules. The majority of the justices flatly endorsed the state-rights interpretation of the Tenth Amendment: It recognized a reserved area of state jurisdiction that the federal government could not invade. Even though the Constitution expressly delegated the power to levy taxes and spend for the general welfare to Congress, it could not use that power to regulate agriculture. Not only did the *Butler* decision destroy the government's program to help farmers, it jeopardized the just-passed Social Security system, which also relied on the taxing power to achieve a goal not expressly authorized by the Constitution.

In *Carter v. Carter Coal Co.* (1936), the Court voided the Bituminous Coal Conservation Act of 1935, which had set up an agency to make codes for the coal industry. Once again the majority of the justices denied that Congress could regulate a business that only "indirectly" affected interstate commerce. Their approach was entirely formalistic, depending on their definition of "direct" and "indirect." It did not matter how big the coal mining company was, that the coal was intended for interstate commerce, or that it was impossible for a state to limit the production of its coal industry or to impose the costs of improved safety or working conditions when its neighbors refused to do so. "The extent of the effect [on interstate commerce] bears no logical relation to its character," the Court declared. "If the production of one man of a single ton of coal intended for interstate sale and shipment . . . affects commerce indirectly, the effect does not become direct by multiplying the tonnage, or increasing the number of men employed." Once again the liberal justices dissented, and even Hughes criticized the rigidity of the majority. Nonetheless, the Supreme Court had reconfirmed the state-rights view of federalism articulated in the *E.C. Knight* case and the Child Labor cases. Under it, the federal government was hamstrung in trying to deal with the Depression. Poorly drawn federal laws poorly defended in court had led the Supreme Court's majority to reaffirm the most conservative version of its constitutional jurisprudence.

The constitutional crisis was made worse by the Court's decision in *Morehead v. New York ex rel. Tipaldo* (1935). The *Morehead* case was a challenge to New York's new minimum-wage law, passed in a desperate effort to stabilize wages. New York's lawyers argued that wage regulation was as vital to its citizens' interests as the regulation of the price of milk. But although they had sustained other state efforts to combat the Depression, on this issue Hughes and Roberts swung back to the conservative side. A bare majority of the justices overruled the minimum-wage law on the same "due process" grounds that the Court had used in *Adkins v. Children's Hospital* in 1923. Roberts later insisted that he would have voted to overturn *Adkins* if New York's lawyers had asked the court to do so.

Instead they had futilely tried to reconcile the minimum-wage law with the Court's precedents. If true, his silence at the time was a colossal blunder. Observers concluded that the Supreme Court was now set against all New Deal legislation to fight the Depression.

The Election of 1936 and the New Deal Constitutional Revolution

Armed by the decisions of the Supreme Court, in the presidential election of 1936 conservatives charged Roosevelt with subverting the Constitution. They claimed that the New Deal agencies were creating a tyranny in which government controlled everything. Roosevelt's policies were "socialistic," encouraging class war and hostility between business and labor.

Roosevelt occasionally blasted back at those who "steal the livery of great national constitutional ideals to serve special interests." But in general he avoided making a direct issue of constitutional interpretation. He considered proposing constitutional amendments to affirm federal power to enact New Deal legislation, but advisors urged him to wait. If the Supreme Court ruled such popular legislation as the Wagner Act and Social Security unconstitutional, all would see the necessity for amendments. Until then, it was dangerous to provide ammunition for the conservative attack.

It was Republicans who made the Constitution an issue. Their platform opened, "America is in peril." It warned voters that "political liberty" and "their character as free citizens" were in jeopardy and pledged the party to "constitutional government and free enterprise." Republicans nominated a longtime progressive, Kansas governor Alfred H. Landon, for the presidency, but on the campaign trail he credited the Supreme Court with saving America from New Deal legislation, while former President Hoover urged Americans to reject Roosevelt and "this challenge to liberty." The Republicans waged a tough and bitter campaign. But Americans reelected Roosevelt and other Democrats by overwhelming majorities. The great liberal victory of 1936 forced Republicans to concede that reversing the New Deal was impossible. The basic shape of the "general-welfare state" thus became an accepted part of American life.

After his victory, Roosevelt again thought about suggesting constitutional amendments but instead decided to push for a law enabling him to "pack" the Supreme Court with new members who would support his programs. The legislation authorized the president to nominate an additional justice to the Court for every justice over seventy years of age. Although he claimed that he was merely trying to facilitate the business of the Court, everyone knew his real purpose. The proposal aroused vocal opposition, even among supporters of the New Deal. Many liberals worried that curbing the independence of the Supreme Court would set a precedent so dangerous that not even saving the New Deal could justify it. The liberal members of the Court joined conservative brethren in opposition. Southern Democrats, already restive because of the New Deal's limited efforts to help African Americans and its support for union organization in the South, almost unanimously opposed the measure. Republican progressives, who had supported many of Roosevelt's initiatives, returned to the party fold.

At issue was the Court's role in American public life. At its extreme, the court-packing plan represented the legal realist view that judges could not help but impose their own economic, social, political, and ethical values. Given that reality, judicial review was entirely inconsistent with democracy; it allowed "nine old men," as one critic described the justices, to impose their ethical and political views on the millions. A less extreme view conceded the legitimacy of judicial review, but insisted that the constitutional system provided for checks upon it. Not only could the people amend the Constitution, but Congress and the president had their own resources for combating judges who went too far in obstructing their legitimate authority. Among these resources was the power that the Constitution gave to Congress to alter the size of the Supreme Court. Had Congress acted on this view, it is almost certain that the Supreme Court would have played a far less active role in constitutional adjudication in the years following the New Deal.

In the end, Congress rejected the president's plan, confirming the widely held belief that the Supreme Court had a special role in the American constitutional system. The Court itself made the court-packing measure unnecessary. The overwhelming sentiment in favor of liberalism, the lessons of years of depression, and the damage their vacillating course had done the Court convinced Hughes and Roberts to join Brandeis, Stone, and Cardozo in a five-justice liberal majority. Cynical observers called it "the switch in time that saved nine," although it is clear the two justices had made their decision before Roosevelt submitted his plan.

The new, liberal majority emerged in March and April of 1937, just months after Roosevelt's reelection, encouraged by more carefully drawn legislation and more carefully considered constitutional arguments from better prepared government lawyers. In *West Coast Hotel Co. v. Parrish,* the Court repudiated the laissez-faire constitutionalism doctrines of "liberty of contract" and "substantive due process of law," explicitly reversing its decision in the *Adkins* case. Although the majority reiterated the old dichotomy between legitimate exercises of the police power and arbitrary infringements of economic rights, it was clear that the decision marked a turning point. No longer would the Court consider freedom the rule and restraint the exception in cases involving government regulations of the economy and employment. The fact that the case involved a female employee no longer mattered. "Liberty under the Constitution is . . . necessarily subject to the restraints of due process, and regulation which is reasonable in relation to its subject and is adopted in the interests of the community is due process," the Court held. Since that decision, no law regulating the economy has ever again been overturned by the Supreme Court for violating substantive due process of law. Any "reasonable" regulation satisfies the requirements of due process—a very easy standard to meet.

A little over two weeks later, the Court began the process of repudiating dual federalism and state-rights constitutionalism. In *National Labor Relations Board v. Jones & Laughlin Steel Corp.* (1937), it sustained the constitutionality of the National Labor Relations Act against charges that it violated the Tenth Amendment. Abandoning the effort to draw a strict line between federal and state jurisdiction over the economy, the Court declared, "Although activities may be intrastate in character when separately considered, if they have such a close and substantial relation to interstate commerce that their control is essential or appropriate to protect that commerce from burdens or obstructions, Congress cannot be denied the power to exercise that control." Thus the Court obliterated the distinction it had drawn between production and commerce in the *E.C. Knight* and *Carter Coal* cases. The regulation was an appropriate effort on the part of the federal government to prevent strikes and labor unrest that could affect the whole nation. "[I]t is idle to say that the effect [of such unrest] would be indirect or remote. It is obvious that it would be immediate and might be catastrophic." A month later the Court sustained the Social Security Act.

Nor did the Court again rule a statute unconstitutional for delegating too much legislative discretion to an administrative agency. In part this was because Congress took care to observe the Court's cautions in the *Schechter* case. In part it was because Congress would within a decade establish rules to secure due process in administrative proceedings. But a good part of the reason was the Court's abandonment of laissez-faire constitutionalism.

From 1937 to 1939 the appointment of four new justices, two of them replacing conservatives, strengthened the liberal majority on the Court. In 1941 the Court capped the New Deal revolution in federalism. In *U.S. v. Darby Lumber Co.* it explicitly overruled *Hammer v. Dagenhart* and repudiated the concept of "state rights," or "dual federalism." The Tenth Amendment did not set a limit on national power. It merely restated the "truism" that powers not delegated to the federal government remained with the states. It did not define what those powers were. The degree of the change was dramatized a year later in *Wickard v. Filburn.* The Court upheld wheat production limits applied to an Ohio dairy farmer under the second Agricultural Adjustment Act. Although Filburn used his wheat solely to feed his livestock and family, not selling a single bushel on the open market, the justices unanimously agreed that such activities, when undertaken by thousands of farmers, would affect the national market and therefore were subject to federal regulation.

As the Court ratified the New Deal's revolutionary expansion of federal power, it also abandoned one of the oldest sources of national power over the states. In *Erie Railroad Co. v. Tompkins* (1938), it reversed the nearly one-hundred-year-old decision in *Swift v. Tyson* (1842). Under the *Swift* rule, the Court had created a uniform, national law of contracts, torts, employment, and a host of other areas, most of it serving conservative business interests. Reacting against such judicial activism, the liberal justices announced that they would henceforth follow state law except where the situation required uniformity, a vague rule that remains hard to apply even today.

Since both federal and state courts were bound to follow Supreme Court interpretations of the Constitution, the change in the Court's position made it almost impossible to overturn government economic regulations on due process or state-rights grounds. Laissez-faire constitutionalism was dead. Constitutional interpretation no longer imposed conservative economic philosophy on the state and federal governments. The way was open for the massive regulation of the economy that came to characterize the United States for the rest of the twentieth century.

TIMELINE

1929	The stock market crash marks the beginning of the Great Depression.
	Congress creates Federal Farm Board to lend money to farmers.
1932	Congress creates the Reconstruction Finance Corporation to lend money to banks, insurance companies, and other financial institutions.
	Congress creates the Home Loan Bank System to lend money to homeowners.
	Democrat Franklin D. Roosevelt elected president, inaugurated in 1933.
1933	Ratification of the Twentieth Amendment moves the inauguration of presidents from March 3 to January 20 of the year following their election.
	Roosevelt declares a "Bank Holiday"; solvent banks reopen under the Emergency Banking Act.
	The "Hundred Days": Congress passes New Deal measures creating the Civilian Conservation Corps, the Federal Emergency Relief Administration, and the Agricultural Adjustment Administration.
	Congress creates the Tennessee Valley Authority.
	Federal Securities Act passed.
	Ratification of the Twenty-First Amendment ends Prohibition.
	Congress creates the National Recovery Administration.
1934	The Supreme Court permits states to suspend the collection of debts in *Home Building and Loan Association v. Blaisdell.*
	Nebbia v. New York expands the definition of businesses affected with a public interest, permitting a broader range of state regulation.

Securities Exchange Commission (SEC) created.

Congress passes the Indian Reorganization Act.

1935   *Schechter Poultry Corp. v. U.S.* rules the National Industrial Recovery Act unconstitutional.

1935   The National Labor Relations Act creates the National Labor Relations Board (NLRB); labor unions begin a series of successful organizing drives.

Congress passes the Social Security Act.

The National Housing Act creates the Federal Housing Administration (FHA).

1936   *U.S. v. Butler* rules the Agricultural Adjustment Act an unconstitutional invasion of state rights.

Carter v. Carter Coal Co. strikes down the Bituminous Coal Conservation Act.

The Supreme Court overturns state minimum-wage laws in *Morehead v. N.Y. ex rel. Tipaldo.*

Roosevelt reelected president.

1937   *West Coast Hotel v. Parrish* sustains the constitutionality of minimum-wage legislation, overruling *Adkins v. Children's Hospital* (1923).

In *NLRB v. Jones & Laughlin Steel Co.,* the Supreme Court signals a reversal of its New Deal adjudication by upholding the constitutionality of the National Labor Relations Act.

1938   In *Erie Railroad Co. v. Tompkins,* the Supreme Court reverses *Swift v. Tyson* (1842).

The Fair Labor Standards Act defines minimum wages and maximum hours of labor.

1939   The Reorganization Act authorizes the president to begin rationalizing the executive branch.

1940   Roosevelt reelected to an unprecedented third term as president.

1941   The Supreme Court sustains the Fair Labor Standards Act, overturning *Hammer v. Dagenhart* (1918), in *U.S. v. Darby Lumber Co.*

1942   *Wickard v. Filburn* indicates the Supreme Court will sustain federal economic regulations that affect businesses remote from interstate commerce.

FURTHER READING

The best overview of the Great Depression is Robert S. McElvane, *The Great Depression* (1984). For a comprehensive chronicle, consult Arthur M. Schlesinger, *The Age of Roosevelt* (3 vols., 1957–1960). Alfred U. Romasco covers Hoover's unsuccessful effort to fight the Depression in *The Poverty of Abundance* (1965). Good, brief surveys of the New Deal are Paul Conkin, *The New Deal* (3d ed., 1992) and Justus D. Doenecke, *The New Deal* (2003). More detailed is Conkin's *FDR and the Origins of the Welfare State* (1967). Another good, brief summary is Alan Brinkley's essay "The New Deal Experiments," in *The Achievement of American Liberalism: The New Deal and Its Legacies,* ed. William H. Chafe (2004). William E. Leuchtenburg's *Franklin D. Roosevelt and the New Deal* (1960), is an excellent, readable discussion, summarized in "The Achievement of the New Deal" in *Fifty Years Later: The New Deal Evaluated* Harvard Sitkoff ed. (1985). Ballard Campbell puts the New Deal in a long-range context in *The Growth of American Government* (1995). Alan Brinkley discusses "The New Deal and the Idea of the State," in *The Rise and Fall of the New Deal Order,* ed. Steve Fraser and Gary Gerstle (1989).

For the basics of constitutional history during the New Deal era, see Paul L. Murphy, *The Constitution in Crisis Times, 1919–1969* (1972). For the increased power and responsibility of the Executive Branch, see Ellis W. Hawley's essay "The Constitution of the Hoover and F. Roosevelt Presidency and the Depression Era," in *The Constitution and the American Presidency,* ed. Martin Fausold and Alan Shank (1991). Barry D. Karl studies the background and process of *Executive Reorganization and Reform in the New Deal* (1963), while John A. Rohr writes about the development of the administrative state in *To Run a Constitution* (1986). Political scientist Sidney M. Milkis points out the political implications of the shift to an administrative state in "New Deal, Party Politics, and the Administrative State," in *American Political Parties and Constitutional Politics,* ed. Peter W. Schramm and Bradford P. Wilson (1993). For the relationship between this development and legal realism, see chapter 8 of Morton J. Horwitz's *The Transformation of American Law, 1870–1960* (1992).

Alice Kessler-Harris shows how the traditional assumptions about gender roles led New Dealers to shortchange women in *Pursuit of Equity: Women, Men and the Pursuit of Economic Citizenship in 20th Century America* (2001). See also Gwendolyn Mink's *The Wages of Motherhood* (1995) and Suzanne Mettler's *Dividing Citizens: Gender and Federalism in New Deal Public Policy* (1998). In *Public Pensions* (2003) Susan M. Sterett puts in historical context the New Deal's offer of social insurance to mostly male workers, while treating wives and mothers as dependent objects of charity.

John Hope Franklin and Alfred A. Moses Jr. summarize the impact of the New Deal on the African American community in the standard history of African Americans, *From Slavery to Freedom* (7th ed., 2000). For more detail, look at Harvard Sitkoff's *A New Deal for Blacks* (1978) and Raymond Wolters's *Negroes and the Great Depression* (1970). David E. Bernstein points out the negative practical effects New Deal legislation had on African Americans, because of the racist heritage of labor unions, in *Only One Place of Redress* (2001). Robert C. Lieberman thoughtfully and more optimistically assesses New Deal administrative agencies and race in "Race, Institutions, and the Administration of Social Policy," *Social Science History* 19 (Winter 1995): 511–542. For an innovative argument about how Roosevelt's long-term vision for the country ultimately led to the expansion of civil rights for African Americans, see Kevin J. McMahon, *Reconsidering Roosevelt on Race* (2004).

For a critique of the "Indian New Deal," see Lawrence C. Kelly, "The Indian Reorganization Act: The Dream and the Reality," *Pacific Historical Review* 44 (August 1975): 291–312. James Wilson argues for a more positive evaluation in his history of Native Americans *The Earth Shall Weep* (1998)

For overviews of the constitutional transformation inaugurated by the New Deal, see Michael E. Parrish, "The Great Depression, the New Deal, and the American Legal Order," *Washington Law Review* 59 (October 1983): 723–750, and Lawrence M. Friedman, "The Welfare and Regulatory State Since the New Deal," in *The New Deal Legacy and the Constitution,* ed. Harry N. Scheiber et al. (1984). Bruce Ackerman builds an innovative general theory of American constitutional history around his account of the constitutional transformation of the New Deal era. See part 3 of his *We the People,* vol. 2: *Transformations* (1998). Marian C. McKenna provides a thorough, long but readable account of the constitutional conflict from a somewhat conservative perspective in *Franklin Roosevelt and the Great Constitutional War* (2002).

For the revolutionary nature of the change in judicial doctrine, see Edward S. Corwin, "The Passing of Dual Federalism," *Virginia Law Review* 37 (February 1950): 1–24 and Howard Gillman, *The Constitution Besieged* (1993). See also Leuchtenburg's essays collected in *The Supreme Court Reborn* (1995). In contrast, Barry Cushman minimizes the New Deal transformation in constitutional law in *Rethinking the New Deal Court* (1998). In *The Constitution and the New Deal* (2000) the eminent legal historian G. Edward White concedes that a transformation in constitutional doctrine occurred, but he places it later than traditional accounts.

The best traditional account of the Supreme Court in the New Deal era is in William F. Swindler, *Court and Constitution in the Twentieth Century,* Vol. 2: *The New Legality, 1932–1968* (1970). The chapter "Hughes: The Court in Retreat," in Alpheus T. Mason, *The Supreme Court from Taft to Warren* (rev. ed., 1968) is a lively analysis. Drew Pearson and Robert S. Allen's *The Nine Old Men* (1937) was written in part to support Roosevelt's court-packing campaign, but it offers incisive, trenchant portraits of the justices. In contrast, Peter H. Irons argues that the Supreme Court overturned New Deal legislation in part because it was poorly drawn and defended. See his study of the Justice Department under Roosevelt, *The New Deal Lawyers* (1982). Cushman and White reaffirm this perception in their works cited above. Richard Cortner's *The Jones and Laughlin Case* (1970) goes behind the case to make clear how the Court's decisions brought key parts of the New Deal to a standstill. It gives a wonderful sense of how public policy, politics, economics, and constitutional law interact.

Leuchtenburg describes the constitutional issue in the elections of 1936 in "When the People Spoke, What Did They Say?," *Yale Law Journal* 108 (June 1999): 2077–2114. For an account of the court-packing controversy generally sympathetic to Roosevelt, see Leuchtenburg, "The Origins of President Franklin D. Roosevelt's 'Court-Packing' Plan," *Supreme Court Review* 1966: 352–399. McKenna is more critical in *Franklin Roosevelt and the Great Constitutional War,* noted above.

Stephen Gardbaum discusses how the New Deal constitutional transformation empowered the states in "New Deal Constitutionalism and the Unshackling of the States," *University of Chicago Law Review* 64 (Spring 1997): 482–566. James T. Patterson's *The New Deal and the States* (1969) discusses how the New Deal inaugurated an era of cooperation between state and federal government.

15

Liberal Constitutionalism

The triumph of liberalism in the New Deal era transformed American constitutional law. Armed with the broad doctrines of nationalism that the Supreme Court had endorsed in U.S. *v. Darby Lumber Co.*, and *Wickard v. Filburn,* the federal government took control of the economy and exercised ever-greater national police powers. As the court repudiated the doctrine of "substantive due process of law," both the state and federal governments felt free to limit property rights in any manner rationally connected to promoting the general welfare. The result was a radical increase in legislation designed to promote the social and economic well-being of Americans and to soften the rigors of free-market competition, culminating in the Great Society programs of the 1960s.

Commitment to civil liberties and toleration of differences were important elements of the liberal constitutionalism that triumphed in the New Deal era. Groups that had been excluded full acceptance in the community and equal access to economic opportunity—Roman Catholics, African Americans, Jews, southern and eastern European ethnic groups, organized labor, and others—were all part of the liberal New Deal coalition, and they expected public policies that secured their rights.

Constitutional law began to reflect these commitments as early as the 1930s. After a period of retrogression during World War II and the Cold War they burst into full flower in the civil-liberties decisions of the Warren Court era, which extended from 1954 to the early 1970s. The social ideals of toleration and individual autonomy manifested in the opinions of the Warren Court evolved into a wholesale rejection of the limitations American communities traditionally had placed on individual freedom.

The Triumph of Liberal Constitutionalism

Liberal ideas in philosophy, education, art, literature, economics, law, and politics had been growing stronger since the 1880s, but the 1930s marked the clear turning point in their acceptance. When the Depression discredited conservative ideas about economics and the proper role of government, conservative ideas in other areas were inevitably tainted as well. Conversely, liberal ideas in all areas benefited from their successful application to government and the economy. The result was a general shift towards liberalism. Pragmatism became the dominant philosophy, affecting thought in all areas of American life. Most Americans accepted the ideas of "progressive education," articulated by the influential pragmatic philosopher, John Dewey. Modernism triumphed in art, music, and literature. Reinforced by a pervasive, government-backed consumer culture that encouraged Americans freely to indulge their desire for material goods, liberalism stressed individual happiness and self-fulfillment as the ultimate goal, not only of the American economy but of the American constitutional order.

Liberalism viewed the ultimate end of society to be the fullest possible freedom of the individual, but liberals believed that the active aid of government was needed to reach this goal in the modern world. Only government could offset the tendency of powerful private institutions, especially business interests, to circumscribe the freedom of ordinary people. Therefore liberals wanted to maximize popular control of government and to minimize the ability of powerful interests to influence it. They wanted government to have the power to promote individual liberty and equal opportunity, while at the same time they wanted to limit government's power to restrict them.

In the 1960s a large number of younger people reacted against the materialism of the consumer culture. Taking individualism to its logical conclusion, they rejected societal restrictions on personal and sexual behavior, exalting an anarchic hedonism, at the same time that they urged a return to simpler lives, more in tune with nature.

The Growth of Federal Power and Nationalist Constitutionalism

Commitment to the nationalist interpretation of the federal system was a key element of liberal constitutionalism. Between 1930 and 1980 the national government became involved in nearly every facet of American life. It accepted the primary responsibility for maintaining economic stability and prosperity; in the process, nearly all aspects of the economy came under government regulation.

In order to foster economic growth and set standards of business behavior, Congress added ever more regulatory agencies to those that dated from the Progressive Era and the New Deal. New federal agencies set guidelines for the communications industry, the airline industry, and the nuclear power industry. Older agencies expanded their regulation of banking, the stock market, agriculture, interstate transportation, public utilities, and almost every other business activity.

All these agencies operated according to procedures that mixed legislative, executive, and judicial elements. They encouraged suggestions and comments from the public, held hearings and heard opinions, and invited formal testimony on tentative proposals. The agencies also investigated compliance. But legal realists failed to achieve their goal of replacing cumbersome judicial approaches to regulation with modern administrative procedures. Too many Americans identified traditional legal procedures with due process of law. This tendency was strengthened as the United States struggled against fascist totalitarianism in World War Two and Communist totalitarianism afterwards. Critics of bureaucratic power hammered home the idea that the administrative state threatened the rule of law. In 1946 Congress passed the Administrative Procedure Act, which set procedural requirements for administrative agencies. Those accused of violating administrative regulations were entitled to quasi-judicial hearings, with a right of appeal to the courts. Reassured that they retained the power to overturn abuses of administrative power, the courts acquiesced to this new hybrid branch of government.

Intimately connected to particular industries, the agencies became focal points for business lobbying and quasi-legal proceedings. The number of lawyers and lobbyists in Washington exploded. The agencies relied not only on their own staffs but on the businesses they regulated for information and ideas. Often policies were determined in struggles among various interest groups rather than according to a clear vision of the general welfare. The losers frequently complained that the regulatory agencies served special interests rather than the public good. Small businessmen particularly resented this growth of what they called "big government" and consistently opposed it.

The government played an ever-increasing role in labor relations. More industries were brought under the jurisdiction of the National Labor Relations Board. Congress continued to update the Fair Labor Standards Act to regulate minimum wages, working hours, and other aspects of labor relations, expanding its coverage to ever more workers. In 1970 it created the Occupational Safety and Health Administration to improve safety and health conditions for American workers. These agencies also earned the enmity of small businesspeople, who were less able than large corporations to pass on the costs of higher wages and compliance with new rules.

The government also slowly accepted the obligation to maintain a minimum standard of living for working Americans and retirees. Acceptance of this responsibility had begun with the social security, workmen's compensation, minimum-wage, and employment programs of the 1930s. World War II provided Roosevelt and his Democratic successor Harry S. Truman with the opportunity to expand the government's effort to create a broad, financially comfortable middle class. In 1944 Congress passed the Servicemen's Readjustment Act, or "G.I. Bill," which established a "G.I. Bill of Rights" to decent jobs, housing, and education. The federal government authorized the Veterans Administration (V.A.), originally created in 1930, to establish a program guaranteeing mortgage loans to veterans, thereby fueling a tremendous postwar housing boom. To maintain it, the government directly subsidized housing construction and allowed homeowners to deduct the cost of mortgage interest and property taxes from the income on which they paid federal taxes.

Like the New Deal, the goal of these programs was to enable men to provide a home and comfort for their families. Until the revival of feminism in the 1960s, few thought about how the G. I. Bill and the V.A. mortgage-guarantee program privileged men over women, only small numbers of whom had been able to serve in the armed forces. Giving preferences to veterans applying for federal, state, and local government jobs was more obviously discriminatory. But it did not seem unfair to most Americans, who still thought men needed jobs while women took care of the home.

The federal government created a huge boom in college education after World War II by subsidizing university research relating to national defense, public health, and agriculture, and by paying veterans' tuition expenses under the G. I. Bill. Similar benefits were extended to veterans of succeeding wars. Afraid that the Soviet Union was overtaking the United States in science, in the 1960s the government subsidized the education of another generation of young Americans with student scholarships and loans. It also dramatically increased spending on scientific research. At the same time, it began to subsidize elementary and high school education. By 1965 the federal government was spending $25 billion dollars to help schools around the nation.

The government continually increased the social security pensions that aided older Americans. Although described as old-age insurance, in reality social security was a wealth-transfer program through which younger, working Americans supported older, retired ones. In 1965 the government established the Medicare program, which dramatically reduced the financial burden of caring for the elderly. These old-age welfare programs were immensely popular and successful, dramatically reducing the poverty rate among senior citizens.

A large number of government agencies were mandated to protect the interests of consumers. In certain industries, such as transportation and communications, the government controlled prices and business practices. In the decades following the New Deal, the government continually expanded its regulation of the ingredients in food, drugs, and other products, often imposing significant costs on business in order to protect the public. With the passage of the Truth-in-Packaging Act in 1966, federal agencies also began to regulate advertising. In 1972 Congress created the Consumer Products Safety Commission, empowered to recall unsafe products from the market.

The government was also heavily involved in protecting public health. The Food and Drug Administration and various agencies in the Agriculture Department monitored the safety of food and drugs. The National Institutes of Health, created in 1930, supported medical research. Other agencies of the Public Health Service fought epidemic disease. In 1947 Congress passed the Hill-Burton Act, which subsidized the construction of hospitals and extended-care facilities until the 1970s, bringing high-quality care even to remote areas of the country. In 1969 Congress and the president established the Environmental Protection Agency to protect Americans from health hazards caused by pollution of the air, water, and soil.

By the 1960s most Americans fully accepted such governmental activities. In 1965 President Lyndon B. Johnson, another Democrat in the tradition of Roosevelt and Truman, promised that government would create a "Great Society" in which all Americans would share. To carry out that promise, he undertook what he called a "War on Poverty"—an expansion of payments to the poor; food, housing, and medical subsidies; a program of legal services; a free lunch program for schools in poor areas that augmented the subsidized lunch program offered everywhere; special education programs for children and occupational training for adults; and a host of urban and rural economic development programs. Buoyed by two decades of prosperity and economic growth, most Americans seemed willing to allow a larger part of the country's expanding wealth to be used to alleviate poverty; they seemed to accept the premise of the general-welfare state that such a redistribution of resources ultimately served the interests of the whole society.

The Great Society program also promoted artistic and intellectual life. The National Endowment for the Humanities provided aid for research in humanistic disciplines and for transmitting the results to the general public. The National Endowment for the Arts provided similar support for painters, sculptors, dancers, orchestras, museums, theaters, and other artists and cultural institutions.

As a matter of constitutional law, these programs could be sustained only by the nationalist view that the federal government's power to regulate interstate commerce, collect taxes, spend money, and fulfill its other functions was "plenary" and "sovereign"; and they presumed an expansive reading of the Necessary and Proper Clause and the concept of "implied powers." The Supreme Court upheld such general-welfare laws against all challenges to their constitutionality, following the view established in the *Darby Lumber* case that the Tenth Amendment imposed no special limits on national power. Much of the regulation was justified under the Interstate Commerce Clause, the reach of which seemed almost unlimited under the precedent set by *Wickard v. Filburn*. As time went on, Congress rarely even considered whether the national government might be exceeding its authority with such legislation. Debates over federal power and state rights, which used to thunder through Congress, virtually disappeared. Except for a few die-hard Southerners, the doctrine of "state rights" seemed dead.

The Roosevelt Court and the Protection of Civil Liberty

As the national government expanded its role in American society, the Supreme Court began to establish national standards of civil rights and liberties, reflecting dominant liberal ideals of toleration, freedom of speech, and personal autonomy. In *Stromberg v. California* (1931), the Court for the first time ruled a state law limiting free speech unconstitutional, overturning a statute that made it illegal to display a red flag as a symbol of anarchism. In *Near v. Minnesota* (1931), it overturned a law suppressing "malicious" and "scandalous" newspapers. The proper remedy for any wrongs committed by such a newspaper was for private individuals to sue for libel, the Court said, not for the government to put it out of business. In *Powell v. Alabama* (1932), it reversed the conviction of a group of black teenagers who had been denied legal counsel in their trial for raping two white girls. The court ruled that the Due Process Clause of the Fourteenth Amendment guaranteed a defendant's right to a lawyer in state trials where the death penalty might be imposed.

The trend towards more vigorous protection of civil liberties accelerated as President Roosevelt appointed more members of the Supreme Court. As early as 1938 the Court clearly reflected the liberal constitutionalism associated with the New Deal and the Democratic party; in effect, it was already "the Roosevelt Court." As the Court stopped ruling economic regulations unconstitutional for violating due process of law, it began to watch closely for infringements of non-property rights. The Court made its intentions clear in a famous footnote to its opinion in *U.S. v. Carolene Products Co.* (1938). In the opinion the Court affirmed that respect for the democratic process required it to uphold legislation unless it clearly violated the words of the Constitution. The words "due process" alone were too vague to justify ruling economic regulations unconstitutional. But, the justices added in the footnote, "There may be narrower scope for the operation of the presumption of constitutionality where legislation appears on its face to be within a specific prohibition of the Constitution, such as those of the first ten amendments, which are deemed equally specific when held to be embraced within the Fourteenth." These were what legal scholars came to call "the preferred freedoms."

Acting on the "preferred freedoms" principle, from 1937 to 1941 the Court overturned many state laws that limited the right of radicals, labor organizers, and minority religious groups to speak and organize freely. Freedom of speech was explicitly protected by the First Amendment, which applied to the states through the Fourteenth Amendment, the Court said, citing the 1925 *Gitlow* case. The Court expanded the definition of "speech" to include picketing, passing out leaflets, demonstrating, and other forms of behavior linked to the expression of ideas. It revived Holmes's Clear and Present Danger Rule to decide what conditions would justify the restriction of such activities. The lower federal courts limited government's authority to censor literature that offended orthodox morality.

In 1936 a circuit court finally ruled that the federal Comstock Act was not intended to ban birth-control information or devices when intended for distribution by medical professionals. Although the decision was narrow, it reflected both widespread public support for birth control and an erosion of sexual prudery.

Freed from the Comstock Act's restrictions, state and federal welfare agencies began to incorporate birth-control programs into their activities. However, such government programs were designed more to discourage births among the poor than to enhance women's reproductive freedom.

Manifesting a new sensitivity to racial discrimination, the Court also indicated in the *Carolene Products* footnote that it would look closely at laws that targeted "discrete and insular minorities." In *Missouri ex rel. Gaines v. Canada* (1938) it ruled unconstitutional Missouri's program that sent black students out of state for legal training rather than creating a law school to serve them or admitting them to the state's whites-only law school. With this decision the Court made clear that it would require strict equality in all segregated, "separate but equal" educational systems.

Encouraged by the Supreme Court's new concern for protecting civil rights and liberties, organizations like the American Civil Liberties Union, the National Association for the Advancement of Colored People, the American Jewish Congress, as well as labor unions, turned to litigation. The Communist party and other radical groups organized sympathetic lawyers to join the fight. New rights-advocacy bodies proliferated. The flood of talent and cases, in turn, reinforced the judiciary's attention to such issues. In the Supreme Court, the proportion of cases raising questions of civil liberty and equality doubled to nearly 20 percent by the mid-1940s. (By 1970 they would make up more than half the docket.)

The Fourteenth Amendment "Incorporates" the Bill of Rights

In the late 1930s the Supreme Court began to refer to some provisions of the Bill of Rights as having been "absorbed" or "incorporated" into the Fourteenth Amendment and applied to the states, in effect creating a national Bill of Rights. This development paralleled the growth of national legislative power. The justices struggled over how far to go in imposing such national rules: Did the Fourteenth Amendment incorporate all the provisions of the Bill of Rights? If not, which ones did it incorporate? In *Palko v. Connecticut* (1937), the Court ruled that the Amendment incorporated only those provisions of the Bill of Rights that were "implicit in the concept of ordered liberty," or which embodied the "fundamental principles of liberty and justice which lie at the base of all our civil and political institutions."

Lawyers and constitutional scholars called this doctrine "selective incorporation." The selectively incorporated rights included the political freedoms of speech, press, and association; religious freedom; and the most important procedural rights in criminal trials, such as the right to a jury. But the Fourteenth Amendment did not incorporate less significant provisions of the Bill of Rights, nor did it require the states to follow the same rigid rules that applied to the federal government. It did not incorporate the Second Amendment's guarantee of the right to bear arms, for example. In the *Palko* case, the Court held that it did not bar a state from retrying a defendant after successfully appealing a previous acquittal, despite the Fifth Amendment's Double Jeopardy Clause.

Some justices rejected the majority view. In *Adamson v. California* (1947) and for years afterwards, Justice Hugo Black insisted that the Fourteenth Amendment imposed the entire Bill of Rights upon the states exactly as it applied to the national government. The majority view left the justices free to decide for themselves what was "implicit in the concept of ordered liberty," he complained. These words were as vague as "due process of law." If it had been wrong for the Supreme Court to impose its economic views on the country through its interpretation of the meaning of "due process," then it was equally wrong for it to impose its ideas of "fundamental principles of liberty." Legal scholars called Black's position "total incorporation." A few justices went even further, arguing that the Fourteenth Amendment required the states to honor not only the rights listed in the Bill of Rights but others as well. Analysts sometimes called this view "total incorporation plus."

At the other extreme, a few justices, most notably Felix Frankfurter, wanted only the minimum national standardization of rights. They argued that the Due Process Clause of the Fourteenth Amendment did not refer to the Bill of Rights at all. In later years Justice John M. Harlan would say that the Due Process Clause "rested on its own bottom." Only state violations of rights that "shocked the conscience" violated the Fourteenth Amendment.

The same argument arose over questions of judicial procedure: If the Fourteenth Amendment was held to incorporate a provision of the Bill of Rights, did the states have to follow all the rules the federal courts had established to protect the right? When the national government violated one of the procedural protections of the Bill of Rights, for example, the federal courts excluded the tainted evidence from the trial. But in *Wolf v. Colorado* (1949), the majority of the justices held that this "exclusionary rule" need not apply to the states. It was not "implicit in the concept of ordered liberty." Here too Justice Black and others dissented, insisting that there should be a single standard of justice for both state and federal courts. The states should not be subject only to a "watered-down" version of the Bill of Rights.

Disagreements over federalism were closely related to disagreements over how actively the courts should intervene in lawmaking and law enforcement in general. When the state and federal courts had ruled economic regulations unconstitutional during the 1920s and 1930s, many liberals had blasted judicial activism and urged judicial restraint. Several of Roosevelt's appointees (especially Frankfurter, a protégé of former Justice Brandeis) continued to support that position. Rejecting the "preferred-freedoms" justification set out in the *Carolene Products* footnote, Frankfurter insisted that judges had no more business citing vague phrases of the Constitution to impose their views of civil liberty than they had to impose their economic philosophies.

Justice Black also wanted to limit judges' discretion, but insisted on doing so by holding them to what he and other activists thought were the clear mandates of the Constitution. Judges had no business picking and choosing among constitutional limitations in order to defer to legislative decisions, Black averred. Other judicial activists, like William O. Douglas, rejected the concept of judicial restraint altogether. Judges should energetically promote the values of liberty and equality they thought implicit in the Constitution; the whole purpose of constitutional protections was to limit the power of legislatures, they argued, no matter how large or adamant the majority that sustained unconstitutional laws.

The doctrine of "selective incorporation" was a compromise, steering a middle course between Black and Douglas's judicial activism and Frankfurter's judicial restraint on civil-liberties issues. But although most justices adhered to it, the number of rights they believed essential to liberty increased steadily as Americans became more liberal on these issues from the 1930s to the 1970s.

World War II, the "Cold War," and Civil Liberty

Although the trend from the 1930s to the 1970s was to expand the definition and protection of rights, World War II (1941–1945) and the so-called "Cold War" between the United States and the Soviet Union (1947–1956) witnessed a temporary pause.

As fascist and Nazi influence spread in Europe in the 1930s, Roosevelt asked Federal Bureau of Investigation director J. Edgar Hoover to investigate whether fascism or communism presented a threat in the United States. Hoover interpreted the invitation to justify a broad intelligence program aimed at labor unions; communist, fascist, and affiliated organizations; schools; and even the army. Keeping his boss happy, he used the FBI to investigate Roosevelt's political enemies as well.

Wartime generally evokes powerful sentiments of patriotism, accompanied by hostility to those who do not seem fully committed to victory. The Supreme Court dealt with this reality in the Flag Salute cases. Desiring to promote American nationality in a polyglot country, many school boards had established the practice of saluting the flag and reciting the pledge of allegiance in classrooms every morning. The requirement ran counter to the beliefs of several religious minorities, especially the Jehovah's Witnesses, a fundamentalist sect that compared saluting the flag to worshipping idols. Already disliked by members of other fundamentalist denominations, Jehovah's Witnesses became the targets of real hatred as the world plunged into war. Their children were expelled from schools for refusing to participate in the flag ceremony, rendering the parents liable for violation of school-attendance laws. Aided by the ACLU, the Witnesses brought several court challenges against school rules mandating or permitting such expulsions. When the first of the Flag Salute cases reached the Supreme Court in 1940, the justices rejected the appeal. Speaking through their lone Jewish colleague, Frankfurter, the justices held that the state's interest in promoting patriotism justified a slight infringement of religious beliefs.

People around the country took the Court's decision as an endorsement of anti–Jehovah Witness sentiment. School after school made saluting the flag mandatory and expelled recalcitrant children. Mortified by the consequences of the decision, several justices announced a change of heart. Three years later, as the nation came to see the struggle against Germany, Italy, and Japan as a war for freedom against tyranny, the Court reversed its position. In the Second Flag Salute case, *West Virginia State Board of Education v. Barnette* (1943), the Court forbade state and local governments from making such patriotic activities compulsory. The Court's opinion manifested the justices' increasing concern with protecting free choice and individual autonomy, as well as political freedom. "If there is any fixed star in our constitutional constellation, it is that no official, high or petty, can prescribe what shall be orthodox in politics, nationalism, religion, or other matters of opinion, or force citizens to confess by word or act their faith therein," they wrote. Encouraged, Jehovah's Witnesses created their own legal defense team and brought dozens of freedom of speech and religion cases to the courts in succeeding decades.

The antipathy to Jehovah's Witnesses paled in comparison to that faced by people of Japanese descent after Japan bombed Pearl Harbor. White Americans who lived on the Pacific Coast had a long history of hostility towards Asian immigrants. The Japanese attack on Pearl Harbor in December 1941 reinforced this heritage of bigotry to create a wave of anti-Japanese feeling. Responding to pressure from the Pacific Coast, President Roosevelt ordered all people of Japanese descent to leave the area. The government forcibly relocated over one hundred thousand people to remote camps and only slowly allowed some of them to move to cities in the interior. Consequently tens of thousands of Japanese and Japanese Americans lost their jobs and property.

International law permits a belligerent to intern enemy nationals in wartime. However, the government interned not only Japanese nationals, but American *citizens* of Japanese descent, without any trial and for no reason other than the origins of their parents or grandparents, whom the naturalization laws still barred from becoming citizens because of their race. Moreover, the government took no similar action against German or Italian Americans. With the exception of slavery, this internment was the most massive violation of civil rights in American history.

Many civil libertarians attacked these actions. But the Supreme Court proved unwilling to challenge the president in wartime. In *Korematsu v. U.S.* (1944), the Court's rhetoric reflected the concern for "discrete and insular minorities" that it had expressed in the *Carolene Products* footnote. For the first time, the Court stated that only compelling government interests could justify racial discrimination. Yet the justices upheld the constitutionality of the order excluding Japanese Americans from the coast. Relying on skimpy evidence that investigators now agree would not have withstood scrutiny, they accepted the government's claim that Japanese Americans presented a serious enough danger to justify the exclusion order. In *ex parte Endo* (1944), the Court did mandate the release of a young woman from one of the internment camps after the government conceded that she was a loyal American citizen. But the Court avoided ruling on the government's power to detain people without trial where it did not make such an admission.

Americans expected an era of peace and harmony to follow the defeat of the Germans, Italians, and Japanese in 1945. But instead the victory ushered in an era of bitter hostility between the United States and the Soviet Union. The Cold War rekindled the old American fear of radicalism and socialism. During the 1930s, socialists and even communists had joined the forces urging radical social and economic change in the United States and a firm stand against fascism. Communists played an important role in helping labor unions to organize and in fighting for civil liberties in the courts. After Germany invaded the Soviet Union, the Roosevelt administration worked to defuse suspicion of America's communist allies. As relations between the United States and the Soviet Union deteriorated after the war, many blamed American conservatives for the growing hostility. Evidence grew that a number of Communist party members who had secured positions in labor unions and government agencies, alienated by what they saw as the illicit revival of conservatism, were passing information to Soviet agents. People began to suspect that the United States was infiltrated by communist agents working to weaken American defenses and overthrow the government.

Powerful economic and political interests in the United States tried to use postwar anticommunism to their advantage. Businesses hoped to weaken labor unions by accusing them of being socialistic and influenced by communists. They also hoped to convince Americans to oppose regulatory "big government" by identifying it with radical foreign ideologies. In the South, opponents of the growing movement to end racial segregation tried to discredit it by charging that it was controlled by communists. Republicans hoped to regain political power by charging that Democrats were "soft" on communism.

In this intellectual climate, businesses began to fire workers charged with being "radical," especially leaders of labor unions. Conservatives began to attack companies that traded with communist countries. They boycotted movies and sponsors of television and radio programs whose stars, guests, or writers were known to have liberal or radical political views, or who had once been associated with radicals or radical causes. Businesses began to create "blacklists" of people whom they would not employ because of their political views. The "blacklist" was especially strong in the television, radio, and movie industries.

Politicians increased the anticommunist feeling by staging well-publicized investigations into communist influence in labor unions and the communications media. Especially spectacular was the House Un-American Activities

Committee's investigation of the movie industry. Hollywood celebrities charged their colleagues with being or having been communists or leftists, or having associated with radicals, while others denied the right of Congress to investigate their political beliefs and associations.

Americans divided bitterly over the fairness of accusing people publicly of being "un-American" without the protections guaranteed in an actual trial. But most seemed to think that suspects had nothing to fear if they were innocent. Therefore anyone who protested against the investigations became suspect. Partly in self-defense and partly because they believed communists presented a real danger, many liberal groups themselves began to purge their radical members.

By the late 1940s the anticommunist movement was having a strong effect on government. Building upon internal security laws passed in 1939 and 1940, President Truman instituted a program to screen the loyalty of government employees. The attorney general was empowered to make a list of organizations he considered "subversive," and membership in any of them constituted grounds for dismissal. But Republicans went even further. Hoping to discredit the Democrats, they charged that under Roosevelt and Truman, the government had become filled with communist agents and sympathizers. Only Republicans could be trusted to weed them out. The anticommunist feelings grew even more intense when communist forces took over China in 1949 and when the United States went to war to block communist North Korea's invasion of South Korea the following year.

The leader of the Republican attack on the loyalty of Democrats was Joseph R. McCarthy, United States senator from Wisconsin. Without any significant evidence, McCarthy announced that he knew the names of many communists in government. Republicans put him in charge of a Senate subcommittee to investigate his accusations. From 1950 to 1954, McCarthy's committee badgered witnesses and made accusations, without permitting the accused to cross-examine their accusers or to see the information McCarthy claimed to have about them. McCarthy and other anticommunists charged anyone who had worked with communists in the 1930s with being disloyal "fellow-travelers" unless they publicly recanted. Civil libertarians denounced this "guilt by association," but most Americans seemed to sympathize with McCarthy's attacks. By 1952 McCarthy was one of the most powerful men in the United States, and the charge that the Democrats had engaged in "twenty years of treason" played a significant role in electing the Republican war hero, Dwight David Eisenhower, to the presidency.

In the midst of this Second Red Scare, the government began to bring leaders of the American Communist party to trial under the Smith Act of 1940, which made membership illegal in any organization that taught or advocated the forcible overthrow of the government. The party leaders, who were not accused of taking any overt action towards overthrowing the government, appealed their convictions to the Supreme Court. Civil libertarians argued that under the First

Amendment they could not be punished for merely teaching and advocating communism; there had to be a "clear and present danger" of serious, illegal activity. But in *Dennis v. U.S.* (1951), the majority of the justices (with the two most liberal justices, Black and Douglas, dissenting) measured the immediacy of the danger against its gravity. They admitted that the danger was remote but argued that the overthrow of the government was so serious that the country could not wait until the danger was at hand.

After this decision, the government felt free to bring indictments against almost all the activists of the Communist party. At the same time, the Supreme Court sustained the constitutionality of state and national rules barring employment of "subversives" in any government job, even as elementary school teachers or bus drivers. State and local governments began demanding that all employees and even students attending state colleges and universities take loyalty oaths, swearing that they had never belonged to any organization advocating the overthrow of the government.

As the Supreme Court became more conservative on loyalty questions, it became more conservative in other areas as well, in part because Truman had named four relatively conservative justices since becoming president in 1945. The court sustained laws limiting the right of labor unions to picket employers in labor disputes. It ruled that speakers could be silenced if there was a danger of violence *against* them; rather than protecting the speakers from violence, the police could arrest them if they refused to keep quiet. The Court decided that the government could suppress "group libel," that is, language that fostered dislike or hatred of ethnic, religious, racial, or social groups. It maintained that pornography was not protected by the First or Fourteenth Amendments, permitting government to suppress whatever literature or art a jury of twelve people felt was obscene.

Given this conservatism, it is not surprising that in *Everson v. Board of Education of Ewing Township* (1947) and *Zorach v. Clausen* (1952), the Court majority sustained laws providing indirect state support to religious education. Justice Douglas's majority opinion in the *Zorach* case echoed the "Christian Nation" decision of sixty years before, stating that "We are a religious people whose institutions presuppose a Supreme Being." Yet in *Everson* the Court set the groundwork for imposing a stricter separation of church and state in the future. Black's majority opinion for the first time applied the First Amendment's Establishment Clause ("Congress shall make no law respecting an establishment of religion") to the states through the Fourteenth Amendment. The clause was designed to erect, as Black quoted Jefferson, "a wall of separation between Church and State." Such language suggested that the Court's tolerance of government support for religion was limited.

In the mid-1950s the trend towards reading liberalism and toleration into the Constitution revived and the liberal counterattack against the Second Red Scare began to have an effect. McCarthy and other anticommunists helped to discredit themselves by carrying their attacks too far. Americans watched on television as the senator bullied witnesses and made unsubstantiated charges that the United States Army was infiltrated by communists. McCarthy's attack on the army angered Eisenhower, turning Republicans against him. In 1954 the Senate censured McCarthy for abusing his position in the course of his investigations. "McCarthyism" became a term of opprobrium, describing anyone who made repeated, unsubstantiated charges based on guilt by association.

The Warren Court and Civil Liberties

Several of the justices that President Eisenhower appointed to the Supreme Court turned out to be surprisingly liberal in their views, especially the new chief justice, Earl Warren (1953–1969). The Warren Court, the spirit of which persisted beyond Warren's retirement into the early 1970s, proved the most liberal in American history. Its new members soon joined Black and Douglas to modify and reverse the more conservative decisions of the previous decade. In *Yates v. U.S.* (1957), the new majority overturned the convictions of a second group of lower-ranking Communist party activists in trials begun after the *Dennis* decision. The justices held that it was not enough to show that the communists merely advocated and taught the doctrine of revolution; to be convicted they had

The Warren Court in 1964. Standing, from the left: Byron White, William J. Brennan, Potter Stewart, and Arthur Goldberg. Seated, from the left: Thomas C. Clark, Hugo Black, Chief Justice Earl Warren, William O. Douglas, and John Marshall Harlan.

to take practical steps to achieve this goal. Then in a series of cases, the Court made it virtually impossible for either the states or the national government to prosecute anyone for mere membership in a "subversive" organization, to require people to swear that they did not belong to such organizations, or to force anyone to register as a member of such an organization. The cases culminated in *Brandenburg v. Ohio* (1969), in which the Court ruled that advocating the violent overthrow of the government was protected by the Constitution, except where it was designed to produce immediate illegal action. Thus people could no longer be prosecuted merely for advocating the doctrines of communism or any other antidemocratic philosophy.

The reaction against the McCarthyite "Red Scare" of the early 1950s led to a powerful drive throughout American society to protect political freedoms. Civil libertarians argued that Americans should have complete freedom of expression. Teachers' associations demanded the right to speak, write, and teach freely in schools—what came to be called "academic freedom." Students denied that school administrators could prevent unpopular people from speaking on college campuses, or that they could prevent students from organizing groups to promote unpopular causes.

Newspaper reporters claimed special privileges that they insisted were necessary to preserve freedom of the press. They refused to give police material collected in news investigations or to name secret sources of information. To do so, they insisted, would have a "chilling effect" on freedom of the press. Artists likewise insisted on the freedom to write, paint, sculpt, or photograph whatever appealed to their artistic sensibility, even if their work offended many in the community. Librarians and museum administrators were severely criticized if they tried to censor artistic works, and most American intellectual leaders came to accept the idea of complete artistic freedom.

The majority of the justices on the Warren Court shared these liberal values, and they defined the First Amendment's protection of free speech and free press accordingly. The Warren Court strictly limited how the national or state governments could limit political expression. Influenced by the tactics of the Civil Rights Movement, to be discussed in the next chapter, the Court protected not only speech itself, but actions designed to express opinions, known as "symbolic speech." The Court had begun to protect "symbolic speech" in the 1940s, when it overturned state laws that restricted the right of people to speak in public places or to pass out political and religious literature. In the 1960s, impelled by the mass demonstrations of the civil rights and anti–Vietnam War movements, civil libertarians challenged all sorts of laws that prevented people from speaking or demonstrating publicly. Judges in both state and national courts regularly ruled such laws unconstitutional for being too vague or for having a "chilling effect" on free speech. In *Tinker v. Des Moines School District* (1969), the Supreme Court held that even school children could symbolically protest government policy—in

Furious with the Warren Court's decisions promoting racial equality and expanding civil liberties, conservatives called for Warren's removal.

this case they wore black armbands to protest the Vietnam War—and that school administrators could not prevent it.

Again influenced by events connected with the civil rights movement, the Warren Court also rigorously protected freedom of the press. Furious at northern television and newspaper coverage that sympathized with civil rights demonstrators, Alabama officials successfully sued the *New York Times* and local civil rights leaders for libel in the Alabama courts, alleging minor errors in an advertisement that the leaders had placed in the newspaper. The all-white jury levied damages of $500,000. Recognizing the danger that government officials might use local courts to intimidate the news media, the Supreme Court overturned the decision. In the great case of *New York Times v. Sullivan* (1964), the justices ruled that public officials could sue the news media for libel only if they could show actual malice—that is, knowledge that a statement was false or reckless disregard of whether it was true or not. A few years later, the Court extended a similar but less strict rule to news coverage of private individuals. If a person was a "celebrity" he or she had to prove "highly improper" conduct by a newspaper to win a libel judgment; merely proving the falsehood of a news report was not enough.

By the late 1960s, the liberal belief in toleration was reaching its logical extreme. The Supreme Court's desire to protect the individual's right to hold and express even the most unpopular opinions both reflected and contributed to this development. More and more people felt that society had no right to impose standards of behavior on individuals as long as no one was being physically harmed. Many young people gravitated towards a "counter-culture" that challenged social norms of behavior, rejecting traditional standards of dress and grooming, listening to new forms of music, developing new dances that shocked their parents. They experimented with illegal drugs; they rejected traditional sexual behavior and questioned the value of marriage. Stressing, somewhat inconsistently, both the right of the individual to maximum freedom and the necessity for communal life and responsibility, they criticized older Americans as selfish and materialistic.

These attitudes spread to adults as well and by the late 1960s, the whole nation seemed to be undergoing a revolution in morals and behavior. People demanded that states repeal laws that made divorce difficult and that criminalized sexual promiscuity and adultery. They called for the end of laws punishing homosexuality and "unnatural" heterosexual acts. In many parts of the United States, adult behavior and dress changed almost as much as that of young people.

Since people believed that they had a *right* to behave in such individualistic ways, they believed that the courts were obligated to protect it. In the idiom of the1960s and 1970s, they were demanding their own "space"; in legal terms, they were demanding an expanded zone of privacy, free of government intrusion. Influenced by this environment, the Warren Court made it increasingly difficult for national, state, or local governments to impose community moral standards on individuals who rejected them.

One of the most important ways in which the Court limited government's power to establish moral codes was by restricting the ability of local governments to promote religion, especially among children. In the key case *Engel v. Vitale* (1962) the Court ruled that teachers could not lead children in prayer in the public schools. In *School District of Abington Township v. Schempp* (1963) and later cases, the Court made it almost impossible for public schools to encourage prayer or to provide children with religious instruction. At the same time, it set firm limits on how much help government could provide to private religious schools.

The Warren Court also began to limit the ability of government to censor artistic activity. In *Roth v. U.S.* (1957), it ruled that an artistic work could not be suppressed only because some parts of it were obscene. Rather, "the dominant theme of the material as a whole" had to "appeal to prurient interests." In *Memoirs v. Massachusetts* (1966), the Court ruled that suppressed material must not only be obscene, but "utterly without redeeming social value." By the late 1960s, there were hardly any limits to the sexual explicitness or language permitted in books or the visual arts. Great latitude was permitted in the performing arts as well. It was not at all unusual for dance, theater, and movies to include nudity and sexually explicit material. The collapse of government authority to promote good morals through political and artistic censorship was almost complete.

The Court also responded to expanded ideas of privacy, identifying areas of individual autonomy that the Constitution protected against government intrusion. Since the Bill of Rights nowhere mentions a right to privacy, the Court protected it primarily by the way it interpreted other constitutional provisions. For example, the justices made it difficult for public officials to impose rules of moral behavior on their employees by holding that such rules must relate directly to job performance. They thus interpreted the First Amendment as securing a broad area of individual freedom of expression and religious belief.

In *Griswold v. Connecticut* (1965), the Court for the first time declared that the Constitution directly protected privacy itself. The majority of the justices agreed that the Fourteenth Amendment incorporated various provisions of the Bill of Rights that, when combined, created a zone of privacy into which government could not intrude. Others argued that the Ninth Amendment, which recognizes the existence of rights beyond those specified in the Bill of Rights, justified the Court in protecting privacy. Even some of the justices who denied that the Fourteenth Amendment incorporated the Bill of Rights agreed that general principles of due process required the protection of some degree of privacy.

Justice Black trenchantly dissented, denouncing the judicial activism of his liberal colleagues just as he had formerly denounced the judicial activism of conservatives. As always, he insisted that the Fourteenth Amendment incorporated all of the provisions of the Bill of Rights. But it did not go any further. His liberal colleagues' discovery of zones of privacy in the Constitution was no different from conservatives' discovery of freedom of contract in the days before the New Deal. Judges had no business imposing their own beliefs in this way, he argued.

Convinced that the Constitution did protect privacy, the other justices ruled in the *Griswold* case that government could not outlaw sexual education for adults or the sale of contraceptives. The intimacies of sexual relations, especially among married couples, were beyond government's power to regulate. In 1972, three years after Warren himself had left the bench, the Court extended similar rights of privacy even to unmarried couples, demolishing just about the last of the old Comstock laws. The following year the Court's commitment to privacy and individual autonomy culminated in *Roe v. Wade,* in which it ruled state laws against abortion unconstitutional for violating women's right to privacy.

Roe v. Wade clearly illustrated liberal constitutionalism's preference for individual autonomy over state enforcement of traditional moral codes and sexual roles. Looking over the broad history of the conflict between community standards and individual self-determination, the abortion decision seemed to mark the final victory of the deviant culture Victorians had fought in the nineteenth century. For people who retained conservative values, the abortion case seemed a victory for selfishness and self-indulgence. Feminists were quick to point out that critics of the decision seemed to believe that women had a special obligation to put the well-being of others ahead of their own. When it came to motherhood, critics demanded a selflessness inconsistent with the competitive individualism that conservatives approved of in other areas of American life.

In case after case the justices had expanded the area of civil liberty. By the

1970s the Supreme Court had "selectively incorporated" nearly every provision of the Bill of Rights into the Fourteenth Amendment. (The most significant unincorporated provision was the Second Amendment's right to bear arms; the Court did not revisit a 1939 case, *United States v. Miller*, that had held the right to be a collective one exercised by the state militia.) As indicated by the privacy and abortion cases, the Court had gone beyond the language of the Bill of Rights as well. In doing so, it imposed the liberal value of toleration upon the whole society.

The Court also increased its supervision of administrative agencies. In *Goldberg v. Kelly*, decided in 1970, the justices ruled that agencies were constitutionally required to provide hearings and other elements of due process when determining eligibility to government entitlements. Justices would disagree in the future about just what procedures would satisfy the constitutional requirement, but the principle was firmly embedded in the law.

Sharing liberals' perception that government agencies often were more concerned with protecting the interests of those they were supposed to regulate than those of the public, courts abandoned the deference with which they had treated administrative decisions since the New Deal. Consumer advocates, environmentalists, and labor lawyers flocked to the courts to challenge bureaucratic decisions. The Court facilitated their activities by broadening the circumstances under which people and groups not directly damaged by bureaucratic decisions could claim standing to sue. Congress too encouraged private individuals and public-interest groups to act as "private attorney generals," specifically authorizing them to bring suits in federal courts against states and state agencies.

The Court's liberal activism encouraged increasing numbers of attacks on laws and administrative procedures that liberals believed violated individual rights. With the judiciary sympathetic to their arguments, civil libertarians relied on the courts rather than the myriad city councils, the fifty state legislatures, or even Congress. The new importance of the judges was reflected in the number of cases filed each term, which went up from about 1250 in the early 1950s to over 3600 in the early 1970s. (The number would reach 6800 in the mid 1990s.) Conservatives reacted with outrage. "Impeach Earl Warren" billboards sprouted along roadsides. Conservatives throughout the nation complained bitterly about judicial imposition of alien values on their communities.

Civil libertarians strenuously defended judicial activism, reversing the scorn with which liberals had regarded it before the New Deal. Real democracy required judicially enforced limitations on majority rule, they insisted. Law school professors devoted tens of thousands of pages in books and law reviews to the problem of reconciling judicial activism with democracy and to developing principles to guide judges in their grave responsibility. More and more, liberal constitutionalism came to identify the judiciary as the guardian of constitutional liberty.

Toleration of dissenting ideas and behavior was related to another of liberalism's central values—"equality." Decisions protecting political and artistic freedom and the right to behave in unorthodox ways may be seen not only as sustaining individualism but as guaranteeing equal rights for those whose views differed from the majority's. This commitment to "equality" was the second great theme of American constitutional history in the era of liberal consensus.

TIMELINE

1925   In *Gitlow v. N.Y.,* the Supreme Court rules the First Amendment's protection of freedom of speech is also protected against state infringement by the Fourteenth Amendment.

1931–1932 The Supreme Court begins to protect civil liberties in such cases as *Stromberg v. California* (1931), *Near v. Minnesota* (1931), and *Powell v. Alabama* (1932).

1933   Ratification of Twenty-First Amendment ends national prohibition.

1937   *Palko v. Connecticut* articulates the doctrine of "selective incorporation" of the Bill of Rights into the Fourteenth Amendment.

1938   The Supreme Court asserts it will actively protect noneconomic civil liberties in the *Carolene Products* footnote.

1940   The First Flag Salute Case upholds laws requiring school children to salute the flag of the United States.

The Smith Act makes it illegal to advocate or to belong to any organization advocating the overthrow of the government of the United States.

1941–1945 U.S. participation in World War II.

1941   Japanese and Japanese Americans are expelled from the West Coast and relocated into detention camps.

1943   The Supreme Court reverses its decision in the First Flag Salute Case, in *West Virginia State Board of Education v. Barnette.*

1944   The Serviceman's Readjustment Act, known as the "G.I. Bill of Rights" or "G.I. Bill," establishes programs to secure housing and education to veterans.

In *Korematsu v. U.S.,* the Supreme Court rules only "compelling" government interests can sustain racially discriminatory government action, but nonetheless sustains Japanese relocation.

1946   Congress passes the Administrative Procedures Act, setting up administrative courts and requiring due process in the application of administrative regulations.

1947   President Truman issues an executive order establishing a National Security Program; Congress formalizes it by passing the National Security Act.

1947	Supreme Court debates "selective incorporation," "total incorporation," and "non-incorporation" of the Bill of Rights into the Fourteenth Amendment, in *Adamson v. California*.
1950–1954	Second Red Scare; Senator Joseph R. McCarthy investigates communists and communist sympathizers in government.
1951	In *Dennis v. U.S.*, the Supreme Court sustains convictions of leading communists under the Smith Act of 1940.
1953	Earl Warren named chief justice.
1955–1966	The Civil Rights Movement protests racial discrimination in America, leading to widespread civil liberties litigation.
1958	The National Defense Education Act provides low-cost, partly nonrepayable loans for college education.
1962	The Supreme Court bars state-written prayers in public schools in *Engel v. Vitale* (1962).
1963	The Supreme Court forbids organized prayer in public schools in *Abington School District v. Schempp*.
1964	In *N.Y. Times Co. v. Sullivan,* the Supreme Court rules that under the First Amendment, public officials can secure damages for libel only where defendants have made false statements with reckless disregard for the truth.
	President Johnson announces a "War on Poverty."
	The Economic Opportunity Act provides funds for youth programs, a "Job Corps," and other antipoverty programs.
1965	President Johnson announces programs designed to achieve "The Great Society."
	Griswold v. Connecticut rules that laws prohibiting the distribution of birth-control devices and information violate the constitutional right to privacy.
	Medicare established as part of Social Security to guarantee health care for the elderly.
1966	The Supreme Court rules that to be suppressed, pornography must be "utterly without redeeming social value," in *Memoirs v. Massachusetts*.
	Congress passes the Truth-in-Packaging Act.
1969	*Brandenburg v. Ohio* marks the culmination of cases in which the Supreme Court eviscerates state and federal loyalty programs.
	Warren E. Burger succeeds Earl Warren as chief justice of the Supreme Court.
1970	The Environmental Protection Act creates the Environmental Protection Agency.

1970   The Supreme Court rules in *Goldberg v. Kelly* that the Constitution requires administrative agencies to provide due process when deciding who is eligible for the benefits of government programs.

The Occupational Safety and Health Act creates the Occupational Safety and Health Administration to regulate workplace safety and health.

1973   In *Roe v. Wade,* the Supreme Court rules that laws barring abortions violate the right to privacy.

FURTHER READING

For the history of the ideology of the general-welfare state, see Alonzo L. Hamby's *Liberalism and Its Challengers: F. D. R. to Bush* (1992). Lizabeth Cohen describes how the government fostered a consumer culture as the engine of economic prosperity in *A Consumer's Republic* (2003).

For a brief, interpretive characterization of the post–New Deal state, see Lawrence M. Friedman, "The Welfare and Regulatory State Since the New Deal," in *The New Deal Legacy* Harry N. Scheiber et al. ed., (1984). Morton J. Horwitz describes the judicialization of the administrative state in *The Transformation of American Law, 1870–1960* (1992). William E. Nelson analyzes the impact of new ideas on judicial interpretations of law in *The Legalist Reformation* (2001). See Joseph A. Califano, *The Triumph and Tragedy of Lyndon Johnson* (1991) for a discussion of The Great Society and the War on Poverty by a judicious insider. Two retrospectives of The Great Society appeared in 1986, *The Great Society: A Twenty-Year Critique, ed.* Barbara G. Jordan and Elspeth D. Rostow, and *The Great Society and Its Legacy*, ed. Marshall Kaplan and Peggy L. Cuciti. Joseph F. Zimmerman sees the story of *Contemporary American Federalism* (1992) as one of ever-increasing centralization.

William L. O'Neill describes the "counter culture" that challenged conventional morality and behavior in his nearly contemporaneous survey of the 1960s *Coming Apart* (1971). In *America Divided: The Civil War of the 1960s* (2d ed., 2004), Maurice Isserman and Michael Kazin likewise attend to what they call "The Making of a Youth Culture." The essays in *Imagine Nation*, ed. Peter Braunstein and Michael William Doyle (2002) look at the counterculture from every angle.

The standard survey of the constitutional history of the period is Paul L. Murphy, *The Constitution in Crisis Times, 1918–1969* (1972). Murphy's essay *The Constitution in the Twentieth Century* (1986) is a brief overview. Tony A. Freyer's *Hugo L. Black and the Dilemma of American Liberalism* (1990) is a brief, readable survey, focusing on the Supreme Court's role. The best general review of the Supreme Court in the age of liberal constitutionalism is Alpheus T. Mason, *The Supreme Court from Taft to Burger* (1979). More detailed is William F. Swindler, *Court and Constitution in the 20th Century: The New Legality, 1932–1968* (1970).

C. Herman Pritchett discusses the transformation of the Supreme Court from the protector of business and property interests to the guardian of civil liberties in the decade following 1937, as well as the conflict over judicial activism, in his standard *The Roosevelt Court* (1948). Fred W. Friendly describes one of the harbingers of the transition, *Near v. Minnesota,* for a general readership in *Minnesota Rag* (1991). Dan W. Carter does the same for another in *Scottsboro: A Tragedy of the American South* (1969). Melvin I. Urofsky recounts the controversies that engaged the so-called Roosevelt Court from the late 1930s to the 1950s in *Division and Discord* (1997). His "The Roosevelt Court," in *The Achievement of American Liberalism*, ed. William H. Chafe (2004) provides a summary.

For fights over the expansion of civil liberty in general through the 1950s, see John P. Roche's engaging *The Quest for the Dream* (1963). Samuel Walker describes the role of the American Civil Liberties Union in *In Defense of American Liberties* (1990). For the importance of rights-advocacy organizations to liberal constitutionalism, see Charles R. Epp, *The Rights Revolution* (1998). For the gradual application of the Bill of Rights to the states, consult Richard C. Cortner's concise *The Supreme Court and the Second Bill of Rights* (1981). Mason explicates the Preferred Freedoms doctrine in "The Core of Free Government: Mr. Justice Stone and 'Preferred Freedoms,'" *Yale Law Journal* 65 (April 1956): 597–628. For the conflict among Black, Frankfurter, and the other justices over judicial activism, see James F. Simon, *The Antagonists* (1989), as well as Cortner's *The Supreme Court and the Second Bill of Rights*, noted above.

David F. Manwaring describes the events surrounding the Flag Salute Cases in *Render unto Caesar* (1962). Chuck Smith's "The Persecution of West Virginia's Jehovah's Witnesses and the Expansion of Legal Protection for Religious Liberty," *Journal of Church and State* 43 (Summer 2001): 539–577 is an informative brief account. Shawn Francis Peters discusses the subject in more detail in *Judging Jehovah's Witnesses* (2000). For the sobering story of the grossest violation of civil liberty in modern American history, see Testuden Kashima, *Judgment without Trial* (2003); Wendy Ng, *Japanese Internment during World War II* (2002); and Peter Irons, *Justice at War* (1983). Page Smith's *Democracy on Trial* (1995) is less condemnatory. Lillian Baker defends the Japanese relocation, charging critical historians with *Dishonoring America* (1994).

For a general account of the Second Red Scare, consult David Caute, *The Great Fear* (1978). Ellen Schrecker's *Many Are the Crimes* (1998) focuses on McCarthyism. Stanley I. Kutler adds discussions of individual cases in *The American Inquisition* (1982). Arthur J. Sabin discusses the Supreme Court's reaction in *In Calmer Times: The Supreme Court and Red Monday* (1999). A judicious analysis, which takes the communist threat seriously but distinguishes between responsible and irresponsible anticommunism, is John E. Haynes's *Red Scare or Red Menace?* (1996). Painting on a much larger canvass is Richard Gid Powers in his well-written history of anticommunism, *Not Without Honor* (1995).

For an overview of the Warren Court's expansion of civil-liberties protection, see Melvin I. Urofsky, *The Continuity of Change: The Supreme Court and Individual Liberties, 1953–1986* (1989). Morton J. Horwitz's *The Warren Court and the Pursuit of Justice* (1998) is a slim but wide-ranging study. In *The Warren Court and American Politics* (2000), L. A. Scott Powe, Jr. places the Warren Court's decisions within the context of contemporaneous political events. The essays in Mark Tushnet, (ed.), *The Warren Court in Historical and Political Perspective* (1993), deal with the individual justices, while those in Bernard Schwartz (ed.), *The Warren Court: A Retrospective* (1996), deal with the issues as well.

For the law of free speech in the age of liberal constitutionalism, see Frank R. Strong, "Fifty Years of 'Clear and Present Danger,'" *Supreme Court Review* 1969: 41–80. Anthony Lewis tells the story of how the Warren Court radically restricted the use of libel suits to chill freedom of speech in *Make No Law: The Sullivan Case and the First Amendment* (1991). Charles Rembar discerns *The End of Obscenity* (1968) in the pornography trials of *Lady Chatterley's Lover, Tropic of Cancer,* and *Fanny Hill.* David J. Garrow discusses the development of the constitutional right to privacy and the abortion decision in *Liberty and Sexuality: The Right to Privacy and the Making of* Roe v. Wade, *1923–1973* (1994). N. E. H. Hull and Peter Charles Hoffer take an even longer view in Roe v. Wade: *The Abortion Rights Controversy in American History* (2001). For liberals' efforts to reconcile democracy with such judicial activism, see Kalman, *The Strange Career of Legal Liberalism* (1996).

Robert B. Horwitz describes the changing criteria by which courts have reviewed administrative decisions in "Judicial Review of Regulatory Decisions," *Political Science Quarterly* 109 (Spring 1994): 133–169. See also Ruel E. Schiller, "Enlarging the Administrative Polity," *Vanderbilt Law Review* 53 (October 2000): 1389–1453.

16

Liberal Constitutionalism and Equality

The triumph of liberalism encouraged the development of a great Civil Rights Movement designed to make its principles of toleration and equality a reality. The decisions of the Warren Court played a key role in that movement, but it took congressional legislation and vigorous law enforcement by the executive departments and agencies to break down legally sanctioned racial discrimination. Individual prejudices and institutional racism proved even harder to combat.

Growing awareness of discrimination and inequality led to constitutional attacks on their various manifestations. The Supreme Court limited the power of public officials to obstruct the free exercise of religious beliefs. It significantly changed the political landscape by imposing the rule of one person, one vote on the states. It transformed law enforcement by expanding the rights of people accused of crime and reducing the effect of race and poverty on investigations, arrests, and trials.

African American and white radicals found the pace of change too slow, becoming impatient with liberal constitutionalism, criticizing its reliance on courts to remedy injustices and its stress on civil rather than economic equality. They concluded that establishing meaningful equality required mass political action, even violence, rather than appeals to courts and judges.

The Civil Rights Movement

The trend towards liberalism in the 1930s led people to challenge inequalities in American society, the most egregious of which was the system of racial segregation that had developed in the South and spread to parts of the North. As liberalism grew stronger, black and white liberals began to organize. But they had little success until the New Deal, and even then progress came slowly. They failed to secure federal antilynching legislation, for example. But the New Deal energized southern liberals, who believed that overcoming the region's endemic poverty required it to address the debilitating effects of state-enforced segregation.

Relations between African Americans and organized labor also improved during the New Deal. Employers had often used black workers to break strikes or to undercut wages. Elimination of black competition had often been one of organized labor's first demands. But during the New Deal, the Congress of Industrial Organizations (CIO) decided instead to welcome black members, unlike the unions affiliated with the more conservative American Federation of Labor (AFL). Rank-and-file hostility to black workers remained, but membership in CIO unions was open to all, and when unions won improvements in wages and working conditions, black as well as white workers benefited.

The production boom that accompanied World War II fostered a huge black migration to the North between the 1940s and the 1960s. Millions of African Americans established their homes in the great industrial cities of the Midwest, where they benefited from New Deal programs. Improved relations with organized labor, which was closely allied with the Democratic party, encouraged African Americans to transfer their allegiance from the now-conservative Republican party to the more liberal Democrats. This shift strengthened the Democrats in the North, where the growing African American population was able to vote freely. But it identified liberalism with racial equality in the South, and the once strong support for progressive and New Deal legislation there eroded, ultimately making the white South a bastion of political and constitutional conservatism.

Black Americans were not the only group to suffer from discrimination in the United States. Asians and Native Americans faced hostility in the West. There was also significant discrimination against religious minorities, like Jews and Catholics, and against minority ethnic groups. All these groups gravitated towards the political representative of toleration, the northern Democratic party. By the end of the New Deal, it represented a great coalition of the formerly disadvantaged, united in their belief that the power of the federal government should be used to promote economic equality and prosperity.

America's participation in World War II powerfully reinforced the commitment of American liberals to racial and religious toleration at the same time that it exacerbated black impatience with Americans' racial hypocrisy. Proud of their military service, albeit in segregated units, many black soldiers returned determined to secure respect if not equality. Meanwhile, Americans recoiled from the atrocities committed by the Nazis of Germany, who murdered millions of Jews, Gypsies, and Slavs in a mad effort to establish "Aryan" racial purity. For many Americans, ethnic, racial, and religious discrimination were no longer tolerable; it became increasingly less acceptable for people openly to express prejudices against Jews, Irish Catholics, or other white minority groups. With China fighting alongside the United States against Japan, Congress repealed the Chinese Exclusion Act in 1943. A new immigration law in 1952 eliminated the ban on Japanese immigration and removed the white-only provision of the naturalization laws, although it continued quotas that favored European over other immigrants.

The Cold War reinforced the change. The role of the United States as leader of the "free world" militated against state-sanctioned denials of freedom. American leaders became acutely conscious that white racism alienated the colored peoples of what was called the "Third World," where the United States and the communist Soviet Union competed for influence.

In this environment, civil rights organizations began to press for laws to end legal discrimination against black Americans and to use the courts to challenge the constitutionality of laws upholding white supremacy. In 1941 President Roosevelt issued an executive order banning racial discrimination in government hiring and established the Fair Employment Practices Committee. Civil rights lawyers persuaded the Supreme Court to overturn the most blatantly discriminatory voting laws, and in some parts of the South the number of black voters began to grow.

Civil-rights lawyers concentrated especially on laws requiring separate schools. With more and more liberal judges sitting in the courts, these attacks began to succeed. In the 1938 case of *Missouri ex rel. Gaines v. Canada,* the Supreme Court ruled unconstitutional state laws that gave only approximate equality, if that, to African Americans who wanted to go to law school by paying for their tuition in other states. The decision clearly applied to all similar situations. The Gaines case had been brought by the National Association for the Advancement of Colored People (NAACP) and won by its counsel Charles Hamilton Houston, dean of the law faculty at Howard University, the nation's leading African American university. Armed with the *Gaines* precedent, the NAACP used the courts to put ever-increasing pressure on segregation.

After World War II, the NAACP's legal team, led by Houston's student Thurgood Marshall, began to break down racial barriers further. In *Sweatt v. Painter* (1950), the Court ruled the Texas law-school system, which provided separate black and white law schools, unconstitutional. Not only were the black law school's facilities inferior, but the white school alone provided the prestige and contacts that led to success in the legal world. Clearly, only truly equal public facilities would now meet the Court's separate-but-equal test. Southern states and northern cities with segregated school systems frantically began to upgrade black facilities. But the Court now began to question whether any separate facility could be truly equal. In *McLaurin v. Oklahoma State Regents for Higher Education* (1950), the justices overturned a law that admitted black Oklahomans to the state university's graduate school but segregated them within the classrooms, library, dining halls, and residences. Despite the superficial equality in the facilities, the separation denied the black students the benefit of interaction and discussion with their white colleagues; it stigmatized them and increased the difficulty of their studies, the Court said. The Supreme Court seemed slowly to be concluding that racially separate facilities could never really be equal, and Marshall and his lawyers saw the opportunity to attack the constitutionality of segregation itself.

Marshall and the NAACP leadership used the cases to build mass support for the organization. They brought cases only where they had broad backing from the local black community. Challenges to segregation began in a trial court, with local people testifying about conditions. Black crowds thronged the segregated courtrooms, enjoying the spectacle of black lawyers cross-examining white local school officials. Membership in the NAACP soared from 40,000 in 1940 to 400,000 in 1946. Slowly but surely, the organization spread back into the South.

Buoyed by their successes in higher education, the NAACP determined to challenge educational segregation in general, bringing cases against segregated public school systems in Washington, D.C., Charleston, South Carolina, Topeka, Kansas, and other cities. They won in several of the lower federal courts and lost in others. In 1952 Marshall and his legal team squared off against the lawyers for more than a dozen states and cities led by John W. Davis, one-time Democratic presidential nominee and now the leading conservative lawyer in Washington.

Awed by the magnitude of a decision outlawing segregation, the Court hesitated. But in 1954 the Court finally delivered its opinion in the great case of *Brown v. Board of Education of Topeka, Kansas,* unanimously ruling that government-enforced racial segregation in schools violated the Equal Protection Clause of the Fourteenth Amendment, effectively overruling *Plessy v. Ferguson.* In the years following, the Court ruled that any government-enforced segregation, whether in public or in private facilities, was unconstitutional. Legal support for segregation was slowly dismantled.

Where it was relatively easy to do so, the Court simply ordered state and local governments to stop designating facilities as white- or black-only. But desegregating the schools was a far more difficult problem. White southerners supported racial separation in schools more strongly than any in any other facet of life except marriage. The justices knew that they had trodden into an explosive area. Having ruled school segregation unconstitutional, they took more than a year to hear further arguments about how to dismantle it. Finally, in a second *Brown v. Board of Education* decision in 1955, they instructed local courts to use whatever powers necessary to achieve integration "with all deliberate speed."

Where local authorities decided to conform to the Court's ruling, they did so reluctantly. Attempting to do only the minimum, they were often aided by local federal judges. Interpreting the Court's instruction to move with "all deliberate speed" to mean "cautiously," they accepted local plans for "token integration," by which a few black students would be permitted to enroll in white schools where seats were available. Most would continue in all-black schools. Even these programs would proceed slowly, often one grade at a time.

Furious at the desegregation decisions, most white Southerners determined to resist them. Southern congressmen called for the impeachment of the Supreme Court justices and proposed constitutional amendments to recognize segregation. They proposed to create a new court, made up of the chief justices of all the state courts, with the power to reverse Supreme Court decisions. Although they claimed to be defending "state rights," in reality white Southerners were trying to revive the doctrine of state sovereignty. Empowering state justices to over-rule Supreme Court decisions would have given the states the final judicial authority Spencer Roane and other state-sovereignty advocates had sought 150 years earlier. Southerners revived the old doctrine of Nullification, calling on the sovereign states to interpose their authority to block the enforcement of federal court decisions. Several southern state legislatures followed a policy of "massive resistance" to desegregation, making it illegal for local officials to integrate schools, repealing the laws that established the public school system, selling gov-ernment facilities to private individuals who would maintain racial segregation, and closing public facilities ordered to integrate.

Some southern government officials cooperated with white supremacist groups to intimidate local black communities. Local law-enforcement officials were often members of the White Citizens Council or the Ku Klux Klan, which was revived once again to fight racial equality. Police and special intelligence units worked with the Council, Klan, and similar groups, identifying civil rights lead-ers who could be targeted for reprisals.

The governors of Arkansas, Alabama, and Mississippi defied the federal courts, hoping that President Eisenhower and his successor, John F. Kennedy, would refuse to enforce their orders. A key test came in Little Rock, Arkansas in 1957. There, Arkansas governor Orval Faubus prohibited the enforcement of a school integration order issued by the federal circuit court, claiming his action was necessary to prevent violence that he himself encouraged. President Eisen-hower reluctantly backed the court, putting state units of the National Guard un-der federal orders to enforce the law. The Supreme Court responded to the challenge in *Cooper v. Aaron*. With each justice separately signing the opinion, the Court held that government officials were bound to obey judicial decrees enforc-ing constitutional obligations as the Court defined them. Neither state governors nor any other institution of government could defy court orders based on a con-trary interpretation of the Constitution. Mississippi's Governor Ross Barnett is-sued a similar challenge to John F. Kennedy by resisting the court-ordered integration of the University of Mississippi in 1962. After a day of mob attacks on the school's lone black student and the U.S. marshals who had accompanied him to the university, Kennedy finally federalized the Mississippi National Guard and ordered it to enforce the court's order.

The Supreme Court's opinion in *Cooper v. Aaron* was the most far-reaching claim the Court had ever made that other government officials had to defer to its interpretations of the Constitution. The Court had always had *final* authority over interpreting the Constitution, because in the end all laws and governmental acts in the United States can be appealed to the judiciary. But in the crisis over integra-tion, the Court was claiming *preemptive* authority; once the Court interpreted the

Constitution, it claimed, all other branches of government were bound not only to enforce its immediate decision but to accept its interpretation as binding.

Traditionally it had been conservatives who had exalted the role of the courts as the protectors of liberty. Jeffersonians, Jacksonians, antislavery Republicans, Progressives, and New Deal Democrats had all claimed that the people, through their elected representatives, had equal authority to construe the Constitution and to carry out its provisions. But a newly libertarian Supreme Court, checking the majority's efforts to deny liberty and equality to dissenters and minority groups, led liberals too to see the judiciary as the main defender of constitutional rights. As conservatives began to criticize the judges for undermining democracy, liberals rushed to defend them. Judicial supremacy became a major tenet of liberal constitutionalism.

But despite its claim of final authority, it was clear that the Supreme Court alone could not force an end to segregation. Individual lawsuits took too long and were too expensive to combat segregation effectively. Massive resistance was proving hard to overcome. "Token integration" would take years to challenge. Moreover, there was still little legal basis for challenging private discrimination in businesses, housing, or public accommodations. By the late 1950s desegregation was stalled, and neither President Eisenhower nor President Kennedy seemed willing to face the problem boldly.

Inspired by the Court's denunciation of segregation but frustrated at inaction, black college students and church groups throughout the South turned to nonviolent public protest to force changes in discriminatory policies and to pressure the federal government for laws against racial discrimination. They were joined by northern college students, churches and religious groups, and labor unions. As older civil rights organizations like the NAACP hammered at discriminatory laws in the courts, new civil rights groups organized demonstrations and economic boycotts. These protests were led by a new generation of able leaders, of whom the best known was the charismatic apostle of nonviolent protest, Reverend Martin Luther King Jr., who came to prominence in one of the first peaceful protests of the Civil Rights era, the Montgomery Bus Boycott of 1955–1956. Victory in that campaign came only with a court order to desegregate the buses, but the idealism and sacrifice that sustained the successful boycott galvanized the African American community.

White southerners reacted to the protests with stubborn hostility and often with violence, beating and even killing protesters. Northerners, who could now witness the petty viciousness of southern white supremacy on television, were shocked by the brutal response to peaceful but highly visible protests: King's desegregation campaign in Birmingham, Alabama, which was met with police dogs, water hoses, and truncheons; the assaults on "sit-in" demonstrators who tried to integrate southern diners and cafes; the attack on the "freedom riders" who tried to travel through the South on integrated buses; the riot that threatened the lives

Thurgood Marshall, the first African American justice of the Supreme Court. Marshall earlier made his reputation as the leading lawyer for the NAACP.

of the first black student to desegregate the University of Mississippi and the U.S. marshals sent to protect him.

The violence led to a powerful reaction in the North. Northerners demanded that the national government pass laws to end segregation and guarantee the right to vote. The massive March on Washington in 1963, was followed in 1965 by a riveting march from Selma to Montgomery, Alabama, to demand voting rights. Southern police met the Alabama protest with water cannons, police dogs, and clubs, once more shocking Northerners and solidifying support for federal action. The Supreme Court in effect encouraged the protests, often bending legal precedents to overturn convictions of demonstrators on trespass, contempt-of-court, and breach-of-the-peace charges.

The demonstrations ultimately resulted in a series of civil rights laws, including the Twenty-Fourth Amendment, which banned the payment of poll taxes as a requirement for voting in national elections, the Civil Rights Act of 1964, and the Voting Rights Act of 1965. The Civil Rights Act was an extremely comprehensive effort to end most discrimination in the United States. It authorized the federal government to bring suits to desegregate public facilities as well as to withhold federal funds from discriminatory public programs—an extremely

Martin Luther King, the great proponent of nonviolent protest at the March on Washington.

effective tool. Title II prohibited racial, ethnic, and religious discrimination in public accommodations, and it overturned any state or local law that required such segregation in any place whatsoever. Title VII prohibited any business affecting interstate commerce from discriminating in employment, not only on the basis of race, religion, or ethnic background but sex as well.

The Voting Rights Act barred literacy tests wherever fewer than 50 percent of adults were registered to vote, a provision that primarily affected the South but also some districts with large Hispanic populations elsewhere. It required all such jurisdictions to submit future changes in election procedures to the Justice Department for pre-clearance. The act also gave the national government the power to register voters whenever twenty residents alleged that state officials were discriminating against them because of their race.

Southerners bitterly resisted the passage of the Civil Rights and Voting Rights Acts, arguing that the states had final jurisdiction over race relations, and that the national government could not exercise its delegated powers to usurp that jurisdiction. But the Supreme Court rejected this state-rights argument in *Heart of Atlanta Motel v. U.S.* (1964), declaring the Civil Rights Act an appropriate exercise of the national government's plenary power to regulate interstate commerce. Likewise, in *South Carolina v. Katzenbach* (1966), the justices upheld the Voting Rights Act as a valid exercise of Congress's power to enforce the Fifteenth Amendment.

It was the enforcement of the Civil Rights Act, the Voting Rights Act, and their amendments, along with the active pressure of federal agencies, rather than the decisions of the Supreme Court, that finally broke down state-enforced segregation and the customs that had denied educational and employment opportunities to African Americans and other minority groups. The Voting Rights Act led to a dramatic increase in black political power in the South. African–American voter registration ultimately came to equal that of whites. In the decades following passage of the act, thousands of African Americans were elected to local offices in the South and several to Congress. Black Southerners also helped to elect a new generation of moderate white Southern leaders, including future presidents Jimmy Carter and Bill Clinton.

But the Civil Rights Movement also polarized the South. As white Southerners resisted desegregation, they also abandoned other elements of liberal political philosophy. As early as 1964, the Republican party capitalized on this alienation by nominating archconservative Barry Goldwater for the presidency. Repudiated in the North, Goldwater carried several southern states. Alabama governor George C. Wallace led conservative insurgencies within the Democratic party in 1968 and 1972, and many of his followers deserted the party in national elections. Although moderate southern candidate Jimmy Carter did well in 1976, Democratic presidential candidates would rarely carry southern states thereafter. Conservative Republicans slowly but consistently gained ground in southern congressional delegations, state legislatures, and governors' mansions. Nonetheless, in the 1960s the events associated with the Civil Rights Movement reinforced constitutional nationalism and liberal constitutionalism in general. The New Deal had already discredited the doctrine of state rights. The identification of state rights with segregation, intolerance, and violence further tarnished the doctrine in the eyes of most Americans. It seemed as dead as the doctrine of state sovereignty.

"Affirmative Action" and "Equality of Result"

By the 1970s, the Civil Rights Movement had achieved its original aims. Legally enforced segregation was almost entirely eliminated from the United States. The Civil Rights Act of 1964 and later laws and court decisions had made it illegal even for private individuals to discriminate on account of race in employment, schooling, or housing. African Americans throughout the South were registering to vote and beginning to elect black government officials.

Many people, however, were disappointed with the results. Government action against outright segregation had been effective. But it proved very difficult to end discrimination in employment, schooling, and housing, in part because it was difficult to prove that decisions in these areas were motivated by racial prejudice. It was also difficult to end discrimination because the effects of racial prejudice were so deeply imbedded in American life and history. Decades of discrimination had left many African Americans poorer and less educated than whites, and therefore ill equipped to compete for jobs and good schools. Moreover, jobs and promotions were often dependent on personal relationships from which most African Americans were still excluded. Liberals came to call this persistent inequality "institutionalized racism," because it resulted from long-term realities of American society rather than from individual decisions to discriminate.

Many people began to demand that the government take positive steps to correct the results of this inequality. Liberty meant more than freedom from government oppression; people had rights to certain things that government was bound to provide, such as decent jobs, housing, and food. The government responded positively to many of these demands. The War on Poverty, designed to secure economic well-being for all people, was one of the clearest examples.

Already sensitive to racial discrimination, the Supreme Court became sensitized to more subtle, "institutional racism" by its first black justice, the NAACP's Thurgood Marshall, appointed by Lyndon Johnson in 1967. The judges now required government officials to take positive steps to remedy past discrimination in hiring and schooling. State and local governments that had discriminated in the past had to take "affirmative action" to remedy the situation, even if the remedy meant discriminating against whites. Various departments of the national government issued similar rules for companies doing business with the government and institutions seeking government financial aid. These administrative actions were more effective than court orders in promoting affirmative action, since they applied to businesses and other institutions generally and did not require case-by-case litigation. Likewise, judges said that it was not enough for school systems to end legally enforced segregation. They must create racial balance in each school, even if this goal required children to be taken to schools outside their neighborhoods. Many state and local governments established programs that encouraged contractors to hire minority-owned firms to perform some of their government work. Colleges and universities set targets for recruiting minorities to their student bodies. Only through such "benign discrimination" could the effects of years of exclusion be overcome, the programs' advocates argued.

Federal administrative agencies and the courts also looked closely at neutral tests that had a discriminatory effect in employment, promotion, student admission, and other areas of life. The Supreme Court led the way in *Griggs v. Duke Power Co.* (1971), ruling that such tests were permissible only if they directly related to job performance. Otherwise, superficially neutral tests, such as literacy or general intelligence tests, could be used to eliminate minority applicants, who for years had been by law denied equal educational opportunities. The ruling not only helped African Americans; it ultimately opened millions of jobs to women and other minorities who could not meet irrelevant height, weight, strength, and endurance tests. These developments suggested a change in the idea of "equality." Originally the Civil Rights Movement had demanded "equal opportunity"—the right to compete freely in American society without the handicap of unfair laws. But after decades of state-supported discrimination, equal opportunity alone could not change the great disparity in the economic condition of whites, African Americans, and other minority groups. Now people were demanding "equality of result"—a guarantee that African Americans and other minorities would succeed in about the same numbers as white people.

The Ferment of Civil Rights

The success of the Civil Rights Movement had a profound impact on other groups who suffered from discrimination in the United States. Group after group organized to use the same tactics, including Hispanic Americans, women, homosexuals, handicapped people, and others. The efforts of these groups were also quite successful, and the national government began to act vigorously to secure their rights under the Civil Rights Act of 1964. Where that law was inadequate, Congress passed new ones, such as the Age Discrimination in Employment Act of 1967. At the same time, the new sensitivity to racism led Congress to pass the Immigration Act of 1965, which eliminated the quotas that had favored Europeans over others. Immigrants from Latin America and Asia soon outnumbered those coming from Europe.

Native Americans faced peculiar complexities in the civil-rights era, seeking equal rights on the one hand and special status on the other. In 1953 Congress had formally adopted termination of special status for Indians as a national goal and gave prior consent to any state that extended legal jurisdiction over Indians and Indian reservations. Terminated tribes would lose their common land, reservation health and education facilities, and the ability to manage resources as a community. Some states interpreted termination to abrogate all privileges secured to Native Americans by treaties.

Termination had been driven by a humanitarian commitment to integrating Native Americans fully into American society and a less altruistic desire to open natural resources on Indian reservations to exploitation. But termination proved disastrous for most of those it was intended to benefit. No new termination acts passed Congress after President John F. Kennedy took office in 1961, which limited the policy's impact to about 200 tribes and 12,000 people. Conceding the permanence of tribal government, Congress determined to secure the basic rights of individuals subject to tribal authority. In 1968 it passed the Indian Bill of Rights, extending many of the protections of the Bill of Rights to those under tribal jurisdiction.

After the government closed the prison on Alcatraz Island in San Francisco Bay, members of the American Indian Movement occupied it, demanding changes in government treatment of Native Americans. Over 5,500 Indians participated in the protest, which lasted from 1969 to 1971.

Reacting against the assimilationism that inspired the termination policy, a new generation of radical activists worked to revive Native American customs and to invent new ones based on older traditions. A series of high-profile actions electrified Indians across the country. Activists established the American Indian Movement and other advocacy and action groups. Appealing to liberal principles of toleration and respect for cultural differences, the Native American rights movement won broad support. In 1975 Congress passed the Indian Self-Determination and Education Assistance Act of 1975, authorizing tribes to enter into their own contracts for educational and other services. In 1978 it formally declared a federal policy of protecting Native American traditional religious beliefs, ordering agencies to revise their policies accordingly. This was followed by a series of laws to help Native Americans maintain control of their institutions, land, and cultural artifacts and even to discourage adoptions of Indian children by outsiders.

In the same years the Supreme Court began to protect tribal rights. Not only did federal courts order the federal government to reimburse tribes for property taken in violation of treaties, they ruled that tribes were entitled to the *return* of lands states had taken from them without federal authorization. Tribes prepared to claim rights over property long distributed to private non-Indian landowners, forcing property owners, states, and the federal government to negotiate financial settlements. When the Court ruled that treaties limited the operation of state laws on reservations, tribes took advantage of the situation to open gambling casinos. In 1988 Congress passed the Indian Gaming Regulatory Act, requiring states and tribes to negotiate agreements to govern such activities.

Like the African American Civil Rights Movement, the Native American movement fell short of its aspirations. Poverty remained endemic among Indians, whether in cities or on reservations. They faced the obstacles of institutional discrimination that defied solution by civil rights laws. But Indian pride had been boosted immensely. Respect for traditional customs had grown among Indians and non-Indian Americans. Tribal authority was no longer under attack, and coerced assimilation had been repudiated.

The Women's Movement of the 1970s and 1980s rivaled the Civil Rights Movement in its impact. Revitalized by the Civil Rights Movement, feminists demanded equal access to all areas of social and economic life, the elimination of laws limiting women's reproductive freedom, and an end to sexual exploitation and the denigration of women as "sex objects." A new generation of feminists worked assiduously to awaken their sisters to the inequities of gender relationships and to make men conscious of sexist assumptions and behavior. Many women (perhaps the majority) rejected the label "feminist," but the practical consequences of discrimination in employment led to rapidly growing support as economic pressure forced ever-greater numbers of women into the job market. In 1972 Congress responded to women's demands by sending the Equal Rights Amendment, which would bar discrimination based on sex, to the states for ratification.

The changed perception of women's place in society soon affected the courts. Beginning with the 1971 case of *Reed v. Reed*, the Supreme Court invalidated state laws that "irrationally" discriminated against women. In *Craig v. Boren* (1976), the Court struck down an Oklahoma law that set a higher minimum drinking age for men than for women, indicating that it would look with heightened scrutiny at laws discriminating on the basis of sex. Such laws would have to serve important public interests, rather than be merely "rational." *Roe v. Wade* (1973), which recognized women's right to control reproduction through abortion, was also a response to the Women's Movement. At the same time, the justices began to enforce Title VII of the Civil Rights Act, which banned sexual discrimination in employment. As women began to break down traditional barriers in employment and social organizations, federal agencies established affirmative-action programs to combat sexual discrimination similar to those combating racial discrimination.

American participation in the Vietnam War energized younger Americans in a similar way. Inaugurated by an older generation, the war disrupted the lives of the young men called upon to fight it. Alienated young people questioned the un-thinking patriotism of their elders and charged that powerful business interests dominated the government and determined its policies. The so-called New Left at-tacked liberalism in general for compromising with a fundamentally inequitable system that needed radical restructuring rather than piecemeal reform. Adopting the tactics of the Civil Rights Movement, young people demonstrated against the war. In 1969, over 200,000 protesters imitated the earlier March on Washington with a huge antiwar demonstration. When President Richard M. Nixon expanded the war by sending troops into Cambodia in 1970, student protests closed down colleges across the nation. In Ohio, the demonstrations ended in tragedy when National Guardsmen fired upon protesters, killing four of them.

Among the most compelling of the protesters' grievances was the complaint that while they were eligible for the draft at age 18, nearly all states set the voting age at 21. In response, Congress proposed the Twenty-Sixth Amendment, enfran-chising citizens over 18 years of age, which the states ratified in 1971. The change hardly reconciled young people to the war, but as the Nixon administration wound down the hostilities and ended the draft, the antiwar protests petered out. Without the grievance of the war to excite masses of young Americans, the New Left tide slowly ebbed.

Nonetheless, by the 1970s, civil rights activity had led to a great expansion of the definitions of "rights." Many people demanded as their "right" things which in earlier years would have been seen only as in their "interest"; they engaged more and more in what legal scholars came to call "rights talk." Older people or-ganized to demand an end to discrimination against them in employment. They argued that it violated their rights to require them to retire at age 65 or to prefer younger applicants for jobs. They succeeded in having the antidiscrimination provisions of the Civil Rights Act of 1964 extended to age discrimination and having the retirement age increased to 70. People with physical disabilities claimed a right to equal access. Responding to their demands, the government re-quired that nearly all public places and services be modified, no matter what the cost, to enable disabled people to use them freely. The antidiscrimination provi-sions of the Civil Rights Act were extended to them as well in new legislation such as the Americans with Disabilities Act of 1990.

One Person, One Vote

The justices of the Supreme Court shared the growing sensitivity to inequality. As Congress expanded the civil rights laws to cover more and more groups, the na-tional courts enforced the laws vigorously. The Court also acted boldly to make certain that all people were fairly represented in the political process. It was cus-tomary for states to apportion one branch of their legislatures by geographic unit, like counties, or according to some rule other than simple population. In many cases states did not reapportion representation in either branch to keep up with population changes. As a result, conservative rural and small-town voters controlled the state legislatures even though they were a minority of the state's population. They blocked liberal legislation supported by urban legislators.

The Supreme Court had avoided controversies arising from this issue on the grounds that they were inherently political rather than judicial questions. But given the Court's liberalism and its concern with equality, pressure grew for it to intervene. In the 1962 case of *Baker v. Carr*, the justices ruled that Tennessee's malapportionment of its state legislature was an issue that they could consider after all. The Equal Protection Clause of the Fourteenth Amendment required that the basis of apportionment at least be rational, the Court held. Tennessee's apportionment failed even that minimal test; Tennessee's own constitution required reapportionment every ten years, and the legislature had not fulfilled this responsibility since 1901.

The Court soon went further. Almost immediately, plaintiffs challenged the apportionment of legislatures in fifteen more states. In *Reynolds v. Sims* (1964) and other apportionment cases, the Court ruled that the Equal Protection Clause required that representation in the state legislatures conform generally to the rule of "one man, one vote." "Legislators represent people, not trees," Chief Justice Warren wrote in his majority opinion. In another series of cases, the Court ruled it unconstitutional to create districts or establish procedures that had the effect of preventing minority groups from electing representatives to office. Particularly suspect were changes from district to at-large elections—for example, a change from electing members of a city council from individual districts to electing all of them from the city as a whole. Such a system often prevented voters in mostly African American districts from being able to elect black officials to represent them. Not only did the Court look closely at such changes, but it ruled that they had to be cleared by the Justice Department under the Voting Rights Act of 1965. The Justice Department, watching closely for proposals that diluted the impact of black votes, regularly struck such proposals down.

The Rights of People Accused of Crime

The Supreme Court showed its sensitivity to inequality in yet another very important area, criminal law. Leaders of the Civil Rights Movement had complained bitterly that the police and courts treated poor people and members of minority groups unjustly. They were more likely to be stopped, searched, arrested, and abused. They often were not aware of their constitutional rights and too poor to afford lawyers. Civil libertarians pointed out cases where terrible injustices had been committed.

The Supreme Court attempted to guarantee the same rights to all people in criminal investigations. In *Gideon v. Wainwright* (1963), the Court ruled that in serious cases the government must provide lawyers to defendants unable to afford counsel themselves. A few years later they extended the rule to cover even minor cases. In the famous case of *Miranda v. Arizona* (1966), the Court required the police to inform suspects of their rights: the right not to answer questions, to know that anything they said could be used against them in court, and to have a lawyer. The Court also tried to prevent police from stopping people and searching their property without reasonable cause to suspect them of a crime. In *Mapp v. Ohio* (1961), the justices reversed the old rule of *Wolf v. Colorado* and forbade state courts from admitting evidence secured in violation of these rules.

The justices were also concerned about prejudice in sentencing. Civil libertarians had complained for years that poor people and members of minority groups were far more likely than others to receive severe punishment. In *Furman v. Georgia* (1972), the Court ruled that the death penalty was unconstitutional as it was being applied in most states. The justices did not overturn the death penalty because it constituted "cruel and unusual punishment" prohibited by the Eighth Amendment, as Thurgood Marshall and Justice William Brennan wanted. Instead they held that it was being imposed arbitrarily and that this injustice, not the death penalty itself, was cruel and unusual.

These decisions reinforced a law-and-order reaction to increased crime. In 1968 Republican presidential candidate Richard M. Nixon blasted activist judges for coddling criminals. Law enforcement officials lamented that dangerous criminals were released on technicalities. Popular books and movies glorified rogue policemen and vigilantes who scorned the rules as they made sure the bad guys got what they deserved. But the key reforms stuck. Poor defendants received legal aid, however limited the skills of the lawyers dragooned to help them. "*Miranda* warnings" became as much a staple of popular culture as disdain for the suspects who benefited from them.

Religious Toleration

Just as growing racial tolerance affected how the Supreme Court interpreted the Constitution, so did the growing national commitment to religious toleration. Concern for the feelings of racial minorities had played an important part in leading the Court to ban government-sponsored prayer from the schools. It also led the Warren Court to limit the power of government to obstruct the free exercise of religious beliefs.

The traditional legal rule dated back to the days when the government had suppressed Mormon polygamy. In *Reynolds v. U.S.* (1879) the Court had ruled that while government could not punish religious beliefs, it could pass laws prohibiting conduct as long as those laws were reasonably related to the public welfare. But the Supreme Court had undercut that rule during World War II in the Second Flag Salute Case when it ruled that schools could not force children to salute the flag. Now, with the growing stress on toleration and individual autonomy of the 1960s, members of religious minorities demanded that local governments take account of their religious convictions when passing regulations. When state and local governments failed to do so, they turned to the courts.

The Warren Court soon jettisoned the *Reynolds* rule that regulations of mere behavior were constitutional as long as they were rationally connected to the public welfare. Faced with a state requirement that those receiving unemployment compensation agree to take any job that did not require work on Sunday, the justices ruled that such regulations violated the First Amendment's guarantee of religious liberty to those who observed the Sabbath on other days. A decade later the Court ruled that states must exempt people who objected to secondary education on religious grounds from compulsory education requirements. Encouraged by such decisions, the federal courts strictly enforced the Civil Rights Act's ban against religious discrimination in employment, forcing public and private employers to accommodate religious beliefs in their work policies.

By the 1960s and 1970s, the principles of American liberalism were being applied in ways that had not been imagined in the early years of the twentieth century. They were imposed throughout the country by the national government, including the president, Congress, and the courts. Areas of the country where people remained more conservative had been unable to resist. But a growing number of Americans were signaling opposition to many of these liberal policies and court decisions. Slowly, a conservative reaction began that by the late 1970s would undermine the liberal consensus.

TIMELINE

1936   For the first time, most African American voters support the Democratic party in a national election, helping to reelect Franklin D. Roosevelt.

1938   In *Missouri ex rel. Gaines v. Canada* the Supreme Court orders Missouri to admit a black applicant to its only state-supported law school.

1941–1945 The United States fights Nazism and fascism in World War II, increasing sensitivity to religious and racial intolerance.

1950   The Supreme Court requires Texas to integrate its leading state-supported law school in *Sweatt v. Painter.*

1952   Congress eliminates racial restrictions from immigration and naturalization laws.

1953   Congress declares the goal of terminating special tribal status of Native Americans and authorizes states to extend jurisdiction over Indian reservations.

Earl Warren becomes chief justice of the Supreme Court.

1954	The Supreme Court rules racially segregated schools unconstitutional in *Brown v. Board of Education of Topeka, Kansas;* in following years the Court rules segregation unconstitutional in all public facilities.
1955	The Supreme Court requires segregated school systems to be dismantled "with all deliberate speed" in *Brown v. Board of Education II.*
1955–1964	Many southern states oppose desegregation with "interposition," "massive resistance," and "token integration."
1955–1956	Montgomery Bus Boycott inaugurates the Civil Rights Movement and brings Rev. Martin Luther King to prominence.
1957	The Little Rock Crisis forces President Eisenhower to use the National Guard to enforce desegregation orders issued by federal courts.
1961	In *Mapp v. Ohio,* the Supreme Court rules that the "Exclusionary Rule" applies to states as well as to the federal government.
1962	In *Baker v. Carr,* the Supreme Court rules malapportionment of state legislatures unconstitutional; later cases announce the principle of "one man, one vote."
	Violence forces President Kennedy to call out the National Guard to enforce federal court orders desegregating the University of Mississippi.
1963	In *Gideon v. Wainwright,* the Supreme Court rules persons accused of felonies must be provided lawyers; later cases extend the ruling to serious misdemeanors.
	The March on Washington brings over 200,000 demonstrators to the capital.
1964	The Twenty-Fourth Amendment is ratified, forbidding states from requiring citizens to pay poll taxes in order to vote.
	The Civil Rights Act of 1964 bars racial, religious, and ethnic discrimination in public facilities and employment; the act also bars sexual discrimination in employment.
	The Supreme Court sustains the constitutionality of the Civil Rights Act of 1964 in *Heart of Atlanta Motel v. U.S.*
1960s–1980s	The Women's Rights Movement demands equal opportunity and treatment in employment and raises sensitivity to sexism in all areas of American life.
1965	The Selma-Montgomery March against racial discrimination in voting is met by local police violence, increasing pressure for national legislation to secure voting rights.
	The Immigration Act eliminates quotas by country of origin from the immigration laws.

1965 The Voting Rights Act bars literacy tests in districts with low voter registration and authorizes the federal government to register voters where local registrars refuse to do so.

1966 The Supreme Court sustains the Voting Rights Act in *South Carolina v. Katzenbach.*

   In *Miranda v. Arizona,* the Supreme Court requires that criminal suspects be informed of their rights before being questioned.

1967 Thurgood Marshall becomes the first African American justice on the Supreme Court.

   Congress prohibits age discrimination in employment.

1968 The Indian Civil Rights Act requires tribal authorities to observe the provisions of a bill of rights.

1969 Warren E. Burger succeeds Earl Warren as chief justice.

1971 The Supreme Court rules that the Civil Rights Act of 1964 requires that job-qualification tests with discriminatory effects must be directly related to job performance, in *Griggs v. Duke Power Co.*

   The states ratify the Twenty-Sixth Amendment, which enfranchises citizens over 18 years of age.

1972 Congress sends the Equal Rights Amendment, barring discrimination based on sex, to the states for ratification.

   The Supreme Court rules the death penalty, as presently administered in most states, unconstitutional in *Furman v. Georgia.*

1973 In *Roe v. Wade,* the Supreme Court rules that laws barring abortions violate women's constitutional right to privacy.

1976 In *Craig v. Boren,* the Supreme Court rules that the Equal Protection Clause requires sexually discriminatory laws be subjected to "heightened scrutiny."

1978 Congress declares a policy of preserving and protecting traditional Native American religious practices.

FURTHER READING

John P. Roche's *Quest for the Dream* (1963) brings the story of American tolerance and intolerance through the 1950s. Robert J. Norrell, *The House I Live In* (2005) provides an overview of race relations in the 20th century. For changes that prefigured the Supreme Court's desegregation decision, see Michael J. Klarman, "*Brown,* Racial Change, and the Civil Rights Movement," *Virginia Law Review* 80 (February 1994): 7–150. Mary L. Dudziak points out the impact of competition with Soviet communism in *Cold War Civil*

Rights (2000). For the Civil Rights Movement, see Donald G. Nieman, *Promises to Keep* (1991) and Harvard Sitkoff, *The Struggle for Black Equality, 1954–1980* (1981). There are two splendid accounts of Martin Luther King's leadership of the movement: Taylor Branch, *Parting the Waters* (1988), which he followed with *Pillar of Fire* (1998), and David Garrow, *Bearing the Cross* (1986). Juan Williams's *Eyes on the Prize: America's Civil Rights Years* (1987) is the well-written, highly illustrated companion to the outstanding Public Broadcasting System documentary of the same name.

For the NAACP-led legal assault on segregation before *Brown v. Board of Education*, see Mark Tushnet, *The NAACP's Legal Strategy Against Segregated Education* (1987). Jack Greenberg, who became director-general of the NAACP Legal Defense Fund, tells the story from the perspective of a key participant in *Crusaders in the Courts* (1994). He carries the story beyond *Brown*, as does Tushnet in his study of the impact of Thurgood Marshall, *Making Civil Rights Law: Thurgood Marshall and the Supreme Court* (1994).

Michael Klarman synthesizes the insights of his influential law review articles on the history of law and race in the U.S. in *From Jim Crow to Civil Rights* (2004), a must-read. For his thesis that *Brown* was more important for the political controversy it engendered than its direct effect on law, see "How Brown Changed Race Relations: The Backlash Thesis," *Journal of American History* 81 (June 1994): 81–118. Richard Kluger presents the story of *Brown v. Board of Education* on an epic scale in *Simple Justice* (1975). More manageable are Robert J. Cottrol et al., *Brown v. Board of Education* (2003), and James T. Patterson, *Brown v. Board of Education* (2001). Patterson carries the tale through the end of the twentieth century.

Numan V. Bartley chronicles *The Rise of Massive Resistance* (1969) in the South. Dan T. Carter chronicles the career of Alabama segregationist George Wallace in *The Politics of Rage* (2d ed., 2000).. For federal judges' reaction, read Jack Bass's *Unlikely Heroes* (1981) and his study of Judge Frank M. Johnson, *Taming the Storm* (1993). For an earlier, more general study, see Jack R. Peltason, *58 Lonely Men: Southern Federal Judges and School Desegregation* (1961). Tony A. Freyer analyzes a crucial turning point in *The Little Rock Crisis* (1984). William H. Chafe's *Civilities and Civil Rights* (1980) is the tale of the sit-in movement in Greensboro, North Carolina. J. Mills Thornton III tells the story of the struggle in Montgomery, Birmingham, and Selma, Alabama, in *Dividing Lines* (2002). In *Federal Law and Southern Order* (1987), Michal R. Belknap argues that ultimately it was the rise of southern moderates, rather than pressure from the federal government, that ended violent resistance to desegregation in the South.

Hugh Davis Graham describes the development of federal legislation and law enforcement in *The Civil Rights Era* (1990). Nick Kotz writes compellingly about *Lyndon Baines Johnson, Martin Luther King Jr., and the Laws that Changed America* (2005). Dean J. Kotlowski concentrates on the Nixon administration's enforcement of equal rights in *Nixon's Civil Rights* (2001). In *The Minority Rights Revolution* (2002) John D. Skrentny emphasizes how government agencies championed equal rights for some groups while excluding others. Michal Belknap describes how commitment to federalism inhibited the national government's response to southern violence in *Federal Law and Southern Order*, noted above. See also Carl M. Brauer, *John F. Kennedy and the Second Reconstruction* (1977). For federal enforcement of voting rights, see Stephen Lawson, *Black Ballots* (1976). Donald S. Strong chronicles the foot-dragging of southern federal judges in *Negroes, Ballots, and Judges* (1968). See William Bradford Huie's *Three Lives for Mississippi* (1968) for the moving story of three civil rights workers murdered during the Mississippi voter registration drive of 1964.

Samuel Leiter and William M. Leiter provide a thorough description *Affirmative Action in Antidiscrimination Law and Policy* (2002). Herman Belz argues that the courts and the federal bureaucracy illicitly transformed the principle of equal opportunity into one of equal results by insisting on "affirmative action." See Belz, *Equality Transformed* (1991). Melvin Urofsky does not find the change as radical in *A Conflict of Rights* (1991).

The rise of Hispanic consciousness in 1960s and 1970s California is chronicled in Ian F. Haney Lopez, *Racism on Trial* (2004). Manuel G. Gonzales provides a briefer overview in his general history of *Mexicanos* (1999) in the United States. Sharon Barnartt and Richard Scotch analyze the rise of organized protest among Americans with disabilities from the 1970s through the end to the twentieth century in *Disability Protests* (2002). Duane Stroman sketches a brief history as part of his *The Disability Rights Movement* (2003).

The termination policy is described in James Wilson's general history of Native Americans *The Earth Shall Weep* (1998). The rise and triumph of the principles of Indian "self-determination" from 1960 to 1975 is the subject of George Pierre Castile's *To Show Heart: Native American Self-Determination and Federal Indian Policy* (1998). John R. Wunder's study of Indian rights in American history *"Retained by the People"* (1994) discusses the Indian Bill of Rights in historical context. The essays in *Native Americans and the Law*, ed. John R. Wunder, (1996) offer more specifics, as does *American Indian Policy in the Twentieth Century*, ed. Vine DeLoria (1985).

Leila Rupp and Verta Taylor describe the quiescent period of the women's movement from 1945 to the 1960s in *Survival in the Doldrums* (1987). Dorothy Sue Cobble draws attention to *The Other Woman's Movement* (2004) that worked with organized labor to improve working conditions from the 1930s into the 1960s. Barbara Sinclair Deckard's *The Women's Movement* (3d ed., 1983) surveys the 1960s and 1970s as part of a longer study, as does William Chafe, *The Paradox of Change* (1991).

Richard Cortner discusses the background of *The Apportionment Cases* (1970), while Ward Y. Elliott's *The Rise of Guardian Democracy* (1974) provides a general history of the Supreme Court and voting rights from 1845 to 1969. David J. Bodenhamer discusses the expansion of due-process rights during the Warren years in *Fair Trial* (1992). See also Samuel Walker, *Taming the System* (1993). Anthony Lewis recounts the story of *Gideon v. Wainwright* in his readable classic, *Gideon's Trumpet* (1984). For a sobering illustration of why the Warren Court established the Miranda Rule, see Bernard Lefkowitz and Ken Gross's gripping tale of a near-miscarriage of justice, *The Victims* (1969). Yale Kamisar discusses the relationship between the expansion of suspects' rights in criminal investigations and the Civil Rights Movement, as well as the public reaction to the decisions, in his contribution to *The Warren Court: A Retrospective*, ed. Bernard Schwartz (1996).

For the Warren Court's decisions protecting the rights of religious minorities and imposing a rigid separation of church and state, see Frank J. Sorauf's *The Wall of Separation* (1976) and the relevant chapters of Richard E. Morgan's *The Supreme Court and Religion* (1972).

For the growing pervasiveness of the rhetoric of rights and entitlements in the 1970s and 1980s, see Kristin Bumiller's *The Civil Rights Society: The Social Construction of Victims* (1988) and Mary Ann Glendon's very influential *Rights Talk* (1991).

17

Curbing Presidential Power

The prestige and power of the presidency began to grow when Theodore Roosevelt revitalized the office during the Progressive Era. But the dynamic Franklin Delano Roosevelt, father of the New Deal, architect of victory in World War II, established a precedent for presidential leadership that transformed American government. From the New Deal onward, Americans looked to the president rather than Congress to inaugurate public policy. Washington, Jackson, Lincoln, and the Roosevelts became the models of political leadership, rather than the great congressmen Webster, Clay, or Sumner.

Presidential power expanded dramatically between the 1930s and the 1970s. As utilized by the driven and manipulative President Richard M. Nixon, it came to threaten the constitutional system itself. The Watergate Scandal awakened Americans to the danger of misuse of power and drove Nixon from office. But the declining prestige of the presidency was not complemented by any rise in respect for Congress. By the mid-1970s, the national government itself seemed to be in growing disrepute.

The Growth of Presidential Power

The New Deal bred new respect for the presidency. Roosevelt's example convinced most liberals that a strong presidency was essential to active government and the general-welfare state. This perception was reinforced by the fact that from 1938 through the early 1960s liberal presidential proposals were often defeated in Congress by a coalition of conservative Republicans and southern Democrats, who held a disproportionate number of congressional committee chairmanships and leadership positions

State legislatures had similar obstructionist reputations. In most states, seats in at least one house of the legislature, and usually both, were apportioned to give conservative, rural voters greater representation than liberal voters living in the cities and suburbs. Thus in the states as well as in national government, energetic, progressive governors often faced intransigent conservative lawmakers. By the

1960s many Americans had come to see both Congress and the state legislatures as obstacles to efficient government.

The 1962 Supreme Court ruling that all voting districts had to be equal in population weakened the ability of rural, conservative state legislators and congressional representatives to block legislation. At the same time liberals were able finally to end conservative control of key congressional committees. As a result of these developments, and aided by a landslide Democratic victory in the election of 1964, President Lyndon Johnson was able to secure passage of almost all of his Great Society, War on Poverty, and civil rights proposals from 1964 to 1968. Since these were presidential initiatives, their passage increased the prestige of the Executive more than that of Congress.

Conservatives grew to dislike presidential leadership for the same reasons that liberals approved of it. They worried that presidential influence in the political system had grown too great, citing the reelection of Franklin Roosevelt to a third and fourth term in office in 1940 and 1944. No previous president had ever violated the precedent George Washington had set when he retired after his second term. In the short-lived conservative reaction that followed the end of World War II, Republicans successfully amended the Constitution to limit presidents to two terms. But although the change did weaken presidents' influence during their second terms, it did not reverse the general flow of power to them.

Because the Constitution makes the president commander-in-chief and gives him prime responsibility for conducting foreign relations, presidents became especially formidable in these areas. In 1950, for example, President Harry S. Truman sent American military forces to fight in Korea without securing a declaration of war from Congress. He argued that he was merely meeting American obligations under the United Nations treaty, which Congress had ratified. In 1958 President Eisenhower sent troops to the Middle East without congressional authorization, and in 1962 President Kennedy sent American military advisers to Southeast Asia in the same way. From 1965 to 1968, President Johnson increased the number of soldiers in Southeast Asia and sent troops to the Dominican Republic. By the 1960s, American presidents claimed that they had the primary responsibility to protect national security and that this trust implied a broad range of presidential powers in the areas of war and foreign relations.

The Supreme Court generally endorsed this proposition when it was challenged. The key case dated to 1936, when the Court declared that the president had inherent, plenary power to conduct foreign policy in *U.S. v. Curtiss-Wright Export Corporation.* The government regularly relied on this case when people challenged presidential foreign-policy decisions affecting them. In the years preceding World War II, President Roosevelt entered into agreements that in effect allied the United States with the British against Germany even though Congress had not declared war. By executive agreement, without the Senate confirmation required of treaties, Roosevelt supplied the British with armaments and undertook to defend shipping on the American side of the Atlantic against German interdiction. Roosevelt was able to cite many previous executive agreements and the *Curtiss-Wright* case to support his argument that presidents possessed the inherent power to make such arrangements. Despite criticism that some of these agreements amount to treaties that require Senate ratification, succeeding presidents have continued to enter into them.

Presidents began to declare that they could enact domestic policies without congressional approval when necessary for national security. Truman claimed such power in 1952 during the Korean War. Knowing that the government could not permit a strike to interrupt steel production during the war, the steel companies had taken a hard line in negotiations over wages and working conditions with the steel unions. In case of a strike, steel company executives expected the president to intervene under the terms of the Taft-Hartley law, which authorized the president to order strikers back to work in cases threatening the national welfare. Unwilling to serve as a strikebreaker on behalf of the steel industry and allied politically with organized labor, Truman instead seized control of the industry entirely. When the steel executives went to court, Truman justified his action by citing his inherent power to protect national security.

In *Youngstown Sheet and Tube Co. v. Sawyer* (1952), a closely divided Supreme Court denied that a president could take such a step without the sanction of a congressional law, especially since Congress had refused to incorporate such a provision into the Taft-Hartley Act. While four justices argued that the Korean War emergency justified such extreme measures, the majority held that Truman had gone too far. The Constitution placed the lawmaking power in Congress; only the direst emergency, if any, could justify such an exercise of presidential power.

The Steel Seizure Case not only indicated the limits of presidential power; it also demonstrated that the Court would intervene in a highly politicized case involving a coordinate branch of government. This determination was perhaps more important than the actual decision. If the Court had avoided a decision, the issue of presidential power would have been left to the political process alone. The only effective restraints on presidential claims of authority would have been the power of the people to defeat a president's bid for reelection or the power of Congress to affect presidential actions by withholding money to pay for them or by instituting impeachment proceedings.

The "Imperial Presidency" and the Watergate Scandal

Although support of a strong presidency had been a characteristic of liberal constitutionalism since the New Deal, that tenet eroded quickly during the Vietnam War. At first that conflict resembled small-scale military interventions in Latin America and the Caribbean that presidents had undertaken without declarations of war. But as the situation deteriorated, President Lyndon B. Johnson escalated American involvement. Rather than secure a declaration of war, he seized upon an attack upon U.S. naval forces off the coast of North Vietnam to secure a congressional resolution authorizing him "to take all necessary measures to repel any armed attack against the forces of the United States." Armed with the Tonkin Gulf Resolution Johnson sent hundreds of thousands of American soldiers into combat.

Opponents of the war challenged its legality, insisting that military action of this magnitude required a congressional declaration of war. They charged that Johnson had manufactured the attack. Nothing, critics said, better showed the detrimental effect of Congress's reliance on the executive branch for information. But the Tonkin Gulf Resolution proved to be a turning point in American constitutional history. No president has since asked Congress for a formal declaration of war, and every president has claimed the right to send troops into combat without one.

The antiwar movement grew as the Vietnam war wore on with ever-greater American casualties and no sign of victory. Employing the tactics of the Civil Rights Movement, antiwar activists organized marches, demonstrations, and civil disobedience. The Democratic party divided sharply over the issue, and Johnson was forced to give up his hopes for reelection. In 1968, the Republican Richard M. Nixon narrowly won the presidency.

Despite his disdain for liberal leaders, Nixon recognized the power of the liberal consensus on many national issues, and in many areas he worked within its framework. Assailing vulnerable aspects of liberalism rhetorically, he moved the administrative state in a more conservative direction, but he did not really challenge its fundamental commitments. Nonetheless, liberals saw him as a conservative intent on dismantling the achievements of the 1960s, a perception he encouraged with rhetorical attacks on what he and Vice President Spiro Agnew identified as an elitist, liberal establishment.

Nixon's claims for executive power confirmed liberals' fears that he presented a threat to constitutional liberty. Although expanded executive power had been identified with the liberal presidents Roosevelt, Truman, Kennedy, and Johnson, Nixon willingly utilized it to pursue his more conservative goals. Claims of inherent presidential power reached their highest point during his presidency. Faced with a generally liberal and Democratic Congress that opposed many of his foreign and domestic policies, Nixon was convinced that he nonetheless represented the views of the majority of Americans. He considered Congress obstructionist and beholden to special interests.

Nixon not only continued the war in Vietnam, but he claimed sole responsibility for prosecuting it. Without informing Congress, he authorized the mining of North Vietnam's chief harbor, the bombing of neighboring Cambodia, and finally an invasion of Cambodia as well. He also instructed the Central Intelligence Agency (CIA) to undertake secret operations without informing the congressional committees responsible for overseeing it.

When Congress sought information about American activities in Southeast Asia and elsewhere, Nixon ordered his subordinates to lie, claiming that as president he was authorized to mislead Congress when necessary to protect national security. He also ordered subordinates to refuse to testify before Congress or to provide documents to it, saying that withholding information about discussions in the executive branch was an "executive privilege" inherent in the separation of powers ordained by the Constitution. Not only was it essential that his aides remain confident that their advice was confidential, Congress had no right to demand testimony from the officials of a coordinate branch of government. As the president's subordinates, they were bound to obey when he instructed them not to speak.

President Nixon also claimed that he could ignore rules governing criminal investigations in the interests of national security. He ordered government agencies to infiltrate and disrupt groups that opposed the Vietnam War and ordered surveillance of many Americans without securing the warrants required by law. Civil libertarians went to court to stop this practice, and in 1972 the Supreme Court held that the president could not ignore the law in this way. Nixon responded by creating a special, secret investigating group, responsible only to him and his closest aides.

Nixon argued that the government had the power to prevent the publication of information that would compromise national security. When newsmen secured secret documents—soon called "the Pentagon Papers"—demonstrating that government officials had misled the public and Congress while expanding the war in Vietnam, Nixon asked for a court order forbidding their publication. This effort violated the rule dating back to seventeenth-century England that the government could not impose "prior restraint" on publication, even if the publication were illegal. Illegal publication could be punished; but it could not be stopped ahead of time. This rule had long been considered the essence of freedom of the press. Publishing the Pentagon Papers violated no law, and Nixon argued that the government did not even have to prove that the material would damage national security. The courts had to accept the president's opinion without question, he insisted, because he had the chief responsibility for protecting the nation.

The Supreme Court disagreed. In the Pentagon Papers Case, *New York Times Co. v. U.S.* (1971), the Court held that the government had to demonstrate to a judge that there was actual danger to national security. Angered by this and other court decisions limiting his legal power to suppress damaging information, Nixon authorized his subordinates to do whatever necessary to stop newsmen from getting it. His aides called these lower-level operatives "plumbers," because they were supposed to stop information from leaking. The "plumbers" assumed that the president could authorize them to break the law.

As the presidents claimed broader powers over national defense and foreign relations, they also claimed ever more power to carry out domestic programs without congressional authorization. For example, in 1948 President Truman, without securing Congress's approval, issued an executive order ending racial discrimination in federal government employment. In 1949 he ordered an end to segregation in the armed forces, claiming authority to do so as commander-in-chief. Presidents also claimed the power to declare "national emergencies" when they thought events threatened national security. To meet these emergencies, they argued, they could issue orders and rules without waiting for congressional action. When he became president, Roosevelt had declared such an emergency to combat the Great Depression. Truman had declared one when he sent troops to Korea. Numerous statutes also authorized presidents to take action only after declaring an emergency. Nixon relied on one of them when he imposed wage and price controls to combat inflation in 1972.

Congress had cooperated in this expansion of presidential power by continuing to give government agencies wide discretionary power to carry out general policies. Since presidents appointed the leaders of these agencies, they could influence how forcefully policies were carried out. Unable to secure a conservative, Republican majority in Congress, from 1969 to 1974 President Nixon used these powers to obstruct the execution of liberal programs, claiming an inherent "executive power" to control spending and administration of the laws. He ordered the Justice Department to oppose lawsuits seeking further desegregation in the South. He ordered the Department of Health, Education, and Welfare to soften the rules barring federal support for discriminatory institutions and businesses.

When federal judges ordered the reinstatement of the old rules, Nixon ordered his subordinates to ignore them. He instructed the director of the Office of Economic Opportunity, responsible for the War on Poverty, to dismantle the agency he was appointed to administer. The administration refused to enforce a variety of environmental, occupational safety, and education laws. Nixon politicized the Office of Management and Budget (OMB), which previously had coordinated agency requests for funding in light of available resources. Now he used it to control expenditures. Pointing to earlier precedents, Nixon used the OMB to "impound" money Congress appropriated for programs that he opposed. But whereas his predecessors had sought congressional approval after impounding expenditures because of changed circumstances, Nixon claimed an inherent presidential authority to cut funds.

Finally, Nixon used his power over the executive branch to intimidate his enemies. Even before Franklin Roosevelt's administration, presidents had discreetly used their influence to weaken their opponents. On one memorable occasion, President John F. Kennedy had "jawboned" the steel industry into rolling back a price increase, by threatening it with special tax audits and strict enforcement of potentially hamstringing regulations. Lyndon Johnson encouraged the director of the Federal Bureau of Investigation to keep him informed of the indiscretions of powerful economic and political leaders in order to help give him some leverage over them. But Nixon went further. Convinced that politics was a kind of warfare, certain that his opponents were as ruthless as he was (and in some cases they were), he created an "enemies list" and ordered federal agencies to investigate the people and institutions on it. He ordered the Internal Revenue Service to audit the income taxes of opponents and to review the tax-exempt status of nonprofit institutions that opposed his policies. He authorized "dirty tricks" to disrupt the activities of his opponents and of the Democratic party itself. His subordinates used their political positions to pressure businesses for political contributions to Nixon's reelection campaign in 1972.

Many observers began to worry that the growth of an "imperial presidency" was challenging constitutional government itself. When American voters reelected Nixon overwhelmingly in 1972, it seemed it would be impossible to control him. However, in 1973 the illegal activities of Nixon's agents became public as a result of their unsuccessful attempt to burglarize the headquarters of the Democratic party in the Watergate apartment complex. As Congress and law-enforcement officials investigated the "Watergate Scandal," Nixon and his aides tried to cover up their involvement by lying, refusing to testify, and withholding incriminating documents and tape recordings. When Congress learned that Nixon had taped conversations in his office, he argued that it was his "executive privilege" to withhold such evidence, both from Congress and from the special prosecutor that his attorney general named to investigate the burglary. When the special prosecutor insisted on securing the tape and other information, Nixon ordered the attorney general to fire him. Both he and his deputy resigned rather than do it. Nixon finally got Solicitor General Robert Bork to carry out his order. Shocked observers thought that the future of constitutional government hung in the balance. The furious public reaction to the "Saturday Night Massacre" forced Nixon to name a completely independent special prosecutor, who continued to argue in court that the president must turn over the tapes. When lower courts agreed, Nixon's lawyers appealed to the Supreme Court. Many worried that if even a few of the justices sustained his position, Nixon would claim an inherent right to refuse to obey a Supreme Court decision diminishing the presidency.

Like the special prosecutor, Congress rejected Nixon's claim to executive privilege. The House of Representatives prepared to impeach him both for the crime of obstructing justice and for withholding the documents and tapes. At the same time, the Supreme Court rejected Nixon's argument and ordered him to make all materials available to law-enforcement officials, in *U.S. v. Nixon* (1974). Recognizing that the president might defy a divided Court, the justices overcame differences and delivered a unanimous decision. The executive privilege did not extend to refusing materials needed in a criminal investigation, the Court ruled. It was up to the courts to look at the material and decide whether its relevance to a criminal investigation outweighed the president's executive privilege. Recognizing that a refusal to obey would lead to another article of impeachment, Nixon acquiesced.

As the House of Representatives considered impeachment, President Nixon's lawyers insisted that he could be impeached only for an actual crime, echoing the position President Andrew Johnson's defenders had taken a century earlier. But most scholars and lawyers concluded that impeachment could be used to remedy abuses of power, even if no laws were violated. The issue was never decided, however, because it became clear that Nixon had in fact broken the law. The tapes showed plainly that he had conspired with his aides to cover up their connection to the Watergate burglars. The discovery forced him to resign before the House of Representatives could vote to impeach him.

Restraining Presidential Power

Both Presidents Gerald Ford (1974–1977) and Jimmy Carter (1977–1981) reduced the imperial trappings of the presidency, eschewing the pomp and ostentation associated with President Nixon. Carter walked part of his inauguration parade route, waving to spectators along the street. He made one famous televised address to the nation in a sweater. Both Ford and Carter avoided relying on executive privilege to withhold information from Congress, aiming for more transparency and using other justifications when they believed secrecy essential.

Congress was able to regain some of the power that it had lost in previous decades. In a major reorganization, Congress added greatly to its staff and its ability to collect information, so that it no longer had to rely on the executive branch. It passed legislation regulating the way in which presidents could impound funds, and in 1975 the Supreme Court ruled that presidents had to acquiesce. There was no "inherent" presidential "impoundment power." In 1976 Congress passed the National Emergencies Act, setting up procedures that the president had to follow to declare national emergencies and giving Congress clear power to terminate them.

To limit presidents' power to go to war without congressional approval, Congress passed the War Powers Act in 1973. It required the president to notify Congress when committing troops to possible combat. It limited to sixty days the time he could do so without securing specific congressional approval. And even within the sixty days, the law provided that Congress could rescind his action by a majority vote of both houses. Nixon denied the constitutionality of this limit on executive power, as has every president since, but Congress passed it over his veto.

Congress also began to exercise greater power over the administrative state. Before 1974 Congress had occasionally required agencies to secure approval for specific actions from congressional committees or their senior members. But after 1974 it became much more common for Congress to impose such requirements, or to require agencies to get approval from Congress as a whole. Most controversial were laws authorizing congressional vetoes of executive actions. These laws authorized the president or administrative agencies to take actions subject to being rescinded by a vote of Congress, or either house of Congress, or even congressional committees. Presidents had objected to such provisions from the time

Congress first invented them in the 1930s, explicitly pronouncing them void even as they signed the laws in which they were embedded. But Congress had rarely passed such laws. Now, in response to Nixon's grandiose claims of presidential power, they proliferated. By 1976 Congress was considering a bill that would have authorized either chamber to veto any bureaucratic regulation, a revolutionary aggrandizement of congressional power over the administrative state.

Presidents Ford and Carter encountered great difficulty in securing passage of their legislative programs, and for the first time in many years Congress began to initiate and pass some programs of its own. In 1978, with the support of President Carter, Congress passed the Ethics in Government Act. One of the act's provisions created a system for appointing independent counsels, who would be independent of the president, to investigate charges of wrongdoing in the Executive Department. In the following decades numerous independent counsels aggressively investigated the activities of executive officers. Critics charged that their tactics exceeded propriety, took on a partisan cast, and seriously embarrassed the operations of government—a charge that would reach a crescendo when Independent Counsel Kenneth J. Starr's investigations led to the impeachment of President William J. Clinton.

As a consequence of the Watergate Scandal, the activities of independent counsels, and the limitations Congress imposed on executive discretion, the prestige of the presidency declined for a time. That decline became even more precipitous as Ford and Carter proved unable to cope with new economic problems or crises in foreign relations. Yet the reputation of Congress, after initial improvement during the Watergate Crisis, did not increase. By the late 1970s, it seemed that many Americans were losing confidence in their government.

TIMELINE

1933–1945   The New Deal and World War II increase the power of the presidency and the executive branch.

1936   The Supreme Court recognizes inherent, plenary presidential power to carry out foreign policy in *U.S. v. Curtiss-Wright Export Corp.*

1950   Without securing formal congressional approval, President Truman sends U.S. troops to Korea as part of United Nations "police action."

1951   The states ratify the Twenty-Second Amendment, which limits presidents to two terms.

1952   President Truman seizes control of the steel industry to avert a strike during the Korean War; in *Youngstown Sheet and Tube Co. v. Sawyer,* the Supreme Court rules Truman's action unconstitutional.

1964	Congress passes the Gulf of Tonkin Resolution authorizing President Johnson to take whatever actions necessary to protect U.S. forces in Southeast Asia.
1969–1970	President Nixon wages a "secret war" in Cambodia.
1971	President Nixon attempts to prevent publication of the secret Pentagon Papers; in the Pentagon Papers Case (*N.Y. Times v. U.S.*), the Supreme Court rules that the First Amendment forbids prior restraint on publication except in extraordinary circumstances.
1972	Nixon authorizes formation of a secret surveillance group nicknamed the "plumbers."
	Employees of the Committee to Re-Elect the President arrested while breaking into offices of the Democratic Party at the Watergate housing complex.
	Nixon reelected.
1973	The Nixon administration impounds funds for various programs mandated by Congress.
	President Nixon and aides obstruct the investigation of the Watergate break-in.
	The War Powers Act, passed over Nixon's veto, limits the power of the president to commit U.S. troops abroad.
1974	The Supreme Court orders Nixon to turn tape recordings over to the special Watergate prosecutor, ruling in *U.S. v. Nixon* that executive privilege is superseded by duty to make evidence available in a criminal investigation.
	Nixon resigns after the Judiciary Committee of the House of Representatives votes to impeach him.
1976	The National Emergencies Act regularizes the declaration of national emergencies by the president and subjects them to congressional termination.
1978	The Ethics in Government Act establishes procedures for appointing independent counsels to investigate alleged wrongdoing in the executive branch.

FURTHER READING

The standard study of the growth of presidential power in the twentieth century is Arthur M. Schlesinger Jr.'s *The Imperial Presidency* (1973), which, however, reflects the anti-executive sentiments of the Vietnam War–Watergate era. Barton J. Bernstein takes a similar point of view in "The Road to Watergate and Beyond: The Growth and Abuse of Executive Power Since 1940," *Law and Contemporary Problems* 40 (Spring 1976): 58–86. For a historical assessment of presidential power that is more sympathetic to executive claims, see Forrest McDonald, *The American Presidency* (1994).

Clinton Rossiter surveys the Supreme Court's views of presidents' national-defense responsibilities in *The Supreme Court and the Commander-in-Chief* (expanded ed., 1976). Maeva Marcus's *Truman and the Steel Seizure Case: The Limits of Presidential Power* (1977) is a full and insightful discussion of the classic controversy over presidential war powers.

Michael A. Genovese, *The Nixon Presidency* (1990), is a judicious, balanced description of a controversial presidency. Joan Hoff's *Nixon Reconsidered* (1994) is a bit more sympathetic to the president. Richard P. Nathan describes Nixon's efforts to gain control over the bureaucratic state in *The Plot that Failed: Nixon and the Administrative Presidency* (1975).

Louis Fisher discusses Nixon's unprecedented use of impoundment in his study of *Presidential Spending Power* (1975). Mark J. Rozell discusses how President Nixon abused *Executive Privilege* (2002) in his history of the doctrine. Raoul Berger discusses—and rejects—President Nixon's broad claims of inherent presidential power in *Executive Privilege: A Constitutional Myth* (1974). The best account of the Watergate Scandal and Nixon's forced resignation is Stanley I. Kutler, *The Wars of Watergate* (1990). Fred Emery's *Watergate* (1994) is also excellent and more journalistic in approach. Read it instead of Kutler's book if you hate footnotes. Keith W. Olson's *Watergate* (2003) is a briefer, straightforward chronicle. Michael A. Genovese, *The Watergate Crisis* (1996) is an excellent short account intended for classroom use. The Watergate scandal has been the subject of a number of conspiracy theories. You can read about them and how President Nixon's reputation has fared in David Greenberg, *Nixon's Shadow: The History of an Image* (2003). In *Shadow: Five Presidents and the Legacy of Watergate* (1999), Bob Woodward, who along with Carl Bernstein first exposed the scandal, describes the way it affected succeeding presidents.

Thomas E. Cronin discusses how the Watergate Scandal weakened the presidency in *The State of the Presidency* (2d ed., 1980). James L. Sundquist chronicles *The Decline and Resurgence of Congress* in his 1981 study, while Edward B. Firmage recounts Congress's efforts to restrain presidential war-making power in *To Chain the Dogs of War: The War Power of Congress in History and Law* (1989). Barbara Hinkson Craig discusses legislative vetoes of presidential and administrative action in her excellent study of the court case that challenged them, *Chadha* (1988).

18

The Revival of Conservative Constitutionalism

The New Deal coalition of unionized workers, ethnic groups who had been excluded from full citizenship, African Americans, and intellectuals began to fray as early as the 1960s. The strains were made worse by economic stress in the 1970s. By the late 1970s many Americans received conservative ideas with renewed interest. In 1980 they elected conservative Republican Ronald Reagan to the presidency and supported a political program that repudiated many of the liberal policies inaugurated since the 1960s.

The renewed vigor of American conservatism was manifested in a revitalized conservative constitutionalism, which criticized liberalism's stress on individual autonomy and toleration, denounced the Civil Rights Movement's turn towards "affirmative action," attacked judicial activism, promoted a strong presidency, and defended state rights. By the 1990s the conservative movement, reinforced by the growing influence of religious fundamentalism, would dominate politics, while its constitutional ideas were aggressively promoted by government lawyers and legal academics.

Conservatism from the 1960s to the 1990s

Despite the ascendancy of liberalism from the 1930s to the 1970s, many Americans still adhered to older, conservative views about economics, morality, society, and government. In many parts of the country, a large majority felt this way; if final decisions had been left to local and state governments in those regions, many of the changes of the post–New Deal era would not have taken place. In fact, much of the national legislation and many of the court decisions expanding government services, protecting civil liberty, and promoting equality were specifically aimed at changing the customs of these communities.

Most white Southerners strongly resented the court decisions and civil rights legislation enforcing racial equality. By the late 1960s the resentment was spreading beyond the South. In part this hostility was fueled by continuing racism, both North and South. But as the national government demanded that local governments, schools, colleges, and businesses take "affirmative action" to secure more positions for members of minority groups, many Americans began to complain that this policy was itself a form of discrimination. Affirmative action seemed like a revival of quota systems that had limited opportunities for minority groups. Many members of ethnic groups that had been subject to quotas opposed affirmative action bitterly. The situation was exacerbated by the fact that affirmative action was applied especially to education and to blue-collar jobs, where disproportionate numbers of Jewish Americans and Americans of Irish, Italian, and eastern European origins were employed. As conservatives denounced affirmative action, the old alliance among African Americans, unionized blue-collar workers, and white minority groups began to crumble.

Even more people were angered when courts ruled that children must be transported to schools outside their neighborhoods in order to secure racial balance. In a crucial decision, the Supreme Court ruled that suburbs with no history of legally encouraged segregation were not subject to integration orders, even though many of their white residents had moved to them to escape school integration. This meant that among whites, "forced busing," like affirmative action, disproportionately affected urban, working-class, ethnic communities. In many cities, even bastions of liberalism like Boston, Massachusetts, the school busing orders precipitated boycotts and violence. Again, conservatives outspokenly denounced the remedy. Busing and other court-mandated desegregation orders fueled a flight of white people to the suburbs, leaving African Americans once more isolated in inferior educational environments, sustained by shrinking tax bases.

In many parts of the country, people reacted angrily to court rulings barring religious observances from the public schools. Some districts ignored them, forcing those who did not share the majority's beliefs to suffer in silence or to turn for a remedy to the federal courts, which often came to be seen as the agent of an alien power. Many people were appalled at the *Roe v. Wade* decision overturning state laws against abortion. In the view of some, premarital pregnancy was the natural consequence of reckless sexual behavior. Abortion freed young women from taking personal responsibility for their actions. Worse, it did so through taking a life, which of course was no more justified in the case of married women's pregnancies. Fundamentalist Protestants, traditionalist Catholics, and Orthodox Jews were especially adamant. Believing an unborn fetus to be a human being, in their view *Roe v. Wade* condoned murder on a massive scale. Nothing more strongly symbolized the way that liberalism privileged individual autonomy over community well-being, selfishness over sacrifice. This perception in turn related directly to older notions of gender, which deemed women to have a special obligation to sacrifice their happiness for others.

Critics believed Supreme Court decisions expanding the rights of criminal defendants were destroying the government's ability to protect citizens from crime. Many people disagreed with the limits that the Supreme Court put on local government's power to censor pornography. They were repelled by proposals to extend the provisions of the Civil Rights Act to homosexuals. Altogether, it seemed to many that the liberal legislation and court decisions of the 1960s and 1970s had undermined the moral standards of the nation. As crime and social unrest increased, conservatives blamed liberals for destroying the basic harmony of society by concentrating too much on the rights of individuals and minority groups and too little on the needs of the community.

The very idea of shared national standards and ideals seemed to be eroding. Conservative voices demanded an end to teaching school subjects in the languages of immigrant children; they proposed making English the official language of the United States. They blasted schoolbooks for covering the histories of minority groups and women at the expense of more traditional approaches. Those who defended multiculturalism interpreted such concerns as an effort to define American citizenship in terms of white European origins and culture.

Local interests also opposed the federal government's efforts to protect the environment. Environmental restrictions increasingly limited how people could develop their own property, sometimes reducing its value and disrupting business and family plans. Antipollution rules made high-sulfur coal mined in Ohio, Pennsylvania, West Virginia, and Kentucky uneconomical, virtually destroying the mining industry there. Laws protecting endangered species of animals and expanding the national park system inhibited the mining, oil, lumber, farming, and ranching industries of the West. Resentment over environmental regulations was exacerbated by Native Americans' success in persuading courts to recognize hunting, fishing, and other economic rights reserved in old treaties. Even more controversial were revived claims to Indian land that had been illicitly distributed to white landowners long ago. A so-called "Sagebrush Rebellion" against federal regulation erupted in the western states, which had once been politically among the most liberal in the nation. Everywhere property owners, large and small, complained that they were being deprived of their rights.

Conservatives increasingly denounced "big government." Local communities should be free to decide questions about morals themselves, they insisted. By the 1970s, conservatives backed constitutional amendments to permit prayer in the schools, to make abortion illegal, and to ban busing to achieve racial balance in the schools.

As early as 1968 conservative politicians, such as President Richard M. Nixon and Alabama governor George C. Wallace, had some success appealing to growing conservatism on social and economic issues. An articulate and combative new group of conservative intellectuals, often called the "New Right," insisted that most Americans embraced conservative values but were overborne by a liberal elite that controlled the nation's intellectual life. They revitalized or remade journals, established university centers, and created conservative think tanks and foundations to counteract liberal ones, putting liberalism clearly on the defensive.

Nonetheless, most Americans still held liberal economic views, approving of government intervention in the economy and redistribution of resources. As long as this support for economic liberalism remained, the traditional Democratic majority of voters persisted despite the strains. But economic problems began to erode this majority. Inflation caused by spending on the Vietnam War, the dramatic increase in the price of energy in the mid-1970s, and new trade competition from Japan and other nations led to an economic stagnation that lasted into the early 1980s. American living standards began to decline for the first time since the end of the Depression.

Popular support for liberal programs that redistributed wealth had peaked during the 1960s, when the economy was growing, everyone's living standards were improving, and jobs were plentiful. Improvements for the poor and for minorities came out of the increase in national wealth; no one actually gave up what one already had. Now, in harder times, improvements for the poor had to come from the wealth of the more successful. When a minority candidate received a job because of "affirmative action," it meant that someone else would remain unemployed. With their standard of living declining, Americans grew ever more resentful of the taxes necessary to maintain social programs, some of which seemed to have created a permanent welfare class. More and more Americans concluded that such programs contributed to crime, poverty, and other social problems by undermining personal responsibility. The connection between the general welfare and antipoverty programs had become tenuous. People rarely spoke of the "general-welfare" state; they spoke of the "welfare" state, and to many people "welfare" simply meant payments to the poor, doled out of the taxes paid by everybody else. These criticisms increased as the Democratic party failed to reverse the economic decline or to deal effectively with its consequences. As they continued to work to improve the opportunities available to minority groups and women, the Democrats seemed to do little for the working people who had made up an essential part of the New Deal coalition.

In the late 1970s a strong conservative political tide set in. One manifestation was the failure to secure ratification of the Equal Rights Amendment in the time Congress allotted, even after the deadline was extended. An even clearer signal came in 1978, when voters in several states forced severe reductions in taxes, beginning a rebellion against government taxation that became a perennial element of American politics. In 1980 the Republicans nominated a committed conservative, Ronald Reagan, for the presidency. Electing him, Americans put the most conservative president into the White House since Herbert Hoover. Republicans gained control of the United States Senate. Although Democrats would retain control of the House of Representatives until 1994, Reagan's forceful personality, the power of his convictions, and his ability to communicate them enabled him to change the direction of American social and economic policy. The Republican party became more and more ideologically cohesive and confident. This gave conservative Republicans a great advantage over the ideologically fractured and demoralized Democrats, who were inhibited by the conviction that they were running against the conservative tide.

Conservatives cut social programs for the poor, at the same time greatly lowering taxes on those with higher incomes. They severely curtailed government regulation of business and weakened the power of labor unions. The result was a dramatic and permanent loss of income among the poorest fifth of the population and a large increase in the wealth of the richest fifth. Unemployment and homelessness increased significantly.

President Reagan was hostile to efforts to remedy past racial discrimination by giving benefits to other than the immediate victims. Racial discrimination was an offense against the individual person who suffered it, his legal advisors insisted. The remedy should be "victim specific." Insisting that the law should make no racial preferences of any kind, Reagan's Department of Justice tried to persuade the Supreme Court to reverse its position on affirmative action programs and to rule them unconstitutional. It challenged out-of-court settlements and voluntary plans establishing quotas for hiring and promotion. It defended the right of private schools to discriminate. It denounced use of the Voting Rights Act to create election districts with African American or other minority-group majorities. All these remedies increased attention to race rather than diminishing it, conservatives complained. They treated people as members of groups rather than as individuals. Complaining that the courts had "turned our civil rights laws on their heads," Reagan at first opposed renewing the Voting Rights Act of 1965, although he finally relented. Politically, Republicans succeeded in labeling the Democrats as the party of racial and other minorities, and of "special interests" of all sorts.

The American people overwhelmingly reelected President Reagan in 1984. In 1988 they elected Vice President George Herbert Walker Bush to succeed him. In both elections Republicans harshly attacked the liberalism of the Democratic candidates, charging that liberalism meant high taxes, wasteful spending, and government by special interests and minority groups. Even Democrats accepted the Republican victories as mandates in favor of conservatism. They offered few counterproposals and devoted their energy to protecting existing general-welfare programs as well as they could. The result was a significant shift toward conservatism in general and conservative constitutionalism in particular.

Encouraged by their leaders, Americans became more and more strongly opposed to special efforts to help the disadvantaged. Many returned to the conservative view that people lived in poverty because they had not been properly inculcated with the "family values" of religious faith, self-respect, self-discipline, hard work, and sacrifice. From this standpoint, expensive social programs could not cure the problems of poverty; only a return to traditional moral values could do so. Motivated by such beliefs, conservatives tried to reimpose traditional moral standards on the nation. They received strong support in this effort from a powerful political movement among Christian fundamentalists,* who re-emerged in politics in the 1970s and 1980s in response to the secularist threat that liberal control of the media, the courts, and other institutions of government seemed to pose to religious values.

The "Religious Right" called for a renewed commitment to what it called the Judeo-Christian tradition. Strong movements developed to secure government support for private religious and secular schools that stressed old-fashioned values and teaching methods, and to bring religious observances back into the public schools. Claiming to represent "the moral majority," the Religious Right pressed for a constitutional amendment to overturn the decisions of the Warren Court requiring strict separation of church and state, and especially for an amendment to permit prayer in the public schools. Conservatives pressured the national government to withhold financial support from artists whom conservatives found obscene or blasphemous. In response Congress radically cut funding for the National Endowment for the Arts and instructed it to withhold support from artists and exhibits that offended public morality. Republican politicians, seeing a powerful new potential ally, encouraged the movement. President Bush enthused that faith-based organizations provide "a thousand points of light" in the fight against social problems. He issued executive orders instructing federal agencies to change rules that had precluded faith-based programs from applying for federal funds designated to combat social ills.

The "Pro-Life" movement, fighting to reverse the *Roe v. Wade* decision, was especially powerful. Although it failed to push an anti-abortion constitutional amendment through Congress, it won federal policies that made abortions much more difficult to procure. Presidents Reagan and Bush named justices to the Supreme Court who disagreed with *Roe v. Wade,* raising hopes that the decision would be reversed. Many more states passed laws making abortions difficult to procure, hoping that a more conservative Supreme Court would sustain their constitutionality. By the 1990s they had made the procedure virtually unavailable in large areas of the country.

In the 1990s and after, gay Americans' demands for equality, respect, and acceptance created a new flashpoint for religious and social conservatives. Local communities began to bar discrimination against gays in public employment. Local governments, colleges, and private businesses began to accord gay couples (sometimes called "domestic partners") the same employment benefits as married couples. By the turn of the century some state courts and city governments were recognizing the right of gay couples to marry.

Conservatives charged that the institution of the family itself was under siege and fought for legislation and constitutional amendments to stem the tide. They

---

*Christian "fundamentalism" refers to the belief that the Bible is literally true and contains no errors, and to the conviction that one must have a personal experience of Christ's presence—that one must be "born again" in Christ—to achieve salvation.

proposed referenda to prohibit state or local authorities from protecting homosexuals from discrimination. Colorado voters passed a constitutional amendment banning such laws in 1992. Several states limited marriage to heterosexual couples and banned laws that recognized domestic partnerships; again conservatives organized popular referenda on the subject. Conservatives pressed for a constitutional amendment to bar both the states and the federal government from permitting gay marriages or extending to gay couples benefits similar to those extended to married heterosexuals.

Conservatives complained that religious groups were denied the use of government facilities and access to school children for fear of breaching the "wall" between church and state. As they gained political strength, they won the passage of laws requiring schools to provide religious groups the same facilities as nonreligious groups. Several state governments tried to restore religious observances in the public schools; others passed laws giving financial support to private secular and religious schools.

Conservative Constitutionalism in the Reagan Era

As the nation became more conservative, the consensus that had supported liberal interpretations of the Constitution broke down. Many judges and lawyers, encouraged by President Reagan's close adviser and attorney general Edwin Meese, began to complain that liberal judges had imposed their own values on society under the guise of enforcing constitutional requirements. They argued that this practice was inconsistent with democracy, and they called upon judges to exercise "judicial restraint." A revived conservative constitutionalism emerged in law schools and among judges, articulated by legal academics such as Robert Bork, Richard Posner, and Richard Epstein, whom Reagan appointed to federal judgeships. The principle of democracy took precedence over the principle of judicial review, conservatives insisted. Judges should never simply impose their idea of what was right and wrong on the pretense of upholding the Constitution. All decisions should be clearly grounded in specific constitutional language.

Many advocates of conservative constitutionalism argued that judges should apply the specific language of the Constitution according to its "original intent" or "original understanding." By this they meant that judges must apply constitutional provisions as they were understood by the people who framed and ratified the Constitution and the amendments to it, not as they might be understood in more recent times. They attacked the notion of a "living Constitution" articulated by liberals who said that the framers intended the Constitution to be adaptable to changing circumstances. Conservatives complained that the liberal Supreme Court decisions of the 1960s and 1970s were merely the arbitrary imposition of liberal ideas on the nation. Decisions protecting criminal defendants; barring states from censoring offensive literature, art, and movies; and prohibiting prayer in the schools and other forms of government accommodation of religion were egregious instances. They pointed to *Roe v. Wade* as the clearest example of liberal justices abusing the power of judicial review to impose their own ideas of morality. No specific language in the Constitution denied the states the power to make abortions illegal, conservatives insisted. No language specified a general right to privacy. The framers of the Constitution, the Bill of Rights, and the Fourteenth Amendment had not understood them to establish such a right. And they certainly had not intended them to limit the power of the states to make abortions illegal. In these circumstances, judges had to defer to the decisions of state legislatures, which represented the views of the majority.

But despite their commitment to judicial restraint, some conservative jurisprudents urged the courts to take a closer look at laws that shifted wealth from one segment of the community to another. They began to argue that such laws amounted to a taking of property, in violation of the Takings Clause of the Fifth Amendment, which says that no property "shall . . . be taken for public use, without just compensation." Encouraged by such arguments, landlords petitioned courts to declare rent controls unconstitutional for taking their property without just compensation. Landowners claimed that environmental restrictions on their property were unconstitutional "takings" as well. In effect, some conservatives were advocating a return to laissez-faire constitutionalism, basing their views on the Takings Clause of the Fifth Amendment rather than on the Due Process Clause of the Fifth and Fourteenth. Supported by lumber, mining, and real-estate development companies, property owners formed organizations, modeled on civil-liberties groups like the ACLU, to press for the recognition of property rights in the courts.

Although judges held that only a complete deprivation of the use and value of a property required compensation under the Fifth Amendment, in 1988 President Reagan issued an executive order taking a broader view and instructing government agencies to take account of property owners' rights under the Takings Clause when considering regulations. From the 1990s onwards property-rights advocacy groups pushed a wide range of bills to restrict environmental limitations on property development. Conservatives were sustained by a new approach to law that applied the techniques of economic analysis to legal questions. The Law and Economics movement insisted that the purpose of law was to increase the total wealth of society by maximizing individual freedom to choose among economic and other alternatives. Laws governing working conditions, setting rigid quality standards for products, and imposing controls on prices and rents all limited the range of choices and inhibited prosperity. Unlike most legal conservatives, Epstein, Bork, Posner, and other advocates of Law and Economics implicitly encouraged judicial activism in order to impose their vision of freedom and economic efficiency.

Conservative Constitutionalism, the Administrative State, and Federalism

Conservatives criticized regulatory agencies for imposing arbitrary rules that deprived businesses and other institutions of the freedom to respond efficiently to the market. Less economically developed states, especially in the South, lured businesses by promising a friendly regulatory environment, putting pressure on other states to loosen restrictions and thus raising the old problem of "federal effects." But in the antiregulatory environment, representatives of states with stronger regulatory institutions had little chance of persuading the federal government to impose regulations uniformly across the country, as they had in the Progressive and New Deal eras.

Business people complained that relations between themselves and federal administrative agencies were adversarial rather than cooperative. Anecdotes of picayune regulations and punishments proliferated. President Reagan responded with Executive Order 12291, issued within a month of taking office in 1981. It required executive agencies to submit proposed regulations to the OMB, which would okay them only if the benefits outweighed the economic costs.

As early as the 1970s Democratic President Jimmy Carter had begun to dismantle agencies regulating transportation. Reagan continued the pressure. States too began to deregulate transportation and public utilities. The termination of the Interstate Commerce Commission in 1995 symbolized the magnitude of the change, as Congress reduced regulatory oversight of whole industries. While state and federal agencies remained the backbone of American governance, they were consistently underfunded and limited in their ability to regulate effectively. In many areas, such as law and medicine, government relied on business and professional associations to establish and enforce regulatory standards.

To make up for the weak enforcement of existing regulations, consumer and environmental groups increasingly turned to class-action lawsuits. Hoping to affect business and professional behavior, victims sought punitive damages for injuries they might not have suffered had administrative agencies established and enforced protective rules. Such suits enraged doctors, small business people, and even local governments as insurance rates soared and the costs of doing business became less predictable. They responded by demanding "tort reform" to make it harder to bring lawsuits, secure large awards, and impose punitive damages. They wrote provisions into employment and service contracts requiring employees and clients to forego legal remedies if disputes arose, requiring arbitration instead.

Conservatives also demanded a return to what they called the values of federalism. Reviving the idea that the Tenth Amendment limited the way the federal government could use its delegated powers, they complained that the national government was passing laws that invaded the rights of the states. Publishing a tidal wave of articles on "federalism" in the nation's law journals, conservatives succeeded in converting the term to their own use. "Federalism" no longer meant the concept of divided governmental authority; it meant the state-rights understanding of how that authority was divided.

State governors and city mayors echoed the call to reduce federal authority. With taxpayers in revolt, local officials resented expensive new rules the federal government imposed on them. Local officials called such regulations "unfunded mandates" because they imposed duties on the states without providing money to pay for them. For example, federal environmental regulations required costly improvements to local sewage and waste disposal systems; they forced states to undertake expensive new antipollution initiatives. In 1974 Congress extended the Fair Labor Standards Act to cover government employees, subjecting state and local governments to the same minimum-wage and maximum-hour regulations that applied to private employers. Facing a dramatic increase in labor costs, the National League of Cities (NLC) went to court to prevent the enforcement of the law, claiming it violated state rights. The NLC and the Council of State Governments passed resolutions calling on Congress to revitalize the Tenth Amendment and to end the imposition of unfunded mandates.

Conservatives argued that federal judges should respect the right of states to make their own policies unless they clearly violated the Constitution. They especially insisted that the justices should not interpret the Fourteenth Amendment as imposing uniform standards of justice on the states. Many conservatives criticized the view that the Due Process Clause of the Fourteenth Amendment incorporated the provisions of the Bill of Rights. Led by Attorney General Meese and Chief Justice William H. Rehnquist, they said that only the clearest violations of human rights—laws or practices that violated fundamental American concepts of justice—violated the Due Process Clause.

In general, conservative jurisprudents rejected what they saw as excessive support for individual rights at the expense of the common standards of faith, behavior, and courtesy that they believed necessary to maintain a moral and civilized society. They denied that the First Amendment contemplated a strict separation between church and state. On the contrary, conservatives insisted, government ought to "accommodate" religious beliefs, as long as it did not favor any particular sect nor impinge on anyone's religious freedom. Likewise, government had the right, indeed the obligation, to maintain minimal standards of decency by suppressing pornography. The First Amendment's protection of free speech and press ought not to be construed to protect obscenity.

Similarly, conservatives attacked constitutional doctrines that protected the rights of suspected criminals at the cost of undermining law and order. They especially objected to the Exclusionary Rule, which barred evidence secured by unconstitutional means from being used in trials of suspected criminals. They complained that it allowed criminals to escape conviction on mere technicalities. The Reagan and Bush administrations pressed for comprehensive crime bills that

A conservative political cartoonist praises President Reagan for promoting state rights. Is the Tenth Amendment paraphrased accurately?

would establish sentencing guidelines, impose harsher sentences for drug traffickers, restrict the insanity defense, widen exceptions to the exclusionary rule, increase the number of federal crimes subject to the death penalty, permit preventive detention of accused criminals, and make it more difficult to secure federal writs of *habeas corpus* to contest procedures and convictions in state courts. Although Congress refused to pass the comprehensive bills, it agreed to a number of their provisions individually.

Conservative Constitutionalism and Presidential Power

Impressed by the aggressive conservatism of the Reagan presidency, conservative jurisprudents claimed broad powers for the president and warned against actions and legislation that violated the principle of "separation of powers." They forcefully challenged the constitutionality of the War Powers Resolution. President Reagan paid minimal attention to the War Powers Resolution when sending troops to Lebanon and Grenada in 1982 and 1983 and none at all when he authorized U.S. naval vessels to protect Kuwaiti oil tankers during the war between Iraq and Iran, blasting Iranian oil rigs and destroying half the Iranian navy.

Conservatives denied the constitutionality of the law creating special prosecutors to investigate misconduct in the executive branch, although the Reagan administration did not dare to veto reauthorizations of the law in 1983 and 1987. A year later the Supreme Court upheld the constitutionality of the Independent Counsel Act in *Morrison v. Olson,* but dissenting Justice Antonin Scalia made a powerful argument that the law corroded the political system by giving extraordinary power and discretion to an officer who inevitably would measure success in terms of prosecution rather than exoneration. Armed with so strong an argument from a respected judge, Republicans successfully prevented reauthorization in 1992.

Conservatives attacked congressional efforts to limit the discretion of executive officials and to establish commissions independent of the president. They insisted upon a broad definition of the "executive privilege" to withhold information from Congress, although the Reagan administration avoided confronting Congress over the issue. They urged that presidents be authorized to make "line-item vetoes" of specific parts of legislation so they wouldn't have to accept or reject legislation on an all-or-nothing basis. Just as liberals had championed presidential power in the face of a conservative Congress after the New Deal, conservatives now championed a conservative presidency against an obstructive Congress fighting a rearguard action to save liberal programs.

This contempt of Congress culminated in a scandal reminiscent of Watergate. Committed to ousting a communist-oriented government from Nicaragua, the Reagan administration orchestrated a local anti-communist guerrilla resistance, which took the name *Contra* to signify its opposition to the Nicaraguan authorities. However, Congress prohibited the expenditure of funds to sustain the adventure. Reagan and other members of the administration then raised money from sources outside the government to continue financing the *Contra* guerillas. Some of the money came from Iran in exchange for weapons that the United States supplied in violation of its own embargo on trade with that country. Throughout the episode, the president's subordinates lied to Congress about their activities. When they first became public, Reagan's aides, like Nixon's before them, tried to cover up the politically embarrassing illegalities.

In contrast to the Watergate Scandal, however, Reagan and Vice President Bush successfully obstructed the ensuing criminal investigation, and Congress never even considered impeachment or other steps to check executive abuse. The officer at the center of the operation, Lt. Col. Oliver North, briefly became a popular hero for the sincerity with which he justified lying to Congress. When he became president, Bush pardoned many of those involved, and his administration refused to release documents necessary to prosecute others. The courts overturned the criminal convictions of the key operatives on procedural technicalities. Although some of the participants were forced to resign and the so-called Iran-Contra scandal seriously weakened the Reagan administration, it marked an erosion of both official and popular commitment to the rule of law that would become more pronounced in succeeding decades.

President Bush continued Reagan's battle for expanded presidential power. He created an executive Council on Competitiveness to review all proposed administrative regulations for potentially adverse effects on business. In 1992 he ordered moratoriums on regulations except for those exempted by the Council. He claimed that the Constitution authorized him to "pocket veto" bills whenever Congress adjourned rather than only when a session ended—repudiating the understanding of more than two hundred years. Claiming this absolute veto power as a constitutional right, he denied that Congress had the authority to regulate the subject.

The Bush administration redoubled efforts to secure a line-item veto. Failing in that effort, the president turned to formal statements denying the constitutionality of portions of bills as he signed them. In these "signing statements" and elsewhere Bush claimed extensive presidential power over foreign relations and national defense. In four years, Bush issued 116 such statements. Announcing that he would ignore provisions he objected to, Bush in effect created a line-item veto of measures that he thought trespassed on presidential power.

Bush reiterated his broad interpretation of presidential power over foreign policy and national defense when Iraq invaded and purported to annex Kuwait, an oil-rich American ally, in 1990. Bush moved forcefully and with no formal congressional input. Securing a United Nations resolution authorizing the use of force against the aggressor, Bush, like Truman forty years earlier, claimed inherent authority to act, denying the constitutionality of the War Powers Resolution. Public pressure finally forced the president to request a congressional resolution of support in January 1991, although he insisted that he was not bound to do so; by the time Congress debated the matter he had built up a multinational force including 400,000 American soldiers. Although Congress cited the War Powers Resolution in authorizing the use of the force, advocates of expanded presidential power argued that Bush had in fact ignored it.

Despite the bold commitment to conservative principles that Reagan and Bush brought to the presidency, continued economic pressure on most American families eroded confidence in conservative solutions. Democrats maintained control of Congress, and while they eschewed the liberal label, they defended traditional liberal policies. By the 1990s Americans were complaining of "gridlock" in the government system, which seemed chronically unable to cope with the challenges of the oncoming twenty-first century. Frustrated voters began to demand limits on the number of terms state legislators and congressional representatives could serve. By 1995, twenty-three states would impose such term limits on their representatives. An independent presidential candidate, businessman Ross Perot, blasted both parties in 1992, gaining broad support and ultimately winning nearly 20 percent of the presidential vote.

Disregarding his success in forcing Iraq out of Kuwait, voters blamed Bush for the malaise. Acknowledging the growing dominance of conservative ideas, in 1992 the Democratic party nominated two southerners for president and vice president, both of whom were identified as leaders of the party's moderate-to-conservative wing. Self-consciously distancing himself from traditional liberalism, William J. (Bill) Clinton defeated Bush to become president of the United States

---

TIMELINE

1968   Alabama governor George Wallace gains nearly 15 percent of the popular vote as a conservative, anti–civil rights, independent candidate for president, carrying five Deep South states.

1970s   Opposition to regulations closing public lands to various business activities leads to the "Sagebrush Rebellion" in the western states.

1973   Arab oil boycott and subsequent increases in energy prices begin a long-term decline in the American standard of living.

1974–1975 Violent antibusing protests shake Boston; opposition to "affirmative action" and busing to fully integrate schools grows in the North and South.

1978   The "Taxpayers' Rebellion" forces tax reductions in several states.

1980s   Rise of the Religious Right and the anti-abortion "Pro-Life" movement.

1980   Conservative Republican Ronald Reagan elected president; Republicans win control of the Senate.

1981   Executive Order 12291 requires executive agencies to submit proposed regulations to the Office of Management and Budget for cost-benefit analysis.

1981–1982 Congress cuts taxes and spending on welfare and antipoverty programs.

1982   Attorney General Edwin Meese argues that courts should enforce only the "original intent" of the framers of the Constitution and the Civil War constitutional amendments when protecting rights.

          Democrats regain control of the Senate, beginning a long period of stalemate between liberals and conservatives.

1984   President Reagan overwhelmingly reelected in an apparent victory for conservative political and constitutional philosophy.

1988   President Reagan issues Executive Order 12630 instructing federal agencies to take account of property owners' rights under the Takings Clause when promulgating regulations.

1990–1991 President George H. W. Bush claims inherent authority to carry out a United Nations resolution authorizing force to counteract Iraq's occupation of Kuwait; Congress passes a resolution authorizing the use of troops under the War Powers Resolution.

1995   Termination of the Interstate Commerce Commission signals the trend away from the regulatory state.

FURTHER READING

William C. Berman tells the straightforward story of *America's Right Turn* (1994), while Jonathan M. Schoenwald's *A Time for Choosing* (2001) is a detailed and insightful analysis of how the conservative political movement organized from the ground up to capture control of the Republican party.

For general accounts and assessments of the Reagan presidency and the conservative agenda in the 1980s, see Joseph Hogan (ed.), *The Reagan Years: The Record in Presidential Leadership* (1990) and Dilys M. Hill et al. (eds.), *The Reagan Presidency: An Incomplete Revolution?* (1990)—especially the essays by Hill ("Domestic Policy in an Era of Negative Government") and Louis Fisher ("Reagan's Relations with Congress"). *The Reagan Presidency: Pragmatic Conservatism and Its Legacies* (2003), edited by W. Elliot Brownlee and Hugh Davis Graham, provides recent reflections by historians, political scientists, and economists. William E. Pemberton's *Exit With Honor* (1997) offers a well-balanced assessment of Reagan as president. For Reagan's efforts to influence the federal bureaucracy to carry out policies he was unable to get through Congress, see Richard P. Nathan, *The Administrative Presidency* (1983).

For insight into the philosophy of modern American conservatism, consult Alonzo Hamby, *Liberalism and Its Challengers* (1992); J. David Hoeveler Jr., *Watch on the Right* (1991); Gillian Peele, "The New Right Agenda," in *The Reagan Presidency: Pragmatic Conservatism*; and Nigel Ashford, "The Conservative Agenda and the Reagan Presidency," in *The Reagan Years*. Gareth Davies describes how the income-entitlement programs Democrats fashioned in the 1970s undermined support for liberalism in *From Opportunity to Entitlement* (1996). For a discussion of the property-rights movement and the Sagebrush Rebellion, see R. McGreggor Cawley, *Federal Land, Western Anger* (1993). Nancie G. Marzulla offers a briefer, sympathetic account "The Property Rights Movement: How It Began and Where It Is Headed," in *Land Rights*, ed. Bruce Yandle (1995). Alfred M. Olivetti Jr. and Jeff Worsham's *This Land Is Your Land, This Land Is My Land* (2003), a primer for property-rights advocates, has a good deal of historical information.

James Davison Hunter puts the struggle between conservatism and liberalism in a cultural context in *Culture Wars* (1991). William Martin describes the rise of the religious right in *With God on Our Side* (1996). Michael Lienesch describes the ideas and political impact of Christian fundamentalism in *Redeeming America* (1993). Bruce Nesmith explains its importance to *The New Republican Coalition* (1994). For the controversy over abortion, see Eva R. Rubin, *Abortion Politics and the Courts* (1987).

Terry H. Anderson's *The Pursuit of Fairness* (2004) provides a good description of the backlash against affirmative action. Raymond Wolters, *The Burden of Brown* (1984), pays special attention to the problem of school busing. For the divisive impact of the controversy on two northern cities, see Ronald P. Formisano, *Boston Against Busing* (1991) and Gregory S. Jacobs, *Getting around Brown: Desegregation, Development, and the Columbus Public Schools* (1998). Wolters approvingly describes the Reagan administration's opposition to affirmative action and other race-based government action in *Right Turn* (1996).

For the Reagan administration's efforts to change the direction of the federal courts, see "Reaganizing the Judiciary," chapter 8 of Sheldon Goldman's *Picking Federal Judges* (1997). More trenchant is Tinsley E. Yarbrough, "Reagan and the Courts," in *The Reagan Presidency: An Incomplete Revolution?*, noted above. There are as yet no objective historical descriptions of conservative constitutionalism. Readers must peruse polemics on both sides. Bernard Schwartz offers a critical examination in *The New Right and the Constitution* (1990). Robert Bork's splenetic *The Tempting of America* (1990) and Charles Fried's more measured *Order and Law* (1991) represent conservative constitutional thought.

Gary L. McDowell argues for judicial restraint in *Curbing the Courts* (1988), as does Christopher Wolfe in his less polemical *The Rise of Modern Judicial Review* (1986). Briefer is Nathan Glazer, "Towards an Imperial Judiciary?" *The Public Interest* No. 41 (Fall 1975): 104–123. For an influential argument that courts should be governed by the original understanding of those who framed constitutional provisions, see Raoul Berger, *Government by Judiciary* (1977). Justice Antonin Scalia defends "Originalism: The Lesser Evil," in the *University of Cincinnati Law Review* 57 (1989): 849–865. For originalism's challenge to liberal constitutionalism and its advocates' response, see chapter 5 of Laura Kalman's *The Strange Career of Legal Liberalism* (1996).

See Richard A. Epstein's seminal *Takings* (1985) for the legal argument sustaining the current revival of laissez-faire constitutionalism. Laissez faire is also implicit in the conservative school of "Law and Economics," advocated most influentially by Richard A. Posner in *The Economic Analysis of Law* (6th ed., 2003).

Martha Derthick and Paul J. Quirk describe *The Politics of Deregulation* (1985) from 1975 to the early 1980s. Susan J. Tolchin and Martin Tolchin take a dimmer view in *Dismantling America* (1983). Barry Friedman describes how presidents tried to exercise greater control over administrative agencies in *Regulation in the Reagan-Bush Era* (1995). For the revival of state-rights federalism, see Vincent Ostrum, "The Contemporary Debate over Centralization and Decentralization," *Publius* 6 (Fall 1976): 21–32, and Raoul Berger's argument for a return to dual federalism, *Federalism: The Founders' Design* (1987). Terry Eastland argues for a stronger presidency in *Energy in the Executive* (1992). Charles Tiefer launches a jeremiad against such claims in *The Semi-Sovereign Presidency* (1994). David Locke Hall discusses *The Reagan Wars* (1991) in the framework of controversy over presidential war-making power and the War Powers Resolution. For the Persian Gulf War in a similar framework, see John Lehman's *Making War* (1992).

19

The Supreme Court and Conservative Constitutionalism

The Supreme Court slowly responded to the revival of conservative constitutionalism. There was no immediate constitutional revolution, however. After expanding the Warren Court precedents in its early years, the Burger Court (1969–1986) began to limit their application without overturning them. In some areas, such as the rights of criminal suspects, it quickly proved far more restrictive. But in some others, such as the right of women to reproductive freedom, it went far beyond its predecessor. Most of all, the Burger Court worked on regularizing and establishing rules for applying the precedents established by preceding courts.

The Burger Court was more concerned than the Roosevelt and Warren Courts with maintaining a balance between state and nation. It applied the restrictions that the Bill of Rights imposed on the states more flexibly, and it reduced the ability of federal courts to intervene in state-court proceedings. Having played an important role in the downfall of President Nixon, the Burger Court later showed some interest in maintaining the separation of powers among the various branches of the federal government. But after experimenting with a rigid formula, it settled on a more flexible approach.

The Rehnquist Court (1986–) promised to be far more conservative than its predecessor and appeared poised to reinterpret the fundamental law in accordance with conservative constitutional doctrines.

The Burger Court, Civil Rights, and Liberties

Most of the justices appointed during the era of liberal consensus retired by 1975. Republican presidents named replacements, and the Supreme Court slowly responded to the changed intellectual and political climate. President Nixon named Warren E. Burger chief justice in 1969. President Reagan named William H. Rehnquist, for many years the most conservative justice on the Court, to replace Burger in 1986. Despite Nixon's and Reagan's efforts, however, there was no quick, wholesale reversal of the liberal constitutionalism of previous decades.

There were several reasons for the slow progress of conservative constitutionalism. A few liberal justices, such as Thurgood Marshall and William J. Brennan Jr., remained on the Court through the 1980s. Not all of the replacements took consistently conservative positions. Justice Harry Blackmun, a Nixon appointee, slowly shifted from moderate conservatism to moderate liberalism on most questions. Sandra Day O'Connor, the first woman justice, chosen by President Reagan for her hard-line stand against expanding the rights of criminal defendants, turned out to be a firm advocate of state-rights-oriented federalism as well. But she tried to strike a balance on many other issues. Brennan, whose contribution to the Warren Court had been underappreciated, proved surprisingly adept at cobbling together opinions that led some of the more conservative justices to join him in sustaining and even expanding the application of liberal precedents. Most important, the principle of *stare decisis*—the obligation to apply the law established in prior cases—carries great weight with judges. Although some of the conservative justices argued that the principle was less relevant in constitutional cases, most justices' commitment to it limited their freedom to disregard precedents that had been followed for decades.

Thus, the change from liberal to conservative court decisions took place very slowly. The first years of Chief Justice Burger's tenure were an extension of the liberal Warren Court, with Burger and his fellow Minnesotan Blackmun often dissenting. However, by the mid-1970s the Court generally stopped expanding the liberties of Americans into new areas. Instead, the justices focused on organizing and explaining legal principles underlying the decisions of the previous decades.

The Bill of Rights and the Due Process Clause of the Fourteenth Amendment recognize certain "fundamental liberties," the justices explained. When government laws or actions touched on these basic rights, the Court would scrutinize them closely. Only "compelling government interests" could justify infringements of fundamental liberties, and the laws or actions that met this requirement had to be "narrowly tailored" to serve those interests. Laws affecting other, less basic liberties need only be reasonably designed to serve a legitimate public interest.

The Court used similar language to explain the rules governing application of the Equal Protection Clause of the Fourteenth Amendment. That clause rendered certain kinds of classifications suspect, among them those classifying people according to race, religion, national origin, the legitimacy of their birth, or their status as aliens or citizens. The courts would subject laws or government actions that classified people along such lines to "strict scrutiny." The Court would uphold such classificationss only if they served compelling government interests and were "narrowly tailored" to achieve them. The justices treated gender as a "semi-suspect" classification that could be justified only by an "important" or "substantial" government interest.

The justices also tried to rationalize the application of the First Amendment. Following the precedent established in *United States v. O'Brien* (1968), the Court distinguished between "pure speech" and conduct designed to make a statement, such as burning a draft card or picketing. Government limitations on speech or publication could be justified only by a compelling government interest. However, officials could limit conduct, even where it was designed to make an intellectual statement, whenever the limitation served a legitimate governmental interest. In the *O'Brien* case, for example, the Court upheld the conviction of a protester who had burned his draft card; the government's legitimate interest in administering the draft justified its requirement that young men maintain their draft cards.

In cases where plaintiffs complained that the government was supporting religion, the Court applied the test established in *Lemon v. Kurtzman* (1971). A law that appeared to support religion could be sustained only if it had a secular purpose, if its primary effect neither advanced nor inhibited religion, and if it did not involve "excessive entanglement" of government and religion.

Utilizing such terms of analysis, the Burger Court applied the precedents of the liberal Warren Court era in a restrained way that satisfied neither liberals nor conservatives. As the number of conservatives on the Court increased, Justice Rehnquist gained more support for his trenchant criticism of the Warren Court decisions and the Burger Court's rationalization of them. Dissents grew in number and in bitterness, and many important cases were decided by only one vote. In some areas a majority of the justices quickly took conservative positions. But in others a small majority sustained liberal principles. None of the landmark decisions of the Warren Court were overturned. Conservative justices often were able to prevent the application of the principles of those decisions to new situations, but they were unable to muster enough justices to repudiate them.

The turn towards conservatism took place most quickly in cases involving the rights of criminal defendants. As early as the 1970s it was clear that the Burger Court was much less sensitive to the effects of poverty and prejudice on the criminal law system than the Warren Court had been. The justices expanded the discretion permitted to police in stopping and searching suspects and began to limit the application of the Exclusionary Rule. In *U.S. v. Leon* (1984), they ruled that evidence secured in violation of the Fourth Amendment right to be free of unreasonable searches could still be used in trials if the police had acted in "good faith" and inadvertently made a "reasonable mistake" while executing a warrant. The new rule indicated the justices' impatience with technicalities that freed suspects. The Exclusionary Rule was designed to deter wrongdoing by law enforcement agents; it was not itself a constitutional right, the Court held. It need not be imposed in case of good-faith mistakes. Several of the justices began measuring the benefit of excluding evidence in particular situations compared to the cost of releasing suspects. The result was to undermine the Exclusionary Rule without overturning it, while Rehnquist boldly urged abolishing the rule altogether.

In a series of cases, the Burger Court carefully delimited the situations in which suspects had a right to legal counsel. The Court also limited the circumstances in which it applied the Miranda Rule excluding improperly secured confessions. According to a new "harmless error" doctrine, the courts would not reverse convictions of defendants in cases where tainted confessions were admitted into evidence if it was clear that the defendants would have been convicted anyway. The conservative majority dismissed the objection that this approach allowed the justices rather than the jury to decide what evidence was important. Other exceptions undermined the rules guarding against coerced or fraudulently secured confessions. The rules were not violated when a suspect admitted her guilt to a fellow prisoner, for example, or before the investigation focused on her, or when the public safety required quick apprehension and questioning. In *Oregon v. Elstad* (1985), the Court held that a confession secured in violation of the Miranda Rule could be made valid simply by informing the suspect of his rights and having him repeat the same confession.

To enable law enforcement agencies to run "sting" operations, the justices relaxed rules against entrapment (encouraging people to commit crimes); defendants could be convicted based on such operations if the evidence showed that they were "predisposed" to the crime. The Burger Court was much more likely than the Warren Court to dismiss constitutional violations as "harmless errors" that did not justify reversal of convictions. Sympathetic to prosecutors and plea-bargaining to avoid trial, the justices saw no constitutional problem with allowing them to coerce confessions by threatening to seek longer sentences if a defendant refused to cooperate. In *Gregg v. Georgia* (1976) the Supreme Court sustained the constitutionality of the death penalty. Only Brennan and Marshall held out for the proposition that execution was a "cruel and unusual punishment" forbidden by the Eighth Amendment. In the opinion of the majority, death-penalty statutes that set clear standards to guide judges and juries obviated the discrimination and arbitrariness that had led the Court to rule them unconstitutional in *Furman v. Georgia*. Nor did the other justices share Brennan and Marshall's concern that the death penalty fell disproportionately on the poor and members of minority groups.

Many cases reflected conservatives' rejection of the view that poverty led to unjust discrimination in the United States. In the key case of *San Antonio School District v. Rodriguez* (1973), the Supreme Court sustained state laws that distributed tax money in such a way that wealthier communities received more than poor ones. When Congress banned the federal government from paying the expenses of abortions for poor women, the Court rejected the argument that the ban discriminated against the poor by effectively denying them a right that wealthier people could enjoy.

The Burger Court proved somewhat less sensitive than the Warren Court to the effects of discrimination in American life. In *Washington v. Davis* (1976) it ruled that the Fourteenth Amendment did not itself forbid government agencies from using job tests that led to the rejection of applicants from minority groups at a higher rate than whites. Such tests were permissible unless there was an intention to discriminate. On the other hand, the Court conceded that civil-rights laws might set more stringent standards.

The Court divided badly over affirmative action. It held race-conscious remedies appropriate where an intention to discriminate had been proven. But many laws and administrative guidelines sought to overcome "institutional racism" as well. Government agencies conditioned federal contracts and financial support for schools on the establishment of affirmative-action programs. Universities, law schools, and medical schools voluntarily took affirmative action to increase the diversity of their faculties and student bodies. Businesses and unions, threatened with lawsuits charging intentional discrimination, often did the same, sometimes as part of out-of-court settlements.

Arguing that the Fourteenth Amendment precluded any racial discrimination whatsoever, critics attacked the constitutionality of such programs. In the landmark case of *Regents of the University of California v. Bakke* (1978), a sharply divided Court upheld affirmative action in higher education. The concurring opinion of the crucial fifth justice, Lewis Powell, held that although quotas were forbidden, promoting diversity in the student body was a compelling justification for taking applicants' race into account. Across the country schools adopted Powell's reasoning and fashioned programs to take affirmative action without quotas.

In areas outside of education, however, the justices ruled that only past discrimination justified racial preferences. Still, narrow majorities affirmed voluntary efforts to eliminate racial imbalances in areas where discrimination had been customary or where gross imbalances in the distribution of benefits raised a presumption of intentional discrimination.

The Court decided not to apply the same approach to voting. Although they made up 35 percent of the local population, no African American had ever served on the city commission of Mobile, Alabama, which was elected at large rather than from districts. That disparity did not prove a discriminatory intent, the justices held in 1980. Congress quickly moved to amend the Voting Rights Act to make the disparate impact of election districts evidence of discriminatory intent. To the dismay of the Reagan administration, in *Thornburg v. Gingles* (1986), the Court interpreted the law to require that election districts be drawn so as to assure the election of minority candidates in numbers reflecting the minority proportion of the general population. All over the South civil-rights lawyers brought cases challenging election districts for school boards, city councils, county commissions, state legislatures, and congressional representatives that did not meet the new standard.

The Burger Court scrutinized laws that discriminated by sex less strictly than it did those that discriminated by race. Some conservatives argued that sexual classification should be permitted wherever the government showed a rational basis for it, but the majority held that it was constitutional only if it served important government objectives. This ruling did not subject such classifications to the same "strict scrutiny" as racial classifications, as liberals wanted; instead it permitted the Court to sustain a number of laws that discriminated *in favor* of women while reserving the power to overturn those that discriminated against them. The Court sustained provisions of the Social Security Act that gave higher old-age benefits to women than men, for example, because the provisions served the important purpose of remedying past economic discrimination.

While the Court was willing to give women some protection against discrimination, it refused to provide similar protection to homosexuals. The Court's birth-control and abortion decisions clearly suggested that government officials were precluded from scrutinizing the private sexual behavior of consenting adults. As traditionalists and liberals fought over extending civil rights protection to homosexuals, gay activists sought to have the courts rule that laws punishing "sodomy," or gay sex, were unconstitutional. But in *Bowers v. Hardwick* (1986), a sharply divided Court rejected their claim to privacy. Given the long history of sodomy laws in the United States, it was preposterous to say that they violated the fundamental principles of American liberty, the conservative justices insisted. The issue was not about sodomy laws, the liberal minority responded acidly. It was about "the most comprehensive of rights and the right most valued by civilized men, . . . the right to be let alone."

Conservatives attacked the Supreme Court decisions that mandated strict separation between the government and religion. Liberal justices urged strict judicial scrutiny of any government activity that suggested that the government endorsed religion; the government had to remain neutral not only among different religions but between religion and irreligion. A growing number of justices rejected this position, arguing that the government should be permitted to accommodate and even encourage religious belief, as long as it did not discriminate among religions.

As in other areas of constitutional law, conservative justices were not able to overturn the rules established in *Lemon v. Kurtzman*. The Burger Court continued to look askance at indirect government support for religious education, because of the entanglement between government and religion that such programs inevitably involved. Nor could governments get around the problem by reimbursing parents for the costs of sending children to faith-based schools. But conservative justices were able to establish exceptions to the generally adverse results of applying the *Lemon* test. In a harbinger of the future, the Court ruled that the Establishment Clause did not obligate universities and colleges to deny religion-based student groups access to university facilities. More than that, failing to provide faith-based groups with the same access to facilities given to nonreligious groups violated their right to freedom of speech. And while it might be unconstitutional to reimburse parents for the children's religious education, giving them tax deductions was not.

In *Lynch v. Donnelly* (1984), a majority of the justices declared that some religious symbols had lost their religious meaning and were now secular, including symbols associated with Christmas and the Jewish wintertime holiday of Hanukkah. Government display of such symbols did not violate the *Lemon* tests. This decision inevitably led to others in which courts tried to distinguish between symbols and rituals that retained religious significance and those that did not. In the end, the rule emerged that the government could endorse the display of religious symbols as long as they shared space with secular symbols and those of other religions. As a practical matter, it became impossible for local governments to resist calls for religious displays made by those trying to promote a return to spiritual values.

With some exceptions, the Burger Court adhered to principles of free speech and freedom of the press established during the Warren years. The justices refused to rule that the First Amendment barred law-enforcement officials from subpoenaing reporters' notes and film for use in criminal cases, and they refused to extend free-speech and free-press principles to student activities in grade and high schools. Over liberal dissents, the justices permitted stringent zoning regulations of bookstores and theaters specializing in erotic books and films. But the Burger Court remained solicitous of free expression. Moderates and liberals joined to rule that the First Amendment precluded firing government employees for their political affiliations, a decision that reversed centuries of political practice. A nearly unanimous Court reversed its tradition of upholding any reasonable regulation of "commercial speech." It overturned laws passed at the behest of professional associations that barred pharmacists, doctors, lawyers, and other professionals from advertising their services and prices, for example. As usual, the Burger Court tried to establish rules: Misleading or deceptive commercial speech was not protected from regulation at all. While "pure" speech could be limited only to serve a "compelling" public interest, "commercial speech" could be regulated when the government's interest was "substantial."

The Burger Court questioned state and federal efforts to limit corporate influence on the political process. Corporations had the same right to participate in that process as individuals, a majority of the justices held. They overturned state restrictions on corporate political activity and in *Buckley v. Valeo* (1976) rejected limits on what corporations and individuals could spend to make their own views known. Spending to promote one's own views was "pure speech" and restrictions had to meet the exacting standards of "strict scrutiny."

While some liberal justices dissented from opinions that protected commercial speech and overturned political spending limits, some of the court's conservatives became trenchant defenders of free speech. As a result commitment to freedom of expression remained strong. In the later 1980s and the 1990s even the conservative Rehnquist Court would overturn laws that made "hate speech" (speech insulting people based on their race, religion, sex, or national origin) illegal, that prohibited criminals from profiting from books about their crimes, and that made it a crime to deface the American flag.

Despite their general commitment to judicial restraint, there were indications that the conservative justices were inclined to protect business and property rights. Relying on the Bill of Rights, the Court made it more difficult for government agents to investigate businesses for wrongdoing or to check upon work conditions. Upholding corporations' right to spend money to affect politics was as much a protection of property rights as freedom of speech. The Court scrutinized government restrictions on the use of property more closely, flirting with the idea that some environmental and other restrictions amounted to "takings," for which owners must be compensated. Landlords and other property owners took heart, bringing numerous suits against zoning and environmental restrictions in the lower courts.

To conservatives, the abortion decision *Roe v. Wade* remained the greatest symbol of the abuses of constitutional liberalism. Throughout the 1970s and 1980s, conservative justices attacked it, but although they were able to restrict its scope somewhat, they could not secure a majority to reverse its principles. No issue was more divisive. Justices Rehnquist and White denounced the decision ever more stridently. Burger switched sides to join them, and the appointment of Justice O'Connor added another dissenter. As state after state passed law after law trying to limit the decision's impact, the remaining justices and pro-choice activists bitterly resisted every regulation touching abortion as a wedge aimed at reversing the decision. By ever-shrinking majorities the remaining justices from the Warren and early Burger Courts fended off the assaults.

The Burger Court, Federalism, Separation of Powers, and the Administrative State

Conservatives had a similarly mixed record in their efforts to reverse the heritage of constitutional nationalism. The principle that the Fourteenth Amendment applied key provisions of the Bill of Rights to the states ("selective incorporation") came under continuous attack. By the 1990s it was unclear whether a majority still adhered to it, but despite the efforts of the Reagan administration and Justice Rehnquist, no decision clearly jettisoned it. However, conservatives did persuade the Court to apply different rules for observing the Bill of Rights in the states than those that applied in federal courts. For example, the Court agreed that juries in state courts need not consist of twelve people and that defendants might be convicted by less than unanimous verdicts.

The Supreme Court also showed its respect for state authority by limiting federal court intervention in state judicial proceedings, reversing the oversight encouraged by the Warren Court. The Court itself refrained from hearing appeals from state court decisions until all state legal remedies were exhausted.

The Court also demonstrated a respect for localism in the area of censoring pornography. As early as 1973, in *Miller v. California,* it rejected the Warren Court requirement that a pornographic work be "utterly without redeeming social value" before it could be censored. Instead, the majority said, pornographic work could be banned if it lacked "serious artistic, political or scientific value" and depicted sexual conduct in a way patently offensive to local community standards. Taking advantage of this interpretation, many communities took action against purveyors of pornographic literature and movies. Over time they succeeded in driving out the most offensive materials. But community standards had clearly changed. Few local juries thought that nudity or explicit sexual references transgressed local standards; federal courts made clear that those that did still could not act against material that had significant social value. Upholders of traditional moral standards continued to complain that federal judges abetted movies and magazines in undermining "family values."

The Court expressed the idea that the federal courts must respect "federalism" most dramatically in the 1976 case of *National League of Cities v. Usery*. This was the case in which city governments challenged Congress's authority to extend the protections of the Fair Labor Standards Act (FLSA) to their employees (see page 352). In a decision that amazed constitutional lawyers, the Court agreed that the extension was unconstitutional, reviving the doctrine of state rights. The Court conceded the national government's authority under the interstate commerce power to apply the FLSA to private businesses. But the act could not be extended to cover state or local government employees, because the unfettered right to manage its own workers was essential to state sovereignty. For the first time since the New Deal, the Court held that the Tenth Amendment and the spirit of federalism limited how Congress could exercise a delegated power.

Conservative lawyers immediately began to argue that many national laws unconstitutionally violated states' sovereignty. They brought cases challenging the application of federal employment laws to states and cities, including laws against age discrimination. They challenged the right of the federal government to require states to agree to various conditions in order to receive federal money; they challenged the constitutionality of laws that required state officials to cooperate in making and enforcing environmental and business regulations. To preserve the power of the federal government to make environmental and antidiscrimination regulations, the justices were forced to make one exception after another to the rule they had established in the *National League of Cities* case. Finally, in *Garcia v. San Antonio Metropolitan Transportation Agency* (1985), the Court reversed itself and overruled the decision. However, four of the nine justices dissented and declared their intention to restore the *National League of Cities* rule.

The justices also divided on how to apply the principle of Separation of Powers. In a key case, *Immigration and Naturalization Service v. Chadha* (1983), the Court ruled that congressional vetoes over administrative decisions amounted to legislation by procedures other than those specified in the Constitution. While conservative justices wanted to protect executive power, they were joined by liberals who wanted to defend regulatory agencies against special interests with influence in Congress.

Several other cases indicated that the Court was moving towards freeing the president from the restraints Congress had imposed after the Watergate Scandal. Conservatives hoped especially that the Court would overturn the law providing for special prosecutors to investigate executive wrongdoing, but the Court disappointed them in *Morrison v. Olsen* (1988) and *Mistretta v. U.S.* (1989) by holding that the concept of Separation of Powers must be applied flexibly in order to secure effective government.

The Court also limited President Reagan's effort to control administrative agencies through the Office of Management and Budget. Endorsing the president's right to influence administrative rule making, the Court nonetheless affirmed that it was statutes rather than executive orders that determined what factors agencies had to take into account. The justices overturned the president's imposition of cost-benefit analyses where Congress had mandated other standards, and it barred the OMB from delaying the promulgation of regulations beyond deadlines Congress had set.

At the same time the Court turned down invitations to more actively police the administrative state through the judiciary. As President Reagan's appointees narrowly construed their obligations to regulate business, consumer advocates and environmentalists turned to judges to force them to adhere to what they said was the intent of the laws. The justices unanimously declined, maintaining the Supreme Court's tradition of judicial deference to administrative decisions and reining in those lower federal courts that become more active in monitoring administrative actions. The courts must defer to administrative rule making as long as it was not "arbitrary and capricious," the justices ruled. Where Congress expressed its intentions clearly, judges should insist that agencies fulfill them. But where Congress's intentions were unclear, judges must defer to an agency's reasonable construction of the laws.

The Rehnquist Court and Conservative Constitutionalism

Despite the success of the liberal holding-action, by the mid-1980s the attitude of the federal courts had clearly shifted towards conservatism, and the Supreme Court seemed on the verge of a wholesale repudiation of liberal constitutionalism. In 1986 President Reagan named Rehnquist chief justice. He then appointed another committed conservative, Antonin Scalia, to join him and in 1987 tried to add another of the country's leading conservative jurisprudents, Robert H. Bork. Conservatives considered Bork the living embodiment of their constitutional vision. They were confident his appointment would transform American constitutional law. Recognizing the stakes, liberals fought it with all their strength. After a bruising and bitter battle, Bork was forced to withdraw and Reagan nominated a more moderate conservative, Anthony M. Kennedy, in his place. Following the appointment of the little-known New Hampshire Supreme Court justice David

Souter to replace Brennan in 1990, President Bush precipitated a similar battle by nominating a reactionary African American government lawyer and federal judge, Clarence Thomas, to replace Thurgood Marshall in 1991. This time conservatives pushed the nomination through, over desperate opposition that focused on Thomas's private life rather than on his ultraconservative opinions.

Those who opposed the Bork and Thomas nominations were reluctant to admit that the Supreme Court was a product of the political process; they continued to insist that the judge's job was to rise above personal values and apply the law. Thus they criticized both nominees' judicial temperaments. Yet they also made a point of the value of maintaining "balance" on the Court. They began to speak of the importance of the "judicial philosophy" of the nominees. Slowly it was becoming clear that the appointment of Supreme Court justices, and thus the Court's articulation of constitutional law itself, was a part of the political process.

By 1991 Chief Justice Rehnquist presided over a Court with five other justices who had been appointed by Presidents Reagan and Bush. An overwhelming majority of the federal judges had been appointed by conservative Republican presidents, carefully chosen for their legal conservatism. As the Rehnquist Court went on the offensive, liberal defenses of the landmark decisions of the Warren and early Burger courts grew more and more desperate. The liberal justices, defending decisions that themselves had overturned decades of precedent, urged the importance of *stare decisis*—adhering to established principles and prior rulings; the conservatives, long the advocates of judicial restraint—now argued

A liberal political cartoonist worries about the effect of Clarence Thomas's appointment on the Supreme Court's interpretation of the Constitution.

that *stare decisis* was less appropriate in constitutional law than in other areas, because mistakes could be corrected outside the Court only through the amendment process.

Conservative views triumphed almost completely on questions relating to the rights of defendants in criminal trials. By the mid-1980s, the Court was imposing rigid rules limiting when defendants could raise objections to the procedures through which they were convicted. The objection had to be timely, made at the appropriate point in the original trial. The Court refused to bend the new rule even if one could show that her lawyer had been incompetent. Once the opportunity to object was missed, it was lost forever, except in a circumstance so egregious that the Court was unable to give an example.

The Court expanded the ability of the police to engage in warrantless searches by limiting the circumstances in which one could expect privacy. Wanting to protect child witnesses in molestation cases, it opened the door to balancing defendant's rights with the state's compelling interests. It found police conduct acceptable in instance after instance in which officers evaded the spirit of the *Miranda* rules. In 1987 a bare majority had ruled that testimony by victims of crime about the impact it had on them was too inflammatory to be permitted in the sentencing phase of criminal trials; in 1991 a six-justice majority overturned the precedent.

The Rehnquist Court was likewise unsympathetic to the claims of prison inmates to basic constitutional rights. Where incarcerated criminals were concerned, there was no need for the state to have a compelling interest to deny rights, five conservative justices held in *Turner v. Safely* (1987). Any regulation is valid "if it is reasonably related to penological interests." On that standard, the Court sustained prison authorities' refusal to allow Muslims to worship and wardens' decisions to curtail prisoners' reading matter, even when the main objection was that it criticized prison conditions.

The Court manifested its increasingly hard line in defendants' rights cases, as well as its insensitivity to racial inequities, in *McClesky v. Kemp* (1987). In *McClesky* the Court again upheld the constitutionality of the death penalty, even though statistics showed that African Americans accused of murdering white victims were eleven times more likely to receive it than whites who murdered blacks. The Court insisted that a defendant's rights were violated only if he showed that the particular jury that sentenced him had been motivated by racial prejudice. No amount of statistical or other evidence demonstrating a more general prejudice would suffice. The Court also rejected challenges to the execution of sixteen- and seventeen-year-old defendants and of mentally retarded defendants, although centrist justice O'Connor joined the four liberal members of the Court in rejecting the execution of a fifteen-year-old.

The Court became much less supportive of legislation designed to remedy racial discrimination. During its liberal period, the Court had interpreted the Civil War–Era Civil Rights Act of 1866 (now section 1981 of the federal code) to

The Rehnquist Court in 1994. From the left: Clarence Thomas, John Paul Stevens (seated), Antonin Scalia, Chief Justice William H. Rehnquist, Sandra Day O'Connor, Anthony Kennedy, David H. Souter, Ruth Bader Ginsburg, and Harry Blackmun.

bar people from discriminating against African Americans in a broad range of areas, in some ways going beyond the legislation of the 1960s. It had interpreted the Civil Rights Act of 1964 to require employers to provide a business-related reason for business practices that led to a great disparity in the number, wages, or position of a company's white and minority-group employees, or between its male and female work force. In 5-4 decisions the conservative majority of the Rehnquist Court cut back on both interpretations. In 1987 it limited the application of the 1866 law to hiring and not discrimination or harassment on the job; employees alleging on-the-job discrimination would have to rely on the more limited remedies afforded by the Civil Rights Act of 1964. In *Wards Cove Packing Company v. Atonio* (1989), the justices overturned *Griggs v. Duke Power Co.* and reinterpreted the Civil Rights Act of 1964 to require plaintiffs to prove that challenged employment practices were intended to discriminate against them and did not serve any reasonable business purpose. The new requirement imposed an almost impossible burden on people attacking discrimination, since discriminatory employers could easily concoct plausible explanations for decisions in any individual case. Moreover, business practices such as laying workers off according to seniority often were not motivated by an intention to discriminate, even though their effect was to protect white men hired in the days before many kinds of jobs opened to African Americans and women. The decision discouraged businesses and other organizations from entering into voluntary affirmative-action agreements, since they would be liable for discriminating against white men unless they admitted that racial and gender disparities were due to earlier purposeful discrimination.

As in *McClesky v. Kemp*, the Rehnquist Court seemed to minimize the persuasiveness of statistical evidence indicating a general pattern of discrimination. It wanted specific evidence of discrimination in the particular case. Over-reliance on statistics raised the specter of quotas for minorities and for women, a remedy that gave special advantages to members of racial minorities and women who had not personally been the victims of discrimination at the expense of innocent white men who had not themselves engaged in it. To Rehnquist, Scalia, and the soon-to-be-appointed Clarence Thomas, the Fourteenth Amendment mandated color-blind public policy, in which only clear evidence of discrimination justified policies that took account of race.

Despite conservatives' avowed support of judicial restraint, the *Wards Cove* case indicated a disposition for greater activism now that they held a majority of the Supreme Court's seats. The *Wards Cove* decision was probably inconsistent with the original intent of Congress when it passed the civil rights laws, and it overturned the interpretation that the Supreme Court had followed, without congressional complaint, for nearly twenty years. Congress responded to the decision by passing the Civil Rights Restoration bill to reinstate the standard of evidence the Court had rejected, but President Bush vetoed it. Under intense pressure, Republicans joined Democrats to pass a slightly modified version in 1991.

In *Richmond v. J. A. Croson Co.* (1989), the Court made clear its antipathy towards affirmative action. It ruled that state and local laws requiring that certain amounts of business be given to minority-owned businesses violated the Equal Protection Clause of the Fourteenth Amendment. The conservative majority rejected the dissenters' argument that "benign" discrimination on behalf of groups that had long suffered oppression should be judged differently. Any program that made racial classifications must be scrutinized strictly, the majority insisted, and only compelling state interests could justify narrowly tailored plans to serve them.

Such decisions reinforced the hostility of the Reagan and Bush administrations to civil rights legislation, and seemed to mark the end of the national commitment to eliminate the economic effects of racial discrimination. Yet in *Metro Broadcasting, Inc. v. Federal Communications Commission* (1990), Justice Brennan once more managed to stitch together a five-to-four majority that ruled that the federal government could require affirmative action in the same situations in which states could not. The decision was one of several occasions when Brennan was able to put together a narrow majority in a civil liberties or equal rights case: In 1986 the Court had interpreted the Civil Rights Act to bar not only discrimination in employment but sexual harassment as well. In 1989 and 1990 the Court overturned state and federal laws making it a crime to burn the flag as a political protest. But the decisions seemed no more than temporary holding actions. The aging liberals Brennan and Marshall could not remain on the bench much longer.

It seemed only a matter of time before the Supreme Court accepted government "accommodation" of religion in the schools and other institutions, as conservative justices bitterly attacked the tests for constitutionality that the early Burger court had established in *Lemon v. Kurtzman*. Several justices insisted that the Court had already rejected those tests in recent decisions and insisted that they be formally overturned. The most conservative justices seemed willing to permit government to go beyond accommodation to flat-out endorsement of religion.

Paradoxically, while conservative justices pressed for an interpretation of the First Amendment that permitted accommodation of religion, they seemed indifferent to the concerns of religious minorities. The Warren Court's rejection of the *Reynolds* rule, which had permitted regulation of religious practice as distinct from mere belief, had caused tensions from the beginning, as religious minorities demanded exemptions from more and more regulations. Jewish soldiers demanded the right to wear skullcaps; Muslim prisoners demanded special food and exemption from dress codes; Amish farmers refused to pay social security taxes; Native Americans tried to block roads from crossing their holy places. Unable to find a clear rule to distinguish demands that must be granted from those that need not be, the Rehnquist Court returned to the *Reynolds* rule in *Employment Division v. Smith* (1990).

Employment Division v. Smith was one of a number of cases in which newly assertive Native Americans protested state and federal actions that hurt tribal religion and culture. All over the country different tribes had challenged government programs that disrupted and even destroyed Indian religious sites to promote tourism, encourage mining and oil production, clear timber, and build highways. After a lower court finally sustained an Indian objection, the Court took up the case. In *Lyng v. Northwest Indian Cemetery Protective Association* (1988) a narrow majority had overturned the lower court decision, upholding a logging program and the construction of a federal highway, even though the justices acknowledged they could have devastating effects on local tribes' religious practices. In *Employment Division v. Smith* a state refused to give unemployment compensation to two Native Americans fired from their jobs for smoking peyote as part of a religious ceremony. The Court ruled that the state's decision did not violate the Native Americans' First Amendment right to worship freely. Governments could enforce any regulations, no matter what their effect on religious practice, as long as these rules were not demonstrably intended to discriminate against a religious group.

Employment Division v. Smith created a powerful reaction because its effects would be felt far beyond a small and relatively powerless religious and racial minority. Politically influential religious minorities and many mainstream Christian denominations lobbied Congress to pass a law protecting religious practices from being inhibited by such regulations, and Congress complied by passing the Religious Freedom Restoration Act of 1993.

Gay couples demonstrate to demand the right to marry.

Given the conservatism of the Rehnquist Court, it was not surprising that it rejected the argument of gay-rights activists that sodomy and other anti-homosexuality laws violated their right to privacy. In fact, the right to privacy itself, and especially to abortion, was also in jeopardy. Clearly, a majority of the justices no longer fully supported *Roe v. Wade*. But rather than overturn the decision, the Court continued to restore state power to regulate abortion piecemeal. The justices sustained state laws that required delays in performing abortions, that required patients to be informed of alternatives, and that required minors to secure parental consent. Despite the implications for free speech, they sustained regulations that prohibited clinics receiving federal support even to provide information about abortion. They denied that blockades of abortion clinics were conspiracies to deprive women as a class of their rights; therefore anti-abortion protesters were not liable to prosecution under federal laws enforcing the Fourteenth Amendment. The most conservative justices chafed at the reluctance of their colleagues to overrule *Roe v. Wade,* while the decision's remaining defenders on the Court gloomily accepted the inevitability of its reversal.

Among the clearest signs of an emerging conservative constitutionalism was the continued trend towards protecting property rights. In 1987 the justices bitterly disappointed landlords in *Pennel v. City of San Jose* by refusing to accept their argument that laws designed to keep rents affordable for poor people were unconstitutional "takings" of private property without compensation.

Surprisingly, Rehnquist himself wrote the majority opinion. But the Court finally accepted the "takings" argument in *Dolan v. City of Tigard* in 1994. With four justices dissenting, the Court ruled that cities could not require real estate developers to set aside land for public purposes, as they were accustomed to doing, unless the taking was roughly proportional to some harm done by the new development itself. The Takings Clause would no longer be "relegated to the status of a poor relation" to the other provisions of the Bill of Rights, Chief Justice Rehnquist announced. Although no one knew how far the Court might take the new precedent, the decision clearly jeopardized the government's power to bar the development of property, without compensating the owners, in order to protect the environment. Jubilant landowners prepared to attack zoning and environmental laws in federal courts around the nation.

State Constitutionalism

With success so doubtful in the federal courts, civil libertarians turned to the state courts for support. A new activism on behalf of civil liberty developed in many of them. Cheered on by Justice Brennan, state supreme court justices interpreted their state constitutions to protect liberties that the Supreme Court said the United States Constitution did not secure. This was easily justified when state constitutions explicitly protected rights, such as privacy, not mentioned in the United States Constitution. But a number of state courts began to interpret state constitutional protections more broadly even when the language of the two constitutions was identical. Since the Supreme Court had long declined to review decisions decided on "adequate and independent" state grounds, state court decisions protecting rights on the basis of state constitutions rather than the United States Constitution were final.

The result was a significant transformation in American constitutional law. Many state courts revisited their state constitutions with enthusiasm. In all of the 1950s only three civil liberties cases had been decided on independent state constitutional grounds. By the 1980s there were hundreds, and state constitutional jurisprudence emerged as one of the most vibrant areas of American constitutional law.

The supreme courts of California, Florida, New Jersey, and New York led the way, but many others followed. State courts interpreted their constitutions to protect the rights of criminal defendants more fully than did the federal Constitution. They did the same in the area of free speech. Many state supreme courts held that their state constitutions guaranteed the right to choose an abortion, insulating their states from the consequences of a possible reversal of *Roe v. Wade*. Many cited special language relating to education in their constitutions to require reform of state funding. As the Rehnquist Court made it easier for government to channel public funds to religious schools and their students, state courts applied stricter provisions of state constitutions to prevent it.

In the 1990s state supreme courts began to rule that privacy or equal protection provisions of state constitutions protected the right of all persons, gay or straight, to engage in consensual sexual relations. One of them was the supreme court of Georgia, which in *Powell v. The State* (1996) overturned on state constitutional grounds the sodomy law that the U.S. Supreme Court had sustained in *Bowers v. Hardwick*. Overall, in the 1980s and 1990s state appellate courts, relying on state constitutional provisions, sustained gay and lesbian parties claiming rights in a stunning two-thirds of the cases they decided; in the federal courts gays and lesbians lost 75 percent of the time. By the turn of the twenty-first century, state courts would begin to hold that equal protection provisions of state constitutions required states to provide gay couples many of the benefits accorded married heterosexuals, and in 2004 the Massachusetts supreme court would rule that its state constitution forbade discrimination against gays in marriage itself.

Conservatives outspokenly protested these decisions. Massachusetts legislators struggled to come up with language for a constitutional amendment that would overturn their supreme court's gay marriage decision. Citizens of New Jersey overturned a supreme court decision barring the release of the names and addresses of child molesters who had served out their sentences. Florida voters amended their constitution to forbid state courts from applying the Exclusionary Rule more strictly than the U.S. Supreme Court. In 2004 the voters of eleven states endorsed initiatives to ban gay marriages. All over the nation conservatives continued to protest judicial activism.

Some conservative analysts argued that the U.S. Supreme Court should insist on uniform interpretation when state and federal constitutional language was substantially the same. In *Michigan v. Long* (1983), the Court reversed its long-standing rule that it would avoid reviewing cases that might have been decided on independent state grounds. To avoid review, state courts were now required to state clearly that they had relied solely on their own constitutions. The response was a big increase in the number of state-court opinions that took care to do so. In effect *Michigan v. Long* valorized independent state constitutionalism.

The explosion of state constitutional law led to a growing federalization of civil liberty, with the citizens of some states accorded significantly different rights than citizens of others. This result was consistent with conservative justices' appreciation of state-rights-oriented federalism. In contrast to libertarian U.S. Supreme Court decisions, those of New York and California did not impose liberal constitutional views on the citizens of more conservative states. Since liberal constitutionalism holds that the purpose of constitutional rights is to protect liberty and equality from majority tyranny, its adherents could not be satisfied that rights received broad protection in New York while they were being denied in Kansas. That philosophy would have left white supremacy intact in the South. No matter how liberal the rulings of state supreme courts, liberals agonized over conservative control of the Supreme Court of the United States.

A Moderate Constitutionalism?

Had President Bush been reelected to the presidency in 1992, he would almost certainly have replaced the last of the liberal Supreme Court justices, finally giving the conservatives, led by Chief Justice Rehnquist, complete control. Instead, Americans elected Bill Clinton. Just when it seemed that the federal courts would finally apply the tenets of constitutional conservatism to their full extent, the political tide of conservatism appeared to ebb.

The Court appeared to reflect the change when it refused to overturn *Roe v. Wade,* even though a majority of the justices had criticized the decision in different opinions. In *Planned Parenthood v. Casey* (1992), three conservatives, led by Sandra Day O'Connor and the newly appointed Justice Souter, argued that reversing *Roe* would violate the principle of *stare decisis* and discredit the Court. They joined two more liberal justices in sustaining *Roe,* although they continued to relax its application.

President Clinton was determined to shore up the moderate justices on the Supreme Court. To do so, he avoided naming pronounced liberals when vacancies opened, turning instead to lower federal court judges with middle-of-the-road records. When a vacancy appeared shortly after his inauguration, Clinton appointed the second woman justice, Ruth Bader Ginsburg, who had played a leading role in the fight for women's rights, but who had established a moderate record as a federal judge. He followed that appointment with a similar one the following year—Judge Stephen Breyer. Clinton succeeded in creating a bloc of at least four moderate justices—Ginsburg, Breyer, Souter, and Justice John Paul Stevens—who were often joined by O'Connor to counteract the three extreme conservatives, Rehnquist, Scalia, and Thomas.

The Court's decision in *Board of Education v. Grumet* (1994) indicated that Clinton's strategy might work. The case challenged a New York law creating a special school district to accommodate the special needs of an ultra-Orthodox Jewish religious sect. Chief Justice Rehnquist and the more extreme conservatives on the Court saw this as an ideal opportunity to repudiate the *Lemon* test that precluded "excessive entanglement" between church and state, and to substitute the principle that the First Amendment permits support of religion as long as the government does not discriminate among different sects. But they were frustrated once again by the moderate coalition led by O'Connor and Souter, who ruled New York's law unconstitutional. The First Amendment requires not only government neutrality among religious groups, but no preference between religion and irreligion, the majority reiterated; it permits no delegation of state power to religious institutions. Still, the opinion paid almost no attention to the *Lemon* test, leaving its status in doubt.

The election of Democrat Bill Clinton and his appointment of moderates to the Supreme Court appeared to stall the march of conservative constitutionalism. Elected as a moderate dubious about big government programs, Clinton would prove committed to diversity, toleration, and individual autonomy. His policies in those areas, combined with the challenge his personal conduct posed to moral values that most Americans adhered to, would deepen the divide between the worldviews that underlay constitutional liberalism and conservatism.

TIMELINE

1969   Warren Burger becomes chief justice.

1971   In *Lemon v. Kurtzman,* the Supreme Court articulates a "three-prong test" to determine whether laws involving religion violate the Establishment Clause of the First Amendment.

1973   *San Antonio School District v. Rodriguez* sustains the constitutionality of Texas's school funding system, holding that laws affecting rich and poor differently do not violate the Equal Protection Clause of the Fourteenth Amendment.

　　　　 Miller v. California holds that sexually explicit material can be banned if it lacks "serious artistic value" and is inconsistent with local standards of decency.

1976   The Supreme Court overturns provisions of the Federal Election Campaign Act limiting corporate and individual political expenditures in *Buckley v. Valeo.*

　　　　 National League of Cities v. Usery rules the extension of the Fair Labor Standards Act to state and local government unconstitutional as a violation of state sovereignty.

　　　　 The Supreme Court sustains the constitutionality of the death penalty in *Gregg v. Georgia.*

1978   *Regents of the University of California v. Bakke* sustains "affirmative action" to promote racial diversity, as long as rigid quotas are not established.

1983   The Supreme Court rules "legislative vetoes" unconstitutional in *Immigration and Naturalization Service v. Chadha.*

　　　　 Michigan v. Long reconfirms that state courts may interpret state constitutions' protections of liberty more broadly than the U.S. Supreme Court interprets similar provisions of the U. S. Constitution but requires an explicit statement that the decision rests on independent state constitutional gounds.

1984   *Lynch v. Donnelly* rules that Christmas displays on government property are constitutional if shown in a secular context.

1984	The Supreme Court establishes a "good-faith" exception to the Exclusionary Rule in *Leon v. U.S.*
1985	The Supreme Court reverses *National League of Cities v. Usery* in *Garcia v. San Antonio Metropolitan Transportation Authority.*
1986	Justice Rehnquist succeeds Burger as chief justice.
1987	The Senate rejects the nomination of leading conservative Robert H. Bork to the Supreme Court.
1989	*Richmond v. J. A. Croson Co.* holds state and local regulations requiring "affirmative action" unconstitutional in the absence of a showing of prior racial discrimination.
1990	The Supreme Court rules in *Employment Division v. Smith* that governments can enforce rules that burden religious practices as long as they were not intended to discriminate against a religious group.
1991	Congress passes the Civil Rights Restoration Act to counteract Supreme Court decisions narrowly interpreting civil rights legislation.
1992	In *Planned Parenthood v. Casey*, the Supreme Court reaffirms *Roe v. Wade*, citing the importance of *stare decisis.*
	Democrat Bill Clinton elected president.
1993	Congress passes the Religious Freedom Restoration Act to counteract *Employment Division v. Smith.*
1993–1994	President Clinton names two moderate justices to the Supreme Court.
1994	In *Board of Education v. Grumet*, the Supreme Court reaffirms strict separation of church and state.
	Dolan v. City of Tigard rules that the Fifth Amendment's Takings Clause forbids local governments from requiring property owners to set aside land for public purposes unrelated to the property's use.
1998	In *Powell v. State*, the Georgia supreme court rules the state's anti-sodomy law violates the privacy protected by the state constitution's guarantee of due process of law.

FURTHER READING

Legal scholars offer perspectives on the Burger Court in Bernard Schwartz (ed.), *The Burger Court* (1998), surveying the Court's decisions topic by topic. Earl M. Maltz provides thorough discussion of the Burger Court's constitutional holdings in *The Chief Justiceship of Warren Burger* (2000). Like Maltz, Melvin I. Urofsky finds continuity between the Burger and Warren Courts in *The Continuity of Change* (1989). Bob Woodward and

Scott Armstrong provide an unusually intimate look at the Burger Court in *The Brethren* (1979), based on the reports of talkative clerks; be aware that its gossip should be seasoned with more than a few grains of salt.

Ethan Bronner's *Battle for Justice* (1989) is a balanced account of the Bork nomination that makes the stakes clear. Mark Gitenstein has also written an insightful, balanced account, *Matters of Principle* (1992). *Capitol Games* (1992), by Timothy M. Phelps and Helen Winternitz, is a good journalistic account. Christopher E. Smith limns a theory of "critical nominations" in his analysis of the struggle over confirming Clarence Thomas. Constitutional theorist Bruce Ackerman puts the Bork nomination in a similar context in an academic article, "Essays on the Supreme Court Appointment Process: Transformative Appointments," *Harvard Law Review* 101 (April 1988): 1164–1184.

The Burger Court's hard line on crime is described and criticized in John F. Decker, *Revolution to the Right* (1992). Herman Belz and Melvin I. Urofsky, respectively, describe the Court's record on affirmative action in *Equality Transformed* (1991) and *A Conflict of Rights* (1991). On women's rights, see the survey Earlean McCarrick prepared for a general audience, "The Supreme Court and the Evolution of Women's Rights," *This Constitution* 13 (Winter 1986): 4–11. Dan Drucker exhaustively covers the Burger Court's abortion decisions in *Abortion Decisions of the Supreme Court, 1973–1989* (1990). The relevant chapters of Donald P. Judges, *Hard Choices, Lost Voices* (1993) are more manageable.

Civil libertarian Gregg Ivers laments the Burger Court's freedom-of-religion decisions in *Lowering the Wall* (1991). Leo Pfeffer discerns a shift towards accommodation of religion in the middle years of the Burger Court in *Religion, State, and the Burger Court* (1984). For the revival of protection for property rights, see William W. Van Alstyne's prescient "The Recrudescence of Property Rights As the Foremost Principle of Civil Liberties: The First Decade of the Burger Court," *Law and Contemporary Problems* 43 (Summer 1980): 66–82, and Martin Shapiro, "The Supreme Court's 'Return' to Economic Regulation," *Studies in American Political Development* 1 (1986): 91–141.

Henry P. Monaghan analyzes the rebirth of state rights/dual federalism in "The Burger Court and 'Our Federalism,'" *Law and Contemporary Problems* 43 (Summer 1980): 39–50. Barbara Hinkson Craig describes a key case in the Burger Court's renewed attention to Separation-of-Powers issues in *Chadha* (1988). For the return to judicial deference to administrative decisions, see Robert M. Horwitz, "Judicial Review of Regulatory Decisions: The Changing Criteria," *Political Science Quarterly* 109 (Spring 1994): 133–169.

Peter Irons describes the early career of the Rehnquist Court in *Brennan vs. Rehnquist* (1994), coming down firmly on the side of the former. For the growing conservatism of the Rehnquist Court in its early years, see Sue Davis, *Justice Rehnquist and the Constitution* (1989); Stanley H. Friedelbaum, *The Rehnquist Court* (1994); Christopher E. Smith, *Justice Antonin Scalia and the Supreme Court's Conservative Moment* (1993); and David S. Savage, *Turning Right* (1992). While Savage saw the confirmation of Justice Clarence Thomas as signifying the triumph of constitutional conservatism. David J. Garrow perceived the emergence of a centrist coalition in "Justice Souter Emerges," in the *New York Times Magazine*, September 25, 1994. Garrett Epps chronicles *Employment Division v. Smith* with great clarity in *To an Unknown God* (2001).

G. Alan Tarr discusses "State Constitutional Interpretation" in chapter 6 of *Understanding State Constitutions* (1998). Daniel R. Pinello provides statistics demonstrating the degree to which state constitutionalism sustained gay and lesbian rights in the 1980s and 1990s in *Gay Rights and American Law* (2003).

20

The Clinton Impeachment and the Erosion of Constitutional Comity

The bitterness of political disputes in the 1990s and early 2000s put the American constitutional system under ever-increasing strain. The Republican and Democratic parties, once amalgams of liberals, moderates, and conservatives that sought votes from a largely middle-of-the-road electorate, became increasingly polarized. Benefiting from a powerful conservative political current that slowly made them the majority party for the first time in more than half a century, Republicans appeared to question the very legitimacy of William J. (Bill) Clinton's presidency after his election in 1992. The civility and mutual respect necessary to operate a government of checks and balances eroded dramatically in the 1990s and early 2000s. Dogged political warfare culminated in an effort to remove the president through a bitterly divisive impeachment that presaged the disputed election of 2000.

Culture War and the Election of 1992

Recognizing the declining appeal of liberalism, in 1992 the Democratic party platform and presidential nominee Bill Clinton claimed to present an alternative to it and to conservatism. Insisting that the economy was their first priority, the Democrats relegated the issues of civil rights and liberties to a secondary position. Clinton and the Democrats claimed to repudiate reliance on government to solve economic and social problems.

Although they focused the campaign on economic issues, Democrats continued to regard free choice as central to liberty, including women's right to choose an abortion to terminate a pregnancy. They urged toleration and praised multiculturalism. But Clinton turned this difficult issue into one of simply sympathizing with others. He expressed apparently heartfelt concerns for all Americans who faced unemployment, lacked health insurance, lived in dangerous neighborhoods, or worried about the many other problems of recent American society, telling them, "I feel your pain." To the dismay of leaders of the Religious Right, Clinton's deep southern roots gave him a remarkable facility with religiously charged language.

381

While Democrats stressed the economy, Republicans stressed "values." Democrats endorsed "moral relativism," their platform charged. Democrats "deny personal responsibility, disparage traditional morality, denigrate religion, and promote hostility towards the family's way of life." Republicans promised to appoint judges who would sustain traditional values. They called for a constitutional amendment to ban abortion, defended prayer in the schools, and promised to end government subsidies of art and literature that brought religion and traditional morality into contempt. At the Republican convention, Patrick Buchanan, a conservative newspaper columnist who had contested Bush's renomination in the primary elections, rallied conservatives to a "culture war." The election was "about who we are," he told the delegates. "It is about what we stand for as Americans. There is a religious war going on in our country for the soul of America." In that struggle, Buchanan insisted, Democrats "are on the other side."

Such vitriolic language alienated many people, but it expressed the deep conviction of many conservatives about what was at stake. Few observers noted the ominous implications for American democracy. What would be the effect of interpreting elections not as contests over public policies but as contests between good and evil for the very soul of the nation?

To Republicans, candidate Bill Clinton represented both liberal immorality and Democrats' ability to gull voters. Furious at his ability to evade responsibility for a number of questionable past actions and his success at cloaking his liberalism in conservative, even religious rhetoric, Clinton's enemies dubbed him "Slick Willie." Republicans were frustrated and angry at Democratic efforts to blur the meaning of liberalism and their connection to it. "The voters would shun them if their true markings were revealed," the Republican platform insisted. Many conservatives saw Clinton's victory as a fundamental miscarriage of the political system.

Nonetheless, the voters appeared to have broken the stalemate in government. For the first time in twelve years one party controlled both Congress and the presidency. Democrats had an opportunity to change the direction of American constitutional development.

The Breakdown of Constitutional Comity

President Clinton's earliest initiatives confirmed conservatives' conviction that he had deceived American voters about his social and political philosophy. He issued executive orders overturning a number of policies limiting federal support for those seeking abortion. He announced his intention to order the armed forces to stop trying to ferret out gays in the military and to end the practice of ousting them with dishonorable discharges. Nothing could more clearly manifest liberalism's stress on freedom of choice, personal autonomy, and privacy; its toleration of various cultures and lifestyles; and its opposition to enforced orthodoxies than so radical a departure from military tradition. That the order was to come from a commander-in-chief who had himself avoided service in the Vietnam Era made it even more controversial.

So did Clinton's claim that as commander-in-chief he could institute so radical a change in social policy by an executive order rather than through congressional legislation. In promising to do so Clinton was following the precedent Harry S. Truman had set when he desegregated the armed forces. The symbolism was obvious: The movement to end discrimination against gay Americans paralleled the movement to end discrimination against African Americans. Conservatives reacted with utter fury. After a bitter struggle, Clinton and the military compromised on a "Don't ask, don't tell" policy designed to end inquests into soldiers' sexual orientations but that still left gays subject to court martial and dishonorable discharge upon discovery. Supported by Congress, which reacted strongly to evidence of sexual harassment in the military academies, Clinton also was largely successful in eliminating limitations that the military imposed on women's service.

Conservatives insisted that Clinton had hidden his true agenda during the campaign. Pointing out that he had secured only 43 percent of the vote, they asserted that the voters who had backed Bush and third-party candidate Ross Perot opposed his liberal philosophy. Conservative activists outside government—radio talk-show hosts, journalists, and literary polemicists—were particularly outspoken. The freedom with which anyone can post items on the Internet opened a huge new medium for attacks, not subject to any kind of policing for accuracy or taste. Conspiracy theories abounded, linking Clinton and his wife Hillary to all sorts of nefarious doings, extending even to murder.

Republicans in various ways refused to accord Clinton the respect the opposing party normally shows the elected president. The Constitution's system of checks and balances provides the opportunity for determined leaders of the different branches of government to obstruct the operation of the others and the government as a whole. The rules and customs within branches can be utilized the same way, as for example the right of senators to *filibuster*—that is, to obstruct legislation by speaking without time limits unless a super-majority (at present sixty votes) votes to cut off debate. There must be a measure of mutual respect, self-restraint, and cooperation—of *comity*—among the branches for the system to work. In the heat of the passionate struggle over fundamental moral values this comity began to break down. As their hostility to Clinton increased, Senate Republicans made use of the rules permitting filibusters to prevent the passage of a number of Clinton initiatives. Traditionally, minorities had resorted to filibusters only on questions of the deepest political, moral, and constitutional concern. But Republican senators used filibusters and the threat of filibusters to kill a number of Clinton's proposals that were hardly revolutionary and fulfilled promises the people had endorsed by electing him. Observers worried that if such tactics became customary, it would be impossible for simple majorities to enact public policy, presenting a basic challenge to the democratic system.

Conservatives' suspicions about the character of Bill and Hillary Clinton were confirmed by a number of minor unseemly scandals and by recycled accounts of questionable land and bank dealings in Arkansas. Charges flew wildly on the Internet and on conservative radio talk shows. Some established conservative newspapers were almost as inflammatory. Because Congress had allowed the Independent Counsel Act to lapse in 1992, Attorney General Janet Reno in January 1994 arranged for the appointment of John B. Fiske Jr., a moderate Republican lawyer to undertake an investigation of the allegations. The Clintons and their aides dragged their feet in complying with requests for documents and began to claim an executive privilege even broader than that claimed by Reagan and Bush.

Conservatives criticized Fiske's careful approach, willingness to compromise on access to evidence, and dismissal of some of the wilder charges. Congress reauthorized the Office of the Independent Counsel in August 1994, reenacting the provision authorizing a three-judge panel to appoint special prosecutors. The panel replaced Fiske with a far more conservative Republican, Kenneth W. Starr.

As Starr turned to his investigation, Clinton faced charges that he had harassed a young woman named Paula Jones while governor of Arkansas. Aided by the president's bitterest critics, Jones brought suit as Clinton vehemently denied the charges. Jones's accusations renewed speculation about Clinton's sexual behavior, adding fuel to conservative charges that he represented the dangers that liberalism posed to traditional American moral values.

Liberal Constitutionalism in Retreat

Despite their campaign rhetoric, Clinton and the Democratic majority in Congress were, as Republicans had claimed, committed to harnessing the power of the national government to solve economic and social problems. They rolled back a portion of the Reagan-era tax cuts. They promised a new burst of government activism to combat the economic decline of the United States, in particular pledging to insure the availability of reasonably priced health care to all. This promise was a major extension of the social welfare programs that had characterized the New Deal and Great Society. Both Democrats and Republicans knew that it had the potential to firmly reestablish the old liberal coalition and restore public faith in liberal constitutionalism. With the Democratic majorities in both houses of Congress, enactment of some health insurance reform seemed certain.

Despite Democratic control of Congress, Clinton decided to keep responsibility for the reform in the executive branch. Meeting largely in secret, with little congressional input, Clinton's advisors, with the first lady presiding, developed an unwieldy, confusing program. As public opinion turned against the proposal, Democrats in Congress wavered. The Senate Republican leadership made clear its intention to filibuster, forcing Democrats to seek 60 votes to pass any bill. In the end they did not even bring it to a vote. Instead of reaffirming the relevance of liberalism to the solution of social and economic problems, the health-insurance debacle seemed to confirm the bankruptcy of liberal ideas.

Meanwhile conservatives continued to stress moral issues. They promoted local and state referenda to bar the enactment of laws protecting gay citizens from discrimination. They continued to rally against abortion and for restoring prayer to the schools. During the 1994 congressional campaign Republican candidates for the House of Representatives took the unprecedented step of pledging to pass a fully articulated conservative program in the first hundred days of Congress; they called it "a contract with America." Many of the proposals had significant constitutional implications, including term limits for elected officials, stronger child pornography laws, measures to strengthen the influence of individual parents over what schools taught their children, tougher uniform sentencing of criminals, further "good faith" exceptions to the Exclusionary Rule, and measures to strengthen the death penalty. Alienated by Democrats' failure to deliver on their promises and fearful of continued economic decline, in 1994 voters drove them from office at every level of the federal system. Republicans took control of both houses of Congress for the first time in forty years.

The 1994 election marked a major realignment in American politics—the emergence of a permanent Republican majority in the nation to replace the party equilibrium of the previous twenty-five years. Triumphant conservative Republicans interpreted the result as a mandate to dismantle the general-welfare state and the liberal constitutionalism that sustained it. They moved boldly to enact key elements of conservative constitutionalism, including legislation to ban "unfunded mandates" and a Private Property Protection Act to require that the government compensate property owners for economic losses due to environmental and other federal regulations. They pressed a constitutional amendment requiring a balanced budget and moved to cut funding for a wide array of federal social programs. They proposed to fund policies with simple block grants, turning their administration over to the states. Congress passed a bill giving the president a line-item veto over appropriations. The Republican majority leader in the Senate promised to open each day's proceedings by reading the Tenth Amendment.

Conservatives pressed cutting-edge issues in the states even harder. Where state constitutions permitted, they proposed statewide referenda to bar affirmative action, passing a constitutional ban in California in 1996; elsewhere they demanded that legislators force an end to the practice. Several states passed legislation that harkened back to state-sovereignty notions of federalism, forbidding the enforcement of federal environmental regulations within their boundaries. This environment encouraged private intimidation of government officers. At the extreme, right-wing opponents of the registration and control of firearms organized armed militia, prepared to fight what they thought was a conspiracy to deprive Americans of the weapons necessary to resist government tyranny.

Republicans regarded the courts as the primary engine through which liberal values had been imposed on the country, and they worried that Clinton-appointed judges might continue to do so long after Clinton himself left the scene. Now in control of the Senate, Republicans cited Democrats' war on the Bork and Thomas nominations to justify delays and refusals to confirm nominations at all levels of the federal judiciary. They forced the president to make acceptable nominations, or even to trade confirmation of a nominee he favored for the nomination of a judge desired by Republicans. Senate committees froze consideration of appointees to government agencies they supervised, forcing Clinton to "package" his nominees with others preferred by Republicans. While partisan opposition to the Clinton administration played a large role in this aggressive assertion of congressional authority, it also represented an effort to exercise greater control over the agencies of the modern administrative state. With a Democrat in the White House, conservative solicitude for presidential prerogatives temporarily receded.

Resurgent conservatives naturally expected to regain control of the White House in 1996. Faced with a new political reality, Clinton returned to his notion of an alternative to both liberalism and conservatism. He backed continued deregulation of industry. He worked to extend international free-trade agreements that overrode American labor, safety, and environmental regulations. He relied on Republican votes to refashion the welfare system, forcing long-term beneficiaries back into the work force. Rather than proposing new social programs, he applied increased tax revenues to eliminate the huge national debt he inherited from his tax-cutting predecessors. In his 1996 State of the Union Address to Congress, he announced, "The era of big government is over."

To his critics' dismay, Clinton's readjustment worked. In 1996 he easily won reelection. From Republicans' standpoint, Clinton had once again demonstrated his lack of principle.

The Clinton Impeachment

Even as the president's popularity rebounded, Independent Counsel Kenneth Starr and his staff proceeded with their investigations. Starr interpreted his mandate broadly. He reopened investigations that had been completed by his predecessor. He turned to matters only tangentially linked to the original questions he had been authorized to look into. When in doubt, he secured expanded mandates from the Justice Department and the three-judge panel. Starr's staff engaged in the techniques typical of criminal investigation, promising reduced sentences or immunity from prosecution to those willing to testify that Clinton had helped to cover up corrupt real estate and banking activities while governor of his home state. Finding no material evidence of a crime (from financial records, for example), they pressured his associates to corroborate the accusations. Appointed for the sole purpose of investigating the president, Starr's goal was to make a case. He

In this Halloween cartoon, Pat Oliphant links Kenneth Starr's course in the Clinton impeachment to the demands of the Religious Right for the re-imposition of conservative sexual morality. What does Oliphant mean by "sexual McCarthyism"?

would exonerate the Clintons only if he found that the charges against them could not be sustained.

Both the Paula Jones case and the Independent Counsel investigations raised significant constitutional issues about the presidency. Clinton's lawyers moved to quash Jones's case, arguing that a sitting president must be immune from private lawsuits. Otherwise a president could be continually distracted by frivolous suits brought by political enemies. Unable to persuade the trial court judge to dismiss Jones's suit, Clinton's lawyers did win a postponement until he left office. But in *Clinton v. Jones* (1997) the Supreme Court unanimously disagreed with the delay. The president is not above the law, the Court affirmed, and the obligation to answer lawsuits is not inherently so onerous as to impair his ability to do his job. If a particular case did have such an effect, the trial judge could adjust the proceedings to take account of it, but a categorical delay until the president left office went too far.

The Clinton administration's claims of executive privilege also led to judicial proceedings. Clinton's lawyers made extremely broad claims of privilege. The administration tried to withhold notes involving discussions between the White House staff and the first lady, who held an informal position never before covered by the privilege. They tried to withhold "talking points" given to sympathetic

Democrats. They claimed a privilege for anyone, official or private, upon whom the president called for advice. They claimed a similar privilege for his staff. Conceding that the privilege gave way to judicial and legislative necessities in some instances, Clinton argued that Congress had a weaker claim to privileged communications when engaged in oversight than it did when devising legislation. He argued that secret agents guarding the president could not be called on for information; presidents had to have absolute confidence in their discretion lest they dispense with protection in order to maintain privacy. His lawyers called it a "protective function privilege."

The courts dismissed all of these claims. Relying on the Watergate tapes case *U.S. v. Nixon*, they reiterated that executive privilege could be outweighed by the needs of Congress and the judiciary to fulfill their functions. The need to investigate possible criminal activity carried particular weight. The administration gave way rather than appeal these decisions, but the delays worked to slow Starr's investigation, giving Clinton's allies time to make devastating political attacks on its integrity.

The Clintons' refusal to cooperate in the investigation, the orchestrated political attacks on the Office of the Independent Counsel, belated discoveries of important pieces of evidence earlier said to be missing all led Starr's staff to conclude that the Clintons were guilty of something, despite the dubiousness of the charges and the uncertain reliability of those making them. Among themselves, they likened the behavior of Clinton's partisans to those of an organized crime family. The comparison persuaded them to cooperate with Paula Jones's lawyers in a "sting" operation. They caught Clinton lying in a sworn deposition and in testimony to a grand jury about a tawdry sexual relationship with a presidential intern, breaking the law in a matter unrelated to anything Starr had been authorized to investigate. It was a tactic justifiable in an anti-organized crime operation but questionable in other circumstances.

In accordance with the Independent Counsel Act, Starr transmitted evidence of Clinton's perjury and attempted cover-up to Congress. Although Starr and Republican congressional leaders insisted that they were only concerned with Clinton's lies under oath and his obstruction of justice, their protests were belied by Starr's report, which recounted the sexual encounters in salacious detail, and innumerable comments from congressional Republicans. For many conservatives, Clinton's offenses demonstrated the link between private and public immorality. That Clinton should violate both his marriage oath and his oath to tell the truth in a legal proceeding was the natural consequence of his beliefs—or lack of them. As a leading House Republican put it, Clinton's conduct was "a sign of moral decline in society that had to be checked."

Public opinion reacted strongly against the impeachment effort. Republicans lost ground in congressional elections in 1998. But they pushed ahead, despite widespread complaints of excess partisanship. After a bitterly acrimonious debate the House passed two impeachment resolutions on nearly straight party-line votes, one accusing the president of perjury and the second of obstructing justice.

In the Senate, the issue was never in doubt. With popular opinion strongly against removing the president and Republicans outnumbering Democrats by only 55 to 45, no one expected the House impeachment managers to secure the 67 votes need for removal. Although Clinton's legal counsel argued that he had not committed the offenses, only the rankest circumlocution could absolve him of having committed perjury. For most Americans, the key legal question was whether perjury committed in the particular circumstances, a lie about private sexual conduct in a deposition taken in a civil suit, amounted to the "high crime and misdemeanor" that the Constitution required for impeachment and removal. Many of those who opposed impeachment insisted that it lay only for offenses connected to the president's official duties, not for private conduct. Others argued that a lie designed to spare oneself and one's family the embarrassment of admitting to an extramarital affair did not rise to the level of an impeachable offense, even if a lie on another subject might. Still others said that removal was too extreme a sanction for the offense. By rejecting the alternative of censure and bringing an impeachment, the House had given the Senate no alternative between acquittal and removal, and many senators, including some Republicans, resented it.

The managers responded that such a lie—a criminal (although rarely prosecuted) offense under United States law—went to the heart of the president's constitutional obligations and merited removal. How could the United States be a "nation under law" if the person with the ultimate responsibility for enforcing the law was not obligated to obey it? One after another the managers made powerful appeals to senators to uphold the principle of the rule of law. In the view of many of them the popular opposition was a sign of the moral degeneration of the nation. One senator pleaded with his colleagues: "We must simply summon our courage and yell, 'Stop tampering with the soul of America.'" But he failed to persuade. On February 12, 1999, the Senate refused to convict on the perjury article by a vote of 45 to 55, with ten Republicans joining the Democrats in opposition. Five Republicans joined Democrats in the 50 to 50 vote on the obstruction-of-justice article.

In the view of many Americans, Republicans had been as guilty as Clinton of undermining the rule of law. They viewed the impeachment in the context of six years of harassment of the president, refusal to accept the legitimacy of his election, failure to accord him the respect due the elected representative of the American people, wild charges and reckless invective, and a special prosecutor chosen by the president's political enemies. Few Americans had much good to say about the character of William Jefferson Clinton, but removing the president after such a campaign would not represent the rule of law; it would vindicate a stubborn refusal to accept the results of the democratic process. In a final comment on the events, Republicans and Democrats agreed to allow the Independent Counsel Act expire without authorization in 1999. The fiasco led analysts to wonder whether the impeachment process, which had been credited with preserving the integrity of the constitutional system during the Watergate scandal, had been discredited.

The polarized reaction to the Clinton presidency and the impeachment boded ill for American democracy. Leading Republicans seemed to have refused to concede the legitimacy of a democratic election. Democrats had defended a president who had clearly violated the laws he was sworn to uphold. Clinton himself offered the barest apology for his misconduct, instead claiming credit for standing up to a partisan impeachment. Americans were dividing more and more starkly on what they saw as issues of deepest principle. As conservatives questioned the integrity of those who rejected moral absolutism, liberals were coming to doubt the commitment of conservatives to democracy and constitutional liberty.

The Presidential Election of 2000 and the Constitution

The Republican presidential candidate in 2000, George W. Bush, the son of Clinton's predecessor, appeared to share the concern that many Americans expressed about the bitter divisiveness. As governor of Texas, he had worked closely with Democrats on a number of issues. He promised to raise the tone of political debate, avoid negative attacks on his critics, and to be a unifier rather than a divider as president. Making a special point of his fundamentalist Christian faith, he nonetheless eschewed the bitter rhetoric of the Religious Right and kept its fiery spokespeople from taking prominent roles in the campaign. Softening the hard edges of Republican ideology, he promised a "compassionate conservatism."

Constitutional issues were central to the Republican campaign. The platform promised smaller government, less regulation, and lower taxes. It promised Republicans would "restore the force of the Tenth Amendment, the best protection the American people have against federal intrusion and bullying." In regulating education and health care, Republicans stressed local responsibility, expressing their respect for the traditional authority of local school boards over education and of the states to regulate health insurance, health care professionals, and health care guidelines. Republicans avowed their intention to "reform" the judiciary in a conservative direction, pointing approvingly to their candidate's pledge to nominate judges "who have demonstrated that they share his conservative beliefs and respect the Constitution." Throughout the campaign Bush expressed his admiration for Justices Scalia and Thomas and promised to nominate people who shared their philosophy to the Supreme Court and federal judiciary. At the same time Republicans endorsed restrictions on lawsuits in a variety of areas, to "break the grip of the trial lawyers on our legal system."

The platform pledged to work for the return of voluntary prayer to the schools and pledged that a Republican administration would vigorously enforce legislation that guaranteed religious groups equal access to school facilities. It

Some Americans were dismayed that the Supreme Court would step in to decide the winner of the presidential election of 2000. Others were relieved. What does this political cartoon indicate about the Supreme Court's role in American political and constitutional life?

warned of "the pollution of our culture," attacking violence, drugs, and pornography in the media and on the Internet. The platform in effect endorsed the accommodationist position on church and state. Besides endorsing prayer in the schools, Republicans promised to open programs to secular and faith-based institutions equally. They endorsed the right of schools, courthouses, and other public buildings to display copies of the Ten Commandments.

The platform also echoed conservative constitutional positions on race and equal protection, explicitly opposing quotas and implicitly opposing affirmative action. Likewise, Republicans cautioned against excessive multiculturalism, supporting formal recognition of English as the nation's official language. Promoting tough policies to fight crime, Republicans pledged to "reform" the Exclusionary Rule and to secure a constitutional amendment to protect victims' rights in the criminal process. Affirming their commitment to protecting the environment, Republicans argued that protecting property rights was the best way to do it. "We will safeguard private property rights by enforcing the Takings Clause of the Fifth Amendment," they promised.

Democrats nominated Clinton's southern-born vice president, Al Gore, like Clinton a centrist and critic of his party's liberal wing. Stressing the economic prosperity of the Clinton years and the administration's success in eliminating chronic federal deficits, Gore ran on a platform that continued Clinton's policy of co-opting conservative rhetoric to frustrate much of the conservative program.

Democrats eschewed the kinds of programs characteristic of liberalism from the 1930s through the 1960s. Rather than promise new regulations or ambitious social welfare programs, they turned almost entirely to tax incentives and financial subsidies to encourage individual and business decisions that would increase access to education, help provide health insurance, encourage saving for retirement, and facilitate other desirable goals. In effect, the platform and campaign abandoned key elements of constitutional liberalism—active government and the constitutional nationalism that it relied on.

While the Republicans made the appointment of judges with conservative philosophies a central plank of their platform, Democrats soft-pedaled constitutional issues. Rather than confront Republicans on the specifics of constitutional conservatism, the Democratic platform spoke in generalities. "Unlike Republicans," it stated, "Al Gore will appoint justices to the Supreme Court who have a demonstrated concern for and commitment to the individual rights protected by our Constitution, including the right to privacy." Only politically sophisticated observers could perceive this bare sentence to articulate the deep differences in constitutional philosophy that separated Democrats from Republicans. It was hardly a confident restatement of liberal constitutionalism.

The party's most explicit constitutional commitments were to "the right of every woman to choose, consistent with *Roe v. Wade*," and to continue to fight for the inclusion of all, including racial and other minorities, women, and gays and lesbians, as equal members of the American community. Trying to balance multicultural diversity with the widespread desire to defend a central definition of Americanism, the Democratic platform concluded, "In the years to come, we must celebrate our diversity and focus on strengthening the common values and beliefs that make us one America—one nation, under God, with liberty and justice for all." The affirmation of the Pledge of Allegiance's reference to a nation under God was striking.

Although their presidential candidate softened their rhetoric and blurred the hard edge of their beliefs, many Republicans believed that the election of 2000 was a referendum on a political and constitutional philosophy that they were sure a large majority of Americans shared. More than that, it was a campaign to repudiate the fundamental amorality of liberalism, illustrated concretely, they thought, in the person of Bill Clinton. "The rule of law, the very foundation for a free society, has been under assault, not only by criminals from the ground up, but also from the top down," their platform warned. In the view of many Republicans, liberalism threatened the most fundamental American values and the rule of law itself. In the view of many Democrats, Republicans had been unwilling to accept defeat in the previous two presidential elections.

When the election resulted in a virtual tie, this mutual suspicion and distrust challenged the ability of the constitutional system to resolve the crisis. Democratic candidate Gore led in the popular vote by only 500,000 votes out of over 105 million cast; in a number of states the margin between the candidates was razor-thin. The result of the election would turn on who would receive Florida's votes in the Electoral College. There Bush had a lead of about 1500 out of more than 5.5 million votes.

A number of factors led Democrats to believe that a majority of Florida voters had intended to vote for Gore. Because ballot problems seemed to have occurred more in counties that tended to return Democratic majorities than Republican ones, Democrats believed that if the votes were properly recounted, Gore would overcome Bush's lead. Although Florida's laws governing recounts were poorly drawn and inconsistent, earlier interpretations by previous secretaries of states and the Florida courts provided the leeway necessary to ascertain the true will of the people. If she had wanted to, Florida's secretary of state could have devised a recount that would have legitimized the state's election. Instead she interpreted the law in the interest of her candidate, declaring him the winner by 537 votes.

It is difficult to know whether a less partisan course on the part of Florida's state election officials would have encouraged compromise between the candidates' camps in the interest of democracy and constitutional government. It is doubtful. From the beginning Bush's allies claimed the election was over and that there was nothing to concede. The Republicans' adamant position left Gore little choice, and both camps turned to the courts to try to secure the presidency.

To preserve his margin of victory, Bush's lawyers did everything possible to persuade the courts to stop all recounts. Gore's lawyers insisted that Florida law required manual recounts and that the state's judicial precedents required that all processes be geared to determining the true intent of the voters, rather than merely observing the technicalities of the statutes. Gore's lawyers were correct about the precedents, but those precedents were pitted against statutory language that mandated a return within seven days. Turning to the courts to evade the statutory language, no matter how firmly based in the state's legal precedents, looked to Republicans like trying to go outside the rules. The fact that Florida's supreme court was made up of Democratic justices made things appear even worse. Already convinced of the perfidy of the Clinton administration and the immorality of liberalism in general, Republicans were certain that Democrats intended to steal the election. But this conviction in turn meant that Republicans would not rely on the state's judicial processes to resolve the dispute. Controlling the legislature, Republicans prepared to have it simply declare Bush the victor and appoint the people to cast the states electoral votes. At the same time, Bush's lawyers petitioned the predominantly Republican federal judiciary to intervene to prevent the state courts from ordering the recounts Gore wanted.

It was hard to see on what basis the federal courts could take jurisdiction. The Constitution specifies that the president of the Senate—that is, the vice president—shall count the electoral vote in the presence of both houses of

Congress and then indicates how to proceed if no candidate has a majority. It does not indicate how to resolve disputes about contested electoral votes, leaving Congress to fill in those details. In the years after the Hayes-Tilden debacle of 1876, Congress had established a procedure designed to encourage states to resolve such disputes and to reduce the danger of a partisan result in Congress. If a state failed to settle the dispute, a complex set of rules came into play, all designed to minimize the freedom of choice of Congress by specifying which set of electoral votes would be accepted in what circumstances.

As the Supreme Court had recognized, the Constitution leaves a number of "political questions" to the discretion of other branches of government. Impeachment was one; counting the electoral vote had always seemed to be another. But the crisis was more acute than most Americans realized. The newly elected House of Representatives remained under Republican control while Democrats had secured control of the Senate in the election of 2000. This fact would play a large part in determining the outcome if Florida's votes remained disputed, as seemed likely. Democrats would control the Senate only because Vice President Gore would cast the deciding vote.* Worse, Gore's running mate, Joseph Lieberman, was also part of the Democrats' one-vote Senate majority. Thus, unless Gore and Lieberman recused themselves, turning the election over to the Republicans, the count would turn on the votes of the Democratic presidential and vice-presidential candidates themselves. With Republicans already convinced that Democrats were out to steal the election, it was impossible that they would accept the legitimacy of a Democratic presidency secured under such circumstances. Indeed, it was unlikely that most Americans would be prepared to do so. The breakdown in constitutional comity between the president and Congress and between the parties would only grow worse and perhaps reach crisis proportions.

Such a delicate situation called upon both candidates and their parties to exercise the utmost restraint and moderation, to seek compromise in the interest of the public good. Instead each side had turned to the courts in an adversarial legal system. Each side insisted upon its interpretation of law and fact. Each side considered the other to be acting in bad faith. Even though few Americans understood how dire the prospects were, most knew enough to turn to the institution they believed most likely to eschew partisanship for law—the Supreme Court of the United States. But the Court itself no longer seemed above the partisan fray. In the bitter dispute between constitutional liberalism and conservatism, the Court itself had divided. Could it rise above its own divisions and the bitter partisanship that was so closely connected to them?

---

*The law specified that the Congress elected the previous November count the electoral votes on January 3. At that time there would be 50 Democratic and 50 Republican senators. The Twentieth Amendment to the Constitution specifies that the president and vice president remain in office until January 20. So Vice President Gore would be presiding over the Senate, able to break a tie vote.

TIMELINE

1992   William J. (Bill) Clinton elected president.

1994   Attorney General Janet Reno appoints Robert B. Fiske Jr. special counsel to investigate various allegations of wrongdoing on the part of President Clinton and Hillary Rodham Clinton.

Congress reauthorizes the Independent Counsel Act; Kenneth W. Starr appointed independent counsel in place of Fiske.

1994   Republicans capture control of the House of Representatives for the first time in over fifty years.

1995   The Private Property Protection Act gives owners the right to compensation when regulations reduce the value of their property.

1996   Bill Clinton reelected president.

1997   Supreme Court rules that the president is not immune from private lawsuits during his term of office (*Clinton v. Jones*).

1998   Independent Counsel Starr refers evidence of impeachable offenses to the House of Representatives.

The House of Representatives passes articles of impeachment to present to the Senate.

1999   The Senate votes against convicting Clinton on the articles of impeachment.

Congress declines to reauthorize the Independent Counsel Act.

2000   The election of 2000 results in a virtual tie.

FURTHER READING

Essays in Gerald Pomper (ed.), *The Election of 1992* (1993), discuss the campaign and the issues. For the breakdown in comity between the president and Congress, see Peter Shane, "When Inter-Branch Norms Break Down," *Cornell Journal of Law and Public Policy* 12 (Summer 2003): 503–542. Charles O. Jones, *Clinton and Congress* (1999) describes the details of Clinton's failure to pass a health insurance reform act and the following impasse, stressing the role of the separation of powers on American government.

By far the best and most judicious analysis of the impeachment is by the influential federal judge Richard A. Posner, *An Affair of State* (1999). Journalist Bob Woodward devotes the largest part of his nonpartisan *Shadow: Five Presidents and the Legacy of Watergate* (1999) to the Clinton scandals. A number of more partisan books expose the activities of right-wing extremists and Clinton's personal and political enemies in inventing and exaggerating stories. Overly dismissive of Clinton's misconduct, they nonetheless make sobering points about the credulity of the mainstream media. For a manageable example, see James D. Retter, *Anatomy of a Scandal* (1998). Susan Schmidt and Michael Weisskopf describe developments from Independent Counsel Kenneth Starr's perspective in *Truth at Any Cost* (2000).

The essays in David Gray Adler and Michael A. Genovese (ed.), *The Presidency and the Law: The Clinton Legacy* (2002), provide excellent scholarly surveys of presidential immunity, executive privilege, the independent counsel, and impeachment, as do those in Mark J. Rozell and Clyde Wilcox (ed.), *The Clinton Scandal and the Future of American Government* (2000). On the special danger Clinton faced after adopting a "preemptive" strategy to counter Republicans in a conservative age, see Stephen Skowronek, *The Politics Presidents Make* (1993), and Mark Tushnet, "The Constitutional Politics of the Clinton Impeachment," in *Aftermath: The Clinton Impeachment and the Presidency in the Age of Spectacle*, ed. Leonard V. Kaplan and Beverly I. Moran (2001), which also has insightful essays on the prosecutorial approach of independent counsels (Tuerkheimer), declining respect for the rule of law (Solan), and the relation of conservative views of liberalism to the impeachment (Novak).

Historian John Milton Cooper Jr. stresses the ideological makeup of the political coalitions that confronted each other in the campaign of 2000, in "Leaving It: The Election of 2000 at the Bar of History," in *The Unfinished Election of 2000*, ed. Jack N. Rakove (2001). In the same volume, Henry E. Brady describes the polarization of the American electorate on economic and moral issues in "Trust the People: Political Party Coalitions and the 2000 Election." John Kenneth White stresses the depth of *The Values Divide* (2003) in politics. For an eminent legal scholar's assessment of the relationship between Republican conservatism and the constitutional decisions of the Supreme Court, see Cass R. Sunstein, "Does the Constitution Enact the Republican Party Platform? Beyond *Bush v. Gore*," in *Bush v. Gore*, ed. Bruce Ackerman (2002), which suggests the constitutional stakes of the election.

There are innumerable books and essays about the dispute over which candidate carried Florida and the way the issue was resolved. Many are partisan, and the controversy was so bitterly contested that even those that attempt a nonpartisan assessment are certain to be seen as taking one side or another. The political staff of the *Washington Post* provides a well-written inside account of the dispute, titled *Deadlock* (2001). Jeffrey Toobin's gripping popular description *Too Close to Call* (2001) tends to sympathize with Gore but is nonetheless judicious and even-handed. Abner Greene provides the clearest and most succinct explanation of the legal issues in *Understanding the 2000 Election* (2001), but not everyone would agree with his suggestions of how they should have been determined. The best scholarly analysis of how the courts handled the issues is Howard Gillman, *The Votes That Counted* (2001). Gillman praises most of the Florida judges for rising above simple partisanship. His verdict on the U.S. Supreme Court is something else again.

21

The Rehnquist Court, Judicial Supremacy, and the Constitution

The renewed energy and confidence among conservative politicians after the congressional elections of 1994 was mirrored by a renewed conservatism on the Supreme Court. No centrist-liberal majority emerged. Instead Justices Kennedy and O'Connor more and more often joined Justices Rehnquist, Scalia, and Thomas to form narrow conservative majorities. Justice Souter, in contrast, firmly allied with the more liberal bloc, making the Rehnquist Court the most persistently polarized court in American history, with O'Connor still the swing vote.

With conservative Republicans in control of the House of Representatives and soon to gain control of the Senate, the justices no longer had to worry that Congress would challenge conservative decisions as they had with the Civil Rights Restoration Act in 1991 and the Religious Freedom Restoration Act in 1993. Flexing its institutional muscles, the Court ruled the latter unconstitutional in *City of Boerne v. Flores* (1997). In the end, conservative justices, who not long before had urged judicial restraint and adherence to the original understanding of the framers, proved as intent as liberals on proclaiming judicial supremacy.

Arrogating to itself the preemptive authority to interpret the Constitution, the Court tended to treat the other branches with growing condescension. Nowhere was the Court's dominance demonstrated more forcefully than in the disputed presidential election of 2000. The Court's course in that controversy, compared to its role in the disputed Hayes-Tilden election 124 years earlier, clearly indicated the degree to which Americans had conceded ultimate authority over constitutional issues to the justices.

The Rehnquist Court and the Instability of Conservative Constitutionalism

A number of factors still prevented the Rehnquist Court from completely reconstructing constitutional law in the image of conservative constitutionalism. First, Clinton's moderately liberal appointees joined Souter and Stevens to form a solid base of four justices committed to preserving the jurisprudence of the Warren

397

and Burger Courts. Second, Justice O'Connor's approach to constitutional law was significantly different than that of fellow-conservatives Scalia and Thomas. Committed to formalistic reasoning and to establishing clear rules to guide lawmakers and lower courts, Scalia and Thomas often criticized O'Connor's preference for balancing competing interests and applying standards of reasonableness. O'Connor conceded that her approach meant that each case required searching inquiry, but again and again she made clear her suspicion of categorical, mechanistic thinking and her distrust of sweeping judgments. Usually O'Connor came down on the conservative side in specific cases, often providing the deciding vote. But her case-by-case, minimalist approach did not lend itself to establishing fixed and widely applicable conservative rules.

Third, the conservative justices disagreed among themselves over the principle of *stare decisis*—the respect to be given legal precedents. O'Connor and Kennedy remained far more committed to that principle than their conservative allies, who continued to argue that it had less justification in matters of constitutional law, where only the Court itself could reverse an erroneous prior decision, than in other areas. This commitment to *stare decisis* made O'Connor, especially, more inclined to contain or reinterpret the landmark decisions of the Warren and Burger Courts than to overturn them.

Beyond differences of jurisprudential style, there also were serious disagreements among the five more conservative justices on matters of law. Scalia, Thomas, and Rehnquist rejected the liberal values that underlay the precedents of the Warren. Despite coming down on the conservative side in most specific cases, O'Connor's basic values often seemed more similar to those of the dissenters than her conservative allies. She was willing to reinterpret the great Warren and Burger–Era cases in a more conservative direction, but she was not willing to jettison them. Kennedy's divergence from the three hard-line conservatives was less marked, but it clearly existed on a number of issues.

The result was that decisions supported by the five more conservative justices rarely were accompanied by opinions to which all of them subscribed, much less opinions softened enough to attract the support of any of the moderates. A confusing welter of concurring opinions proliferated, with justices agreeing with one part or another of the main opinion of the Court and indicating disagreement with other parts. It became an art to figure out what parts of opinions had the support of a majority of justices. This incoherence added to the sense that conservative decisions were unstable in many areas and had not established firm law. The weight of constitutional law had clearly shifted rightward. But the most salient characteristic of the Rehnquist Court was not its conservatism but its factionalism.

"Fundamental Liberties" and "Suspect Classifications"

The Court continued to distinguish between most government laws and actions and those that affected fundamental liberties or involved "suspect" classifications. The Court still subjected these to "heightened scrutiny." Even if justified by compelling or important state interests, they still had to be "narrowly tailored" to impose as slight a burden as possible. "Fundamental liberties" continued to be defined in terms of the Bill of Rights. Other rights, which the Rehnquist Court referred to as mere "liberty interests," could be infringed on a mere showing of reasonability. Some lower federal courts began interpreting the right to bear arms as a fundamental liberty specified in the Bill of Rights, and there were indications that some of the justices agreed. But the Supreme Court did not yet reconsider its old position that the Second Amendment secured only a collective right to bear arms in the state militia rather than establishing a fundamental individual right.

Despite the aversion of some of the justices to fixed rules and formalistic categorization, the Rehnquist Court tended to elaborate rules and categories that complicated the basic principles. For example, the Court distinguished public forums, dedicated to communication and discussion, from nonpublic areas. Only a compelling government interest could justify free-speech restrictions in a public forum; but authorities could institute reasonable, content-neutral restrictions in other spaces. The Court distinguished between content-neutral regulations of speech and regulations that instituted preferences for particular speech. It distinguished between religious beliefs and religiously motivated action, and between neutral government regulations that incidentally burdened believers and those that appeared to target them. Different levels of scrutiny applied to actions fitting within the different categories.

The Rehnquist Court and Freedom of Expression

The Rehnquist Court had a decidedly mixed record on civil liberties. It was surprisingly protective of freedom of speech and press. For liberals, freedom of speech had long been seen as more than merely a tool necessary to democratic politics. It had become "freedom of expression," an aspect of the autonomous, searching individualism liberals believed in. As long as this value was not implicated, the liberal justices were willing to sustain restrictions that served other compelling interests, such as campaign finance reform and protecting racial minorities from harassment. The conservative justices were particularly concerned to assure broad rights of political speech against such restrictions. The consequence was that shifting coalitions among justices generally sustained freedom both of political and nonpolitical expression, as well as freedom of association.

The key rule remained that government not discriminate against speech based on its content. A rule adversely affecting all speech could be sustained if it served other legitimate interests, but not a rule that inhibited the expression of some points of view but not others. The touchstone case was *Rosenberger v. University of Virginia* (1995), in which the Court overturned the university's policy of withholding subsidies from religiously oriented publications. For the conservative majority, the policy amounted to forbidden content-based discrimination, while the dissenters sustained it as a legitimate effort to avoid subsidizing religion. Even laws against symbolic representations of hate, such as Nazi swastikas and burning crosses, had to be content-neutral; they had to bar intimidation of all kinds aimed at any group, the Court ruled in *R.A.V. v. City of Minneapolis* (1992). Indeed, some justices opined in a subsequent case that cross burning inevitably carried a particular message and therefore could not be singled out for banning.

However, both liberal and conservative justices evaded the rule mandating strict scrutiny of content-based discrimination by making categorical exceptions or redefining the issues. For example, the conservative majority exempted grade schools and high schools from free-speech requirements, sharply cutting back on the free-speech rights secured to students in the Vietnam War era. The conservative wing of the Court adhered to the rule established in *Rust v. Sullivan* (1991), in which the Court had sustained a regulation that barred clinics receiving federal funds from informing clients about abortion services. The government had the right to prefer some public policies to others, and in doing so it could specify how funds were to be spent and the conditions under which they could be received; the general rule that government could not discriminate against speech on the basis of its content did not apply. Therefore, the government could tell libraries that they had to install devises on computers to filter out material unfit for children, if they wanted to receive government grants. The government could also set moral standards for recipients of awards supporting the arts.

But in general it was the more liberal justices who tended to categorize free-speech cases in ways that permitted limitations. Liberals were willing to permit government restrictions on commercial speech. They were less inclined to protect the speech of anti-abortion demonstrators. In the much-watched case of *Hill v. Colorado* (2000), Justices O'Connor and Rehnquist joined the more liberal justices in upholding a state law precipitated by ever more confrontational demonstrations around abortion clinics. The law limited the ability of demonstrators, whatever their viewpoint, to disrupt the activities of medical clinics by picketing and confrontation. This was merely a regulation of the place and manner in which people could exercise their free-speech rights, the liberals argued; because the protests took place in a "nonpublic forum" the law had only to be reasonable and content-neutral. While those committed to women's right to choose abortions celebrated, some civil libertarians worried that the case provided a template for suppressing demonstrations everywhere. Indeed, a definite trend began for officials to limit political demonstrations to particular, often remote locations, claiming such regulations were justified by the *Hill* decision.

The most powerful disagreement came over campaign finance reform. The liberals, sustained by O'Connor, the only justice with significant political experience, consistently upheld laws limiting corporate and party campaign contributions. They insisted that limits on contributions did not significantly inhibit free speech. The four conservatives charged the majority with diluting free-speech protections.

The struggle grew more intense as Americans became more disenchanted with the influence of money in politics and the proliferation of negative campaign advertising. In 2002 Congress responded to public pressure by passing the McCain-Feingold law to bar the political parties from raising cash not subject to the rules imposed on contributions to specific candidates. Republican leaders, who tended to benefit more than Democrats from the outlawed system, challenged the law. The battle culminated in *McConnell v. Federal Communications Commission* (2003). Advocates of change worried that the Court might rule against the law and impose a free-speech straightjacket that would make reform impossible. But O'Connor again joined the more liberal justices to sustain campaign finance reform, while the rest of her conservative colleagues blasted away at the erosion of free-speech guarantees.

The difference between the conservative and liberal justices stood out clearly when it came to regulating nonpolitical expression. For liberal justices, even erotic dancing was a form of expression. Government needed a compelling reason to suppress it, and a mere desire to promote the predominant moral code did not satisfy that test. Conservatives disagreed. Dancing was conduct rather than speech, and it could be regulated for the purpose of promoting morality and fighting prostitution. By 2000 a middle ground had emerged, with most of the justices agreeing that exotic dancing had some expressive content that must receive a degree of protection. But the Court held that local authorities could ban the dancing, and even regulate the location of erotic booksellers, to combat the "secondary effects" of erotic businesses, such as prostitution, increased crime, and violence. Controlling such "secondary effects" became a major justification for wide ranging attacks on erotic businesses.

However, the Rehnquist Court overturned congressional efforts to impose controls on television and the Internet to protect children from exposure to "indecent" material. It likewise rejected laws that banned explicit Internet depictions of sex appearing to involve minors. Merely "indecent" material was not "obscene" material, and protecting children could not justify limiting adults' access to it, however offensive to most people.

The Rehnquist Court and Religion

Similar divisions characterized the Rehnquist Court's approach to issues involving religion. These issues mattered deeply to conservatism's powerful constituency on the Religious Right. Four justices—Rehnquist, Scalia, Thomas, and Kennedy—assailed the notion that the First Amendment established a wall of separation between church and state. It mandated neutrality among different religions and denominations but not hostility to religion in general. They pointed out that the government had a long history of endorsing religious belief, citing such practices as pledging allegiance to a nation "under God," minting coins saying "in God we trust," and observing Christmas. The Court had avoided ruling such practices unconstitutional by calling them "secular." This violated both common sense and logic, the conservatives argued. They vigorously attacked the tests of constitutionality the Burger Court had established in *Lemon v. Kurtzman*—that government acts have a secular rather than religious purpose, that they not have a primary effect of promoting religion, and that they avoid "excessive entanglement" between church and state.

On occasion the conservatives suggested that government had the right to prefer religious values and standards of conduct over secular alternatives, but usually they conceded that government programs could not be designed to promote religion. Instead of using the *Lemon* tests, the Court should ask only whether a challenged regulation had a secular purpose and was neutral between religion and secularism, they urged. The fact that it might have the incidental effect of promoting religion did not render it unconstitutional.

Overturning *Lemon* would have constituted an immense symbolic victory for conservative constitutionalism, but the conservatives could not secure O'Connor's vote. O'Connor agreed that government should accommodate religion; in a nation where religious belief ran so deep, it was impossible not to. But she shared liberals' commitment to pluralism and like them worried about the propensity of school boards and other government officials to treat those holding unorthodox beliefs as outsiders rather than respected members of the community. For her the issue was whether a reasonable person would feel excluded, and that required an evaluation of each particular circumstance rather than the application of a fixed rule.

With the acquiescence of the more liberal members of the Court, O'Connor refashioned the *Lemon* tests. Downplaying the entanglement issue, she held that the key questions were whether a challenged government regulation or action had the purpose or effect of endorsing or inhibiting religion, and whether it would lead reasonable people to believe they were somehow considered less than full members of the community. Kennedy expressly rejected this formulation, worrying that its application would render many accommodations of religion unconstitutional. Doesn't pledging allegiance to a nation "under God" signal atheists that they are not fully part of the community?, he asked. Doesn't treating "In God We Trust" as a national motto do the same? He insisted that the correct test was whether government actions coerced religious beliefs or participation, either directly or subtly. No matter how conceived, however, these concerns led O'Connor and Kennedy to join the liberals in guarding carefully against officially sanctioned prayers and other religious activities in schools. Even programs allowing students themselves to decide whether to open ceremonies with formal religious invocations could not withstand their scrutiny. Thus the Rehnquist Court disappointed religious conservatives in an area of deep concern to them.

But in other areas the Rehnquist Court substantially altered church-state law. Fear of forbidden "entanglement" with religion had led school administrators and other local officials to exclude religious groups from access to public facilities and programs. Not only did the Rehnquist Court rule such exclusions unnecessary, but as the Court held firmly in the *Rosenberger* decision noted above, such discriminations violated freedom of speech, press, and association.

Kennedy's stress on coercion meant he had no problem with government programs that allowed individuals freely to choose whether to support religious institutions. Voucher programs that let parents choose to send their children to private religious schools raised no issue of coercion in his view. O'Connor's reformulation of the *Lemon* test likewise undermined the limitations the Warren and Burger Courts had put on state support for religious schools. Administrators and teachers in religious schools could be trusted to honor restrictions on aid, she insisted. Therefore strict monitoring was not required, and one need not fear over-entanglement between church and state. As a result, in *Agostini v. Felton* (1997) Kennedy and O'Connor joined the other conservative justices in reversing a key, twelve-year-old case that had precluded sending public school specialists into religious schools to help with remedial education. Civil libertarians worried that the same reasoning would justify direct public support for any teacher of a secular subject.

As *Agostini* made clear, one of the most significant consequences of the conservatives' dominance on the Rehnquist Court was the elimination of constitutional barriers to government subsidies for religious institutions and religious indoctrination. One by one the Rehnquist Court broke down the barriers that had inhibited such subsidies. The conservatives articulated their position most trenchantly in *Mitchell v. Helms* (2000), upholding the public purchase of computers, books, and other material for religious schools. Of course, computers could easily be diverted to religious uses, but as long as the purpose was secular— to aid education—and the support was available equally to secular and religious institutions, the fact that the purchases amounted to a direct subsidy of religious schools made no difference. O'Connor accepted the result, but not the reasoning. Shocked at her colleagues' aggressive rejection of the most basic principles that governed the constitutional law of church-state relations, she sustained the program because she trusted the recipients not to divert the material to religious uses, not because the diversion would make no difference.

But the effect was the same. *Agostini v. Felton* and *Mitchell v. Helms* opened the door to massive public support of religious education. Given these precedents, it was no surprise that in 2004 the Court sustained a school voucher program subsidizing the decisions of parents to pull their children from underperforming public schools and enroll them in private schools, 96 percent of which were religious in orientation. (The case was *Zelman v. Simmons-Harris.*) In this case the money went to underwrite both religious and secular activities, but as long as the subsidy was the result of the free choice of the parents and the primary purpose was secular, Kennedy and O'Connor were satisfied.

As the *Boerne* case demonstrated, the Rehnquist Court believed that the Free Exercise Clause of the First Amendment required no religious exemption from the operation of neutral laws. Any such exemptions would have to be the result of democratic decisions to accommodate religious beliefs. At first consideration, this narrow reading of the Free Exercise Clause seemed inconsistent with conservatives' desire to accommodate religion. But observers pointed out that the consequence of the conservatives' decisions was to enhance the position of mainstream religious denominations. With their large followings they could secure legislation to subsidize religious institutions while securing exemptions from legislation that affected them adversely. It was religions with small numbers of adherents, especially those whose beliefs offended the majority, that would be unable to secure needed exemptions from general laws.

The Rehnquist Court and Defendants' Rights

In the area of defendants' rights, the Burger and early Rehnquist Courts had already created so many exceptions to the general principles enunciated by the Warren Court that the whole edifice seemed ready to crumble. In 1999 the Fourth Circuit Court of Appeals gave the Court the opportunity to strike the blow. Taking the view that the *Miranda* rules were merely a suggested procedure for making sure confessions were voluntary, the court of appeals held that they had been superseded by the long-ignored law Congress had passed in 1968 to counteract the decision. Given the opportunity to cast off the symbol of the Warren Court's revolution in the criminal law, the Rehnquist Court desisted. The parallel between the anti-*Miranda* law and recent efforts of Congress to counteract conservative Court decisions may have made the justices cautious. In *Dickerson v. United States* (2000) Rehnquist—once one of *Miranda*'s most trenchant critics—wrote the decision reaffirming *Miranda*'s vitality. Only Scalia and Thomas dissented.

Nonetheless, the Court remained supportive of the police and skeptical of claims that suspects had been denied constitutional rights. It continued to limit the circumstances in which criminal defendants could appeal convictions based on constitutional error. The justices made it especially hard to secure writs of *habeas corpus* to bypass appeals through the state judicial systems. Since the Supreme Court hears few appeals from state courts, restricting *habeas corpus* petitions had the effect of closing the only practical way to challenge state decisions. The Court was untroubled by a thirty-year sentence for stealing a bag of golf clubs, based on a state law mandating such sentences for habitual criminals, or a fifty-year sentence for stealing $150 worth of video equipment. In fact, some justices denied that the Eighth Amendment's ban on cruel and unusual punishment required any proportionality at all between crime and sentence.

The Court was cold to prison inmates' claims to freedom of speech and religious freedom. Reversing a Burger Court precedent, a five-justice majority denied inmates' rights to legal materials and excoriated lower federal courts for interfering with prison administrators. Encouraged by the Court's tirade, in 1996 Congress passed a new law severely limiting the circumstances in which federal prisoners could initiate litigation.

The justices continued to narrow the application of the Exclusionary Rule by broadening the situations in which warrantless or mistaken searches constituted "harmless error." It continued to reduce the circumstances in which people could claim the privacy that made search warrants necessary. It expanded the situations in which police were allowed to stop and search ordinary citizens. It limited the right to refuse to obey police instructions and widened the scope of what police could consider suspicious conduct. Such broad discretion left police virtually free to stop anyone on any number of pretexts. One consequence was allegations that police disproportionately singled out black men for stops and searches based on minor infractions. Scandals involving such "racial profiling" damaged the reputation of several police agencies.

The Rehnquist Court was so firmly identified with law-and-order skepticism about defendants' rights that it came as a surprise when the Court took a more liberal position on any major issue involving crime, as when it ruled that "evolving standards of decency" made executions of severely mentally retarded murderers unconstitutional under the Eighth Amendment. The Court followed that decision with one holding that similar evolving standards precluded imposing death sentences on adolescents younger than eighteen.

The federal courts also demolished key elements of the guidelines states and Congress have passed over the last two decades to toughen criminal sentences. In 2004 a federal judge revived the widespread criticism of the federal guidelines, ruling them unconstitutional for giving too much power to prosecutors. The harshness of the mandated penalties enabled them to force plea bargains on defendants, who were forced to plead guilty to lesser charges for fear of the drastic sentences judges would be required to impose if they were found guilty on greater ones. In a number of states, these laws required judges to impose harsh sentences after considering the nature of the crime and the record of the criminal; some states permitted judges to impose the death sentence if they found aggravating circumstances after a murder conviction. The Supreme Court overturned these procedures, ruling that the Sixth Amendment's requirement of jury trials precluded judges from imposing stiffer sentences based on facts not put before juries. The ruling put in doubt the constitutionality of the federal guidelines as a whole.

The Rehnquist Court and Property Rights

While the conservative majority of the Rehnquist Court generally cut back on judicial protection of civil liberties, it began to revive protection for property rights, although more cautiously than its decision in *Dolan v. City of Tigard* had portended. Out since the area of land-use regulations, the Court proved hesitant to accept the notion of a "regulatory taking"—the idea that the government ought to compensate owners when regulations diminish the value of their property. But the Court did gradually increase surveillance of government actions that affected real estate, especially the widespread practice of exacting some community benefit from developers in exchange for granting permits and licenses. The Court disappointed advocates of property rights, who hoped it would require broad compensation for environmental regulations, perhaps making them too expensive to enforce. Instead the Court elaborated complex rules that somewhat limited the governments' range of options. Conservatives were more likely than liberals on the Court to find that land-use restrictions constituted a "taking." Moreover, the Court suggested that landowners were entitled to jury trials, with juries deciding whether a contested regulation actually served a public purpose at all.

Paradoxically, arch-conservatives Scalia and Thomas objected when a mixed majority of liberals and conservatives held that excessive punitive damages in civil suits might violate the Takings Clause or amount to deprivation of property without due process of law. They objected to interfering with so traditional a power of juries.

Affirmative Action and Equal Protection

Few issues divided the conservative and liberal justices on the Rehnquist Court more decisively than the Court's approach to racial issues. In the view of the liberals, racism persisted, deeply embedded in American life and institutions, requiring continued judicial intervention and race-conscious remedies to combat it. In the view of conservatives, the door was largely open to members of racial minorities to take responsibility for their own lives. No one more clearly resented the stigma that racial preferences imposed on African Americans who did not need them than Justice Thomas.

The Court signaled the sea change in *Missouri v. Jenkins* (1995) in which it ruled that district courts must surrender jurisdiction over school districts once school officials had dismantled racially discriminatory systems, demonstrated their good faith, and established a situation similar to what would have existed had they not engaged in discriminatory behavior. The fact that schools remained segregated and underperforming did not matter. All over the country school districts petitioned for release from judicial oversight. Relieved judges agreed. The dissenters assailed the decision for its failure to recognize how deeply and persistently racial discrimination affected communities.

The Rehnquist Court, with Justice O'Connor writing the key opinions, insisted that the Fourteenth Amendment created a "color-blind Constitution," as the first Justice Harlan had advocated a century earlier. The right to be free of racial discrimination belonged to individuals not to groups, and thus to whites as much as to people of color. According to O'Connor, government could deviate from this principle only in the clearest cases of prior discrimination or for the most compelling of reasons. Rehnquist seemed to come around to her view, while the other members of the conservative majority seemed to believe that no circumstances whatsoever could justify violating it.

Few affirmative action programs could survive O'Connor's test. Nor could Justice Brennan's distinction between federal programs and state programs survive his departure from the bench. In *Adarand Constructors, Inc. v. Pena* (1995) the Court overturned Brennan's *Metro Broadcasting* decision sustaining federal minority-preference programs. Trying to encourage the development of minority-owned businesses, city and state governments all over the nation had established affirmative action programs like the federal government's. The Court's decision was a deathblow. Construction companies filed suits to block them everywhere. Local efforts to tailor affirmative action plans more carefully all failed, as district courts struck them down. Prospects for government-sponsored affirmative action in other areas were equally dire.

The conservative majority's commitment to a color-blind Constitution also doomed efforts to assure minority representation in government by consciously drawing election districts in which they made up the majority. In a series of cases beginning with *Shaw v. Reno* (1993) the Court recognized a new individual right to vote in a district that was not shaped primarily on the basis of race. Such districting, like any other government action that made racial classifications, could survive strict scrutiny only if it served a compelling state interest and was narrowly tailored to achieve it. Assuming that voters' color outweighed all other characteristics was the rankest sort of racial stereo-typing, the majority insisted. The justices warned that treating race as the most important aspect of people's identities would lead to the "balkanization" of American society. Therefore assuring minority representation in proportion to their numbers could never be a compelling state interest, especially if minor-ity representation meant representation by an official of the same color. No amount of statistical evidence that black officials could win election only in largely black districts, especially in the South, could shake the majority's convictions. The answer to that sad fact, if it were one, was to overcome voters' bigotry, not accommodate it by segregating voters into election districts by race.

Critics pointed out the overwhelming evidence that southern election dis-tricts had been racially gerrymandered in the past to reduce or eliminate African American's political influence. In other areas the Court had agreed that counter-ing past discrimination was a compelling state interest, but in these cases the

Court insisted that past bigotry could be addressed in other ways and therefore could not satisfy strict scrutiny.

However, on this issue the conservative bloc proved more fragile than the moderate-liberal one. Most African American voters were Democrats, and there was no constitutional inhibition against shaping election districts to secure partisan advantage. So how was one to know whether the predominant purpose for combining black voters into a single district was racial or partisan? The conservative justices tried to work up criteria upon which to base a determination, but none seemed very persuasive. O'Connor finally bolted, joining the moderate bloc in *Hunt v. Cromartie* (1999) to sustain a redistricting that created black majority districts as the consequence of permissible partisan gerrymandering rather than impermissible racial gerrymandering. To her former allies' dismay, she did so even though the district court had found race to be the predominant basis for the redistricting. To reject a lower court's finding of fact on a disputable question clearly signaled her concern that the Court was undermining the authority of the legislature. The decision meant that every case would turn on evidence presented to the trial court regarding politicians' motivations in districting, but astute trial judges would realize that as long as O'Connor remained on the Court, they could not ignore legislators' assurances that their motives were partisan rather than racial without risking an embarrassing reversal on appeal.

O'Connor's role as a crucial swing vote was manifest again when the Court considered affirmative action in higher education. Ever since the *Bakke* decision of 1976, colleges and universities had justified affirmative action programs as necessary to achieve their compelling interest in maintaining diverse student bodies. With the Rehnquist Court's increasing hard line against racial preferences, proponents of college affirmative action programs worried that their days were numbered. In 1996 the Third Circuit Court of Appeals held the University of Texas's program unconstitutional. District courts in California followed the third circuit precedent. The Supreme Court finally addressed the issue in 2003 and O'Connor again proved the decisive vote. Reconfirming Justice Powell's reasoning in *Bakke*, O'Connor's opinion in *Grutter v. Bollinger* sustained the University of Michigan Law School's affirmative action program. Colleges and universities had a compelling interest in maintaining a diverse student body. The law school's procedures were narrowly enough drawn to accomplish the goal without unduly burdening other applicants. They considered every applicant individually rather than simply giving an arbitrary number of points based on race; they eschewed quotas in favor of attempts to secure a "critical mass" of minority students. In a companion case she found the freshman admissions policy at the University of Michigan's College of Literature, Science, and the Arts wanting in this regard; it simply gave extra points to minority applicants. Only two of the liberal justices continued to argue that "benign discrimination" ought to be treated differently than hostile discrimination. While the decisions preserved affirmative action in educational institutions, it did not seem likely that the Court would consider promoting diversity a "compelling state interest" in any other context.

While the Court's affirmative-action decisions inhibited gender preferences as certainly as racial preferences, the justices remained sensitive to gender discrimination. Over Scalia's and Thomas's objections, the Court interpreted federal civil rights laws broadly to protect women from sexual harassment. It interpreted the concept to include not only actions that caused actual psychological damage but hostile work environments, and the justices held employers generally accountable for harassment of their employees. (The Court was much less willing to give a broad reading to the Americans with Disabilities Act, designed to protect handicapped Americans from discrimination, however.) Although the Court had held that laws making gender classifications were subject only to "intermediate" rather than "strict" scrutiny, the majority interpreted that scrutiny to require "exceedingly persuasive justification" of gender discriminations. In *United States v. Virginia* (1996) the Court held that the state's justifications for its 157-year tradition of limiting admission to the prestigious Virginia Military Academy failed that test.

Only Scalia dissented, in a cogent articulation of conservative constitutional values: "In my view the function of this Court is to *preserve* our society's values regarding (among other things) equal protection, not to *revise* them; to prevent backsliding from the degree of restriction the Constitution imposed upon democratic government, not to prescribe, on our own authority, progressively higher degrees." Court tests of constitutionality "cannot supersede—and indeed ought to be crafted *so as to reflect*—those constant and unbroken national traditions that embody the people's understanding of ambiguous constitutional texts."

Naturally, Scalia, this time joined by Rehnquist and Thomas, dissented even more trenchantly from the Court's decision in *Romer v. Evans* (1996), which struck down a voter-imposed amendment to Colorado's constitution that prohibited laws to protect homosexuals from discrimination. Such a "broad and undifferentiated disability" imposed on a single group failed even the simple rationality test required of classifications that were not suspect, the Court held. The point was simply to deny protection to a disfavored group, with no independent justification. Scalia's dissent reflected social conservatives' feeling that their ideas of morality were under siege. In an opinion notable for its resentment of "the elite class from which the Members of this institution are selected," he described the amendment as merely "a modest attempt . . . to preserve traditional sexual mores against the efforts of a politically powerful minority to revise those mores through the use of the law."

Scalia, Rehnquist, and Thomas were equally dismayed seven years later, when the Court overturned *Bowers v. Hardwick*, which had upheld laws against homosexual sex. In *Lawrence v. Texas*, the Court once again found no rational reason for the law other than enforcing a moral code. The Court conceded that the law reflected "profound and deep convictions accepted as ethical and moral principles" to which many "aspire and which thus determine the course of their lives." But the issue was "whether the majority may use the power of the State to enforce these views on the whole society through operation of the criminal law." The answer demonstrated the continuing hold of liberal constitutionalism. "Our obligation is to define the liberty of all, not to mandate our own moral code."

Scathingly, Scalia pointed out the inconsistency between the decision and *Planned Parenthood v. Casey*, in which Kennedy, Souter, and O'Connor had insisted on the need to uphold the principle of *stare decisis* against the political pressure to overturn the abortion-rights decision *Roe v. Wade*. In *Lawrence*, Scalia complained, the Court was reversing a decision that had been just as controversial, against which powerful groups had brought as much political pressure as right-to-lifers had brought against *Roe*. It was hard to argue with his observation that "state laws against bigamy, same-sex marriage, adult incest, prostitution, masturbation, adultery, fornication, bestiality, and obscenity are likewise sustainable only in light of *Bowers'* validation of laws based on moral choices. Every single one of these laws is called into question by today's decision."

The Rehnquist Court and Federalism

The most dramatic triumph of Rehnquist-Court conservative constitutionalism came in the area of federalism. Repudiating the nationalism that had dominated the Supreme Court and American life since the New Deal, the Rehnquist Court revitalized the principles of state rights. Marshall, Story, Webster, and Lincoln had identified the federal government as instrument of the whole people of the United States. In *U.S. Term Limits, Inc. v. Thornton* (1995), four of the conservative justices rejected that notion. "The people of the several states are the only true source of power," they insisted. "The Constitution simply does not recognize any mechanism for action by the undifferentiated people of the Nation."

Justice Kennedy rejected so extreme an articulation of state rights, joining the liberal bloc in a more traditional description of the Union. But in other cases involving federalism issues, he joined the conservatives, establishing a solid majority of justices adhering to state-rights doctrines. The conservative justices held that respect for state judiciaries limited the circumstances in which federal courts could grant writs of *habeas corpus* to criminal defendants who claimed their rights were being violated. They developed what they called the "anti-commandeering" principle. The principle of "dual sovereignty, . . . reflected in numerous constitutional provisions," meant that the federal government could not require state and local authorities to administer federal laws. The states were independent and sovereign entities and could not be turned into agencies of the United States.

In the 1997 case *Prinz v. United States* the Court overturned a federal requirement that sheriffs and other chief local law-enforcement officers undertake background checks of applicants for gun licenses. The United States had "two political capacities, one state and one federal, each protected from incursion by the other," the majority insisted. A requirement that state officials administer a federal regulatory scheme undermined the states as "independent and autonomous political entities." Thus the Court repudiated the nationalist doctrine of *Darby Lumber Company* that the Tenth Amendment stated but the "truism" that what was not delegated was reserved. The majority revived the pre–New Deal interpretation that the Amendment imposed state-rights limitations even on delegated powers.

At the same time, the Court circumscribed federal authority by narrowing the reach of the interstate commerce clause, under which Congress long had exercised a national police power over safety, health, and the environment. Since the New Deal, the Court had sustained a wide range of federal legislation as long as it could perceive some connection, often tenuous, between the regulation and interstate commerce. In 1990 Congress responded to what became a wave of school shootings with a law making it a crime to carry a firearm within a thousand feet of a school, claiming that the violence affected interstate commerce. In *U.S. v. Lopez* (1995) the Court ruled the law unconstitutional. Congress's authority over interstate commerce extended only to whatever "substantially" affected it. Congress had not demonstrated any such substantial effect on commerce, nor had it made a connection to interstate commerce part of the crime. (Congress quickly amended the law to limit prosecutions to those bearing a firearm that had "moved in or otherwise affects interstate or foreign commerce.")

The full implications became clear in 2000, when the Supreme Court overturned a provision of the Violence Against Women Act of 1984 that authorized the victim to sue the perpetrator in federal court. "Gender motivated crimes of violence are not, in any sense of the phrase, economic activity," the Court said in *United States v. Morrison*, and even though Congress had taken pains to document its effect on employment, production, and travel, the justices were not satisfied. Although they phrased their objection in terms of the reach of interstate commerce, it was clear that the justices' real concern was with maintaining a separate sphere of sovereign state authority. Upholding the law "would allow Congress to regulate any crime as long as the nationwide, aggregated impact of that crime has substantial effects on employment, production, transit, or consumption"—that is, the very "substantial" effect on interstate commerce that the Court had said was necessary to justify regulation. "The regulation and punishment of intrastate violence that is not directed at the instrumentalities, channels, or goods involved in interstate commerce has always been the province of the States," the Court said. "Indeed, we can think of no better example of the police power, which the Founders denied the National Government and reposed in the States, than the suppression of violent crime and vindication of its victims."

The *Boerne* case carried similar implications for congressional enforcement power under section 5 of the Fourteenth Amendment. Section 5 empowers Congress to enforce the Amendment by "appropriate legislation"—the gloss on the meaning of "necessary and proper" advocated by Hamilton, Marshall, and other proponents of broad national power. According to the nationalist rule, most famously articulated in *McCulloch v. Maryland*, legislation is "appropriate" when it is "plainly adapted" to achieving a constitutional end. But in *Boerne* the Court held that enforcement measures not only had to meet this criterion, they had to be congruent with and in proportion to the state action being remedied, and the justices reserved for themselves the decision as to whether Congress had gone too far. It was clear that the Court was imposing a restrictive standard of "congruence" and "proportionality" in order to protect states from the potentially far-reaching power that the Fourteenth Amendment delegated to Congress.

Authors of constitutional law casebooks queried whether the most potent congressional voting and civil rights legislation could survive scrutiny based on the rules the Court had specified in *Boerne*—for example, laws that supplemented state remedies for private discrimination with federal ones, that subjected states to private lawsuits over discrimination, or that required state and local governments with a history of discrimination to get advance federal approval for changes in election procedures and districting.

The Rehnquist Court's most aggressive and far-reaching defense of state rights limited the power of Congress to authorize private lawsuits against states and localities. Although the Eleventh Amendment simply bars citizens of one state or a foreign state from suing another state in the federal courts, in the 1890s the Supreme Court had interpreted it to mean that citizens could not sue their own state in federal court. The Court ameliorated this interpretation by allowing suits against state officers, and it had recognized the power of Congress to subject states to suits in order to enforce the Fourteenth and Fifteenth Amendments and to regulate interstate commerce. During the era of constitutional nationalism Congress had authorized private lawsuits against states as an alternative to administrative regulation.

The state-rights majority of the Rehnquist Court, however, saw such laws as affronts to state sovereignty. In *Seminole Tribe v. Florida* (1996) it overturned a key provision of the Indian Gaming Regulatory Act. The act had authorized tribes to bring suits in federal court to force states to negotiate agreements governing Native American gambling casinos. "Even when the Constitution vests in Congress complete law-making power over a particular area, the Eleventh Amendment prevents congressional authorization of suits by private parties against unconsenting States," the justices ruled, reversing a seven-year-old precedent to the contrary. In 1999 the Court ruled that state employees could not sue to secure withheld overtime pay under the Fair Labor Standards Act. "Congress has vast power," but it "may not treat these sovereign entities as prefectures or corporations," the Court insisted.

Only where the Constitution explicitly authorized Congress to enforce limits on state power, as in the Fourteenth and Fifteenth Amendments, could Congress breach sovereign immunity, the majority held, and even there it had to make its intention clear and explicit. But the justices soon made clear that the power of Congress to authorize lawsuits against state governments was severely restricted even when enforcing those Amendments. Congress's decision to abrogate state sovereign immunity to enforce Fourteenth Amendment rights had to meet the "congruence and proportionality" test specified in *Boerne v. City of Flores*, the Court ruled. Legislation permitting copyright-infringement lawsuits against state authorities failed to meet this test. So did laws authorizing victims to sue the states for age discrimination and for discriminating against people with disabilities, rejected in *Kimel v. Florida Board of Regents* (2000) and *Board of Trustees of the University of Alabama v. Garrett* (2002) respectively. Disregarding the evidence Congress had gathered to prove the pervasiveness and seriousness of the discriminations, the Court held the abrogation of the states' sovereign immunity from lawsuits too extreme a remedy. Only where laws combated the grossest and most pervasive cases of state abuse, such as racial and perhaps gender discrimination, would the majority of the justices sustain such an affront to the states.

The Rehnquist Court's sovereign-immunity jurisprudence threatened to eliminate the private lawsuit as a tool for enforcing federal mandates upon the states. It left victims of state action without a practical remedy, and it forced Americans to rely on generally overworked and underfunded federal administrative agencies to assure state compliance with federal laws. The trend reflected not only the Court's commitment to a state-rights conception of federalism but its distaste for using private lawsuits as a tool to effectuate public policy. For the same reason, the Court tightened the rules giving plaintiffs standing to bring cases, limited class-action suits, and sustained contracts substituting arbitration for legal remedies against arguments that they violated public policy and deprived people of rights without due process.

One might expect a commitment to state rights to lead the Court to defer to state policy judgments and court decisions, but only O'Connor seemed to fulfill that expectation. Both the liberal and the conservative justices tended to praise state autonomy when state decisions conformed to their ideological commitments and to override it when they did not.

The Court and the Administrative State

In light of conservative complaints about over-zealous and arbitrary bureaucrats, many observers expected the Rehnquist Court to enforce more stringently the principle that Congress cannot delegate its legislative powers to the Executive branch, and especially to administrative agencies. The chief justice had indicated his sympathies lay in this direction in dissents from Burger Court decisions that had upheld broad delegations of rule-making authority. Conservatives were excited by the grounds on which the trendsetting conservative D.C. Court of Appeals overturned the Environmental Protection Agency's claim of broad freedom to set pollution standards. If Congress had intended to give the agency such broad discretion, the judges said, the law doing so would have constituted a forbidden delegation of legislative power. If the Supreme Court affirmed the decision, it would signal a new era of judicial review of congressional delegations of authority to administrative agencies. But in *Whitman v. American Trucking Association* (2001) the Court unanimously reversed the decision. The Court maintained its post–New Deal record of never having overturned a congressional delegation of power as overly broad.

In a public talk a few years' earlier, Scalia, who authored the Court's opinion, probably explained why. "Broad delegation to the Executive is the hallmark of the modern administrative state," he said. "Agency rulemaking powers are the rule rather than, as they once were, the exception." For the conservative justices, traditionally sympathetic to the broad exercise of executive power, administrative agencies—especially when guided by executive orders issued by conservative presidents—may well have been preferable to reliance on Congress, whose conservative majorities were tenuous and subject to direct political pressure.

However, the long tradition of judicial deference to administrative expertise began to fray. The Court began to protect the free-speech rights of business against administrative regulations, and lower federal courts energetically followed suit. The Court stressed that it did not owe deference to agencies' interpretations of their own power. In 2000, for example, the Court dismayed health reformers by rejecting the Food and Drug Administration's claim that Congress had authorized it to regulate tobacco products. Observers wondered whether the overwhelmingly conservative judges in the lower federal courts would take this as a signal for more aggressive review of bureaucratic claims of authority.

The Court constrained both presidential and congressional power in 1998 when it ruled that the line-item veto measure Congress had passed in 1996 was unconstitutional. The Court held that the Constitution's mode of presenting legislation for the president's signature precluded alternatives. But its most stinging blow to the presidency came when it rejected President Clinton's appeal to delay the lawsuit Paula Jones brought against him alleging sexual harassment and sexual imposition while he was governor of Arkansas. Lawsuits alleging private misconduct would distract a president from the business of government; such suits could be trumped up to harass any president and disrupt any administration, he warned. But in *Clinton v. Jones* (1997) the Court unanimously rejected Clinton's argument. The justices were naively confident that the Jones case would take little of the president's personal time and attention.

Contempt of Congress and the Disputed 2000 Presidential Election

As the Court acted ever more boldly to put its stamp on constitutional interpretation, it seemed to exercise less restraint in dealing with the other branches of government, especially Congress. In *Boerne v. Flores* the court had circumscribed Congress's power to enforce the Fourteenth Amendment. The fifth section of the Fourteenth Amendment, which authorizes Congress to enforce its provisions, gives it only the power to enforce the Amendment as interpreted by the Court, the justices insisted. The Religious Freedom Restoration Act went beyond that authority. Although they disagreed about the specific case, liberal and conservative justices alike opined that the Supreme Court has preemptive authority to decide the authoritative meaning of provisions of the Constitution—an authority so complete that it excludes all other alternatives and binds the other branches of government.

Many critics blasted the Court's reasoning. The Court *had* recognized freedom of conscience to be a fundamental American liberty. The Religious Freedom Restoration Act had merely specified the general circumstances in which that liberty must give way to governmental necessities, reinstituting the rule the Court itself had originally established. But the justices disagreed. Not only did the law redefine religious liberty itself, they insisted, but even if it were merely an enforcement measure, it was disproportional to the problem it was designed to solve. In effect, the Court was claiming the power not only to define constitutional rights but to second-guess the decisions of Congress about how to enforce them, despite the Fourteenth Amendment's explicit delegation of that authority. It is inconceivable that Reconstruction-Era Republicans intended such a result. Observers noted that the Court's majority no longer appeared to treat Congress as a co-equal branch of government. The Court insisted that Congress demonstrate in its deliberations that subjects of its regulations were "substantially" related to interstate commerce. It demanded evidence that laws enforcing the Fourteenth Amendment were "congruent" and "proportional" to the state deprivation of rights they were designed to remedy. Applying this test to laws passed years and even decades before the Court had articulated this requirement, the justices of course found the record wanting. When Congress did supply such a record, the Court second-guessed whether the evidence was sufficient, giving Congress less deference than it did mere administrative agencies or the factual records developed by lower courts.

When Congress reached policy decisions of which the majority approved, however, such as extending the terms of copyrights in materials about to pass into the public domain, the Court stressed the broad discretion the Constitution gave Congress. The contrast with the Court's treatment of Congress when its policies collided with the majority's constitutional values made the Court's arrogance all the more apparent.

Nowhere did the Court make its contempt of Congress clearer than in its course in the disputed presidential election of 2000. Counting the electoral vote was a preeminent example of what were called "political questions"—constitutional issues that the courts declined to decide because the Constitution had assigned their resolution to other branches. These had included matters such as the recognition of rival claimants to state government authority, the right of representatives to their seats in Congress, issues surrounding the impeachment of federal officials, and controversies over election districting and the apportionment of state legislatures.

But the Supreme Court had been claiming an ever more predominant role in the settlement of constitutional issues. During the high point of liberal constitutionalism, the Warren Court had curtailed the "political question doctrine," intervening in apportionment and districting cases and going so far as to overturn a decision by the House of Representatives over who was entitled to a seat, despite the provision of the Constitution declaring that "Each House shall be the Judge of the Elections, Returns, and Qualifications of its own Members." Nonetheless, some constitutional issues apparently remained "political questions" left to others to decide. For example, no one seriously suggested going to court to stop the Clinton impeachment or that Clinton could appeal a conviction to the Supreme Court.

The Rehnquist Court had taken the Supreme Court's claim to be the guardian of the American Constitution to new heights, acting as if it and it alone was the final arbiter of the constitutional system. Almost nothing seemed beyond its purview. Most Americans hoped that the Supreme Court might settle the disputed election in a nonpartisan application of the law. Bush's lawyers had appealed to it to stop the Florida supreme court from ordering a recount; Gore and Democratic leaders openly declared they would abide by any decision. While the justices would split badly over issues, the original decision to intervene was unanimous. No justice, liberal or conservative, suggested that the "political question" doctrine precluded jurisdiction. Normally, federal judges conceded that it was up to a state's judiciary to interpret state laws. Nonetheless, the Supreme Court, in an unprecedented exercise of federal judicial power, intervened to stop the recount and in effect decided who would be president of the United States.

The justices divided bitterly on the merits, with the five conservative justices stopping the recount on the grounds that the Florida supreme court's approach violated the Equal Protection Clause of the Fourteenth Amendment, and the four liberal justices dissenting.* It was just the kind of apparently partisan result that most people had hoped the Court would avoid. Nonetheless, most Americans acquiesced in the result, anxious to end the dispute and fearful of a crisis if events continued in the direction they seemed to be headed. Vice President Gore imme-

---

*The Court ruled that by failing to establish a standard to govern the recount any more specific than the statute's direction to determine the "intent of the voter," the Florida supreme court had violated the Equal Protection Clause of the Fourteenth Amendment. So vague a standard permitted different county election boards to apply different standards, denying the uniformity that equal protection of the voters required; those whose votes were disregarded by boards applying stricter standards would suffer in comparison to those whose votes were counted under looser standards.

The decision was inconsistent with the hitherto unquestioned practices of virtually every state in the nation. It ignored the fact that there had been a wide disparity in how ballots were cast in Florida in the first place. The decision made sense, however, if the majority of the justices, like most Republicans, believed that the Florida supreme court was intentionally trying to cheat Bush out of the election. Cheating, of course, would constitute a flagrant denial of equal protection, and the language of several of the justices indicated that this was precisely what they thought. But deciding the case on such an assumption violated all the rules of mutual respect between state and federal courts.

diately announced that he accepted the decision and conceded the election. Nothing could better illustrate the dominance the Supreme Court had acquired over the American constitutional system.

What troubled critics most about the Supreme Court's decision was that it seemed inconsistent with much of the judicial philosophy of the justices who made it. It was a bold exercise of judicial power on the part of justices who generally advocated restraint. It was a decision patently inconsistent with the original intent of the framers of the Constitution and the federal law governing the electoral count on the part of justices who claimed that original intent was of prime importance. It was a dramatic assertion of federal power on the part of justices committed to state rights. Justices who were generally unsympathetic to claims based on the Equal Protection Clause relied on it in circumstances in which it had never been applied. Most damning, in the critics' view, was the Court's explicit statement limiting the application of the clause to the specific circumstances, so that the case would not be a precedent for challenging other aspects of the voting process on equal protection grounds. The Court seemed to mandate equal protection for Bush voters and no one else.

Hardly an observer defended the Court's reasoning in *Bush v. Gore*. Many denounced it as damaging to the Court and a perversion of the rule of law. Those who defended it did so primarily on the ground that the Court had to step in to resolve a developing constitutional crisis. That justification raised the question about whether Americans still regarded the rule of law, essential to constitutionalism, to be their most fundamental value.

TIMELINE

1993	*Shaw v. Reno* begins a series of cases overturning "racial gerrymandering" of election districts.
1995	*Missouri v. Jenkins* establishes rules encouraging the release of once discriminatory school districts from judicial supervision.
	Adarand Constructors, Inc. v. Pena rules federal minority-preference programs unconstitutional.
1996	The Supreme Court limits the power of the federal government to breach states' sovereign immunity from lawsuits in *Seminole Tribe v. Florida*.
	Romer v. Evans overturns an amendment to the Colorado state constitution that forbids laws to protect homosexuals from discrimination.
	In *United States v. Virginia* the Supreme Court forces Virginia Military Institute to accept women applicants.

1997	The Supreme Court refuses to recognize a presidential immunity from lawsuits alleging private misconduct in *Clinton v. Jones*.
	The Supreme Court overturns the Religious Freedom Restoration Act in *City of Boerne v. Flores*.
	Printz v. United States overturns a provision of the federal gun control law on the grounds that it unconstitutionally "commandeers" state officers to administer federal laws.
1999	In *Hunt v. Cromartie* the Supreme Court says election districts drawn to secure partisan majorities are constitutional even if they result in racially homogeneous districts.
2000	*Kimel v. Florida Board of Regents* rules that provisions of the Age Discrimination Act authorizing victims to file suits against states and localities unconstitutionally abrogate states' sovereign immunity. In the following year, the Court overturns similar provisions of the Americans with Disabilities Act.
	United States v. Morrison says the Violence Against Women Act exceeds the powers of Congress to regulate interstate commerce.
	The Supreme Court upholds laws limiting the right of protesters to picket outside abortion clinics in *Hill v. Colorado*.
	The Supreme Court stops the recount of the presidential vote in Florida in *Bush v. Gore*, in effect deciding the disputed 2000 presidential election.
2002	The Supreme Court rules school voucher programs constitutional in *Zelman v. Simmons-Harris*.
2003	*Grutter v. Bollinger* upholds affirmative action programs to promote racial diversity among college students.
	Lawrence v. Texas overturns *Bowers v. Hardwick*, ruling unconstitutional laws criminalizing homosexual relations in private between consenting adults.
2004	The Supreme Court upholds the McCain-Feingold campaign reform act against a challenge based on the free-speech provision of the First Amendment (*McConnell v. Federal Elections Commission*).

FURTHER READING

Influential constitutional analyst Kathleen M. Sullivan suggests factors that have constrained the ability of the Rehnquist Court to impose conservative constitutionalism consistently across constitutional law in "The Jurisprudence of the Rehnquist Court," *Nova Law Review* 22 (Spring 1998): 743–761. Like Sullivan, Linda Greenhouse, the chief Supreme Court correspondent of the *New York Times*, stresses different jurisprudential styles among the justices in "Between Certainty & Doubt: States of Mind on the Supreme Court Today," *Green Bag* 6 (2d series) (Spring 2003): 241–252. Cass R. Sunstein praises

Justice O'Connor's case-by-case approach to decision making in *One Case at a Time* (1999), which criticizes the justices who favor more sweeping judgments. Justice Scalia favors clear rules in his essay "The Rule of Law as a Law of Rules," *University of Chicago Law Review* 56 (Fall 1989): 1175–1188.

For the Rehnquist Court generally, see Tinsley Yarbrough's *The Rehnquist Court and the Constitution* (2000) and the essays in Herman Schwartz (ed.), *The Rehnquist Court* (2002). *Rehnquist Justice* (2003), edited by Earl M. Maltz, discusses the jurisprudence of each of the justices of the later Rehnquist Court. In *Morality Imposed* (2000) Stephen E. Gottlieb attributes the course of the Rehnquist Court to the desire of its conservatives to sustain an intolerant traditional moral order.

Amy E. Black, Douglas L. Koopman, and David K. Ryden discuss the constitutional issues and litigation over school vouchers and other programs that permit faith-based oganizations to receive public funding in chapter 6 of *Of Little Faith* (2004). For the Rehnquist Court's affirmative-action and redistricting decisions and the political and legal maneuvering that led up to them, see Samuel Leiter and William M. Leiter, *Affirmative Action in Antidiscrimination Law and Policy* (2002), and Tinsley E. Yarbrough, *Race and Redistricting* (2002). Historians Stephan and Abigail Thernstrom have written prolifically and polemically criticizing racial preferences, providing good historical background. See their *America in Black and White* (1997) and Abigail Thernstrom's *Whose Votes Count?* (1987). J. Morgan Kousser responds to the Thernstroms's argument against race-conscious redistricting in *Colorblind Injustice* (1999), which also provides a thorough historical context.

Alfred M. Olivetti Jr. and Jeff Worsham devote a chapter to the Supreme Court and property rights in *This Land Is Your Land, This Land Is My Land* (2003). Michael S. Greve concludes in *The Demise of Environmentalism in American Law* (1996) that the courts now treat environmentalism as incompatible with common-law property rights. His conclusion seems exaggerated at the moment, but his work raises interesting questions about the relationship between the two sets of values.

A good deal has been written about the Rehnquist Court's devotion to "federalism." Mark Killenbeck describes clearly what is at stake in his essay "Revolution or Retreat?" in *The Tenth Amendment and State Sovereignty*, ed. Mark R. Killenbeck (2002). Deeply critical is Judge John T. Noonan Jr. in *Narrowing the Nation's Power* (2002). Compare Marci A. Hamilton's "Nine Shibboleths of the New Federalism," *Wayne Law Review* 47 (Fall 2001): 931–943. Daniel A. Farber offers a sensitive analysis of the Supreme Court's federalism in "Pledging a New Allegiance: An Essay on Sovereignty and the New Federalism," *Notre Dame Law Review* 75 (March 2000): 1133–1144.

For the Court's increasing condescension towards Congress, see Ruth Colker and James J. Brudney, "Dissing Congress," *Michigan Law Review* 100 (October 2001): 80–144.

Bush v. Gore has been widely analyzed by legal academics in books and articles. Nearly all, including those generally sympathetic with conservative constitutionalism, have found the decision unprincipled. For the best defense of *Bush v. Gore*, see *Breaking the Deadlock* (2001) by the eminent conservative jurist Richard A. Posner, which is full of interesting insights and information. The influential, outspokenly liberal constitutional scholar Bruce Ackerman secured essays from a number of highly regarded American legal scholars, of whom only President Reagan's solicitor general defended the decision. They are published in *Bush v. Gore* (2002). The best investigation of the role of partisanship in the decision is Howard Gillman, *The Votes That Counted* (2001).

22

American Constitutionalism in a Changing World

The elections of 2000 confirmed the dominance of conservative constitutionalism not only because the Republican candidate, George W. Bush, succeeded Bill Clinton as president but also because his opponents did not dare to advocate the sorts of broad government programs associated with liberalism. Instead it appeared that the conflict between rival views of American constitutionalism would be over the role of religious institutions and values in public life—how far popular majorities could go in giving their moral convictions the force of law.

Eight months after President Bush's disputed ascendance to the presidency, on September 11, 2001, the United States suffered the first enemy attack on its soil since Japan's attack on Pearl Harbor. Seizing control of civilian airliners, terrorists affiliated with an anti-Western Islamic organization called Al-Qaeda crashed into the twin towers of the World Trade Center in New York City and the Pentagon headquarters of the United States armed forces in Washington. Had courageous passengers not sacrificed their lives to force down a fourth airliner, it likely would have devastated either the Capitol building or the White House.

The prospect of further terrorist attacks raised the question of whether a compelling public interest in security justifies actions that Americans and their courts might not have tolerated before the disasters. The very openness of American society made it more difficult to counter terrorism, and it was understandable to ask whether some interpretations of liberty were no longer appropriate. Since conservative constitutionalism traditionally justified restrictions on civil liberties in the name of national security, the events of September 11 added to its attraction. One manifestation was the widespread support for the so-called USA Patriot Act, which significantly expanded the power of government to engage in domestic intelligence and eliminated barriers between surveillance for national security purposes and for criminal prosecution. The actions of the Bush administration raised the question of how far Americans and the Supreme Court, which now claimed a near-monopoly over defining what the Constitution meant, would go in reconsidering the boundaries of constitutional liberty.

420

In response to the attacks, the administration declared a "war on terrorism." Presidential power always increases in wartime, and President Bush claimed broad authority to act on behalf of national security. The attacks led the United States to invade Afghanistan, whose leaders had provided a haven for Al-Qaeda. The Bush administration also cited the September 11 attack as justification for a second invasion of Iraq. But the process by which America went to war raised serious questions about the balance of power between president and Congress. Moreover, the administration's assertion of a unilateral right to engage in pre-emptive military actions, its treatment of prisoners, and its antipathy to collective international action to deal with global problems raised concerns among critics about America's fidelity to international law and its commitment to the rule of law generally.

A deeply divided electorate confirmed the conservative direction of American constitutionalism by reelecting President Bush in 2004 despite harsh attacks on his competence and bitter criticism of the principles he embodied.

The George W. Bush Administration and Conservative Constitutionalism

The commitments of the second President Bush assured continued conflict over fundamentals of American constitutionalism. Making his personal faith a central element of his political appeal, the president firmly supported initiatives that reflected his belief that the First Amendment permits the government to recognize the central place religion plays in American life. Failing to persuade Congress to eliminate rules that precluded faith-based organizations from receiving government grants for social programs, he effected much of the change through an executive order. The administration backed constitutional amendments to reintroduce prayer into the public schools; campaigned for vouchers to subsidize private education, including at religious schools; and provided financial support for religiously oriented programs to combat social ills. Reelected after a hardfought, close campaign in 2004, it was certain that the president would continue to throw the legal weight of his administration behind efforts to repudiate the notion of a wall between church and state.

The Bush administration also made a point of championing the moral values advocated by social conservatives and the Religious Right. It backed further limitations on abortions and a constitutional amendment to define marriage as the union of a man and a woman, limiting the ability of government to offer gay couples the legal benefits they give to married heterosexuals. After the Massachusetts supreme court ruled gays entitled to marry under the state constitution, the president made defense of traditional marriage a key element of his reelection campaign. Conservatives put referenda banning gay marriages on the ballot in eleven states. Pointing to the tradition of liberal religious activism dating back to the

Civil Rights era, Bush's political advisors urged conservative religious leaders to encourage their followers to support the Republican party as the agent of moral reform. A significant number responded, creating "moral action teams," publishing political newsletters, and sponsoring voter-registration drives among congregants. In the election of 2004 fundamentalist Christians voted in record numbers, passing the anti–gay marriage proposals in every state where they were on the ballot and taking credit for the Republican victory. Leaders of the Religious Right prepared to use their political muscle to secure moral legislation in the states as well as to pressure federal officials. Many critics worried that encouraging religious institutions to take such a direct role in politics would erode separation of church and state.

Another major presidential initiative was "tort reform," which the administration hoped would reduce the cost of health care and unshackle entrepreneurial energy. This program had two main thrusts—to shield businesses and professionals from what they believed was unreasonable liability for trumped-up injuries, and to substitute arbitration for lawsuits to settle disputes. Frustrated in his first term, President Bush pledged to make tort reform a priority of his second. Such proposals raised questions not only about the meaning of due process of law but also about government's obligation to protect the public, because in the absence of governmental regulation, the main constraint on corporate and professional behavior had become civil liability for actions that put the public at risk.

During the campaign of 2004 the president made a point of promising to reform social security by enabling American workers to invest a portion of the money that they would otherwise pay into the system. After his reelection he promised to make this proposal his top priority. If he were to succeed, nothing would better illustrate the triumph of conservatism, with its stress on individual responsibility, over liberalism's ideal of shared responsibility for the general welfare.

The President, Congress, and Control of the Administrative State

In pressing their political program, President Bush and his advisors consistently worked to expand the power and influence of the executive department. One element in the effort was a dramatically broader claim to confidentiality. The administration defied the efforts of the nonpartisan General Accounting Office (GAO), Congress's key investigatory agency, to obtain the names of business people and lobbyists who helped to devise the administration's energy policy. The GAO decided not to appeal when a federal district court dismissed its suit to obtain the names, acquiescing in a major limitation on its power to investigate executive actions on behalf of Congress. Environmental groups were no more successful. The Supreme Court backed the administration, stressing the president's special need for confidentiality. The outcome of all this maneuvering has been to enhance the president's ability to withhold information about executive branch deliberations from public scrutiny and to set the stage for further claims of confidentiality.

President Bush also issued a new executive order vastly increasing presidential authority over the distribution of presidential papers in apparent contravention of the Presidential Records Act of 1978. The result is to seriously inhibit the work of journalists and historians. But even more important, the broad grounds upon which President Bush claimed the right to confidentiality implied that all congressional efforts to open executive communications to scrutiny would meet the same objections. Similarly, the administration denied Congress's authority to demand any documents relating to federal prosecutions, even with regard to closed cases. Both Republican and Democratic members protested vigorously, and the administration voluntarily made a number of documents available. But it did not abandon its legal position.

As part of its campaign to maintain the confidentiality of deliberations in the executive branch, the Bush administration fought against the creation of a commission to investigate the effectiveness of government antiterrorist activities prior to the September 11 attacks. It refused to provide internal documents to congressional committees looking into executive decisions that led to the Iraq War. As Congress worked to turn the new Homeland Security Administration into a full-fledged executive department, the president invoked executive privilege to withhold information and forbid testimony from its director. The administration stonewalled requests from civil liberties advocacy groups for documents relating to the detention and abuse of war prisoners, and refused to provide the names of people held in connection with antiterrorist investigations.

The government also classified a much broader range of material as secret, thus limiting access to it under the Freedom of Information Act (FOIA). Moreover, it assigned only limited funds to pay for declassification and for responses to FOIA inquiries, creating a substantial backlog that substantially delayed the release of information

Trying to take advantage of Republican control of the legislative branch and the crisis atmosphere following September 11, the Bush administration also sought to persuade Congress to give it much more discretion over the allocation of spending. In both the Patriot Act and in the proposed budget for operations in Iraq, the administration asked for a virtually free hand in shifting allocated funds from one area to another. In both cases, the Senate refused to surrender Congress's control of the public purse, giving the president only limited flexibility.

Facing stiff resistance to his political initiatives in the closely contested Congress, Bush continued the trend towards an "administrative presidency," trying to effect changes in energy, environmental, and other policies by appointing loyal partisans to key positions in the executive departments and directing executive orders to administrative agencies. The president quickly reversed prior presidential directives regarding environmental protection, conservation, abortion and birth control, and other areas of public policy. He just as quickly issued his own order instructing executive departments and agencies to promote energy and resource development and to consult local governments and property owners before promulgating regulations affecting property rights. Moving forcefully to exert executive control over administrative agencies, in only two years the administration's Office of Information and Regulatory Affairs sent back over twenty regulations for reconsideration; it had returned only nine during the whole eight years of the Clinton administration.

While the president worked to expand executive influence through political appointments and executive directives, Congress exercised influence through controls on spending and by specifying goals and procedures in statutes. Administrative agencies worked closely with Congress on spending and budgetary issues. Even though Congress generally appropriated money in lump sums, agencies adhered carefully to the preferences Congress expressed in accompanying reports. At the same time, post-Watergate congressional legislation continued to limit the president's power to impound or shift spending.

The Supreme Court seemed likely to play an important role in looming conflicts between president and Congress over influence in the administrative state. Although the *Chadha* case had eliminated the power of Congress to overturn regulations through one-house legislative vetoes, it generally required agencies to fulfill congressional intent expressed in statutes, even if the agency had to disregard presidential directives to do so. But a pro-executive Supreme Court could change constitutional directions, and it certainly could interpret statutes in a way that would harmonize more with presidential preferences.

With a Supreme Court already strongly tending towards conservative constitutional doctrines, future appointments could have great significance. Social and religious conservatives expected President Bush to nominate justices who would sustain the constitutionality of laws reflecting their moral values. Business interests likewise looked for nominees who would sustain administrative decisions that limited the impact of environmental, consumer-information, product safety, antimonopoly, and employment laws. Property rights advocates looked for nominees that agreed with their broad notions of what constituted "takings."

Concern about conservative Supreme Court nominees likewise motivated a good deal of the support that civil liberties groups, environmentalists, and women's-rights organizations gave the president's Democratic opponents. With the stakes so high, Democrats began to filibuster* judicial appointments. Although they too had used Senate rules to prevent the confirmation of unacceptable judges, Republicans insisted that engaging in filibusters to do so went too far. They argued that unless it specified otherwise, the Constitution required the Senate to give "advice and consent" to presidential actions by simple majority votes. They warned that if Democrats persisted in their course, they would ask the vice president, as presiding officer of the Senate, to rule a filibuster out of order and then sustain his

---

*Senate rules permit individual senators to speak as long as they can hold the floor unless a supermajority, presently sixty senators, vote to close debate. This rule enables even a single senator to "filibuster" legislation in an effort to prevent its passage. In recent times a mere announcement of an intent to filibuster has triggered the requirement of sixty votes to go forward.

ruling by a majority vote. Justice O'Connor's resignation in 2005 and Rehnquist's illness raised the stakes. Democrats threatened to respond by bringing the Senate to a standstill. Nothing more dramatically illustrated the collapse of comity between the parties and the stress it was placing on the constitutional system.

The President, Congress, and the "War on Terror"

Americans' response to the terrorist attacks of September 11 again illustrated the ambiguity over presidential authority to commit the United States to war. Congress continued to claim final authority and to insist that the process conformed to the War Powers Act. The president continued to insist that he was not obligated to obey the act and had not done so.

As a practical matter, the ability of a president to shape public opinion in a time of crisis again seemed to render Congress powerless to resist. Within days of the September 11 attack Congress passed a resolution authorizing the president to use whatever force he thought appropriate against any nation, organization, or person that he concluded had aided it. Although he denied that he needed the resolution to act, like his predecessors President Bush voluntarily conformed more or less to the War Powers Act's requirements when he authorized the invasion of Afghanistan.

However, Bush was also intent on overthrowing the regime of Iraqi dictator Saddam Hussein. He claimed that American intelligence information indicated that Iraq was developing nuclear, chemical, and biological weapons of mass destruction. These weapons posed an "imminent" threat, the president insisted. By "imminent," the administration did not mean immediate in time, however, but something more like clear and likely in the future. Presented with such a danger, the president argued, the United States had a unilateral right to launch a preemptive war. At the same time, he justified the use of the American military as measures to enforce existing United Nations resolutions aimed at forcing Iraq to readmit UN weapons inspectors he had expelled. After Saddam grudgingly let the inspectors back in, however, the UN Security Council refused to pass a new resolution authorizing the use of force until they had a chance to report.

Many Americans, UN officials, and observers around the world warned that an American attack on Iraq in these circumstances would violate international law. The Security Council had rejected the American resolution authorizing force. Moreover, in the years before their expulsion, the weapons inspectors had found no evidence that the Iraqis were continuing to develop weapons of mass destruction. But the United States determined to push ahead despite these concerns. No outside authority ought to be able to dictate how it responded to threats to its national security, Bush insisted. Most Americans appeared to agree, although dissenters pointed out that if every nation took the same position, it would mean an end to the concept of collective security and perhaps even to the international rule of law.

Although President Bush denied that he was required to secure the consent of Congress to commit American forces to battle, like presidents before him he finally decided to seek a congressional resolution of support. Although many congress people expressed strong reservations about the administration's evidence and aggressiveness, hardly any challenged the legality of a pre-emptive war. In October 2002 both Houses of Congress authorized the president to use the armed forces "as he determines necessary" to protect the United States against the Iraqi threat. In effect Congress turned responsibility for declaring war over to the president, much as it had when it passed the Tonkin Gulf resolution during the Vietnam War era. Despite the failure to secure broad international support, in March 2003 the United States launched its preemptive attack.

President Bush's unilateralism reflected his administration's pervasive suspicion of multilateral agreements designed to establish and enforce international law. The administration ended American support for treaties to protect the environment, control the exploitation of resources, fight arms trafficking, limit biological weapons, and halt nuclear testing. Bush withdrew President Clinton's signature from the treaty establishing an International Criminal Court, refusing to allow an international body to exercise authority over the actions of American military forces and civilian peacekeepers. The administration's legal advisors prepared arguments that a number of doctrines of international law, including provisions of the Geneva Convention forbidding torture, no longer were appropriate in a world fighting terror.

The Bush administration challenged conventional notions of international law in other ways as well. It developed a new category of "unlawful enemy combatant" to describe suspected terrorists seized in Afghanistan or elsewhere, applying the designation to Al-Qaeda and Afghan fighters who had been captured on the battlefield. (President Bush later limited the designation to Al-Qaeda fighters.) Even an American citizen arrested in the United States could be classified an "unlawful enemy combatant" if he were engaged in terrorism. The government held that "unlawful enemy combatants" were not entitled to the protections of the 1949 Geneva Convention Relating to the Treatment of Prisoners of War. Unlike prisoners of war, who had to be released when hostilities ceased, unlawful enemy combatants could be tried and sentenced to prison by military commissions. Traditional American rules of evidence did not pertain in such cases, the administration argued, and there was no right to appeal to civilian courts.

As of 2005, the administration had held over five hundred enemy combatants for more than two years at the American base at Guantanamo Bay, Cuba, and in other foreign locations, where it claimed that American constitutional protections did not apply. It rejected the complaints of the Red Cross about the conditions under which the prisoners were held. Administration officials ignored protests from FBI and CIA agents about the severe and possibly brutal interrogations to which prisoners were subjected. The government indicated that some detainees would be tried by military commissions while others would be released when they no longer presented a risk and had no further value as potential sources of information.

Keeping identities and locations secret, the administration was generally able to prevent civil-rights lawyers from acting on behalf of detainees to challenge its actions. Finally, the father of an American citizen detained in Afghanistan petitioned for a writ of *habeas corpus* on his son's behalf. The government insisted that the courts must accept its unsupported statement that he was an enemy combatant. Rejecting that position, the Supreme Court ruled in 2004 that American citizens have the right to challenge such an assertion before a "neutral decisionmaker." But it conceded that the proceeding could be shaped so as not to burden the government inordinately in a time of military conflict, and it agreed that if the allegation were sustained, citizens could be held as long as hostilities continued. Moreover, it was doubtful that the right to challenge one's designation as an enemy combatant applied to non-citizens. In response to the decision, the government established a procedure for all prisoners to convince army officers that they were being held by mistake, denying any right to appeal an adverse decision and claiming that this process should meet the Court's concerns. To many critics the government's claims seemed extreme and dangerously corrosive of American values and international law.

Events seemed to justify their concern: Scandals over sadistic mistreatment of prisoners in Iraq shocked Americans and damaged the nation's reputation around the world, with news reports indicating that similar abuses had occurred in Afghanistan and at the prison at Guantanamo Bay. While cabinet officers took formal responsibility for actions they claimed to know nothing about, no American policymaker was held accountable.

Although it put forward legal arguments defending its positions, the administration's course as a whole raised questions about whether Americans would maintain their commitment to the rule of law under the pressure of the terrorist threat. By 2005, federal judges were beginning to deny the administration's arguments, but it was unclear whether appellate courts would sustain their decisions or whether the administration would acquiesce if they did.

Relying on recent federal laws and Supreme Court precedents that vested the government with broad discretion to fight illegal immigration, the Bush administration treated aliens dramatically different than citizens in the "war on terror." Urging people to refrain from retaliating upon Muslim and Arab Americans, the government was far less concerned about the rights of Muslim and Arab aliens. The government held people suspected of possible terrorist connections incommunicado for weeks and months, not even notifying immediate families of their whereabouts. Just as with "unlawful enemy combatants," evidence of widespread physical abuse has emerged, encouraged, critics worried, by a sense that the government condoned it.

A Surveillance State?

The treatment of aliens after the September 11 attacks portended a growing acceptance of intrusive security measures and surveillance in the United States. A "surveillance state," in which the government keeps a close watch on visitors and citizens, is not incompatible with freedom. While every authoritarian state is a surveillance state, closely monitoring its citizens to prevent political opposition, not every surveillance state is authoritarian. Because the Irish Republican Army for a time presented a grave risk of terrorism, security cameras are everywhere in Great Britain, for example. Citizens of Japan tolerate pervasive surveillance. Although some Japanese complain about invasions of privacy, Japan is nonetheless a free and democratic country.

After the September 11, airports instituted pervasive inspection of travelers, with similar measures to be extended to other forms of transportation. The government mandated background checks of transportation personnel; checking ongoing activities seemed a natural next step. Security personnel stopped and questioned suspicious persons; in the circumstances a degree of "ethnic profiling"—considering Middle Eastern features and names as one of the factors triggering suspicion—seemed inevitable. Such security measures spread to public buildings as well. Airlines, telephone companies, and other businesses were quick to turn over information about customers when requested by government officials.

THE CHRISTIAN SCIENCE MONITOR

Can Americans have both privacy and security?

These were blanket precautions not linked to specific threats other than vague color-coded alerts. Fear of terrorism was pervasive. Even rural areas and small towns considered themselves targets. The newly created Department of Homeland Security, with control over what had been disparate agencies responsible for immigration, foreign intelligence, and crime fighting, considered a wide array of proposals that would provide the government with extensive information about American citizens and alien residents.

The USA Patriot Act was the legislative embodiment of the new direction. Hard-line law-enforcement officials and intelligence agents had long chafed at the restrictions court decisions and federal statutes imposed on the exchange of information among government agencies and the limits in placed on the surveillance of United States citizens and resident aliens. After September 11 the terrorist threat convinced many Americans that these limitations were no longer appropriate. The main purpose of the Patriot Act was to eliminate them and give law-enforcement and surveillance agencies the same power to investigate American citizens that they had to investigate foreigners. The new law not only permitted but encouraged the exchange of information between intelligence and law-enforcement agencies. To the delight of criminal investigators, it said that protecting national security had to be only one of the goals of an investigation rather than the primary one. This meant that all the tools Americans wanted to use against potential terrorists might be used against people suspected of ordinary crimes as well.

The Patriot Act authorized surveillance not only of non-citizens but of American citizens suspected of supporting terrorist activities. It defined both the activities and "support" broadly, leading civil liberties groups to worry that acts of civil disobedience and even mere political endorsement of suspect organizations would qualify. A special panel of judges could now authorize secret surveillance and searches of American citizens as well as foreigners, and any evidence secured this way could be used in any criminal prosecution. The Act also required providers of telephone, Internet services, other businesses, and even libraries to provide information on users and subscribers at the request of any government agency.

A surveillance state is incompatible with the stress on privacy and personal autonomy central to liberal constitutionalism, as well as with the widespread fear of big, intrusive government among conservatives. Congress did respond to these concerns. For all its breadth, the Patriot Act actually restricted government far more tightly than the legislation the Bush administration originally asked for. Moreover, legislators set a five-year moratorium on many of its provisions. Nonetheless, urged on by both liberals and many conservatives, over three hundred cities and towns around the country formally voted to condemn the law. A few courts began to find parts of it unconstitutional. But the Bush administration pressed for yet broader authority and to make the law's provisions permanent.

The Future of American Constitutionalism

The presidential election of 2004 indicated that Americans are bitterly and almost evenly divided over issues that have profound implications for the Constitution. Conservatives and traditionalists continue to press for further changes to bring constitutional law into harmony with their vision of a society informed by principles of Christian morality. Americans struggle over the proper balance between freedom and security in a new age of vulnerability to terrorism. The "administrative presidency" claims that it rather than Congress has the right to control the federal bureaucracy. The Supreme Court claims that the other branches are bound to surrender their own interpretations of the Constitution when they conflict with the justices'; in response, legal academics argue for recognition of the role of the people in construing American constitutionalism, while conservative politicians urge judicial restraint and propose legislation to strip the courts of jurisdiction over sensitive issues. Americans' desire to be free of outside constraints in protecting our national security strains our deep commitment to the rule of law. A bitter fight looms over filling Supreme Court vacancies.

A history of the Constitution published at any time in the past would have ended with a similar reference to ongoing controversies. In the United States, nearly all issues can be, and ultimately are, argued in constitutional terms. Constitutional principles reinforce or undercut efforts to secure our economic interests or to give our moral convictions the force of law. Rival understandings of human nature, of liberty, and of the role of the state assure continued conflict over the meaning of the Constitution itself. Therefore there can be no end to a history of constitutional government in the United States. The story is never complete. Future chapters remain to be written by the people of the United States, as we continue to engage each other in our efforts to secure the blessings of liberty.

TIMELINE

2001   On September 11, Al-Qaeda terrorists hijack commercial airliners and crash them into the World Trade Center in New York City and the Pentagon in Washington, D.C.

Congress authorizes the president to take measures necessary to counteract terrorist activities aimed at the United States. President Bush organizes an invasion of Afghanistan, location of Al-Qaeda's headquarters and training bases.

Congress passes the USA Patriot Act.

2001   President Bush issues a military order authorizing the detention of "unlawful enemy combatants" and their trial by military commission.

2002   Congress passes a resolution authorizing the president to use American armed forces as he determines necessary to protect the United States from the threat of Iraqi weapons of mass destruction.

The United States organizes an international force to invade Iraq, claiming authority under earlier UN resolutions.

2004   Reports and photographs of abuse of detainees held in Iraq are published in the American and world press.

The Supreme Court rules that American citizens alleged to be "enemy combatants" have the right to challenge the allegation before "a neutral decisionmaker."

FURTHER READING

It is still early for historical assessments of the George W. Bush presidency. For some early analysis by political scientists, see the essays in Fred I. Greenstein, ed., *The George W. Bush Presidency: An Early Assessment* (2003), and Gary L. Gregg and Mark J. Rozell, eds., *Considering the Bush Presidency* (2004). Several essays in *The George W. Bush Presidency: Appraisals and Prospects,* edited by Colin Campbell and Bert A. Rockman (2004) make clear how the ideological cast of the Bush administration has fanned already bitter divisions in the United States. See those by Campbell and Rockman.

Amy E. Black, Douglas L. Koopman, and David K. Ryden discuss the politics of the Bush administration's faith-based initiatives in *Of Little Faith* (2004). Lewis D. Solomon writes sympathetically of efforts to use faith-based organizations to solve social programs in *In God We Trust?* (2003). He addresses the constitutional issues in chapter 8.

Joel D. Aberbach describes Bush's use of executive orders and other executive resources to promote his policies through an "administrative presidency." See his essay in *The George W. Bush Presidency: Appraisals and Prospects,* noted above. For the development of the "administrative presidency" in a longer historical perspective, see Kenneth R. Mayer, *By the Stroke of a Pen* (2001). On confidentiality and secrecy, see Mark J. Rozell, "Executive Privilege in the Bush Administration," in *Considering the Bush Presidency,* noted above. Louis Fisher blasts Bush's justifications for the Iraq invasion as well as Congress's surrender of its authority to the president in chapter 9 of *Presidential War Power* (2d ed., 2004).

A good deal has been written about the Bush administration's rejection of constraints upon the exercise of American power. For a brief introduction, see Ivo H. Daalder and James M. Lindsay, "Bush's Foreign Policy Revolution," in *The George W. Bush Presidency: An Early Assessment.* For the full version, see their critical *America Unbound* (2003), which concentrates on the Iraq War. For a more general criticism of American tendencies to undermine international law, see Nicole Deller, Arjun Makhijani, and John Burroughs, *Rule of Power or Rule of Law?* (2003). Jennifer Elsea, *Treatment of "Battlefield Detainees"*

(2003) explains the laws governing prisoners of war and their application to Taliban and Al-Qaeda fighters.

The essays in *American National Security and Civil Liberties in an Age of Terrorism*, edited by David B. Cohen and John W. Wells (2004) place the challenges wrought by American vulnerability to international terrorism in a historical context. For essays debating proposals to promote "homeland security" at the expense of privacy rights, see James D. Torr (ed.) *Homeland Security* (2004).

Quinn H. Vandenberg describes the way that Congress has made immigration law an engine of oppression in "How Can the United States Rectify Its Post-9/11 Stance on Noncitizens' Rights?" *Notre Dame Journal of Law, Ethics & Public Policy* 18 (2004): 605–646. For a harrowing account of an FBI investigator's effort to rescue a Nepalese alien he had mistakenly brought under suspicion, see Nina Bernstein, "In F.B.I., Innocent Detainee Found Unlikely Ally," *New York Times*, June 30, 2004, Section A, p. 1.

In *The Soft Cage* (2003), Christian Parenti describes the Patriot Act as the culmination of a long, slow drift towards greater surveillance in the United States. Donald J. Musch's *Civil Liberties and the Foreign Intelligence Surveillance Act* (2003) provides a historical context focusing on statutes and cases. For a concise, chronological description of the law of surveillance, see G. Stevens and C. Doyle, *Privacy: Wiretapping and Electronic Eavesdropping* (2002). In a detailed analysis of the Patriot Act, *No Greater Threat* (2002), C. William Michaels worries that the law portends the rise of a national security state, something more threatening than the "surveillance state" described in this chapter.

Articles of Confederation and Perpetual Union

Between the states of New Hampshire, Massachusetts Bay, Rhode Island and Providence Plantations, Connecticut, New York, New Jersey, Pennsylvania, Delaware, Maryland, Virginia, North Carolina, South Carolina, Georgia.*

Article 1.

The stile of this confederacy shall be "The United States of America."

Article 2.

Each State retains its sovereignty, freedom and independence, and every power, jurisdiction, and right, which is not by this confederation expressly delegated to the United States, in Congress assembled.

Article 3.

The said states hereby severally enter into a firm league of friendship with each other for their common defence, the security of their liberties and their mutual and general welfare; binding themselves to assist each other against all force offered to, or attacks made upon them, or any of them, on account of religion, sovereignty, trade, or any other pretence whatever.

Article 4.

The better to secure and perpetuate mutual friendship and intercourse among the people of the different states in this union, the free inhabitants of each of these states, paupers, vagabonds, and fugitives from justice excepted, shall be entitled to all privileges and immunities of free citizens in the several states; and the people of each State shall have free ingress and regress to and from any other State, and shall enjoy therein all the privileges of trade and commerce, subject to the same duties, impositions, and

---

*This copy of the final draft of the Articles of Confederation is taken from the *Journals of the Continental Congress,* 9:907–925, (November 15, 1777).

restrictions, as the inhabitants thereof respectively; provided, that such restrictions shall not extend so far as to prevent the removal of property, imported into any State, to any other State of which the owner is an inhabitant; provided also, that no imposition, duties, or restriction, shall be laid by any State on the property of the United States, or either of them.

If any person guilty of, or charged with treason, felony, or other high misdemeanor in any State, shall flee from justice and be found in any of the United States, he shall, upon demand of the governor or executive power of the State from which he fled, be delivered up and removed to the State having jurisdiction of his offence.

Full faith and credit shall be given in each of these states to the records, acts, and judicial proceedings of the courts and magistrates of every other State.

Article 5.

For the more convenient management of the general interests of the United States, delegates shall be annually appointed, in such manner as the legislature of each State shall direct, to meet in Congress, on the 1st Monday in November in every year, with a power reserved to each State to recall its delegates, or any of them, at any time within the year, and to send others in their stead for the remainder of the year.

No State shall be represented in Congress by less than two, nor by more than seven members; and no person shall be capable of being a delegate for more than three years in any term of six years; nor shall any person, being a delegate, be capable of holding any office under the United States, for which he, or any other for his benefit, receives any salary, fees, or emolument of any kind.

Each State shall maintain its own delegates in a meeting of the states, and while they act as members of the committee of the states.

In determining questions in the United States, in Congress assembled, each State shall have one vote.

Freedom of speech and debate in Congress shall not be impeached or questioned in any court or place out of Congress: and the members of Congress shall be protected in their persons from arrests and imprisonments, during the time of their going to and from, and attendance on Congress, except for treason, felony, or breach of the peace.

Article 6.

No State, without the consent of the United States, in Congress assembled, shall send any embassy to, or receive any embassy from, or enter into any conference, agreement, alliance, or treaty with any king, prince, or state; nor shall any person, holding any office of profit or trust under the United States, or any of them, accept of any present, emolument, office or title, of any kind whatever, from any king, prince, or foreign state; nor shall the United States, in Congress assembled, or any of them, grant any title of nobility.

No two or more states shall enter into any treaty, confederation, or alliance, whatever, between them, without the consent of the United States, in Congress assembled, specifying accurately the purposes for which the same is to be entered into, and how long it shall continue.

No State shall lay any imposts or duties which may interfere with any stipulations in treaties entered into by the United States, in Congress assembled, with any king, prince, or state, in pursuance of any treaties already proposed by Congress to the courts of France and Spain.

No vessels of war shall be kept up in time of peace by any State, except such number only as shall be deemed necessary by the United States, in Congress assembled, for the defence of such State or its trade; nor shall any body of forces be kept up by any State, in time of peace, except such number only as, in the judgment of the United States, in Congress assembled, shall be deemed requisite to garrison the forts necessary for the defence of such State; but every State shall always keep up a well regulated and disciplined militia, sufficiently armed and accoutred, and shall provide, and constantly have ready for use, in public stores, a due number of field pieces and tents, and a proper quantity of arms, ammunition and camp equipage.

No State shall engage in any war without the consent of the United States, in Congress assembled, unless such State be actually invaded by enemies, or shall have received certain advice of a resolution being formed by some nation of Indians to invade such State, and the danger is so imminent as not to admit of a delay till the United States, in Congress assembled, can be consulted; nor shall any State grant commissions to any ships or vessels of war, nor letters of marque or reprisal, except it be after a declaration of war by the United States, in Congress assembled, and then only against the kingdom or state, and the subjects thereof, against which war has been so declared, and under such regulations as shall be established by the United States, in Congress assembled, unless such States be infested by pirates, in which case vessels of war may be fitted out for that occasion, and kept so long as the danger shall continue, or until the United States, in Congress assembled, shall determine otherwise.

Article 7.

When land forces are raised by any State for the common defence, all officers of or under the rank of colonel, shall be appointed by the legislature of each State respectively, by whom such forces shall be raised, or in such manner as such State shall direct; and all vacancies shall be filled up by the State which first made the appointment.

Article 8.

All charges of war and all other expences, that shall be incurred for the common defence or general welfare, and allowed by the United States, in Congress assembled, shall be defrayed out of a common treasury, which shall be supplied by the several states, in proportion to the value of all land within each State, granted to or surveyed for any person, as such land and the buildings and improvements thereon shall be estimated according to such mode as the United States, in Congress assembled, shall, from time to time, direct and appoint.

The taxes for paying that proportion shall be laid and levied by the authority and direction of the legislatures of the several states, within the time agreed upon by the United States, in Congress assembled.

Article 9.

The United States, in Congress assembled, shall have the sole and exclusive right and power of determining on peace and war, except in the cases mentioned in the 6th article; of sending and receiving ambassadors; entering into treaties and alliances, provided that no treaty of commerce shall be made, whereby the legislative power of the respective states shall be restrained from imposing such imposts and duties on foreigners as their own people are subjected to, or from prohibiting the exportation or importation of any species of goods or commodities whatsoever; of establishing rules for deciding, in all cases, what captures on land or water shall be legal, and in what manner prizes, taken by land or naval forces in the service of the United States, shall be divided or appropriated; of granting letters of marque and reprisal in times of peace; appointing courts for the trial of piracies and felonies committed on the high seas, and establishing courts for receiving and determining, finally, appeals in all cases of captures; provided, that no member of Congress shall be appointed a judge of any of the said courts.

The United States, in Congress assembled, shall also be the last resort on appeal in all disputes and differences now subsisting, or that hereafter may arise between two or more states concerning boundary, jurisdiction or any other cause whatever; which authority shall always be exercised in the manner following: whenever the legislative or executive authority, or lawful agent of any State, in controversy with another, shall present a petition to Congress, stating the matter in question, and praying for a hearing, notice thereof shall be given, by order of Congress, to the legislative or executive authority of the other State in controversy, and a day assigned for the appearance of the parties by their lawful agents, who shall then be directed to appoint, by joint consent, commissioners or judges to constitute a court for hearing and determining the matter in question; but, if they cannot agree, Congress shall name three persons out of each of the United States, and from the list of such persons each party shall alternately strike out one, in the petitioners beginning, until the number shall be reduced to thirteen; and from that number not less than seven, nor more than nine names, as Congress shall direct, shall, in the presence of Congress, be drawn out by lot; and the persons whose names shall be drawn, or any five of them, shall be commissioners or judges to hear and finally determine the controversy, so always as a major part of the judges who shall hear the cause shall agree in the determination; and if either party shall neglect to attend at the day appointed, without shewing reasons which Congress shall judge sufficient, or, being present, shall refuse to strike, the Congress shall proceed to nominate three persons out of each State, and the secretary of Congress shall strike in behalf of such party absent or refusing; and the judgment and sentence of the court to be appointed, in the manner before prescribed, shall be final and conclusive; and if any of the parties shall refuse to submit to the authority of such court, or to appear or defend their claim or cause, the court shall nevertheless proceed to pronounce sentence or judgment, which shall, in like manner, be final and decisive, the judgment or sentence and other proceedings being, in either case, transmitted to Congress, and lodged among the acts of Congress for the security of the parties concerned: provided, that every commissioner, before he sits in judgment, shall take an oath, to be administered by one of the judges of the supreme or superior court of the State where the cause shall be tried, "well and truly to hear and determine the matter in question, according to the best of his judgment, without favour, affection, or hope of reward": provided, also, that no State shall be deprived of territory for the benefit of the United States.

All controversies concerning the private right of soil, claimed under different grants of two or more states, whose jurisdictions, as they may respect such lands and the states which passed such grants, are adjusted, the said grants, or either of them, being at the same time claimed to have originated antecedent to such settlement of jurisdiction, shall, on the petition of either party to the Congress of the United States, be finally determined, as near as may be, in the same manner as is before prescribed for deciding disputes respecting territorial jurisdiction between different states.

The United States, in Congress assembled, shall also have the sole and exclusive right and power of regulating the alloy and value of coin struck by their own authority, or by that of the respective states; fixing the standard of weights and measures throughout the United States; regulating the trade and managing all affairs with the Indians not members of any of the states; provided that the legislative right of any State within its own limits be not infringed or violated; establishing and regulating post offices from one State to another throughout all the United States, and exacting such postage on the papers passing through the same as may be requisite to defray the expences of the said office; appointing all officers of the land forces in the service of the United States, excepting regimental officers; appointing all the officers of the naval forces, and commissioning all officers whatever in the service of the United States; making rules for the government and regulation of the said land and naval forces, and directing their operations.

The United States, in Congress assembled, shall have authority to appoint a committee to sit in the recess of Congress, to be denominated "a Committee of the States," and to consist of one delegate from each State, and to appoint such other committees and civil officers as may be necessary for managing the general affairs of the United States, under their direction; to appoint one of their number to preside; provided that no person be allowed to serve in the office of president more than one year in any term of three years; to ascertain the necessary sums of money to be raised for the service of the United States, and to appropriate and apply the same for defraying the public expences; to borrow money or emit bills on the credit of the United States, transmitting, every half year, to the respective states, an account of the sums of money so borrowed or emitted; to build and equip a navy; to agree upon the number of land forces, and to make requisitions from each State for its quota, in proportion to the number of white inhabitants in such State; which requisitions shall be binding; and, thereupon, the legislature of each State shall appoint the regimental officers, raise the men, and cloathe, arm, and equip them in a soldier-like manner, at the expence of the United States; and the officers and men so cloathed, armed, and equipped, shall march to the place appointed and within the time agreed on by the United States, in Congress assembled; but if the United States, in Congress assembled, shall, on consideration of circumstances, judge proper that any State should not raise men, or should raise a smaller number than its quota, and that any other State should raise a greater number of men than the quota thereof, such extra number shall be raised, officered, cloathed, armed, and equipped in the same manner as the quota of such State, unless the legislature of such State shall judge that such extra number cannot be safely spared out of the same, in which case they shall raise, officer, cloathe, arm, and equip as many of such extra number as they judge can be safely spared. And the officers and men so cloathed, armed, and equipped, shall march to the place appointed and within the time agreed on by the United States, in Congress assembled.

The United States, in Congress assembled, shall never engage in a war, nor grant letters of marque and reprisal in time of peace, nor enter into any treaties or alliances, nor coin money, nor regulate the value thereof, nor ascertain the sums and expences necessary for the defence and welfare of the United States, or any of them: nor emit bills, nor borrow money on the credit of the United States, nor appropriate money, nor agree upon the number of vessels of war to be built or purchased, or the number of land or sea forces to be raised, nor appoint a commander in chief of the army or navy, unless nine states assent to the same; nor shall a question on any other point, except for adjourning from day to day, be determined, unless by the votes of a majority of the United States, in Congress assembled.

The Congress of the United States shall have power to adjourn to any time within the year, and to any place within the United States, so that no period of adjournment be for a longer duration than the space of six months, and shall publish the journal of their proceedings monthly, except such parts thereof, relating to treaties, alliances or military operations, as, in their judgment, require secrecy; and the yeas and nays of the delegates of each State on any question shall be entered on the journal, when it is desired by any delegate; and the delegates of a State, or any of them, at his, or their request, shall be furnished with a transcript of the said journal, except such parts as are above excepted, to lay before the legislatures of the several states.

Article 10.

The committee of the states, or any nine of them, shall be authorized to execute, in the recess of Congress, such of the powers of Congress as the United States, in Congress assembled, by the consent of nine states, shall, from time to time, think expedient to vest them with; provided, that no power be delegated to the said committee for the exercise of which, by the articles of confederation, the voice of nine states, in the Congress of the United States assembled, is requisite.

Article 11.

Canada acceding to this confederation, and joining in the measures of the United States, shall be admitted into and entitled to all the advantages of this union; but no other colony shall be admitted into the same, unless such admission be agreed to by nine states.

Article 12.

All bills of credit emitted, monies borrowed and debts contracted by, or under the authority of Congress before the assembling of the United States, in pursuance of the present confederation, shall be deemed and considered as a charge against the United States, for payment and satisfaction where of the said United States and the public faith are hereby solemnly pledged.

Article 13.

Every State shall abide by the determinations of the United States, in Congress assembled, on all questions which, by this confederation, are submitted to them. And the articles of this confederation shall be inviolably observed by every State, and the union shall be perpetual; nor shall any alteration at any time hereafter be made in any of them, unless such alteration be agreed to in a Congress of the United States, and be afterwards confirmed by the legislatures of every State.

These articles shall be proposed to the legislatures of all the United States, to be considered, and if approved of by them, they are advised to authorize their delegates to ratify the same in the Congress of the United States; which being done, the same shall become conclusive.

Constitution of the United States of America

PREAMBLE

We the people of the United States, in order to form a more perfect union, establish justice, insure domestic tranquillity, provide for the common defense, promote the general welfare, and secure the blessings of liberty to ourselves and our posterity, do ordain and establish this Constitution for the United States of America.

Article I

Section 1.   All legislative powers herein granted shall be vested in a Congress of the United States, which shall consist of a Senate and a House of Representatives.

Section 2.   The House of Representatives shall be composed of members chosen every second year by the people of the several States, and the electors in each State shall have the qualifications requisite for electors of the most numerous branch of the State Legislature.

No person shall be a Representative who shall not have attained to the age of twenty-five years, and been seven years a citizen of the United States, and who shall not, when elected, be an inhabitant of that State in which he shall be chosen.

Representatives and direct taxes shall be apportioned among the several States which may be included within this Union, according to their respective numbers, which shall be determined by adding to the whole number of free persons, including those bound to service for a term of years and excluding Indians not taxed, three-fifths of all other persons. The actual enumeration shall be made within three years after the first meeting of the Congress of the United States, and within every subsequent term of ten years, in such manner as they shall by law direct. The number of Representatives shall not exceed one for every thirty thousand, but each State shall have at least one Representative; and until such enumeration shall be made, the State of New Hampshire shall be entitled to choose three, Massachusetts eight, Rhode Island and Providence Plantations one, Connecticut five, New York six, New Jersey four, Pennsylvania eight, Delaware one, Maryland six, Virginia ten, North Carolina five, South Carolina five, and Georgia three.

When vacancies happen in the representation from any State, the Executive authority thereof shall issue writs of election to fill such vacancies.

The House of Representatives shall choose their Speaker and other officers; and shall have the sole power of impeachment.

Section 3.   The Senate of the United States shall be composed of two Senators from each State, chosen by the legislature thereof, for six years; and each Senator shall have one vote.

Immediately after they shall be assembled in consequence of the first election, they shall be divided as equally as may be into three classes. The seats of the Senators of the first class shall be vacated at the expiration of the second year, of the second class at the expiration of the fourth year, and of the third class at the expiration of the sixth year, so that one-third may be chosen every second year; and if vacancies happen by resignation or otherwise, during the recess of the legislature of any State, the Executive thereof may make temporary appointments until the next meeting of the legislature, which shall then fill such vacancies.

No person shall be a Senator who shall not have attained to the age of thirty years, and been nine years a citizen of the United States, and who shall not, when elected, be an inhabitant of that State for which he shall be chosen.

The Vice President of the United States shall be President of the Senate, but shall have no vote, unless they be equally divided.

The Senate shall choose their other officers, and also a President *pro tempore,* in the absence of the Vice President, or when he shall exercise the office of the President of the United States.

The Senate shall have the sole power to try all impeachments. When sitting for that purpose, they shall be on oath or affirmation. When the President of the United States is tried, the Chief Justice shall preside: and no person shall be convicted without the concurrence of two-thirds of the members present.

Judgment in cases of impeachment shall not extend further than to removal from the office, and disqualification to hold and enjoy any office of honor, trust or profit under the United States; but the party convicted shall nevertheless be liable and subject to indictment, trial, judgment and punishment, according to law.

Section 4.   The times, places and manner of holding elections for Senators and Representatives shall be prescribed in each State by the legislature thereof; but the Congress may at any time by law make or alter such regulations, except as to the places of choosing Senators.

The Congress shall assemble at least once in every year, and such meeting shall be on the first Monday in December, unless they shall by law appoint a different day.

Section 5.   Each house shall be the judge of the elections, returns and qualifications of its own members, and a majority of each shall constitute a quorum to do business; but a smaller number may adjourn from day to day, and may be authorized to compel the attendance of absent members, in such manner, and under such penalties, as each house may provide.

Each house may determine the rules of its proceedings, punish its members for disorderly behavior, and with the concurrence of two-thirds, expel a member.

Each house shall keep a journal of its proceedings, and from time to time publish the same, excepting such parts as may in their judgment require secrecy; and the yeas and nays of the members of either house on any question shall, at the desire of one-fifth of those present, be entered on the journal.

Neither house, during the session of Congress, shall, without the consent of the other, adjourn for more than three days, nor to any other place than that in which the two houses shall be sitting.

Section 6.   The Senators and Representatives shall receive a compensation for their services, to be ascertained by law and paid out of the treasury of the United States. They shall in all cases except treason, felony and breach of the peace, be privileged from arrest during their attendance at the session of their respective houses, and in going to and returning from the same; and for any speech or debate in either house, they shall not be questioned in any other place.

No Senator or Representative shall, during the time for which he was elected, be appointed to any civil office under the authority of the United States, which shall have been created, or the emoluments whereof shall have been increased, during such time; and no person holding any office under the United States shall be a member of either house during his continuance in office.

Section 7.   All bills for raising revenue shall originate in the House of Representatives; but the Senate may propose or concur with amendments as on other bills.

Every bill which shall have passed the House of Representatives and the Senate, shall, before it become a law, be presented to the President of the United States; if he approve he shall sign it, but if not he shall return it with objections to that house in which it originated, who shall enter the objections at large on their journal, and proceed to reconsider it. If after such reconsideration two-thirds of that house shall agree to pass the bill, it shall be sent, together with the objections, to the other house, by which it shall likewise be reconsidered, and, if approved by two-thirds of that house, it shall become a law. But in all such cases the votes of both houses shall be determined by yeas and nays, and the names of the persons voting for and against the bill shall be entered on the journal of each house respectively. If any bill shall not be returned by the President within ten days (Sundays excepted) after it shall have been presented to him, the same shall be a law, in like manner as if he had signed it, unless the Congress by their adjournment prevent its return, in which case it shall not be a law.

Every order, resolution, or vote to which the concurrence of the Senate and House of Representatives may be necessary (except on a question of adjournment) shall be presented to the President of the United States; and before the same shall take effect, shall be approved by him, or being disapproved by him, shall be repassed by two-thirds of the Senate and House of Representatives, according to the rules and limitations prescribed in the case of a bill.

Section 8.   The Congress shall have power

To lay and collect taxes, duties, imposts, and excises, to pay the debts and provide for the common defense and general welfare of the United States; but all duties, imposts and excises shall be uniform throughout the United States;

To borrow money on the credit of the United States;

To regulate commerce with foreign nations, and among the several States, and with the Indian tribes;

To establish an uniform rule of naturalization, and uniform laws on the subject of bankruptcies throughout the United States;

To coin money, regulate the value thereof, and of foreign coin, and fix the standard of weights and measures;

To provide for the punishment of counterfeiting the securities and current coin of the United States;

To establish post offices and post roads;

To promote the progress of science and useful arts by securing for limited times to authors and inventors the exclusive right to their respective writings and discoveries;

To constitute tribunals inferior to the Supreme Court;

To define and punish piracies and felonies committed on the high seas and offenses against the law of nations;

To declare war, grant letters of marque and reprisal, and make rules concerning captures on land and water;

To raise and support armies, but no appropriation of money to that use shall be for a longer term than two years;

To provide and maintain a navy;

To make rules for the government and regulation of the land and naval forces;

To provide for calling forth the militia to execute the laws of the Union, suppress insurrections, and repel invasions;

To provide for organizing, arming, and disciplining the militia, and for governing such part of them as may be employed in the service of the United States, reserving to the States respectively the appointment of the officers, and the authority of training the militia according to the discipline prescribed by Congress;

To exercise exclusive legislation in all cases whatsoever, over such district (not exceeding ten miles square) as may, by cession of particular States, and the acceptance of Congress, become the seat of government of the United States, and to exercise like authority over all places purchased by the consent of the legislature of the State, in which the same shall be, for erection of forts, magazines, arsenals, dock-yards, and other needful buildings and

To make all laws which shall be necessary and proper for carrying into execution the foregoing powers, and all other powers vested by this Constitution in the government of the United States, or in any department or officer thereof.

Section 9.   The migration or importation of such persons as any of the States now existing shall think proper to admit shall not be prohibited by the Congress prior to the year 1808; but a tax or duty may be imposed on such importation, not exceeding $10 for each person.

The privilege of the writ of habeas corpus shall not be suspended, unless when in cases of rebellion or invasion the public safety may require it.

No bill of attainder or ex post facto law shall be passed.

No capitation, or other direct, tax shall be laid, unless in proportion to the census or enumeration herein before directed to be taken.

No tax or duty shall be laid on articles exported from any State.

No preference shall be given by any regulation of commerce or revenue to the ports of one State over those of another; nor shall vessels bound to, or from, one State, be obliged to enter, clear, or pay duties in another.

No money shall be drawn from the treasury, but in consequence of appropriations made by law; and a regular statement and account of the receipts and expenditures of all public money shall be published from time to time.

No title of nobility shall be granted by the United States: and no person holding any office of profit or trust under them, shall, without the consent of the Congress, accept of any present, emolument, office, or title, of any kind whatever, from any king, prince, or foreign state.

Section 10.   No State shall enter into any treaty, alliance, or confederation; grant letters of marque and reprisal; coin money; emit bills of credit; make anything but gold and silver coin a tender in payment of debts; pass any bill of attainder, ex post facto law, or law impairing the obligation of contracts, or grant any title of nobility.

No State shall, without the consent of Congress, lay any imposts or duties on imports or exports, except what may be absolutely necessary for executing its inspection laws: and the net produce of all duties and imposts, laid by any State on imports or exports, shall be for the use of the treasury of the United States; and all such laws shall be subject to the revision and control of the Congress.

No State shall, without the consent of Congress, lay any duty of tonnage, keep troops or ships of war in time of peace, enter into any agreement or compact with another State, or with a foreign power, or engage in war, unless actually invaded, or in such imminent danger as will not admit of delay.

Article II

Section 1.   The executive power shall be vested in a President of the United States of America. He shall hold his office during the term of four years, and, together with the Vice President, chosen for the same term, be elected as follows:

Each state shall appoint, in such manner as the legislature thereof may direct, a number of electors, equal to the whole number of Senators and Representatives to which the State may be entitled in the Congress; but no Senator or Representative, or person holding an office of trust or profit under the United States, shall be appointed an elector.

The electors shall meet in their respective States, and vote by ballot for two persons, of whom one at least shall not be an inhabitant of the same State with themselves. And they shall make a list of all the persons voted for, and of the number of votes for each; which list they shall sign and certify, and transmit sealed to the seat of government of the United States, directed to the President of the Senate. The President of the Senate shall, in the presence of the Senate and the House of Representatives, open all the certificates, and the votes shall then be counted. The person having the greatest number of votes shall be the President, if such number be a majority of the whole number of electors appointed; and if there be more than one who have such majority, and have an equal number of votes, then the House of Representatives shall immediately choose by ballot one of them for President; and if no person have a majority, then from the five highest on the list said house shall in like manner choose the President. But in choosing the President the votes shall be taken by States, the representation from each State having one vote; a quorum for this purpose shall consist of a member or members from two-thirds of the States, and a majority of all the States shall be necessary to a choice. In every case, after the choice of the President, the person having the greatest number of votes of the electors shall be the Vice President. But if there should remain two or more who have equal votes, the Senate shall choose from them by ballot the Vice President.

The Congress may determine the time of choosing the electors and the day on which they shall give their votes; which day shall be the same throughout the United States.

No person except a natural-born citizen, or a citizen of the United States at the time of the adoption of this Constitution, shall be eligible to the office of President; neither shall any person be eligible to that office who shall not have attained to the age of thirty-five years, and been fourteen years a resident within the United States.

In case of the removal of the President from office or of his death, resignation, or inability to discharge the powers and duties of the said office, the same shall devolve on the Vice President, and the Congress may by law provide for the case of removal, death, resignation, or inability, both of the President and Vice President, declaring what officer shall then act as President, and such officer shall act accordingly, until the disability be removed, or a President shall be elected.

The President shall, at stated times, receive for his services a compensation, which shall neither be increased nor diminished during the period for which he shall have been elected, and he shall not receive within that period any other emolument from the United States, or any of them.

Before he enter on the execution of his office, he shall take the following oath or affirmation:—"I do solemnly swear (or affirm) that I will faithfully execute the office of the President of the United States, and will to the best of my ability preserve, protect and defend the Constitution of the United States."

Section 2. The President shall be commander in chief of the army and navy of the United States, and of the militia of the several States, when called into the actual service of the United States; he may require the opinion, in writing, of the principal officer in each of the executive departments, upon any subject relating to the duties of their respective offices, and he shall have power to grant reprieves and pardons for offenses against the United States, except in cases of impeachment.

He shall have power, by and with the advice and consent of the Senate, to make treaties, provided two-thirds of the Senators present concur; and he shall nominate, and by and with the advice and consent of the Senate, shall appoint ambassadors, other public ministers and consuls, judges of the Supreme Court, and all other officers of the United States, whose appointments are not herein otherwise provided for, and which shall be established by law; but Congress may by law vest the appointment of such inferior officers, as they think proper, in the President alone, in the courts of law, or in the heads of departments.

The President shall have power to fill up all vacancies that may happen during the recess of the Senate, by granting commissions which shall expire at the end of their next session.

Section 3. He shall from time to time give to the Congress information of the state of the Union, and recommend to their consideration such measures as he shall judge necessary and expedient; he may, on extraordinary occasions, convene both houses, or either of them, and in case of disagreement between them, with respect to the time of adjournment, he may adjourn them to such time as he shall think proper; he shall receive ambassadors and other public ministers; he shall take care that the laws be faithfully executed, and shall commission all the officers of the United States.

Section 4. The President, Vice President and all civil officers of the United States shall be removed from office on impeachment for, and on conviction of, treason, bribery, or other high crimes and misdemeanors.

Article III

Section 1. The judicial power of the United States shall be vested in one Supreme Court, and in such inferior courts as the Congress may from time to time ordain and establish. The judges, both of the Supreme and inferior courts, shall hold their offices during good behavior, and shall, at stated times, receive for their services a compensation which shall not be diminished during their continuance in office.

Section 2. The judicial power shall extend to all cases, in law and equity, arising under this Constitution, the laws of the United States, and treaties made, or which shall be made, under their authority—to all cases affecting ambassadors, other public ministers and consuls—to all cases of admiralty and maritime jurisdiction—to controversies to which the United States shall be a party—to controversies between two or more States—between a State and citizens of another State;—between citizens of different States—between citizens of the same State claiming lands under grants of different States, and between a State, or the citizens thereof, and foreign states, citizens or subjects.

In all cases affecting ambassadors, other public ministers and consuls, and those in which a State shall be party, the Supreme Court shall have original jurisdiction. In all the other cases before mentioned, the Supreme Court shall have appellate jurisdiction, both as to law and fact, with such exceptions, and under such regulations, as the Congress shall make.

The trial of all crimes, except in cases of impeachment, shall be by jury; and such trial shall be held in the State where said crimes shall have been committed; but when not committed within any State, the trial shall be at such place or places as the Congress may by law have directed.

Section 3.   Treason against the United States shall consist only in levying war against them, or in adhering to their enemies, giving them aid and comfort. No person shall be convicted of treason unless on the testimony of two witnesses to the same overt act, or on confession in open court.

The Congress shall have power to declare the punishment of treason, but no attainder of treason shall work corruption of blood, or forfeiture except during the life of the person attainted.

Article IV

Section 1.   Full faith and credit shall be given in each State to the public acts, records, and judicial proceedings of every other State. And the Congress may by general laws prescribe the manner in which such acts, records, and proceedings shall be proved, and the effect thereof.

Section 2.   The citizens of each State shall be entitled to all privileges and immunities of citizens in the several States.

A person charged in any State with treason, felony, or other crime, who shall flee from justice, and be found in another State, shall on demand of the executive authority of the State from which he fled, be delivered up, to be removed to the State having jurisdiction of the crime.

No person held to service or labor in one State, under the laws thereof, escaping into another, shall, in consequence of any law or regulation therein, be discharged from such service or labor, but shall be delivered up on claim of the party to whom such service or labor may be due.

Section 3.   New States may be admitted by the Congress into this Union; but no new State shall be formed or erected within the jurisdiction of any other State; nor any State be formed by the junction of two or more States, or parts of States, without the consent of the legislatures of the States concerned as well as of the Congress.

The Congress shall have power to dispose of and make all needful rules and regulations respecting the territory or other property belonging to the United States; and nothing in this Constitution shall be so construed as to prejudice any claims of the United States, or of any particular State.

Section 4.   The United States shall guarantee to every State in this Union a republican form of government, and shall protect each of them against invasion; and on application of the legislature, or of the executive (when the legislature cannot be convened), against domestic violence.

Article V

The Congress, whenever two-thirds of both houses shall deem it necessary, shall propose amendments to this Constitution, or, on the application of the legislatures of two-thirds of the several States, shall call a convention for proposing amendments, which, in either case, shall be valid to all intents and purposes, as part of this

Constitution, when ratified by the legislatures of three-fourths of the several States, or by conventions in three-fourths thereof, as the one or the other mode of ratification may be proposed by the Congress; provided that no amendments which may be made prior to the year one thousand eight hundred and eight shall in any manner affect the first and fourth clauses in the ninth section of the first article; and that no State, without its consent, shall be deprived of its equal suffrage in the Senate.

Article VI

All debts contracted and engagements entered into, before the adoption of this Constitution, shall be as valid against the United States under this Constitution, as under the Confederation.

This Constitution, and the laws of the United States which shall be made in pursuance thereof; and all treaties made, or which shall be made, under the authority of the United States, shall be the supreme law of the land; and the judges in every State shall be bound thereby, anything in the Constitution or laws of any State to the contrary notwithstanding.

The Senators and Representatives before mentioned, and the members of the several State legislatures, and all executive and judicial officers, both of the United States and of the several States, shall be bound by oath or affirmation to support this Constitution; but no religious test shall ever be required as a qualification to any office or public trust under the United States.

Article VII

The ratification of the conventions of nine States shall be sufficient for the establishment of this Constitution between the States so ratifying the same.

Done in Convention by the unanimous consent of the States present, the seventeenth day of September in the year of our Lord one thousand seven hundred and eighty-seven and of the Independence of the United States of America the twelfth. In witness whereof we have hereunto subscribed our names.

Amendments to the Constitution

Article I*

Congress shall make no law respecting an establishment of religion, or prohibiting the free exercise thereof; or abridging the freedom of speech, or of the press; or the right of the people peaceably to assemble, and to petition the government for a redress of grievances.

---

*The first ten Amendments (Bill of Rights) were adopted in 1791.

Article II

A well-regulated militia being necessary to the security of a free State, the right of the people to keep and bear arms shall not be infringed.

Article III

No soldier shall, in time of peace, be quartered in any house without the consent of the owner, nor in time of war, but in a manner to be prescribed by law.

Article IV

The right of the people to be secure in their persons, houses, papers, and effects, against unreasonable searches and seizures, shall not be violated, and no warrants shall issue but upon probable cause, supported by oath or affirmation, and particularly describing the place to be searched, and the persons or things to be seized.

Article V

No person shall be held to answer for a capital, or otherwise infamous crime, unless on a presentment or indictment of a grand jury, except in cases arising in the land or naval forces, or in the militia, when in actual service in time of war or public danger; nor shall any person be subject for the same offense to be twice put in jeopardy of life or limb; nor shall be compelled in any criminal case to be a witness against himself, nor be deprived of life, liberty, or property, without due process of law; nor shall private property be taken for public use without just compensation.

Article VI

In all criminal prosecutions, the accused shall enjoy the right to a speedy and public trial, by an impartial jury of the State and district wherein the crime shall have been committed, which district shall have been previously ascertained by law, and to be informed of the nature and cause of the accusation; to be confronted with the witnesses against him; to have compulsory process for obtaining witnesses in his favor, and to have the assistance of counsel for his defense.

Article VII

In suits at common law, where the value in controversy shall exceed twenty dollars, the right of trial by jury shall be preserved, and no fact tried by a jury shall be otherwise reexamined in any court of the United States, than according to the rules of the common law.

Article VIII

Excessive bail shall not be required, nor excessive fines imposed, nor cruel and unusual punishments inflicted.

Article IX

The enumeration in the Constitution, of certain rights, shall not be construed to deny or disparage others retained by the people.

Article X

The powers not delegated to the United States by the Constitution, nor prohibited by it to the States, are reserved to the States respectively, or to the people.

Article XI

[Adopted 1798]
The judicial power of the United States shall not be construed to extend to any suit in law or equity, commenced or prosecuted against one of the United States by citizens of another State, or by citizens or subjects of any foreign state.

Article XII

[Adopted 1804]
The electors shall meet in their respective States, and vote by ballot for President and Vice President, one of whom, at least, shall not be an inhabitant of the same State with themselves; they shall name in their ballots the person voted for as President, and in distinct ballots the person voted for as Vice President, and they shall make distinct lists of all persons voted for as President, and of all persons voted for as Vice President, and of the number of votes for each, which lists they shall sign and certify, and transmit sealed to the seat of government of the United States, directed to the President of the Senate—the President of the Senate shall, in the presence of the Senate and House of Representatives, open all the certificates and the votes shall then be counted—the person having the greatest number of votes for President shall be the President, if such number be a majority of the whole number of electors appointed; and if no person have such majority, then from the persons having the highest numbers not exceeding three on the list of those voted for as President, the House of Representatives shall choose immediately, by ballot, the President. But in choosing the President, the votes shall be taken by States, the representation from each State having one vote; a quorum for this purpose shall consist of a member or members from two-thirds of the States, and a majority of all the States shall be necessary to a choice. And if the House of Representatives shall not choose a President whenever the right of choice shall devolve upon them, before the fourth day of March next following, then the Vice President shall act as President, as in the case of the death or other constitutional disability of the President.

The person having the greatest number of votes as Vice President shall be the Vice President, if such a number be a majority of the whole number of electors appointed; and if no person have a majority, then from the two highest numbers on the list the Senate shall choose the Vice President; a quorum for the purpose shall consist of two-thirds of the whole number of Senators, and a majority of the whole number shall be necessary to a choice. But no person constitutionally ineligible to the office of President shall be eligible to that of Vice President of the United States.

Article XIII
[Adopted 1865]

Section 1.   Neither slavery nor involuntary servitude, except as a punishment for crime whereof the party shall have been duly convicted, shall exist within the United States, or any place subject to their jurisdiction.

Section 2.   Congress shall have power to enforce this article by appropriate legislation.

Article XIV
[Adopted 1868]

Section 1.   All persons born or naturalized in the United States, and subject to the jurisdiction thereof, are citizens of the United States and of the State wherein they reside. No State shall make or enforce any law which shall abridge the privileges or immunities of citizens of the United States; nor shall any State deprive any person of life, liberty, or property, without due process of law; nor deny to any person within its jurisdiction the equal protection of the laws.

Section 2.   Representatives shall be apportioned among the several States according to their respective numbers, counting the whole number of persons in each State, excluding Indians not taxed. But when the right to vote at any election for the choice of Electors for President and Vice President of the United States, Representatives in Congress, the executive and judicial officers of a State, or the members of the legislature thereof, is denied to any of the male inhabitants of such State, being twenty-one years of age and citizens of the United States, or in any way abridged, except for participation in rebellion, or other crime, the basis of representation therein shall be reduced in the proportion which the number of such male citizens shall bear to the whole number of male citizens twenty-one years of age in such State.

Section 3.   No person shall be a Senator or Representative in Congress or Elector of President and Vice President, or hold any office, civil or military, under the United States, or under any State, who, having previously taken an oath, as a member of Congress, or as an officer of the United States, or as a member of any State legislature, or as an executive or judicial officer of any State, to support the Constitution of the United States, shall have engaged in insurrection or rebellion against the same, or given aid and comfort to the enemies thereof. Congress may, by a vote of two-thirds of each house, remove such disability.

Section 4.   The validity of the public debt of the United States, authorized by law, including debts incurred for payment of pensions and bounties for services in suppressing insurrection or rebellion, shall not be questioned. But neither the United States nor any State shall assume or pay any debt or obligation incurred in aid of insurrection or rebellion against the United States, or any claim for the loss or emancipation of any slave; but all such debts, obligations, and claims shall be held illegal and void.

Section 5. The Congress shall have the power to enforce, by appropriate legislation, the provisions of this article.

Article XV
[Adopted 1870]

Section 1. The right of citizens of the United States to vote shall not be denied or abridged by the United States or by any State on account of race, color, or previous condition of servitude.

Section 2. The Congress shall have power to enforce this article by appropriate legislation.

Article XVI
[Adopted 1913]
The Congress shall have power to lay and collect taxes on incomes, from whatever source derived, without apportionment among the several States, and without regard to any census or enumeration.

Article XVII
[Adopted 1913]

Section 1. The Senate of the United States shall be composed of two Senators from each State, elected by the people thereof, for six years; and each Senator shall have one vote. The electors in each State shall have the qualifications requisite for electors of voters for the most numerous branch of the State legislatures.

Section 2. When vacancies happen in the representation of any State in the Senate, the executive authority of such State shall issue writs of election to fill such vacancies: Provided, that the Legislature of any State may empower the executive thereof to make temporary appointments until the people fill the vacancies by election as the Legislature may direct.

Section 3. This amendment shall not be so construed as to affect the election or term of any Senator chosen before it becomes valid as part of the Constitution.

Article XVIII
[Adopted 1919; repealed 1933]

Section 1. After one year from the ratification of this article the manufacture, sale, or transportation of intoxicating liquors within, the importation thereof into, or the exportation thereof from the United States and all territory subject to the jurisdiction thereof, for beverage purposes, is hereby prohibited.

Section 2. The Congress and the several States shall have concurrent power to enforce this article by appropriate legislation.

Section 3.   This article shall be inoperative unless it shall have been ratified as an amendment to the Constitution by the legislatures of the several States, as provided by the Constitution, within seven years from the date of the submission thereof to the States by the Congress.

Article XIX
[Adopted 1920]

Section 1.   The right of citizens of the United States to vote shall not be denied or abridged by the United States or by any State on account of sex.

Section 2.   The Congress shall have the power to enforce this article by appropriate legislation.

Article XX
[Adopted 1933]

Section 1.   The terms of the President and Vice President shall end at noon on the 20th day of January, and the terms of Senators and Representatives at noon on the 3d day of January, of the years in which such terms would have ended if this article had not been ratified; and the terms of their successors shall then begin.

Section 2.   The Congress shall assemble at least once in every year, and such meeting shall begin at noon on the 3d of January, unless they shall by law appoint a different day.

Section 3.   If, at the time fixed for the beginning of the term of the President, the President-elect shall have died, the Vice President-elect shall become President. If a President shall not have been chosen before the time fixed for the beginning of his term, or if the President-elect shall have failed to qualify, then the Vice President-elect shall act as President until a President shall have qualified; and the Congress may by law provide for the case wherein neither a President-elect nor a Vice President-elect shall have qualified, declaring who shall then act as President, or the manner in which one who is to act shall be selected, and such persons shall act accordingly until a President or Vice President shall have qualified.

Section 4.   The Congress may by law provide for the case of the death of any of the persons from whom the House of Representatives may choose a President whenever the right of choice shall have devolved upon them, and for the case of the death of any of the persons from whom the Senate may choose a Vice President whenever the right of choice shall have devolved upon them.

Section 5.   Sections 1 and 2 shall take effect on the 15th day of October following the ratification of this article.

Section 6.   This article shall be inoperative unless it shall have been ratified as an amendment to the Constitution by the Legislatures of three-fourths of the several States within seven years from the date of its submission.

Article XXI
[Adopted 1933]

Section 1. The eighteenth article of amendment to the Constitution of the United States is hereby repealed.

Section 2. The transportation or importation into any State, Territory, or Possession of the United States for delivery or use therein of intoxicating liquors, in violation of the laws thereof, is hereby prohibited.

Section 3. This article shall be inoperative unless it shall have been ratified as an amendment to the Constitution by conventions in the several States, as provided in the Constitution, within seven years from the date of submission thereof to the States by the Congress.

Article XXII
[Adopted 1951]

Section 1. No person shall be elected to the office of President more than twice, and no person who has held the office of President, or acted as President, for more than two years of a term to which some other person was elected President shall be elected to the office of President more than once. But this article shall not apply to any person holding the office of President when this article was proposed by the Congress, and shall not prevent any person who may be holding the office of President, or acting as President, during the term within which this article becomes operative from holding the office of President or acting as President during the remainder of such term.

Section 2. This article shall be inoperative unless it shall have been ratified as an amendment to the Constitution by the legislatures of three-fourths of the several States within seven years from the date of its submission to the States by the Congress.

Article XXIII
[Adopted 1961]

Section 1. The District constituting the seat of Government of the United States shall appoint in such manner as the Congress may direct:

A number of electors of President and Vice President equal to the whole number of Senators and Representatives in Congress to which the District would be entitled if it were a State, but in no event more than the least populous State; they shall be in addition to those appointed by the States, but they shall be considered for the purposes of the election of President and Vice President, to be electors appointed by a State; and they shall meet in the District and perform such duties as provided by the twelfth article of amendment.

Section 2. The Congress shall have the power to enforce this article by appropriate legislation.

Article XXIV
[Adopted 1964]

Section 1.   The right of citizens of the United States to vote in any primary or other election for President or Vice President, for electors for President or Vice President, or for Senator or Representative in Congress, shall not be denied or abridged by the United States or any State by reason of failure to pay any poll tax or other tax.

Section 2.   The Congress shall have the power to enforce this article by appropriate legislation.

Article XXV
[Adopted 1967]

Section 1.   In case of the removal of the President from office or of his death or resignation, the Vice President shall become President.

Section 2.   Whenever there is a vacancy in the office of the Vice President, the President shall nominate a Vice President who shall take office upon confirmation by a majority vote of both Houses of Congress.

Section 3.   Whenever the President transmits to the President pro tempore of the Senate and the Speaker of the House of Representatives his written declaration that he is unable to discharge the powers and duties of his office, and until he transmits to them a written declaration to the contrary, such powers and duties shall be discharged by the Vice President as Acting President.

Section 4.   Whenever the Vice President and a majority of either the principal officers of the executive departments or of such other body as Congress may by law provide, transmit to the President pro tempore of the Senate and the Speaker of the House of Representatives their written declaration that the President is unable to discharge the powers and duties of his office, the Vice President shall immediately assume the powers and duties of the office as Acting President.

Thereafter, when the President transmits to the President pro tempore of the Senate and the Speaker of the House of Representatives his written declaration that no inability exists, he shall resume the powers and duties of his office unless the Vice President and a majority of either the principal officers of the executive departments or of such other body as Congress may by law provide, transmit within four days to the President pro tempore of the Senate and the Speaker of the House of Representatives their written declaration that the President is unable to discharge the powers and duties of his office. Thereupon Congress shall decide the issue, assembling within forty-eight hours for that purpose if not in session. If the Congress, within twenty-one days after receipt of the latter written declaration, or, if Congress is not in session, within twenty-one days after Congress is required to assemble, determines by two-thirds vote of both Houses that the President is unable to discharge the powers and duties of his office, the Vice President shall continue to discharge the same as Acting President; otherwise, the President shall resume the powers and duties of his office.

Article XXVI
[*Adopted 1971*]

Section 1. The right of citizens of the United States, who are eighteen years of age or older, to vote shall not be denied or abridged by the United States or by any State on account of age.

Section 2. The Congress shall have power to enforce this article by appropriate legislation.

Article XXVII
[*Adopted 1992*]

No law, varying the compensation for services of the Senators and Representatives, shall take effect, until an election of Representatives shall have intervened.

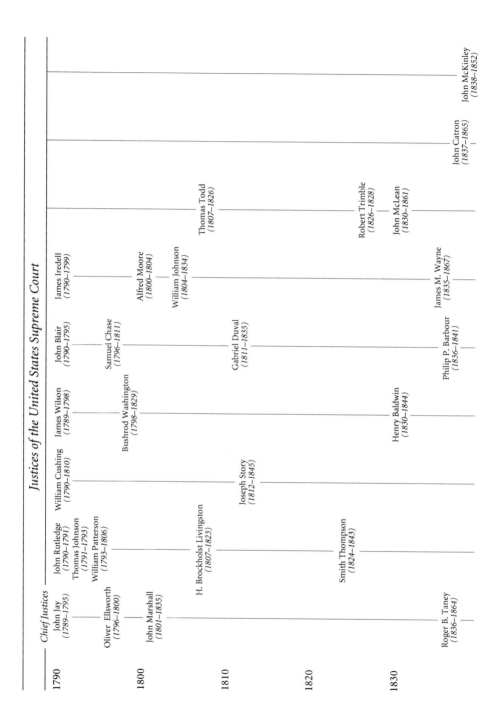

Justices of the United States Supreme Court

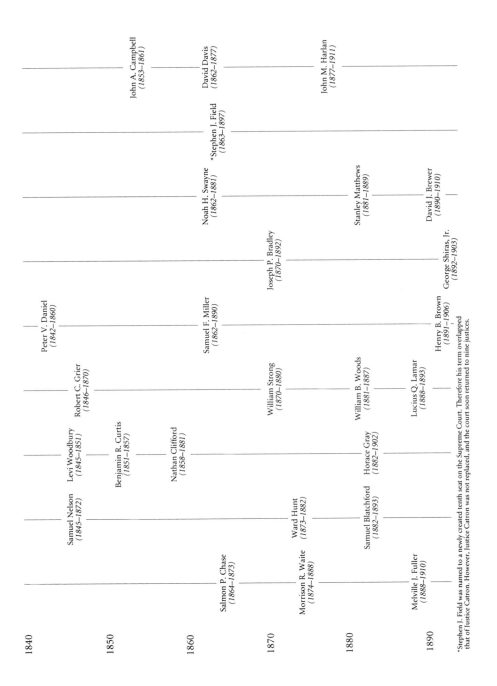

John A. Campbell
(1853–1861)

David Davis
(1862–1877)

John M. Harlan
(1877–1911)

Noah H. Swayne
(1862–1881)

*Stephen J. Field
(1863–1897)

Stanley Matthews
(1881–1889)

David J. Brewer
(1890–1910)

Joseph P. Bradley
(1870–1892)

Peter V. Daniel
(1842–1860)

Samuel F. Miller
(1862–1890)

George Shiras, Jr.
(1892–1903)

Robert C. Grier
(1846–1870)

William Strong
(1870–1880)

Henry B. Brown
(1891–1906)

Levi Woodbury
(1845–1851)

Benjamin R. Curtis
(1851–1857)

Nathan Clifford
(1858–1881)

William B. Woods
(1881–1887)

Lucius Q. Lamar
(1888–1893)

Samuel Nelson
(1845–1872)

Horace Gray
(1882–1902)

Ward Hunt
(1873–1882)

Samuel Blatchford
(1882–1893)

Salmon P. Chase
(1864–1873)

Morrison R. Waite
(1874–1888)

Melville J. Fuller
(1888–1910)

1840

1850

1860

1870

1880

1890

*Stephen J. Field was named to a newly created tenth seat on the Supreme Court. Therefore his term overlapped
that of Justice Catron. However, Justice Catron was not replaced, and the court soon returned to nine justices.

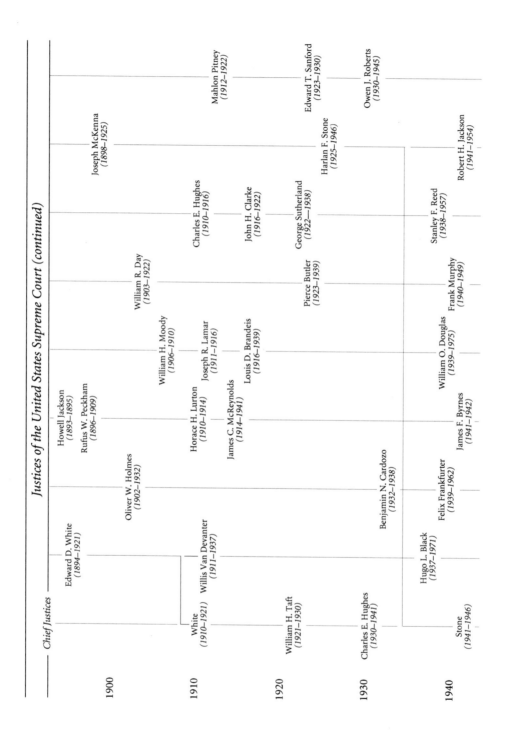

Justices of the United States Supreme Court (continued)

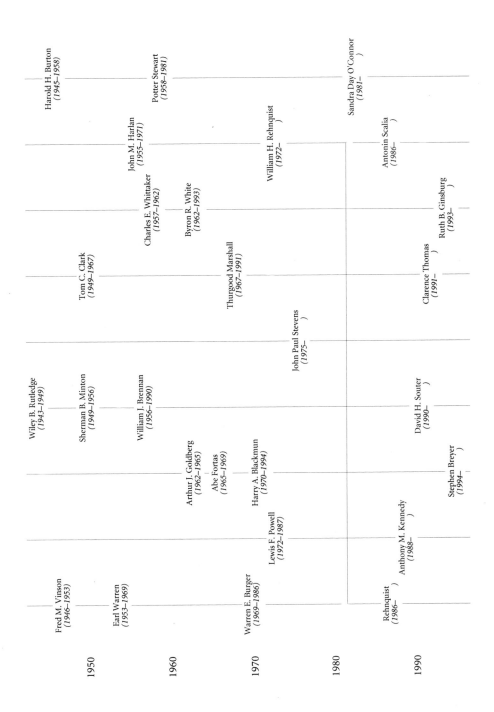

Table of Cases

NOTE: The form of the citations below follows *A Uniform System of Citation* (18th ed., Cambridge, Mass.: Harvard Law Review Association, 2005), modified somewhat for the benefit of students and scholars outside the law. The abbreviation "U.S." refers to the official *United States Reports*. Boldface page numbers are cross-references to this text.

Photo Credits

p. ii: State Museum of Pennsylvania, Pennsylvania Historical and Museum Commission; p. 82 (left): © Stapleton collection/Corbis; (right): Reunion des Musees Nationaux/Art Resource, New York; p. 94: Stock Montage; p. 111: *John Marshall*, 1755–1835, 1859 engraving by Johnson, Fry Co. Publishers, New York. Courtesy of The Library of Virginia; p. 134: Courtesy of the Metropolitan Museum of Art, New York; p. 135: © Stapleton Collection/Corbis; p. 136: Courtesy of The New York State Historical Association; p. 159: © Bettmann/Corbis; p. 162 (left): engraving by A. H. Ritchie, photo by Hulton Archive/Getty Images; (right): Cincinnati Museum Center—Cincinnati Historical Society Library; p. 190 (left): Stock Montage; (right): Stock Montage; p. 194: © Corbis; p. 195: Courtesy of Picture History; p. 196: 1869 cartoon, photo by MPI/Getty Images; p. 220: Stock Montage; p. 236: photo by MPI/Getty Images; p. 244 (left): Courtesy of Art and Visual Materials, Special Collections Department, Harvard Law School Library; (right): © Bettmann/Corbis; p. 271: *The Nine Old Men of the Supreme Court*, Hirschfeld. Art Reproduced by Special Arrangement with Hirschfeld's Exclusive Representative, The Margo Feiden Galleries Ltd., New York, www.alhirschfeld.com / photo provided by the Franklin Delano Roosevelt Library, Hyde Park, New York; p. 300: ©Bettmann/Corbis; p. 302: © Danny Lyon/Magnum Photos; p. 317: © Bettmann/Corbis; p. 318: photo by Hulton Archives/Getty Images; p. 322: photo by Ralph Crane/Time Life Pictures/Getty Images; p. 353: Eugene Craig cartoon courtesy of *The Columbus Dispatch*; p. 369: Mike Peters cartoon courtesy of *the Dayton Daily News*; p. 371: photographed by Richard Strauss, Smithsonian Institution. Collection, The Supreme Court Historical Society; p. 374: photo courtesy of the Gay Literation Network, www.CABN.org; p. 387: OLIPHANT © 1998 UNIVERSAL PRESS SYNDICATE. Reprinted with permission. All rights reserved; p. 391: Ed Stein cartoon ©*The Rocky Mountain News*/Distributed by Newspaper Enterprise Association, Inc./United Media; p. 424: Clay Bennett cartoon ©2001 *The Christian Science Monitor* (www.csmonitor.com). All rights reserved.

Index